THE CRISIS OF
CONSERVATISM

THE CRISIS OF CONSERVATISM

The politics, economics and ideology of the
British Conservative party, 1880–1914

E.H.H. Green

London and New York

First published 1995
by Routledge
11 New Fetter Lane, London EC4P 4EE

Simultaneously published in the USA and Canada
by Routledge
29 West 35th Street, New York, NY 10001

© 1995 E.H.H. Green

Typeset in Palatino by
Florencetype Ltd, Stoodleigh, Devon
Printed and bound in Great Britain by
T.J. Press (Padstow) Ltd, Padstow, Cornwall

British Library Cataloguing in Publication Data
A catalogue record for this book is available from the British Library

Library of Congress Cataloging in Publication Data
Green, E.H.H.
The crisis of conservatism: the politics, economics, and ideology of the British
Conservative Party, 1880–1914/E.H.H. Green.
p. cm.
Includes bibliographical references and index.
1. Great Britain–Politics and government–1837–1901. 2. Great Britain–Politics
and government–1901–1936. 3. Conservatism–Great Britain–History–19th
century. 4. Conservatism–Great Britain–History–20th century. 5. Conservative
Party (Great Britain)–History. I. Title.
DA560.G74 1994
324.24104–dc20 94–10882

ISBN 0–415–01255–4

To my mother and
in memory of my father

CONTENTS

ACKNOWLEDGEMENTS

My chief feelings on completing this book are relief and gratitude. Relief because there were times when I thought this project would never end, gratitude because over the years a number of friends, colleagues and institutions have combined to ensure that it did. As a cinema fan I cannot help but be struck by the similarity between acknowledgement sections in books and Oscar acceptance speeches, but, although I have no desire to outdo Greer Garson and Sally Field, I have incurred many debts which I would like to record. My initial research on Edwardian Conservatism was funded by a Department of Education and Science Major State Studentship, and I received further essential support from St John's College, Cambridge. The Institute of Historical Research elected me to a Research Fellowship for the session 1984–5, and enabled me to bring the first phase of the project to completion. In 1986 the Principal and Fellows of Brasenose College, Oxford elected me to an Edward White Bate Junior Research Fellowship in history, and allowed me to extend the scope of my research on both this and other projects to a degree which would not otherwise have been possible. At the same time my experiences teaching in Oxford, as a College Lecturer at Magdalen College in 1987 and as Radcliffe Lecturer in Modern History at St Hugh's College between 1988–90, were also invaluable. At St Hugh's in particular the necessity of broadening and deepening my understanding of European history served to strengthen the comparative aspects of my research. The importance of the link between teaching and research has been confirmed at the History Department at the University of Reading, which appointed me to a Lectureship in Modern British History in 1990 and provided a congenial and secure academic home in which to finish this book. Without the scholarly and financial support that these institutions have provided, *The Crisis of Conservatism* would not have been written, and I am very grateful for their confidence in both me and my work.

An historian is dependent upon his or her sources, and for providing me with access to these crucial materials I am grateful to the Librarians and Archivists at the following institutions: the University Library, the

Seeley Library, the Marshall Library, the libraries of St John's College, Corpus Christi College and the Churchill College Archive Centre in Cambridge, the Bodleian Library (especially the staff of Room 132), the History Faculty Library and the libraries of Brasenose College and Rhodes House in Oxford, the Senate House Library of London University, the libraries of the University of Birmingham, University of Reading, and University of Sheffield, the House of Lords Record Office, the Public Record Office, the Scottish Record Office and the local Record Offices of West Sussex (Chichester), Devon (Exeter), West Kent (Maidstone), Guildford, Gloucester and Liverpool. I must also express particular thanks to Mr Robin Harcourt-Williams, the archivist of Hatfield House, and to Mr R.D. Freeman, who granted me access to the papers of H.S. Foxwell.

For permission to quote from manuscript sources I am grateful to all of the above institutions and to the following individuals: Admiral Sir Ian Hogg (Gwynne papers), Mrs R.M. Stafford (Steel-Maitland papers), Dr Benedict Benedicz (Chamberlain papers), the Marquis of Salisbury (Salisbury papers), Mr R.D. Freeman (Foxwell papers).

I have benefited from the support of many who I now feel able to call fellow historians. My greatest debt is to Peter Clarke, who has been a constant source of inspiration and encouragement from the beginning of my academic career. On a very practical level he has given freely of his time to read and offer detailed comment on my work as it has progressed. In particular his comments on the final manuscript were invaluable. Less tangible, but equally important, his sympathy and friendship during the academic recession of the 1980s was crucial to my remaining in the historical profession. During those grim years I was also fortunate enough to enjoy the support of Jimmy Burns and Michael Thompson, and I will always be grateful for the counsel and encouragement they offered. Friends and colleagues in Cambridge, London, Oxford and Reading have also provided both intellectual and moral support over the years. Duncan Tanner, Mary Short, Leah Rosen, Tony Morris, Miles Taylor, Lawrence Goldman, Margaret O' Callaghan, Dave Feldman, John Lawrence, John France, John Parry, Simon Bromley and Steve Pumfrey shared the pains of the early 1980s but also shared their time and scholarship with great generosity. I benefited from Stefan Collini's advice when I began work on the historical economists, and Michael John helped guide me through the minefields of European history in the late nineteenth century. John Rowett, Ross Mckibbin, Jose Harris, Colin Matthew, Peter Ghosh, Keith McClelland, and Dave Jarvis have, through discussion of both their own work and mine, greatly assisted in the development of this project at various stages. Myfanwy Lloyd and Roy Wolfe rendered invaluable service in helping me prepare the Tables and Appendices. In a period when research in the humanities has been undervalued and undermined

I have been fortunate in the determination of my contemporaries to provide, in spite of the Government's relentless philistinism, a stimulating and generous intellectual environment.

My publishers have proved both patient and supportive. I am grateful to my initial commissioning editor, Tony Morris, for taking the project on, but above all I extend my thanks to my current editor Claire L'Enfant for her kindness and good humour as she waited (and waited) for this book to be delivered. Heather McCallum and Sue Bilton have taken the book through its development stages with consummate professionalism, and the suggestions and corrections made by the readers of the manuscript were of great assistance.

I also owe a big thanks to those 'non-historical' friends, Rob Hughes, Zoe Penn, Alex Holdcroft, Tom Kuhn, Debbie Pain, Charlie Arden-Clarke, Charlie Jenne, Caroline Sampson, John Rouse, Pauline Cook and Edith Hall, who have put up with my whinges and helped me to live with this project over the years. Individually and collectively they have helped preserve my good humour and my sanity. I feel I must also record the contribution of my 'best friend', Cadbury, who died shortly after this book was completed. Her loyalty and affection were always a great tonic, and my many walks with her provided periods of calm and reflection that helped me to think through many a difficult question. I greatly miss her influence. To any readers who might feel sceptical about this canine contribution, I can only say that she was infinitely more helpful to my studies, and certainly talked more sense, than any education minister of the past fifteen years.

My family have, on all sides, provided critical support for my scholarly endeavours. My brother, Simon, has, more than he realizes, been a source of inspiration as well as sympathy. Colin and Jean Brant helped to make difficult times much easier, and have often revived my flagging spirits with their warmth and affection. Their kindness has only underlined my good fortune in meeting Clare Brant, without whom my life and (the) work would not have been completed. Our partnership at work and play has been a source of inspiration and delight. Her own standards of scholarship made her a demanding reader, and her copy-editing skills sharpened my prose style and helped turn an unwieldy manuscript into a book. All of this was matched by a patience, supportiveness and love that was unbounded and which makes me feel very lucky. My debt to my parents is immeasurable. They supported my academic career through thick and thin, and it was often very thin. It is a matter of great sadness to me that my father died before this book was completed. My parents helped to type up my doctoral thesis in the days before I could afford a computer, and I would have liked more than anything for both of them to see the finished project.

Oxford, February 1994

ABBREVIATIONS

MANUSCRIPT SOURCES AND PUBLISHED DIARIES

ACP	Austen Chamberlain papers
ADP	Akers-Douglas papers
ALP	Alfred Lyttelton papers
BLP	Bonar Law papers
BP	Balfour papers
CARP	Carnarvon papers
CP	Crawford papers, J. Vincent (ed.), *The Crawford Papers: The Journals of David Lindsay 27th Earl of Crawford and 10th Earl of Balcarres 1871–1940 during the years 1892–1940* (Manchester 1984)
CPA	Conservative party archive
COCP	Cecil of Chelwood papers
CROP	Cromer papers
EHP	Edward Hamilton papers
FP	Farrer papers
GP	Gibbs papers
HAGP	H.A. Gwynne papers
HSFP	H.S. Foxwell papers
IFLP	Imperial Federation League papers
IP	Iddesleigh papers
JCP	Joseph Chamberlain papers
JSSP	J.S. Sandars papers
KP	Kidd papers
LCCP	Liverpool Chamber of Commerce papers
LJMP	L.J. Maxse papers
MP	Milner papers
NP	Northcliffe papers
RCP	Randolph Churchill papers
RDBP	R.D. Blumenfeld papers
RSD	Robert Sanders Diary, J. Ramsden (ed.), *Real Old Tory Politics* (London 1980)

SP	Salisbury papers
SELP	Selborne papers
SMP	Steel-Maitland papers
STRP	Strachey papers
TCP	Tariff Commission papers
WARP	Wargrave papers
WASHP	W.A.S. Hewins papers
WDBP	Willoughby de Broke papers
WLP	Walter Long papers

PERIODICALS

AgHR	*Agricultural History Review*
BIHR	*Bulletin of the Institute of Historical Research*
CR	*Contemporary Review*
EcHR	*Economic History Review*
EHR	*English Historical Review*
EJ	*Economic Journal*
ER	*Economic Review*
FT	*Fair Trade*
HJ	*Historical Journal*
HR	*Historical Research*
IF	*Imperial Federation*
JBS	*Journal of British Studies*
JCH	*Journal of Contemporary History*
JHI	*Journal of the History of Ideas*
JMH	*Journal of Modern History*
NR	*National Review*
P and P	*Past and Present*
TCBH	*Twentieth Century British History*

MISCELLANEOUS ORGANIZATIONS AND OFFICIAL TITLES

BCA	British Constitutional Association
ASU	Anti-Socialist Union
CCA	Central Chamber of Agriculture
CCO	Conservative Central Office
CLA	Central Land Association
FTL	Farmers' Tariff League
IFL	Imperial Federation League
IML	Imperial Maritime League
LPDL	Liberty and Property Defence League
NFTL	National Fair Trade League

NFU	National Farmers' Union
NHCA	North Hampshire Conservative Association
NL	Navy League
NSL	National Service League
NUCA	National Union of Conservative Associations
PRO	Public Record Office
RCDTI	Royal Commission on the Depression of Trade and Industry
RCC	Royal Commission on Currency
RCAD	Royal Commission on Agricultural Depression
TC	Tariff Commission
TRL	Tariff Reform League
USRC	Unionist Social Reform Committee
WHCA	West Hampshire Conservative Association

INTRODUCTION
The peculiarities of
Edwardian Conservatism

The British Conservative party has been the most successful political party of the modern era. Between 1881 and 1990 the Conservative party won sixteen of the twenty-eight general elections held, and, under a variety of electoral systems, their share of the vote rarely fell below 40 per cent. This electoral success ensured they were in government, either alone or in coalitions dominated by their party, for seventy of the 109 years separating Benjamin Disraeli's death and Margaret Thatcher's resignation. Even when the Conservatives did not gain office, their electoral strength was often great enough to deny their opponents a working Parliamentary majority,[1] whereas Conservative electoral success resulted for the most part in Parliamentary dominance.[2] No other European party of the Right operating within a mass electoral system has equalled this achievement, and on the Left only the Swedish Social Democrats have come close. In the light of this record the Conservative party could be forgiven for considering itself to be Britain's natural party of government.

In this century of Conservative success there is, however, a period which Conservatives would prefer to forget. Soon after their triumph at the 'Khaki' election of September 1900, the Conservatives fell into an electoral slump. A series of poor by-election results led up to the January 1906 general election, in which the Conservative Parliamentary contingent was reduced to its lowest-ever level of 157. In the two general elections of 1910 the Conservatives recovered ground, but they remained pinned in opposition by an unprecedentedly cohesive anti-Conservative bloc. Thus when the Great War broke out the Conservatives had lost three general elections and had been in opposition for eight years, and there were few signs that the party was in a position to break out of this enclave.[3]

How was it that the Conservative party, which had enjoyed great electoral sucess in the late nineteenth century, and which was to reestablish its dominance in the inter-war years, was so weak in the Edwardian period? One apparently plausible answer is that the Conservatives caused their own downfall. In the early years of the century the Conservatives adopted a controversial policy that seemed to alienate

1

the electorate. The policy in question was tariff reform, and on this basis the problems of Edwardian Conservatism appear to have begun at Bingley Hall, Birmingham on 15 May 1903, when Joseph Chamberlain launched the tariff reform campaign.

In retrospect it seems self-evident that tariff reform would cause nothing but trouble for the Conservative party. To argue for tariffs meant attacking free trade. This had the effect of reinvigorating the Liberal party, which in itself was a blow to the Conservatives. After the Liberal split over Home Rule in 1886, the Conservatives had benefited from facing a divided and demoralised opposition, but after 1903 the internal divisions which had so weakened the late nineteenth-century Liberal party were largely forgotten as Liberals rallied to defend the altar of free trade. By a huge irony Joseph Chamberlain seems to have helped repair the damage which his own defection from the Liberal ranks in 1886 had caused.

The Conservative assault on free trade had other, deeper ramifications. In the early twentieth century there was a widespread tendency to see free trade more as an article of faith than an economic policy. The introduction of free trade, generally associated with the repeal of the Corn Laws in 1846, had coincided with an extended up-turn in Britain's fortunes, and the political-economic orthodoxy of mid- to late-Victorian Britain was that peace, prosperity, and social progress were linked to free trade. For over fifty years both Liberal and Conservative governments had avowed that all the economic, political and moral arguments were in favour of free trade, with Disraeli himself famously declaring protectionism 'not only dead but damned'. By seeking to resurrect this supposedly irredeemable cause, Edwardian Conservatives condemned themselves to overturning a revered wisdom.

The historical record is full of heretics whose ideas ultimately triumphed, but history is also full of heretics who sparked only the flames of their own destruction, and the Conservative party's commitment to tariff reform seems to fall into this last category. To many contemporaries (and to many historians) the Conservative party's adoption of tariff reform as its 'first constructive work' was at best foolhardy and at worst an act of self-immolation. What made tariff reform so difficult and ultimately so damaging, it was claimed, was the core tariff policy – a proposal to secure imperial markets for British producers through preferential tariff agreements with the Colonies. This proposal faced two seemingly insurmountable obstacles. First, the self-governing Colonies, the only worthwhile markets, were lukewarm about imperial economic unity. These Colonies had begun to develop their own industrial base and were not keen to face a flood of British imports. Second, and more important, the only agreement in which the Colonies were interested entailed the Conservatives advocating duties on imported foodstuffs. These 'food taxes' were seized upon by the Liberal and Labour parties as, literally, a bread and butter issue to deploy against the Conservatives. Throughout the Edwardian period the Conservative party's apparent willingness to impose a 'dear loaf' upon the British people was contrasted with their opponents' defence of 'the free breakfast table'. In an electoral system dominated by low earners the Conservatives appeared to be threatening to raise the cost of living, and three general election defeats provide strong *prima facie* evidence that the Conservatives paid a heavy price for their advocacy of 'food taxes'.

The Edwardian Conservative party's general conduct, and its commitment to tariff reform in particular, seem all the more peculiar in the light of the party's previous and subsequent behaviour.[4] From the 1880s to the 1990s the Conservatives have enjoyed a reputation for political sagacity and for closing ranks in the face of adversity. The history of the Conservative party is the history of an institution that has placed a high value on avoiding controversial initiatives and maintaining unity. This pattern of behaviour was established under its archetypal practitioner Lord Salisbury, but it was also a feature of Conservative politics for the greater part of the period between 1918 and 1990, and undoubtedly contributed to the party's success.[5] This is not to say that Conservative politics and policy have lacked drama. The Conservative party has proved quite capable of pursuing novel policy directions, but such innovations have almost invariably been tempered by careful political calculation and electoral experience, and some have been quickly jettisoned as a result of adverse party or public reaction. Furthermore, although the Conservatives have had their share of internal disagreements, the party has tended to settle such disputes relatively quickly. The events of 1922 (ending the Coalition with Lloyd George), 1929, 1945, 1966 and 1974 (the implications of electoral defeat) and 1990 (poll tax) saw the Conservative party engage, both publicly and privately, in quite bitter internal feuds, but in each case the 'crisis' was followed by electoral victory. The Conservative party's reputation for careful manoeuvre, discipline and unity is historically merited, especially when contrasted with the behaviour of rival parties. In the Edwardian period, however, the Conservative party appears to have been anything but sagacious and disciplined. Not only did the Conservatives commit themselves to a new and controversial policy, but they persisted with it in the face of electoral adversity. Moreover, the new initiative provoked opposition within the party, and caused internal disputes of the kind previously (and subsequently) associated with the Conservatives' opponents. The Edwardian Conservatives seem to have set aside all the lessons handed down by Lord Salisbury in a most cavalier fashion, and this at a time when one would have thought that respect for Salisbury's legacy would have been at its height.

Whether the Edwardian Conservative party's own behaviour, and in particular its commitment to tariff reform, was to blame for all its difficulties is open to question. What is clear, however, is that any attempt to understand 'the peculiarities of Edwardian Conservatism' must address the issue of why the party became embroiled in the tariff debate. It may well be that the Conservatives were wrong, or even insane, to adopt tariff reform, but to criticize or ridicule the party's decision does not explain it. The historical issues that must be faced are why the Conservative party turned to tariff reform, why at that time, and why the tariff debate dominated Conservative politics for so long. Here it must be stressed that tariff reform was not some passing fad or a minority taste for Conservatives. The National Union of Conservative Associations (NUCA), representing the party's grass roots, was a haven of pro-tariff sentiment through the Edwardian period, passing motions in favour of tariff reform and other tariff-related policies from 1903 to 1913. In 1905 Arthur Balfour was informed that 172 of his Parliamentary contingent of 374 were committed to 'the full Chamberlainite programme', and that a further seventy-three agreed with Chamberlain but were waiting for the party to adopt his policy 'officially' before declaring themselves publicly.[6] Thus only two years after Chamberlain launched his controversial initiative he appears to have secured the open or tacit support of two-thirds of Conservative MPs. Indeed in December 1905, *before* the Conservatives were decimated by the 'Liberal landslide', the Conservative Chief Whip warned Balfour's Parliamentary Secretary that 'all our men want a definition from the Chief. If they don't get it the majority will follow Chamberlain'.[7] After 1906 the Conservative party's commitment to tariff reform grew still more pronounced. Balfour accepted tariff reform as the party's 'first constructive work', and in 1907, first in a speech at Hull in February and than at the close of the NUCA Conference in November, gave official sanction to tariff reform as a policy of imperial preference, industrial protection and as a means of gathering revenue for unspecified social reforms. By 1909 even, some Conservatives who opposed tariff reform had conceded that tariffs had both tactical and even intrinsic merits,[8] and in the general election of January 1910 every Conservative candidate placed tariff reform at the head of his election address.[9]

After 1906, moreover, the Conservatives developed broader aspects of the tariff campaign that Chamberlain had raised but then largely ignored. In particular tariffs played a central part in the Conservatives' attempt to shape a clear response to the Liberal government's labour and social policies. The only Liberal measures the Conservatives did not mutilate in the House of Lords between 1906 and 1910 were the Trades Disputes Act, the School Meals and School Health measures and the introduction of Old Age Pensions, and they were equally reluctant to voice opposition to such legislation in the Commons or in the country.[10] At the same time the Conservatives brought forward their own positive policy suggestions. The most ambitious ideas were presented in an 'Unauthorized

Programme', which appeared in the *Morning Post* in the autumn of 1908 and called for an extension of the pensions system, a national insurance scheme, land reform, regulation of sweated labour and other measures. Many of these suggestions were taken up by the NUCA Conference that year and by the party hierarchy, and thus even before the founding of the Unionist Social Reform Committee (USRC) in 1911 the Conservatives had a clear social policy agenda.[11] At all levels in the party, however, it was stressed that the only efficient and equitable method of funding such reforms was through revenue from tariffs. This link between tariff reform and social reform had been suggested by Joseph Chamberlain in 1903, but he had not, to the chagrin of many of his followers,[12] developed the theme. In this key area of policy, therefore, the Conservative party adopted and pursued Chamberlain's ideas with a vigour and urgency that the man himself had not matched.

Edwardian Conservative party politics were dominated by tariff reform. Between 1903 and 1906 the party was increasingly under the sway of tariff reformers at most levels and in most regions, and between 1906 and 1910, dissenting voices at both central and local level were isolated. Between 1910 and the outbreak of the Great War the party's commitment weakened, but the tariff campaign and the issues surrounding it remained central to Conservative politics. In many ways the Conservatives became more of a 'tariff reform party' after Joseph Chamberlain was removed from active politics by a stroke, and although his lingering charisma was certainly great it cannot explain the party's overwhelming acceptance of a tariff-based strategy between 1906 and 1910 nor the continued importance of the tariff question thereafter.

One possible explanation for the Conservative party's prolonged interest in tariff reform is that it seems foolhardy only in hindsight, in that whilst the difficulties of tariff reform are obvious to historians, perhaps they were not so clear at the time. But this can hardly have been the case. In the 1880s the National Fair Trade League (NFTL) had campaigned for tariffs on both manufactured and agricultural imports,[13] and had attracted enough Conservative support for sixty Conservative MPs to be known as fair traders.[14] Furthermore, the NUCA had, in the 1880s and 1890s, passed several motions calling for retaliatory tariffs and/or imperial preference. Yet the Conservative party had never made fair trade a frontline issue, in part because the Liberals had raised a 'dear food' cry and the Conservative leadership had considered fair trade an electoral liability. Indeed, after the Conservative defeat at the general election in 1892, Joseph Chamberlain, no less, complained to Arthur Balfour that 'Lord Salisbury's unfortunate allusion to Fair Trade cost us a dozen seats in the counties'.[15] Likewise, the problems of finding an agreement with the Colonies had been very apparent. In the late nineteenth century proposals for closer inter-imperial trade and defence relations had been made at successive Imperial Conferences, but they had foundered on the rocks of Colonial nationalism.[16] The Conservatives' 'persistence . . . in a cause that was so politically disastrous'[17] cannot be explained by their having blundered through ignorance of the possible consequences.

A seemingly more promising line of interpretation is that the Conservative party's adherence to tariff reform was a product of changing social and political alignments within the Conservative party. Here Joseph Chamberlain's prominence in the tariff campaign appears to offer important clues. Chamberlain, of course, was not a Conservative but a Liberal Unionist – one of the renegades of 1886 who had joined forces with the Conservative party in a Unionist alliance, but who were not part of the Tory tradition. If the tariff campaign was Chamberlain's brainchild then perhaps tariff reform was not an authentic Conservative policy, but a radical Liberal Unionist idea.[18] There is some apparently powerful evidence to support this interpretation. A number of the most prominent spokesmen of the tariff campaign, such as Joseph Chamberlain himself, his son Austen, and Alfred Milner, were Liberal Unionists, whilst some of the most vocal opponents of tariff reform were Lords Hugh and Robert Cecil, who, as sons of the great Lord Salisbury, could claim to represent the voice of 'authentic' Conservatism. But above all 'out of their own mouths do we condemn them', for in July 1912 one ardent tariff reformer, Richard Jebb, remarked to the sacked editor of the *Morning Post* that

> the ultimate cause of the trouble at the Morning Post was that we were running a Radical Policy in the name of Conservatism, trying to twist the principles of Conservatism – if it ever had any principles and is not simply temperament – to suit our programme, which was Liberal Unionist. We did it in good faith, but it was a fraud all the same.[19]

Here, surely, is eloquent confirmation that tariff reform was not 'genuine' Conservative politics, but the product of an alien ideology that gained a brief but damaging supremacy over the forces of Conservatism.

The thesis that tariff reform was, in essence, a Liberal Unionist policy is initially compelling, but does not bear close inspection. It is based on two assumptions: first, that the division between the Liberal Unionist and Conservative wings of the Unionist alliance was still significant enough to determine developments on the Right of British politics; second, that Liberal Unionists were the driving force behind tariff reform. But both assumptions are false. The division between Liberal Unionists and Conservatives did not formally end until 1912, when the party organizations were amalgamated, but there was a blurring of distinctions long before the official fusion. Writing to Alfred Lyttelton in December 1894, H.H. Asquith declared 'I confess I regard the nominal distinction between Liberal Unionists and the Conservatives as one which has quite ceased to have any practical meaning'.[20] Asquith was not an unbiased observer, but even at this stage, his views were not unsupported. In 1895 one Conservative writer was arguing that the erosion of differences between the two groups had reached the stage where a formal coalition was desirable,[21] and that very year the Liberal Unionists formed a government with the Conservatives. Some Conservatives did complain that Liberal Unionists received too many Cabinet and junior ministerial positions in 1895. However, Arthur Balfour, commenting on the appointment of the Liberal Unionist Sir Robert Finlay as Solicitor General, told one such complainant that

> so far as opinions are concerned, there is no distinction whatever between an L[iberal] U[nionist] like Finlay and a C[onservative] U[nionist] like, for example, yourself. Indeed, my private opinion is that you would probably be tempted to describe Finlay's opinions as those of a 'bigoted old Tory'.[22]

Balfour concluded by stating that the division was now only a 'difference of name'.[23] Oscar Wilde's Lady Bracknell drew a still finer distinction between the two groups. When she enquired about Jack Worthing's politics he replied 'I really have none. I am a Liberal Unionist'. 'They count as Tories', Lady Bracknell declared, 'They dine with us, or come in the evening at any rate'. Of course all of these commentators had, in one way or another, good reason to play down the differences between Liberal Unionists and Conservatives, and they could be regarded as unreliable witnesses. Simply to take their comments at face value is to risk playing the arbitrary parlour game of whose quotation do I prefer. Rather than depend on this approach it is preferable to examine the evidence, or the lack of it, for serious differences between Liberal Unionists and Conservatives.

In the early 1890s there was some tension between Liberal Unionists and Conservatives. There were a number of disputes at local level over representation,[24] but perhaps more worrying were the religious differences between the two groups. For example, in 1892 Austen Chamberlain's candidacy for East Worcestershire provoked alarm amongst local Conservatives on the grounds that he was not a member of and did not seem to support the Established Church. Arthur Balfour attempted to assuage these concerns, but confessed that 'there are admitted differences', and felt obliged to call for 'forbearance'. At the same time, however, Balfour pointed out, quite rightly, that 'some of the most distinguished members of the Liberal [Unionist] section . . . are among the most strenuous of its [the maintenance of Establishment] advocates'.[25] Whether Balfour's argument won the day, or whether Conservative fears were not that important after all, Austen Chamberlain was returned unopposed and held the seat with no problems for many years. Even on the most potentially divisive religious issue, education, the Liberal Unionists and Conservatives avoided a major split. In both 1896 and 1902 there was significant Liberal Unionist opposition to the education reforms proposed by first Salisbury's and then Balfour's administrations, and there was some evidence of a leakage of Liberal Unionist votes in the constituencies.[26] But on neither occasion did a Liberal Unionist resign from the Cabinet, nor did any Liberal Unionist MP 'cross the floor'. What is more, Joseph Chamberlain publicly defended the 1902 Education Bill and told Balfour that he would resign rather than see the measure dropped.[27]

Arthur Balfour's claim in 1895 that the Liberal Unionist–Conservative divide was only a difference of name was perhaps an exaggeration, but on the evidence of working relations between the two groups it was not wholly misplaced. It is difficult to find points of contention that drew a hard and fast line between Liberal Unionists and Conservatives over policy, and through the 1890s they enjoyed cordial relations.[28] The 'forbearance' demanded by Balfour was one reason for this lack of conflict, but it is also the case that on many issues divisions of opinion cut across the Liberal Unionist–Conservative divide.[29] As Balfour pointed out Church Establishment was one area where the nuances of opinion defied any simple reduction to a Liberal Unionist–Conservative split, and in the 1890s Joseph Chamberlain's suggestions for a more positive social policy gained as much sympathy on the Conservative as on the Liberal Unionist side, and likewise were greeted with as much hostility by some Liberal Unionists as by some Conservatives.[30] In many respects this lack of major disagreement should not come as a surprise. After all, if points of agreement had not outweighed differences the two sides would not have got together in the first place and their alliance would hardly have lasted. Relations between Liberal Unionists and Conservatives were not always easy, but arguably they were often easier than relations *within* the two groups. In the early twentieth century there were still differences between Liberal Unionists and Conservatives, and they should not be ignored, but they were less important than they had once been and were fading fast.[31] Certainly the Liberal Unionists were remarkably careless about maintaining a separate identity. In the 1890s little or no attempt was made to strengthen the Liberal Unionist presence in the constituencies, and in the House of Lords Liberal Unionist and Conservative identities had effectively merged by the turn of the century.[32] The Liberal Unionist–Conservative divide was not meaningless, but one must get the division in perspective, and the difference was simply not significant enough to determine events in and after 1903.

Apart from the fact that the Liberal Unionist–Conservative divide will not bear the explanatory weight demanded of it, there are other problems with seeing tariff reform as a Liberal Unionist policy. To begin with radical Liberal Unionists were not the driving force of tariff reform, and its most enthusiastic supporters were drawn from a cross-section of the Unionist alliance. In particular Joseph Chamberlain found some of his most committed support amongst the most traditional sector of the Conservative party, the aristocracy,[33] and if many leaders of county society threw their weight behind tariff reform so too did much of the farming community, with the old 'Squire', Henry Chaplin, emerging as one of the most ardent tariff protagonists.[34] But doubts about the Liberal Unionist credentials of the tariff campaign are not only prompted by the personnel involved. Even more important, it is difficult to see tariff reform emerging from a distinctive Liberal Unionist ideology. In this context it is helpful, in the first instance, to take up the views of Richard Jebb. Jebb's correspondence with Fabian Ware, as noted above, has been seen as a confession of Liberal Unionist responsibility for tariff reform, but, as is frequently the case, an uncorroborated confession and a failure to disclose all the evidence have led to an unsafe conviction. Jebb, it will be remembered, argued in July 1912 that the *Morning Post*, by supporting tariff reform, had been running a Liberal Unionist policy in the name of Conservatism, and that this 'fraud' had led to Ware being replaced as editor. Indeed, Jebb had stated these views at an earlier date, arguing in January 1912 that 'the Morning Post, having changed its editor, last spring, has reverted to machine Conservatism'.[35] And yet, Ware's replacement at the *Morning Post*, H.A. Gwynne, was equally committed to tariff reform, and both he and the paper were critical of the party leadership when the tariff policy was softened in the winter of 1912–13 – strange manifestations of 'machine Conservatism'.[36] Similar problems surround yet another piece of evidence that at first glance portrays tariff reform as 'unequivocally' Liberal Unionist. In February 1906, following the Liberal landslide in which Balfour lost his seat, there was an intense debate in the Conservative ranks over both policy and the party leadership.[37] Lord Balcarres noted, however, that there was no chance of Joseph Chamberlain replacing Balfour as leader because 'the Conservative party, to use Walter Long's words, "will not be led by a bloody Radical" '.[38] Yet in the same diary entry Balcarres also noted that 'His [Chamberlain's] policy is clearly more acceptable than Balfour's to the party', but that '[t]he majority of Tariff Reformers ... prefer A.J.B. as leader'.[39] In other words the Conservative party distinguished between Chamberlain's person and his policy. A moment's reflection on the Conservative party's long-term history, and in particular the sub-cultures of late-nineteenth-century Conservatism, indicates why Chamberlain's policy was popular with the party. The Conservatives had, of course, defended the Corn Laws in 1846, and protectionist sentiments had continued to lurk beneath the surface of mid-Victorian Conservative politics. Disraeli was the first leading politician to advocate some form of economic union to bring about imperial federation, whilst in the 1880s and 1890s the NUCA had expressed overwhelming support for tariffs, and many Conservative MPs had openly declared their sympathy for fair trade, imperial preference and even a return to agricultural protection. If tariffs were part of a distinctive political tradition it was a Tory tradition.

A simple party-political divide on the Right cannot explain the advent and longevity of tariff reform, but perhaps a socio-economic division offers a more promising avenue of interpretation. Here, once again, Joseph Chamberlain stands as a paradigm case, in that his background, as a Birmingham businessman, seems to indicate that tariff reform was a manufacturers' policy.[40] This was certainly a view common at the time. As well as Liberal and Labour party propaganda about the 'tariff millions' provided by business support,[41] some Conservatives characterized tariff reform as an industrial policy, with Lord Robert Cecil remarking in his memoirs that one of his main objections to tariff reform had been that with the tariff campaign '[t]he dominance of the landowner was at an end ... his place was taken by the business man'.[42] That the tariff campaign was inaugurated by a man who had made his reputation as a representative of provincial, industrial interests, and ended with an aristocratic patrician, Arthur Balfour, being replaced as Conservative leader by a tariff-reforming Glasgow ironmaster, Andrew Bonar Law, appears to confirm this interpretation. Tariff reform, it seems, was indicative of the rising power of the urban, industrial middle classes and their villa-dwelling clientilists in Conservative political circles – a symbol of the *embourgeoisement* of British Conservatism.

However, the idea that tariff reform was a manufacturers' policy is deeply flawed. In particular, the deep commitment of many aristocratic and rural Conservatives to the tariff cause makes it very difficult to accept tariff reform as the result of pressure from urban Conservatives. Indeed, membership of the most fanatical tariff reform grouping within the Conservative party, the Confederacy,[43] was deliberately kept 'wholly free from ... manufacturers'.[44] Nor are the diverse social origins of tariff reform personnel the only problem with the 'industrial' thesis. The actual structure of the tariff policy itself demonstrates a strong agricultural input. The range of duties on agricultural produce incorporated in the tariff programme between 1903 and 1913 went far beyond that required for imperial preference, for the simple reason that these duties were explicitly advocated as assistance for Britain's agricultural sector. Moreover, a broad range of non-fiscal agricultural initiatives were tacked on to the tariff programme, and debate on rural policy and rural needs played a central role in the work of various tariff reform committees and pressure groups.[45] Neither in terms of personnel nor substantive content can the tariff campaign be described as a policy designed by or for industrialists.

That the 'industrial' and 'Liberal Unionist' theses are open to many of the same objections is in part a product of their being based on similar premises. In particular, both see the events of 1886 as essential to an explanation of tariff reform. The 'industrial' thesis emphasizes the changing socio-economic basis of the Conservative party, and in this context the gravitation of the Liberal Unionists to the political Right appears as a critical point in a more general shift of urban and middle-class wealth to Conservatism in the late nineteenth and early twentieth century. The 'Liberal Unionist' thesis places greater emphasis on the specifically political aspects of the realignment of 1886, although there is an implicit assumption that the the changing socio-economic base of Conservatism created a more receptive climate for 'Liberal Unionist' ideas. The contention of this study is that neither of these interpretations does justice to the origins and development of the tariff debate. The 'industrial' thesis presents what is essentially an economically determinist explanation of tariff reform, in which the changing social base of the Conservative party determines the emergence and structure of tariff reform. In the 'Liberal Unionist' thesis the changing political base of Conservatism determines the tariff superstructure. This study would agree that developments in the 1880s were indeed crucial in shaping the tariff debate, but it will also argue that only a more subtle examination of the relationship between the politics and economics of tariffs allows one to grasp fully why tariff reform became the dominant issue in Conservative politics in the early twentieth century.

UNDERSTANDING TARIFF REFORM: THE CRISIS OF CONSERVATISM

Ultimately, the reason the Conservative party embraced the politics of tariff reform in the early twentieth century is the one usually given by miscreant teenagers – it seemed like a good idea at the time. This stemmed not from the party being influenced by a charismatic individual, or by an alien ideology, or by a new social elite, or even by sheer stupidity. Rather tariff reform, a multifaceted policy structure, seemed to the bulk of the Conservative party to offer solutions to a set of difficulties which reached their peak in the Edwardian period, but which had their roots in the way the Conservative party's identity interacted with and was affected by changes in the patterns of British economic, social and political life in the late nineteenth and early twentieth century.

In the last quarter of the nineteenth century Britain's position in the world underwent a major change. The almost unrivalled imperial and economic supremacy which Britain had enjoyed in the mid-Victorian period was challenged by the emergent military and industrial might of Germany, the United States and other powers. What troubled many contemporaries was the question of whether Britain was equal to this challenge. In *The Expansion of England* J.R. Seeley argued that 'For establishing the stability of an Empire there are certain plain tests which the political student ought to have at his fingers' ends. Of these some are applied to its internal organization and some to its external conditions'.[46] In applying these 'plain tests' many late-nineteenth-century commentators drew the conclusion that the British Empire was faced with severe difficulties. Concern about Britain's apparently deteriorating military position was manifested in a number of ways. To begin with there were the findings of the 1879 Royal Commission on Imperial Defence, which were considered too alarming to be made public.[47] What could not be kept secret, however, were Britain's reversals during the Boer War, which confirmed many misgivings about Britain's military organization and pushed military reform into the realm of public debate.[48] If the army was the subject of the greatest criticism the navy did not go unscathed. Rapid advances in naval technology raised questions about the obsolescence of Britain's ageing fleet, and in the 1890s a series of disastrous naval exercises seemed to indicate that most barn doors were safe from the guns of the Royal Navy whilst British ships were not safe from each other.[49] The cost of maintaining the Navy, let alone bringing it up to date, was constantly increasing and doubts were cast on the financial viability of maintaining a 'two-power' standard.[50] The navy race with Germany only served to exacerbate and publicize Britain's naval difficulties, whilst a combination of aggressive journalism, the activities of the Navy League, and the celebrated dispute between Admirals Fisher and Beresford, served to keep naval questions before the public. Given the depth of official and public concern about Britain's military situation it is hardly surprising that the genre of 'invasion literature' flourished at this time.[51] Whether authors like G.T. Chesney, Erskine Childers or William Le Queux, who poured a variety of invaders into a Britain bursting at the seams with foreign agents, helped to create or simply fed off these concerns is a moot point,[52] but it is perhaps enough to note that anyone with a tale to tell about Britain's military-imperial insecurity found a receptive audience.

Concern over Britain's economic performance was also rife in the late nineteenth and early twentieth century.[53] Two Royal Commissions on Agriculture (RCAD) produced gloomy conclusions about the state of British agriculture, and even the 1885 Royal Commission on the Depression of Trade and Industry (RCDTI), noted, as a rider to its fairly optimistic general conclusion, that 'there is one important branch of industry which must be excepted. We refer of course to agriculture'.[54] British industry too was thought to have its problems. As with agriculture, contemporary concern about industry prompted both official and unofficial investigation and alarm, ranging from the setting up of the RCDTI to the 'Made in Germany' scares of the 1890s. Whether or not the developments in both agriculture and manufacturing indicated that the British economy was in *decline* was, and indeed still is, a matter of debate. Recent studies of the period have tended to see structural change rather than decline as the chief characteristic of the British economy in the late nineteenth and early twentieth century. In particular Sir John Clapham's idea of a 'great hinge', which swung wealth, economic activity and also population away from the industrial North and Midlands towards the tertiary sector and the South and South-East, has been confirmed. However, as this study will seek to demonstrate, some contemporary observers felt that the changes described by modern scholarship were themselves evidence of decline, insofar as they felt that such changes were neither welcome nor healthy.

Concern over Britain's economic performance was complemented by disquiet over social problems, especially poverty, but also old age, health, conditions of work and housing. To some degree the poor and deprived made their presence felt through direct action, in the shape of the publicity that surrounded the riots and strikes in London in the mid- to late 1880s. Likewise the emergence of Socialist organizations and more widespread trade union activity seemed to indicate that the poorer elements of society were seeking to find an independent, militant voice to express deep-seated grievances. It was also the case that a series of investigations of poverty produced some alarming results, the most famous being Charles Booth and Seebohm's Rowntree's studies, which indicated that almost one third of, respectively, London's East End and York were living in poverty. Such 'revelations', coupled with the fact that the franchise was extended to a large section of the poorer classes, propelled social policy towards the centre of politics.[55] From the early 1880s, the 'condition of the people' was an issue that few in public life could avoid hearing about or addressing.

These varied but widespread concerns over apparent flaws in Britain's international and domestic situation led to doubts being raised over maxims of policy, especially economic policy, that had seemed set during the mid-Victorian boom. As confidence in Britain's imperial and economic ascendancy receded, and as social progress, prosperity and peace no longer seemed assured, so a broad spectrum of opinion expressed doubts over the infallibility of liberal economics, and it is partly within this context that the genesis and development of tariff reform must be set. The tariff debate was one strand in a more general questioning of Britain's adherence to liberal economics that marked political and economic debate in the late nineteenth and early twentieth century, which emerged from a general sense that all was not well with Britain's imperial, economic and social life.

But if tariff reform can be seen as emerging from a general debate this still leaves the question as to its prominence in a particular political context. It is here that tariff reform must be seen as the product of a dynamic relationship between questions of decline and the question of Conservative identity. A number of general problems were prompted by Britain's changing external and internal situation in the late nineteenth and early twentieth century. Could or should the Empire survive? Was the British economy unhealthy or sound? Should the State play a greater role in promoting the material well-being of its citizenry, especially the poorer classes? If the State was to play a more active role where was its assistance most needed, and who amongst the citizenry would pay for this enhanced role? Did the concept of citizenship itself need to be redefined? Could British society and the British polity adjust to the problems of a maturing economy without major or violent upheaval? These problems faced politicians of all hues and provoked debate within as well as between the major political parties. The break-up of the Gladstonian Liberal party, the Liberals' prolonged internal crisis of the 1880s and 1890s, and the emergence of the New Liberalism were products of the Liberal party's effort to produce a distinctively *Liberal* answer to these questions. Likewise, the Conservatives had to find answers that were recognizably *Conservative*, and the tariff debate was a symptom of the party's ongoing effort to produce them. In the Edwardian period, just as the New Liberalism and indeed Liberal Imperialism were part of the Liberal party's attempt to recast its identity and produce a positive solution to the problems outlined above, so the tariff debate was part of a similar Conservative project.

In the last quarter of the nineteenth century the Conservative party's identity was clear – it was the party of property, the party of Empire and the party of the Church. This study will concentrate most of its attention on the Conservatives' position as party of property and Empire. That it devotes relatively little attention to the Church aspect of the Conservative identity is a quite deliberate omission. It may have been the case that the Church of England remained 'the Tory party at prayer', but there were growing doubts, not least amongst Conservatives themselves, as to whether they could remain 'the Church of England at politics'. One of the most interesting features of Conservative politics in the Edwardian period is that, after 1902 at any rate, religious issues loomed very small. Even Welsh disestablishment was treated as a matter of primary importance by only a small minority of Conservatives, and certainly the tariff debate, apart from the metaphor of heresy, was free of the theological undercurrents that had characterized debates on free trade in the early nineteenth century.[56] Rightly or wrongly, but in any case understandably, the Conservative party, especially in the Edwardian period, looked primarily to the secular aspects of its identity to define its political *raison d'être*, and this study will seek to explain why this was the case and why the tariff debate was symptomatic of this development.

The Conservative party began to establish itself as the party of property under Disraeli, but consolidated this position in the early years of Salisbury's leadership. This development was essential for the party to remain a viable political force. Until the 1870s the Conservatives had been associated with the land, but economic and demographic change, especially migration from rural areas after 1850, shifted the balance of population and ultimately political representation from the countryside to urban areas. If the Conservative party had remained the political arm of the landed interest it would have been marginalized. Thus in the last quarter of the nineteenth century the Conservatives reached out to new urban and suburban interests and became the party of property in general.[57] In an age when property and power were closely related, the construction of an alliance between landed and urban property made sense, but it also posed problems. To begin with there was the issue of the status of urban elites and supporters in the Conservative structure. Landed snobbery and fear of usurpation was often matched by urban resentment of aristocratic 'dilettantism' and the 'booby' squirearchy. This was not just a question of bridging social distinctions; the questions of how the Conservative party was managed and by whom were at issue. In addition there was the problem of whether the demands of the various sections of propertied society could be reconciled and satisfied by the Conservative party. Had not rural and urban interests fought out the great set-piece battle over free trade in the 1840s? Such was the common perception of relations between town and country, aristocracy and 'millocracy' embedded in British political mythology. Could the different and sometimes conflicting interests of Britain's propertied elites be balanced? This problem was complicated by the 'Great Depression' and the maturing of the British economy. During the mid-Victorian boom most sectors of the economy had seemed to prosper without assistance and hence without envy, but the cyclical downturns and increased foreign competition of the late nineteenth and early twentieth century saw demands for State aid from both rural and urban interests. An ongoing task for the Conservative party was thus to construct a strategy that pulled together the various and sometimes conflicting elements and interests of propertied society.

A further difficulty for the 'party of property' was that successive electoral reforms led, by the mid-1880s, to the creation of a mass, propertyless electorate. In the first place this necessitated a new approach to politics. The secret ballot (1872), limits on personal expenditure by candidates (1883) and the impact of redistribution (1885) meant that the electorate was less open to 'influence' than in former times. As a consequence informal networks of patronage and personal authority were increasingly ineffective as the sole basis of political organization: new structures and a professionalized party bureaucracy at both central and local level were requirements for coping with 'the democracy'. The 'age of the masses' also raised question marks over the political utility of the link between Conservatism and Anglicanism. A major concern of the Conservative party and its propertied supporters was that class rather than community or religious allegiance would shape voting behaviour as the masses sought to improve their material existence. Revelations about the poor condition of the people strengthened this belief that mass enfranchisement would result in the secularization and class polarization of politics. The Conservative party thus faced the questions of how the party of property was to appeal to a propertyless electorate on secular terms and how to defend property against a major secular enemy, Socialism, which first raised its head in the 1880s but emerged as a serious challenge in the Edwardian period. Hence another ongoing task for the Conservative party was to construct an effective 'top-down' appeal to the masses and secure popular support for, or at least acquiesence in, the prevailing distribution of power and resources.

The Conservatives' role as the party of Empire was also begun under Disraeli and confirmed under Salisbury. This process saw the Conservatives equate the interests of the nation with the Empire and defence of the Empire with their party. The Conservatives thereby identified themselves as the guardians of nation and Empire, in deliberate contrast to Liberal 'sectionalism', as epitomized by the Liberal party's support for Irish Nationalism, Home Rule and an assault on the integrity of the heart of Empire. This role seemed to offer the Conservatives a means of addressing both propertied and non-propertied audiences. To begin with it allowed them to appeal to groups who saw their social, economic and political interests as linked, directly or indirectly, to imperial expansion or consolidation. At the same time the appeal of Empire was potentially cross-class, and held out the possibility of both garnering mass support and forestalling the development of class politics through popular patriotism. However, being the party of Empire also brought problems. First, there was the question of how the party of Empire was to cope with the challenge of the rival imperial powers and the apparent relative decline in Britain's military, economic and imperial status. Second, there was a problem of costs in terms of maintaining imperial defence and boosting development in new territories. Third, there was the issue of the imperial structure itself, and in particular how the aspirations of the self-governing dominions could be satisfied within the imperium. Finally, there was the issue of what British interests wanted from Empire, and whether they all wanted the same thing. These questions confronted all politicians, but they had a particular resonance for the self-appointed guardians of national and imperial interests.

The difficulty for the Conservatives was not that they were unable to produce answers to these questions, but that they produced too many.

Between 1880 and 1900 the Conservative party's internal debate over how it should respond to the problems arising out of Britain's seeming relative decline, the advent of the mass electorate, the condition of the people, and the emergence of Socialism was kept to manageable proportions. That the Liberal party was thrown into a prolonged identity crisis by the same problems was of considerable assistance to the Conservatives. This, along with Lord Salisbury's skills, an excellent party organization, and the survival, much against expectation, of some traditional forms of associational politics, enabled the Conservatives to secure a string of political and electoral triumphs.[58] As a consequence the values, institutions and interests with which Conservatism was associated seemed secure from internal disruption. The Empire at its moment of danger was safe from unsympathetic 'Little Englander' management, and property was secure from Socialism. The external challenge to British imperial and economic interests from foreign competitors was another matter. Here there was growing disquiet by the end of the century. But even in this more troubled area Salisbury's skilful diplomacy both at home and abroad, coupled with a general confidence in the competence and sympathy of Conservative governments kept debate over the party's outlook and strategy within close confines. Thus although there were competing conceptions of the Conservative identity in the Salisburyian era they rarely produced significant disruptions, largely because the challenges and problems posed to the Conservatives' position as the party of Empire and the party of property seemed by a mixture of good management and good luck to have been kept at an acceptable level.

After 1900 the question of how to express the Conservatives' identity as party of Empire and property, and thereby hold together the coalition of forces that had sustained it in power in the Salisburyian years, became more problematic. With regard to the Empire a key episode was the Boer War. When in 1900 L.T. Hobhouse described the Boer War as 'the test issue of this generation' his central concern was to draw a line through the Left of British politics. But the Boer War had even greater significance for the Right. Conservatives had few qualms about whether the war was 'wrong', but what did concern them was the fact that the mightiest Empire ever known took four years, lost thousands of lives and spent millions of pounds subduing 'a little people, few but apt in the field'.[59] Given the growing concern over Britain's ability to defend the Empire against other great powers the Boer War was hardly reassuring: as one of H.G. Wells's characters put it 'our Empire was nearly beaten by a handful of farmers amidst the jeering contempt of the world ... [and] we felt it acutely for several years'.[60] It is difficult to overstate the sense of inadequacy which the Boer War induced. Alfred Milner, who, as High Commissioner, had, along with Joseph Chamberlain, done most to shape

British policy in South Africa before and during the war, argued in January 1902 that

> the condition of South Africa today is a most bitter commentary on our supposed imperial strength. Here is a single Colony, not by any means one of the largest in the Empire, in which a bare majority of disaffected people is able to disorganize our whole South African policy ... and threaten the foundations of the Empire itself.[61]

Besides military reversals and administrative inadequacies, the much-publicized fact that the great 'imperial race' had had many of its potential army recruits rejected on medical grounds sent a further shock-wave through the British body politic.[62] The British Empire had been tested and found wanting, and whilst the sense of crisis the war engendered affected all sections of political opinion it had a special significance for the self-professed party of Empire.

In the wake of the Boer War many Conservatives questioned the way their party had governed the Empire in the late nineteenth century, with the result that there was a proliferation of views about how to make up for various shortcomings. At the highest level the 'diplomatic revolution' of 1902–4, which saw the alliance with Japan and entente with France, represented an acknowledgement that Britain's isolation was no longer so splendid and that there was a need to reshape Britain's world role.[63] The army reforms proposed by the Conservative War Ministers St John Brodrick and H.O. Arnold-Forster between 1902–5, and the enquiries into the nation's food supply and physical deterioration, were also attempts by the 1900–5 Conservative government to deal with criticisms, not least from their own back benches, supporters and newspapers, about their governance and defence of the Empire.[64] But in spite of these developments there were many who felt that the Conservative party needed to go further, and the early twentieth century witnessed a proliferation of organizations arguing for a strengthening of both Britain's and the Empire's structure and defences. For example the National Service League (NSL) campaigned for the introduction of compulsory military service, whilst a reinvigorated Navy League (NL) and a splinter movement, the Imperial Maritime League (IML), called for an expansion and modernization of the navy.[65] From several quarters, but notably from within its own ranks, the Conservative party was pressed to act decisively to restore its credibility as the party of Empire.

Nor was the Conservatives' position as the party of property stable. In the 1880s and 1890s relations between the Conservatives' new urban elites/supporters and their traditional allies in the counties were for the most part fairly cordial. Towards the end of the century the party faced particularly strong pressures to give more assistance to British agriculture, which presented a dilemma. If assistance was not granted it could upset the farming community; if it was, urban interests might be equally upset at the 'special status' enjoyed by rural communities. Indeed with both farming and industrial lobbies becoming better organized and more assertive the problem of harmonizing the interests of the Conservatives' core constituents was becoming more arduous. There were no signs of an imminent crisis at the turn of the century, but the question of how to integrate a set of stratified propertied interests was a constant constraint on Conservative politics. In part Salisburyian Conservatism was able to hold the ring for its varied propertied interests because the party fulfilled its defensive role very well, in that it seemed to control the mass electorate and forestall a Socialist threat. However, in the Edwardian period the situation changed. The Conservative party's electoral performance was poor and it faced new and more threatening opponents. The 1906 general election was a key episode here. It was not simply that the Conservatives lost, or even the dramatic reduction in their Parliamentary contingent, that was so worrying, but rather the trends in British politics which the election was taken to indicate. Arthur Balfour, not normally given to hyperbole, told Lady Salisbury that 'CB [Campbell-Bannerman, the Liberal leader] is a mere cork bobbing on a torrent that he cannot control. The result of the recent election is part of the same phenomenon which has led to demonstrations in Berlin and riots in St Petersberg'.[66] The election of fifty-four Labour representatives was seen as bad enough in itself, but between 1906 and 1910 the Liberal party's willingness to introduce social reforms for the poor at the expense of the rich, and its appeal to the mass electorate in class terms, indicated that Socialism had become a real threat.[67] In the 1880s and 1890s Salisbury's adroit political management and electoral success had seemed to defend property effectively, but in the early years of the twentieth century Salisburyian Conservatism, even in the subtle hands of Arthur Balfour, no longer seemed able to control the masses. Confidence in the Salisburyian approach thus receded, and many Conservatives felt compelled to search for a new strategy that would appeal to the mass electorate and stem the rise of Socialism.

As with the Empire, the challenge to property saw a cluster of new organizations and some rejuvenated older groups press for greater vigilance in dealing with the 'Socialist menace'. The Anti-Socialist Union (ASU), the British Constitutional Association (BCA) and the Middle-Class Defence League (MCDL) joined the Liberty and Property Defence League (LPDL) and the London Municipal Society (LMS) in the war against Socialism. This 'legion of leagues' that emerged on the Right is worth dwelling upon. Many of these organizations referred to themselves as 'non-party', in that they defined their aims as 'national' or 'imperial' and above mere party politics.[68] In fact it is clear that these organizations had an overwhelmingly Conservative membership, and that they can be

19

regarded as attempts to increase public interest in and support for values, interests and institutions associated with Conservatism. Likewise the timing of their appearance can be explained on the grounds that prior to the early twentieth century 'the Conservatives had no need of recourse to such pressure groups because they already possessed access to institutions adequate for the defence of their interests within the existing sociopolitical framework'.[69] In other words, the Conservative party became interested in new forms of appeal and organization when it became apparent that support for, and hence the security of, the Empire and property could no longer be ensured by older forms of social and political control. This is to describe the 'legion of leagues' from the top down, and to identify them as part of a 'technique of rule' through which the Conservative party attempted to confront new challenges. Another way of viewing them, however, is from the bottom up: as expressions of concern about the ability of the Conservative party adequately to meet new challenges to the Empire and property. That there should have been a Navy League or an Anti-Socialist Union at all is significant, given that the Conservative party was supposed to be the party of the Navy and the party of anti-Socialism. That these leagues were filled with Conservatives is evidence that there were many Conservative supporters who felt that the party was not doing its job properly. On this basis there is reason for taking the 'non-party' claims of these groups seriously, for they were frequently critical of the Conservative party and often expressed strong reservations about its effectiveness. There were occasions when the leagues assisted the party, and hence they often received money from Conservative Central Office (CCO), but it was not always easy to control their activities and their relationship with the party was often ambivalent and sometimes hostile.[70] The 'legion of leagues' were as much a symbol of confusion as innovation in Conservative politics, and reflected the Edwardian Conservative party's basic problem of constructing a new definition and defence of its political identity and its core and potential constituency.

It is within the context of the Conservative party's efforts to reconstruct its identity and redefine its constituency that the tariff reform campaign must be understood. As the party of Empire the Conservatives had to confront Britain's apparent imperial weakness, as the party of property they had to confront the most serious challenge yet faced from the Left, and if they were to be the effective party of anything they had to win elections. As the Conservative party confronted these problems tariff reform came to be regarded as almost a *deus ex machina*. To understand how and why this happened it is essential to appreciate that tariff reform was not a unitary or unchanging policy. Between May 1903, when Chamberlain first propelled tariff reform to the centre of British politics, and January 1910, when the Conservative party fought a general election on a tariff

20

reform ticket, the shape of the tariff campaign changed dramatically. It evolved over time, gathering new aspects and different emphases as it was used to address different audiences and problems.

When Joseph Chamberlain first hit upon and then launched the tariff campaign, between May 1902 and May 1903, the focus was on imperial issues. This is understandable given, first, that Chamberlain's own career had been tied to the Empire since his acceptance of the Colonial Secretaryship in 1895, and, second, that in the wake of the Boer War strengthening the Empire's economic, diplomatic and military position was considered, particularly by the Conservative party, a matter of prime importance. In this respect tariff reform, in its first phase, offered a way of restoring the Conservatives' credibility as the party of Empire. Furthermore, Chamberlain argued that these proposals would win broad electoral support, in that popular enthusiasm for the Empire, and the employment benefits gained from imperial markets, would ensure mass support, whilst the profits from secure and expanding imperial trade would ensure business support. However, by the autumn of 1903, when Chamberlain 'carried the fiery cross' to the constituencies, the tariff policy had been broadened from the suggestion for a preferential duty on corn to a programme that included an all-round tariff on manufactures, and duties on meat, dairy produce and vegetables. The political logic of this expanded programme followed its economic logic. Preference by itself could only have a direct interest for employers and employees in the export sector: it offered no benefits to those industries concerned about import penetration and had little or nothing to offer agriculture. Chamberlain was aware of the opposition a 'lop-sided' programme could generate, and the tariff schema that emerged in the autumn of 1903 was an attempt to avoid such an imbalance. Similar motives were at work in the setting up of the Tariff Commission in early 1904. Its task was to structure a 'scientific' tariff, but in effect this meant designing a tariff that would attract as many and alienate as few interests as possible.[71] There was, however, a widely-recognized flaw in the tariff structure. The 'food taxes', incorporated for the sake of both preference and British agriculture, were acknowledged, even by Chamberlain himself, to be electorally dangerous. Hence could tariffs be used to offer any 'compensation' to the masses for the 'dear loaf'? Secure employment was one thing, but in the summer of 1903 Chamberlain hinted that revenue from tariffs could be used to pay for social reforms. Chamberlain seemed to abandon this idea almost as soon as he raised it, even though many of his 'followers' did not, but after 1906 it was resurrected with a vengeance, and revenue tariffs as a means of funding social reform became a central part of both the tariff and Conservative policy agenda. In addition tariffs, both as protective and revenue devices, were presented as the basis of a Conservative land reform project to halt and even reverse rural depopulation by the creation of small holdings.[72] Agricultural workers were to have an opportunity to escape their position as 'wage slaves', whilst urban workers, perhaps migrants from the country themselves, were to have the opportunity to escape the over-supplied labour markets of Britain's industrial centres.[73]

From an argument for uniting the Empire, tariff reform burgeoned into a programme that also encompassed policies for the defence of British industry, the implementation and funding of social reform and the defence and indeed regeneration of British agriculture. That the tariff programme evolved in this way was a result of a dialectic between the internal dynamics of Conservative politics and developments on the Left. In the summer of 1903 the call for imperial preference had an immediate appeal to a substantial section of Conservative opinion that desired to see the imperial system strengthened against external threats and internal weakness. At the same time the possibility that a crusade for imperial unity could boost the Conservatives' already flagging electoral fortunes increased its purchase. But there were obvious objections too, in that the policy as initially announced had the potential to alienate the mass vote and divide propertied interests. The last problem was partially overcome by the broadening of the tariff programme in the autumn of 1903 and the work of the Tariff Commission, but the problem of the mass vote remained. Indeed, some Conservative opponents of tariff reform blamed the Conservatives' catastrophic defeat in 1906 on the 'food taxes'. However, it was at this juncture that developments on the Left strengthened the appeal of tariffs. The Liberal government, in alliance with the Labour party, appeared committed to the politics of class jealousy, introducing social reform and promising material benefits to the masses at the expense of the propertied classes. This was threatening and, even more worrying, it seemed popular. In the face of this challenge tariff reform offered the Conservatives a positive alternative to 'Socialist' social reform. In part this was simply because tariffs were a 'non-confiscatory' means of raising revenue, but there was more to it than that. The full tariff programme, as it had evolved by circa 1909, had become an alternative *system* of political economy which was to unite different economic sectors, different social classes and different branches of the imperial race under the umbrella of a national–imperial economic structure.

The full tariff programme was an economics of political integration, and as such it appeared to offer a solution to the key problems the Conservative party faced. For the party of Empire the imperial aspect of the tariff programme offered three things. First, and most straightforward, it held out the prospect of imperial strength through unity in an increasingly hostile world of large-scale States. Second, imperial preference was to reconcile the economic aspirations of Mother country and Colonies, and thereby avoid the necessity for greater Colonial independence. Third, it was to demonstrate the benefits of Empire to broad sections of the electorate and convince them that the Conservatives were still the only true party of Empire. For the party of property the tariff programme offered two things. First, the balanced tariff benefits offered to industrial and agricultural interests were to cement town and country in a joint campaign against liberal political economy. Second, tariffs were to demonstrate the unity of capital and labour in defence of national production, provide revenue for social reforms, and compensate employers for any additional input costs that social or factory legislation caused. In other words they were to provide a positive alternative to counter the appeal of Socialism. Ultimately, the tariff programme, as it evolved between 1903 and 1910, represented a *Radical Conservative* strategy for restructuring the Conservative party's identity. The term Radical Conservative has been used here in preference to Radical Right in order to differentiate developments on the British Right from those on the continent.[74] In the European context the term Radical Right has been used to describe proto-Fascist groups and ideas that flourished in the period before 1914.[75] A characteristic feature of these patterns of thought was that they viewed the existing condition of society as flawed, corrupt and in need of fundamental revision, if necessary by violent action.[76] Such extreme views were not part of the political project envisaged by supporters of the full tariff programme.[77] It was certainly a Radical project in that its policy proposals represented a break with established patterns of economic and imperial policy and in that it sought to mobilize mass support, but it was explicitly Conservative in that it sought to defend existing institutions and the prevailing distribution of social, economic and political power.

The 'peculiarities of Edwardian Conservatism' were the product of the Conservative party's attempt to reconstruct its identity in a period when older strategies and traditional forms of political and social authority were thought to have failed. In retrospect the Conservative party may seem to have acted in a misguided or even irrational way, but then the values, interests and institutions with which the party was most closely associated seemed to be seriously threatened, and desperate times call for desperate remedies. To Edwardian Conservatives a Radical Conservative strategy, based on tariff reform in its various guises, seemed for a time the most effective weapon they could summon to deal with the difficult issues confronting them. That it ultimately provided no remedy for the party's problems and may even have worsened them simply indicates, thankfully for historians, that outcomes do not always match intentions.

Part I
QUESTIONS OF DECLINE

1

THE POLITICAL ECONOMY
OF DECLINE

The immense echo of my father's speech in May 1903 is inexplicable
unless it is appreciated that the train was already laid.
(A. Chamberlain to B. Dugdale, 4 March 1931)[1]

The question of 'fiscal reform', which has now burst into so violent
a flame, is not new: it has feebly smouldered for many years.
(A.J. Balfour to Devonshire, 27 August 1903)[2]

The circumstances in which Austen Chamberlain and Arthur Balfour
produced these statements could not have been more different.
Chamberlain's reflection came at the end of a long career, whereas
Balfour's was produced at the height of the Cabinet crisis sparked by the
opening of the tariff debate. Yet both statements offer insights into the
genesis of the tariff reform campaign. As Chamberlain argued, the train
of the tariff debate was ignited long before 1903: the issues, as Balfour
told Devonshire, had been part of the sub-culture of British politics and
economics for some years. Indeed, one of the most important aspects
about the nature and timing of the tariff controversy is that it was not a
random development, but the culmination of a political and economic
debate rooted in the 1880s and 1890s, which focused on the question of
the continued prosperity and security of Britain and the Empire.

Military concerns should not be underestimated as a contributory factor
in creating the climate of opinion which shaped the tariff controversy. The
Conservative party sought to contrast its concern for Britain's military
effectiveness with the neglect of such matters by 'Little Englander'
Liberals.[3] Consequently it was effected by the *fin de siècle* sense of
impending doom which saw unpleasant comparisons with Rome become
commonplace.[4] The argument for imperial organization, which was such
a vital part of the tariff campaign, must be viewed as emerging from a
general sense of imperial insecurity which had a particular resonance for
British Conservatives. It will not be the task of this study to explore in full
the military or 'external' aspects of the question of decline.[5] Instead this
book will concentrate on the internal aspect of decline, and in particular

on how contemporary analysis of Britain's economic situation in the late nineteenth century helped set the tariff controversy alight.

AN ECONOMIC CRISIS?

Between 1870 and 1914 the British economy underwent a number of changes. The most obvious was in the agricultural sector.[6] Agriculture's share of Britain's GNP fell from 20 per cent in 1860 to a mere 7 per cent by 1914. This decline was matched by the fact that agricultural output did not increase in absolute terms over the period. But import penetration of the British market increased markedly, with imports of grain, for example, showing a fourfold rise. The Royal Commissions which investigated the condition of agriculture painted a portrait of decay. Even the 1885 RCDTI, which produced a fairly optimistic *Final Report*, noted that 'In stating this general conclusion there is one important branch of industry which must be excepted. We refer, of course, to agriculture'.[7] The rural community gave eloquent expression to their views on the situation by voting with their feet – Britain's farm population fell by one-quarter between 1860 and 1914 and the rural population as a whole by one-third.[8] There were regional variations in agricultural fortunes and in the circumstances the agricultural sector showed remarkable resilience,[9] but the 'golden age' of high farming had passed.

For the rest of the British economy a complex picture emerges. Between 1870 and 1914 Britain slipped from a dominant first to an uneasy third place in respect of percentage share of world manufacturing production. Britain's share of the world market for manufactured goods also declined from 41.4 per cent in the late 1870s to 29.9 per cent by 1913.[10] In the same period there was a substantial increase in import penetration by foreign manufacturers. These facts seem to support claims made by many contemporaries, that the late nineteenth-century British economy was in decline.

In the light of reassessments by economic historians it can be argued that contemporary concerns were misplaced and that, on the whole, Britain's economic performance in the period 1870–1914 was fairly good.[11] But if the British economy is no longer portrayed as being in decline it is seen as undergoing structural changes as adjustments were made to an increasingly competitive international economy. This process of adaptation witnessed the British economy moving towards a concentration on those areas where it enjoyed a comparative advantage, namely in services and in the old staples of coal, textiles and heavy engineering. In other areas of manufacture, particularly in the chemical and electrical industries, Britain's competitors are seen to have enjoyed a comparative advantage as a result of their greater concentration, economies of scale and technological lead.[12]

28

The process of adaptation described above was slow and painful for the British economy, made more so by the fact that in the period of the mid-Victorian boom Britain had been a major producer and exporter of all manufactured and consumer goods. As one recent survey of the period has argued, the main problem for the British economy was that it had enjoyed a 'free lunch' during the 1850s and 1860s which was taken away in the late nineteenth century.[13] Thus increasingly frequent cyclical downturns after the mid-1870s, and the fall in prices between about 1873 and 1895, hit Britain harder than other countries because Britain's position as the leading manufacturing and trading nation made her economy more vulnerable. Similarly, the emergence of strong competition and the revival of protectionism also hit Britain harder because of its reliance on international trade. The verdict of economic history is that, for the most part, there is little evidence to suggest that the closure of markets by tariffs or the upswing in competition had any drastic effect on the volume of British trade or on the British economy in general. On a disaggregated level it is not denied that some areas of manufacturing, notably the Birmingham and Black Country metal trades, the silk industry, and some elements of the iron and steel sector, suffered,[14] but, it is argued, this was more than compensated for by developments in other sectors. Services enjoyed substantial growth, and trade was, it seems, successfully switched to the supply of capital goods and basic manufactures to primary-producing areas, with the result that by 1914 Britain still held a powerful position in the world economy.[15]

In the cold light of retrospect economic historians conclude that the British economy had its problems between 1870 and 1914 but that, overall, it faced up to them quite well.[16] This was not, however, the verdict of much late nineteenth-century opinion. This clash of opinion between economic historians and contemporary observers has been attributed to the fact that contemporary analysis 'had very little to do with any objective assessment of Britain's needs as a great industrial power',[17] but this misreads the economic arguments advanced by those who felt the economy was in decline. The important factors to be considered are the *assumptions* the analysis is based upon and the criteria used to judge the economy's performance, for they determine which facts are seen as of particular relevance and also how they are interpreted.

This chapter will outline the assumptions underpinning the arguments of those who depicted the British economy in the late nineteenth century as in decline. It will examine three movements which emerged as a direct result of the contemporary sense of crisis, the campaigns for imperial federation, fair trade and bimetallism. It will also examine aspects of the contemporary response to the late nineteenth-century 'fiscal crisis' of the British State, and look briefly at contemporary views of 'the condition of the people'. By examining these varied aspects of the 'political economy of decline' this study will show that contemporary concern about the condition of the British economy generated criticism of established liberal orthodoxies regarded as the governing maxims of British economic policy, and that the triptych of liberal economics, free trade, the gold standard and the balanced budget, and the broader set of assumptions which underpinned them, were all threatened by the contemporary response to what was once termed 'the Great Depression'.

FAIR TRADE

> The protective tariffs of other countries, and even of our own colonies, have much to do with the present depression.
>
> (Huddersfield Chamber of Commerce
> to RCDTI, November 1885)[18]

The National Fair Trade League (NFTL) came into existence on 17 May 1881. The immediate cause of its appearance was the break-down of the 'Cobden' Treaty, and the apparent willingness of the Liberal government to negotiate a new, less favourable commercial agreement with France.[19] But both the demise of the Cobden Treaty and the emergence of the NFTL were symptomatic of broader developments. The Cobden Treaty was a casualty of the wave of economic nationalism and resurgent protectionism which swept the industrialized world in the late nineteenth century; the NFTL was the most important early manifestation of this phenomenon in Britain.

The starting point for the fair trade campaign was the contention that the British economy was facing severe difficulties. Speaking in the House of Lords in November 1884 Lord Dunraven, a prominent member of the NFTL, outlined the fair traders' view of the British economic situation when he argued that Britain's staple industries, in particular cotton, iron and steel and shipbuilding, were all stagnating, whilst other industries, including coal-mining, wool and engineering were all experiencing lengthy periods of either complete idleness or short-time work. Dunraven argued that agriculture's plight was more serious than that of any other industry, but 'that the whole commercial, trading, mining, manufacturing community was suffering'.[20] Such an argument found much support in the reports sent to the RCDTI by various Chambers of Commerce and trade assocations. Of fifty Chambers of Commerce sent questionnaires by the RCDTI, thirty-eight replied that in their area industry was in a state of deep depression.[21]

It being fair trade wisdom that British industry and agriculture were in the throes of depression, the next questions were why and how this had come about. Fair traders pointed to foreign competition and foreign tariffs as the central problems.[22] Foreign competition, and in particular the influx of foreign grain, was depicted as the essential cause of the miserable condition of British agriculture. The difficulties facing British industry were seen to stem from a more complex set of problems. Industrialization of the continental powers and the USA had, it was argued, reduced the market for British goods. The fair traders contended that this 'natural' process was, however, being unnaturally hastened by tariff barriers which prevented British producers from competing in these markets on equal terms.[23] Once again this argument was confirmed by complaints from the business community. The Sheffield iron and steel industry had been complaining about the impact of US tariffs as early as the mid-1870s, and these complaints escalated during the 1880s.[24] Nor was Sheffield a lone voice. Thirty-two of the Chambers of Commerce mentioned above, and eight of the trade assocations, saw the closing of foreign markets by tariffs as a major cause of the difficulties facing industries in their districts. The fair trade diagnosis of the basic cause of Britain's industrial malaise seemed to be one with which many British businessmen agreed.

The fair traders were unequivocal in defining a solution. The basic elements of their programme were outlined in the NFTL's 'manifesto', published in *The Times* on 3 August 1881. The formula was simple: just as foreign competition and foreign tariffs were seen to be the main cause of Britain's economic difficulties, so British tariffs were to be the means of reestablishing Britain's competitive position. 'Retaliatory' tariffs were to be placed on imports from countries which imposed tariffs on British goods, in order to force them to reduce their tariffs and allow fair competition. At the same time a system of preferential duties was to be established between Britain and the Empire, the key impost at the British end being a 'moderate corn duty'.[25] Retaliatory tariffs were to force open markets which had been closed by protectionist regimes, whilst imperial preference was to give British producers privileged access to untapped colonial markets. Protective tariffs were not a part of the 'official' NFTL programme, and only appeared infrequently in impromptu statements by some leading fair traders.

Given that the fair trade analysis of the causes of 'the present discontents' was in harmony with the views of many British businessmen, one could be forgiven for assuming that their proposals would have gained their support. However, this was not the case. Certainly, all those Chambers of Commerce and economic groups which had complained about the impact of foreign tariffs and foreign competition agreed that it would be a good idea if both could be either reduced or removed, but that was the extent of their unanimity. The different sectors, industries and localities offered diverse and often conflicting suggestions for solutions.

The simple fact of the matter was that different aspects of the fair trade programme necessarily appealed to different sectors of the economy. One particularly obvious division was between agriculture and industry. The RCAD, which reported in 1896, concluded that between 1876 and 1894 grain prices had fallen by an average of 30–40 per cent, and foreign competition was clearly marked out as the main cause of this precipitous drop.[26] British farmers made a market response to the influx of grain by diversifying into dairy farming and market gardening,[27] but even here foreign competition exerted a downward pressure on prices. This emphasis on the impact of foreign competition ensured that the only tariffs to which British farmers demonstrated any commitment were *protective* tariffs. During the 1880s a large number of Chambers of Agriculture, especially those in the hard-hit arable districts of Lincolnshire, East Anglia and Essex, advocated corn duties of varying levels of severity, and in 1886 the Central Chamber of Agriculture made the first of a series of pronunciations in favour of a tariff on corn.[28] The corollary of the agricultural sector's enthusiasm for protection was indifference or hostility towards retaliatory tariffs. Such tariffs posed a possible threat to farmers' economic interests. British farmers were not exporters; their only concern was with import penetration of the home market. The imposition of retaliatory tariffs on, say, imports of agricultural machinery threatened farmers with increased costs. Thus the only benefit the fair trade movement offered agriculture was a general reopening of the debate on free trade. This was welcomed by the most hard-pressed elements of the agricultural community, but those farmers who had been hoping for a protectionist campaign were disappointed. Many farming spokesmen also expressed concern about proposals for imperial preference, especially those based on 'free admission' of colonial grain: it was of little relevance to farmers whether they were ruined by foreign or colonial imports.[29]

A rural–urban divide was not the only difference of opinion which handicapped the fair trade campaign. Within Britain's manufacturing sector there were considerable divergences of opinion over tariffs. Six of the fifty Chambers questioned by the RCDTI were in favour of retaliation in its purest form, whilst nine others proposed a watered-down version. Fifteen Chambers argued in favour of opening new markets and bringing about closer commercial relations with the Colonies, but the question of preferential tariffs, except in the case of the Birmingham Chamber, was almost wholly avoided. Several Chambers not only avoided the question of preferential tariffs but insisted that the Colonies should abolish all tariffs and that Empire free trade be established. Nine Chambers were clear that no legislative action, apart from government assistance in the opening of new markets, could help improve the situation, and the Nottingham Chamber pointedly remarked that 'any interference with the principle of free trade would induce results disastrous to our commerce'.[30] A number of other suggestions, such as reduction of taxes and lowering of railway rates, received support. However, several

Chambers noted that they could make no suggestions as to ameliorative legislative action because 'opinion is so divided that it is impossible to arrive at a satisfactory conclusion'.[31] It seems likely that even those Chambers which put forward positive suggestions were far from unanimous in their support for them.[32]

The fair traders found it virtually impossible from the start to appeal to or forge a coherent constituency, for divisions of opinion over tariffs were symptomatic of a deeper difficulty: a desire to avoid the label of protectionism. Deference to the principles of free trade was a hallmark of many of Britain's complaining Chambers of Commerce. Only three Chambers, Birmingham, Newark-on-Trent and Macclesfield, actually repudiated free trade by demanding straightforward protective tariffs, whereas virtually all the other Chambers argued that what they really wanted was 'genuine' free trade. The fair trade movement was constrained by the fact that few business centres were convinced that the abandonment of free trade was a good idea. In this sense it is wrong to say that 'retaliation' was simply a clever way of disguising the protectionist stance which lay underneath the rhetoric of 'genuine free trade'.[33] This may have been true for some advocates of retaliation, but even if it was the case that 'retaliationists' were simply clever protectionists then it is significant that they chose the mask of 'genuine free trade' for their disguise, for this acknowledged that free trade was still the ruling deity. Equally, the emphasis on retaliation can be seen as a product of market rationality. The complaint of most businesses, agriculture aside, was market closure not import penetration. Consequently the appeal of 'genuine' free trade was understandable. But whilst economic rationalism was certainly at play one should not underestimate another powerful force, namely the grip of free trade on British economic and political culture. Free trade was a concept treated with almost biblical reverence, and the vocabulary which was used by both critics and defenders of the 'altar' or 'gospel' of free trade is significant. The conflict which surrounded the fair trade programme was as much a product of the confused attitudes, as well as the differing interests, which the breath of economic 'heresy' brought into the open.

The fair trade campaign achieved little but illustrated much. Having emerged in 1881 in a blaze of publicity the NFTL thereafter enjoyed mixed fortunes. In October 1881 Edward Hamilton noted that Gladstone was devoting a great deal of time to repudiating fair trade, and yet only a year later he could record that 'one hears no more of "fair trade". That little bubble has effectively busted'.[34] The devout free trader Hamilton provided the best explanation for the varied fortunes of fair trade, when he remarked in October 1884 that 'trade is bad generally: and it has given rise to a revival of the cry for disguised protection under the name of 'Fair Trade'.[35] But whilst the resonance of fair trade was linked to the business cycle it remained a part of political and economic debate for fifteen years, and was emphatically not an ephemera. This was because 'periods of depression had become of more frequent occurrence and longer duration . . . [whilst] the recoveries had become more transitory'.[36] In short the cyclical down-turns of the late nineteenth century were regarded as severe enough to engender, as C.T. Ritchie stated, a 'want of confidence . . . in the commercial policy of the country'.[37] The ascendancy of free trade was never seriously threatened, and it would be a mistake to over-estimate the power of a fair trade challenge which was neither coherent nor well-organized. Yet it would also be a mistake to under-estimate the importance of fair trade as a symptom of unease about Britain's economic standing.

Sir John Clapham wrote of the fair trade movement that 'its strength lay less in its economics . . . than in its sense of a changing world and in its nationalism',[38] a view which has not been altered by the few studies which have been made of fair trade since. However, the fair traders' economics, nationalism, and sense of a changing world were inseparable. In the first issue of *Fair Trade* it was stated that the fair traders' questioning of Britain's prevailing commercial policy, particularly with regard to relations with the Colonies, was a sign that 'The revolt of Nationalism against the spirit of Cosmopolitanism was . . . forcing its way to the front'.[39] What fair traders meant by this was that economic rationality was, throughout the industrialized world, increasingly being defined by the needs of the *res publica* rather than by the needs of indi-vidual 'economic men'. That other nations had closed their doors to British goods in order to foster domestic production, and that the Colonies were Britain's best per capita customers, indicated to fair traders that nationalism was exerting a powerful influence. Fair trade challenged free trade not simply because it necessitated the advocacy of tariffs but because it questioned its assumptions about international trade.

Incorporated within the fair traders' 'nationalist' critique of free trade was their argument that market decisions were not necessarily rational for a particular national economy. Speaking in the House of Lords in November 1884 Lord Dunraven noted that 'the decline of any particular trade might mean merely the transference of capital and labour from an unprofitable to a profitable undertaking, an operation which, although it might cause temporary distress might eventually be beneficial to the nation. But', he went on, 'if all industries are languishing, and if in each case the decline was owing to the fact that in that particular trade capital could no longer be profitably employed, the inference was very different'.[40] The implications of this argument were quite far-reaching. In giving his 'private evidence' to the Macmillan Committee in February 1930 J.M. Keynes pointed out that 'Free Trade . . . assumes that if you threw men out of work in one direction you re-employ them in another. As soon as that link is broken, the whole Free Trade argument breaks down'.[41] Keynes spoke of unemployment, Dunraven spoke of

34

unprofitable capital, but both were making the same case against free trade, namely that an unrestrained market did not necessarily lead to a beneficial allocation of resources for a particular national economy. Britain's invisible earnings from overseas investment, Dunraven suggested, were not an unmixed benefit. If such earnings were the result of Britain having 'surplus capital' then well and good, but Dunraven and other fair traders contended that such income represented 'profits on capital invested abroad which had been or might have been invested at home'.[42] That capital had gone abroad was, the fair traders argued, because domestic investment had been made less profitable by Britain's refusal to safeguard its national productive base. The cosmopolitan tendencies of British investors were therefore seen as inextricably linked to Britain's cosmopolitan trade policy.

The fair trade campaign's significance outweighed its achievements. For the first time in forty years important questions had been asked about Britain's commitment to free trade, and it was clear that the 'protectionists' were moving onto the offensive. The difficulties which confronted many sectors of the British economy in the late nineteenth-century economy were evidently serious enough to convince many that all was not well with the world. Fair trade was a manifestation of doubt, the well-known first sign of a weakening faith.

IMPERIAL FEDERATION

... the most useful course to adopt would be to take steps to ... create new markets wherever possible ... [and] to cultivate closer commercial relations with our colonies.
(Dewsbury Chamber of Commerce to RCDTI, 30 October 1885)[43]

Speaking at Birmingham in January 1889 Joseph Chamberlain announced that Britain was entering a new era in terms of the way people thought about the Empire. There had been, Chamberlain argued, two previous eras characterized by very different views of Empire. The first era, which he placed in the eighteenth century, Chamberlain decribed as an 'age of selfishness' in which Britain had looked on the Colonies as possessions fit only for exploitation. This selfish age had, according to Chamberlain, given way to 'the period of apathy and indifference' lasting from the early nineteenth century to the late 1870s, when, under the influence of liberal political economy, Britain had regarded the Colonies as of little or negative value. In the 1880s, however, Chamberlain saw a new conception of the Empire developing in opposition to the 'Little Englandism' of liberal political economy, a concept based on notions of imperial partnership which acknowledged that without the Colonies Britain would slip to the rank of a 'fifth-rate nation'.[44]

Whatever the merits of Chamberlain's historical typology, his speech elucidated important aspects of British imperialist thought as it developed in the late nineteenth century. It is certainly true that only in the last quarter of the nineteenth century did a self-conscious British imperialism emerge. It is also true that the chief exponents of and apologists for this 'new imperialism', such as Chamberlain himself, saw themselves as having to face down a prevailing economic orthodoxy which questioned the value of Empire. Finally, the new imperialism in Britain was both in theory and practice profoundly defensive – the product of growing anxiety about Britain's imperial and economic security.

The defensive tenor of the new imperialism in Britain is very apparent from its timing and format. It emerged *after* the period of Britain's unrivalled supremacy, and its central goal was *consolidation* not expansion. The increase in the amount of territory encompassed by Britain's *formal* Empire after 1880 was matched by a decrease in the level of Britain's *informal* control over a much wider area of the globe.[45] Britain's annexation of territory on a grand scale was an acknowledgement that Britain was no longer unchallenged. In economic terms Britain's acquisition of territory was particularly defensive. If one accepts Gallagher and Robinson's formula that British policy before the 'new imperialism' was 'trade with informal control where possible, trade with formal control where necessary'[46] then it is clear that many contemporaries felt formal control was 'more necessary' in the last quarter of the nineteenth century. The upswing in interest in imperialism amongst British businessmen in the late nineteenth century was a product of fear over the threatening implications of colonial expansion by rival powers. With rival nations protecting trade with their newly-acquired Colonies with tariffs, the 'fear of the closing door' was widespread. Britain remained a free-trade nation, but British business interests campaigned strongly for pre-emptive colonial expansion.[47]

The degree of business interest in imperialism tended to fluctuate with the business cycle. Thus in 1884–5, a period which witnessed a bad downturn, the Liverpool Chamber of Commerce expressed great concern to the Foreign Office about German annexations in West Africa, whilst a concerted business lobby attacked the then Liberal government's supposed general neglect of Britain's commercial interests in the tropics.[48] The RCDTI thus expressed a common business response to economic downturn when it concluded 'we must display greater activity in the search for new markets'.[49] An upswing in the economy from early 1886 to late 1887 saw business enthusiasm for an expanded Empire fall away, but interest was reawakened by further downturns, and from early 1888 through to the bottoming-out of the economic trough in the mid-1890s the commercial aspect of the Empire was a central business concern. During this latter period, the Liverpool Chamber of Commerce demanded that the British government 'exercise more settled control' over such areas as Bechuanaland and Swaziland[50] and that it further move to 'secure the boundaries of the West African colonies and ... the system of British influence adjacent'.[51] Meanwhile, the Glasgow, Manchester and London Chambers of Commerce all advocated the opening up of 'new countries under the British flag' as a means of relieving the related problems of over-production and the closure, by tariffs, of traditional markets and territories colonized by protectionist powers.[52]

Fears about Britain's economic security which impelled many to urge an expansion of formal Empire also prompted efforts to discover some way of making better use of those territories over which Britain already exerted influence. The Imperial Federation League, founded in 1884, represented the most important effort to draw commercial and general interest in the Empire into a coherent movement for imperial consolidation. It argued that as traditional markets for British manufactures in the United States and Europe had become difficult to penetrate, so Britain had to look to the colonial markets as an outlet for British goods.[53] Specifically concentrating on the white, self-governing 'dominions', the IFL made a statistical case for the greater relative value of these markets. Although in terms of volume of trade the USA and the continent were still the largest markets for British products, the increase in exports to the self-governing Colonies was larger and their per capita consumption of British manufactures higher.[54] This had profound implications in the 1880s and 1890s, when depression and the reemergence of protection threatened to restrict outlets for British producers.[55]

The IFL had reason to hope that their arguments would carry weight in business circles. A consistent plea registered by the various Chambers of Commerce who sent detailed replies to the RCDTI was for the development of stronger commercial bonds with the Empire, even after the Commission's inconclusive Report was produced. In January 1887 *Imperial Federation* remarked that 'If we can induce associations of business men ... to perceive that they will gain permanently by Federation and suffer from the want of it, then we shall have made a successful appeal to an irresistible motive power'.[56] In March 1887 the annual gathering of the Associated Chambers of Commerce welcomed a motion extolling the commercial value of imperial federation, and endorsed similar motions over the next decade.[57] Individual business associations were equally vocal. In October 1888 the IFL journal noted that the Cutlers' Feast at Sheffield had been 'practically an Imperial Federation meeting',[58] whilst between 1889 and 1894 the Liverpool Chamber organized several special meetings to stress the importance of colonial commerce.[59] In the 1890s the Birmingham Chamber passed motions annually arguing that 'the future prosperity of British commerce must depend on increasing our commercial relations with our colonies',[60] and these sentiments found frequent echo in Chambers as diverse as Blackburn, Bradford and London.[61]

With business support for its aims seemingly so widespread and, with 100 MPs being members of the League, it may appear strange that the IFL did not achieve tangible results. The IFL's early years seem to have been a success, with branches springing up across the country, literature widely disseminated, and influential sections of the business and political world expressing enthusiastic support. Furthermore, the IFL played a major role in the calling of the first Colonial Conference in 1887. But this apparent success hid a major weakness in the IFL's position. Many people were in favour of imperial federation in the same way that many are against sin, that is to say as a general position. Whilst the IFL spoke in generalities they could appeal on a broad front, but difficulties began to emerge over how imperial federation was to be achieved.

The IFL realized the difficulties of framing a specific policy from the start. At a meeting of the General Committee of the IFL in February 1885 an attempt to hasten the development of a specific programme was shelved on the grounds that the IFL should concentrate its energies on 'educative' work.[62] At a Special Meeting of its Executive Committee in July 1886, a division of opinion emerged which was subsequently to dog the organization. Sir Alexander Galt declared that he hoped that 'the Colonies would enter into a Commercial League for mutual tariff concessions' which Britain would enter 'sooner or later'. Sir Rawson W. Rawson argued that it was necessary to create 'a condition of things in which the Colonies within the Empire would exchange their goods without duty, like countries or provinces within the same nation'.[63] Although the IFL managed to play down this division at the time, they remained aware of the problems involved in presenting a definite policy. In December 1886, when the editor of *Imperial Federation* asked for instructions from the Executive Committee as to the line the journal should adopt on commercial federation, he was told to 'encourage discussion' but 'without expression of opinion editorially'.[64] Similarly, Lord Rosebery, the IFL's Chairman, told the Leeds Chamber of Commerce in October 1888 that imperial federation was 'in the first place ... a commercial question', but that it was not 'fit or proper' for the IFL to propose a definite scheme for commercial federation.[65]

The main reason for the IFL's reticence was outlined by the rival, or perhaps complementary, organization the NFTL. In July 1886 *Fair Trade* pointed out that

The Imperial Federationists ... talk loudly and plausibly ... but any reference to the fiscal or commercial question is carefully tabooed ... in private conversation many who are deep in the councils of the Imperial Federation League fully agree that it is through fiscal union that the great question may be solved ... [but] they are afraid to come near the holy altar of Free Trade, for fear of internal divisions.[66]

This was precisely the case, for the tariff issue crippled the IFL's efforts to find a universally acceptable policy.

With regard to harmonizing colonial and British ambitions, the IFL's predicament was made clear by one British proposal for an imperial trade policy. This was for a system of Empire Free Trade, forcefully expressed in Joseph Chamberlain's argument for an 'Imperial Zollverein' at a meeting of the Chambers of Commerce of the Empire in 1896.[67] This certainly satisfied the demands of British producers, for it offered the entire Empire market as a unit in which they would enjoy preferential treatment. At the same time it did not threaten 'the holy altar of Free Trade', because its implementation would have meant the creation of a larger free-trade zone than had previously existed and no new British tariffs. What were not satisfied by this proposal, however, were the Colonies' own national aspirations. In 1895, soon after taking on the Colonial Office, Chamberlain had launched an investigation to discover how British exports to the colonial markets could be increased.[68] His deputy, Lord Selborne, pointed out that unless such an investigation was handled with delicacy the Colonies might 'think that we are not caring for their interests but only for those of British producers'.[69] The proposal for a 'Zollverein' would have forced the Colonies into the role of suppliers of raw materials and food-stuffs in exchange for British manufactures; this could not satisfy their wish to develop their own manufacturing sectors. The Colonial Premiers appear to have agreed with Edward Hamilton's conclusion that 'the Colonies ... would have a great deal to lose'[70] from a 'Zollverein', for at the 1897 Colonial Conference they dismissed the idea.

With inter-imperial free trade a non-starter, it became clear at an early date that the only way to forge closer commercial links was through a more complex system of reciprocal tariff agreements. Such a system necessitated that the Colonies retain tariffs against all manufactured imports but offer preferential treatment to British goods, whilst Britain found some way of offering preferential treatment to the Colonies. There were, however, important difficulties. Many of the Chambers of Commerce advocating closer commercial relations with the Colonies in their replies to the RCDTI had avoided making any comment about pref-erential tariffs. Once again specifics presented problems. In addition it was generally acknowledged that the only possible system under which Britain could offer preference to the Colonies would be under a British tariff system which taxed either imported raw materials, which was unac-ceptable to British manufacturers, or food, which raised the spectre of a 'dear food' cry.

In spite of the obvious difficulties the bolder spirits of the IFL became increasingly willing to take up the cause of imperial preference. Speaking in Manchester in January 1887 the Secretary of the IFL H.O. Arnold-Forster stated his belief that 'there is . . . reason to hope for a differential tariff, which would give favourable treatment to anything coming from any part of the British Empire'.[71] Such statements received short shrift from the free traders in the IFL. For example in December 1891, commenting on the call for imperial preference which had been made at the Birmingham meeting of the NUCA the preceding November, Sir Lyon Playfair, himself a member of the IFL General Committee, remarked 'Here is our old friend protection in the thinnest disguise. The Colonial Fiscal Federation is simply the horse put forward for show . . . The dark horse . . . is Protection for English corn and cattle'.[72] Matters were only made worse by the increasing emphasis placed on imperial preference by the fair traders, a trend which served to damn the IFL as 'protectionist' through guilt by association.[73]

Ultimately the division over tariffs destroyed the IFL. The beginning of the end came in 1892, when Lord Salisbury charged the IFL to produce a concrete policy in order for the public and the government to judge whether imperial federation was in the realm of 'practical politics'. Unable to hide its internal divisions the IFL became 'a house divided against itself'.[74] In November 1893, in a special statement to the IFL Council, the Secretary, Arnold-Forster, stated that with the IFL being

> compelled by . . . public demand . . . to give an indication of what is meant by the Federation of the Empire . . . at once lines of cleavage have shown themselves in a manner which cannot be mistaken . . . There is a party in the League which holds that a commercial union of the Empire is essential . . . and there is a party which holds that such a union would not constitute a Federation, or that, in any case, a change in the fiscal policy of this country would be too high a price to pay.[75]

The net result of this division of opinion was that the IFL disintegrated, leaving a rump organization, the Imperial Federation (Defence) Committee, to discuss the less controversial issue of military cooperation within the Empire. Discussion of imperial commercial policy devolved into a conflict between two splinter groups largely made up of ex-IFL members. The British Empire League took its stance on the maintenance of free trade whilst the United Empire Trade League raised the banner of preference,[76] with the former gaining its strongest support from the commercial and financial interests in the City of London, and the latter finding its chief protagonists in Birmingham and Sheffield.[77]

In spite of its somewhat ignominious end and its lack of obvious achievements the IFL's brief life illuminates British responses to the

'Great Depression'. From the beginning the IFL had implicitly subverted the assumptions of liberal political economy. In 1864 J.E. Cairnes wrote that 'We do not ask – we certainly do not receive – any commercial advantages from the Colonies which are not equally open to the whole world, which we should not equally command though the political connection were severed tomorrow'.[78] His view outlined a tradition of liberal economic thought on the commercial value of Empire expressed in the work of Smith, Senior, and J.S. Mill, and which was to be reiterated by Fawcett, Thorold Rogers, Goldwin Smith, Hobson and even by Jevons and Marshall.[79] The IFL occupied an antithetical position. Its central contention was that Empire markets were not only of basic value but were of ever increasing value given the circumstances of the late nineteenth century. Thus, contra Cairnes, the IFL contended that Britain did receive commercial advantages from the Colonies which were not on offer in the wider world, so it was worthwhile Britain asking the Colonies to confirm and extend these advantages. The IFL made a qualitative distinction between types of market, whereas for liberal political economy a market was just a market and was only to be analysed in quantitative terms. The IFL justified its arguments by reference to the relatively higher per capita consumption of British goods in the Colonies, but the Colonies were seen as a better market because they were *Colonies*, influenced by or better disposed towards Britain.

The other major area in which the IFL came into conflict with liberal political economy was, of course, on the question of tariffs. Writing in 1887 W.J. Courthope, a member of the IFL Executive Committee, told Lord Carnarvon that there was 'a great change coming over men's minds about free trade'.[80] There was more to Courthope's statement than hyperbole or self-deception. The IFL as an organization never proposed imperial preference as part of an agreed programme, but the discussion which it helped to provoke drew the issue of preference to the centre of the debate over Britain's commercial future. Although the IFL never actually campaigned for tariffs it served to galvanize discussion of the most heretical aspect of anti-liberal economic thought.

BIMETALLISM[81]

... among the subjects to which our attention has been called in the course of our enquiry there is one which seems to us to require special consideration, both on account of its actual importance, and because of the anxiety expressed with regard to it in many mercantile quarters, as having a direct and peculiar bearing upon the trade and industry of the country, and upon the prices of commodities. We refer to the important subject of the currency.

(RCDTI, *Final Report*)

Bimetallists attributed the depressed state of agriculture and many of Britain's manufacturing industries to the worldwide fall in prices which hit the international markets after 1874. Thus far bimetallists differed little from much contemporary opinion, but they blamed the acuteness of the depression not on real factors, such as over-production or foreign competition, but on the international monetary situation. Bimetallists argued that the root of the problem of falling prices was the almost universal adoption of the gold standard by the industrialized nations, with the major turning point the demonetization of silver by Germany in 1873. This was thought to have had had two detrimental effects on the industrialized economies. First, it had caused an appreciation in the price of gold. Second, it had brought about an increase in the amount of work gold had to do in the international economy as a result of its being the only acceptable standard of exchange for the major powers. This, it was argued, had created a severe relative contraction in the world's money supply, and, following the quantity theory of money, a concomitant fall in prices.[82]

If the widespread adoption of the gold standard was blamed for the general deflation of the late nineteenth century it was also blamed for another problem affecting particular trading interests. The corollary of the more widespread adoption of the gold standard was the demonetization of silver and a divergence in the relative values of the two metals as the price of silver plummeted. Whilst most of the industrialized world had adopted the gold standard some of the world remained on silver, and trade between the two areas was, according to the bimetallist analysis, gravely dislocated. Silver's depreciation was seen to have substantially diminished the purchasing power of nations with silver-based currencies, like India, for the goods of nations on the gold standard. The depreciation of silver was seen to have had two further harmful effects on trade between gold and silver regions. The first was that whilst the purchasing power of silver had fallen in relation to goods produced in gold regions, its purchasing power with regard to goods produced in silver-using nations had necessarily remained constant. This was deemed to have given producers in silver-using countries an enormous competitive advantage over producers operating under the gold standard, with the growth of Indian cotton exports to China at the expense of Lancashire being seen as a prime example.[83] At a time when British manufacturers, and particularly cotton manufacturers, were seeking to expand their exports to markets such as those in the Far East in order to compensate for the closure by tariffs of the American and many European markets, the bimetallists were drawing attention to the possibility that currency difficulties could prevent the development of the full potential of these trading areas.

The bimetallists produced a monetary solution to the world's and Britain's economic difficulties: they proposed an international agreement for a bimetallic standard in which both gold and silver would be freely convertible and in which their relative value would be fixed at a legal ratio.[84] By abandoning gold and adopting a joint standard, so it was argued, the shortage of money caused by the increased demand for gold was to be overcome, and, hence, so was the problem of falling prices in gold-using nations. At the same time the remonetization of silver, and the action of the fixed ratio was to remove the disjuncture between gold- and silver-using nations and destroy the competitive advantages enjoyed by the latter.

Support for the bimetallic solution came mainly from those sectors of the economy which felt most hard pressed by falling prices and trade problems with silver states. One such sector was British agriculture. When the *First Report* of the RCAD was presented in 1894, bimetallism featured prominently as one of the two solutions most favoured by farmers; and the leading agricultural members of the Commission, Walter Long and Henry Chaplin, produced a special section of the *Report* pressing for currency reform.[85] With falling prices a major problem for the agricultural sector, only two possible avenues of escape seemed plausible, a reduction of costs or increased prices. The farming community's greatest desire was to bring about a rise in prices, and the favoured means for achieving this was protection. However, the farmers' yearning for protection was acknowledged to be a love that dared not speak its name. Bimetallism had the important advantage that, even though it was avowedly inflationary, it was not protection as such. Furthermore, bimetallism, because its effect on prices was to be a general one, could not be portrayed as a measure designed to give the farming interest any special advantage.

Sectors of British manufacturing industry provided the other main pro-bimetallic lobby, and one industry, cotton, showed a particular interest in bimetallism. When the forerunner of the Bimetallic League was founded in 1881 its first office was established in Manchester and Stephen Williamson, the one-time President of the Liverpool Chamber of Commerce, declared that Lancashire, as in the 1840s, had to lead the country to a new economic outlook.[86] By 1888 the Manchester Chamber had came out in support of bimetallism, and the Annual Conference of the Bimetallic League held in that year was dominated by the cotton interest.[87] In 1887 and 1888 the Royal Commission on Currency took evidence from a number of mill owners and bosses from the cotton trade and its related industries describing the hardships they were suffering as a result of the currency crisis.[88] Nor was it simply the bosses who spoke out. By the early 1890s the United Textile Factory Workers Association, the main cotton operatives union, was calling on its members not to vote for any Parliamentary candidate who was not a bimetallist.[89] As the price fell towards its lowest trough in the mid-1890s the cotton industry provided the bimetallic campaign with some of its most vocal supporters.[90]

With sections of both industry and agriculture blaming the currency situation for falling prices, a form of 'producers' alliance' emerged on the issue of bimetallism. Certainly a conscious attempt was made to foster such an alliance, for when H.H. Gibbs spoke of the damage the currency problems inflicted on the British economy he was very careful to state that he was 'speaking of productive British industry, and I mean thereby agriculture and the industries that produce goods'.[91] In the bimetallist analysis the fact that Britain's productive sectors were suffering without relief was no accident. Rather this situation was seen to have developed because, as the cotton boss J.C. Fielden put it, 'The capitalist class may be divided into the fixed investment class and the Industrial capitalist' and that whereas 'The former gains by every fall in prices ... the latter suffers'.[92] That the financial community benefited from a fall in prices whilst the productive sector suffered was inevitable, so the bimetallists contended, because 'A fall in prices ... involves the transference from the active producers of wealth a larger proportion of production in satisfaction of the "fixed charge" due to the passive owners of wealth'.[93] As a result the bimetallic campaign represented their fight as 'a struggle between Lombard Street and the industrial interests of England'[94] and identified the City of London as the common enemy of farmers and industrialists alike,[95] and for much of the 1880s and 1890s poured vitriol on the despised 'money power'.[96]

Beneath the bimetallists' rhetoric about cosmopolitan rapacity and the conspiracy of 'Goldbugs' lay a crucial point – they wished to prevent Britain from becoming a nation of 'mortgagers and rentiers'. To the bimetallists it was vital to arrest this development on two counts. First, it was felt to be impossible for a national economy to live on finance alone, because in the end the financial sector was itself dependent on productive wealth. Indeed, the conclusion of the bimetallists was that 'England may have derived some ... particular gain from acting as the broker of the world', but that 'at the best' it was 'a very small part of what has made England rich', and that, ultimately, it was 'the profits on her exports that have made her the creditor of the world'.[97] Bankers 'only held the counters' whilst the manufacturers and merchants 'play the game'.[98]

At no point did the bimetallists contest the fact that Britain's net wealth as a creditor nation was, through invisible earnings, increasing throughout the period of 'monetary disorder'. What they sought to establish, however, was that whilst there was 'no reason to suppose that the depreciation of silver has caused any diminution of wealth in the United Kingdom' it had 'certainly altered its distribution',[99] and that those who had benefited from this redistribution – bankers – were the ones whose increase in wealth benefited the nation *as a whole* least. The heart of the bimetallists' case here was their description of the employment effect of the monetary situation. In 1881 H.S. Foxwell declared that 'irregularity of employment is the root evil of the present industrial system' and that 'interruptions of employment are to a great extent caused by disturbances originating in prices'.[100] Over the next decade bimetallists pressed home their argument that 'prolonged depression of prices ... due to ... the continuous change in the value of money' could only 'unsettle relations and injure the weak'.[101] In contrast a depreciation in the value of money was to provide 'a period of higher and somewhat rising prices ... favourable to trade', which in turn would raise production and increase employment.[102]

The bimetallic campaign did not obtain its ends, but its importance should not be underestimated as one more illustration of the discontent engendered by the economic downturn of the late nineteenth century and concern about Britain's economic development. That a downturn in the fortunes of Britain's 'productive' sector coincided with rapid growth in the service sector, raised questions as to whether the two things were related, and whether such a structural shift was either necessary or desirable. The bimetallists' assault on the gold standard meant more than an attack on a single aspect of economic policy. The gold standard was one part of the interlocking mechanism which made up a supposedly self-regulating economy; to question the gold standard was to question the rationality of accepting 'natural' market decisions. The bimetallic argument was that the existing market structure was biased in effect, and that its allocative bias was damaging the British economy by diverting resources from the productive sector. The 'scientific' case for retaining the gold standard was seen as a cloak for the normative interests of the financial community, since preservation of the status quo served the 'cosmopolitan' interests of the banking community.

The bimetallists' concern at the growing importance of the 'invisible' sector extended into a critique of Britain's general economic position, and this was appreciated at the time. Writing in 1898 Robert Chalmers, one of the Permanent Secretaries at the Treasury, told Lord Farrer

> The more I have to do with these heterodox people [bimetallists], the more I realise the unity of the principles which lead you to maintain the two things – free trade and sound currency. One is the obverse of the other, the reverse of the same coin.[103]

There was, of course, a strong historical link between the two, in that the campaign for 'sound currency' had gone hand in hand with the campaign for free trade in the decades after the Napoleonic Wars, and both had reached successful conclusions in the 1840s.[104] But free trade and the gold standard also shared a common purpose. The rationale of the gold standard was not only to ensure that the domestic currency was 'sound', but that domestic prices and interest rates moved in harmony with Britain's international trade position. In short, free trade and the gold standard were complementary parts of a mechanism linking the British economy to the international economy. To question the gold standard was to question the wisdom of maintaining an open, internationally-orientated economy. Furthermore, the gold standard was, in effect, a sterling-exchange standard and, by establishing the primacy of sterling, had helped, with Britain's open markets and dominant merchant marine, to make Britain, and in particular London, the commercial mart of the world. Anything which threatened Britain's link with the international economy thus threatened Britain's invisible earnings, and any criticism of the invisible sector implied a willingness to undermine Britain's 'cosmopolitical' economy.

THE CONDITION OF THE PEOPLE

> While the problem of 1834 was the problem of pauperism, the problem of 1893 is the problem of poverty.
> (Alfred Marshall, Evidence to the Royal Commission on the
> Aged Poor, 1893)

In 1890 William Booth, founder of the Salvation Army, published his most celebrated work, *In Darkest England and the Way Out*. Booth chose the theme of his book carefully. The opening sentence referred readers to H.M. Stanley, the frontispiece was a map of 'darkest England', and Booth portrayed Britain's poorer districts as *terra incognita* suporting an un-Christian, semi-savage population in need of spiritual and material help. The whole book was, in short, an extended metaphor of discovery, highlighting the argument that in Britain as in Africa there were 'lost tribes' and 'startling revelations'. *In Darkest England* was one of many publications and projects that 'revealed' Britain's 'hidden continent' of poverty in the last quarter of the nineteenth century. In the early 1880s journalists, such as G.R. Sims of the *Pictorial World* and W.T. Stead of the *Pall Mall Gazette*, sensationalized London's poor, again drawing parallels with the 'imperial mission'. Seebohm Rowntree and Charles Booth sought to study the problem 'scientifically', and determined 'objectively' that 30 per cent of the populations of, respectively, York and London were living in poverty. At the same time, however, the processes of investigation, identification and classification that Rowntree and Booth deployed were very similar to those that have been linked to the 'science culture' of imperialism. Rowntree and Booth's studies were in this respect also part of the 'discovery' of the poor by Britain's middling and upper classes.

It is, however, inaccurate to say that poverty was 'discovered' in the 1880s and 1890s: rather it was 'invented'. Throughout the early and mid-Victorian period a large section of the population had experienced severe deprivations, and this had been acknowledged not only by the Poor Law, but also by philanthropists, novelists and social investigators. But to say that the later Victorians simply put a new label on an existing phenomenon would be to ignore the importance of naming to the way a problem is defined. The switch from the language of pauperism to the language of poverty was signficant, because it was symptomatic of the creation of a new discursive field which shaped the way in which the 'condition of the people' was observed and addressed.[105]

The critical new departure in the 1880s and 1890s was the conception of poverty as a systemic problem caused by social circumstance rather than individual failings. The *Oxford English Dictionary* notes, for example, that 'unemployment' was first used in its modern sense as an abstract noun in 1888. The timing of this definition may be over-precise or even arbitrary, but the *OED* is correct in saying that this meaning of unemployment was 'common usage after 1895'. In the 1880s and 1890s commentators from all walks of life and from across the range of political opinion discussed unemployment in terms of external causes rather than as an individually-generated problem. H.S. Foxwell attributed it to money-supply rooted price fluctuations, Lord Dunraven blamed foreign tariffs and Britain's free trade system, J.A. Hobson argued that maldistribution of income leading to underconsumption was the cause.[106] Particular analyses of the causes of unemployment varied, but there was general agreement that it was a *social* problem in terms of both its causes and effects and thus that it required and indeed demanded a social solution. What was true for unemployment was equally true for other problems – insecurity in old age, poor working conditions, ill health, insanitary housing – all of which were increasingly seen as having structural roots and an impact on society in general as well as on particular individuals.[107]

That the workings of the economy could result in systemic deprivation for significant sectors of society was a blow to classical liberal economics. According to that orthodoxy such systemic problems could not occur, in that the free operation of economic forces was supposed to produce an optimum distribution of resources at a full employment equilibrium. Thus, along with the issues raised by the fair trade, imperial federation and bimetallic campaigns, the 'condition of the people' question destabilized the concept of a natural, self-sustaining economic equilibrium that had flourished in the mid-Victorian era. This in turn generated debate about the proper role of the State. If one assumed that social problems were individually generated or extra-ordinary then one could either deal with them on a case by case basis or simply wait for a peculiar situation to right itself. However, if one assumed structural defects then there was a case for structural repairs carried out by society's central agency, the State. The 'Chamberlain Circular' of 1885, through which the government empowered local authorities to use public works to counter unemployment, is thus rightly seen as a watershed, for in terms of content and context it represented a break from the concept of the 'nightwatchman' State that had informed mid-Victorian social policy.[108]

However, it was not simply the logic of the new social analysis that led to an interest in Collectivist ideas and strategies. Concern about the nation's social and economic equilibrium also prompted fears about its political equilibrium. The demonstrations and riots by the unemployed in 1886 and 1887, the great strikes of 1889, and the continued industrial conflicts of the 1890s seemed to indicate that the lower orders were no longer willing to accept the authority of their betters without question. Indeed, the situation in London in the mid-1880s provoked what has been likened to a *'grande peur'* on the part of the capital's middling and upper classes.[109] At a broader level it was no coincidence that the 'condition of the people' emerged as an issue at the same time as the Third Reform Act made working-class voters the majority. Social investigation and 'the social problem' were part of the climate which brought about the 'transition to high politics in English social policy'.[110] Investigation of working-class life was in a manner of speaking intelligence gathering, part of a general curiosity about the mass electorate, and the 'discovery' of poverty indicated to politicians of all hues that so far as the masses were concerned social reform was the stuff of politics.[111] The debate on 'the condition of the people' was thus tied not only to questions of the proper realm of State activity, but to concerns about the survival of the State and the ability of political actors to gain access to its powers.

THE FISCAL CRISIS OF THE STATE

That W.E. Gladstone chose, in 1894, to resign over the issue of the Navy Estimates was very fitting. Gladstone had taken great pride in his skills as Chancellor of the Exchequer, an office he held for more years than any politician before or since; it was Gladstone who had turned the Budget into a major political event, and it was the principles of public finance which Gladstone had done so much to establish that defined Victorian budgetary orthodoxy. The basics of Gladstonian finance, as eulogized by F.W. Hirst,[112] were to reduce taxation as far as possible, to ensure an even incidence of taxation on individuals and classes and, above all, to balance the budget. The necessary corollary of all this was that expenditure had to be kept to a minimum – 'economy' was the central edifice of Gladstonian finance. In 1894, however, Gladstone had found himself ranged against his Cabinet colleagues on the issue of economy. His decision to resign thus marked not only the need of his own career but indicated that the Gladstonian era was drawing to a close.

If it was the case that Gladstone was the patron saint of fiscal rectitude it was equally true that the Treasury was the temple of the faithful and its permanent staff the guardians of the altar. Gladstone left behind him in the Treasury Chambers a number of personal and professional protégés, men like Robert Chalmers, Francis Mowatt, Reginald Welby and Edward Hamilton, and this 'Gladstonian garrison'[113] sought to ensure that successive Chancellors kept to the paths of fiscal righteousness. But fiscal and political developments in the late nineteenth century placed the Treasury on the defensive, whilst the heresiarchs in the spending departments grew ever more assertive.

The underlying cause of the budgetary problem was simple: a massive increase in public expenditure. In 1870 expenditure by central and local government had totalled £93,000,000 or 9 per cent of GNP, by 1895 it was £157,000,000 or 19 per cent of GNP.[114] Four years of war in South Africa between 1898 and 1902 pushed central government expenditure alone over the £200,000,000 mark. But the Boer War was not in any sense the main cause of the fiscal crisis or controversies of the Edwardian age. The first clear indication that balancing the books was becoming a problem had emerged in the late 1880s, with Edward Hamilton noting in April 1888 that even with such a parsimonious Chancellor as Goschen at the Exchequer there was the threat of a deficit of £1,100,000.[115] That such problems existed in peace-time, ten years before the outbreak of the conflict in South Africa and when such a pillar of orthodoxy as Goschen occupied Number Eleven, puts the problems caused by the Boer War in perspective. As the Conservative Chancellor Sir Michael Hicks-Beach pointed out in his last Budget speech in April 1901, the increase in *ordinary* expenditure was at the root of the fiscal crisis, and military, social and local government spending was, even in the normal course of events, moving on an apparently inexorable upward curve.[116]

With deficits becoming a perennial fear the Treasury fought tenaciously to control the ambitions of spending Ministers and to demonstrate to 'spendthrift' Cabinets the consequences of their actions. In April 1894 Edward Hamilton noted that Sir William Harcourt's budget, with its graduated death duties, could but damage the propertied classes, but, he remarked, this served the propertied classes right – having demanded a big navy they had to pay for it.[117] Two days later Hamilton was writing in similar vein about the Commons' discussion of old age pensions, bemoaning the fact that 'it is extraordinary how politicians can in a light hearted way advocate proposals which would involve a colossal expenditure, and then ... holler out at having to pay the bill!'.[118] In late 1894 Hamilton was informed that Goschen was not to be Chancellor if the Conservatives came back into power, and this he attributed to the fact that Goschen's 'orthodox principles of finance do not chime in with those entertained by some of the Unionists'.[119] In June of 1895 Hamilton was relieved to learn that his new Tory 'chief' was to be Hicks-Beach – 'a very straight man ... no *fads* or heterodox notions'[120] – but he still felt obliged to fire his Memorandum on public finance across the bows of an incoming Government which, to his evident disgust, had 'given plenty of promises'.[121]

With the Conservative government established, Hamilton and his Treasury colleagues busied themselves in trying to curb any propensity to 'extravagance'. Hamilton noted in October 1895 that he was going to have his 'work cut out resisting some of the demands which Chamberlain and co. are sure to press, and are beginning to press – like development of Crown Colonies and the further support of voluntary schools'.[122] By January 1896 Hamilton's concern had turned to exasperation as he described how 'Members of the Cabinet press proposals on the Chancellor ... from which they derive or hope to derive credit for the expenditure involved thereby, and never take into account the discredit which he may get for having to provide the money'.[123] What made matters worse for the Treasury was that well-known 'spendthrifts' like Chamberlain were joined by men like Goschen who, on arriving at the Admiralty, was transformed from his Exchequer incarnation as Goschen the miser into Goschen the prodigal. A characteristic feature of Salisbury's third administration was, therefore, a battle between the Treasury and the spending departments, with many disagreements over a range of policy areas. The frustrations could not be contained, and in January 1900 Lord Salisbury of all people lauunched a scathing attack on the Treasury, likening its attempt to impose financial constraints on government action to the worst excesses of the Stuart monarchy.[124]

The increasing demands which the spending departments placed on the public purse were a product of the increasingly complex problems which faced late nineteenth-century Britain. For the defence departments, matching the growing strength of rival powers and policing Britain's imperial territories necessitated a rapid and substantial increase in expenditure on both men and material;[125] to reduce Britain's imperial commitment was unthinkable. Other departments faced similar difficulties. The scale of Britain's social problems, coupled with the assumption that the provision of material comfort was the best method to secure social peace and attract votes, led, as noted earlier, to a number of expensive social reforms: free education, housing and sanitary reforms, and workmen's compensation, all placed additional burdens on the Exchequer. That much of the cost of social reform and social administration fell upon local government or other locally elected authorities did not ease the financial problems of central government. The localities found it equally difficult to shoulder increased expenditure and, as a result, the fiscal crisis of the local state became as pronounced as that affecting the central authority.[126] The problems of the localities then fed back into the centre, for in the late nineteenth century grants-in-aid to local authorities proved to be one of the fastest-growing areas of government expenditure.[127] Additional demands were made by industry and agriculture, especially the latter, for the lowering of local rates to reduce costs during the depression, demands which could only be met by further recourse to central funds.[128] Joseph Chamberlain's early schemes for extending the market for British goods in the Empire demanded considerable investment in imperial infrastructure, sums which the Treasury clearly regarded as unacceptable.[129] Whichever way the British government turned, and whichever problem it sought to address, increased expenditure beckoned.

The growth of both normal and extra-ordinary expenditure made the threat of a chronic budget deficit very real. The fiscal implications of this situation, as many contemporaries realised, were far-reaching. The idea of even a short-term budgetary deficit was regarded in the pre-Keynesian era as unacceptable on all sides of the political spectrum. At the same time though, the financial burden of governing a highly-urbanized society experiencing the problems attendant on a maturing economy, let alone the cost of administering and protecting a vast territorial empire, meant that even the most sincere exponents of 'economy' were on a hiding to nothing. With retrenchment untenable there was only one option left, namely to increase the government's income. The question was, could this be done without breaking the mould of the existing tax structure.

In April 1889 Edward Hamilton, commenting on Goschen's reaction to a potential deficit, had noted that the Chancellor had considered imposing a 'small registration duty on all imports and exports'.[130] Much to Hamilton's relief Goschen instead turned to the Estates Duty. For Chancellors in the 1890s, the constant test of their ingenuity was to balance the books with resorting to fiscal novelties. Goschen, and his Liberal successor Harcourt, managed to keep the Exchequer in the black and to avoid decisive breaks from fiscal orthodoxy, but they tested the limits to the extreme. Whilst Goschen had flirted with revenue tariffs, Harcourt looked to direct taxation in his famous 1894 Budget.[131] This led Edward Hamilton, in July 1895, to warn the incoming Conservative government that 'unless the brake is applied to the spending propensities of the State . . . the Government may ere long find themselves confronted with a choice of evils involving serious changes in our fiscal system'.[132] Hamilton evidently agreed with Harcourt that the nation had 'reached the limits of tolerable taxation'.[133] State expenditure was not curtailed, however, and by 1899 an alarmed Hicks-Beach gave notice of an impending deficit of £4,000,000. Having insisted that neither a loan nor a raid on the sinking fund could be used to remedy the situation, and with his colleagues still unwilling to accept economies, Hicks-Beach concluded that 'the deficit . . . must therefore . . . be met by increased taxation'.[134] The question as to what kind was postponed for two years. Between 1899 and 1901 Hicks-Beach was able to conceal his problems under the cover of the financial exigencies of war, resorting to borrowing and a substantial increase in the income tax, but with peace looming in 1901 Hicks-Beach's difficulties resurfaced.

Writing to Salisbury in September 1901 Hicks-Beach described his problems in terms of the expenses and debt incurred not as a result of the war, but rather in terms of the fact that he could no longer resort to war taxation and borrowing. The core of the problem, he explained, was that 'normal expenditure has increased ... 40 per cent or more than 42 millions in ... six years' and that he could 'conceive no financial methods which could long provide for such a rate of increase in time of peace'.[135] Without massive reductions in expenditure, Hicks-Beach concluded, the only route to a balanced budget was to break from the established tax regime. He noted that there were only two possible strategies, both of which were unpalatable. The government could continue with war-time levels of direct taxation or draw more more revenue from indirect taxation, but Hicks-Beach suggested that the existing indirect duties were at the limit of effectiveness. He concluded that 'the only possible indirect taxes which would produce any important income without a complete return to a Protectionist policy, would be small duties on corn, or meat, or petroleum'.[136] Hamilton's prediction of 1895 had been borne out, the Conservatives could either resort to sustained, high levels of direct taxation, with all the redistributive implications that involved, or they could impose import duties which symbolically represented an abrogation of free trade. In the end the Conservatives opted to impose a one shilling registration duty on imported corn, the repeal of which in April 1903 ignited the tariff debate.

In the mid-Victorian era successive Chancellors, as a result of buoyant revenues attendant on an expanding economy, had enjoyed almost effort-less, budgetary surpluses. Budgetary policy itself had become essentially non-controversial, but the late nineteenth-century fiscal crisis of the British State changed all that. By threatening to undermine the balanced budget, the cardinal principle of 'sound' public finance, the fiscal crisis forced British chancellors towards radical new paths of fiscal policy and brought to an end the effective fiscal consensus which had been estab-lished by Peel, accepted by Disraeli and brought to the peak of refinement by Gladstone.[137]

The most immediate contact between the citizen and the State is the payment of taxation, and tax policy is the realm of economic policy for which the government of the day is held to be most responsible. The fiscal crisis brought the question of the distribution of the tax burden, and the distribution of wealth to the centre of British political decision-making. But in addition the fact that the fiscal crisis led the Conservative government to impose a revenue tariff illustrates its broader impact on British political and economic debates. Throughout the nineteenth century one of the main reasons for the Treasury's insistence on rigorous economy was their knowledge that any tendency towards a budget deficit could force or, even worse, tempt Governments to resort to tariffs.[138] Indeed, in 1899, Edward Hamilton had feared that the arch-protectionist Henry Chaplin was going to press for the introduction of pensions precisely because it would lead the government to introduce tariffs.[139] For Hamilton and the Treasury, one of the great beauties of Britain's liberal economic orthodoxy was that it was 'knave proof'.[140] Just as the gold standard prevented governments from tinkering with the currency, so the balanced budget thwarted knavery in two ways: first it prevented the incumbent administration from irresponsible acts of legislation aimed at 'bribing' the electorate and, second, it kept the British fiscal system clear of the need for tariffs, thereby precluding the clamour of special interests for protection. The danger of the deteriorating budgetary position was, in effect, that it was creating too much space for such 'heterodox' characters as Chaplin.

DEPRESSION, ECONOMICS AND ECONOMIC INTERESTS: SOME CONCLUDING REMARKS

The period of the 'Great Depression' marked an important turning point in British economic development – upon that much all commentators, contemporary and modern, are agreed. However, whereas for many contemporary observers the last quarter of the nineteenth century was a period in which the British economy was showing clear signs of decline, the verdict of modern economic history is that the emphasis should be placed not on decline but on *change*. Britain it seems experienced a relative decline in terms of share of world trade and manufacturing production – the inevitable result of moving from a quasi-monopoly to a competitive market – but the late nineteenth century was not a time of depression. Rather it was a period which saw the onset of structural changes, most notably the rapid growth of the tertiary sector, a decline in the international competitiveness of some sectors of British industry, and the decay of the most uncompetitive element of the agricultural sector. But a careful examination of contemporary opinion shows that these changes and developments were recognised at the time. It is true that they may not have been analysed with the sophistication of modern economic analysis, but comtemporary observers were able to grasp the most important trends in the British economy. In fact the essence of the contemporary analysis of Britain's economic situation was that the economy was in decline precisely because these structural changes were taking place. For example, H.H. Gibbs pointed out to W.H. Smith that the foundation of the bimetallist contention is *not that the country is not growing richer*, but that the goods of fortune have been unequally distributed [and that] . . . the classes who live upon realised capital have grown richer whilst those who have lessened their capital and income are the industrious producers.[141]

Similarly, even the doyen of economic orthodoxy in Oxford, F.Y. Edgeworth, conceded to the fair trade cause that 'pure preservation of agriculture *might* furnish sufficient motive for protection'.[142] Those who depicted the British economy as in decline, and the advocates of bimetallism, fair trade and imperial preference were by far the most pessimistic commentators, *equated* decline with the structural changes described by late twentieth-century observers, because they saw these structural changes as unhealthy. The differences between the contemporary and modern interpretations are the product not of a disagreement over basic facts, but of differing views as to whether the changes taking place in the late nineteenth-century economy were either necessary or helpful.

Once it is realized that the question of the 'myth' or 'reality' of the 'Great Depression' is not the basic issue at stake between contemporary and modern observers, it is much easier to grasp the significance of economic developments in the late nineteenth century and the debates which they generated. Rather than concentrating on the 'real' impact of the cyclical downturns of the late nineteenth century it is better to examine the pyschological and ideological ramifications of the depression years. The onset of structural change, the difficulties of British industry, the decline of agriculture, and the strength of foreign competition confirmed the worst fears of Britain's farmers and shook the confidence of many of Britain's manufacturers. The campaigns for bimetallism, fair trade and imperial federation were simply the most extreme symptoms of growing uncertainty about Britain's economic future and, more particularly, were indicative of a creeping doubt about the wisdom of Britain's increasingly unilateral commitment to economic internationalism.

The fundamental issue which emerged during the period of the 'Great Depression' was the question of Britain's role in the world economic order. The most important issue which the movements for imperial federation, fair trade and bimetallism brought to the fore was whether Britain was sensible, or indeed strong enough, to allow the structure of the British economy to be shaped by developments in the international economy. But although the issue itself was clear enough, the most interesting feature of the British business community's response was that they could not produce a coherent answer because they were not in any sense a community. The economic debates generated by the Great Depression revealed that the stratification of British finance, industry and agriculture was remarkably extensive. One division was over the relative merits of 'production' and 'finance and commerce', an issue raised most obviously by the bimetallic debate, but also present in the argument over fair trade and in the split between free trade/liberal imperialists and advocates of imperial preference. Industry and agriculture were seen as in conflict, such as over local rating relief. Divisions were, however, just as pronounced within as between sectors. British agriculture was marked by disputes between farmers and landlords, and also by conflicts of opinion between the predominantly mixed and cattle-farming areas of the North and West and the arable East and South.[143] The British manufacturing sector was also divided by geography, by different market perspectives, by scale and by organization. The financial sector demonstrated a stronger sense of unity, mainly because it was more a genuine community of interest, geographically concentrated in London and largely committed to the defence of Britain's links to the international economy.

The fragmentation of industrial and agricultural opinion was not helped by the fact that there were no institutional mechanisms to assist in promoting a common front. For the manufacturing sector the Associated Chamber of Commerce could not co-ordinate strategic thinking about the economy; its annual meetings brought local representatives together to air views, but this often exacerbated differences of opinion. With no effective central voice for industry, local chambers went their own way.[144] The agricultural sector suffered from the same problem, in that neither the Central Land Association nor the Central Chamber of Agriculture spoke for the industry as a whole. The CLA was generally, and rightly, regarded as a landowners' club, and although the CCA was supposedly more representative of the tenant farmers it too became increasingly associated with landowners. Both organizations tended to be dominated by representatives of the corn-growing belt, which caused resentment, especially in North-Western agricultural circles, in the 1890s.[145] A forum to bring industry and agriculture together appears never to have been seriously considered.

For anyone in Britain seeking 'the business response' to the 'Great Depression' life was made very difficult by the babel of voices with which the British business community spoke. Reflecting the highly individualistic structure of British economic activity, this helps explain why dissent against economic orthodoxy tended to be inchoate and ineffective. But in spite of the wide divergences of opinion there were common arguments emerging from the various economic interests in the late nineteenth century. The general tenor of the replies sent to the RCDTI and the other Royal Commissions which examined the state of the British economy, and the attention paid to the campaigns for fair trade, bimetallism and imperial federation, indicated a significant groundswell of economic discontent building up during the period of the 'Great Depression'. It is also clear that much of this discontent was critical, either implicitly or explicitly, of Britain's liberal economic policy structure. Nor did this discontent and criticism simply evaporate with the cyclical upswing which began in the mid- to late-1890s. Not all sectors benefited equally from this upswing, but the frequent and severe downturns of the previous fifteen to twenty years, and the fact that foreign competition had come to stay, engendered lingering doubts about the wisdom of Britain's established economic policies. A large part of British industry and agriculture fretted over its future, and the State fretted over its finances and the 'fitness' of its citizens. The question which occupied the minds of many contemporaries was whether the doubts and discontents which marked the period of the 'Great Depression' had important political ramifications, and it is to this question that this study will now turn its attention.

Part II

THE NATURE
OF THE
POLITICAL PROBLEM

2

CONSERVATISM AND THE EMPIRE

> If you look to the history of this country since the advent of Liberalism. . . you will find that there has been no effort so continuous, so subtle, supported by so much energy and carried on with so much ability and acumen as the attempts of Liberalism to effect the disintegration of the Empire.
>
> (Benjamin Disraeli at the Crystal Palace, 24 June 1872)[1]

Benjamin Disraeli's assertion that the Liberals could not be trusted with Britain's imperial interests, and that the Conservatives were the only sincere party of Empire, represented an important staging post for the Conservative party. Disraeli seized the nationalist strains of Palmerstonian diplomacy, gave them an imperial twist and sought to establish a Conservative monopoly over 'patriotic' issues.[2] The purchase of the Suez Canal shares, the aggressive stance adopted in Southern Africa and Afghanistan, the creation of Queen Victoria as Empress of India, and the encouragement of 'jingoism' over the Eastern Question made up elements in a process which saw the Conservative party in the 1870s attempt to annex the language of patriotism and Empire.[3] From then on the Conservative party sought to present the Liberal party as unpatriotic and anti-imperial and itself as the guardian of national and imperial interests.

BECOMING THE PARTY OF EMPIRE

The Conservatives did not find it easy to monopolize the Empire and patriotic issues, for the Liberal party had strong grounds for contesting Conservative claims. Palmerston had, after all, been an idiosyncratic Liberal, and patriotism had been an important part of the Radical vocabulary since the eighteenth century.[4] In the 1870s there was no obvious reason to suppose that Palmerston's party had abandoned an active foreign policy, nor to assume that Liberals and Radicals had ceased to articulate a powerful, non-chauvinist patriotic appeal. The bulk of Whig opinion was publicly committed to defend British imperial interests: the two most influential publicists of the cause of Empire in the late 1870s and early 1880s, Charles Dilke and J.R. Seeley, were both Liberals.[5] Even the rising star of Radicalism, Joseph Chamberlain, noted with dismay after the Congress of Berlin that the Liberal party had been harmed by a minority 'peace at any price' grouping in its ranks, and he told W.T. Stead that

> It is our business to show that we are as keenly alive to the respon-
> sibilities and duties of a great nation as our opponents; that we also
> have 'imperial instincts', but that we desire that these should be
> devoted to worthy objects.[6]

Liberal criticism of Disraeli's imperial policy was based not on anti-imperialism but on a different conception of Empire.

In the run-up to the general election of 1880 the Conservatives' brand of imperialism seemed more of a hindrance than a help. The depression of trade and agriculture between 1877 and 1880 may have been the underlying cause of hostility to the incumbent Conservative administration,[7] but the government's foreign and imperial policy also rendered it vulnerable. Disraeli's 'forward' policy in South Africa and Asia had been all very well when cheap and successful, but in the late 1870s losses, both human and financial, dimmed the policy's appeal. Likewise, although the government's bellicose stance on the Eastern Question may have seen the emergence of 'jingoism' as a popular phenomenon[8] it also allowed Gladstone to mobilize the Liberal-Nonconformist conscience in a crusade against the iniquities of 'Beaconsfieldism'.[9] In the Midlothian campaign of late 1879 Gladstone placed foreign and imperial issues at the heart of his assault on Disraeli's administration. On the one hand Gladstone argued that the Conservative government's aggression was leading Britain into unnecessary and expensive conflicts. At the same time Disraeli's support for a Turkish Empire that had massacred Bulgarian Christians was condemned as against the values of liberty, justice and Christianity upon which the British Empire was supposedly based. In short, Gladstone trumped the Conservatives' patriotic-imperial card by presenting the Liberal party as the only right-minded trustees of Britain's imperial heritage and interests. This was a remarkable but double-edged success. It was certain that this realm of policy would be used as a measure of the new Liberal government's performance, and Liberal failings in this sphere were quickly exploited.

Imperial problems dogged Gladstone's second administration from the outset. Soon after the Liberals took office Britain's deteriorating relationship with the Boer territories led to an outbreak of hostilities which provoked concern about British paramountcy in South Africa. As the aim of this study is to examine the domestic political ramifications of the

Liberals' imperial problems I will not enter into a detailed discussion of the 'First Boer War'.[10] Briefly it is fair to say that after the Boers had inflicted a number of defeats on British troops in minor skirmishes, culminating with the British débâcle at Majuba Hill, the Liberals managed to avoid a full-scale conflict by constructing a compromise in the shape of the Pretoria Convention of April 1881. In theory this agreement established British 'suzerainty' over the Transvaal and Orange Free State, but in practice it acknowledged the independence of the Boer Republics.[11] This settlement looked suspiciously like a climbdown: the Tory press denounced the Liberals' 'weak' defence of British interests, whilst Salisbury pointed out that 'A suzerainty over a Republic is merely a diplomatic invention' and concluded that the Convention was 'a device to cover surrender'.[12] These barbs were well aimed, for the crisis in Southern Africa had threatened to divide both the Liberal Cabinet and the Liberal party at large. On the one hand the Whig/Right of the Liberal party had taken the view that the government, and the Colonial Secretary Kimberley in particular, had been less than competent in dealing with the situation and thus, by implication, neglectful of British interests. On the other hand the Radical/Left had argued that the government and Kimberley had adopted an excessively interventionist stance when no obvious British interest was threatened, and had thus contravened the principles of self-determination which Gladstone had extolled during the Midlothian campaign.[13] In the end a crisis was avoided, but the controversy over South Africa showed that the Liberal party's imperial flank could be turned.

The Liberals enjoyed no respite in their second year of government. In the summer of 1882 the Egyptian nationalist rising led by Arabi propelled the government, in spite of Gladstone's reluctance, into another military expedition to 'restore order' in Egypt. On this occasion the defeat of the nationalist forces at Tel-el-Kebir ensured that criticism of the government was muted, until the situation in North Africa deteriorated in the Sudan, where Islamic fundamentalism 'represented in an extreme form that militancy which Britain thought she had seen in Arabi'.[14] In 1883, with Mahdist activism on the increase, the Liberal government agreed to William Hicks commanding what was in formal terms an Egyptian expedition into the Sudan, but in November Hicks and his force were destroyed. This setback provided the Conservatives with ammunition: in March 1884 Gladstone noted that 'Egypt is worked relentlessly for purposes of mischief, and it pays'.[15] In an attempt to cut their losses the government ordered the evacuation of the Sudan, but unfortunately the individual they chose to carry out this task – General Charles Gordon – took it upon himself to stay on in Khartoum, in what was, in every sense, a vain attempt to restore quiet to the Sudan. In February 1885 Khartoum fell to the besieging Mahdists and Gordon was killed.

Even before Gordon's death Gladstone had complained that 'The Egyptian flood comes on us again and again, like the sea on the host of Pharaoh';[16] following the fall of Khartoum, Gladstone was more like Noah without his ark. In the Lords Salisbury blamed government indecision, and argued that if the Liberal Cabinet opted to abandon the Sudan after the conclusion of military operations it would be 'dangerous to Egypt and inconsistent with the interests of the Empire'.[17] Salisbury also raised the issue of confidence over future Liberal management of the Empire,[18] and, in a clear appeal to Whig/Right opinion, portrayed Gladstone as a prisoner of 'his extreme supporters' on the Radical side of the Liberal party who looked upon him as 'the apostle of absolute negation in foreign affairs'.[19] Pointing to general Liberal 'incompetence' in imperial affairs, the Duke of Richmond, seconding the Conservative censure motion in the Lords, declared that

> When the present ministry came into power one of their first acts was an apology to a great and friendly power . . . offered needlessly . . . A little later we had to deplore the humiliating defeat at Majuba . . . Ireland . . . is at the present moment on the verge of rebellion. They have tried the patience of our Colonies. They have jeopardized India . . . and they have deluged the Soudan with the blood of our brave soldiers.[20]

In the Commons Henry Chaplin similarly linked Ireland and the Sudan, and argued that Britain's imperial crises were the product of Liberal doctrine, claiming that the situation in the Sudan, like the government's other imperial difficulties, was 'the outcome – the natural and inevitable outcome – of the madness of the Midlothian campaign'.[21] For the Liberals to have lost one imperial skirmish could be deemed unfortunate, that they had lost two seemed like carelessness.

The Conservative critique of the Liberal government was part of a campaign to bring about the defection of 'moderate' Liberal opinion – the strategy being to portray the Liberal government as the 'prisoners' of a Radical Little Englander phalanx. In developing these arguments Conservatives mined a rich vein of concern in the Liberal ranks. An analysis of Liberal party voting patterns in the House of Commons between 1880 and 1885 has revealed a group of Liberal MPs who consistently supported Conservative criticisms of the government's imperial and military failures;[22] during imperial crises government majorities fell to their lowest levels. Many individual Liberals became disillusioned with the party over imperial issues. For example in July 1884 the young Alfred Milner, soon to be an unenthusiastic Liberal Parliamentary candidate, told H.S. Foxwell that with regard to the government's Egyptian policy 'I should have been heartily glad to see them turned out for it'.[23] In 1885 H.O. Arnold-Forster, the adopted son of W.E. Forster, the former

Liberal Education and Irish Secretary, resigned his Liberal candidacy in Devonport in protest at the Liberals' 'betrayal' of Gordon and mismanagement of the Sudanese crisis.[24] By mid-1885 it was not only in the domestic sphere that the spectre of Radical influence was causing concern in Liberal circles.

It was, however, the Irish Question which allowed the Conservatives the fullest scope to exploit Liberal divisions over imperial issues.[25] To understand the full resonance of the Irish problem in late-Victorian politics it is essential to acknowledge that it was regarded as 'Britain's closest, most apparent and intractable Imperial problem'.[26] Although Ireland was part of the United Kingdom the essence of the Irish problem – a conflict between a privileged 'settler' class and a nationalist movement founded on native peasant grievances – gave it a distinctly colonial form. Contemporaries certainly saw resemblances. In the early 1880s Afrikaners opposing the British in South Africa were labelled 'Fenians' by Cabinet Ministers and officials at the Foreign and Colonial Offices,[27] and it is not difficult to see why the parallels were drawn. Groups like the 'Fenians', the Boers, and Arabi's supporters were all nationalist challenges to the legitimacy of British control. The links were further confirmed by the fact that the Irish Nationalist party at Westminster consistently supported opposition to British rule wherever it emerged. When, in 1880, the Queen's Speech announced the British government's intention to suppress the Boer rebellion the Irish Nationalists moved a hostile amendment condemning the policy. They also gave support to Arabi, opposed intervention in Egypt, and even had the temerity to express sympathy for the Mahdists.[28] In the light of their demands for self-government and their opposition to any extension or strengthening of the British Empire elsewhere, the Irish Nationalists represented the closest and most constant challenge to Britain's imperial rule.

To many disgruntled Liberals the Irish Question came to embody everything they disliked about the government's administration of the Empire and the general tenor of Liberal politics. Between 1880 and 1885 Radicals habitually joined forces with Irish Nationalists to harry the government over imperial questions, and appeared to support the view that the Empire dealt with the Irish as unjustly as it dealt with the Boers, Egyptians, Sudanese and other oppressed natives.[29] In contemporary eyes Radical Little Englandism and Irish Nationalism showed a common hostility to the maintenance of the integrity of the Empire, and Ireland was increasingly depicted as the focus for those who sought to disrupt the Empire. Of course Whigs and moderate Liberals were accustomed to finding Radical views objectionable, but what was particularly alarming in the early 1880s was the idea that Radical opinion made the government too attentive to Irish grievances and too neglectful of the task of governance in Ireland. The government's policy was seen to veer between concessions to Irish demands and coercive efforts to enforce the rule of law and the rights of property, and Whig and moderate opinion was clearly apprehensive about the effect of government policy on British authority in Ireland and also further afield. Sir A.C. Lyall, the Liberal Governor of the Indian North-West Provinces, told John Morley in 1882 that the murder of the Irish Secretary, Lord Frederick Cavendish, and his deputy in Phoenix Park had undermined his confidence in Gladstone and the government, on the grounds that 'assassins' in India and Afghanistan would follow the Irish example.[30] Likewise, the depth of controversy over the Ilbert Bill of 1883 arose from a more general anxiety generated by Ireland's seeming descent into ungovernability. The Ilbert Bill, designed to extend the role and powers of 'native' officials in India, was denounced as an abdication of responsibility, and the proposal to give Indian magistrates the power to judge Europeans was met with particularly fierce resistance.[31] Once again the Irish analogy was drawn, with the disaffected Liberal jurist James Fitzjames Stephen announcing in *The Times* that his opposition to the Ilbert Bill was akin to, even a consequence of, his opposition to Irish Home Rule.[32] The Irish Question was constantly cross-referenced with other imperial problems: it was not *sui generis* but regarded as part of the main policy agenda of the period.

Writing to Lord Spencer in December 1883 Gladstone argued that 'Experience convinces me . . . that whilst Ireland has plenty of power to vex this great Empire, she has no power at all to wound it'.[33] Many Liberals disagreed. How far Home Rule threatened the unity of the Empire was crucial to the 'Great Separation' of the Liberal party on that issue. Home Rule for Ireland *was* clearly an imperial issue. Gladstone himself saw the vital question: 'is this, is Home Rule, a thing compatible or incompatible with the unity of the Empire',[34] and his supporters were convinced that Home Rule gave Ireland the fullest measure of self-government 'consistent with the unity and integrity of the Empire'.[35] Thus Lord Spencer informed the Queen Empress that although 'we deeply regret to learn that the Queen considers that the Irish measures of the government are dangerous to the Union of the Empire . . . we venture to take a different view of the proposal'.[36] Likewise Spencer told Lord Monck that even with the creation of a separate Irish legislature he would 'deny that . . . Parliament will lose its character as Imperial'.[37] In the House of Commons too Home Rule Liberals upheld imperial integrity; they merely denied Home Rule was a threat to the Empire.[38]

Opponents of Home Rule saw it as incompatible with the security of the Empire. Salisbury of course had linked the Irish question to the threat of imperial disintegration in 1883, and in 1886 the Conservatives simply asserted that his fears had proved justified. Walter Long claimed Conservatives were as anxious as anyone to see Ireland at peace, but he added that 'there was a price that was too heavy for such a benefit and that was to give up the integrity of the Empire', and that 'the Government scheme . . . would lead to the dismemberment of the Empire'.[39] In developing the imperial case against Home Rule the Conservatives found support from Whig and moderate Liberal opinion time and again. Leading the way was Hartington, who ended his long protest against Home Rule with the appeal that MPs opposed to the measure 'sink all minor differences, and . . . unite as one man for the maintenance of this great Empire . . . compact and complete'. Another Liberal ex-Cabinet Minister, G.J. Goschen, declared 'the effect of surrender' would send a signal to Europe and India that Britain could no longer resist challenges to its imperial interests.[40] By attacking Home Rule in terms of the integrity of the Empire the Conservatives brought their six-year campaign to destroy the Liberal government's imperial credentials to a climax. The events of 1886 allowed the Conservatives to establish themselves as the only committed defenders of the rights of property[41] and the most committed guardians of the Empire.

After 1886, Liberal Imperialism was not destroyed: it found ample expression in the constituencies and was represented in the highest echelons of the party by Lord Rosebery, H.H. Asquith, R.B. Haldane and Edward Grey.[42] Furthermore, even those Liberals who were identified as 'Little Englanders' were for the most part not hostile to the Empire in any straightforward sense.[43] Yet no matter how hard and with what justice the Liberals, especially the Liberal Imperialists, argued their case, the Conservatives had succeeded in identifying Conservatism with the defence of the Empire and Liberalism with its disintegration. The Imperial Federation League, founded in 1884, first declared itself to be non-partisan, and attracted support from Liberals and Conservatives alike.[44] However, after 1886 a majority of MPs most involved in IFL activities were Conservatives; Conservatives and Liberal Unionists together outnumbered Liberals by over four to one.[45] It is true that the longest serving President of the IFL after 1886 was the future Liberal Prime Minister Lord Rosebery, but in 1890 he confessed to the IFL's secretary

> I have heard it stated . . . that members would join in greater numbers or with greater confidence if the President were one of different politics to mine. I dare say this is so, and for that and other reasons, I think there would be a great advantage in the selection of a Conservative President.[46]

That such a committed Liberal Imperialist as Rosebery could make such an admission bears eloquent testimony to the Conservative party's success in annexing the realm of imperialist discourse.[47]

The time and effort the Conservative party devoted to establishing its claim to be *the* party of Empire prompts the question as to why they bothered. All too frequently it is taken as read that the Conservatives were the party of Empire, but it is a development which needs to be explained. A vulgar Marxist analysis would look to the social make-up of the Conservative party, in that a complex lattice of material interests appears to have linked Conservatives to the Empire. In the period between 1880–1914 over half the Parliamentary party had some form of connection with Britain's military establishment. Many Conservative MPs were or had been officers in the regular army, and many others were high-ranking members of local volunteer forces and the county yeomanry. Although military duties did not necessarily guarantee enthusiasm for the Empire the obvious connections between military careers and the Empire made it likely. For the aristocracy and gentry the Empire seems to have provided new investment and employment opportunities to bolster incomes hit by the agricultural depression. Comprehensive surveys are not yet available, but there is evidence that landed families diversified their asset holding in order to reduce their dependency on a depressed agricultural market, and that colonial stocks and real estate were a favourite (and patriotic) alternative.[48] At the same time the expansion of the Empire also saw an expansion of the Imperial Service. New colonies meant new colonial governorships and a host of other posts, all of which, in addition to the positions already available, offered suitable employment for scions of Britain's traditional elite.[49] In the newer Conservative world of provincial manufacture the Empire and its markets were regarded as important assets in the depressed and highly competitive environment which existed from the mid-1870s on.[50] Likewise Britain's burgeoning service sector, which fuelled the development of suburbia – the home of 'Villa Toryism' – owed much of its growth, especially in London, to the increasing market for Indian, dominion and colonial loans, stocks and insurance.[51] That the jingo crowds which filled Trafalgar Square on Mafeking night were largely made up of clerks is thus unsurprising, for such celebrations acknowledged the bread and butter which the Empire provided for these yobbish Pooters.[52]

It would, however, be an over-simplification to assert that imperialism can be read off from Conservative material interests in the Empire. The Conservative constituency was highly stratified and there was plenty of room for disagreement: a clerk from Camberwell did not necessarily see imperialism in the same way as an aristocrat, and neither necessarily shared the same vision of Empire as a Birmingham screw manufacturer, whose views could in turn differ from those of a City financier.[53] A crude materialist analysis simply looks at the problem in the wrong way. One should ask not simply whether the Conservative party was imperialist because its constituency was imperialist, but whether the constituency was imperialist because it was Conservative. This acknowledges that ideological constructions are as 'real' as any material factor in shaping political behaviour. However, it is an approach which throws up problems of its own. Imperialism may have been part of a matrix of shared values and assumptions intrinsic to being a Conservative in the late nineteenth century, but this was neither 'natural' nor well-established. The creation of Conservative imperialism was just that, a creation and not some innate process. Likewise it was only in the 1870s and 1880s that the Conservatives worked hardest to present themselves as the imperial party, which poses the question as to why it was so important for a Conservative to be an imperialist then.

The vital clue to establishing why imperialism was so important to the late nineteenth-century Conservative party lies in the transformation of Britain's imperial position. Britain's annexations in the late nineteenth century were essentially defensive, frequently prompted by the fear that rival powers would seize territories and close them to British trade. Furthermore, the extent of Britain's imperial commitment caused concern over whether Britain had the resources to defend its possessions.[54] Unrest within Britain's formal and informal Empire also threatened to disrupt British imperial interests, even in the most settled parts of the Empire. In Canada especially, but also in the Australian territories, the assertion of independent policies necessitated a reassessment of Britain's relationship to its Dominions. In short, the late nineteenth century witnessed a graphic change in the structures of British imperialism.

One result of Britain's 'crisis of imperialism' was that it sparked a wide-ranging debate about future conceptions of Britain's imperial role and its domestic implications. The majority of participants accepted the importance of maintaining the Empire, but a cluster of arguments contended that without the Empire Britain could not maintain either power or prosperity. The central assumption of the strong imperialist positions was an argument about size. J.R. Seeley provided the canonical reference here with his remark in *The Expansion of England* that the trend to political unification and the emergence of great continental states like Germany, the USA and Russia indicated that 'states which are on the old scale of magnitude are unsafe, insignificant, second rate'.[55] Informed by vogue metaphors from Darwinism many imperialists saw the message of the age to be that only the Empire possessed resources on a scale to match the evolving continental powers with which Britain had to compete.[56] In hard-pressed industrial and commercial districts, many looked to the Empire's existing and potential markets as a secure and expanding outlet for British capital and goods. Proposals put forward by the various Chambers of Commerce to the RCDTI indicated that there was disagreement as to the best manner of exploiting the Empire, but agreement on the Empire's commercial importance.[57] This had further potential in terms of overcoming social problems, especially unemployment. The markets of the Empire would, it was argued, maintain high levels of trade, output and employment.[58] In addition, the Colonies were depicted as settlement areas capable of absorbing Britain's surplus and unemployed population, with the added bonus that these settlers would then become colonial customers for British goods and help provide stable employment for those left behind.[59] Closer co-operation with the Colonies on matters of imperial defence, especially military expenditure, was put forward as a means of avoiding what is now known as 'imperial overstretch'.[60] In other words, the Empire itself was to be the chief instrument of maintaining Britain's imperial status.

The imperialist arguments which emerged in the late nineteenth century signalled a potential constituency for the Conservative party. The economic value of Empire discerned by British businessmen presented an opportunity for an appeal to specific interest groups, but broader aspects were even more important. All the arguments in favour of Empire were concerned about stability. The Empire's resources and markets were to stabilize the British economy, and this, in tandem with the export of surplus population as colonial settlers, was to guarantee prosperity and social peace. This could appeal not only to those who had a direct interest in imperial land, stocks, mines and markets but to those with a stake in maintaining the social and political status quo. It was very important that the Empire could be presented as a *national* rather than a sectional or class interest. In the Home Rule debate the Empire was deployed as a means of tapping anti-Irish prejudice, but imperialism seemed to hold out the possibility of a more general cross-class appeal to national solidarity. The Conservative party constantly implied that the lower orders would put loyalty to country and Empire above loyalty to class.[61] Some Conservatives felt the Empire could provide their party with genuine popular appeal, particularly if imperial patriotism was linked to material benefits provided by an imperial economy.[62] However, the bulk of the Conservative party, following the example of Salisbury himself, fought shy of populist imperialism and were sceptical about its efficacy. Set against the backdrop of the main political aims of Salisburyian Conservatism the appeal of the Empire to the British masses was a secondary consideration. Rather the language of imperialism seemed to be imbued with the potential to prevent popular politics from becoming class politics. Salisbury's speech about the importance of Empire at Carnarvon in April 1888 illustrates perfectly the ideological work of Empire in this context. Salisbury acknowledged Britain's difficulties,

> We have a population constantly growing in a limited island. We
> have all the difficulties of vicissitude in prosperity and adversity, the
> increasing claims of the poor, the increasing difficulties of the rich.
> We have looming before us political questions such as were never

presented to the world to settle before, the relations between capital and labour and the like.[63]

Salisbury's sense of Britain as a 'limited island' was in keeping with the imperialist emphasis on using the scale of the Empire to help solve Britain's problems. However, the chief function of imperialism for the Salisburyian party was not to proselytize the masses but to reassure and rally those frightened by the masses. This does indeed relate to the Conservative constituency in the late nineteenth century. But rather than being the *result* of a consensus, the Conservative stress on imperialism expressed a *desire to construct* a consensus between an existing and a broader potential constituency. The essence of the Conservative position was that Conservatism was synonymous with imperialism and imperialism synonymous with stability. For contemporaries the main critics of Empire within the British polity – Radicals, Irish Nationalists, and Socialists – were the groups most associated with threats of social upheaval and political change. By identifying Conservatism with imperialism, and imperialism with stability Conservatives simultaneously presented imperialism as central to their domestic *raison d'être*.

THE PARTY OF EMPIRE AND THE BURDEN OF EMPIRE

The Conservative party's success in establishing itself as the party of Empire brought problems as well as benefits. After 1886 they had to defend their claim to this title and hold together the pro-Empire coalition of forces which they had constructed in the 1870s and early 1880s. This task was eased somewhat by the behaviour of the Liberal party. Until Gladstone's retirement in 1894 the Liberals remained committed to Irish Home Rule, the quintessential anti-imperial policy. The tenure of Gladstone's successor Rosebery, a Liberal Imperialist, was short-lived and he was followed in quick succession by Sir William Harcourt, a renowned 'Little Englander', and Sir Henry Campbell-Bannerman, a man whose attitude to the Empire was as difficult to fathom as the rest of his political outlook. Moreover, in the 1890s the Liberals' low morale and poor organization prevented their co-ordinating an appeal on a subject as divisive as the Empire.

The Conservatives' political opponents may have done their best to make life easy for the 'imperial' party, but the same could not be said for Britain's imperial rivals.[64] The Conservatives, in government for twelve of the last fifteen years of the century, bore the responsibility of shaping the British response to a series of external challenges. But any attempt to extend, defend or develop territories under British control raised the unpleasant question of who was to pay for increases in military, administrative and infrastructural outlay. In February 1887 Salisbury warned Sir Evelyn Baring, the Egyptian Pro-Consul, that

> In considering the financial question you must not forget the extreme difficulty . . . in persuading the H[ouse] of C[ommons] to incur any expense about Egypt. The presence of taxation here is very heavy. Motions in the direction of economy will unite many who ordinarily vote apart.[65]

These fiscal worries dogged the Conservatives' imperial policy through the last decade of the century. Joseph Chamberlain's ambitious colonial development schemes of the late 1890s were thwarted by budgetary considerations, whilst even Kitchener's 'reconquest' of the Sudan in 1896–8 drew strong Treasury criticism and raised the spectre of increased taxation.[66] Occasional schemes received government support, but the preferred approach was to leave the extension and consolidation of the Empire to British interests 'on the ground' – hence the so-called partition of Africa 'by company'.[67] But even this could cause expensive or embarrassing problems. In Southern Africa, for example, the activities of the British South Africa Company, culminating in the Jameson Raid, pushed Britain towards renewed conflict with the Boer Republics. Difficulties such as these cast doubts, in terms of expenditure and basic principle, on the practice of using private interests as agents of imperial policy.

There were further internal complications. The strain on British resources raised the question as to whether the Colonies, and especially the self-governing Dominions, could be persuaded to shoulder some of the burgeoning cost of imperial maintenance. This was understandable, for the contribution of British taxpayers to the cost of Empire was much greater than that of Dominion taxpayers, whilst the benefits of the Empire, in terms of capital investment and the provision of imperial defence, were disproportionately enjoyed by the Dominions.[68] It was in part this imbalance which prompted the Cape Premier Jan Hofmeyr to propose, at the first Colonial Conference in 1887, an imperial revenue tariff for the purpose of providing a common fund to pay the costs of imperial defence. No doubt Hofmeyr also saw the revenue argument as the means to open a broader debate on imperial trade policy, but the burden of imperial defence was a major issue, especially in Britain.

Funding imperial defence was linked, almost from the outset, with proposals for an imperial tariff since the Dominions and Colonies were reluctant to raise direct taxation to pay for imperial defence. But from the 1880s on the self-governing Dominions demonstrated an increasing self-assertiveness, particularly in the realm of trade and tariff policy. In pro-imperial circles, both in Britain and the Dominions, this gave rise to concern that a 'centrifugal' tendency was developing which could break up the Empire; hence the slogan of the IFL was 'Federation or Separation'. To link imperial defence and imperial trade would counter potential disruption of the 'imperial bond' from within. As both the party of Empire and the imperial government the Conservatives were thus confronted by the issue of whether to redefine the relationship between Britain and its 'daughter' states in order to preserve the Empire as a meaningful entity.

The problem for Conservative governments in reshaping the Empire was that many of the policy options available seemed likely to disrupt both the Empire and the Conservative political base. Successive Conservative governments, as noted above, sought to avoid ambitious imperial development for fear of increasing the domestic tax burden. Persuading the Empire to take on a greater share of the cost was hampered by the reluctance of the Dominions to do so without the prospect of a broader economic quid pro quo. Unfortunately the favoured British options of Empire Free Trade, or an 'Imperial Zollverein', ran counter to the Dominions' desire for greater economic self-sufficiency. Likewise the Dominions' proposal for preferential, reciprocal tariff agreements, pressed with increasing vigour through the 1890s, divided British imperialist opinion and were thought, as a consequence of the 'food tax' bogey, to be unacceptable to a mass audience. Such difficulties explain why Conservative ideas about Empire, whether outlined by 'great men' like Disraeli or given collective expression by organizations like the Primrose League were mostly vague and even platitudinous. It is significant that in 1891 Salisbury threw the burden of producing a plan for imperial federation on the IFL, thereby steering both his government and his party away from the problem; when the IFL broke under the strain his caution seemed justified. It was much easier for Conservatives to pose as the defenders of Empire rather than present a positive vision of imperial development. Conservative imprecision on imperialism implicitly acknowledged that it could disrupt as well as unify the forces of Conservatism.

In the late 1880s and 1890s the Conservatives avoided difficult decisions on imperial policy, but it was clear these decisions would have to be faced. A Memorandum to the Conservative Cabinet in February 1891 concluded that there were sound economic arguments against imperial preference, but stated that, for two reasons, 'The persistent demand of the colonies for preferential fiscal arrangments may . . . become politically embarrassing'. On the one hand the British government's apparent 'contempt' for imperial preference proposals was, the Memorandum pointed out, 'interpreted in the Colonies as indifference to commercial union itself'. Further refusals were deemed likely to strengthen colonial separatism. Examining the domestic political scene the Memorandum concluded that 'the existence of the Imperial Federation League, and the support given to it, and to the Colonial Institute and the Imperial Institute, show the strength of feeling at home in favour of a consolidation of the Empire' which could not be ignored for ever.[69] Through the 1890s and early years of the twentieth century the resonance of this last point increased for the Conservatives; NUCA meetings carried motions in favour of imperial preference in 1887, 1891, 1892, 1894, 1895, 1896, 1898, 1900 and 1902.[70]

It was this groundswell of opinion, in the Colonies, in Britain at large and in the Conservative party in particular, which, in the mid-1890s, allowed Joseph Chamberlain to reinvigorate his political career. By the early 1890s he had established a cordial relationship with the Conservative leadership, but he was still regarded with some suspicion in the lower party echelons. However, by 1900 Chamberlain was the darling of the rank and file, eulogized in the Conservative press, and cheered on Conservative platforms throughout the country. It has been suggested that Chamberlain's emergence as a dynamic Colonial Secretary and the champion of imperial preference is best understood in the biographical context – 'Brummagem Joe' seeking to turn Britain's imperial realm into 'the British Empire Limited'.[71] There is something to this, but it offers only a partial insight into the significance of Chamberlain's advocacy of Empire. Insofar as residual Conservative suspicions of Chamberlain were in part the product of his social origins, a 'business' view of Empire could have appeased only a section of urban Conservative opinion. Indeed, had he described the Empire in purely business terms Chamberlain would most likely have reinforced Conservative prejudices against him. When Chamberlain focused on the issues of imperial development he spoke the language of the countryside. At Walsall in July 1895, in one of his first major speeches after becoming Colonial Secretary, Chamberlain compared the Empire not to a business enterprise, as one might have expected in this urban, industrial setting, but to an 'undeveloped estate', and, extending the metaphor, he declared 'What would a great landlord do in a similar case with a great estate? ... If he had the money he could expend some of it at any rate in improving the property'.[72] In effect, Chamberlain used a language associated with a landed, Conservative ethos. Furthermore, portraying the 'improving landlord' as a figure to be emulated could but appear as an act of apostasy, given his previous association with urban politics and radical denunciations of the landlord class. Chamberlain presented his interest in Empire in terms acceptable to Conservative sensibilities, and, more important still, brought his renowned energy to bear on the problems of Empire and intra-imperial relations when they were a cause of growing concern to many Conservatives.

THE BOER WAR AND THE GENESIS OF TARIFF REFORM

The mid- to late-1890s thus saw a *process* whereby a dynamic imperial policy had increasing attractions for a Conservative party struggling to justify its claim to be the party of Empire, but the *moment* when the attraction was strongest was during and immediately after the second Boer War. The Boer republics had long been seen as obstacles to British supremacy in Southern Africa and development of their gold fields increased Boer wealth and strength. The attempt by the British South Africa Company to solve this problem ended with the ignominy of the Jameson Raid, an event which exposed the limitations of 'ground level imperialism', and, in the shape of the general European reaction and the German response in particular, demonstrated Britain's isolation at a time of increasing great-power tension. For Joseph Chamberlain, whose own career was briefly threatened by accusations of complicity in the raid, the South African problem was of personal significance, but the situation in South Africa epitomised imperial difficulties, and imbued it with significance for the party of Empire. Thus the needs of Joseph Chamberlain and the needs of the Conservative party intersected on the veld, and as the crisis in South Africa deepened so Chamberlain's stock with Conservative opinion rose. In July 1899 Lord Selborne informed Chamberlain

> I met Bartley ... today. As you know he is ... not fond of L[iberal] U[nionist]s. He came up to me and said 'look here, you know that I am not alone on the Tory benches in not loving this Government too dearly, but if you will only have the pluck to see this Transvaal business through ... we will stick to you through thick and thin'.[73]

That a Tory bigot like Bartley could express such sentiments indicates how far Chamberlain's belligerent stance had won over the Conservative rank and file. As 'Joe's War' progressed, and during the 'Khaki' election of September 1900 Chamberlain enjoyed enormous popularity with Conservative audiences. Just as one imperial problem had brought Chamberlain into an alliance with the Conservatives, so another enabled him first to consolidate his position in the Tory fold and then emerge as a genuine leader of Conservative opinion.

It was in the context of the Conservative response to the shortcomings revealed by the Boer War that the tariff reform campaign, with its emphasis on uniting the Empire, enjoyed such resonance. For the Conservative party, eager to refurbish its image as the party of Empire, a policy which held out the promise of greater imperial security was bound to strike a chord whilst memories of 'Black Week' were still fresh. Here it is important to recognize that although the Conservative party accepted Kipling's verdict that Britain had been treated to 'A Lesson' in South Africa, there were two factors which gave them cause for optimism – the Conservative victory at the 'Khaki' election of 1900, and the level of military and diplomatic support Britain had received from the Colonies.

The question of whether Conservative electoral triumph in September 1900 was the product of mass enthusiasm for an imperial war is still a matter of debate for historians.[74] However, contemporaries of all political shades saw the result as mass support for the war and for imperialism. Writing to Goldwin Smith in January 1900 James Bryce described Britain as 'intoxicated with militarism',[75] and another Liberal, J.A. Hobson, was profoundly impressed, and depressed, by the ease with which he felt the masses had been manipulated by a corrupt, imperialist press playing upon what he referred to as 'the mass psychology of jingoism'.[76] Conservative observations were similarly dominated by references to what Salisbury called 'the jingo hurricane',[77] and for Joseph Chamberlain the war had presented an opportunity to make a strident appeal to the patriotism of the masses and to demonstrate the electoral potential of popular imperialism. Having urged the electorate 'not to think of persons or parties but only of imperial interests',[78] whilst telling voters that a vote for the Liberals was a vote for the Boers, Chamberlain seemed to have been vindicated by the Conservative triumph.

It is easy to appreciate why contemporary opinion was so impressed by the seemingly favourable effect of the Boer War on the Conservative party's electoral fortunes. Since the Second Reform Act no government had retained office; the 'swing of the pendulum' had been elevated to the status of an electoral law. Thus the Conservative victory in 1900 was unprecedented, and Liberal failures submerged as attention focused on explaining Conservative 'success'. As a consequence popular imperialism was established as an electoral trump card for the Conservatives, and those who had argued in the 1890s that the party play this card more frequently had their case strengthened.

The 'popular' response to the Boer War was one 'permissive' factor in creating the space for imperial preference and the tariff reform campaign, but a further impetus came from the assistance which Britain had obtained from the Colonies during the conflict. Writing to Lord Beauchamp in March 1900 Chamberlain argued that 'whatever may have to be recorded in this war there is one great inestimable gain: the bloodshed has cemented the British Empire, and the sense of unity is stronger than it ever has been before'.[79] Three years later Chamberlain restated these wartime sentiments in the opening speech of the tariff campaign, declaring

> we have had a war – a war in which the majority of our children abroad had no apparent direct interest. We had no hold over them,

no agreement with them of any kind, and yet, at one time during this war, by their voluntary decision, at least 50,000 Colonial soldiers were standing shoulder to shoulder with British troops . . . It is something for a beginning.[80]

Looking at the war from this perspective the *National Review* was able to argue that 'the South African War opened a new epoch in our history'; although 'the crisis revealed the unpleasant fact that Great Britain had scarcely a foul weather friend in the civilized world' it had been the case that 'the hostility of the foreigner had been superabundantly compensated by the grit and determination of the Colonies'.[81] The Boer war seemed to show that the Colonies were committed as much as the motherland to the maintenance of the Empire, and that colonial nationalism, which had impeded moves towards closer imperial unity in the 1890s, was an obstacle that could perhaps be overcome.

Displays of imperial sentiment by the 'younger nations' were also evident in the crucial sphere of economic relations. In March 1900, when offering his eulogy on the unifying effects of the war, Chamberlain, conscious of colonial nationalism, had told Lord Beauchamp, 'Knowing as I do the strong feeling of independence which exists in all the self-governing Colonies . . . I would greatly prefer the initiative in any further movement towards closer union should be taken by the Colonies'.[82] Between 1900 and 1903 Chamberlain's wish was fulfilled. At the Colonial Conference of 1902 the resolution was passed that

> with a view to promoting the increase of trade within the Empire, it is desirable that those Colonies which have not already adopted such a policy should, as far as their circumstances permit, give substantial preferential treatment to the products and manufactures of the United Kingdom . . . [and] That the Prime Ministers of the Colonies respectfully urge on His Majesty's Government the expediency of granting in the United Kingdom preferential treatment to the products and manufactures of the Colonies.[83]

This resolution came to be known as 'the Colonial offer', and Chamberlain, again in his Bingley Hall speech of May 1903, referred to this, as to the war, as a 'new chapter in our imperial history'. Launching the tariff campaign was thus designed to exploit the Colonies' imperial enthusiasm and post-war British goodwill towards the Colonies before they began to fade.

The nature and timing of the tariff campaign owed a great deal to the Boer War and the 1902 Colonial Conference, inasmuch as they provided evidence that 'our Colonies are enthusiastically imperialistic'[84] when the survival of the Empire had never seemed more threatened yet more necessary. These circumstances helped to convince Chamberlain that he had grounds to hope, even expect, that imperial preference would be endorsed by the Conservative party. One year before his Bingley Hall 'declaration' Chamberlain had made a very similar speech which had attracted praise but excited little controversy. Prior to his departure for South Africa in the autumn of 1902 Chamberlain, to his satisfaction at least, gained Cabinet approval for imperial preference. In his absence the Treasury dug in its heels over the corn duty, but the underlying Cabinet majority appeared to favour the preference. Chamberlain also knew that on 15 May Balfour was to receive a deputation of Conservative back-benchers arguing in favour of both the retention of the corn duty and imperial preference, and there is circumstantial evidence which suggests that Balfour himself knew and perhaps even approved of the argument Chamberlain was to put forward in May 1903.[85] Against this backdrop Chamberlain personally may have felt less inhibited in giving expression to his 'constructive imperialism' in 1903. The Boer War and the 'Colonial Offer' had increased the political space for a 'new departure' in imperial policy. Whether that space was large enough to accommodate the ambitious initiative launched by Chamberlain was in 1903 unclear, but growing unease at the Empire's condition and its implications for the Conservative future provided the Conservative party with a persuasive reason to find out.

CONCLUDING REMARKS

This chapter concludes that the roots of the tariff reform campaign can be traced to 1886. However, it was not because Joseph Chamberlain deserted to the Conservatives in that year that tariff reform came onto the agenda almost twenty years later, nor was it a result *per se* of the general Liberal Unionist defection. What was important about 1886, and this cannot be overstressed, was the set of issues which underpinned the Conservative success of that year. The accent on the imperial implications of Home Rule, itself an extension of a process of Conservative argument developed under Disraeli's leadership, allowed the Conservatives to construct a political and electoral coalition in which the security and good governance of the Empire were linked to prosperity, social peace and political order at home. But the question as to how Britain's imperial interests were to be secured, and in turn how the Empire was to guarantee prosperity and social and political order, was by no means straightforward. Moreover, the issues involved became more complex and immediate when towards the end of the nineteenth century the Empire was confronted by severe internal and external pressures.

The Conservative party's problems as the party of Empire reached a crisis point with the Boer War. The military weaknesses, administrative incompetence and indeed social problems the war revealed laid the

Conservatives open to the charge that, as the party of Empire, they had not done a particularly good job. On the question of the army and administration the Conservatives could claim that they were as well-equipped as their political opponents to produce thorough reforms, but Asquith's remark that an 'imperial race' could not flourish in 'the rookeries and slums of England' was a well-placed jibe at the inadequacies of Conservative social policy and an implicit critique of the notion that the Empire in itself was either a symbol of or the means to prosperity. With regard to this last issue it was important that the cost of the war exacerbated an already serious fiscal problem,[86] with the result that concern in the City over government borrowing increased, a controversial revenue duty on corn was introduced, and the issue of government finance was brought to the forefront of political debate. For the Conservative governments of the late nineteenth century the problem of financing imperial security had proved difficult enough, but the escalating cost of Empire, which the cost of the Boer War symbolized, enabled the Conservatives' opponents to make political capital. In the late 1890s a number of Liberal and other Left critics attacked the cost of Empire from a variety of viewpoints. The most radical critique, that of J.A. Hobson, presented imperial expenditure as a squandering of resources that could and should have been devoted to domestic social reforms – an argument which signposted a possible Liberal appeal to the mass vote on the basis of popular anti-imperialism. Equally worrying was the kind of attack launched by Sir William Harcourt in 1903, when he pointed out to the Conservatives that 'you perorate about the Empire, but it is not the Empire that pays. It is little England'.[87] Given that the majority of taxpayers were assumed to be Conservative this raised the possibility of the Conservatives being hoist with their imperial petard amongst their own constituency. The Empire had become a focus for rather than a diversion from issues of wealth distribution, not just between social groups and classes but also within them, and not just within Britain but between Britain and its Colonies. The ultimate irony, therefore, was that the very issues which the Conservatives had sought to defer by playing the imperial card in the 1870s and 1880s were made more immediate by the question of Empire itself. Imperial policy became once again contested political terrain, incorporating urgent domestic issues.

3

CONSERVATISM AND THE PROPERTIED

> I think the 'classes' and dependents of class are the strongest
> ingredients in our composition.
>
> (Salisbury to Lord Randolph Churchill, 9 November 1886)[1]

For the greater part of the nineteenth century the social base of the
Conservative party was relatively homogeneous. Drawing its leadership
from the aristocracy and its Parliamentary cohorts from the county
squirearchy, and gaining its most rock-solid and rock-headed support
from the English counties, the Conservative party represented, above all
else, the political arm of the landed interest. The party was never *exclusively* landed, but the interests of the land and British agriculture were the
focus of Conservative politics from the time of Lord Liverpool to the time
of Lord Salisbury. However, in the last quarter of the nineteenth century
urban politics and urban interests took on a new significance for the
Conservative party. In particular, the Conservatives benefited from a
steady gravitation of urban propertied wealth to the political Right,
which provided them with a strong core of support in urban areas and
saw the emergence of a greatly-expanded urban Tory elite. These developments contributed to what has been termed 'the transformation of
Victorian Conservatism',[2] a process which saw the Conservative party
become less the party of the land and more the party of property in
general.

The great climacteric of the Conservative party's emergence as the
party of property came in 1886. Exploiting general unease in the Liberal
ranks at the apparent leftward drift of Liberal politics, and benefiting
from more particular concerns over Gladstone's conversion to Irish Home
Rule, the Conservatives succeeded in drawing the bulk of the Liberal
right wing, and a handful of Radicals, into an alliance with the forces of
Conservatism. For many Conservatives the Liberal split in 1886 was not
wholly unexpected, in that they had worked to secure just such a development. Soon after the Conservative defeat at the general election of
1880, Sir Stafford Northcote noted that 'it is likely enough that a

Conservative cave may be formed on the Liberal side ... [and] if we manage our opposition discreetly we may often join hands with them, and perhaps ultimately bring some of them to take part in a Conservative cabinet'.[3]

Between 1880 and 1886 Conservative efforts to drive a wedge into the Liberal party were focused on two issues in particular, the security of Empire and the security of property. The Conservative critique of Liberal imperial policy, and the importance of Home Rule in the context of that critique, have been dealt with in the previous chapter. This chapter will examine how a critique of Liberal politics in general, and of Liberal Irish policy in particular, allowed the Conservatives to present the Liberals as careless of the rights of property owners and themselves as the true guardians of propertied interests.

BECOMING THE PARTY OF PROPERTY

The Conservative claim that a Liberal government could not be trusted to defend property rights began in earnest with the Ground Game Act of 1880.[4] As will be seen below, the Conservatives found it difficult straightforwardly to oppose this measure, but, in shaping his argument in support of a damaging Whig amendment, Stafford Northcote noted that his approach was based on 'enlarging ... the importance of upholding the doctrine of free contract in view especially of the formidable invasions of the rights of property with which we are threatened in other particulars'.[5] Northcote's position, supported by Salisbury and other leading Conservatives, was that the Ground Game legislation in itself was less damaging than its implications in the context of other issues. Here the particular issue Northcote had in mind was the government's proposed Irish land legislation, which was to reach the statute book in 1881.

The Irish land problem had been brought to the forefront of British politics in the late 1870s by the Irish tenantry's demands for the famous '3 Fs' – fair rent, fixity of tenure, and freedom of sale. On taking office the Liberals had known that this issue would present problems, and in a Memorandum to the Cabinet in December 1880 Gladstone himself pointed out that to accept these demands would 'introduce fundamental changes into the nature of property, which might, in their turn, entail claims for compensation upon the people of the United Kingdom, and might next be found difficult to confine to one only of the three kingdoms'.[6] Gladstone anticipated Conservative arguments, for when his government presented its Irish Land Bill in the spring of 1881 the Conservatives attacked it on the grounds that it conceded the '3 Fs' and established a dangerous precedent for State interference with property rights.[7] Salisbury himself produced a most powerful critique of the Bill in these terms, arguing that the danger of Liberal Irish legislation was that its principles were applicable not just to land in Ireland but to all forms of property in all parts of the United Kingdom.[8]

Between 1881 and 1886 the Conservatives pressed home the argument that property rights were being undermined by Liberal legislation. With regard to the position of landowners Salisbury contended that not only had the property of Irish landlords been 'taken from them under a mockery of judicial forms', but that many an English landowner was justifiably concerned that 'the earthquake wave which has been fatal to his Irish brother ... is travelling slowly towards him'.[9] This statement was made and reiterated against the backdrop of growing agitation on 'the land question' in Britain. The early 1880s saw the ideas of Henry George, the American land tax campaigner, attract a great deal of publicity, and 1883 saw the founding of the 'Georgeite' Land Nationalization League. Within the mainstream of British politics, Joseph Chamberlain singled out the landowning aristocracy for particular abuse with his jibes at a class that 'toils not neither does it spin', and land reform was at the heart of *The Radical Programme* of 1885.[10] The activities of the English Farmers' Alliance, with their demands that looked suspiciously like the '3 Fs',[11] and the Liberals' Scottish Crofters' Act of 1886, which granted fair rents and fixity of tenure to Scottish tenant farmers, seemed to confirm that agitations against landowners and State interference with property rights could not be confined to Britain's traditional social laboratory.

According to Salisbury it was not only landowners who had cause for concern, but that all propertied interests had a right to be worried, for an increasingly radical Liberal party had demonstrated that they sought 'by the action of taxation, of succession laws, and of sundry other devices borrowed from the Socialist armoury ... to attain an absolute level [of equality], first in the ownership of land, and afterwards in all other forms of ownership'.[12] In practice it was difficult for Conservatives to point to any wide-ranging Liberal action which threatened non-landed property. The Employers' Liability Act of 1881, which rendered employers liable to damages suits in cases of workplace injury to employees, was potentially one such case. Conservative coal owners, whose industry was particularly prone to industrial accidents, spoke out against the measure, with Thomas Knowles arguing that 'if the House passes this Bill, they must include something in it that would give mine-owners power to relinquish their leases, or it will confiscate their property'.[13] In addition Conservative spokesmen argued that Employers' Liability would 'promote litigation' and thereby 'widen the differences between employer and employed'.[14] However, this particular case aside, the Conservatives did not point to specific measures when they denounced the Liberals' general assault on property rights. Rather it was the overall tendencies of Liberal politics which provided Conservatives with ammunition.

The main Conservative argument was that Radicalism tainted with Socialism had become the dominant Liberal party ethos. In 1883 Salisbury declared that one of the chief reasons that 'disintegration' was the 'peril of the present time' was because 'the temper that severs class from class is constantly gaining strength'. Salisbury described the situation in Ireland as 'the worst symptom of our malady', but he contended that 'it is beginning to infect us in this country also', and he pointed out that

> Those who lead the poorer classes of this country are industriously impressing upon them, with more or less plainness of speech, that the function of legislation is to transfer to them something – an indefinite and unlimited something – from the pockets of their more fortunate fellow-countrymen.[15]

Salisbury's denunciation of 'That organizer of decay, the Radical agitator'[16] was aimed at an obvious target. A few months before Salisbury published 'Disintegration', Joseph Chamberlain had predicted that future legislation would be directed towards improving the lot of the masses, and he had gone on to make his jibes at Salisbury's class. With Chamberlain and his Radical colleague Dilke in the Cabinet, and with the *Radical Programme* glorying in its 'socialistic' stance,[17] Salisbury was presented with both the opportunity and justification to present the future of Liberal politics as 'spoliation ... painted the colour of philanthropy'.[18]

Raising the spectre of a Liberal party dominated by 'the New Radicalism' was one means of encouraging the defection of propertied Liberal support. A more prosaic, but equally important, aspect of the Conservatives' campaign was their argument that Liberal legislation, especially in Ireland, was undermining the theory and practice of freedom of contract. Once again Salisbury's 'Disintegration' summed up much of the Conservative case. Referring to 'principles which ... we ... once believed to be inviolable ... but which are now freely sold in the market-place of politics', Salisbury took as his prime example 'the sanctity of contracts ... a principle for which our present Parliament takes every opportunity of evincing its contempt'.[19] The idea that Liberal legislation had 'betrayed' freedom of contract was a promising means of turning the Liberal flank, for the notion of free, contractual relationships was at the heart of Victorian Liberal ethics. The canonical reference here is Sir Henry Maine, who famously described the development of civilized, free societies in terms of the progress of social relationships 'from Status to Contract'. To suggest the Liberals had abandoned freedom of contract was, in effect, to suggest that the Liberal party had abandoned Liberalism as understood by many of its most celebrated adherents and theorists. Contract law underpinned not only rights pertaining to real property, it also provided the basis for certainty in financial and commercial transactions, and was at the heart of employment law. In other words the significance of any departure from 'free contract' was appreciated, not only by Liberal jurists like A.V. Dicey and Fitzjames Stephen but by the legally-minded, and often legally-trained, property owners, commercial men and employers who made up an important part of the British Liberal party in Parliament and in the localities. What is more, an emphasis on the issue of free contract enabled the Conservative party to pre-empt contentions that Liberal legislation addressed problems and privileges associated with only one form of property in one region. In 1887 the then Conservative Lord Chancellor, Lord Halsbury, argued that

> If there is to be an attack on property it will be resisted with much greater force if it is possible to say that it includes all property, not merely property which has any peculiar privilege, because then it can be said that an attack on property is an attack on property of all kinds.[20]

It was precisely this notion of a general threat to property that the Conservatives developed through their emphasis on the contractual implications of, in particular, Liberal legislation in Ireland. In the end the Conservatives were able to insist that, if the doctrine of free contract was abandoned, the Irish landlord was not an island unto himself, but that the bell tolled for all property owners throughout the United Kingdom.[21]

Developments within the Liberal party seemed to indicate that the Conservatives were pushing at an open door. As noted above, the existence of a moderate Liberal 'cave' hostile to Radical initiatives was suspected as early as 1880, and in the following years a steady trickle of resignations, and some significant signs of internal dissent, pointed to divisions in the Liberal ranks on the question of property rights. In 1880 Lord Lansdowne and the Duke of Argyll both resigned from the Cabinet in protest at the government's policy in Ireland. In the following year both spoke out against the Irish Land Bill, agreeing with Conservative spokesmen that it undermined free contract and established a dangerous precedent.[22] There was also Liberal opposition to the Employer's Liability Bill. Led by the coal owner W.Y. Craig,[23] thirteen Liberal MPs[24] voted against the Bill's Second Reading, and this quite probably underestimates the degree of disquiet in the Liberal ranks.[25] In January 1882 a by-election in the North Riding of Yorkshire provided further evidence of tensions within the Liberal party, in that the Radical local association endorsed a candidate from the Farmers' Alliance, thereby provoking a revolt by local Whig notables, with the result that the Conservatives won the seat with Whig and moderate Liberal support.[26] By January 1886 there was enough disquiet for eighteen Liberals, including Hartington and Goschen, to vote against a Liberal motion designed to defeat the Conservatives on the

Queen's Speech.[27] With party discipline and loyalty at a premium on such occasions this was a clear indication that all was not well in the Liberal camp.

Liberal defections to the Right were nothing new. In the late 1860s and 1870s the growth of Conservative support in urban areas in particular had been partly due to Liberal desertions.[28] But in the late 1860s and 1870s Liberal desertions appear to have been sparked by specific pieces of Liberal legislation and were not necessarily permanent. For example the 1871 Trade Union legislation clearly offended Liberal employers,[29] whilst Liberal Anglicans, in particular some Whig notables, were upset by the disestablishment of the Irish Church and Gladstone's apparent willingness to make concessions to militant Nonconformity.[30] However, the bulk of Liberal employers and Whig grandees had remained loyal to Liberalism and made a significant contribution to the Liberal victory in 1880. In part this may have been due to the fact that Gladstone's first administration, whilst making concessions to the more Radical and militant elements of Liberalism, had also denied these elements some of their most cherished aims and thereby achieved a balance of disappointment.[31]

In the early 1880s concern amongst Whigs and moderate Liberals was more serious and systematic. In 1882 G.J. Goschen, a leading Liberal moderate, 'hazarded the prediction that compulsory division of property would be the law in the Country five and twenty years hence',[32] and in 1885 he was moved to write at some length about the dangerous turn Liberal politics had taken since the general election of 1880.[33] He did not focus on specific legislative examples of the new Radical trend in Liberal politics: discussing Irish land and Employers' Liability, he argued that 'the greatest force of the new movement has not been seen in legislation so much as opinion'.[34] In particular Goschen contended that whereas the mid-Victorian Liberal party had been concerned with abolishing unacceptable excesses of privilege the 1880s model, under the influence of 'socialistic' thinking, was seeking to improve the lot of the propertyless through a 'constructive' programme based on a disregard for principles that safeguarded property rights.[35] Here Goschen allied himself with some of the earlier deserters from the Liberal camp, such as Sir Henry Maine.[36] In 1885 Goschen, like Maine, concluded that 'various economic principles . . . have died since 1880', and he too noted that

> Among the most conspicuous casualties let us recall the sad fate of freedom of contract. We seem almost to have arrived at this formula – little freedom in making contracts, much freedom in breaking them.[37]

Similar concerns were voiced, both in public and private, by other Liberal notables.[38] On the Right of the Liberal party the conviction grew that 'the New Radicalism' was increasing its strength and authority within the

Liberal movement and fundamentally changing the shape of Liberal politics.

The resignations of Argyll and Lansdowne, and the concerns which prompted Goschen and others to express public disquiet about 'the New Radicalism', were symptomatic of an important aspect of Liberal politics in the early 1880s. Gladstone's second administration was marked by an increasingly tense debate over the future of Liberalism:[39] were Whigs and their moderate allies to be marginalized by an apparently inexorable rise in Radical opinion, or could the traditional Whig approach of providing a moderate leaven to reform politics be continued? Writing to Lansdowne in August 1885 Earl Spencer outlined the essence of this dilemma as he tried to persuade his one-time Cabinet colleague to stay within the Liberal fold. 'I cannot agree with a good deal that the Radicals urge', Spencer wrote, but he argued that

> We who are moderate Liberals can do a great deal to check extreme views. It has not yet been shown that Extreme men are dominant and the Moderate men in a hopeless minority. Possibly the New Electorate may reverse this but I doubt it.[40]

Spencer clearly remained optimistic about the continued relevance of 'moderate' Liberalism, but the fact that he felt obliged to state his case so strongly reflected his concern that others might be less sanguine. In this context Spencer's reference to the new electorate was significant. The enfranchisement of the agricultural labourers in 1884 added impetus to Radical politics, but the Redistribution Act that accompanied Reform made electoral life more difficult for Whigs and moderates. The creation of single-member constituencies and, as a necessary corollary, the abolition of a large number of two-member seats, had removed a structural prop of the Whig/moderate–Radical alliance. The prevalence of two-member seats before 1885 had facilitated the classic Liberal electoral formation of a Whig/moderate running in tandem with a Radical. The reduction in the number of two-member constituencies removed this basis of co-operation between Spencer's 'Extreme' and 'Moderate' men. By 1885 Whigs and moderate Liberals appeared to be threatened not only by a closure of ideological space within the Liberal fold but also by a squeeze on their physical presence in the party.

The Conservative party sought to exploit this Whig/moderate fear of marginalization.[41] Salisbury was quick to pick up on the Liberals' internal difficulties, arguing that the Whigs found themselves members of a party 'which has recently equipped itself with a brand-new set of opinions, in which individual freedom and the sacredness of property are treated as matters of very light account'.[42] The simple message which Salisbury and the Conservatives broadcast almost continuously between 1880 and 1886 was that there was no room in an increasingly Radical Liberal party for moderate opinion, and that if Whigs and moderate Liberals were serious about defending such things as freedom of contract and property rights, then they were better off joining forces with the Conservatives.

Whig/moderate concern at an apparent Radicalization provided a backdrop for the Home Rule crisis, and it was Home Rule which enabled the Conservatives to bring their campaign to divide the Liberal party on the issue of property rights to a successful conclusion. This does not imply a reductionist interpretation of 'the great separation in the Liberal party' in which Liberal Unionists are described as 'propertied' and Home Rulers as 'non-propertied' – a close analysis of the Liberal division renders such an interpretation untenable.[43] However, it is important not to reject one reductionist argument only to replace it with another. That one can find a modicum of 'propertied' Home Rulers and 'non-propertied' Liberal Unionists does not mean the *issue* of property rights was not at stake in 1886. Prominent Whigs like Spencer, Carrington and Rosebery, who supported Home Rule, recognized all too well that fears about property were a cause of Liberal defections in 1886,[44] and the fact that they remained in the Liberal fold merely indicates that they had a higher boiling point on this issue than many of their colleagues. The Liberal schism in 1886 cannot be reduced to a simple division between 'propertied' and 'non-propertied' Liberals, but it was certainly a division between those who saw Home Rule as intrinsically threatening to property rights and those who did not.

That Home Rule was seen to have a bearing on property rights was in large part due to the way in which the Irish problem was conceptualized and contextualized. Contemporary opinion tended not to mince words in describing the conflict in Ireland as a class war between disgruntled peasants and their (equally disgruntled) landlords, whilst the campaigns of the Irish Land League were often referred to as 'agrarian Socialism'. When the Irish situation was described in these terms Gladstone's conversion to Home Rule, particularly when placed within the context of earlier 'concessions', was characterized as a failure of governance. In 1881 the Duke of Argyll had referred to the Irish Land Act as 'helter-skelter legislation', whilst Lansdowne had portrayed it as 'the reward of past agitation . . . [and] the vantage point of the agitation of the future'.[45] These statements matched comments made by Salisbury when, in 1882, he told Carnarvon 'It does not do for the Lords to accept without resistance . . . attacks on property. It demoralizes the public opinion of the community and makes fresh attacks much more tempting and easy'.[46] The point of contact between Salisbury's thinking and the outlook of disaffected Whigs and Liberal moderates was that good governance consisted of addressing genuine grievances, but within the context of firm government resistance to disruptive agitations. Home Rule for Ireland was presented as the antithesis of good governance. At the same time, Home Rule meant abandoning the Irish landlords to the tender mercies of a Land League-dominated Irish assembly.[47] In effect, a key Conservative argument against Home Rule was that any government willing to make such a concession to such an agitation could not be trusted to defend any institution, in particular private property, against any similar agitation. In the political climate of the early 1880s, with a new propertyless electorate to be faced, this was a powerful argument to deploy, and it was an argument that many Whigs and moderate Liberals echoed in their opposition to Home Rule.

That Home Rule produced a political polarization over the issue of property was of great importance for the future of British politics. Soon after the defeat of the Home Rule Bill Gladstone told R.H. Hutton, editor of the Liberal Unionist *Spectator* that 'your "Unionists" from Dukes downwards are warped by the spirit of class'.[48] Gladstone at this point was on one of his not uncommon quests for moral self-justification, and was writing when his disdainful wrath was at its height, but the language and tone of his denunciations of the Liberal Unionists did not alter a great deal thereafter. In 1889 he told an approving National Liberal Federation that

> For a long time the wealthy and the powerful had been gradually detaching themselves from the body of the Liberal party and finding their most natural associations in Toryism, in stagnation, and in resistance. For some of them it was a perfect Godsend when Home Rule turned up, and supplied them with a plausible excuse for doing ostensibly or even ostentatiously that which in their hearts they had been longing for an excuse to do.[49]

These remarks, coupled with the link the Conservatives established between Home Rule and threats to the security of property, indicate that discussion of the Home Rule controversy in terms of 'class interest' was not a product of modern historical analysis. 'Unionism' was described by both Liberals and Conservatives at the time as bound in with the defence of wealth and property, and this definition of the Home Rule divide was central to the way in which Liberals, Liberal Unionists and Conservatives constructed their identities and potential audiences (both their own and each other's) after 1886. Ironically Gladstone, who had spent much of his political life seeking to prevent the 'spirit of class' from dominating British politics, had, through his commitment to Home Rule, brought the possibility of class politics closer.

In the closing decades of the nineteenth century the changing political allegiance of property owners confirmed the identity of the Liberal and Conservative parties as, respectively, the 'party of the masses' and 'party of the classes'. The trend was especially marked in the make-up of the Parliamentary Parties. In the early 1880s the Liberal party had contained a weakened but still respectable landed contingent, and enjoyed the support of two-thirds of business representatives in Parliament. In the 1890s it was the Conservatives and Liberal Unionists who provided two-thirds of business MPs, whilst the defection of the bulk of the Whigs had led to an even greater concentration of territorial wealth on the Right of British politics.[50] Likewise in the constituencies the Conservatives' ever-increasing strength in middle-class suburban seats in particular provided further evidence of their growing appeal to property owners of all kinds both before and after 1886. All of this serves to confirm that 1886 was as much a symptom as a cause of a realignment which transformed the social basis of Conservative politics. However, in this context it is important to realize that 1886 was indeed *both* a symptom and a cause. It may have been the case that many Whigs had found their position in Liberal politics increasingly uncomfortable from the early 1870s. Equally it may have been the case that sections of the British *bourgeoisie*, once the backbone of Liberalism, had become *les satisfaits* of the mid-Victorian polity, viewed further social or political reforms as potentially threatening, and transferred their allegiance to Conservatism more or less voluntarily. But it is also the case that the Conservative party had worked hard to encourage these developments. But if the Conservative party had to expend a great deal of political energy to become the party of property it was also the case that no small degree of effort was required to maintain that position, for the simple reason that there were disadvantages as well as advantages to being the party of property.

To begin with there was the question of ensuring smooth relations between the old and new Conservative elites. To have drawn all forms of property together in a defensive alliance was one thing, to satisfy their varied needs and aspirations was another. This may seem at first glance to be a non-problem. Table 1 provides four 'snapshots' of the occupational background of Conservative membership of the House of Commons in 1884, 1896, 1904 and 1912. The categories have been deliberately 'blurred' in order, paradoxically enough, to create a clearer picture of the Conservative party's social make-up. To have contrasted the categories more obviously would have been misleading. For example, the cohort of 'aristocratic/gentry MPs' who were also 'lawyers' contained a number who had been called to the Bar but did not practise, or who had spent only a few years active in the profession. A full survey of family lineage and sources of income for all Conservative MPs in the period would clarify the position, but in the absence of comprehensive data the tables on pp. 90–1 avoid arbitrary weighting of particular categories, and provide a fair impression of the often overlapping occupational structures of the Conservative Parliamentary party.

The number of overlaps may seem to undermine the notion of a rural–urban divide. This is *partly* true, for the intersection of rural and urban interests did help smooth the social and political union of 'old' and 'new' wealth. In this sense the Conservative party's 'integration problem' was in part rendered less problematic by the 'amphibious' nature of Britain's wealth and power elite. However, the career of one of the more obviously 'amphibian' Conservative politicians of the period is testimony to the continued significance of the rural–urban divide. David Lindsay, Lord Balcarres, had an impeccable aristocratic pedigree. On succeeding to his father's title in 1913 Balcarres became 27th Earl of Crawford (created 1398): no *nouveau riche* arriviste here. This impressive lineage was an essential qualification for his becoming a Conservative Whip in 1906.[51] Yet Balcarres sat for the Lancashire constituency of Chorley, not on the strength of his aristocratic pedigree but because his family had extensive coal and iron interests in and near that seat. If Balcarres had not been able to present himself as a local 'industrialist' he would not have been accepted as representative of his constituency.[52] Balcarres merged rural and urban interests in his personal activities, but his public career saw different audiences distinguish between the 'aristocratic' and 'industrial' aspects of his life. That the interests of even a single individual could be demarcated in this way indicates that the concept of a rural–urban divide continued to have great meaning in Conservative politics.

THE CONSERVATIVES AND THE RURAL ELITES

Land gives one position and prevents one from keeping it up.
(Lady Bracknell in *The Importance of Being Earnest*)

This country appears to care little, if at all, for the position of the land ... Unquestionably, politicians do mould their conduct upon the wishes of the towns rather than the country.
(*The Estates Gazette*, 14 October 1899)

Between 1880 and 1914 the Conservative party's association with the land remained very strong. Salisbury's Cabinets were not only drawn almost exclusively from the aristocracy but contained a notoriously dispropor-tionate number of his own family.[53] Salisbury's successor, his nephew Arthur Balfour, also presided over an essentially aristocratic Cabinet. It is true that Balfour was succeeded as Conservative leader by a Glasgow-born iron master, but Law remained largely isolated in terms of the social back-ground of his 'Shadow Cabinet'. The rest of the Conservative hierarchy, that is the party managers at Conservative Central Office (CCO) and the Whips in Parliament, also remained solidly landed. In the Salisburyian period CCO was dominated by 'the Kentish Gang' of country gentlemen who took their cue from the Chief Whip Aretas Akers-Douglas. Under Balfour the landed dominance continued, with the Somerset grandee

Alexander Acland-Hood bossing the party organization from the Whips' Room. The reorganization of the party in 1911 separated CCO and Whips' functions, created the new post of party Chairman, and diluted the landed element in CCO.[54] However, the Whips' Room remained a gentry preserve, and Lord Balcarres noted in 1913, when a new Whip was to be appointed, that 'it is desirable that this leading Parliamentary organizer should if possible be drawn from that level of society which is above the prevailing struggle for social distinction'.[55]

What was true of the Conservative hierarchy was true of the Conservative Parliamentary party. Both the numbers and proportion of Conservative MPs drawn from or connected to the aristocracy/gentry remained very high between 1880 and 1914 (see Table 1). There was certainly a marked *embourgeoisement* of the Conservative party over the period, but the durability of the traditional sector catches the eye. The continued prominence of the aristocratic/gentry MP reflected the importance of county seats to the Conservatives. In 1895 the Conservatives won 185 county seats as they swept to an impressive victory, but they also won 125 county seats in losing the January 1910 election. Not all county seats were dominated by landed or rural interests, but the majority were and in such constituencies the presence of a 'carpetbagging' candidate was strongly resented by the traditional sector of the party.[56] As long as the counties continued to be over-represented in Parliament, landed MPs were likely to occupy a large section of the Conservative benches whether the party was in government or opposition.

The prominence of aristocratic/gentry MPs may seem to be simply business as usual for a party which had identified itself as the guardian of rural interests. But this is a most inappropriate term to describe the relationship between the Conservatives and their traditional supporters. In the late nineteenth and early twentieth century, both the upper and lower ends of landed society were politically restive and severely tested the party leadership's management skills.

i. The aristocracy

In the 1870s the British aristocracy, in terms of wealth, power and status, still had the appearance of a ruling class. Aristocratic fortunes, as measured in probate returns, remained mostly larger than those accumulated in industry or commerce.[57] Furthermore, landownership, which conveyed status as well as income, was more concentrated in Britain than in any other European nation, and titled rank was confined to a narrow band of families.[58] Local government in the counties, from the Lords Lieutenant through the Sheriffs to the magistracy, was in the hands of local notables, and reinforcing these formal structures were associations like the hunt and militia. In Parliament the political elite still resembled

Table 1 Occupational cross-categories of Conservative MPs in 1884, 1896, 1904, 1912

1884 245	Totals	Aristoc./land	Manufacture	Brewing	Law	Service sector	Military/ yeoman
Aristoc./land	150		4	1	72	19	103
Manufacture	18			0	13	7	7
Brewing	7				3	2	4
Law	140					21	91
Service sector	38						19
Military/yeoman	154						

1896 399	Totals	Aristoc./land	Manufacture	Brewing	Law	Service sector	Military/ yeoman
Aristoc./land	279		18	2	110	60	117
Manufacture	68			1	47	34	28
Brewing	8				3	3	3
Law	281					107	135
Service sector	159						68
Military/yeoman	204						

Table 1 continued

1904
366

	Totals	Aristoc./land	Manufacture	Brewing	Law	Service sector	Military/yeoman
Aristoc./land	195		16	3	111	36	114
Manufacture	60			0	34	18	19
Brewing	6				2	2	3
Law	226					45	107
Service sector	84						31
Military/yeoman	179						

1912
278

	Totals	Aristoc./land	Manufacture	Brewing	Law	Service sector	Military/yeoman
Aristoc./land	150		13	4	66	57	75
Manufacture	38			0	21	20	12
Brewing	6				3	1	5
Law	158					66	70
Service sector	115						59
Military/yeoman	150						

Disraeli's 'Venetian Oligarchy'. The Conservative party was the aristocratic party par excellence, but the Liberal leadership was also drawn largely from the nobility. The great country Seats provided the setting for high political intrigue, and the rhythms of Parliamentary life were harmonized with those of the 'London Season', the races and the grouse moors.[59] Above all there was the House of Lords, which provided the aristocracy with an institutional identity and authority at the heart of politics.

From the 1880s on, however, the aristocracy was under threat. The agricultural depression, and the fall in rents that it caused, affected most aristocratic families, especially those dependent upon farm rentals and in the Celtic fringe.[60] Legislation to control, tax or eliminate landlord privileges posed a further threat to the value of land as a commodity and landownership as an occupation. The Ground Game Act (1880), along with the Irish Land Act (1881), the Agricultural Holdings Act (1883), and the Scottish Crofters Act (1886), weakened a landowner's authority in dealing with his or her property. In Ireland widespread agitation rendered even the day-to-day management of estates difficult, and some landlords feared for their lives. As a consequence many Irish landlords took the opportunities offered by the Irish Land Acts of 1896 and 1903, and were effectively 'bought out' by the State. In the rest of the United Kingdom too land sales, both distressed and otherwise, increased markedly over the early twentieth century as a prelude to the great break-up of estates in the 1920s. Meanwhile, the electoral reforms of 1883–5 forced the aristocracy to confront a new political world, peopled by a larger, more anonymous electorate who they were forbidden to 'treat' and who were less subject to 'influence'. The creation of County Councils in 1888 and Parish Councils in 1894 also ended the aristocracy's monopoly of local government and forced local notables to 'stand the buffet' of elections. Similarly, military reforms in the early twentieth century, especially those implemented by Haldane, reduced the importance of local militias and yeomanry and the aristocracy's role in another area of county life once seen as its preserve.[61] Finally, the constitutional crisis of 1910–11 led to the Parliament Act which abolished the House of Lords' veto over legislation. Economically, socially and politically the British aristocracy were in retreat.

The aristocracy looked to the Conservative party to defend them in these difficult times. After all the party was led for much of the period by, in the first instance, the most articulate apologist for aristocratic life that British politics had produced, and latterly by a scion of the same family. Furthermore, the Conservatives' critique of Liberal 'extremism' in the early 1880s allowed them to unite the aristocracy politically. Before the 1880s the Conservatives had a majority in the Lords, and after 1886 that majority was even greater as Liberal Unionist defections deprived the Liberals of all but a rump of their grandee support. Thus the aristocracy seemed well placed to influence the Conservative party to defend their interests, and the Conservatives possessed, in their majority in the Lords, a powerful instrument to carry out that purpose.

Yet the Conservatives seemed neither able nor in some instances willing to protect the aristocracy's position. Indeed, on occasion they seemed to collude with attacks on the aristocracy. In spite of the depression Conservative governments offered only limited succour to Britain's agricultural sector.[62] Meanwhile, the Liberals 'anti-landlord' legislation of the early 1880s passed relatively unscathed through the Lords. The Conservatives offered only limited resistance to Parish Councils and Harcourt's Death Duties in 1894, and, more surprising still, were themselves responsible for introducing elected County Councils in 1888, and the Irish Land Acts of 1896 and 1903 that led to the effective disappearance of the great Irish estates. In the latter case the Irish landlords got very good terms, but the Conservatives still seemed to be negotiating a surrender rather than counter-attacking.

The Conservatives' caution is explicable in terms of their desire not to allow their party, or their party's dominance of the House of Lords, to appear as open instruments of class or sectional interest. With regard to agriculture the Conservatives, as will be seen below, had to balance any assistance with the demands of other interest groups, such as manufacturers. They were concerned that a naked display of self-interest by the Lords would undermine the institution's legitimacy and provoke Radical attacks.[63] For example in 1894 Lord Montagu of Beaulieu advised Salisbury against opposing the Parish Councils Bill on the grounds that opposition would allow a disintegrating Liberal government to rally support with a 'Peers versus the People' cry.[64] Conservative strategy under Salisbury was to use the Lords' powers only when Liberal legislation could be portrayed as 'sectional'. This was the Salisburyian 'long game', in which the best defence of aristocratic and indeed propertied interests in general was to secure Conservative rule and deploy the Lords for strategic rather than everyday ends. Often this meant passing legislation which both Salisbury and others of his class regarded as obnoxious, but this allowed the Lords to 'keep their powder dry' for occasions when they could choose the ground on which to fight the Liberals.[65] The defeat of Home Rule in 1894 was one such occasion. Home Rule, as noted earlier, had strong anti-propertied implications, but other issues bound in with it helped disguise the self-interest of its opponents. The key task of bringing down the Liberals was achieved in 1894, and the threat of Radical legislation deferred, but on an issue which left the Liberals groping for a plausible accusation of *parti pris*.

Salisbury's careful statecraft for the most part reassured the aristocracy that their interests were well served by the Conservatives. An interesting barometer of this is the advice drawn up by Earl Carnarvon for his wife in the event of his death. In the early 1880s Carnarvon was so alarmed at trends in British politics that he built up a portfolio of colonial stocks and land and advised his wife to be ready to flee overseas. But by the 1890s Salisbury's successes had reassured him to the point where he felt able to advise the consolidation and even expansion of his home estates. A degree of uncertainty and nervousness remained, but the near panic of the early 1880s was gone.[66] This is not to say, however, that Salisbury always enjoyed smooth relations with his aristocratic supporters as a whole, or even with Carnarvon. In 1888 Carnarvon himself led opposition to the County Councils Bill in the Lords, and the following year the Upper House rejected the Conservative government's Land Transfer Bill. In the 1890s Salisbury had to work hard to keep the Lords in line on Harcourt's 1894 Budget, and in 1896 (as in 1887) his own government faced opposition from Irish aristocrats and landowners over an Irish Land Bill, a development which, according to Edward Hamilton, was 'practical proof that they [the Lords] do not vote at the bidding of Lord Salisbury – that is when their pockets are concerned'.[67] By 1900 the Irish aristocracy in particular were growing increasingly impatient with the Conservative party's apparent readiness to surrender their interests. Some English grandees were willing to accept that Ireland was 'pessimi exempli', on the grounds that 'Irish conditions are such a mess that one breach of principle more or less does not seem to count',[68] but there were bounds, both in Ireland and the rest of the UK, as to what was deemed acceptable.

In the late nineteenth and early twentieth century the aristocracy provided the Conservative party with funds, influence, a number of talented individual politicians, and a majority in the Upper House. However, as a social class 'the loyalty of the Tory peers was far from blind: it was conditional on the party and its leaders defending aristocratic interests as they perceived them',[69] and this was increasingly difficult for the Conservatives. The British aristocracy considered themselves a beleaguered class. Some of the super-rich families had the foresight and resources to make a 'market response' to depression, diversifying their economic interests. However, many were not so imaginative or well-endowed, and suffered accordingly. In these circumstances the threats and taunts of Radical politicians served only to heighten the aristocracy's already pronounced sense of insecurity. Some aristocrats were tempted, even longed, to 'lash out' in defence of titled wealth, status and power, and it was this temptation that Salisbury sought to control, on the grounds that in the long run the interests of his class were best served by a patient war of manoeuvre rather than head-on confrontations. In turn this meant assuaging the aristocracy's sense of insecurity, and here Salisbury, assisted by the Liberal party's internal problems, was largely successful. However, the fact that, even in these largely favourable circumstances, Salisbury could not prevent outbursts of aristocratic spleen did not bode well for the future, and in the early twentieth century their Lordships proved even more difficult to control.

Salisbury's own resignation undoubtedly removed a force for aristocratic moderation. Salisbury had earned the trust of his class and his loss was a great blow to them. Other factors also fanned the fires of aristocratic fear and resentment. After 1900 there was a steady erosion of the aristocratic presence on County Councils,[70] and both Conservative and Liberal army reforms provoked aristocratic concern. Most important, however, the Liberal victory of 1906 meant that for the first time in twenty-six years the aristocracy was confronted with a united Liberal government with a huge majority. As its legislative programme unfolded Lord Lansdowne warned Lord Selborne that 'there must be some limit to our [the Lords'] capacity for swallowing principles'[71] – in 1909 came the People's Budget and the land taxes.

ii. The farmers

If the nineteenth-century Conservative party had always been an aristocratic party it was also 'the farmer's friend', but in the last quarter of the century doubts arose as to whether this relationship would continue to be so cordial. Writing to Carnarvon in October 1881, Salisbury noted that 'We shall have some bother with our agricultural friends',[72] and in the decades that followed his words were to prove prophetic.

The first indications that the Conservatives might have trouble in rural areas surfaced in the 1870s, when it became evident that the 'great depression' was placing a severe strain on rural communities. To begin with there was the impoverished condition, and increasing militancy, of the agricultural labourers. The labourers' position had always been difficult,[73] and relations with their social superiors had always been strained, but Joseph Arch's Agricultural Labourers' Union brought a new dimension to popular rural protest,[74] and household enfranchisement in the counties gave the labourers' grievances a new significance. The concern that the labourers' outlook provoked in Conservative circles will be examined in the following chapter. At this juncture the focus will be the deteriorating relationship between landlords and tenants and the problems this created for Conservative politics.

Differences and indeed open conflict between landlord and tenant had been a feature of rural life in Ireland in particular, but also to a degree in Scotland and Wales, before the 1870s. That the 'Celtic Fringe' saw increased tenant agitation in the last quarter of the nineteenth century was thus not that surprising to contemporaries. More novel, and more directly worrying for the Conservative party, was the appearance of landlord–tenant conflict in rural England. The 'Celtic Fringe' after all had provided the Conservatives with little or no support over the years, but the English counties were the Conservative heartland and English tenant farmers had long been the bedrock of Conservative support in those constituencies. Anything that threatened to alter this situation was of major concern to the Conservative party.

The main cause of tension between landlord and tenant in England was the agricultural depression. From the 1870s on a combination of foreign competition, a long-term fall in agricultural prices and, in 1877 to 1879 and again in 1892 to 1894, poor harvests, caused severe difficulties for English farmers. The most severe problems were in the arable districts of the South and East, but dairy, livestock and mixed farming regions were by no means immune from the effects of the depression. The 'custom of the country' in many rural areas was for landlords to cushion their tenants against hard times through rent reductions and other informal methods of financial and social support.[75] However, landlords were also affected by the depression, and it was difficult for them, especially those dependent on farm rents alone, to provide adequate relief for their tenants. The custom of the country, it seems, could not cope with the scale and duration of the problems emerging in the late nineteenth century.[76] The apparent failure of informal mechanisms of community support led on the one hand to strained relations between landlords and tenants, and on the other to demands from the rural community, but especially farmers, for government assistance.

An early example of tenant agaitation was their demand, voiced in the mid-1870s, for landlords to provide compensation for improvements. Much pressure was brought to bear on the government to legislate on this matter, and Disraeli's government was faced with the dilemma of satisfying the farmers' demands, and thereby implicitly endorsing 'anti-landlord' sentiments, or disappointing the farmers and appearing to be merely a tool of the landlords. The 1875 Agricultural Holdings Act, a compromise measure which created the legal framework for a compensation process but stopped short of compelling landlords to compensate tenants for improvements, epitomised the Conservative dilemma. But it signally failed to square the circle. Only a few months after this legislation was enacted the *Chamber of Agriculture Journal*, mouthpiece of the Central Chamber of Agriculture, remarked that the 'slipshod and pernicious style' with which such 'great questions' had been dealt with by the Conservative government was 'simply contemptible'. In 1879, with farmers countrywide growing increasingly restive, the Farmers' Alliance came into being, and began to agitate for tenant rights that looked like an English version of the '3 Fs'. It seemed that Britain's farmers were no longer predisposed to identify their interests with those of their landlords, that they no longer instinctively deferred to them on political matters, and that there was the potential for conflict within the upper echelons of rural society.

The Conservative party's concern was that the Liberals would exploit these growing differences between landlords and farmers. In the 1880 general election the Liberals secured significant gains in county seats, largely on the strength of support from disgruntled farmers, and the Liberal government's almost immediate repeal of the Malt Tax and introduction of the Ground Game Act seemed to indicate that they intended to extend their farming appeal. The Conservatives were clearly worried by these developments, with Stafford Northcote noting that

> What chiefly disconcerts our men is the audacity with which the Government are putting themselves forward as the true farmers' friends – and the momentary applause they are obtaining from the Chambers of Agriculture and other representatives of the farmers' interests on account of the Hares and Rabbits Bill and the repeal of the Malt Tax.[77]

Moreover, the Conservatives had great difficulty in deciding just how to meet this threat. Stafford Northcote again summed up the problem, recording that

> The difficulty we are placed in by the Hares and Rabbits Bill is a serious one. Four leading Whigs have given notice that they will oppose it ... on the grounds that it interferes with freedom of contract. If we do not act with them on this occasion, we shall disgust them ... On the other hand many of our county members are aware that by voting against this Bill they will risk the loss of their seats.[78]

A special meeting was convened at the Carlton Club to discuss the dilemma, but this resulted only in 'an agreement to differ'.[79] This problem recurred in 1883 as a result of the Liberals' Agricultural Holdings Act, which made it compulsory for landlords to compensate tenants for improvements.[80] For much of Gladstone's second administration the Conservatives were on the defensive in their county strongholds, alarmed by apparent Liberal inroads into Conservative farming support and yet finding it difficult to respond without compromising their defence of landlords.

Much of the farming vote, alarmed by the implications of Chamberlain's antics in the countryside, returned to the Conservative fold in and after 1886, but this did not mean the relationship between the Conservative party and farmers was restored to the relatively comfortable *status quo ante* the 1870s. Far from it. The relationship continued to be intensely problematic. If anything, farming complaints about economic distress deepened in the late 1880s and 1890s, and calls for assistance grew louder. At first glance it seems the farming community was in a good position to make its grievances and policy desires known in the right places. In the late 1880s the Conservative Parliamentary party contained 'an "Agricultural Committee" to which nearly all the county members belong[ed]' which met on the first Wednesday in every month to discuss issues and legislation affecting agriculture.[81] However, this Committee appears to have enjoyed little success.[82] The only occasion on which the 'Agricultural Committee' appears to have gained a receptive audience was in 1887, in the wake of a Liberal victory at the Spalding by-election. Concerned by the Liberals' apparent ability to mobilize the labouring vote the 'Agricultural Committee' pressed for allotments legislation as a popular counter to Liberal appeals.[83] Whether it was the committee's views or a more general concern over Conservative vulnerability in the counties that proved decisive is difficult to assess, but in 1888 the Conservatives introduced legislation to provide allotments in rural areas. Even this 'victory' was double-edged. Allotments were seen as of interest largely to labourers and were an additional cost for rural communities. Likewise, the Conservatives' introduction of free, compulsory education in rural districts in 1892, and their Small Holdings Act of the same year, were aimed largely at the labouring vote and represented new burdens for rural local government. Conservative measures to appease labouring opinion may have been designed to help defend the political future of farming MPs, but they were not without their drawbacks. To begin with there was the cost of such legislation. If rural rates had to rise to fund the new measures there was the certainty of renewed farming agitation over 'the burdens on agriculture'. In addition the fact that government action seemed to be forthcoming only on 'labourers' issues' meant that farming opinion could easily conclude that 'the farmer is nowhere today in considerations of party politicians, and the labourer is the king to whom the leaders of both parties do homage'.[84]

Farming frustration continued to give Conservatives cause for concern through the 1890s. In December 1892 Henry Chaplin attended a special agricultural meeting in London at which 250 representatives of Chambers of Agriculture and farming associations were present. In his report on the meeting Chaplin noted that it had taken a great deal of effort to prevent the farmers passing a '3 Fs' motion by a substantial majority, and he argued that, unless something was done to ease the farmers' plight, ostensibly moderate farmers might join with their labourers to support Radical measures based on anti-landlord sentiment.[85] In the same month Chaplin told the Conservative Chief Whip that 'the agricultural situation ... is grave and ... full of difficulty' and that there was the possibility of farmers forming their own independent party so antagonized.[86] Such a notion may appear fanciful, but the examples of the German Agrarian League, the Farmers' Alliance in the USA, and the political leverage exercised by the Danish co-operatives, provided contemporaries with evidence of often effective independent farming action. Moreover, the founding of the National Federation of Tenant Farmers' Clubs in January 1893, and a more general increase in independent farming action in the 1890s, seemed to herald the possibility of just such a development in Britain.[87] It is also worth noting that when a landowner, Lord Winchilsea, launched a joint landowners and tenants organization he received very little farming support.[88] It seems that English farmers were suspicious of associations linked with or led by a landlord, no matter how sympathetic that landlord might be to farming grievances.

The Conservatives were probably fortunate to be out of office between 1892 and 1895, the period when the agricultural price trough reached its lowest point. The Liberal government established a Royal Commission to investigate the agricultural depression, but otherwise offered no concessions to farming interests. However, in and after the 1895 general election the Conservatives still had to work to convince farmers that their party held farming interests in greater esteem than the 1892-5 Liberal government. A particularly important test was the position of the 'Ministry of Agriculture'. Shortly after the 1895 election Balfour felt obliged to remind Salisbury

> that in any final arrangements [for the new Government], some one will have to be provided in the House of Commons to answer for Agriculture ... More questions are asked of the Minister of Agriculture than of any other except the Irish Secretary.[89]

At first glance this seems a trivial point to raise, but at the heart of the matter was the status accorded the Board of Agriculture. Henry Chaplin had already told Salisbury that 'there is considerable difficulty brewing about Agriculture and the Cabinet'. The problem, Chaplin noted, was that 'many of our County members have made it a handle in their constituencies, that the Minister of A[griculture] was not in the [Liberal] Cabinet' and that their position would 'not be very easy to defend' if the Conservatives did not make the Presidency of the Board of Agriculture a Cabinet post.[90] Whether the exclusion of the Minister of Agriculture from the Cabinet would have sparked a 'farmers' revolt' cannot be stated as certain, but the Conservative leadership took the threat seriously, forestalling any immediate difficulties by making the Board of Agriculture a Cabinet post.[91]

The 'Ministry of Agriculture' question epitomized the relationship between the farming community and Conservative party in the late nineteenth century, in that the farmers became increasingly militant and independent whilst the Conservatives searched for ways to appease them. Nor did this problem disappear after the turn of the century. In 1907 the appearance of the fledgling National Farmers' Union provided evidence of a desire on the part of many farmers to organize themselves as an independent pressure group, and in 1907-8 various motions in favour of establishing a separate agricultural party were produced in agricultural chambers across the country.[92] Likewise in 1910 Austen Chamberlain was informed by a leading Conservative agricultural spokesman, George Courthope,[93] that it was important he attend a dinner organized by the Central Chamber of Agriculture, the Farmers' Club and the Central Land Association, because

> there is a great deal of political activity among agriculturalists all over the country, and there is no doubt that agricultural matters will be forced to the fore in the House . . . the various agricultural bodies are looking to this dinner as an important move in the game, and I am sure it worth an effort to show that our leading men sympathize with the farmers' activity.[94]

Edwardian Conservatives, like their predecessors, were forced to confront the questions of how to cope with disgruntled and disillusioned farmers and hold on to farming support.

In the 'golden age' of British, and especially English, farming between 1850 and the mid-1870s the social and political structures of rural life seemed settled and secure. But the pattern of 'the rich man in his castle, the large tenant farmer with his hunters and the parson in his Church',[95] and, one may add, the Conservative MP returned to Westminster, seemed far less immutable in the late nineteenth and early twentieth century. The 'fixity' of mid-Victorian rural society and politics appears to have been largely dependent upon the prosperity of English agriculture in a period when home as well as foreign producers supplied the needs of Britain's booming industrial towns. In contrast, the agricultural depression made questions such as security of tenure, cost of improvements, and the level of rents openly contentious in a way not known before. The result was that established patterns of authority in Britain's rural communities were disrupted and traditional political allegiances destabilized.[96] The disruption in England was clearly not as deep or as widespread as in Ireland or even Scotland, but it was marked nonetheless. Obviously English farmers were not transformed overnight into 'Boycotters' or even Radical agitators. Established patterns of authority, like all old habits, die hard, especially when they are supported by a network of social and political relations as deep and complex as those that characterized English rural society. But, in spite of the structured hierarchies of the hunt, the county yeomanry and the local magistrates bench, and the pull of local loyalties they both expressed and reinforced, it seems that in the late nineteenth and early twentieth century farmers were generally less willing to accept the economic and political authority of their landlords, and more sceptical about the Conservative party's position as 'the farmers' friend'.

Likewise landlords felt threatened by the militancy of tenant demands whilst the Conservative party fretted for the first time over the reliability of the farming vote.

THE CONSERVATIVES AND THE URBAN ELITES

If only we can pull the Party from under the wheel of mere county and landed influence, & give to urban constituencies a just share.
(A.B. Forwood to Salisbury, 9 June 1885)[97]

The *embourgeoisement* of late nineteenth-century Conservatism was manifest at all levels of party activity. Disraeli, albeit somewhat reluctantly, appointed urban, middle-class figures like R.A. Cross and W.H. Smith to Cabinet posts, and Salisbury continued the practice, promoting Smith to the post of Leader of the House, sending C.T. Ritchie to the Board of Trade, and making W.L. Jackson Financial Secretary to the Treasury and, later, Irish Secretary. The Parliamentary Conservative party experienced an even greater influx of urban representatives (see Table 1). In the early 1880s the great majority of Conservative MPs were landed, but the Parliamentary party at that point was made up of MPs who had retained their seats at the 1880 election defeat, when the Conservatives had been driven back onto their traditional county strongholds. Furthermore, it was a Parliamentary party that reflected the structure of the electoral system before the crucial reforms of 1884–5. From the mid-1880s on, when the Conservatives were frequently in office and a new electoral structure was in place, the Conservative Parliamentary cohort consisted of a large number of MPs with urban roots.

The changing social composition of the Conservative Parliamentary party corresponded to a marked shift in the geography of Conservative support from the counties to the boroughs. Britain was still urbanizing rapidly in the mid- to late nineteenth century, and the electoral system was gradually changing to reflect this fact. The 1885 Redistribution Act produced the most important changes, establishing 230 new constituencies (but only twelve new MPs) by abolishing many double-member constituencies and creating single-member seats based (approximately) on population. The net result was that the electoral weight of the country was shifted from the South to the industrial North and Midlands.[98] The enfranchisement of the agricultural labourers by the 1884 Reform Act served only to underscore the importance of urban support to the Conservatives, in that this reform ensured that the Conservatives could no longer regard the counties as secure electoral territory.[99]

For the Conservatives to attract and keep urban support they required active local Conservative elites who were prepared to expend time, energy and money on organization and propaganda and who could exercise

101

influence in borough seats. The evidence of the late 1860s and early 1870s indicates that the Conservatives were beginning to benefit from the emergence of just such an urban Tory elite. Local Conservative clubs and associations, sponsored and organized by local Conservative notables, multiplied in Britain's urban communities and built a national framework for their activities in the shape of the National Union of Conservative and Constitutional Associations (NUCA). The benefits of this expanded urban presence were made clear by the Conservatives' general election victory in 1874 when there was a large swing to the Conservatives in the boroughs.[100] The next two general elections confirmed the importance of urban support. In 1880 the poor Conservative showing was due largely to losses in the boroughs, whilst in 1885, the first election held after the electoral reforms of 1884–5, the Conservatives' losses in the counties were compensated by gains in the boroughs where they won a majority of seats for the first time. Similarly the Conservatives' electoral victories of 1895 and 1900 saw them secure a majority of borough representation.

Conservative party politics in the boroughs as in the counties was very much a 'politics of local notables'. Taking the example of the Conservative party in Sheffield, the chairman of Sheffield Conservative Association (SCA) in the 1890s was Sir Henry Edward Watson, a solicitor, but also a director of the steelmakers Charles Cammell and Co. and of Allied Insurance. Watson, a Deputy Lieutenant and JP for the West Riding, was also chairman of Sheffield Children's Hospital, a trustee of Sheffield Boys' Charity School and a patron of many other local institutions. The power behind Watson's throne was George Franklin, vice-president of SCA, chairman of its Finance Committee, and Treasurer of the Brightside ward Conservative Association. Franklin was chairman of the Sheffield and Hallamshire Bank and director of the National Telephone Company, as well as chairman of his own accountancy partnership. Franklin was also treasurer of the University College and honorary secretary of the Cherry Tree Orphanage. Publicity for the Conservative cause was provided by Sir William Leng, proprietor-manager of the *Sheffield Daily Telegraph*. Almost without exception the leading Conservative activists in Sheffield in the late nineteenth century were all prominent local businessmen and/or professionals and were active not only in local politics but also in local charities and other civic and voluntary institutions. At present the detailed ground-level structure of late nineteenth-century urban Conservatism is largely historical *terra incognita*,[101] but the fragmentary surveys that are available suggest that the participation and authority of local notables that characterized Conservative politics in Sheffield was repeated elsewhere.[102]

The network of local interests and civic commitment that was the basis for political activity in towns like Sheffield demanded that Parliamentary representatives were genuinely able to represent the locality and its needs. This meant that urban MPs almost invariably needed to be closely associated with the social and economic life of their constituency.[103] In manufacturing districts, especially those dominated by one industry, a typical Conservative candidate would be a large local employer, or failing that a prominent member of the Chamber of Commerce. Thus in the cotton districts of Bolton, Ashton-Under-Lyme, Blackburn, and Manchester North-West one finds the mill-owners, H. Shepherd-Cross, H.J. Whiteley, Harry Hornby, and W.H. Houldsworth. In Burton-on-Trent there was Hamar Bass, in Bury St Edmunds Edward Greene, and in Warrington Gilbert Greenall, all representatives of local brewing concerns. In St Helens there was H. Seton-Karr who by marriage and business association was a representative of the biggest local employer, Pilkington Glassmakers. In Wolverhampton there was the ironmaster, the 'Iron King of South Staffordshire' and sometime president of the Wolverhampton Chamber of Commerce, Alfred Hickman, and in Barrow-in-Furness there was the shipping magnate C.W. Cayzer.[104]

Not all urban seats were industrial or manufacturing districts. The suburbs and residential areas of Britain's major cities represented a new, fast-growing and, especially after the redistribution of 1885, an important cluster of seats. These constituencies were a major element in the Conservatives' urban presence in and after 1885. In the suburbs and residential areas there were few if any major 'local' employers. There may well have been major employers dwelling in these seats, but their 'interests' almost by definition lay elsewhere. A significant proportion of the voting population of these constituencies, the home of 'Villa Toryism', would have been in 'white collar' or at least 'black-coated' occupations, that is to say they were professionals, semi-professionals, members of the 'shopocracy' or clerical workers. Conservative MPs who represented these seats tended to be from the wealthy professions, especially the law, and/or the service sector. (See Table 2 Appendix 2 for lists of Conservative representatives in middle-class London and S.E. suburban seats and their social background.) In London a number of middle-class districts provided homes for scions of landed society,[105] but it was relatively unusual for landed MPs or candidates to stand for provincial towns and cities, for the simple reason that they were not generally welcome. In 1892, for instance, Salisbury was warned of difficulties brewing in Southampton because some members of the local party were 'advocating the candidature of a young and inexperienced nobleman as a representative of a great commercial borough', something which was 'regarded by the burgesses with ridicule and contempt'.[106] If a landed candidate had genuine links with an urban locality that was a different matter. Thus it was acceptable for J.F. Hope, the nephew of the Duke of Norfolk, to sit for Sheffield Brightside, for the simple reason that the Duke was a major landowner in Sheffield and was a patron of local charities and institutions. Likewise the involvement of the Dudley and Dartmouth families in Conservative politics in the Black Country was a result of their commitment to municipal politics and the civic life of their communities.[107]

The significance urban Conservatives attached to their identity, and the importance of satisfying their status requirements was of great importance to Conservative politics in the late nineteenth century. Having played a vital part in their party's electoral triumph in 1874 the urban Tory elites grew resentful of the way their contribution went apparently unacknowledged by the party leadership in terms of a full share of office, patronage, or even polite thanks.[108] In the early 1880s the frustration of the urban Tory elites made itself felt in the shape of 'Tory Democracy'. This represented not a campaign for working-class Conservatives but a campaign by and for people who claimed that they were best equipped to further the Conservative cause with Britain's urban electorate, both working- and middle-class. This, they argued, was to be done through local Conservative associations led 'by cultivated, self-denying, noble-minded men of power and position'[109] – in other words themselves. With its demand for an enhanced role for the NUCA and local party structures Tory Democracy was a form of political insurgency, and it was this insurgent movement which allowed Randolph Churchill to achieve his political successes in the early 1880s. Churchill's power base did not stem from his Parliamentary skills, but from the fact that he appeared as 'the champion of provincial Toryism against the Conservatism based on land, church and metropolitan grandees'.[110] Whether Churchill himself appreciated this is open to question, but his downfall certainly owed much to the fact that Salisbury, unlike Disraeli and Northcote, took steps to ensure that provincial Toryism would not feel the need for another adventurous champion. Salisbury's cultivation of urban Toryism in the early 1880s was less spectacular than Churchill's, but it was equally effective, and when he became undisputed party leader and later Prime Minister, he continued to cultivate provincial Toryism and urban Conservative elites.

Salisbury enjoyed direct political communication with some important urban communities in the shape of members of the 'Hatfield' magic circle sitting for urban seats. Salisbury's heir, Lord Cranborne, sat for Darwen, his nephew Arthur Balfour for East Manchester, and his son-in-law Gerald Balfour for Leeds Central. Of these 'Salisbury scions' only Arthur Balfour was anything like a national figure when adopted for his constituency, and none of them had intimate links with the communities they served. In other words they stood out as exceptions to the general rule of MPs having strong ties to their constituencies. One explanation for this anomaly is that there was no better way for an aristocratic party leader to demonstrate a personal sense of respect for urban Conservatism than for his son and other close relatives to place their electoral survival in the hands of urban Conservative associations. To foist 'young and inexperienced noblemen' on great commercial centres was one thing, but for the party leader to demonstrate a desire to have a close finger on the pulse of urban Conservative opinion was another. It is difficult to be certain that Salisbury designed these candidacies to demonstrate a personal commitment to urban Conservatism, but it seems likely that some such calculation was in play here.

Salisbury, unlike his predecessors, was careful to treat the NUCA with measured respect by addressing its annual meetings on a regular basis. Salisbury, again unlike his predecessors, made frequent speaking trips to the provinces and appeared at numerous (and doubtless tedious) 'urban' functions.[111] As early as 1884 Salisbury was corresponding with prominent Leeds Conservatives about meeting the Chairman of their Association and visiting the city.[112] In 1893, 1895 and 1896 A.K. Rollitt, one of the leading lights of urban Conservatism,[113] urged Salisbury to attend the banquet of the Associated Chambers of Commerce: Salisbury duly appeared.[114] Not every demand or wish was fulfilled. In 1888 W.L. Jackson, another important representative of urban Toryism,[115] requested that Leeds be granted a City charter on the grounds that if this were done by a Conservative government it would greatly help the Conservative cause in Leeds and boost the morale of local party activists.[116] At this point nothing was done, and nine years later Jackson was writing with another request. 'The Leeds City Council', Jackson wrote, 'greatly desires to have conferred upon the City a Lord Mayoralty, as has been done at Liverpool, Manchester, Birmingham and Belfast'. He pointed out that

> Leeds was ... for 60 years governed municipally by an arbitrary and tyrannical, Radical majority; for more than 30 years the Conservatives have striven to gain a foothold ... [and] two years ago, the Conservatives for the first time since 1834 obtained a majority.[117]

On this occasion Salisbury acknowledged the Leeds Conservative party's efforts, and the Lord Mayoralty was granted the following year.

The honours system was also an important means of rewarding and ensuring the loyalty of the urban Tory elites. Salisbury was one of the most active contributors to a trend which saw the post-1880 honours system become an ever-increasing source of reward for political services.[118] In 1885 A.K. Rollitt, the Conservatives' 'municipal' expert was knighted, and in 1887 Howard Vincent, the Sheffield MP also received his 'K'. In 1890 W.L. Jackson, the champion of Leeds Conservatism was made a Privy Councillor and he later became Baron Allerton; in 1897 J.F.S. Rolleston, a leading figure in Leicester Conservatism, was knighted, whilst Alfred Hickman, the Wolverhampton MP, was knighted in 1891 and made a baronet in 1903. Leading honours for MPs were, of course, a traditional reward for individual service. However, these honours were seen not simply as rewards for individuals. In 1892 the Conservative leadership decided to recommend General Goldsworthy, the Hammersmith MP, for a knighthood. There was, however, some doubt as to whether he would accept the honour, but Salisbury's secretary, Schomberg McDonnell, felt that Goldsworthy might be persuaded 'if I make much of the compliment to Hammersmith'.[119] In the end Goldsworthy turned down the honour, but the point that honours for MPs were presented as honours for the community they represented is important.[120] Equally important, it was not just MPs who were recommended for or received such 'baubles'. In 1892 Byron Reed, then chairman of the NUCA, asked Balfour to request an honour for J.B. Stone,[121] who was chairman of Birmingham Conservative Association and also a long-serving and influential figure on the NUCA Council. Stone was a powerful symbol of provincial Conservatism, and he did indeed receive his knighthood in 1892, three years before he became MP for Birmingham East. Likewise Arthur Balfour sent Schomberg McDonnell a lengthy shopping list of honours requests from local party grandees in Manchester,[122] whilst in Sheffield the wholly local figures of William Leng and H.E. Hughes received a knighthood and CMG respectively. Such individual examples of honours for urban Conservative notables are legion. However, the most eloquent testimony to the systematic political use of the honours system is the fact that over half of the voluminous correspondence between Salisbury and the Conservative Chief Agent, Middleton, was concerned with honours. Clearly Salisbury and Middleton, and the Chief Whip Akers-Douglas whose honours correspondence was also vast, felt that the questions of who was to get what, when and why from the honours system was worth a great deal of thought and energy.

Naturally it was not possible to fulfil every request for an honour. To have done so would have undermined the rationale of honours, which is after all to provide people with a distinctive title.[123] A further limitation was that the monarch, whose gifts these honours ultimately represented, did not always co-operate fully – in December 1898 the Queen unilaterally reduced the number of CBs and knighthoods in the New Year's Honours List by one-third, which prompted Schomberg McDonnell to fear that 'there will be many sore backs'.[124] Other problems existed. Creating a peerage could be inconvenient if the candidate was an MP and his elevation would cause an unwanted by-election.[125] Also the elevation of a particular individual could upset the pecking order and cause resentment amongst other 'hopefuls'.[126] Furthermore not every local Conservative activist was deemed of high enough status to warrant a major honour – a certain level of income and social standing was still essential to, for example, the award of a baronetcy. But in such cases the Conservatives had other, lower-level rewards to offer, and other ways of appeasing local Conservative activists.

The Primrose League, which started life as part of the Tory Democratic apparatus, is generally seen as an attempt to foster popular, working-class participation in Conservative politics.[127] This may be the case,[128] but arguably it was just as important as a means of integrating urban Tory elites into the 'social politics' of Conservatism. The 'officers' of the local Primrose League 'habitations'[129] tended to be a mixture of local gentry and middle classes, and many of the League's meetings were not mass affairs but social and business functions for the upper echelons. Here the Primrose League's involvement of upper- and middle-class women takes on a particular significance. It not only provided a (suitably domestic) political role for women, but also a political 'Society' which reinforced male association in the upper echelons of Westminster politics and local Conservative associations and clubs.[130] When these factors are considered, one function of the Primrose League seems to have been to forge closer links not only between the Conservatives and 'the democracy' but also between old and new Conservatives who sought to control 'the democracy'.

Another 'participatory' reward in the gift of the Conservative hierarchy was membership of the Carlton Club or, failing that, the Junior Carlton. A good example, of many available, is provided by Salisbury's son, Lord Cranborne, MP for Darwen, who told Akers-Douglas in July 1886 that

> A Mr William Huntington, one of my constituents, is very anxious to get into the Junior Carlton ... He is a county magistrate for Lancashire and rather an important man in Darwen – being a partner of Potter who stood against me in '85 and brother of Charles Huntington who really came out against me this time ... William Huntington is, however, a Tory and supported me, but it would be very useful to confirm him in the faith. He is not, I take it, a very convinced Tory. I may add that the firm of Potter and Huntington is the most important firm in Darwen and influences a large number of votes.[131]

In many respects all the ingredients of the 'management' of urban Toryism are discussed in this letter: a local notable, from an essentially Liberal backgound, needing to be confirmed in the Conservative faith in order that his local influence will be committed to the Conservative cause – all this to be achieved by holding out a simple but vital symbol of political recognition and social acceptance.

The assimilation of urban Conservatives within the Conservative fold was not achieved simply by letting nature take its course. Relations between the party's traditional wing and their arriviste allies were not always easy, for old prejudices died hard. In the 1870s the Conservative leadership, with Disraeli the most obvious example, failed to offer any real recognition to their urban supporters, and they had been answered with public criticism describing them as a 'superannuated oligarchy' marked by 'indolence and class bias'.[132] The last fifteen years of the century saw a much closer working relationship between old and new Conservatives, but even during Salisbury's leadership there was still ample evidence of socio-political prejudice. Arthur Balfour, who had every reason to be grateful to the urban Conservative elites who ran his local party, often referred to urban Conservatives with cynical contempt. When he suggested W.L. Jackson as a possible Postmaster General in 1891 he stated that

> He has great tact and judgement – middle class tact and judgement I admit, but good of their kind. He justly inspires great confidence in businessmen: and he is that *rara avis* a successful manufacturer who is fit for something besides manufacturing.

Balfour ended this glowing testimonial with the comment that 'A Cabinet of Jacksons would be rather a serious order, no doubt: but one or even two would be a considerable addition to any Cabinet'.[133] This could simply have been Balfour playing on (or even with) his uncle's snobberies, but he expressed similar sentiments to other members of the Conservative hierarchy. In 1888 he wrote to Akers-Douglas about 'a great idiot in my country, who . . . is burning to become a member of the Carlton Club',[134] and in 1892, in forwarding a request for a baronetcy for a Manchester Conservative, he recommended the award on the basis that the man was old and heirless and that the baronetcy would thus lapse with his death.[135] The crucial point here, however, is that Balfour's cynical remarks were made in private. The public face of the Salisburyian leadership was one of appreciation and respect for their urban supporters. The openly disdainful tone and behaviour which had so often characterized the Disraelian hierarchy's outlook was no longer acceptable: urban Conservatism and the urban Tory elites were too valuable to be treated in such a cavalier manner. At the same time the care and effort that the party hierarchy expended on their dealings with the new urban elites shows that this was a relationship that was being managed through an almost constant process of negotiation. The visible hand of skilled party management governed this still problematic relationship.

CONSERVATISM AND THE PROPERTIED: THE PROBLEMS OF A POSITIVE APPEAL

In many ways the Conservative party's difficulties with the rural and urban elites were very similar. Both sought reassurance that the party valued them. The party sought to provide such reassurance, but the question arises as to why the Conservatives did not do so more dramatically. The late nineteenth century produced strong demands for economic assistance from both urban and rural interests. Frequently these carried criticisms of established economic orthodoxies associated with Liberalism. One would have thought this represented a major opportunity for the Conservative party to construct a coalition of economic interests hostile to Liberalism and all its works in the sphere of political economy. However, the Conservatives were understandably reluctant to undertake such an initiative; to have done so might well have fragmented rural and urban economic interests, and endangered the unity of any propertied coalition.

The tariff agitations of the last quarter of the century indicate the constraints on the Conservatives' scope for shaping a more positive appeal to Britain's propertied. The most vocal request for tariff assistance came from Britain's farmers. In his report to Salisbury on the agricultural conference of 1892 Henry Chaplin noted that when he addressed the meeting and 'mentioned the word Protection' the audience were 'like people gone mad – many of them springing up in their places and cheering frantically'.[136] Chaplin, a landowner and MP in the depressed, arable-farming county of Lincolnshire, was a convinced protectionist himself and had strong personal reasons for 'talking up' the degree of protectionist sentiment in the farming community. But Chaplin's view that there was 'no mistaking how deep the [protectionist] feeling is among the large majority of farmers'[137] appears to have been justified. As early as September 1881 William Lowther won a by-election in the hard-pressed arable-farming constituency of North Lincolnshire on a protectionist platform, and Lowther's success was repeated in January 1882 when two protectionists were returned in regions as distinct as Cambridgeshire and North Yorkshire. There were few dramatic electoral successes for protectionists after 1884, but activity in many of the chambers of agriculture and farming clubs of Britain through the 1880s and 1890s meant that J.H. Round did not exaggerate when in 1895 he charted the progress of what he called 'the protectionist revival'.[138] By 1896 the *Digest of Agricultural Opinion* was able to report that 60 per cent of farmers favoured protection as a solution to their difficulties.[139]

Nor was it just in farming districts that tariffs had an appeal. The NFTL was principally an urban movement, drawing its support in the main from those regions that had suffered most from the impact of foreign tariffs or imports. Thus there was particularly strong fair trade sentiment in Sheffield, parts of the Black Country, amongst the Birmingham metal trades and in Bradford. However, fair trade sentiments could also be found, without having to search too hard, in areas renowned for their commitment to free trade, such as Manchester and Lancashire cotton towns.[140] In 1885 prominent Liberals placed much of the blame for their reversals in borough seats on fair trade,[141] and when the RCDTI questioned chambers of commerce and trade associations through the country it discovered that fair trade, or at least a willingness to question the benefits of free trade, was quite widespread in Britain's industrial heartlands.[142]

At times it seemed the Conservative party might try to exploit these anti-free trade sentiments. In 1881 Edward Hamilton noted that Gladstone was 'incensed at the account to which the Tories are turning this wretched hollow Fair Trade cry',[143] and through the 1880s and 1890s the Conservatives often hinted, not always very subtly, that they had some sympathy for a revision of Britain's free trade position. In 1882 C.T. Ritchie moved a Conservative motion in the Commons demanding a Select Committee on the impact of foreign tariffs on British trade. Ritchie stated that the motion was 'animated by no spirit of hostility to free trade principles', but he also spoke of a widespread 'want of confidence . . . [in] the commercial policy of the country',[144] and over the next fifteen years such Conservative-backed motions became almost a Parliamentary fixture.[145] It was also the Conservatives who supported, and in 1885 conceded, the fair traders' demand for a Royal Commission on the 'depression'.[146] After the 1885 general election there were sixty Conservative MPs listed as fair traders, forty-eight from the boroughs and twelve from the counties (see Appendix 1), and grass roots Conservative opinion seemed even more sympathetic to tariff heresies. From 1887 on the NUCA passed motions calling for a revision of Britain's free trade stance on an almost annual basis, and the popularity of tariff heresies with provincial Conservative opinion seems to have prompted Randolph Churchill to toy with fair trade in the early 1880s.[147] Of course some might attribute Churchill's flirtation with fair trade to his lack of political sagacity, but even that supposed paragon of political wisdom Salisbury felt moved to argue, at a regional assembly of the NUCA at Hastings in 1892, that Britain's free trade position might need to be reconsidered in the light of changing circumstances.[148]

Table 2 Occupational cross-categories of Conservative MPs in London, 1880–1910

111	Totals	Aristoc./ land	Manufac- ture	Brewing	Law	Service sector	Military/ yeoman
Aristoc./ land	37		1	0	7	4	20
Manufacture	13			0	2	3	0
Brewing	4				0	1	0
Law	42					4	2
Service sector	34						1
Military/ yeoman	13						

However, the Salisburyian Conservative party refused to commit themselves to a pro-tariff stance. One possible explanation for this is that they did not wish to trespass on the free trade sentiments of their Liberal Unionist allies after 1886. But it is not wholly clear that the Liberal Unionists saw free trade as essential to their identity. In 1887 Hartington announced at Dover that if he had to choose between a Home Rule government and a protectionist government he would choose the latter.[149] Given Hartington's reaction to the tariff reform campaign sixteen years later the Conservatives may have been wise not to take him at his word, but the fact remains that the Liberal Unionists' commitment to free trade is often assumed rather than demonstrated. A more important problem with this explanation is that Conservatives showed a reluctance to come out against free trade before 1886. It may be that they were already concerned about alienating potential Liberal deserters, but this cannot explain why Randolph Churchill dropped his interest in fair trade, for he was the Conservative politician least liked by, and least sensitive towards, 'moderate' Liberals and Whigs.

A more plausible explanation for the Conservatives' drawing back from an assault on free trade is their fear of a 'dear food' cry. Henry Chaplin, hardly the most self-restrained politician, noted that when he addressed the agricultural meeting of December 1892 he had 'the fear of Middleton before my eyes' and had 'dared not respond altogether as ... [the meeting] would have wished'.[150] But the 'dear food' bogey by itself can only explain why the Conservatives rejected *agricultural* protection. Much of the fair trade agitation was concerned with industrial protection and retaliation. Neither of these proposals required a 'food tax', and they appeared to have been popular enough with the urban masses in 1885 to have secured the return of a significant number of Conservative fair trade MPs. At least in principle there seemed to be an opportunity for a powerful Conservative appeal to urban voters of all classes on the basis of providing tariff benefits for British industry. But, as Edward Hamilton was quick to realize, there was a major political objection to such an economic strategy. Remarking on a conversation with Lord Bath, Hamilton noted that Bath was

> hankering after 'fair trade' and imagines that this delusive cry will find a ready response with the new electorate in the towns, forgetting that the protection of manufactured articles in any form, open or disguised, would make matters worse for agriculturists.[151]

Herein lay the rub. British agriculture had nothing to gain and much to lose from industrial protection and retaliation. Likewise imperial preference, also popular with some urban interests, was predicated on the notion of importing colonial instead of foreign foodstuffs, and thus offered no respite to Britain's farmers from the deluge of imports. In 1887 the Conservative fair trade MP Frederick Dixon-Hartland stated that fair trade was a political non-starter 'until manufacturers and agriculturists can agree upon some policy'.[152] Given these (much-discussed) facts the Conservative party was hardly likely to launch a policy initiative directed solely at the towns.

Nor was it simply the rural–urban divide which placed constraints on Conservative action on the tariff front. As was noted earlier in this study there was no clear agreement within Britain's business community as to the most effective kind of tariff, or even as to whether free trade ought to be rejected.[153] Again these problems were well known to the Conservative party. Apart from the fact that many Conservative MPs from industrial and commercial constituencies were themselves active in Chambers of Commerce it was also common practice for urban MPs to be ex-officio members of their local Chamber. As a consequence the Conservative party was filled with representatives who had first-hand knowledge of the complex interests and shades of opinion on these questions held by British businessmen. Sir Michael Hicks-Beach, then Chancellor of the Exchequer, demonstrated his consciousness of the problems involved with tariff questions when, in 1897, he wrote to Salisbury to discuss a proposed countervailing duty on sugar imports subsidized by foreign government bounties.[154] Hicks-Beach stated that he had no free trade objection per se to this course of action, but he felt that the effect of such a duty would be to encourage retaliation, with the result that the price of sugar would increase drastically. Such a result would, Hicks-Beach argued, antagonize 'brewers, the fruit growers and fruit packers (a class as poor as match makers) whose industry means jam, and requires cheap sugar; buscuit makers ... and others.'[155] Given that Conservative MPs represented different regions, different industries and different interests it was almost impossible for the party to hold a consistent, unified outlook on these issues. In 1892 Salisbury himself estimated that, in spite of the vocal presence of tariff enthusiasts, about half the Conservative Parliamentary party remained committed to free trade, in particular he mentioned '1. The representatives of commercial constituencies: 2. The political economists of whom we have a sprinkling: and 3. Those, mainly young men, who are sensitive to the reproach of belonging to the stupid party'.[156] In short, the Conservatives received conflicting signals on tariff questions, which could only presage clashes of interest if any decision on a new departure were taken.

The rural–urban divide was also important when it came to the vexed question of local taxation. The idea of compensating farmers for the loss or unavailability of tariff protection through a reduction of their tax burden was not new. The first Conservative administration after the repeal of the Corn Laws had taken this course of action, and thereafter both Liberal and Conservative governments had introduced numerous adjustments in taxation and deployed central government funds to assist local government (and thus local ratepayers) in general and rural local government in particular.[157] By the late 1880s, during Goschen's period at the Exchequer, the practice of subsidizing local government from central revenues reached new heights, but it also began to arouse concern. Above all the issue of whether town and country were being dealt with on an equal basis became a central question.[158]

The predicament the Conservatives faced in balancing the demands of rural and urban ratepayers is best demonstrated by their attempt to relieve the 'burdens on agriculture' through the Agricultural Land Rating Act of 1896. Having castigated the 1892–5 Liberal administration for 'ignoring' the farmers' plight the Conservatives entered office virtually pledged to do something for the farming community. Salisbury had indicated the probable direction the Conservatives would take in a speech at Trowbridge in 1894.[159] He likened British agriculture to a train pulling up a steep gradient towing two extra burdens, those burdens being foreign competition and high local taxation. With protection beyond the realm of 'practical politics' it was only logical that local taxation became the focus of Conservative efforts to assist agriculture, and in April 1896 the Conservatives introduced a measure to relieve agricultural land of half its local tax burden.

On the face of it the so-called 'Agricultural Relief Act' was a success – at last the Conservatives had given some succour to their oldest friends. But at the same time the Act highlighted some problems. To begin with it was criticized for not giving assistance *directly* to farmers. Strictly speaking relief went to the landowner, with the assumption being that, as farm rents took account of local taxation, the landowners would pass on the savings to their tenants through rent reductions. The fact that this would not *necessarily* happen allowed Liberals to claim that the 1896 Act was simply 'doles for the squire and the parson', and opened up the possibility that, once again, the Liberals would be able to exploit landlord–tenant differences.[160] Also the Act was not as generous as either the farmers would have liked or as the RCAD had recommended. The RCAD had argued in its interim report that agricultural land should only pay one quarter of its rateable value whereas the Act had only conceded one half. The Conservatives thus seemed to be in the position of delivering only half a loaf, which was better than nothing, but still disappointing. That the Conservatives had not been more generous was largely a result of the twin presssures of cost and who was to pay. As it stood the 1896 arrangement meant that central government funds had to provide £3,550,000 additional grant-in-aid to rural authorities, and the main complaint was that urban taxpayers were being forced to subsidize rural ratepayers. The Liberals argued 'that it is inexpedient and unjust that relief granted from Imperial taxation to rateable property should be restricted to one class only of such property',[161] and contended that the government was simply using urban ratepayers' money to bail out not only its own supporters but its own members, with Lloyd George stating that the proposer of the Bill, Henry Chaplin, stood to gain £700 per annum in rate relief and that the Cabinet as a whole would receive £2,250,000.[162] This was all good polemical stuff from the Liberal benches, but there were those on the Conservative side who agreed, with George Whiteley, the cotton-spinner and MP for Stockport stating that 'the Bill was in every respect contrary to the interests of the towns ... [and] a gross and cruel act of injustice to the boards and urban districts of the country'.[163] There was no urban Tory rebellion when Parliament voted on the legislation, but there were neverthless signs that any further 'favouritism' towards rural areas would not be greeted warmly by urban Conservatism.[164]

There was one issue that seemed to offer the Conservatives the possibility of uniting rural and urban interests through a positive appeal – bimetallism. The beauty of bimetallism was that it appealed to all interests concerned about falling prices. It secured support from farming communities, who saw it as a means of achieving a price rise without the stigma that was attached to protection, and it also appealed to a wide variety of manufacturing centres, especially the Lancashire cotton industry. The bimetallic movement held out the rhetoric of a 'producer alliance' which could bridge the differences of town and country.[165]

As with the tariff agitations it seemed on occasion that the Conservatives might throw their weight behind the bimetallic movement. In 1886 one of Randolph Churchill's few significant acts as Chancellor (apart from resigning) was to throw a bone in the direction of bimetallic opinion in the shape of increased silver purchases and coinage by the Royal Mint.[166] It was a Conservative government which set up the RCC in 1887, and in 1892 Churchill's replacement, Goschen, committed Britain to sending a delegation to the International Monetary Conference at Brussels. The NUCA, as with fair trade and imperial preference, provided a ready platform for bimetallists in the Conservative grass roots.[167] Likewise the Parliamentary party was often abuzz with bimetallic activity: between 1892 and 1895 the Conservative opposition forced a number of Parliamentary debates on the currency question, with Joseph Chamberlain arguing in 1895 that such a motion would detach the Liberal government's Lancashire members, exacerbate divisions in Rosebery's Cabinet and hasten the government's downfall.[168] This particular scheme of Chamberlain's came to nothing, but the importance of bimetallism to Lancashire was not overlooked in the 1895 general election campaign, for bimetallism was very prominent in the Conservatives' triumph in the cotton districts that year. In 1895 forty Conservative bimetallists were returned to Westminster, the bulk of them from Lancashire, and the

National Review spoke, with some justification, of Salisbury's new Cabinet as a 'bimetallic Cabinet'.[169]

However, as with tariffs so with the currency question – the Conservative party nodded and winked but in the end adhered to the status quo. In this case it may well have been the case that the Conservatives flattered literally to deceive. In 1887 Henry Chaplin, then sitting as a member of the RCC, told Salisbury that

> A difficulty has arisen at the Chamber of Agriculture which will certainly affect the County Members, and may affect us all . . . There is to be a Protectionist motion at their annual meeting . . . [and] Judging from the marked increase in favour of the movement – in all the local Chambers . . . it is certain to be carried.

Chaplin's 'solution' to this difficulty was to table an alternative motion 'to divert attention – to the subject of this Commission'.[170] Chaplin admitted that he was in fact 'rapidly becoming a Believer' in bimetallism, and over the next ten years he proved to be a persistent lobbyist for the bimetallic cause. But the notion that bimetallism was a means of diverting farming attention away from protection towards a 'safer' issue undoubtedly helps to explain some of the sympathy the Conservative leadership showed to the currency heretics. Such diversionary tactics are all very well, but they can also store up trouble. Having presented farmers with an 'Inevitable Disappointment'[171] over protection, and then persuaded them to look at the currency question instead, the Conservatives faced the danger that farmers might grow restive if their situation did not improve and nothing was done about currency reform. Appointing a Royal Commission and sending delegates to international conferences may have been a way of talking without acting, but they were also a way of raising hopes, not just amongst the farming community but amongst all those groups interested in bimetallism, and at some point those hopes had to be fulfilled or dashed.

The crunch for the Conservatives on bimetallism came after 1895. At that point they had openly played on bimetallic opinion when in opposition, and two senior members of the party, Henry Chaplin and Walter Long had, as members of the RCAD, publicly advocated bimetallism as a solution to agriculture's problems, and the party's Lancashire MPs, led by W.H. Houldsworth, were exerting pressure on the government. In the end Salisbury's administration refused to embrace bimetallism, and effectively brought the debate to an end in 1897–8, first by rejecting proposals from the US and French governments for an international bimetallic agreement and, second, by taking the decision to place India on the Gold Standard.[172] In taking these decisions they were undoubtedly helped by the upswing in the trade cycle that began in 1896, which in particular launched the cotton industry on its long Indian summer, and by their action in providing the farming community with some cheer through the Agricultural Relief Act. It would, however, be unwise to attribute the Conservative government's rejection of bimetallism simply to these factors. Nor is it enough to point to the problems involved in forging a workable international agreement.[173] To understand the Conservatives' decision to eschew currency reform it is essential to take into account the fact that they were constrained by the conflicting signals they received from the various groups involved in the currency debate. It was certainly the case that British agriculture, like its continental counterparts, showed a marked interest in bimetallism. Likewise many sections of British industry were also enthusiastic, but even in areas where bimetallic opinion was strong, like Lancashire, there was still significant support for the currency status quo.[174] More important still there was powerful opposition to bimetallism in Britain's financial and commercial heartland, the City of London. City opposition to bimetallism was expressed not only by organizations like the GSDA, but in direct City lobbying of the Treasury, through the influential voice of the Bank of England, and through the close relationship some prominent City figures enjoyed with Salisbury himself.[175] With the City having become overwhelmingly Conservative in its political allegiance in the late nineteenth century a Conservative government veering to bimetallism would have been a recipe for alienating this most powerful of economic interests. Thus on the one issue where there appeared to be at least a possibility of bringing agricultural and industrial interests together, the leading financial and commercial interests of the country seemed implacably hostile.

In 1881 the Conservative MP Sir Massey Lopes tabled a Commons' motion calling for the creation of a Ministry of Agriculture and Commerce – the idea being that a new economic 'supremo' was necessary if the depressed state of farming and trade was to be effectively dealt with. In a memorandum to Gladstone on this question the then President of the Board of Trade noted that

> The first question which arises is as to the possibility and policy of combining in a single department the business especially connected with both agriculture and commerce. After careful consideration it appears to me impossible that any such arrangement would permanently satisfy the interests concerned. The interests of commerce and agriculture, identified as they frequently are with the interests of town and country, are sometimes inconsistent and antagonistic.

In the light of this division between rural and urban interests the President of the Board of Trade concluded that a Minister of Agriculture and Commerce was out of the question, because no single person could 'enjoy the full confidence of both these great interests'.[176] The evidence of the economic policy debates of the late nineteenth century indicates that this judgement was almost certainly correct. Uniting the various sectors of the British economy behind any policy initiative, if it was to be achieved at all, was clearly going to require a complex and comprehensive policy structure. This was a lesson the Salisburyian Conservative party seems to have learned well, inasmuch as they consciously avoided the task of building such a structure. It was to be an ironic twist of fate, therefore, that the President of the Board of Trade who had so eloquently stated the problem in 1881, one Joseph Chamberlain, was to be instrumental in pushing the Edwardian Conservative party into a more ambitious approach in and after 1903.

CONCLUDING REMARKS

The Conservative party's transformation from political arm of the landed interest to party of property in general was a process which carried immense advantages in an age when property and power were intimately related. But this process was by no means smooth or problem-free. Indeed one of the most important things to grasp about the 'transformation of Victorian Conservatism' is that it was a *process*. In short the relationship between Conservatism and Britain's various propertied elites was in a constant state of negotiation as the Conservative party worked to construct and consolidate its identity as the party of property. That the process was so complex was due to the fact that it was not easy to establish exactly what it meant to be the party of property in the late nineteenth century. On the one hand the urban Tory elites' suspicion and resentment of the social and political exclusiveness of the party's landed hierarchy had to be assuaged. On the other hand the aristocratic leadership had to control its own disdain for their new-found urban friends and at the same time deal with the anxieties of their own class and the farmers' fear that urban politics and politicians were ousting them from the centre of Conservative attention. On top of this the cyclical economic downturn of the late nineteenth century, and the process of structural change it inaugurated in Britain's rural and urban economies, meant that the competing and sometimes conflicting demands of agriculture, industry and commerce had somehow to be comprehended by the Conservative party. None of this was easy. It required skilled party management and deft political judgement to hold the ring of 'propertied' politics in the late nineteenth century.

In terms of the broad aims of this study the Conservatives' problems as the party of property have a threefold significance. First, the fact that the Conservative party had difficulties integrating its support long before 1886, and that this problem continued to exercise the party thereafter, puts into perspective, or more accurately puts in its place, the notion that any internal problems facing the forces of Conservatism after 1886 were

117

a product of tensions between Conservatives and Liberal Unionists. It is noticeable that when the Conservative leadership, or the Conservative grass-roots, or indeed even fair trade and bimetallist activists, discussed constraints on policy options the Liberal Unionist–Conservative divide was rarely if ever mentioned, but the question of balancing rural and urban or other conflicting interests was always well to the fore. Likewise although questions were raised about whether Liberal Unionists were receiving a disproportionate share of honours or office spoils, this represented simply a new subset of a problem that had existed since the 1870s. The formal divide between Conservatives and Liberal Unionists produced only minor complications in a much broader process of socio-political realignment on the British Right.

A second, more important point that emerges here is that the complexity of the Conservative party's most immediate constituency enables one to understand why Conservative governments were so 'unimaginative' in the face of the 'Great Depression'. The conflicting interests of Britain's highly stratified farming and business community placed a crucial political constraint on the Conservatives' room for manouevre. As a consequence the Salisburyian Conservative party's decision to do little or nothing was just that, a *decision* chosen from a number of possible options with the alternatives discarded as too politically risky. In this sense Salisbury's response to the late nineteenth-century situation was very similar to Baldwin's 'Safety First' strategy in 1929 and the policies of the 'National' government in the 1930s. Doing 'nothing' was on each occasion the thing least likely to be divisive of the Tory constituency and thus the most constructive thing to do politically.

The final issue that emerges from the Conservative party's balancing act with the propertied elites is how long it could go on. Albert Einstein once remarked that for someone to walk a tightrope for five minutes was reasonable, but that it was ridiculous to expect them to do it safely for twenty years. The Conservative party's relationship with Britain's propertied classes was not balanced so precariously, but nevertheless its stability could not be taken for granted.

That the Salisburyian Conservative party managed to avoid exacerbating tensions between the propertied elites was not simply due to skilled management of issues likely to cause conflict. It was also a product of the fact that the late nineteenth-century Conservative party fulfilled the task that had brought the propertied elites together under the Conservative banner in the first place, namely it successfully defeated the challenge of the forces of 'anti-property'. In other words the Conservatives fulfilled what one might call the negative role of a political party, in that people support parties not only for the benefits they confer in office but also because they keep opponents out. One of Salisbury's achievements was that he kept the lid on potential differences within the

Conservative structure by constantly accentuating the negative role of the Conservative party and stressing the common ground that all propertied interests shared in keeping the threat to property rights at bay. The question, though, was what would happen if the Conservative party's ability to defend the rights of property effectively was called into question.

4

CONSERVATISM AND THE PROPERTYLESS

The challenge of democracy and socialism

DEFINING THE PROBLEM: 1880–1900

The Reform Bill is a frightfully democratic measure which I confess appals me. Its effect will not be felt at once, but in a few years it will come with a rush. I don't see any hope for the Tories anywhere or anyhow.

(Sir William Harcourt to Lady Harcourt, 2 December 1884).[1]

suppose that the legislative authority is vested in the lowest orders ... those who are possessed of some little property readily find means of regulating the taxes so that they are burdensome to the wealthy and profitable to the poor.

(Alexis de Tocqueville, *Democracy in America*)

In 1884 Britain entered the age of the mass electorate. The 'Third' Reform Act enfranchised approximately 1.76 million new voters, and after 1884 two out of three adult males were, in theory at least, entitled to vote.[2] The social composition and geographical location of the new voters were significant. Extensions of the franchise in 1832 and 1867 had been mostly concentrated in urban areas: in the first instance the vote had been given to Macaulay's 'good shopkeeper' and in the second to a large segment of the urban working class. The 1884 act introduced household enfranchisement in the counties, ensuring that the bulk of those newly enfranchised were agricultural workers. For the first time town and country enjoyed equal levels of enfranchisement, and the electorate as a whole was dominated by the labouring classes.

The general reaction to this expansion of the electorate was that it would cause difficulties for the Conservatives. To begin with the new voters were concentrated in the Conservative electoral heartland – English counties. In addition, the Redistribution Act of 1885 destroyed many of the old electoral communities in the counties which had been vital to Conservative *Honoratiorenpolitik* in those districts throughout the nineteenth century.[3] The problem of defending the party's strongholds was, however, regarded as a subset of a more general Conservative dilemma produced by the changed electoral system. How was the party of property and privilege to survive in a political world in which the votes of the propertyless had become the ultimate arbiters?

To a late twentieth-century observer looking back on the Conservatives' electoral dominance in the period 1918–92, the late nineteenth-century concern over the Conservative party's popular appeal can only appear misplaced, but in 1884 things seemed different. Between 1846 and 1884 the Conservatives had held office for only eight years. It was true the Conservatives had enjoyed an electoral triumph in 1874, but it was widely felt that this had been more a Liberal failure than a Conservative success, and any optimism had been dispelled by a comprehensive defeat in 1880. The party hierarchy seemed ill-equipped to establish a rapport with the mass electorate. Neither Disraeli nor his party had shown much enthusiasm for 'popular Toryism',[4] and the party was led in 1884 by the man who had shown the greatest hostility to the rise of 'democracy'.[5] In describing the 'Third' Reform Act as a disaster for the Conservative party Sir William Harcourt was voicing a commonly held opinion. As soon as it had become known that an extensive measure of reform was to be enacted, Goldwin Smith had told Milner Gibson that 'an exclusive Tory Government is a thing of the past', whilst in December 1886, even after a Conservative election victory, a morose Sir Michael Hicks-Beach told Salisbury that he had 'much doubt whether the country *can* be governed now-a-days by persons holding opinions which you and I should call even moderately Conservative'.[6] In the 1880s the general consensus was that Conservatism and 'democracy' were at best uneasy partners and at worst completely incompatible.

The Conservatives' electoral experiences immediately before and after the 1884–5 reforms intensified their concerns. In 1885 the Conservatives failed to secure a majority of county seats for the first time;[7] a hostile labourers' vote was blamed. It was thought that agricultural labourers were alienated from their social superiors. Here the blame was placed on the bitter struggles of the 1870s that had followed the establishment of the Agricultural Labourers Union by Joseph Arch. In June 1885 Henry Howorth informed Balfour, 'Muller tells me that the reports from the southern counties are anything but reassuring. The squires have allowed Joseph Arch to come between them and their labourers and they may presently reap their reward'.[8] But if Joseph Arch had sowed it was Joseph Chamberlain who was thought to have reaped, in that the newly-enfranchised labourers were reckoned to have voted 'for the man who promised ... all sorts of good things'.[9] Joseph Chamberlain's stumping the country with the small holdings policy devised by his lieutenant Jesse Collings had prompted Lady Salisbury to fear that 'the Radicals are promising three acres and a cow to everybody and if the people believe them it is a bad lookout for us'.[10] To many observers it seemed her fears had been justified. Joseph Chamberlain certainly thought so, arguing that 'the "cow" has done well in the agricultural districts', whilst Reginald Brett told Chamberlain 'you should be congratulated on your success in the counties'.[11] Whether or not it was Chamberlain's policy that won the counties for the Liberals in 1885 or simply, as Edward Hamilton thought, 'the ill will . . . of the new voters for the farmers, parsons and landlords'[12] cannot be stated as certain. What is certain, and what is most relevant, is that the Conservatives were convinced that the economic position of the labourers had predisposed them to radicalism and made the counties no longer safe electoral territory. Nor did this sense of insecurity in the counties evaporate after the Liberal split in 1886. In 1887, when the Conservatives lost a by-election at Spalding Henry Chaplin attributed the defeat to the fact that 'the labourers came up in droves to the booths within the last hour – and voted for Stewart [the Liberal candidate] to a man'.[13] In 1888 the Conservative MP Henry Farquarson warned the Conservative government that they were 'leaving behind them . . . a hostile force capable at the next general election of inflicting serious losses upon the Unionist majority . . . I refer to "rural disaffection"'.[14] Similar warnings echoed around the Conservative press and political circles well into the 1890s, and their message was clear – the counties could no longer be expected to return Conservative MPs.

If Conservatives felt insecure about their relations with the 'Village Labourer' they were also less than comfortable with the 'Town Labourer'. Britain's cities and boroughs, especially working-class districts, had been traditional Liberal territory, and in 1880 the Liberals recaptured much of the ground gained by Conservatives in the boroughs in 1874. Salisbury's negotiations with the Liberals over electoral reform in 1883–4 confirmed the Conservatives' sense of insecurity. Salisbury aimed, wherever possible, to isolate pockets of 'villadom' in Britain's fast-growing suburbia – Mr Pooter rather than Joe Bloggs was looked upon as the best hope for urban Conservatism. In 1885 the young George Curzon, standing in South Derbyshire, expressed the fears of many Conservatives when he noted that 'My electorate is 11,500, over 7,000 new voters. Of these between 4,000 and 5,000 are colliers and manufacturers and I haven't a chance with them. They won't even hear me . . . So certain am I to be beaten that I am planning a tour round the world'.[15] The urban and industrial working class may not have been *terra incognita* to Salisburyian Conservatives, but neither were they regarded as *terra firma*.

This unease with the mass electorate helps to account for Conservative fear of Socialism in the late nineteenth century. In 1882 Alfred Milner stated that 'Socialism has become a word of everyday use',[16] and although Milner was somewhat premature in making this pronouncement, it was at this time that Socialism emerged onto the British political scene. The early 1880s witnessed the emergence of a number of explicitly Socialist groups, such as the Social Democratic Federation, the Socialist League and the Fabian Society. The early 1880s were also the era of Henry George, the Land Nationalization League and, most important of all, Joseph Chamberlain's 'ransom' speech and the *Radical Programme*. All of these developments gave the politics of the British Left a radical twist. With the founding of the Independent Labour Party (ILP) in 1893 Socialist representatives made their first major bid for Westminster, thereby signalling that some elements of the labour movement were no longer content to remain, in Engels' phrase, 'the tail of the great Liberal party'. Sir William Harcourt's well-known remark of 1894 that 'we are all Socialists now' was hardly a literal truth, but it indicates how rapidly the emergence of Socialism ceased to be a novelty in British political debate.

The 'socialist threat' first made a prominent appearance in Conservative politics between 1880 and 1886, when it was cast to great effect in the campaign to bring about the desertion of Whigs and Liberal moderates. Twenty years passed before Socialism occupied centre stage again, but meanwhile Conservatives continued to worry about Socialism. The exact nature of the Socialist threat, however, remained somewhat obscure. In 1892 James Kirkup noted that when people came to define Socialism in Britain they generally meant 'any interference with property ... on behalf of the poor'.[17] This umbrella definition was symptomatic of a general confusion, not least among British Socialists themselves, as to what Socialism stood for, apart from being a doctrine intrinsically subversive of property. Efforts were made, by friend and foe of Socialism alike, to produce a clearer picture of this new political force. Its most obvious trait was seen to be a willingness to extend the power of the State.[18] Consequently Socialism was frequently taken to be synonymous with Collectivism, a point confirmed by the fact that in the British context its antithesis was frequently seen to be *Individualism* and not capitalism.[19] Certainly this was the definitional framework adopted by people like Lord Wemyss, Herbert Spencer and the Liberty and Property Defence League (LPDL),[20] but even those on the Right who were sympathetic to an increased role for the State agreed that *technically* 'we shall be unable to have a State which is not *socialistic* in some respects [because] the very notion of the State implies Socialism'.[21]

Not all Conservatives, however, conceded that State intervention was necessarily *Socialist*. For those who thought thus – undoubtedly a majority – State intervention had to display certain other characteristics to qualify as Socialist. In this context the crucial factor was not State action in itself, but how that action was effected, or as one Conservative writer put it, 'It is the *method* by which Socialism proposes to remedy social evils that constitutes the peculiar essence of Socialism'.[22] Here the most important criterion for judging whether a measure was Socialist was the financing of State intervention. Socialism was thought to use the power of the State to promote the interests of the propertyless at the expense of the propertied. This definition of Socialism, more precise than that offered by extreme Individualists, was the one most commonly used in Conservative circles from the 1880s.[23]

That Socialism had emerged at the same time as the introduction of mass politics did not come as a great surprise to many contemporary, especially Conservative observers, for they assumed there was an almost necessary correlation between 'Democracy' and 'Socialism'. In 1883 Salisbury decorously described a democracy as 'consisting of men who must ordinarily be engrossed by the daily necessities of self-support',[24] alluding to the cross-party consensus that a mass electorate could but be an impoverished electorate. By 1884 newspapers, political journals and social investigators examining the 'condition of the people' had painted a stark picture of Britain's lower orders,[25] and a series of Royal Commissions on Britain's economic and social conditions, as well as further unofficial enquiries, reinforced these impressions of urban 'rookeries' and rural decay.[26] This perception of the *social* make-up of the electorate led to three assumptions about the probable *political* outlook of 'the democracy'. The first was that the mass of voters would wish to improve upon their deprived circumstances. The second was that the masses would be hostile towards those who occupied a more privileged position, or that class jealousy would become a major determinant of political and electoral behaviour. Finally, it was assumed that the masses' desire for material betterment and their incipient class jealousy would emerge into the mainstream of British politics not in the guise of a revolutionary upheaval, but in the form of a demand for social reform to be financed by taxation levied, either centrally or locally, on the propertied classes.

In the early 1880s Joseph Chamberlain appeared to embody the dangerous potential of the 'new politics' when he fused statements like 'the future of politics are social politics'[27] with his demand to know what 'ransom' property would pay to preserve its privileges.[28] The spectre that haunted many Conservatives was described by Salisbury in 'Disintegration' when, with Chamberlain in mind, he spoke of the threat of the radical demagogue exploiting the privations of the poorer classes and 'impressing upon them ... that the function of legislation is to transfer to them something ... from the pockets of their more fortunate countrymen'.[29] Nor did Chamberlain's 'seeing the light' in 1886 remove this threat. Like Sidney Webb, Conservatives felt that the political enfranchisement of the lower orders was bound to be followed by a demand for their social and economic enfranchisement. Like Henry Grattan, they felt that 'If you transfer the power in the State to those who have nothing in the country, they will afterwards transfer the property'.

II. SHAPING THE CONSERVATIVE RESPONSE, 1880–1900: THE TRIUMPH OF QUIETISM AND TRADITION

In the late nineteenth century the scale and scope of the Conservative party's strategy for coping with the twin challenges of the mass electorate and its 'rent-seeking' desires were, at the national level, defined by its leader's pessimistic assumptions about the relationship between Conservatism and the masses. Lord Salisbury had resigned his Cabinet post in 1867 in opposition to the extension of the franchise, arguing that democracy was a threat, because it was bound to lead to a politics of electoral 'bribery'. By the time of the 'Third' Reform Act he still thought there was no possibility of converting 'the democracy' to Conservatism: all that could be done was to discipline the masses on their inexorable march to political ascendancy.[30] Salisbury's view of the future of British politics was almost vulgar Marxist, insofar as he saw the triumph of democracy and radicalism, even Socialism, as almost inevitable. From this perspective, Salisbury saw the Conservative party as a sort of guards' van of the revolution – there to apply the brake where possible but otherwise simply being pulled along by a runaway radical train.

The policy implications of Salisburyian Conservatism were quietist. It conceded that State-sponsored social reforms were probably the most effective form of appeal to the mass electorate. It also conceded that such an appeal could be made on non-Socialist grounds. However, Salisburyian Conservatism eschewed 'constructive' programmes on the grounds that the general outlook of the electorate rendered any such attempt futile. Individual reforms were seen as possible, perhaps even desirable, but a *programme* of social reform was an anathema to the Salisburyian *Weltanschauung*.[31]

Having rejected what was widely thought to be the most effective policy appeal to the mass electorate Salisburyian Conservatism sought to cope with 'the democracy' by organization. The late nineteenth-century Conservative organization, under the control of the party's Chief Agent, R.W. Middleton, was a smooth-running and well-financed machine.[32] This machine was entrusted with the task of securing a sizeable but above all stable vote which would remain largely unaffected by the 'swing of the pendulum'. This meant identifying Conservative voters through intensive canvassing. A great deal of work by local members and volunteers was the key to this process,[33] and it was in gathering information that the Primrose League made one of its most important contributions to Conservative politics. It provided 'an army of unpaid canvassers'[34] which was of course invaluable at election times,[35] but also central to the process of discovering who the faithful were and ensuring that they were entitled to vote. Annual revisions of the electoral register, and the complexities of the post-1884 franchise, made the process of qualifying and registering to vote very difficult.[36] Constant scrutiny of the electoral register was thus vital to ensure that one's supporters were not over-looked. CCO was able to provide advice as to the best methods of dealing with the annual revisions, and many local Conservative associations were, as a result of their wealthy membership, able to afford full-time secretaries to monitor and 'assist' the revising barristers.[37] However, the secretaries of local Conservative associations needed detailed knowledge of local political/voting allegiances to secure an optimum registration. The Primrose League was an ideal mechanism for ascertaining this information via its membership and social functions.[38]

A good party organization could also make life difficult for opponents. As one local party secretary pointed out 'our interest is quite as much to keep radicals off as to get Conservatives on'.[39] Salisbury and Middleton looked to the party machinery to keep the number of adult males registered countrywide below 60 per cent, their maximum for Conservative security.[40] Nor were they alone on this point.[41] The Conservative hierarchy also assumed it was essential to keep as many of those on the register from turning out on polling day – the basic philosophy here being the lower the poll the better the chances of a Conservative victory. An interesting case-study is the Rossendale by-election of 1891. A few weeks before polling Lord Wolmer wrote to Salisbury, 'I believe the poll at Rossendale will be 90 per cent – in which case we cannot lose by less than 200 – on a poll of 85 per cent we should pull it off by about 150'.[42] Wolmer's estimate was supported by CCO, where the secretary, W.H. Rowe, calculated that 'Any percentage less than 89 per cent would be pro rata in the Unionist favour'.[43] If keeping the turnout low was a priority in a constituency like Rossendale, where the urban working-class vote posed the threat,[44] it was still more important in the counties where it was widely thought that 'It is "Hodge" upon whom the Radicals depend'.[45] To achieve low turnouts in the counties the Conservative hierarchy sought to hold general elections at times, such as during the harvest, when the labouring turnout was certain to be low.[46] In both town and country the Salisburyian Conservative hierarchy had very little faith in their ability to attract the labouring vote, and sought by a variety of means simply to reduce the number of working-class voters.

The Conservative leadership's determination to avoid rather than confront the mass electorate shows they did not seek to construct a 'popular' party. Salisbury's strategy was to *control* and not to practise popular politics. This is not to say, however, that popular Conservatism did not exist in the late nineteenth century. Popular Toryism was strong in many mill towns in Lancashire, where a combination of employer paternalism and cross-class religious allegiance underpinned the Conservative cause,[47] and a similar marriage of local employer influence

126

and popular Anglicanism aided Conservative success in parts of the Black Country.[48] In Liverpool, where the large Irish community triggered virulent popular Anglicanism, working-class Conservatism, fostered by the influence of local Tory notables, was also well-established.[49]

The basic mechanisms of popular Conservatism were similar in all these regions. Influence of local employers was always to the fore, but it was mediated by a range of institutions, associations and social practices that produced a communitarian style of politics. A notable's reputation as a 'good' employer, a generous (and conspicuous) local philanthropist, and a patron of local working-men's clubs and leisure activities were vital ingredients of popular politics in industrial constituencies.[50] At the same time groups like the Primrose League, which appears to have been particularly important in involving both middle- and working-class women in the sub-culture of urban Toryism,[51] helped to forge and reinforce cross-class associational links. Community solidarity – the 'Us' of popular Conservatism – was increased by emphasizing 'hostile' communities – the 'Them' of popular Conservatism. In some areas the existence of immigrant populations, such as the Irish in Liverpool and other urban centres in Lancashire, and the Jewish community in London's East End, saw popular Conservatism draw upon ethnic prejudices which were frequently expressed in the form of popular Anglicanism. In this respect to be a member of the Church of *England* was also to be anti-Irish and 'Anti-alien'.[52] But Popular Anglicanism was also directed at British Nonconformists, and especially at militant Nonconformity. Here, as a study of Wolverhampton politics has shown, an emphasis on the 'regulatory' politics of Nonconformity in the spheres of, for example, gaming and licensing, allowed Conservatives to portray Nonconformists, and by association Liberals, as a group of puritanical killjoys who wished to interfere with working-men's pleasures. In contrast the social life of Conservative clubs and associations presented almost an anti-politics of 'beer and bonhomie'[53] as a defence against any threat from a new Parliament of the Saints.

The culture of some of Britain's major urban and industrial areas indicates that working-class Conservatism of the kind described above was an important part of urban politics in the 1880s and 1890s.[54] These areas were important to Conservative electoral success in the period 1880–1900 – especially the strength of the Conservative presence in Lancashire.[55] CCO provided financial assistance at election times, but the mobilization of working-class Conservatism was achieved by local activists utilizing the appeal of local ties, loyalties and interests. It seems that Conservatives 'on the ground' in Britain's provincial urban centres, drawing on their experience of local conditions, had more confidence in their ability to attract working-class support than did the metropolitan leadership. Popular Conservatism appears also to have been based on traditional patterns of local power and authority and on an essentially 'negative' set of issues. It relied on the continued strength of the 'deference community', albeit reinforced by new organizational networks, on the resonance of cross-class appeals over issues such as the defence of national interests and institutions against alien influences, and on the preservation of working-class leisure activities from Liberal moral faddism.

In many ways the popular Conservatism described above and the Salisburyian strategy were complementary. Popular Anglicanism, the fostering of anti-Irish sentiment and the denunciation of Liberal puritanism required no ambitious legislative programme and conformed with the Salisburyian emphasis on the limited, negative role of Conservative politics. That the leadership was prepared to limit ambitious 'popular' Conservative initiatives is demonstrated by the fate of proposals for a more positive, programmatic Conservative appeal to the working-class electorate in the late nineteenth century. There were two areas of policy which were seen to hold potential for a positive appeal, namely social reform and a reform of Britain's broader economic strategy. The first Conservative politician to be credited with the idea of a positive approach to the mass electorate on social issues is Lord Randolph Churchill,[56] who made his case in a number of major speeches and brought forward an albeit inchoate programme at Dartford in 1885,[57] but Conservative discussion of social reform did not really begin and certainly did not end with Churchill.

A number of speakers from the Conservative ranks contended that the only way to make the counties safe was to pursue a positive appeal to the labouring vote. In the wake of the Conservatives' defeat at the Spalding by-election in mid-1887, Henry Chaplin pressed hard for the introduction of Allotments legislation as a means of attracting the labouring vote.[58] The Conservative Government passed such legislation early in 1888 as a direct result of concern over the electoral situation in the counties, but the Allotments Act did not assuage their fears. By 1891 Chaplin was active again, firing off Christmas Day missives concerning his proposed Small Holdings Bill to both Balfour and Salisbury, arguing that it was essential 'to counter-act the efforts of Schnadhorst and co . . . and [to] show to the agricultural labourers that the Radicals have no monopoly of interest in their welfare'.[59] Nor was Chaplin alone in articulating such fears.[60] In 1892 the Conservatives enacted Chaplin and Jesse Collings' Small Holdings proposals, and introduced free education in rural areas in the same year, continuing the debate as to how best to come to terms with a mass rural electorate.

This debate also addressed the urban working class. Salisbury himself called for housing reform in the early 1880s,[61] and his arguments were extended in the 1890s by a number of Conservative proposals for stimulating working-class home ownership. In addition Salisbury's third administration passed the Workmen's Compensation Act, which allowed the Conservatives to further their claim to be the party of 'practical social reform'. Supporting this last measure in the Commons, Edward Goulding[62] voiced the hopes of his party when he declared that 'this measure would be received with great satisfaction by the working class',[63] and Joseph Chamberlain rounded-off the debate by remarking that it was no surprise at all 'that the Tory party should have brought in a Bill of this kind [because] so far as social legislation . . . was concerned the whole credit was due to . . . the Tory party'.[64]

That social reform and social questions were such recurrent themes in late nineteenth-century Conservative politics reflects the party's assumption that a presentable stance on social reform was essential for electoral credibility. This is a point worth emphasizing, for it gives the lie to any suggestion that Conservative interest in social reform post-1886 was a quid pro quo for the support of the Liberal Unionists, especially those of the Chamberlain ilk.[65] In fact it is difficult to find any evidence of Liberal Unionist pressure decisively influencing Conservative social policy. On the one occasion when a prominent Liberal Unionist – Chamberlain – attempted to promote a wide-ranging social programme, his influence proved negligible.[66] Similarly, on those occasions when the Conservatives did enact reforms it was perceived electoral pressures which proved decisive. Interest in allotments, small holdings and free education in rural areas owed far more to the electoral insecurities of rural Conservative MPs than to any wish to appease radical Liberal Unionists.[67] Likewise, in Scotland, where antagonism to 'Tory Democracy' and 'progressive' legislation had been most pronounced in the early 1880s, it was noted in 1892 that 'Conservative opinion has advanced there of late, *under the persuasion of the polls'*.[68]

Neither is it the case that Liberal Unionists were the main proponents and Conservatives the main opponents of social reform. It is true that, in the 1890s, Chamberlain was the most prominent *individual* advocate of positive social policies on the political Right, but it is also true that some of his main opponents were in the Liberal Unionist ranks[69] and some of his most committed supporters were Conservatives.[70] Furthermore, the most radical programme of social reform emanating from the Right was promulgated by the Scottish NUCA;[71] a host of lesser measures were also promoted by Conservatives.[72] The division in the forces of Conservatism on the question of social reform did not follow simple party lines, but split between 'constructive' and 'quietist' approaches, with each outlook being held with varying degrees of strength by Liberal Unionists and Conservatives alike. In this debate the common view was that social reform was indeed popular; the disagreement was over whether or not social reform could perform a Conservative function in either theory or practice. Opinion on this matter was divided into three distinct patterns of thought which criss-crossed the formal Liberal Unionist–Conservative divide. First there were the Conservative Individualists, in particular Lord Wemyss and the LPDL, who saw any extension of State activity beyond the bounds established by 1880 as Socialist.[73] Second, there was the Salisburyian approach, which rejected systematic intervention, but did not see social reform and State intervention as intrinsically Socialist. In the Salisburyian world individual measures, considered on their merits, could enact Conservative ends. Last, there were the advocates of a Radical Conservative strategy, who argued that the mass electorate would indeed be attracted to Socialist State intervention unless they were offered a positive alternative of Conservative reforms. In the 1890s these Radical Conservatives produced some very bold schemes: both their content and their fate are instructive.

The most wide-ranging package was put forward by the Scottish NUCA at the end of October 1894. Calling on the House of Lords to initiate measures 'for the social well-being of the people' the Scottish Tories passed motions in favour of old age pensions, the extension of Employers' Liability to all forms of employment, argued that the immigration of pauper aliens should be halted to defend British jobs, demanded an arbitration service for industrial disputes, and sought to find ways of extending owner-occuppiership amongst the working class.[74] But it was not only North of the border that social reforming proposals were emerging from Conservative circles. In 1892 the English NUCA Conference in Sheffield debated social reform, and a number of proposals on pensions and housing gained widespread support.[75] In response to the general tenor of the Conference proceedings, Arthur Balfour saw fit to mark his key-note speech with a declaration that 'laissez faire is ... completely discredited', going on to state that the Conference had confirmed that the Conservatives were the true party of social reform.[76] Over the course of the 1890s, similar debates and pronouncements were a prominent feature of NUCA Conferences. However, the net effect of these motions, when measured by the ultimate test of legislative results, was limited. To understand why, it is instructive to examine the genesis and failure of the most celebrated effort of the 1890s to infuse Conservative politics with a programme of social reform.

Between 1892 and 1894 Joseph Chamberlain produced a stream of proposals designed to persuade the Conservative leadership to adopt a more adventurous social policy. Chamberlain's programme, which appeared in its most detailed form in the autumn of 1894, called for many of the measures brought forward by the Scottish NUCA, namely pensions, extension of Employers' Liability, housing reform and so forth.[77] In presenting these proposals Chamberlain had two aims: first, to make sense of his own political position; second, to provide the Conservative party with a popular platform. Writing to Henry Chaplin in

1895 he noted, 'my position has been a very difficult one since the split [of 1886]'.[78] The core of his problem was how to reconcile his alliance with the Tories with his 'vehement support of Radical doctrines previously'.[79] But Chamberlain linked his own position with an argument that positive action on social reform was necessary for the Conservatives' own image. In February 1892 Chamberlain was both publishing his views on social legislation[80] and pressing Balfour with a social programme similar to that which he was to produce in a more detailed form two years later – the thrust of his argument being that positive social policies were necessary to avert electoral disaster. Chamberlain's 1894 programme was also supported by these contentions, for he claimed that had it not been for the publicity given to his proposals, the Conservatives would have lost by-elections at Forfar and Brigg.[81] For Chamberlain popularity and social reform were inextricably linked.

The 1894 programme also revealed the problems Chamberlain faced in convincing people both of the necessity and efficacy of his approach. The Conservatives had some sympathy for Chamberlain's personal political objectives, and such social reforms as were enacted gave Chamberlain the chance for some important Parliamentary set-piece self-justification. But his argument about broader electoral needs had limited effect in the 1890s. Salisbury's careful, 'negative' approach to the mass electorate seemed successful. In March 1892 Salisbury reacted to a suggestion that the Conservatives enact leasehold enfranchisement by stating that such a move would 'risk alienating old friends without conciliating any new adherents'.[82] He responded similarly to Chamberlain's more ambitious schemes; he told Balfour in July 1892 that if the party acted on Chamberlain's advice 'we must in so doing alarm a good many people who have always been with us'. He went on to add that although he feared that 'these social questions are destined to break up our Party', he saw no reason 'to incur the danger before the necessity has arisen'.[83]

In the fiscal climate of the late nineteenth century any party seeking to promote social reform had to confront the problem of the distribution of wealth. Most politicians, especially those inclined to caution, like Salisbury, were loath to place additional burdens on taxpayers. Besides the fiscal crisis more particular economic interests had to be confronted if the role of the State was to be extended. For example, any attempt to introduce old age pensions meant impinging on the territory of the Friendly Societies, a powerful and well-entrenched lobby around which Joseph Chamberlain for one trod very warily when he broached the idea of pensions in 1892.[84] Another example of economic obstacles to reform emerged in the debates on the issue of regulating the hours of labour, a perennial question in the 1890s. In a Memorandum on 'The Eight Hours Question', written as a briefing document for Balfour in March 1891, J.S. Sandars argued that an eight-hour day in the mining and other industries would raise wages and other employer costs. In some circumstances, Sandars contended, such increased costs could be borne without complaint, but were insupportable in the 1890s because of the intensity of foreign competition.[85] The case against Eight Hours legislation was put even more strongly by George Wyndham, the Conservative MP for Dover. Writing to his father in May 1892 Wyndham noted that 'the theory of that measure [the Eight Hours Bill before Parliament at that time] is unassailable so long as you exclude foreign competition from the problem'.[86] Over the rest of the decade this argument was wheeled on by prominent industrialists, both in Parliament and behind the scenes, whenever any measure of industrial welfare was proposed,[87] an indication of the constraints which politicians faced when considering social reform.[88]

That Salisbury was able to command support for his quietist approach was due largely to the fact that he appeared to have delivered the political goods for the Conservative party. In terms of *results* the electoral fortunes of the party were good. The bulk of the party, leaving aside the committed Individualists, would have agreed with Balfour's dictum that 'the best antidote to Socialism was practical social reform',[89] but the Socialist threat seemed very remote in the late nineteenth century, and there seemed to be little need to pursue an ambitious social programme on these grounds. In March 1888 the President of the Board of Trade, C.T. Ritchie, told Salisbury that 'Public opinion is a little sensitive on the subject of pauperism and employment at the present moment . . . [and] is also rather inclined . . . to favour . . . unsound and dangerous departures'.[90] But ultimately Ritchie felt that the situation was not sufficiently serious to warrant anything more radical than a committee to investigate the level and effectiveness of poor relief.[91] No matter how hard men like Vincent, Chaplin, Chamberlain and Sir John Rolleston argued that 'the condition of [social and economic] affairs at the present moment . . . is encouraging Socialism . . . [and] if allowed to continue will bring about a social cataclysm',[92] all the evidence seemed to point in the other direction. Salisbury, it seemed, had not only tamed or at least disciplined 'the democracy', he had at the same time, and at minimal cost, seen off the threat of Socialism.

The constraints which acted on Conservative advocates of social reform also hampered those Conservatives who sought to construct an alternative interventionist strategy, for social reform was not the only appeal to the material interests of the working class which was put forward as a means of winning mass support. In the 1880s and 1890s many Conservatives argued that tariffs of one form or another had the potential to attract working-class support. Successive NUCA meetings saw motions in favour of imperial preference, retaliation and protection carried by large majorities.[93] The sponsors were frequently connected with particular economic interests,[94] but in order to 'sell' their arguments it was essential to present them as measures capable of garnering popular support.

In March 1886 the journal of the IFL declared that 'the question of Imperial Federation is as much a working man's question as any, for it is intimately bound up with the question of trade',[95] and it was in this context that arguments in favour of tariffs were developed. At the NUCA Conference at Sheffield in 1892, Sir Howard Vincent sought to 'remind' his colleagues that the most popular of all social reforms would be the provision of secure employment, which, he argued, could only be achieved through protective tariffs, imperial preference, and the halting of alien immigration.[96] This link between tariffs, Empire, employment and social reform offered a form of social policy which avoided the barriers placed in the way of an extensive programme of domestic legislation. This seems to explain Joseph Chamberlain's growing devotion to imperial matters in the 1890s. In May 1895 Chamberlain declared 'we believe in the expansion of Empire ... we desire ... to develop that commerce and that enterprise upon which I am convinced the happiness of the population depends much more than it does upon *any legislative action*'.[97] In July of the same year, having taken the somewhat obscure post of Colonial Secretary, Chamberlain explained that he had taken on the task of developing the resources of the Empire because

> it is only in such developments that I can see any solution of the social problems with which we are surrounded. Plenty of employment and a contented people go together ... old markets are getting exhausted, some of them are being closed to us by hostile tariffs, and unless we can find new countries which will be free to take our goods you may be quite satisfied that lack of employment will continue to be one of the greatest social evils.[98]

There was no mention of social reform, because imperial development itself was to be the true social reform. By equating the Empire and imperial trade with secure employment Chamberlain identified his interest in social questions with the established Conservative interest in Empire and the growing Conservative sub-culture of imperial unity. What imperial 'enthusiasts' realized was that, by adding a social dimension to imperial policy, they could discuss social policy in connection with what were recognized as specifically Conservative interests.

Those who advocated a new approach to commercial policy acknowledged that any hint of tariffs meant confronting the fact that 'no attack is more powerful, no argument more cogent to the popular sense, than the wild clatter of [the] "bread tax" '.[99] For some – for example Empire free traders – the solution was to state that their proposals would simply involve an adjustment of existing tariffs rather than the imposition of new ones. Bolder spirits who argued for either protection, preferential agreements with the Colonies or a mixture of both, contended that tariffs could be used to appeal to the 'producer' interests of the British working population by holding out the promise of secure and indeed growing levels of employment. An appeal on these terms had two great advantages. The first was that it emphasized the 'producer' aspect of working-class life and thereby met the consumer-based 'dear-food' argument on terms which were meaningful to the working-class electorate.[100] The tariff contingent argued if one could get across 'the primary truth in political economy ... that production precedes consumption',[101] then the working class would recognise that regular and stable employment came before cheap bread. The second string to the tariff bow was that an approach based on 'producerism' enabled a broader appeal to be made to economic nationalism. The recurrent metaphor of invasion is significant here. In its crudest form it took the guise of the numerous calls for a halt to 'alien immigration' which almost invariably accompanied motions in favour of protection and/or preference at NUCA meetings. Imports of manufactured goods were also described in similar terms as a foreign threat to British labour. Hence the deliberately xenophobic titles of the literature which emerged from Conservative protectionist circles, such as E.E. Williams' *Made in Germany* and *The Foreigner in the Farmyard* and F.A. Mackenzie's *The American Invaders*. The underlying message such appeals sought to present was that an open, internationally-orientated economy was not beneficial to the 'national labour' interests of the British working man.

The working class seemed not wholly unreceptive to these arguments. In 1886 a representative of the Shop Hours Labour League wrote to Salisbury to complain about 'the ... tantalising gilded mockery ... of dangling a so-called cheap and large loaf before the eyes of the people if they have no settled work',[102] a statement which reinforced the claims of pro-tariff Conservatives that protection of employment could be as potent an appeal as 'dear food'. Nor was it just a case of isolated statements providing a basis for otherwise untenable claims. Advocates of both preference and protection could and did point to the 1885 General Election, when the Conservative success in the boroughs was attributed by a number of observers to the fair trade issue.[103]

Yet, in spite of the claims of the pro-tariff lobby, and in spite of some evidence that working-class opposition to tariffs was not monolithic, the bulk of the Conservative party remained unconvinced. Every time a man like Ellis Ashmead-Bartlett argued that the prolonged economic downturn provided an opportunity to popularize the inadequacies of free trade, a man like Sidney Herbert would express the view that 'hundreds of agricultural workers in the more distant villages believe that the Conservatives want[ed] to abolish the "cheap loaf" and to grind down the labourers'.[104] In the eyes of the Conservative party the electoral potential of tariffs seemed far outweighed by the dangers.

SOME PRELIMINARY CONCLUSIONS

In the late nineteenth century the advocates of a positive Conservative appeal to the mass electorate were always fighting an uphill battle. Their problem was to convince the party that their proposals were, to use a favourite Salisburyian expression, 'practical politics'. Most Conservatives would have conceded that, *in principle*, social reform was popular and could perform a Conservative function: similarly, the bulk of the party were, *in principle*, either open or discreet supporters of tariffs. *In practice*, however, the party was not willing to take a political gamble with what appeared, quite understandably, to be high-risk strategies. The electoral situation gave no immediate cause for concern as the party won three resounding electoral victories in the period 1886–1900. In addition the threat of Socialism seemed to have been thwarted. As an intellectual movement Socialism undoubtedly had some impact in the 1880s and 1890s, but its practical input into British politics was minimal. Individual Socialists played an important part in establishing the militant 'New Unionism' and in leading the great strikes of the late 1880s, but the employers' counter-offensive in the 1890s, and in particular their ability to bring the pressure of the Courts to bear on trade union activity, reduced and in some cases reversed the impact of the unions' early victories.[105] The ILP had failed to make any significant electoral break-through, and the likelihood of Socialist or 'Socialistic' legislation being passed in the period after 1886 was extremely remote. In the wake of the 1895 General Election W.E.H. Lecky, who had deserted the ranks of Liberalism in 1886 as a result of his fears for property (not least his own), wrote that the Conservative victory had shown how 'enormously men had overrated the importance of noisy groups of socialists, faddists, and revolutionists that float upon the surface of English political thought like froth flakes on a deep and silent sea'.[106] In these circumstances advocates of a positive strategy found it difficult to press their case whilst the purchase of quietist arguments in the Conservative ranks increased. Salisburyian Conservatism seemed to have provided the Conservatives with a quite sizeable bird in the hand, and they were reluctant to relinquish this no matter how many were seen lurking in the bush by the advocates of a more positive appeal.

DEFINING THE PROBLEM: 1900–1910

we may be in opposition for half a generation.
(L.J. Maxse to Bonar Law, 29 January 1906)[107]

135

C[ampbell] B[annerman] is a mere cork bobbing on a torrent that he cannot control. The result of the recent election is part of the same phenomenon which has led to demonstrations in Berlin and riots in St Petersburg.

(A.J. Balfour to Lady Salisbury, 17 January 1906)[108]

The Conservatives' 'electoral hegemony' reached its apogee in 1900. In the general election of September 1900 they enjoyed their second crushing victory in succession and became the first government since 1865 to retain office. Furthermore, the 'Khaki' Election gave the Conservatives their third outright victory in four elections held since the political realignments of 1886, and their fourth period of office since the electoral reforms of 1884–5. However, it was to be their last independent triumph before 1922.

Things began to go wrong for the Conservatives after 1902. A series of poor by-election results, with only a brief recovery lasting from late 1903 to early 1904, led the Conservatives to expect defeat at the next general election, but no-one anticipated its scale. In January 1906 the Conservative party 'encountered the most smashing defeat at the polls sustained by any political Party in modern Parliamentary history' and returned 'a broken and impotent remnant'[109] to the House of Commons with its Parliamentary contingent reduced to 157. The Conservatives were unable to reverse the verdict of 1906 at either of the general elections of 1910 – they narrowed the gap but remained in opposition. A close examination of the results of 1910 shows that the Conservatives faced severe difficulties. Both the January and December elections saw high turnouts (January's peak at 87 per cent) and on each occasion the Conservatives polled a higher percentage of votes than ever before under the electoral system introduced in 1884. At the same time the Conservative vote remained remarkably stable over both elections. These two facts indicate that the Conservative vote reached its ceiling in 1910. It seems that, as Edwardian voting stabilized around the party political mould existing in 1910, the electoral system was in danger of condemning the Conservatives to permanent opposition.

Wherein lay the problem? One possible explanation is that weaknesses in the Conservative party's organization were responsible,[110] but at best this can only partially explain their electoral failures.[111] The Conservatives' late nineteenth-century electoral performance was not as solid as it first appears. Two convincing wins in 1895 and 1900 seem to demonstrate Conservative strength. Both resulted in substantial Conservative majorities and both saw them take a very high share of the votes cast – 1900 providing the best result with an overall Conservative majority of 134 on the basis of 50.3 per cent. of the poll.[112] However, on closer inspection these results are less impressive. On both occasions the

Conservatives were almost half way to victory before polling began. A demoralized and ill-organized Liberal party,[113] bereft of funds, left 117 seats uncontested in 1895 and 149 in 1900.[114] By way of contrast the maximum number of unopposed Liberal returns was forty in the unusual circumstances of 1886. Even the 50.3 per cent share of the vote the Conservatives obtained in 1900 is somewhat misleading, for one must ask 50.3 per cent of what? In 1900 the total poll was 3,523,482, with 35.1 per cent of the electorate residing in seats that returned unopposed MPs, the bulk of whom were Conservatives. In 1892, when the Liberals had won, in spite of the Conservatives' careful timing of the election, the total vote had been 4,598,319, with 27.4 per cent of the electorate being represented by unopposed MPs almost evenly divided between Liberals and Conservatives. Similarly, when the Liberals achieved their landslide in 1906 the poll had risen by over 2,000,000 since 1900, the turnout was 82.6 per cent, and only 12.6 per cent of the electorate was represented by unopposed MPs.[115] On the basis of a closer scrutiny of the figures the Conservatives' 'popularity' in the late nineteenth century seems less obvious.

The Conservative success of the 1880s and 1890s was in many ways too much an historical success, that is to say it was dependent on a particular set of conditions; any alteration in those conditions would destroy its basis. In particular the Conservatives were vulnerable to any one of three developments: the more positive challenge which would come from a Liberal revival, an anti-Conservative reaction, and the emergence of a third political party.[116] The electoral difficulties of Edwardian Conservatism came about as a result of the conditions arising for all three factors to occur simultaneously.

The importance of the Liberal revival of the early twentieth century has long been recognized,[117] and it was doubtless abetted by a surge of opinion against the Conservatives.[118] But important as both the Liberal revival and anti-Conservative reaction were it was the emergence of a third force in British politics – the advent of Labour – which was perhaps most important in creating the Conservative party's electoral problems. Certainly it was this factor which created most alarm in the Conservative ranks. The significance of Labour was that it was both a symptom and cause of a widespread collapse of working-class Conservatism. Popular Conservatism in the late nineteenth century, as noted above, was based on a combination of employer influence and cross-class religious and community affiliations, but the foundations of this form of politics were undermined in the late nineteenth and early twentieth century. Developments in Blackburn offer a well-known example.[119] Blackburn's Conservatives, with local employers Harry Hornby and William Coddington in the van, had mobilized Anglican opinion on the Home Rule and education questions, and, fighting elections almost exclusively on these issues, held the borough's two seats from 1885 to 1906.[120] Between 1900 and 1906, however, a strong Labour Representation Committee presence was established, and in 1906 the Labour candidate Philip Snowden captured one of the borough's seats, with Harry Hornby holding the other against the national trend. But with Hornby's retirement in 1910 the borough returned Snowden and a Liberal fighting in tandem on a 'Progressive' ticket, in spite of the fact that the two Conservative candidates were free traders and concentrated their campaign on the traditional, popular Anglican issues of Home Rule and education. Evidence from other Lancashire constituencies, and also from the Black Country, indicates that popular Anglicanism had lost much of its purchase in the early twentieth century.[121] Secular issues, especially those relating to the workplace displaced confessional differences as a focus of political debate. This not only weakened popular Anglicanism but also made the prominence of local employers in the Conservative camp more of an electoral liability than an asset.

The political influence of employers was weakened by the shift away from family-owned, owner-managed businesses to public corporations run by salaried staffs. The 'face-to-face', personal link, so important to the communitarian style of factory life and politics in the mid- to late Victorian age was breaking down, and with it went much of the 'paternal' authority which had been the focus for working-class Conservatism in many areas. Lord Balcarres, whose own influence as a coal owner had been used to good effect in Wigan, noted in 1912, against the backdrop of the miners' strike of that year, that

> we [bosses] are animated by no less generous motives towards our men than Lord Bal. [his father] was ... [but] none the less the personal tie has gradually disappeared, and our men are the servants of a huge, joint-stock company which to them represents but little more than a machine ... Even if I were more free [from political activity] it would be in many ways difficult, simply as a director of a company, to occupy the position we previously held where responsibility was personal.[122]

Two years earlier, in the January election of 1910, the Conservatives had lost the Wigan constituency, which they had held since 1874, to a Labour candidate, and although the seat was regained in December 1910 the political certainties of a generation had been undermined.

Lord Balcarres also noted that even where 'in spite of the organization of modern enterprise, the personal link has been maintained, precisely the same trouble exists, and the strikers are just as fully opposed to their present system of wages'.[123] This general worsening of industrial relations, which was at its most severe in 1912, had emerged with the cyclical downturns of the 1880s and 1890s, and the increasingly vulnerable competitive position of much of British industry. Profit-squeezed employers across a range of industries sought to restore their position by a number of methods, but in particular by reducing input, and especially labour, costs.[124] Struggles over wage rates and working practices provoked some very ugly disputes in the 1890s, and, even where open conflict was avoided, employees were frequently forced to work harder and faster for the same wage.[125] The late 1880s saw organized labour achieve significant successes, but the 1890s saw organized capital strike back, through civil court actions to curb trade union activity and through the action of powerful employer groups like the Engineering Employers' Federation, triumphant in their 1897 lockout of 37,000 workers. As British industrialists sought to maintain their competitiveness in worsening market conditions, British industrial relations took a turn for the worse.

The political and electoral impact of this deterioration in industrial relations was by no means immediate or uniform, but by the early twentieth century its effects were working largely against the Conservative cause. The Conservative party had become identified as a 'bosses party', and was associated with hostility to working-class interests and above all trade union activities.[126] In 1895 the courts had decided that trade union posting of a blackleg blacklist was conspiracy to injure, but the employers' practice of circulating the names of union 'ringleaders' was defined as a legitimate defence of trade interests. Most important of all, the Taff Vale decision of 1901, itself the result of a strike against cost-cutting changes in work practices, had rendered trade unions liable for company losses incurred during strikes, a decision given a warm, public welcome by the Conservative press and by many in the Conservative party.[127] Salisbury's government could protest that these decisions were the result of civil actions and not legislation, but this distinction cut little ice with trade unions who saw a long period of Conservative government and a stream of anti-union court decisions and equated the two.

Labour made most of its gains, in terms of both seats and votes, in old working-class Conservative districts,[128] in part because an electoral pact with the Liberals gave Labour a free run at sitting Conservative members. Likewise, the Liberals benefited from participating in a broad, pro-labour, anti-Conservative alliance in which the Labour party helped to mobilize working-class support for the Liberals. The significance of the Liberal party's independent achievement should not be underestimated, but the factor which gave the New Liberalism its political and electoral bite was the Progressive Alliance with the emergent Labour party.[129] The electoral compact between the Liberals and Labour, sealed by the agreement between Ramsay MacDonald and Herbert Gladstone in 1903, stabilized the working-class vote under the Progressive umbrella. The net effect of this was that Edwardian radicalism coalesced into a united anti-Conservative front, preventing a recurrence of the low turnouts that had so aided the Conservatives in the late nineteenth century.

The emergence of the Labour party and the Progressive Alliance shaped the Conservatives' own assessment of the party's difficulties. Commiserating with Bonar Law, on his defeat in 1906 Joseph Chamberlain remarked 'You have gone down in the Labour wave'.[130] His analysis struck a chord at 'Hatfield', where the new Lord Salisbury declared 'that the Labour movement and organization ... has been of incomparably greater importance than anything else'.[131] Similar conclusions were drawn by the most thorough Conservative analysis of the election, carried out by E.B. Iwan-Muller, the editor of the *Daily Telegraph*. Differentiating between what he termed the 'permanent' and 'special' causes of the Conservative defeat,[132] Muller felt that the major 'permanent' cause was simply the 'swing of the pendulum', and he picked out Chinese labour, a lack of good platform speakers, organizational problems and the alienation of the Nonconformist vote as 'special' problems peculiar to 1906.[133] However, the 'special' cause to which Muller devoted most attention was 'the scientific and unexpectedly complete organization of the Labour vote'.[134] Even more important, Muller argued, was that the election had shown an 'intimate co-operation of the Radical and Labour agents', and whilst he chose Manchester as the best example of this co-operation, he concluded that 'so far as I can ascertain the same is true all over the country'.[135] Arthur Balfour summed up the general Conservative position when he told Joseph Chamberlain that 'the new labour issue' was at the heart of the matter and that 'the smash' had been 'due to a (temporary) alliance between the Independent Labour Party [sic] and the ordinary Radical'.[136]

In stating the view that the electoral co-operation between the Liberal and Labour parties was temporary, Balfour was undoubtedly expressing the most immediate (and most sanguine) Conservative reaction to the strong Labour showing in 1906. As time passed, however, many Conservatives began to take a different view, and to feel that Labour's arrival on the scene had caused an important structural change in British politics. 'I am profoundly impressed', Austen Chamberlain wrote to Balfour in October 1907

> with the dangers of the present situation in the country. It is an entirely novel one. If the struggle were now, as in former times merely a contest between Government and Opposition, I should have no misgiving ... But the advent of the Labour and Socialist Party has changed all this.[137]

Initially worried that the Labour party was deflecting the pendulum from its natural course, from late 1907 Conservatives grew increasingly concerned that the electoral alliance between the Liberal and Labour parties was not temporary. As the social policy of the Liberal government unfolded, and in particular as its budgetary implications became clear, the Conservatives were faced with the prospect of the Liberal and Labour parties drawing closer together both ideologically and electorally.[138] Such a development threatened not to deflect but to arrest the pendulum altogether, a prospect which became a reality by the 1910 general elections. Campaigning against George Lansbury in Bow and Bromley in November 1910, Leo Amery informed Lord Northcliffe that 'the election will turn . . . less on my merits than on the attitude of the Liberal Party'. The difficulty, according to Amery, was that 'Lloyd George has publicly urged them [the Liberals] to support him [Lansbury]. If more than half vote for him I am done'.[139] In the end the local Liberals followed Lloyd George's instructions, and a beaten Amery ruefully informed Northcliffe that 'We did all we could . . . But we had no chance once the Liberals decided to throw in their lot with the Socialists'.[140] What Amery described in microcosm in late 1910 Austen Chamberlain had detected on a larger scale in the January election of that year:

> there is one feature of the situation which causes . . . some anxiety. The combination of the Liberal and Labour Parties is much stronger than the Liberal Party would be if there were no third Party in existence. Many men who would in that case have voted with us voted on this occasion as the Labour Party told them i.e. for the Liberals. The Labour Party has 'come to stay'. It is much stronger than at first appears from the electoral returns for on this occasion it has chiefly served as a catspaw to pull Liberal chestnuts out of the fire . . . the existence of the third Party deprives us of the full benefits of the 'swing of the pendulum', introduces a new element into politics and confronts us with a new difficulty.[141]

The general elections of 1910 seemed to indicate that no matter how well the Conservatives did, the alliance between the Liberal and Labour parties effectively determined the outcome.

In the aftermath of the 1906 general election the Conservative view of the Socialist challenge turned from near complacency to near panic. The Labour vote and the Liberal-Labour alliance were regarded as decisive factors in 1906, but equally important was the Conservative view of what had occasioned this concentration of anti-Tory voting. Lord Stanley spoke for many Conservatives when he remarked that 'I have got the black mark of the Trade Unions against me, and in Lancashire that is fatal'.[142] To those Conservatives who complained of the hostility of trade unions and the working-class vote, the problem was seen primarily as 'the outcome of the Taff Vale decision', which, J.L. Garvin argued, had created the animosity to which 'a great many Radicals owe their seats'.[143] Bernard Holland shared Garvin's opinion, telling Alfred Lyttelton that 'the two great causes of the defeat have been Chinese Labour and the Taff Vale decision'.[144] Holland's reference to Chinese labour was important. However, the Chinese labour issue was significant, Lord Salisbury argued, not as an expression of sympathy for the 'coolies' in South Africa but because 'the question fitted in with the labour fever here'.[145] Likewise any difficulties associated with the tariff campaign were due to that policy appearing, in the guise of 'food taxes', as 'another example of indifference to ... the struggles of the poor'.[146] In effect, the major issues and developments of the 1906 election were all seen to show that the working-class vote had been alienated from the Conservative party.

Had the problem in 1906 been confined to an alienated working class the Conservatives could perhaps have consoled themselves that, sooner or later, mass disillusion with the Liberal party would ensure a return to the status quo ante 1906. But the strength of the Labour vote in 1906, and developments between 1906 and 1910, indicated that they were faced with a more disturbing phenomenon: a broader, positive working-class movement in favour of Socialism. Arthur Balfour summed up the general Conservative reaction to the events of 1906 when he told Lord Northcliffe,

> I regard the enormous increase in the Labour vote ... as a reflection in this country ... of what is going on on the continent, and, if so, 1906 will be remarkable for something much more important than the fall of a Government which had been 10 years in office.[147]

The year 1906 seemed to reveal 'a new distinction of forces between the Pro-Socialists and the Anti-Socialists'.[148]

To begin with many Conservatives felt that the institution most threatened by the advent of Labour and the growth of Socialism was the Liberal party. Arthur Balfour argued that the new developments heralded by 1906 would almost certainly result in 'the break up of the Liberal Party',[149] and on this point even Leo Maxse was in agreement with Balfour, a clear indication of the breadth of the Conservative consensus.[150] However, the direction of political events between 1906 and 1910 forced the Conservatives to reinterpret the significance of Labour's presence. The starting point for this was the Liberal party's commitment to social and economic reform. First came the Trades Disputes Act, which overrode the Taff Vale decision and gave Trade Unions immunity from actions of tort. Then came the provision of free school meals and, most publicized of all, the introduction of old age pensions. All of this indicated to the Conservatives that the Liberal party had shifted decisively leftward. The Conservatives detected an increasing and unholy affinity between the Liberal and Labour parties indicative of the decay of Liberalism and the transformation of the Liberal party into a quasi-Socialist party. This trend was detected by some as early as July 1906,[151] but it was not a commonplace analysis until mid-1907, at which point Austen Chamberlain was able to argue that 'Our danger now is not Liberalism, but "Labour" working with and through Liberalism'.[152] Confirmation of this transfiguration of the Liberal party came in 1909 with the appearance of Lloyd George's 'People's Budget', in which the Conservatives saw 'Socialism ... masquerading as Liberalism' as supposedly Liberal Ministers made 'Socialistic speeches, appealing for Socialistic support for a budget which was Socialistic in spirit'.[153]

That it was in the 1909 *budget* that the Socialist challenge was seen to reach a peak is crucial to understanding how the Conservative party defined the Socialist threat. It was not the growing Liberal commitment to social reform *in itself* which the Conservatives saw as Socialist (only Conservative Individualists took such a line) but the methods by which they were implemented. In 1907 J.L. Garvin stated the key argument when he pointed out that

> the critical struggle of the next decade will be concerned not so much with immediate legislative purposes as with financial means ... the idea of old age pensions contains nothing inherently Socialistic ... All depends upon the method for financing such a scheme.[154]

The political implications attendant on the severe budgetary crisis which had dogged British government since the late 1880s became glaringly apparent after the introduction of the Liberals' old age pensions scheme in 1908 when, partly due to Asquith's underestimation of the scheme's expense, the government found itself facing the prospect of a huge deficit.[155] The Liberal government's revenue problems convinced the Conservative party that Liberalism was abandoning Gladstonian principles of finance in favour of something far more radical and unpleasant. In 1907 Asquith had produced a foretaste of things to come with his graduated super-tax and his differentiation between earned and unearned income.[156] With the budgetary situation worsening in spite of Asquith's innovations, the Conservative *Outlook* declared in June 1908 that 'all indications ... point to a vast development of direct taxation ... Our moribund fiscal system seems likely to expire in the arms of Mr Philip Snowden'.[157] Such fearful premonitions proved well-founded, for in 1909, by introducing an intentionally redistributive tax structure, Lloyd George ushered in a new era of budgetary policy.

To the Conservative party the People's Budget of 1909 represented the quintessence of Socialism. Their response was not simply an hysterical over-reaction to what, in retrospect, looks like a fairly mild innovation. The labelling of the 1909 Budget as Socialist was wholly understandable if one takes into account the peculiar nature of British Socialism. J.S. Mill, Henry George and W.S. Jevons, rather than Marx and Engels, were the true intellectual progenitors of Socialism in Britain, and British Socialism had many more links with the radical Liberal tradition.[158] Socialist economics replaced the labour theory of value with a subjective theory emphasizing social demand as a factor in the creation of wealth. The most radical doctrine which could be constructed on this mode of analysis was the theory of unearned increment, which allowed the State, acting on behalf of society, to appropriate wealth which had been wholly or mainly created by social factors for redistribution for the benefit of society.[159] This concept of 'unearned increment' was common to both New Liberals and Socialists and explains the almost identical nature of Socialist and advanced Liberal social and economic policy before 1914. Thus when in January 1910 one-third of Conservative candidates explicitly referred to Lloyd George's Budget as 'Socialist',[160] and a future Conservative Cabinet Minister was led to declare in 1912 that 'Socialism by instalment ... is now ... the creed of one of the great Parties of the State ... The Radical Party ... has nothing left but Socialism, and no future apart from it',[161] they were in many respects correct. The economic principles which underpinned the government's recourse to progressive taxation on a scale previously unknown were indeed almost inseparable from those espoused by mainstream British Socialists.[162]

Nor was it simply the economic principles of the Budget which marked it out as Socialist. Of equal importance were the social overtones associated with progressive taxation on a broad scale. As far back as 1895 J.A. Hobson, one of the leading New Liberal advocates of the kind of social and economic reforms implemented after 1906, was attacked for his 'Socialism' in the *National Review* on the grounds that his strident advocacy of redistributive taxation entailed his preaching 'the gospel of hatred ... hatred between class and class, between master and men, between rich and poor'.[163] Hobson was being criticized for advocating precisely what Salisbury had criticized in 'Disintegration', that is to say seeking to benefit one class at the expense of the other, which, in Conservatives eyes, represented 'the quintessence of Socialism'.[164] Lloyd George's Budget also fulfilled the criteria for a Socialist measure laid down by contemporary opinion: it was explicitly designed to fund extensive State intervention for the benefit of the poor, it sought to do so by resorting to class-differentiated 'confiscatory' taxation, and at the same time mounted a class-based appeal to the electorate to support these actions. Given such circumstances as this it is perhaps not all that surprising that many Conservatives complained that 'Lloyd George has gone over bag and baggage to Socialism – and has dragged the whole Liberal Party with him'.[165]

SHAPING THE CONSERVATIVE RESPONSE, 1900–10: THE TRIUMPH OF RADICAL CONSERVATISM AND NEW DEPARTURES

It is only Conservatives who can make revolutions nowadays, and they are, if anything, more susceptible to democratic pressure than the Liberals.

(Beatrice Webb, Diary, 26 July 1897).[166]

When Lord Salisbury retired from political life in July 1902 there was little indication that anything more than an individual career had come to an end. Two years on from its great victory at the Khaki election of 1900, there was no clear evidence to suggest that a major reversal of the party's electoral fortunes lay ahead. Yet little over a year after Salisbury's retirement the Conservative party was already beginning to turn its back on Salisburyian Conservatism, and over the course of the next decade they were to reject virtually all of the quietist assumptions and strategies of their old leader.

This rejection of the Salisburyian legacy began in 1903 with the opening of the tariff reform campaign. As in the 1890s Joseph Chamberlain argued that electoral considerations were a driving force of his campaign. Between 1901 and 1903, but especially in the year immediately following Salisbury's retirement, there was a steady erosion of the Conservative electoral position. This was disquieting, and all the more so for a politician like Chamberlain who claimed a special relationship with the mass electorate. Chamberlain also had particular electoral worries, in that grass-roots controversies aroused by the 1902 Education Act seemed to pose a threat to his base in the West Midlands.[167] It should be noted that Chamberlain defended the Act, but the fact that he felt his supposedly impregnable 'Duchy' was no longer secure indicates the seriousness with which he viewed the problem. Although it is too much to say that without the Education Act there would have been no tariff reform, Chamberlain's desire to recover this situation was important in prompting his tariff initiative.

Chamberlain's anxiety to find a new means of securing mass support is clear from the manner in which he shaped and presented the tariff argument. The opening speech of the tariff campaign at Birmingham in May 1903 was almost exclusively concerned with the need to encourage and expand upon the 'imperial sentiment' which the British people had demonstrated during the Boer War. Given the assumption that popular imperialism – 'cheap booze and mafficking' – had been the basis for the Conservative victory in 1900, an imperial cause was a logical choice for a politican seeking to launch a popular Conservative appeal. But it was not only through the call of Empire that Chamberlain sought to appeal to the

145

mass vote. He argued that the extension of trade with the Empire would bring greater and more secure levels of employment for British workers, whilst further improvements in job security were promised in the shape of tariff protection for British industries. Tariffs were also put forward as a means of raising revenue to fund social reforms. These arguments, as well as Chamberlain's choice of cities and localities dominated by industrial workers, revealed his audience priorities. Indeed, after the first month of the campaign Chamberlain told the editor of *The Sun*,

> The working people of this country are more deeply concerned in the question than any other class of the community. Their existence depends upon their employment ... [but] I do not ... base my appeal on material interests alone. I believe that the working classes are eminently alive to the importance of Imperial union.[168]

And in 1905 Chamberlain was still firm in the conviction that 'if our Party were only united [behind our policies] we could keep the artisan vote very generally'.[169]

The 1906 general election result did not dent Chamberlain's belief in the popular potential of a constructive, tariff-based programme. This was partly because Chamberlain felt that the Conservative party had not stood on a clear and positive tariff platform in 1906, owing to indecision on the part of the Conservative leadership. This complaint was understandable. Between 1903 and 1906 Arthur Balfour, faced with serious divisions in his party on the tariff question, had fudged, fudged and fudged again to save the party he loved, desperately trying to find a middle ground between tariff and free trade Conservatives. Balfour had only succeeded in alienating those he had sought to placate. The frustration of the supporters of the 'new departure' had been eloquently expressed in September 1904 when Austen Chamberlain complained to Lord Selborne

> I cannot see what we gain by procrastination, whom we pacify by hesitation, or how we can make a good fight on a half-hearted programme ... We are suffering from weakness and flabbiness which will kill enthusiasm.[170]

and in March 1905 Joseph Chamberlain had declared it 'provoking' that 'our people' could not see the need for greater clarity and conviction.[171] Before 1906 the Radical Conservative contingent had been prepared to accept frustrations as inevitable – Chamberlain himself had argued that an electoral defeat in 1906 was certain and that the important thing was to gain a 'clear run' for the next contest. The 1906 result was seen to have confirmed all the Radical Conservatives' arguments. On the one hand Balfour's 'middle way' had, it was argued, proved disastrous, with Lord Morpeth telling Leo Maxse 'whether A.B. has learned that his late policy

146

is futile ... I imagine that it must be apparent that ambiguity is no good'.[172] In contrast, the little success Conservatives enjoyed was attributed to tariffs – Joseph Chamberlain informing the Australian Prime Minister Deakin that 'the new proposals ... were the only ones that excited keen interest and enthusiasm on the part of our supporters'.[173] Far from being disheartened by the 1906 result Chamberlain and his supporters were invigorated.

This new vigour was manifest in a powerful critique of the party leadership and organization. The essential complaint about Balfour was that his mandarin style was unsuited to the exigencies of democratic politics. Always a remote figure, Balfour was genuinely at ease only in the rarefied atmosphere of Westminster politics where his subtle Parliamentary skills were shown to best effect. To his critics Balfour's strengths seemed like weaknesses after 1906. With their outlook dominated by the idea that 'disregard of opinion outside [the House of Commons] is the chief cause of our overthrow'[174] Radical Conservatives saw Balfour's main failing as that he could not bring himself down from 'the olympian heights of philosophy and golf'[175] and come to grips with popular politics. The net result of Balfour's political style, it was contended, was that 'the democracy understand Mr Balfour as little as he understands the democracy', a situation which ensured that the democracy was alienated from the Conservative party.[176]

The Radical Conservative critique of the party organization argued for an enhanced role and greater autonomy for the NUCA and the local organizations, on the grounds that those sections of the party in immediate contact with the democracy could best respond to its demands. Hence in the spring and early summer of 1906 Chamberlain and his supporters secured a separation of the NUCA from the CCO, achieved autonomy for the Conservative county associations, and brought the party's Literature Department under NUCA control.[177] Historically the NUCA had always shown greater sympathy to both tariffs and a more positive approach to the electorate, and Chamberlain and his supporters knew full well, as did the CCO, that the evidence pointed to a large-scale conversion of the party grass roots to a positive platform based on tariff reform.[178] By bringing the party's propaganda apparatus under NUCA control, the Radical Conservatives knew that they were effectively securing an environment conducive to the development of their policy.

That institutional change was always linked to policy aims in the Radical Tory schema is demonstrated in their critique of CCO. In early January 1906 Joseph Chamberlain told Henry Chaplin that it would be 'terrible' if the Conservatives were to win an election 'with the old lot and the old policy'.[179] In May 1906 Chamberlain, in complaining of Balfour's reluctance to move on organizational reform, remarked that 'the Central Office is as bad as ever, and in all negotiations between it and the country organizations it leans heavily against the tariff reformers and in favour of the free food section'.[180] This link between criticism of the CCO and matters of policy was confirmed by Bernard Wise who, in inviting Lord Milner to join the Confederacy in December 1906, outlined the main aim of this newly-formed secret society as being 'to devise ways of overcoming the antagonism of the Central Office to tariff reform'.[181] Indeed, the activities of the Confederacy represented a clear if somewhat extreme example of the Radical Conservatives' general strategy, in that their answer to the CCO's antagonism was to encourage local party organizations to rebel against Conservative MPs and candidates who refused to adopt the full tariff platform.[182] Thus throughout their manoeuvres the Radical Conservatives' aim was to secure the party's commitment to a positive platform based on tariff reform, and the fact that 'B[alfour] does not seem to take Tariff Reform seriously' and that Balfour's 'hold on the machinery' was 'so strong'[183] were inextricably linked in their analysis of the party's failings. This point was underlined in the wake of the 1910 election defeats, with Fabian Ware, the editor of the *Morning Post*, arguing that 'we shall be no better off if Hughes [the party's Chief Agent] is replaced. What we want is sound policy'.[184]

The Radical Conservatives also concentrated on strengthening the social reforming aspects of the party's programme.[185] Writing to Balfour in October 1907 Austen Chamberlain raised the question of old age pensions, pointing out that it was 'clear this question has reached a position where any Government must be prepared to deal with it', and that as Asquith had 'committed himself to a universal, non-contributory scheme' it was important that the Conservatives announce that 'we are prepared to propose a contributory scheme somewhat on the German model'.[186] In the same letter Chamberlain urged that the Conservatives also outline clear proposals on land reform, housing and sweated labour.[187] In September 1908 the appearance of an 'Unauthorized Programme',[188] dealing with issues such as pensions, sweating, national insurance and land reform, underlined growing concern in Conservative circles that the party was being left behind on social issues. At the same time the 'Unauthorized Programme' stressed that the *sine qua non* for any positive social policy was tariff reform, the policy which was 'the only means of protecting employment, of increasing production, and equitably providing revenue for . . . social reforms'.[189] The relationship between an active Conservative social policy and tariffs, which Joseph Chamberlain had underplayed in his active years as head of the tariff campaign, was firmly re-established, to provide the Conservative party with a platform capable of generating mass support.

After the 1906 election, in the Radical Conservative analysis there was an obvious reason for the growing appeal of Socialism. Writing to Leo Maxse in April 1906 J.L. Garvin argued that 'because there is a lot of froth upon the top of the Labour movement, do not let us forget the bed-rock which is under the movement'.[190] The point Garvin was trying to establish was that the Labour movement had emerged in response to genuine grievances and consequently had a genuine appeal. This argument was pressed home by Austen Chamberlain who told Balfour in October 1907:

> Why does Socialism make such great progress, and why are we not making the progress we ought to do? . . . because Socialism speaks with a decided voice and because it has an attractive and positive policy, which (mischievous as we know it to be) is very attractive to the ignorant and rouses hope and enthusiasm amongst the masses.[191]

The Radical Conservative case was that 'the evils which [the Socialists] discern and against which they protest are real and in urgent need of remedy'[192] and that 'the Socialists' demand for social reform [is] the secret of their success'.[193] The strength of the Labour vote seemed to have demonstrated that 'it is necessary to have a constructive policy if we are to make headway in the country'.[194] The beauty of using tariffs as the underpinning for such a constructive policy, as the 'Unauthorized Programme' made clear, was that it offered an alternative fiscal strategy to confiscatory Socialist taxation as the means of financing social reforms. Radical Conservatism thus offered the party a positive platform which could, so it was argued, confront and defeat Socialism on its own terms.

There are obvious parallels between the arguments for a more positive approach presented during the tariff campaign and those put forward by Joseph Chamberlain and other Radical Conservatives in the 1890s. In Chamberlain's case it is again possible to discern a clear set of personal objectives and policies being presented as essential to the broader political/electoral needs of the Conservative party. There was also a reassertion of the argument that only a positive approach could effectively mobilize the masses. The great difference between the two situations, however, was the Conservative party's response. In the 1890s the bulk of the Conservative party had been unimpressed by Chamberlain's or indeed anybody else's pleas for a positive programme, but in and after 1903 the party, both in Parliament and at large, rapidly accepted tariff reform and the broad constructive programme that went with it.

Electoral circumstances were a key to the party's acceptance of the Radical Conservative strategy. Between July 1902 and August 1903 the Conservatives lost seven by-elections; this apparent erosion of electoral support clearly worried them. As early as March 1903 Beatrice Webb noted that Liberal morale was running high, and that 'the rot has set in severely with the Cabinet. They are panic-stricken . . . they have been . . . shaken by Woolwich and Rye[195] and the rising tide of Nonconformist NUT agitation in London'.[196] Even in September 1902 J.S. Sandars informed Balfour that the position was such that 'Middleton thinks by-elections must, if possible, be avoided',[197] and matters hardly improved in the course of the next twelve months. The string of Liberal by-election victories, and the Progressive triumph at the London County Council elections in 1903, indicated that the Liberal party at both the local and Parliamentary level was back in business. In addition, the loss of Woolwich to a Labour candidate was, as Beatrice Webb argued, a worrying development. Since the Conservatives' electoral base seemed to be narrowing, Chamberlain's brand of popular imperialism, fused with the employment and social reforming elements of the tariff argument, seemed to offer them the hope of a more broadly-based electoral appeal.[198] For a Conservative party which faced a threatening electoral situation this was an offer difficult to refuse.

The 1906 general election, and political and electoral developments between 1906 and 1910, did most to strengthen the hand of those who favoured a positive, tariff-based approach to the electorate. Before 1906 Radical Conservatives had two rivals for the affections of the Conservative party. The most important was the strategy promulgated by Balfour and the CCO. The 'Balfourite' option was not opposed to tariff reform on principle but on the pragmatic issue of party unity. Balfour emphasized party unity as an important issue in its own right whilst simultaneously attempting to construct a workable compromise on the tariff question. He stressed the retaliatory aspect of the tariff argument: this acknowledged the need for a 'reconsideration' of Britain's free trade stance but showed the free trade contingent that he wished to secure a more genuine system of international free trade.[199] The Balfourite position had stood as 'official' Conservative policy before 1906, although there were enormous difficulties in sustaining the complex if not duplicitous logic of this position. As Robert Cecil noted in his memoirs, the result of Balfour's stance was that 'Sometimes both sides ... claimed him as an adherent. At others both rejected him ... If anyone could reconcile the irreconcilable it would be he. But it [could] not be done'.[200]

The difficulty of defending the Balfourite position was, however, not solely confined to the problems of 'reconciling the irreconcilable'. Again, as Robert Cecil pointed out, there were problems in presenting the Balfourite position to a wider audience: 'the body of electors regard[ed] his attitude as either intentionally ambiguous or else motivated by a culpable levity'.[201] Others described the basic problem in less coded terms. Writing to Lord Lonsdale in January 1904 E.H. Currie, the Secretary of the Northern Region NUCA, stated that

in the North, as far as I am able to judge ... there is no use in ... halting at the halfway house of 'Retaliation' as amongst working

men the issues are too complex for them to grasp ... With them it
is just one or the other, Protection or Free Trade.[202]

That Balfour lost his own seat at the 1906 election did not exactly
strengthen his electoral plausibility, and other Balfourites expressed clear
disillusion.[203] In short Balfour's famed subtlety was deemed beyond the
understanding of the mass electorate. But if the ambiguity of the
Balfourite stance was the problem, and a clear-cut choice between tariff
reform and free trade was necessary, why did the Conservative party opt
for tariffs?

Between 1903 and late 1905 George Wyndham, a leading Balfourite,
had expressed reservations about the expediency of the tariff
campaign.[204] In part Wyndham had been concerned about the party's
ethos and unity. Coming as he did from a landed family, Wyndham had
harboured some suspicions about a policy which appeared to have its
origins in 'Brummagem' politics. But more important was his feeling that
Chamberlain's relentless pursuit of the tariff campaign had threatened
Balfour's authority. Wyndham's position might have been expected from
a man who was a close personal friend of 'the Chief'. Yet, during the 1906
election campaign, Wyndham became convinced that tariff reform was
essential. In his election campaign Wyndham ostensibly held to the
Balfourite position on tariff reform, but, as he confessed to his parents, he
had bent the offical programme to breaking point, serving it up 'piping
hot' with a hint of protectionism, a dash of social reform and lashings of
imperialist rhetoric.[205] Convinced that this had contributed to his own
electoral success Wyndham extrapolated, telling his mother that 'we [the
Conservative party] have polled 2,300,000 votes for "Facing facts and
finding a remedy in fiscal reform"'.[206] Hence Wyndham accepted that
tariff reform had been responsible for whatever successes the
Conservatives had experienced.

That the overwhelming majority of Conservative MPs returned in 1906
were tariff reformers supported the claim that tariff reform had been the
Conservatives' only popular cry. However, it was not only this which led
Conservatives to commit themselves to tariffs after 1906: more important
was the reasoning which explained *why* tariff reform had been their only
electoral trump card. Writing to his father soon after the election
Wyndham had argued 'As for the "Liberals" and the "Unionist Free
Traders" – the "Whigs" of our day – Well! Their day is over ... The
Imperialists and Socialists emerge'.[207] The clue to the Conservatives'
vision of post-1906 politics is Wyndham's depiction of the Unionist free
traders and Liberals as wedded in political obsolescence in a new situation dominated by Imperialists and Socialists. For Wyndham, and many
others, 1906 demonstrated that any political group or creed that
was based on *free trade* was destined for the scrap-heap of history.

Contemporaries employed two distinct usages of the term free trade. The narrower usage was confined simply to commercial policy, but in its broadest sense free trade referred to a complete system of social, political and economic thought.[208] This system was also known as 'Cobdenism' or simply 'laissez faire', but it was also referred to by the title most commonly employed by modern scholars to describe it, that is to say Individualism. For George Wyndham, and indeed for the majority of the Conservative party, what the 1906 election had demonstrated was that 'Individualism is doomed'.[209]

It was this 'doom of Individualism', heralded by the advent of Labour, which effectively destroyed the free trade option as a plausible strategy in the eyes of the Conservative party. Before 1906 the Conservative free traders had portrayed tariff reform as a danger to the fabric of British politics. Adamant that the working-class electorate would not accept 'stomach taxes',[210] free traders denounced the tariff campaign as electoral suicide. They also contended that tariff reform aided Socialism. This objection stemmed from their definition of *any* direct State regulation of the economy as Socialist, but it was also a product of their view that the tariff campaign implicitly accepted the Socialist agenda. By attempting to 'bribe' the mass electorate with promises of prosperity the tariff campaign was, according to the free traders, accepting the Socialist premise that the material welfare of the working class could and should be improved by State intervention. Whereas the free Trade system was seen to be largely 'knave proof', in that 'neutral' market decisions could not be manipulated for the benefit of classes or interests, tariff reform threatened to turn politics into a bribery competition which the Socialists, unfettered by any sense of social responsibility or scruples about spoliation, were bound to win.[211]

In the initial stages of the party conflict over the tariff capaign the Conservative free traders had been well placed to influence party policy. The numerical strength of their group was limited,[212] but they enjoyed the support of one of the most important Conservative political journals, Strachey's *Spectator*, and their leadership contained some important party grandees, including the Duke of Devonshire, Lord James of Hereford, the one-time Chancellor C.T. Ritchie, Lord George Hamilton, Lord Balfour of Burleigh and the younger members of the Cecil clan. Free traders had inertia on their side – free trade was the established orthodoxy and tariff reform the dangerous 'new departure'. Although outnumbered free traders possessed important resources representing forces which the party leadership could not ignore.

In the immediate aftermath of the 1906 election the free traders felt vindicated by the extent of the Conservative defeat. In their eyes the voters had sought to defend free trade and destroy tariff reform. But the free traders found it increasingly hard to persuade anyone to accept their analysis. With their Parliamentary contingent reduced to thirty-two they found it difficult to influence party developments, and their problems were compounded by the predominance of tariff reformers in the new Parliamentary party. In addition *anno domini* began to take its toll of their grandee supporters – C.T. Ritchie died in January 1906 and the Duke of Devonshire in 1908, whilst Lords Goschen and James of Hereford went into semi-retirement. With their position at the centre weakened the free traders also faced severe problems at the local level where they came under attack in their own constituencies. In its most extreme form this attack was mounted by the Confederacy, and the activities of this clandestine organization, coupled with the apparent lack of sympathy shown by the Conservative leadership to complaints from harassed free traders, convinced the free trade contingent that they were the victims of a centrally directed conspiracy to drive them from the party.[213] However, an alternative perspective was offered by Walter Long, who told Robert Cecil, the most celebrated victim of a local party rebellion, that

> It is quite evident that the constituencies are becoming more and more determined to have Tariff Reform candidates, and I really think this is the action of the constituencies themselves and is not in any way directed by the Central Office ... in all probability the constituencies will not be prepared to accept you as a candidate. But is not this the result of the spread of Tariff Reform views rather than the action of the Leader of the Party?[214]

Given that neither the Confederacy nor CCO had the resources to enforce conformity on local party organizations, Long was almost certainly correct in arguing that initiatives against the free traders came from the local organizations themselves.[215]

The free traders became increasingly isolated. Assessing their electoral position in February 1908, Lord James of Hereford came to the gloomy conclusion that

> Electorally we are without strength. With the exception of a few constituencies in Lancashire, we can find but slight traces of Free Trade Unionist Electors. Practically they do not exist so as to justify any independent political action.[216]

This was cause for depression, but what made matters worse was the collapse of the broad free trade strategy. The problem here was that the Liberal government's social reform programme undermined the free traders' depiction of the Liberal party as a bulwark against unwanted experiments in State intervention. Writing to Lord Welby in June 1908 St Loe Strachey complained that

> a great many members of the present Government seem to think that Free Trade is nothing but a matter of imports and exports and

keep it in that watertight compartment while they sacrifice Free Trade principles in every other department of Government.[217]

Strachey thus confirmed the view he had expressed to Arthur Elliot earlier in the year, that 'the Liberals have fallen away from what I consider to be true Free Trade principles in such matters as old age pensions and other Socialistic schemes'.[218] Lord Cromer, in a Memorandum of December 1908, stated that whereas only a year earlier he would have advised Conservative free traders to support the Liberals he could no longer do so, for the two sides now had nothing in common besides a too-narrowly defined commitment to free trade.[219]

Initially the free traders hoped that the Liberal party's shift to the Left would see the defection of a large number of moderate Liberals with whom they could form a centrist alliance, but the two Liberal MPs who crossed the floor[220] hardly provided the basis for a mould-breaking realignment – the centre of British politics proved to be all centre and no circumference. The net result was that the Conservative free traders found themselves between the devil of Socialism and the deep sea of Protection. Alliance with or even support for the Liberals could no longer be canvassed as a workable strategy, and the Conservative free traders were forced to accept that much as they hated the Deep Blue Sea the Devil was a worse threat. Even such a devoted free trade Conservative as Lord Cromer was led to argue in May 1909 that

> I am all for adopting a conciliatory, or at all events, not too aggres-sive an attitude towards the Tariff Reformers, for the more I see of the political situation, the more I am inclined to think that Free Trade versus Protection is falling into the background, and that the real fight before long will be Socialist versus Anti-Socialist.[221]

The Conservative free traders were forced to conclude that the only acceptable course was to reaffirm their allegiance to their party, even if this meant swallowing the camel of tariffs.

The collapse of the free trade and Balfourite strategies created political space for the Radical Conservative cause in and after 1906. From all sections of the Conservative party an analysis emerged which linked the 1906 defeat, the advent of Labour and the alienation of the mass vote to the decay of individualism as a political force and the growing appeal and menace of Socialism. Political and electoral developments after 1906 only served to confirm this analysis. In July 1907 Labour candidates won two by-election victories at Colne Valley and North-West Staffordshire, seats which the Conservatives would normally have hoped to gain. With the Liberal party apparently responding to the challenge of Labour by adopting Socialistic measures, it seemed that the Conservative party was being left behind in the competition to reap the potentially rich electoral harvest of social reform. Against such a backdrop it is understandable that the Conservative party should have looked to a Collectivist strategy of its own. To have done otherwise would have been to run the risk of conceding by default the argument that social improvements had to be paid for by the propertied classes. Furthermore, the Conservatives' own electoral mini-revival of 1908 appeared to vindicate Radical Conservative claims. Between January and September 1908 the Conservative party won eight by-elections and came within six votes of achieving another gain in a supposedly safe Liberal seat.[222] In all but one of these contests the Conservative candidate went onto the offensive, denouncing Socialism and pronouncing its commitment to a positive alternative. Small wonder that in September 1908 the opening paragraph of the 'Unauthorized Programme' linked 'the striking success won by the Unionist Party in recent elections and the growing strength of the tariff reform movement',[223] and small wonder that even the most violent opponents of the tariff campaign in the Conservative party felt compelled to admit through gritted teeth that perhaps the advocates of construction had indeed found a popular cry.[224] Events in and after 1906 seemed to indicate that Radical Conservatives were addressing the right issues in the right way.

CONCLUDING REMARKS

Reviewing A.L. Lowell's *The Government of England* for the *National Review* in September 1910 the Conservative publicist W.J. Courthope argued that Lowell's description of British political life had been rendered obsolete. The problem, as Courthope saw it, was that Lowell's survey was based on assumptions drawn from the late nineteenth century, whereas the advent of the Labour party and the emergence of new political issues had transformed British politics. For Courthope the message was clear – the Conservative party had to accept that it could not meet the challenge of the new structure of British political life unless it abandoned Salisbury's approach: 'I am bound to say', Courthope stated

> that, in my opinion, the great leader of the Conservatives . . . was largely responsible for the failure to use *for constructive purposes* . . . the large majorities which the country gave him in 1895 and 1900.[225]

This represented the culmination of almost a decade of criticism, aiming to establish that the Conservative party had to break free from Salisburyian assumptions if it was to confront effectively 'the new forces which have come so unexpectedly into play'.[226]

Whether the Radical Conservatives were correct to be so critical of their old leader's approach is a moot point, but one can understand why the Conservative party found their arguments so seductive. In the late nineteenth century Salisbury had eschewed a positive approach to the electorate on the grounds that organizational efficiency could control the democracy, whilst careful Conservative administration and the agencies of civil society could defend the rights of property against the threat of Socialism. Circumstances had seemed to prove his strategy correct. The Conservatives, with a little help from Liberal divisions, had indeed succeeded in controlling the electorate through the Middleton machine. Likewise the occasional limited concession, coupled with the actions of the law courts and employer organizations, had provided adequate protection against the militancy of the propertyless. Moreover, behind everything stood the watchdog power of the House of Lords, the Conservatives' last and apparently most powerful guardian against radical social and poltical change. However, in the early twentieth century Salisbury's strategy seemed to lose all effectiveness in the face of changed conditions. The Conservative organization could not cope with the mobilization of the mass electorate brought about by a reinvigorated Liberal party in alliance with Labour. The advent of the Labour party, and the Liberal party's leftward shift, indicated that the propertyless had dangerously shifted the campaign against property from the realm of civil society to the realm of the State. Only the House of Lords remained as the last remnant of Salisbury's strategy of defence against the challenge of democracy and socialism, and by 1910, as Liberal fury at the decision of the Upper House to reject the People's Budget grew in intensity, even this no longer seemed secure. Given these circumstances one can readily appreciate why the Conservative party should have turned to a programme which held out the promise of a counter-mobilization of the electorate and a pre-emption of the Socialist threat. The talismanic qualities invested in tariff reform by so many Conservatives were a reflection of how far an increasingly desperate party saw in its various aspects a solution to a problem which Salisbury had defined but not defeated.

Part III

THE NATURE OF THE RESPONSE

5

INTELLECTUAL PRELUDE

There is such a thing as conservative as well as radical Collectivism.
(E. Kelly, *Government or Human Evolution*)

The intellectual history of Britain in the late nineteenth and early twentieth century has tended to see Conservative thought as unimportant.[1] In part this neglect can be attributed to a tradition of regarding the Conservative party as if not 'the stupid party' then an institution lacking a deep interest in ideas. The Conservative party produces few 'great thinkers' and fewer 'great texts' and, as a consequence, has generally been viewed as an unpromising subject for historians of political thought.[2] A comparison with work on the Edwardian Left makes this clear. The volumes devoted to the emergence of British Socialism have been matched only by the thoroughness with which the New Liberalism has been examined, whilst another corpus of research has scrutinized the relationship between them.[3] This work has enriched our understanding of British political and economic development in the late nineteenth and early twentieth century. Yet full understanding will not emerge until a similar degree of attention is paid to the Right.

What has emerged from studies of the intellectual Left is a picture in which Collectivism is the key development in late Victorian and Edwardian political thought, whilst the Socialist 'revival' of the 1880s and 1890s, the emergence of the 'New' Liberalism, and the dialectic of Liberal-Labour relations are the driving force of this intellectual dynamic. In this scenario an increasing awareness of the social problems facing Britain's economy, and the growth of a Labour movement which appeared to owe its existence to working-class resentment of these problems, are seen to have prompted the Liberal party to revise Individualist assumptions and look to Collectivist welfare reforms to reconstruct Liberalism and revitalize the Liberal party's electoral fortunes. The climax of this process is seen to have been reached in the Edwardian period, when the most powerful forces of Progressivism joined hands to promote a breach with the laissez faire assumptions of

159

classical Liberalism – a breach confirmed by the social reforming strategy of the 1906–14 Liberal Governments.[4]

The role of the Conservative party and Conservatism in the debate on Britain's social problems, the advent of Labour, and the rise of Collectivism have, by way of contrast, appeared as passive or oppositional. The problems the Conservative party faced have been considered as 'political' in the narrowest sense, that is to say in terms of the institutional challenge presented by the revival of an old adversary and the entry into the fray of a new one. The fact that the Conservatives, like the Liberals, needed to devise a new conceptual frame to accommodate new issues has been passed by as a non-problem for a party supposedly interested only in the hard realities of politics.[5] There has also been a tendency to assume that the Conservative response to State intervention was broadly opposi- tional: the only 'ideologue' of the Right in the late nineteenth and early twentieth century who has attracted significant attention is A.V. Dicey.[6] Dicey's denunciation of Collectivism has allowed him to appear as the prophetic representative of a Conservatism struggling against State inter- vention. However, the Conservative response to both the 'Individualist versus Collectivist' debate, and to broader issues of the period 1880–1914, was more complex than is generally assumed. The Conservatives did not merely concentrate on the 'practical' aspects of power politics, but concluded that new problems had so altered political life that they must carry out an overhaul of their values and assumptions. They did not rely on a simple negative to place against Collectivist ideas and Progressive strategies. Those Conservatives who adopted an unbending or attenu- ated Individualism were not representative of the general Conservative outlook. Many Conservatives developed their own critique of classical Liberalism and presented a distinctive brand of Conservative Collectivism.

THE ROOTS OF CONSERVATIVE COLLECTIVISM: SOME PREFATORY REMARKS

In 1894 Benjamin Kidd was transformed from an obscure, lower grade civil servant into an intellectual celebrity through the publication of his book *Social Evolution*. Its theme, which Kidd was to reiterate to the point of tedium in later publications, was that man 'grows more and more social',[7] and that contemporary developments were witnessing the inexorable substitution of collective for individual action. Kidd criticized economists and social scientists for having been predisposed in the past to an Individualist approach to the study of social phenomena,[8] but he added that 'one of the remarkable signs of the time in England has been the grad- ually spreading revolt against many of the conclusions of the school of political economy represented by Adam Smith, Ricardo and Mill'.[9]

Soon after the publication of *Social Evolution* Kidd received an invitation from Ramsay MacDonald to join the Rainbow Circle. The purpose of this group, MacDonald informed Kidd, was to discuss '1. The political, economic and ethical shortcomings of Philosophic Radicalism and the Manchester School; 2. The growth from these schools of the new-radical and Collectivist movements in politics and economics; and the ethical, political and economic principles which are to guide us in further social progress'.[10] Kidd declined, and as a result has missed out on historical attention to the Rainbow Circle in recent years.[11] But Kidd continued to develop his critique of Individualist economics and social science throughout his career as a writer and publicist – his 1908 Herbert Spencer Lecture at Oxford, entitled 'Individualism and After', took as its theme that 'Individualism . . . has no final meaning in itself . . . its real significance lies in the fact that it is the doctrine of a transition period preliminary to and preparatory to a more important stage'.[12] In March 1904 Kidd was invited by the rising young Conservative politician Leo Amery to join another discussion group, 'a small League that is being formed of people who are keen on the purely Imperial and constructive side of the Chamberlain movement'.[13] This time Kidd accepted, and became an active participant in the discussions of the Compatriots' Club, which, from 1904 until 1914, functioned as an unofficial Conservative 'think tank' with a membership made up of many prominent Conservative politicians, intellectuals and writers.[14] In spite of the differences of political creed represented by the Rainbow Circle and the Compatriots there was one similarity which explains why Kidd should have received invitations to join both. When, in 1905, the *Compatriots' Club Lectures* were published, one reviewer noted that 'the creed which they advance is consistent and is also comprehensive. It embraces not merely fiscal but other matters . . . In their opposition to laissez faire . . . the contributors to this volume are fully agreed, and their abandonment of this principle is certainly consistent'.[15] Kidd, the Rainbow Circle and the Compatriots shared a hostility to laissez faire and Individualism, and an affinity for Collectivist thought and action.

What divided the Collectivism of the Rainbow Circle from that of Kidd and the Compatriots, and why should this difference have manifested itself in diametrically opposed political forces? A simple answer would be that the Progressive Collectivists retained the free trade element of Manchester and classical economics, whilst their Conservative counterparts rejected free trade and established tariff reform as the basis of their position. This answer is correct, but it leaves unsolved the problem of why tariff reform was so important to the Conservative argument. The development of the Compatriots' Club and its personnel offers a clue. The Compatriots formed in the wake of Joseph Chamberlain's inauguration of the tariff campaign, but the earlier careers of some of the Compatriots show that they were critical of economic 'orthodoxy' before

Chamberlain 'officially' launched the attack. The prime movers in bringing the Compatriots together were Leo Amery, Alfred Milner and Halford Mackinder, who had all been members of the Coefficients' Club, the cross-party society founded by Sidney and Beatrice Webb in 1902 to discuss Collectivist ideas of 'National Efficiency' in an atmosphere of mutual hostility to Individualism.[16] Other prominent Compatriots were the economists W.J. Ashley, W.A.S. Hewins and William Cunningham, all prominent in the late nineteenth-century 'historist' assault on classical economics. Chamberlain himself, and other leading Conservatives, had, since the 1880s and 1890s, been expressing 'unsound' views on free trade,[17] so his break with free trade in 1903 was the occasion, rather than the cause, of the attack on economic orthodoxy. In short, a tradition of Conservative criticism of liberal political economy stretched back to the mid-1880s and even beyond. The formal intellectual challenge was pressed from a number of different directions and disciplines. This essay will concentrate on the most direct Conservative attack on orthodox liberal political economy, and the one which had most input into the tariff campaign – the historical economic critique of the classical and Manchester schools of economic thought.[18]

THE HISTORICAL ECONOMIST CHALLENGE TO ORTHODOX ECONOMICS

In 1887 the Cambridge economist H.S. Foxwell remarked upon a growing dichotomy in British economic thought,

> whereas the older school of English economists contented themselves with deducing, more or less loosely, the consequences which would follow on a given set of assumptions, the new school takes comparatively little interest in the deductions, because they hold that the facts themselves are in a process of evolution and change, and that the nature and direction of this social evolution are a far more important object of study than elaborate and complicated deductions.[19]

The 'new school' was the historical school of economic thought, and its leading lights were Foxwell himself, William Cunningham, W.J. Ashley, W.A.S. Hewins and L.L. Price. Over the course of the late nineteenth and early twentieth century its members engaged in a prolonged 'Methodenstreit' with classical economic thought and the neo-classical succession to the tradition of Ricardo and Mill, and launched a direct assault on 'Manchesterism', which they defined as the most practical manifestation of classical liberal political economy.

The starting point for the historical economists' attack was, as Foxwell implied, the deductive method associated with classical economics.

162

Writing in 1892 William Cunningham argued that 'the very kernel of the difference between the historical school and the "normalists" is that ... the historians isolate a group of facts and try to account for them; the normalists isolate certain motives and measure them, and formulate laws according to which these motives act'.[20] The crux of the historical economists' position was that the fluctuating nature of the socio-economic structure meant that 'no economic principles have this mathematical character of being true for all times and places alike ... they ... become approximately true as statements of the facts of actual life under certain social conditions'.[21]

The adoption of this relativist approach had important implications. Perhaps the most significant was that the historical economists restricted the notion of what constituted economic 'science' but expanded the realm of economic study. In *An Introduction to English Economic History and Theory*, published in 1893, Ashley argued that

> Political Economy is not a body of absolutely true doctrines, revealed to the world at the end of the last century ... No age ... has been without its economic ideas. Political Economy was not born fully armed from the brain of Adam Smith or any other thinker; its appearance as an independent science meant only the disentanglement of economics from philosophical and political speculation.[22]

That the concept of economic science was a comparatively recent and artificial construct was a view reiterated by William Cunningham who remarked that 'Smith ... by isolating wealth as a subject for study ... introduced an immense simplification'.[23] Cunningham felt that Smith had undoubtedly achieved a 'good thing', but he added a warning that 'it must not be forgotten that it [the isolation of economic phenomena] was a tool of convenience'.[24] Any attempt to apply the deductive method to real 'historical' situations, be they past, present or future, was seen as misleading. In his *Introduction* W.J. Ashley stressed that just 'as modern economists have taken for their assumptions conditions which only in modern times have begun to exist, so earlier economic theories were based, consciously or unconsciously, on conditions then present'.[25] In an essay on 'English Economic Doctrine in the Eighteenth Century' William Cunningham took Adam Smith to task for having attacked the English Mercantilists on a-historical grounds – 'the English Mercantilists', Cunningham argued

> were considering how the power of this country might be promoted relatively to that of other nations. The object of their system was not absolute progress anywhere but relative superiority to our political neighbours ... Adam Smith ... assumed that they were trying to

devise means for increasing wealth . . . as an end in itself, while they were doing nothing of the kind.[26]

What Cunningham was trying to show was not that Smith was a bad historian of economic thought, but that he had ignored the logic of the situation behind the Mercantilists' thinking. The significance of this was that if the 'scientific' school could ignore broader elements of past economic life they could commit the same error in the present or the future. And indeed the historical economists' case was that 'the "theoretical" school have . . . lost touch with the actual phenomena of the present day'.[27]

Important evidence that orthodox economic precepts were out of step with contemporary phenomena was, the historical economists argued, provided by the growth of corporate and 'monopolistic' industrial structures. Writing to E.R.A. Seligman in February 1888, H.S. Foxwell stated that

I am with you in believing that the regime of competition has already begun to give place to the regime which we can as yet only dimly apprehend, which is destined to supersede it. In the immediate future it seems to me probable we shall have more and more of monopoly, or of huge corporations.[28]

Later in the same year Foxwell contended that it was 'a mistake to suppose that a state of competition can be a final permanent state – a state of stable equilibrium' and argued that competition's natural result was monopoly. On these grounds Foxwell felt that 'it is competition which is transitorial; and monopoly presents itself, not as something accidental, a stage through which we pass in a backward age, but as something more permanent, more fundamental, than competition itself'.[29] Like Foxwell, W.J. Ashley saw in 'the transition from individual entrepeneurs to great companies'[30] a clear sign that 'the counter movement [to Individualism was] setting in, both in philosophic thought and actual fact'.[31] The growth of trade unions and other collective agencies in a number of countries, and the evolution and consolidation of 'Empire States', were taken to indicate that the development of corporate entities was present in 'everything which is most characteristic of our age'.[32]

This growth of corporate structures was seen to have invalidated classical economic analysis. William Cunningham argued that 'since it deals with the subjective play of motives it is an individualistic not a social science',[33] and hence it was impossible for it to recognize that 'social action and collective bargaining are among the most interesting features of to-day'.[34] According to L.L. Price 'the very raison d'etre of a combination [was] . . . collective action' in that they moved 'by mass, and not by separate parts', with the result that combinations of all kinds were 'the antithesis of individuals competing freely with one another'.[35] In effect, the whole classical model was seen to have been overtaken by events in the real economic world.

The conclusion which the historical economists reached was that

> while there may certainly be an 'Economic Science' which investigates the means of securing wealth at different times and places, such a science must be merely descriptive and classificatory; if we are to have a body of doctrine which lays down maxims in regard to the pursuit of wealth, this body of doctrine can only be a political economy, not a Cosmopolitan Economic Science; for it must devote its attention to the particular needs and ambitions of a particular polity.[36]

With this statement William Cunningham outlined the historical economists' attempt to re-integrate the study of economics with the processes of actual life. The stress on employing economic analysis in a particular time and place was the central tenet of the historical method. Economics could only be a meaningful discipline if it were a 'Political Economy', taking its terms of reference from historically real subjects as opposed to the artificial construct of the economic man. Finally, the nation state appears as the focus of 'meaningful' analysis. Indeed, the fact that 'with the rise of nationalities in modern times the nation has come to be a convenient unit, both for political and economic purposes'[37] led the historical economists to assert not only that 'economics . . . as commonly taught in England has become imperfectly abstract',[38] but also that British economic policy was going in the wrong direction.

THE 'IMPERFECT ABSTRACTIONS' OF ECONOMIC LIBERALISM

For the historical economists the great flaw in Britain's prevailing economic outlook was that free trade and laissez faire had been raised to almost canonical status. They dismissed laissez faire as in any sense a meaningful or helpful doctrine or policy. In their view State intervention in economic matters could not conflict with the material interests of individuals: 'The State', wrote Cunningham,

> is the embodiment of what is common to the different persons in the nation, it expresses the spirit which each shares . . . we cannot represent the State as an abstract entity that is antagonistic to the individual citizens. The State is concerned with the general interest – with what is common to all.[39]

Positing an organic conception of the relationship between the State, Society and the Individual, the historical economists argued that the interests of the individual and society were indivisible. However, whereas the classical and Manchester schools saw social interest as dependent on individual interest, in the historical economists' schema this relationship was inverted. Writing in 1893 Cunningham contended that

in the eager competition of individuals with one another, public objects of general good and for the common advantage, may be overlooked. It is necessary that they should be consciously and deliberately taken in hand by public authority; and there must be some interference with private interests, favourable to some and unfavourable to others . . . In so far as the national resources and the aggregate of individual wealth are distinct, it is desirable that the public authority should occasionally interfere.[40]

Conflict between common and individual interests only arose, Cunningham argued, because future prosperity could be sacrificed by individuals whose desire for immediate gain led them to overlook long-term prospects.[41] To ensure that the interest of the whole, which included the long-term interest of the individual, was not forgotten, the State was to regulate competition. Historical economists thus saw 'the weakness of laissez faire economics' as being that 'it does not formulate any national end as distinct from the interests of particular individuals'.[42]

The historical economists felt that free trade was even more flawed than laissez faire. They argued that free trade assumed, quoting Adam Smith, 'the merchant has no country'. Indeed Cunningham found it ironic that 'though Smith entitled his book *The Wealth of Nations*, he was chiefly concerned in discussing the wealth of the separate citizens ... the thought of the nation as a unit and of the gradual development of its resources was left somewhat in the background'.[43] Because, like laissez faire, it took the individual as its unit of analysis, free trade was seen as laissez faire translated to international economic relations, with the interests of nations being equated with the interests of their individually competing citizens. Hence W.J. Ashley argued that

the repeal of the Corn Laws in 1846 marked the culmination in England of a current of public opinion of far wider range than fiscal policy. It was the most signal triumph of the movement towards political and industrial individualism; towards the removal of restraint [towards] Atomism or Cosmo-politanism.[44]

This 'Cosmopolitan' view of economics saw nations as 'non-competing groups'[45] and 'all . . . contributing to and drawing from the common stock of the world as a whole'.[46]

According to the historical economists there was nothing wrong with the logic of the free trade position. In 1885 Cunningham wrote that 'national co-operation in the pursuit of wealth can only be logically maintained from a Cosmopolitan standpoint: if we want the world to be richer this is the way to do it', but, he added, 'no single government is mainly concerned in the enrichment of the world'.[47] The historical economists agreed that in the mid-nineteenth century, 'so far as England was concerned there was a complete harmony between the cosmopolitan ideal and the national interest',[48] in that free trade had, in the 1850s and 1860s, worked to Britain's benefit. However, they argued that free trade had been successful for Britain because it was a *national* policy,[49] and not a universally valid approach: free trade had simply allowed Britain to take advantage of its manufacturing and trading supremacy. The historical economists then turned this 'success' of free trade in the mid-Victorian period against itself, with Cunningham arguing in 1885 that

> we shall be inclined to question the wisdom of any proposal ... for copying some ... economic method when no other reason can be alleged for doing so than that it worked well in its own day. If it worked well relatively to very different social and political institutions, there must be a strong presumption that it would be unsuitable in the present condition of society.[50]

The reason free trade could no longer be viable in the late nineteenth and early twentieth century had been implicitly outlined by Cunningham in 1885 – world economic conditions had been radically altered by the resurgence of national economic aspirations in Europe and their emergence in the United States. This surge of economic nationalism was seen in the widespread erection of tariff barriers on the Continent and in America, which rejected an international division of labour in which Britain exported manufactured goods to the world and received food and raw materials. This general move back to protectionism, it was argued, had occurred not because protectionist nations were ignorant of the benefits of free trade, but because those nations desired 'to organize [their] economic life ... in independence of [their] neighbours'.[51] These developments were taken as evidence that 'the Cosmopolitan leanings which favour free trade are not now in the ascendant'.[52]

THE PRACTICAL IMPERFECTIONS OF ECONOMIC LIBERALISM

The tendency towards economic nationalism destroyed, in the minds of the historical economists, any possibility that free trade could be useful to Britain. Further, they contended that, in a world in which economic nationalism predominated, Britain's adherence to free trade and its domestic counterpart laissez faire were, as evinced by the parlous condition of the British economy, causing serious damage. 'It is a matter of every day remark', wrote William Cunningham in 1885, 'that our industrial and commercial life in England in the present day is terribly unsatisfactory to those engaged in it'. Cunningham drew a gloomy picture –

> so far as the agricultural industry of this country is concerned, all parties [are] agreed that things [are] in a bad way ... In manufacturing we have similar evils ... [whilst] irregularity of employment is the proximate cause of the miserable conditions of thousands of ... labourers in this country.[53]

This description of Britain's economic condition echoed much contemporary opinion[54] and in this respect the historical economists were simply the academic Cassandras of Britain's economic future.

The historical economists had no doubt about agriculture's chronically depressed condition or the cause of the depression, free trade. For twenty-five years after the repeal of the Corn Laws, argued W.J. Ashley in 1903, British farmers had, through 'high farming', been able to hold their own, but in the 1870s and 1880s the situation had changed. According to Ashley,

> foreign corn began to be placed upon our markets at a price far below what had ever before been deemed likely: the improvement in the means of transportation on land and sea opened up new and virgin soils and cheapened the carriage of their crops ... high farming was no defence against the ... inexpensive farming of the new lands.[55]

In consequence, imports of foreign grain in particular had, it was thought, cut the ground from beneath the British farmer.

The historical economists saw the manufacturing sector as equal cause for concern. British industries, W.J. Ashley argued, had reached their peak of prosperity in the 1870s, and from that point had been steadily declining along with their falling share of the world markets,[56] an analysis which was shared by William Cunningham and W.A.S. Hewins.[57] The explanation of dwindling manufactured exports was that 'other countries, which were expected to remain indefinitely suppliers of food and raw materials, have entered on a large scale career in manufactures'.[58] At the same time the development of other manufacturing nations meant that general market conditions were worsening, as 'trading competition on the part of foreign nations is growing yearly more and more intense [and] ... the commercial and industrial supremacy of this country, once undisputed, is threatened'.[59]

Once again the historical economists singled out free trade as a handicap for Britain's manufacturing sector. Competition they expected, but they felt that Britain's competitiveness was reduced by free trade. As noted above, the historical economists saw the growth of large-scale enterprise, trusts and combines as one of the most important develop-ments of the period, and felt that free trade theory, underpinned by Individualist assumptions, could not possibly comprehend this. Similarly, free trade, because of its Cosmopolitan assumptions, was regarded as incapable of registering the growth of national economic thinking. When put together, these two failures of free trade had, it was contended, disastrous consequences for British industry. The reason, according to L.L. Price, was that in economic matters, God was definitely on the side of the big battalions, and that 'individuals competing freely ... are likely to be worsted in contest by the organized strategy and concentrated strength of a combination'. More important still, experience had shown that 'a Trust, aided and abetted by the active assistance of its State in the protection afforded by a tariff, may be enabled to use tactical devices, which will ensure the defeat of the unprotected individual competitors'.[60] The particular 'tactical device' Price had in mind was 'dumping', or the practice of selling under-cost-price goods in order to undercut competi-tors and drive them out of business. Foreign tariffs were seen not only to have robbed Britain of markets in the protectionist nations themselves, but also to have disadvantaged Britain in 'neutral' markets and the home market. Britain's individualistic industrial structure was, it was thought, defenceless in the face of the tariff-sustained, State-aided power of foreign combines.

The historical economists' pessimistic outlook has been criticized by economic historians, who have tended to see structural change rather than decline as the main characteristic of the late nineteenth- and early twentieth-century British economy. But to dismiss the historical econo-mists as simply 'ill-informed' or 'wrong-headed' is to underestimate them. Perhaps the most important change which economic historians have detected is Britain's marked shift from manufacturing to the tertiary sector and 'services'. As noted in Chapter 1, recognition and criticism of this shift was a central feature of the bimetallist movement of the 1880s and 1890s, and also apparent in the arguments for fair trade and imperial federation. That the historical economists offered support to one or all of these heretical campaigns stemmed in no small part from their agreement with the contention that the shift from manu-facturing to services was unnecessary and fundamentally damaging. Their definition of a healthy economy was based on the premise that 'the creation of productive powers is more important to the nation than possession of values in exchange',[61] and that the service sector scarcely compensated for reduced manufacturing and agriculture. What is more, the historical economists felt the shift from production to services was self-reinforcing, in that the export of capital was both a symptom and a cause of Britain's productive weakness. In 1904 William Cunningham noted that

169

capital goes where it is attracted . . . [and] chronic insecurity and the danger of being exposed to competition with subsidized rivals do not seem to me to be obviously the most favourable conditions for the development of industry in an age when capital has become the dominating influence in production.[62]

The insecurity of British productive enterprise, open as it was to the tactics of State-supported competitors, was thought to have led British investors to foreign enterprises, thereby reinforcing the competitors who were undermining British industry and agriculture.[63]

The dispute between the historical economists and those contemporaries (and more recent scholars) who saw little in the British economy to cause concern is illustrated by their different positions on Britain's trade deficit. In 1898 Edward Hamilton estimated Britain's visible trade gap at £194,000,000, but noted that there was no cause for alarm because,

In the first place, we supply foreigners every year with a huge amount of capital ... the aggregate amount may be put at £2,000,000,000. The interest on this at 4.5% would be £90,000,000, which is being paid in the form of imports without any corresponding exports. In the second place there are also 'invisible' exports to be taken into account in the shape of freights and profits on our vast shipping trade ... [which] may now be put at £90,000,000. When therefore the excess [of imports over exports] goes on increasing, there is no reason to suppose that it is due to other causes than interest due on the increased capital invested abroad and an augmented carrying trade; and such increases are only compatible with a greatly increasing exporting capacity on the part of other nations.[64]

For Hamilton Britain's trade imbalance was the 'natural' outcome of Britain's position as the hub of international trade. For the historical economists this was sheer complacency, insofar as

the substitution of imported manufactures for articles of native production, while it swells the returns of commerce, will ... mean that there is diminished employment and that the increase of commerce has been made at the expense of the prosperity of industrial life.[65]

In other words it was bad for a national economy to lose the balance between productive enterprise and services. The interests of the tertiary sector were seen to be international rather than national; hence the great increase in the returns to this sector were not seen as an adequate measure of Britain's prosperity. The cosmopolitan orientation of finance and commerce ensured that as long as there was an expanding volume of

170

world trade, it was of no particular concern whose trade was being carried, financed and insured, but if one was concerned with the volume of *British* goods traded it was a different story. Whilst the historical economists agreed with Sir Robert Giffen that 'only a Free Trade country, or rather a free imports country, can be the centre of the world's international commerce'[66] their argument was that this was the problem.

The domestic implications of Britain's declining productive base also gave cause for concern. In 1886 H.S. Foxwell, commenting upon the causes of social distress, declared 'uncertainty of employment is the root evil of the present industrial regime'.[67] That unemployment caused social distress was a recurring theme in historical economic writings, with their central complaint being that there had come into existence 'a class of labourers who are chronically unemployed'.[68] Whereas economic heretics on the Left, such as J.A. Hobson, saw chronic unemployment as a product of 'underconsumption', the historical economists believed that 'the problem of the unemployed . . . is necessarily connected with the condition of employment'.[69] Unemployment could not be seen as 'an isolated fact',[70] and as the restoration of Britain's industrial position rested on fitting Britain's trade policies to the rigours of a competitive world so too did the restoration of the unemployed to work. Britain's social problems reinforced the case against free trade, and this 'domestic' failure of free trade also led the historical economists to subject its 'twin' policy, laissez faire, to a considerable pounding.

The historical economists thought laissez faire failed to comprehend the organic relationship between the State, society and the individual. Thus they were predisposed to support social and economic regulation on the grounds that the general good was demonstrably not the aggregate of individual goods. A factory owner who overworked his employees would in the short term make additional profits, but at the expense of the health and well-being of the workforce who, when they retired prematurely and infirm, were bound to become a burden to their families or the community. In such a situation there was, Cunningham argued, 'a strong case for enforcing a restriction'.[71] Cunningham agreed that there could be 'objection taken to class legislation', but at the same time he also felt it was damaging to the interests of the nation as a whole to allow any particular class to suffer.[72] Philanthropy, it should be noted, played a subordinate role in this reasoning. Whilst historical economists did justify State intervention on ethical grounds, the *economic* necessity of such action was emphasized,[73] on the basis that the preservation of national wealth meant the preservation of 'all physical objects which may be used for sustaining and prolonging national life'.[74]

The historical economists argued that unless laissez faire was abandoned the British economy and society would collapse. The social problems resulting from the erosion of Britain's productive base and the general maturing of the British economy were, according to the historical economists, too great to be solved simply by abandoning free trade. As well as seeking to attack the root cause of poverty, unemployment, by overturning free trade, they also supported measures to address the 'symptoms' of social distress. Hence, in the 1880s and 1890s, Cunningham expressed sympathy with Charles Booth's schemes for old age pensions and argued that strong trade unions were essential to the creation of a more secure labour market. L.L. Price became a powerful advocate of industrial arbitration and wages boards, whilst in the early twentieth century Ashley and Hewins advised the USRC which supported the extension of pensions, advocated minimum wages in certain trades, and sponsored several schemes to improve working-class housing and working conditions.[75] For the historical economists it was both logical and necessary that the State should enact social reforms, but what gave their pleas for action greater bite was their contention that 'if the State does not become social reformer it will become Socialist'.[76]

SOCIALISM: THE PRACTICAL AND THEORETICAL CONSEQUENCE OF ECONOMIC LIBERALISM

The extent of social and economic distress in Britain was, the historical economists contended, great enough in its own right to demand an urgent solution, but this was doubly vital because the deterioration of Britain's economic situation had created a climate in which 'an increasing number of persons are inclined to try a desperate remedy and look to some form of Socialism as offering a means of relief'.[77] According to William Cunningham,

> the attraction of Socialism lies not in the reasoning which supports it, but in the hope it holds out . . . with a strong sense of the grinding poverty and degredation in which millions of their fellow men are sunk, the generous spirits of our day can hardly fail to be eager to give every human being the opportunity of developing the best that is in him.[78]

But whilst the historical economists acknowledged the truth of Socialist descriptions of widespread social distress, they argued that both the Socialist analysis and remedy were flawed and counter-productive.

The historical economists saw the errors of liberal political economy repeated by Socialism. Indeed, they viewed Socialists as logical inheritors of the classical approach. In particular they felt that 'it was Ricardo . . . who gave the really effective inspiration to English Socialism'.[79] In 1899 H.S. Foxwell argued,

> I am more and more impressed, as I study the literature on Socialism, with the far-reaching, disastrous consequences of the

unfortunate colour given to economic teaching by Ricardo ...
Ricardo, and still more those who popularized him, may stand as an
example for all time of the extreme danger which may arise from
the unscientific use of hypothesis in social speculations.[80]

Foxwell felt that Ricardo had caused most damage via his labour theory
of value, appropriated by Socialists to justify the redistribution of
wealth.[81] This appraisal of Ricardo's influence was supported by W.J.
Ashley, who took Alfred Marshall to task for 'wrongly' claiming that
Ricardo had been 'misrepresented' by Socialists.[82] The historical econo-
mists conceded that in Britain, unlike on the continent, Socialism had
rejected the revolutionary aspects of the labour theory. However, they still
detected the essence of Ricardo in the gradualist approach of British
Socialism. In 1891, in an article on 'Some Aspects of the Theory of Rent',
L.L. Price stressed the importance of Henry George and the Land
Nationalization movement of the early 1880s to the development of
British Socialism, but at the root of it all, Price argued, was Ricardo:

> just as the more comprehensive form of Socialism, which aims at the
> nationalization of capital, purports to be based on Ricardo's theory
> of value, so the proposal for the nationalization of land is avowedly
> put forward as a practical deduction from Ricardo's theory of rent
> ... these different schemes ... being characterized by the common
> element of the concept of an 'unearned increment'.[83]

Hence the historical economists ranged themselves against the 'People's
Budget' of 1909, which, with its progressive differentiation between
earned and unearned incomes, represented the most practical manifestation of mainstream 'Socialistic' political economy in the period.[84] They
shared Foxwell's view that the 1909 Budget was 'the worst and crudest
Budget of modern times – worthy of the shallow and rhetorical Henry
George, whom our Chancellor, his namesake Lloyd George, much resem-
bles ... it is the the natural result of Ricardo's teaching'.[85]

Although Socialism was thought to have repeated the errors of classical
economics it was also deemed to have committed errors of its own. The
main Socialist fallacy was that it saw social problems as a product of class
inequalities. Socialism, the historical economists argued, saw social
reform as a problem of distribution – the politics and economics of
Socialism were linked by the idea that the poor were denied access to
prosperity by the wealthy. The historical economists accepted that, within
the terms of their own argument the Socialists were correct, and that 'in
the distribution of wealth ... the greater the share of the one party, the
less will be that of the other'.[86] However, they felt the Socialist argument
could not be sustained if social distress was discussed in a broader
context.

The point which the historical economists sought to establish was that whilst the interests of the wealthy and labouring classes were antagonistic when it came to distribution 'they are identical in the production of wealth; for the ultimate source of remuneration of either party is found in the total amount of wealth produced'.[87] The real interest of the labouring classes was seen to lie with security of employment, which would satisfy permanent as opposed to immediate interests. Socialist redistribution was seen to concentrate on immediate concerns without taking note of the future.[88] A further problem the historical economists discerned was that Socialism failed to distinguish between different types of wealth. 'There is', wrote Cunningham,

> a great difference between the rich man who earns a profit by employing labour in any way and the rich man who gains by successful speculation ... The gains which are made out of fluctuations represent very little service rendered to the community ... [whereas] the man who organizes a productive industry helps to meet the needs of consumers, and gives employment to the artisan.[89]

Socialism thus compounded its redistributive fallacies by failing to distinguish between productive and 'parasitic' wealth.[90]

The historical economists thus had good reason to declare that 'it is not by holding to economic orthodoxy ... that the Socialist conclusions can be attacked but by denying the postulates of orthodox economics'.[91] To deny Ricardo and his followers was, implicitly at least, to deny Socialism. Furthermore, Socialism's failure to distinguish between national and cosmopolitan wealth, and its stress on the unity of working-class interests across national boundaries, indicated that, following classical economics, the 'cosmopolitan habit of mind ... [had been] adopted by Socialists' who proposed a system 'which takes no account of differences of race and history'.[92] More important than this intellectual affinity was, however, the emphasis the historical economists placed on 'the message of hope' as the chief weapon in the Socialist armoury. Had it not been for the fact that Britain's out-dated economic policies had rendered British industry and agriculture unable to compete effectively there would, the historical economists argued, have been no chronic unemployment and therefore no chronic social distress. Britain's social problem and the emergence of Socialism were thus taken to be two aspects of the same problem, with the solution being to reject orthodox economic thought and practice.

NEO-MERCANTILISM: THE LODESTONE OF HISTORICAL ECONOMICS

What the historical economists wished to introduce was a new economic praxis. For a model they looked to Germany, where, they felt, 'a revolution had taken place in the whole conception and character of economic study'.[93] The progenitor of the 'revolution' in German economic thinking, according to William Cunningham, was Wilhelm Roscher. The importance of Roscher's work, and in particular his *Grundriss* of 1842, was, Cunningham pointed out, that it had appeared at a time when 'the dogmatism of Ricardo was paramount in Germany as well as in England'.[94] Roscher, he argued, had realized that Ricardo's work did not represent 'a system of national political economy . . . but a mere chrematic dealing with the wealth of individuals'.[95] As a result of this insight Roscher had discarded the 'study of the mere mechanism of competing individuals' and devoted himself to 'the much more important question as to the development of the industrial life of nations'.[96] But although Roscher may have been the prophet of national economics, its patron saint was Friedrich List. Rejecting individualism and rebutting the cosmopolitanism of free trade, List asserted national interest as the central concern for economists. For List their task was not the analysis of the production and distribution of wealth in abstract, but rather the provision of tools for discovering how a particular polity could increase its wealth in relation to competitors. Hence List, in the 1840s, laid the foundations of Neo-Mercantilism, which found its fullest intellectual expression, later in the century, in the work of Gustav Schmoller and Adolf Wagner, and appeared to find practical expression in the economic policies of Bismarck and his Wilhelmine successors; for this reason the historical economists regarded List as 'the only writer to be placed for his influence on the world by the side of Adam Smith'.[97]

The attractions of Neo-Mercantilism, particularly as it had taken shape in Germany, were legion. To the historical economists the 'soulless' Individualism of the classical and Manchester schools lay at the root of Britain's economic and social ills. The essence of Neo-Mercantilism, however, was that it

> defined its object as the creation of an industrial and commercial State in which, by encouragement or restraint imposed by the sovereign authority, private and sectional interests [are] made to promote national strength and efficiency.[98]

Furthermore, Neo-Mercantilism, because it took as its starting point the needs of a given polity, was not bound to conform to any theorem. Rather it was concerned only with the pragmatic task of discovering a particular national policy. It therefore conformed to the historical economists' view that economic ideas had to be related to the particular time and place in which they were conceived, and, equally important, to the specific needs of the late nineteenth and early twentieth century.[99]

If the basic principles of Neo-Mercantilism found favour with the historical economists so too did its policies. Once again, Germany was held up as a model. Bismarckian social reforms of the late 1880s, in particular the introduction of old age pensions, were seen as evidence of the way in which the German State had taken steps to ensure the well-being of all its citizens and, thereby, dilute the appeal of Socialism. But what was regarded as most significant was that German theorists and policy makers had recognized that 'individual competition is only a beneficent force when the conditions under which it acts are carefully regulated'.[100] Furthermore, the use of tariffs in Germany to protect domestic producers and encourage large-scale enterprise was seen to reflect the way in which State intervention had regulated and organized economic activity for the benefit of the nation.

It was this concept of national organization which made Neo-Mercantilism so appealing to the historical economists. Surrounded as they were by evidence that organization, in the shape of trusts, cartels, trade unions and Empires, was the key-note of economic life, the historical economists sought an approach that would equip the British economy with an organizational coherence in keeping with contemporary trends. Indeed, William Cunningham went so far as to argue that industrial trusts themselves provided a model of behaviour for the British Government, declaring that 'in their economic success they [trusts] furnish an example of the policy which our ... political communities might adopt with a view to securing ... prosperity'.[101] A protected national economy was to save Britain from international competition and ensure a 'constructive system under which men and women [could] satisfy their legitimate aspirations',[102] thereby forestalling any demand for Socialism. Only by adopting an organized, national economic structure, which recognized that the State was the defender of 'the ultimate interests of society',[103] could the British economy and polity be saved from both external and internal disruption.

HISTORICAL ECONOMICS AND CONSERVATIVE POLITICS – THE POINT OF INTERSECTION

The 'Methodenstreit' between historical economics and orthodox liberal economics, as it emerged in the 1880s and developed through the 1890s, was largely confined to the academic sphere, with the conflict centred on the traditional academic battle ground of university appointments and syllabus structure. After 1903, however, the debate took on a more public and directly political aspect. It has not passed unnoticed that when Joseph Chamberlain launched the tariff reform campaign in 1903 academic economics split into two camps.[104] On the one hand there were the signatories and supporters of the 'Manifesto' sent to The Times on 15 August 1903, which attacked Chamberlain. Led by Alfred Marshall this group included F.Y. Edgeworth, A.C. Pigou and most other leading figures of orthodox economic thought in Britain. On the other hand there were the historical economists, who answered the orthodox 'Manifesto' by sending a counter letter to *The Times* in support of Chamberlain in September 1903.

For the orthodox economists, especially Marshall, intervention in public controversy was both distasteful and short-lived, but the historical economists' commitment to the tariff debate and the type of Conservative politics which found its focus in the tariff campaign was continuous and complete. W.A.S. Hewins resigned his post as Director of the London School of Economics to become Joseph Chamberlain's chief economic advisor, and from that point his career was dominated by Conservative and tariff politics. In 1904 Hewins was appointed secretary of the Tariff Commission, established by Chamberlain to assist in the design of a 'scientific tariff',[105] and between 1906 and 1910 Hewins also advised Arthur Balfour.[106] In 1912 he became Conservative MP for South Kensington, whereupon he campaigned for tariffs and a more active social policy. W.J. Ashley was hardly less active. As Professor of Commerce at Birmingham University – the educational show-piece of Chamberlain's 'duchy' – Ashley had direct lines of communication with the hub of the tariff campaign. Chamberlain himself praised Ashley's book *The Tariff Problem* as 'the best manual we have'[107] and Ashley's advice on tariff matters was sought by prominent Conservatives, particularly Andrew Bonar Law. Like Hewins, Ashley was a member of the Compatriots Club and devoted most of his work in the early twentieth century to tariffs and social policy. William Cunningham and L.L. Price were somewhat removed from the centre of Conservative politics, but they were both prolific tariff publicists, Compatriots and Chairmen of their University Tariff Reform Associations at, respectively, Cambridge and Oxford.[108] H.S. Foxwell played little or no public role in the tariff debate or Conservative politics. Perhaps his experiences during the bimetallic campaign, which damaged his career, soured his interest in public issues.[109]

The involvement of historical economists in the tariff debate was not simply the common desire amongst academics to strut the public stage. Public controversy certainly offered the historical economists a less cloistered field to confront liberal economics, but many leading Conservative politicians wanted to draw them into the tariff campaign. The rationale for this 'lionization' was made clear by Law when he contacted W.J. Ashley in December 1904: 'There is nothing ... ', Law wrote, 'which tells more against us than the idea that *scientific* authority is against us'.[110] Without the backing of economic 'authority', tariff reform would lack credibility – the appeal to economic 'science' was regarded as a political necessity. But why did Conservative tariff reformers look to the historical economists, rather than to anyone else, to 'supply the economic arguments'?[111]

177

A simple answer would be that they were, in Lenin's phrase, 'hired coolies of the pen', sophisticated propagandists called to provide a prop for the Conservative party's tariff arguments. This is no doubt true, but by itself it is unsatisfactory. Tariff reforming Conservatives required a 'scientific' argument, and to fulfil this specific political end tariffs needed an intellectual verisimilitude. The historical economists were in this sense perfect propagandists because their critique of free trade and liberal economics predated 1903. But besides its consistency why was that *particular* critique so attractive to so many Conservatives? It is helpful here to look, once again, to Germany.

The influence of German economic ideas on the development of British historical economics is difficult to overestimate. The links were in many instances direct and personal. Both Ashley and Cunningham spent periods in the early part of their academic careers at German universities (Göttingen and Tübingen), periods which their biographers believed shaped their mature thought.[112] W.A.S. Hewins also had close contact with the German academic world: his first major essay on British trade was published in Schmoller's *Jahrbuch* in 1899.[113] List's *National System of Political Economy* first appeared in an English translation in Britain in 1885, simultaneous to the emergence of the British historical school. This is not to argue that the British slavishly imitated their German counterparts, but it raises the question of why 'the lessons of Roscher ... went for a quarter of a century unheeded'[114] and yet emerged as a powerful influence in the last two decades of the late nineteenth century. Here, neither personal influences nor pure teleology can answer this question. Rather one must turn to the similarity of context which shaped political and economic thought on both sides of the North Sea.

The broad thrust of German governmental policy in the late nineteenth century was, as noted earlier, the establishment of an essentially Collectivist, anti-Liberal, and anti-Socialist basis for social and economic legislation, which was founded on the notion of a national economic structure. This trend in policy was mirrored in German party politics, in developments in intellectual circles, and in particular in German economic thought. The hostility of Bismarck and his successors to Liberal values and Liberal ideas, and their development of a national economic, Statist counter to Socialism, was most cogently expressed by Gustav Schmoller and Adolph Wagner. That academics were State employees in Germany undoubtedly facilitated the process whereby governments could commission (or pressurize) individuals to produce apologies for Ministerial action, but the work of Schmoller, Wagner and other Neo-Mercantilist economists had particular resonance within governmental circles.[115] Indeed it is possible to discern a general reaction against Liberalism and a pattern of nationalist and anti-Socialist thinking across a broad sphere of German political life. Writers like Treitschke and Gierke as well as the Neo-Mercantilist economists upheld the 'national idea' in explicit opposition to both Liberalism and Socialism. Similarly, Radical Nationalist organizations like the Pan-German League and the Navy League and the development of *Sammlungspolitik* were all aimed at the same targets, as were the policies of Bismarck, Miquel, Tirpitz and Bulow. The movement to protectionism, the enactment of welfare legislation, the great renaissance of mercantilist-type economic ideas and the growth of an assertive and populist nationalism all reflected different, but not essentially differing, parts of a broad debate on the Right of German politics as to the best means of coping with Germany's internal and external problems.

There has only been space in this chapter to examine the German example, but in the United States, France and Italy, as well as Britain, the economic and social problems thrown up by the 'Great Depression' led to a questioning of liberal economics and indeed liberal politics. All of these nations saw Socialist movements challenge the adequacy of liberalism as a force for the social and economic emancipation of the masses. Equally important, however, they all witnessed an assault on economic and political liberalism from the Right, spearheaded by nationalist arguments buttressed by Neo-Mercantilist economics. As a consequence the Right in Europe and even in the United States saw the development of organic conceptions of the nation State which were deployed in specific contrast to the Individualism of classical Liberalism and the class-based analysis of Socialism. The advent of historical economics in Britain can thus be fitted into a broad international pattern of intellectual developments on the Right.

If one examines the British context in more detail one can find further confirmation of historical economics as part of a more general pattern of Conservative intellectual engagement with and criticism of on the one hand classical Liberalism and on the other Socialism. One of the more ironic features of the comparative historical neglect of Conservative ideas is that if one examines the British roots of this brand of Conservative thought they can be found in the same soil which produced the New Liberal crop of Progressive thinkers. Historians of the New Liberalism have rightly stressed the importance of the legacy of Balliol, Benjamin Jowett and T.H. Green in their studies of Progressive thought,[116] but the influence of 'Oxford Collectivism' was just as strongly at work in helping to create the Collectivism of the historical economists. Hewins, Ashley and Price were all at Oxford in the late 1870s through to the 1880s, and, like such pillars of Progressivism as L.T. Hobhouse, Sidney Ball and J.A. Hobson, were part of the intellectual circle which found its focus in the Oxford Economic Society and the general discussion of social reform, Socialism and the reform of classical economic orthodoxies. Similarly, Foxwell and Cunningham, although Cambridge products, were closely associated with the Oxford milieu: Cunningham went so far as to describe T.H. Green as 'the man whom I looked upon as my master in all that I care about philosophy',[117] whilst Foxwell always identified more with the Oxford intellectual climate.[118] Of course some degree of caution must be exercised when examining 'influences' such as these, but the evidence for historical economic Collectivism emerging from a broad discursive field cannot be ignored.

Historical economists shared much common ground with Progressivism in the early stages, but soon diverged. The reason for this, and perhaps the main reason why the historical economists looked to Germany for inspiration, was the historical economists' attachment to nationalism and imperialism. Ashley and Hewins considered themselves Liberals in their early careers, but came to believe that Conservatism was closer to their outlook.[119] Unlike many disillusioned Liberals, Ashley and Hewins did not choose the *via media* of Liberal Unionism to 'go over'. Their 'conversion' stemmed from their belief that the Conservative party's commitment to imperialism made it inherently more constructive than Liberalism.

In the historical economic analysis, Britain's difficulties were the result of the nation being out of step with the evolutionary trend of economic systems. The Empire and 'constructive imperialism' – the term Hewins coined to describe the historical economists' Neo-Mercantilist policy for Britain – had all the requisite attributes to restore Britain's national and international position. In a period when size mattered, the Empire represented the only market and resource base which could match the territorial and material advantages of Britain's major rivals. Economic links with the Empire were thus deemed essential to ensure trading prosperity, profits and employment for British producers, and to escape from Britain's economic decline and the social problems which had attended the loss of trading supremacy. The crucial advantage of the Empire, however, in a period when nationalism mattered, was that it was an extension of the British nation State.[120] For the historical economists any attempt to grapple with Britain's difficulties had to take account of the Empire, and it was Liberal 'anti-imperialism' which drove Ashley and Hewins into the arms of the Conservatives. Both Ashley and Hewins, it should be noted, had become interested in economics through an interest in social reform, and it had seemed natural for them to support a Liberal party supposedly committed to social progress. However, the strong tradition of anti-imperialism in the Liberal party could, given the assumptions of their historical economic analysis, only lead them to question the constructive credentials of British Liberalism. For Ashley and Hewins the only sure cure for Britain's social problems lay in securing Britain's trading position, something which, in their eyes, could not be done if one accepted a Cosmopolitan dismissal of the economic potential of the Empire. It was thus logical that the Boer War, the issue which brought the question of imperialism to the centre of British politics, provided the occasion, although not the essential cause, for the historical economists' en bloc attachment to the Conservatives.

When L.T. Hobhouse described the Boer War as 'the test issue of this generation' his implication was that attitudes towards imperialism which the War revealed defined who was a 'genuine' Progressive and who was not. In 1904, Hobhouse reinforced this test when he launched a critique of those who held that 'a positive theory of the State in domestic affairs [should be] matched by a positive theory of Empire'.[121] Hobhouse was denouncing Chamberlain's efforts to fuse imperialism and social reform in the tariff reform campaign, but was also taking a side-swipe at the Fabians. Bracketing 'reactionary imperialism' with Fabianism may seem paradoxical, but it is quite intelligible given Hobhouse's terms of reference.[122] For Hobhouse, attempting to establish a link between the 'New' and 'Old' Liberalism on the basis of a common 'moral' approach to Empire and foreign policy, imperialism was the 'test' which enabled him to differentiate Liberal Collectivism from other forms of State interventionism. As Hobhouse discerned, there was a link between Fabianism and Conservatives who favoured a 'positive theory of Empire', and, furthermore, the basis of this link was a shared hostility to the 'anti-imperialism' of traditional Liberalism.

The relationship between Fabian Collectivism and so-called 'constructive imperialism' had, for the Progressive writer William Clarke, been discernible as early as 1898. Writing to our old friend Benjamin Kidd, Clarke noted that he could no longer stomach Kidd's views on the grounds that Kidd had become far too much of an imperialist.[123] Clarke also informed Kidd that 'it is precisely my objection to imperialism, which my moral sense revolted at many years ago, that has led me to give up Fabianism, which, like you, is imperialist as being in accord with State Socialism'.[124] This link was further established in the minds of all concerned parties by the Boer War, and the Fabians' support for the imperialist cause.[125] In 1902 the founding of the Co-Efficients Club institutionalized the mutual sympathies of Fabians and constructive imperialists, and in 1903 Sidney Webb remarked on the opening of the tariff campaign that 'Chamberlain has hit on the fundamentally right idea'.[126]

Agreement on the Empire between Fabian Socialism and 'constructive imperialism' stemmed from a shared negative. In *Democracy and Reaction* Hobhouse remarked that Cobden, the *bête noire* of both Fabians and constructive imperialists, saw free trade as 'no isolated doctrine but part of a very compact political system . . . in which the parts were very closely united'.[127] Both Fabians and constructive imperialists would have agreed with this appraisal, and as their object was to renounce Cobden they were also agreed that they should renounce *all* his works. In this sense both

Fabians and constructive imperialists saw imperialism as relevant to their respective outlooks because 'Little Englandism' was an integral part of Cobdenite 'administrative nihilism'. Hence the basis for their rapprochement, which was so marked between 1900 and 1904, was that both were 'in sympathy with the desirability of making the Empire the "Unit of Consideration" rather than the forty millions of this island',[128] and that both saw this as essential to the destruction of mid-Victorian Liberal Individualism.

But although there were points of contact between Fabians and constructive imperialists there were more important differences. Explaining her husband's sympathy for Chamberlain's programme to a hostile Bertrand Russell,[129] Beatrice Webb pointed out that although Sidney was in favour of Chamberlain's general outlook he did 'not agree with the Protectionism of Maxse and Amery',[130] and Webb himself told W.A.S. Hewins that he was 'against taxes on food', the core proposal for uniting the Empire economically.[131] Here was the essential point of departure.[132] For the Fabians imperialism was used to reveal who was or was not a closet Cobdenite. The Fabians had no imperial policy as such, and they had no developed interest in imperial issues. For them imperialism was useful, but only insofar as it served to break up the Individualist position on a front where they were not engaged themselves.

In contrast constructive imperialists regarded the Empire as central to all they stood for, in that imperialism held for them 'all the depth and comprehensiveness of a religious faith'.[133] No doubt this can be attributed to the almost 'Kiplingesque' vision of Empire which they espoused, but there was more to their conception of Empire than simple patriotic idylls of grandeur. Alfred Milner was clear on this point, stating that it was 'a mistake' to think of imperialism 'as principally concerned with painting the map red',[134] and that 'the era of expansion is over . . . the era of organization is only just beginning'.[135] By arguing for a systematic policy constructive imperialists appealed to the Fabian fetishes of good management, 'efficiency' and the rejection of 'ad hoc' structures. At the same time, however, the constructive imperialist demand for a concrete expression of this systematic policy distanced them from the Fabians, as evinced by the formation of the Compatriots' Club in March 1904 when the imperialist faction broke with the Co-Efficients. Expressing the Compatriots' credo in the Club's published *Lectures* J.L. Garvin remarked that 'this Club takes a creed of Empire as its reason of being', and he added that 'the chief object of this Club' was to establish a clear and full *imperial* programme.[136] For the Fabians, imperialism was important as a means of illustrating attitudes; for constructive imperialists it was the central feature of a complete system.

That Collectivist ideas, in the form of constructive imperialism, found their way into the vocabulary of Conservative politics, can be understood if one accepts that historical economics was from the outset a very *particular* brand of Collectivism. The blurring of edges between various strands of Collectivist thought in the 1880s and 1890s, as symbolized by Hewins and Ashley's self-identification as Liberals (and Benjamin Kidd's being invited to join the Rainbow Circle) was an historical rather than a logical problem. That the historical economists emerged as the house intellectuals of the Edwardian Conservative party, and that they used the tariff debate to develop their critique of economic liberalism, was not an intellectual accident. Historical economists did not cease to be historical economists after 1903 and, in a sense, they had been apologists for Radical Conservatism before that date. Throughout the 1880s and 1890s they had systematically and consistently criticized prevailing economic orthodoxies. During the Edwardian period this critique continued on exactly the same lines, except that it was translated from the academic sphere into a highly-charged political arena. That this transfer was achieved seamlessly was a result of the fact that, as Gunnar Myrdal once remarked, the 'perpetual game of hide and seek in economics consists in hiding the norm in the concept',[137] for it was this game which imbued historical economics with its political content from the start.

The historical economists offered a particular definition of Britain's economic problems, and a very particular solution. That they came to be the spokesmen of tariff reform and Radical Conservatism in Edwardian Britain was the result not the cause of their views and ideas. Since the 1880s they had been advancing economic ideas based on a Collectivist, anti-free trade and anti-Socialist thrust, and they saw the tariff-reforming Conservative party as the ultimate expression of the policy aims they approved. The immediate political significance of the historical economists' outlook is explained by the purchase their ideas had within the Conservative party at the time. The historical economists were selected as the ideologues of Edwardian Conservatism because the perspective they offered on Britain's economic problems seemed plausible and helpful to the Conservative party.

6

THE ECONOMICS OF
POLITICAL INTEGRATION

what a tangled web we weave
when first we practice to deceive

(Sir Walter Scott, Marmion)

we are . . . bound to place the clearest emphasis upon our leading
idea – that of the fundamental unity of the whole question.

(J.L. Garvin, 'The Principles of Constructive Economics'
in Compatriots' Club Lectures)

Tariff reform, understandably regarded as the brainchild of Joseph
Chamberlain, did not spring fully formed from the head of its creator.
Between May 1903, when Chamberlain propelled tariff reform to the
centre of British politics, and January 1910, when the Conservative party
fought a general election on a tariff reform ticket, the shape of the tariff
campaign changed dramatically. In the summer of 1903 only one item –
imperial preference – was on the tariff agenda. By 1910, it included
proposals for duties on a wide range of agricultural products and
imported manufactures, and tariffs were also presented as a prerequisite
for some ambitious Conservative schemes of land and social reform.
From an argument for imperial organization, tariff reform had burgeoned
into a programme that encompassed policies for the defence and indeed
regeneration of British agriculture, the defence of British industry and the
implementation of wide-ranging social reforms. It will be the task of this
chapter to explain why and then to examine in detail how this broad
programme developed.

   In Part II of this study it was argued that, in the late nineteenth and
early twentieth century, the Conservative party faced difficulties in terms
of its identity as the party of Empire, as the party of property, and as a
party confronted by the challenge of a mass electorate. The tariff
campaign represented an attempt to grapple with these problems, and
owed much of its appeal to the fact that a large and increasing number
of Conservatives came to regard it as the solution to their difficulties in
all of these problematic areas. The tariff campaign covered such a range

of issues by design. But its breadth was not simply due to the common desire of politicians to be loved. In many respects exponents of tariff reform were forced to be ambitious.

Perhaps the most important feature of the difficulties facing the late-Victorian and Edwardian Conservative party was that it was almost impossible to address one issue without, either explicitly or implicitly, dealing with the others. For example, the most effective appeal to the mass vote was reckoned to be social reform, but in the fiscal climate of the early twentieth century this raised questions of funding, which meant addressing the balance of direct and indirect taxation. Higher direct taxation was an anathema to the Conservatives' propertied support, and so indirect taxation – tariffs – seemed to represent the only means of gathering additional revenue acceptable to the Conservatives' core constituency. However, if indirect taxation was to be increased this raised the question of which goods to tax, and if one or more sectors of the economy were seen to benefit from even an unintended protective effect whilst others did not there was the danger of a clash of interests. At the same time, any increase in the range and incidence of import duties was bound to raise the issue not only of relations with Britain's trading partners, but also of relations with the Colonies. Any point of entry into these problems could only produce a similar chain of complication. If, for example, an attempt was made to shape an appeal to property owners on the basis of rate reductions this entailed, in the first instance, finding a balance between rural and urban rate relief. In addition rate reductions implied either a curtailment of social expenditure at the local level, regarded as difficult to justify to the mass vote, or increased Exchequer grants in aid, which led back to the problem of securing additional revenue from either direct or indirect taxation. Similarly, any attempt to offer tariff benefits to manufacturers or farmers not only raised questions of rural–urban balance and imperial relations, but also whether the mass vote would need or demand compensation for any increase in the cost of living, with the most obvious form of compensation being social reform.

In effect, any attempt by the Conservatives to tackle the problems thrown up by Britain's changing social, economic and political structures could but plunge them into major distributional questions. By this is meant not just the distribution of social and economic benefits, although that was certainly important. Any Conservative decision on these problems could only represent a statement about the priority accorded to particular groups or interests by the Conservative party. In other words the Conservatives would also be distributing power and status by acknowledging or disavowing the importance of various social groups to Conservative politics. It was this ongoing dynamic which dictated the ambitious scope of the tariff programme. The complex structure of Edwardian Conservatism demanded a political calculus that could cope

185

with several parameters, and hence the tariff programme evolved as a formula and language of political integration.

THE TARIFF PROGRAMME: A BALANCED EQUATION

When Joseph Chamberlain launched the tariff campaign imperial considerations appear to have been his main concern: Chamberlain's five major speeches of the autumn of 1903 were published as *Imperial Union*, and Chamberlain told the Duke of Devonshire in September 1903 that 'For my own part I care only for the great question of Imperial Unity. Everything else is secondary or consequential'.[1] However, as Chamberlain himself knew, and as the development of the tariff debate was to demonstrate, a great many issues were 'consequential' on his advocacy of imperial preference.

'If you are to give a preference to the Colonies', Joseph Chamberlain argued, 'you must put a tax on food'.[2] Preference and the 'food tax' may have seemed a logical way of forestalling 'centrifugal' tendencies in the Empire and promoting imperial unity. But food taxes were deemed electoral poison. Few protagonists of tariff reform denied the importance of the 'dear bread' cry, but tariff reform itself was presented as the best means of overcoming the mass electorate's hostility to 'dear food'. To begin with there was some hope, evident in Chamberlain's early pronouncements, that the popular appeal of Empire and the 'Big Idea' of imperial unity would override working-class concern about the cost of living. However, from the outset the tariff campaign sought to soften the 'dear food' problem by expanding the tariff argument to incorporate a number of 'compensatory' proposals. When Chamberlain raised the idea of imperial preference the only issue on the agenda was the duty on imported corn, but at the end of May 1903 Chamberlain was arguing that tariff revenues could be used to fund old age pensions. By September the link between imperial preference and social reform was less prominent,[3] but when Chamberlain 'carried the fiery cross into the constituencies' in October and November he had other compensations to offer the working class, such as reductions in tariffs on tea and cocoa and the promise of protection for British jobs through the introduction of a tariff on imported manufactures. In 1904 the economist W.J. Ashley told Law that the tariff policy would be stronger and more popular 'if you on Mr Chamberlain's side could see your way to associate with it a policy on internal social reform',[4] and the 1906 election defeat confirmed Ashley's view that the Conservatives could not survive 'upon a diet of pure imperialism' and that 'what is required, as a supplement ... is a policy ... of social reform'.[5] Chamberlain's forced retirement from politics seven months later precludes any certainty as to how he envisaged overcoming the 'food tax bogey', but in a speech shortly before his stroke he reactivated the revenue–tariff link between imperialism and social reform.[6] More important still, this link emerged as an integral part of Conservative policy between 1906 and 1910, with Balfour providing official sanction in his speech to the NUCA Conference in Birmingham in 1907. On the one hand the party's official adoption of the tariff reform–social reform link acknowledged that it was difficult to promote imperial preference without social reform, but on the other hand it also contributed to a positive alternative social policy to counter Liberal initiatives.

Given that food taxes were thought to be an electoral millstone, it is worth dwelling on the question of why they became such an important part of the tariff programme. The usual explanation is that there was a general acceptance of Chamberlain's argument that a preferential tariff on imported corn was the best inducement to offer the Colonies in the quest for closer imperial relations. On this reading the seemingly deranged decision of the tariff campaign and Conservative party to saddle themselves with a food tax is explicable in terms of a desire to pursue imperial unity. This is a plausible explanation as far as it goes, but it tells only part of the story. If the food tax was simply a necessary evil it would have been logical to construct a policy which allowed for imperial preference, but which minimized the electoral risks of a 'dear food' cry. However, the tariff campaign produced a very different kind of policy. When Chamberlain spoke in Glasgow in October 1903 he argued for duties on meat, vegetables, dairy produce and flour, and when the Tariff Commission produced its *Agricultural Report* in 1906 it confirmed and extended Chamberlain's proposals.[7] Instead of minimizing the problem the tariff campaign insisted on presenting a programme which could only exacerbate any 'dear food' cry.

There was a method to this madness. The fact that the tariff debate erupted over the 1/- corn duty imposed by Hicks-Beach to pay for the Boer War is important. Chamberlain's opposition to the repeal of this duty may well have been based on his desire to use it for purposes of preference, but others also opposed its repeal. On the very day that Chamberlain spoke at Bingley Hall, Arthur Balfour received a Conservative back-bench deputation, led by Henry Chaplin, demanding that the registration duty on corn be restored for the benefit of British agriculture. A 1/- corn duty could not have helped Britain's farmers in any clear protective sense, but the difficult years of the late nineteenth century appear to have engendered a sense of desperation amongst farmers, especially in the arable districts, and the corn duty symbolized perhaps the last chance for British agriculture to restore its fortunes. Chamberlain himself explained agricultural support for his campaign in these terms, telling the Duke of Devonshire 'it is ridiculous to suppose that 2/- a quarter on corn[8] would restore prosperity to agriculture, although the farmers might possibly support it as drowning men will catch at a straw'.[9]

But were farmers simply 'clutching at straws'? During the second major phase of the tariff campaign in the summer of 1904 Chamberlain, addressing a predominantly farming audience at Welbeck, openly courted rural support. Critically assessing Balfour's concentration on retaliatory tariffs, Chamberlain argued that 'retaliation is a very good thing as far as it goes but where does agriculture come in? The policy will help the manufacturer ... but how does it help the farmer and the [agricultural] labourer?'[10] Chamberlain then went on to argue that the tariffs on corn, flour, dairy produce and meat he had outlined at Glasgow the previous autumn would all encourage farming production and provide fuller employment in rural areas. Thus, in spite of the known dangers of stressing any benefit to agriculture to be gained from his proposals, Chamberlain made a direct appeal to the farming community.

The attention Chamberlain devoted to agriculture, throughout his period as the active leader of the tariff campaign, representated the importance of agriculture – frequently labelled 'the greatest of all our industries' – which marked the first seven years of the tariff debate. From the outset great stress was placed on securing adequate representation of agricultural interests within the tariff movement. When the Tariff Commission was set up in January 1904 its membership included only one leading agriculturalist, but a special sub-committee was organized to deal with agricultural matters, and this committee's work was closely supervised by the Commission's Secretary W.A.S. Hewins.[11] Furthermore, the *Report* produced by this agricultural committee represented, in Hewins' words, 'the most complete and elaborate of all the works of the Tariff Commission',[12] and strenuous, and largely successful, efforts were made to ensure that the Conservative party adopted the committee's proposals. This emphasis on incorporating a strong agricultural policy within the framework of tariff reform recurred throughout the campaign. For example, writing to Leo Maxse in 1906 with regard to an article he was preparing for the *National Review*, Garvin remarked,

> I would have preferred to postpone the agricultural question till we could have dealt with it more thoroughly ... But if you like I shall *leave out the Imperial aspect of food taxation* and devote myself to a hammer and tongs insistence upon the absolute necessity of a tariff in the interests of home agriculture.[13]

Given that the question of agricultural benefits was pressed so hard it seems that many in the ranks of the tariff campaign were more than willing to brave the food tax stigma.

This seemingly strange behaviour is explicable when one appreciates that in political terms it was necessary for a Conservative tariff policy to contain a powerful agricultural aspect. In view of the increasing militancy of the farming community in the late nineteenth and early twentieth century the Conservatives would almost certainly have had to formulate a positive agricultural policy at some point. But it became an absolute imperative within the context of the developing tariff debate. The problem was one of mobilizing support for a tariff-based policy both within the Conservative party itself and in the country at large. With regard to the internal party position the difficulty was how to reconcile a programme based on tariff reform with the traditional base of Conservatism. Here the fact that the tariff campaign was inaugurated by 'Brummagem Joe' was significant, as it meant that its opponents within the party could label it as the policy of an industrial *arriviste*.[14] Even Conservatives who were instinctively sympathetic to tariff reform, such as George Wyndham, expressed concern that a policy which aimed simply at 'naked protection of manufacture' would 'wipe out the *country party*'.[15] In this respect, stress on agriculture arm-in-arm with tariff reform was a clear acknowledgement of the continued importance of the landed element and landed ethos to Conservative politics.

When it came to striking a balance between rural and urban interests what was true for the Conservative party was true for the country as a whole. For farmers tariff reform seemed to offer the hope of a return to protection. The problem with this was of course the 'dear food' cry which had greeted the advocacy of even the small duties necessary for preference and which could be amplified only if those duties did turn out to be the thin end of the wedge. Yet, if the duties were presented as a 'thus far and no farther', non-protectionist measure then there was no basis for arguing that tariff reform would directly help the farming community. But there was even more to the problem than that. If food taxes were deemed an electoral non-starter then perhaps the farmers could have been left in the position they occupied before the opening of the tariff campaign, that is to say suffering from ills for which the favoured cure was politically unacceptable. It is possible that the farmers might have accepted a return to the status quo ante 1903, but this seems highly unlikely, given the bitterness with which the repeal of Hicks-Beach's 1/- duty had been received. But the factor which really prevented a return to the pre-1903 situation was that by the winter of 1903, tariff reform minus the food taxes did not represent a return to normality.

The rapidity with which the tariff campaign developed between May and December 1903 meant that any attempt to overcome the 'dear food' difficulty by abandoning food taxes would have left tariff reform looking distinctly unbalanced in terms of the interests it could serve. Essentially there were only two possible solutions to the 'dear food' problem: food duties either had to be abandoned or successfully presented as non-protective of British agriculture. In the autumn of 1903, however, proposals for protective and retaliatory tariffs against foreign manufactures were added to the original proposals for preference. Thus to have

189

abandoned or denied food taxation would have meant presenting tariff reform as preference plus protection and retaliation against foreign industry, or simply the last two proposals alone. Such a tariff structure could only have been construed as a manufacturers' policy.

This was pointed out by one landed Conservative MP as early as September 1903. Writing to Lord Selborne, E.G. Pretyman accepted that food taxes were probably a vote loser, and he argued that on those grounds Balfour's policy of emphasizing retaliatory tariffs seemed 'absolutely the right one as to choice of battleground *except from the agricultural point of view*'.[16] In Henry Chaplin's mind there was simply no doubt that de-emphasizing the food taxes would alienate the farming vote, for he told Joseph Chamberlain in September 1903 that 'retaliation alone, while offering many advantages . . . to the manufacturer, has none for the agriculturalist . . . and indeed may be said . . . to be opposed to their interests . . . [so] retaliation would quite possibly suffer defeat from Free Traders and agriculturalists combined'.[17] Chaplin's concern seems to have been well-founded. From June to November 1903 amongst the favourable response from thirty Chambers of Agriculture and farming societies from all parts of the country to Chamberlain's proposals are some significant comments. The East Suffolk Chamber commented that it 'cannot support any fiscal changes which exclude the . . . agricultural classes', the Milborne Farmers' Club stated that if a fiscal policy was adopted which raised the costs of agriculture then this would necessitate 'a legitimate and full quid pro quo', and the powerful Lincolnshire Chamber warned that it 'consider[ed] it undesirable to support the proposition of the Prime Minister, to place taxes upon foreign manufactured goods unless there is at the same time an undertaking that corresponding duties shall be placed upon the produce of agriculturalists'.[18]

Food taxes were the most traditional and still the most powerful form of tariff appeal to the farming community, and without an agricultural appeal to match benefits to industry, the tariff campaign clearly had the potential, first, to alienate the farming community from the tariff campaign and the Conservative party and, second, to open a serious split between rural and urban interests. These problems were fully acknowledged at the time and played a very important part in shaping the tariff debate. For example in June 1904 a Tariff Commission sub-committee met to discuss the preliminary report on, and proposed tariffs for, the iron and steel trades, and was reminded that

> We are dealing with the question of the iron and steel trade, and large use is made by the Agricultural interest of iron and steel machinery for a great variety of purposes. If it were laid down as part of a general tariff . . . that a duty was to be imposed upon those articles which are used largely by the Agricultural interests, and

190

which they might think too high before they know what is going to be done with regard to their own particular interests ... it might create unnecessary anxiety, perhaps alarm, and even possibly prejudice our interests with that particular industry.[19]

The problem was summed up by the first meeting of the Tariff Commission's Agricultural Committee, which noted that its task was not simply to design a policy for the farming interest but also to consider 'the best way in which, where there are conflicting interests of the manufacturing and agricultural industries respectively, they can be most satisfactorily harmonized'.[20]

It was not only real or potential differences *between* rural and urban interests that the tariff campaign sought to reconcile. The tariff programme also addressed and attempted to harmonize different interests *within* the rural and urban sectors. On the one hand this meant reconciling employers and employees by positing the dependence of all engaged in a particular industry or trade on the prosperity of that industry. In particular the tariff campaign tried very hard to persuade the working class of the benefits of tariffs. The Trade Union Tariff Reform Association was one illustration of the attempt to attract workers to the tariff cause, and the Tariff Commission expressed the hope that 'we should be able to point in our reports, [to] statements and evidence from people who would be recognized to speak with authority on behalf of the working man'.[21] Here the tariff campaign's stress on job security – 'tariff reform means work for all' – was significant. British labour was depicted as sharing a corporate interest with British capital in the successful continuance of the productive process, and in defending British production against assault by foreign competition. In this sense the notion of class harmony within the productive process of a national economy was intrinsic to the tariff argument. Equally important in this context was the claim, presented with great vigour after 1906, that tariffs would provide revenue for social reforms. This argument deepened the case for the 'unity of capital and labour', in that its underlying premise was that social reform would be counter-productive if financed by a predatory tax assault on British capital.

The reconciliation of capital and labour was, however, only part of the evolving tariff design to secure unity within Britain's productive sectors. The tariff campaign also found itself obliged to expend a great deal of time and money in an attempt to construct a programme which could reconcile or appeal to the different sectors of British capital. With regard to agricultural interests, this meant shaping a policy that was attractive to farmers as well as to landowners, on the basis that some of the more important rural policies of the late nineteenth century, most notably the Agricultural Relief Act of 1896, had been criticized for benefiting

191

landlords rather than tenants. As the agricultural side of the tariff campaign developed, the emphasis on measures to assist small farmers became quite marked. Small holdings proposals especially were developed in tandem with the tariff campaign in order to appeal to agricultural labourers, but they appear also to have reflected a conscious attempt to redress farming grievances about the 'imbalance' of landlord and tenant interests in previous Conservative rural policy.

In similar fashion the diversity of interests within the manufacturing sector shaped the evolution of the tariff programme for industry. In the summer of 1903 imperial preference was the only policy on offer, but this proposal could only appeal to the export sector of British industry, and more particularly to those industries which had strong colonial links. Industries and firms desirous of reopening continental markets or complaining about import penetration and 'dumping' could have little or no interest in imperial preference. By the autumn of 1903 retaliatory and protective tariffs had been added to the tariff agenda, since without this kind of coverage the tariff campaign could not really have hoped to obtain widespread support amongst industrialists.

The most eloquent acknowledgement of the need to construct a tariff programme with as broad an appeal as possible was the creation of the Tariff Commission, set up in the autumn of 1903 with explicit instructions to develop a 'scientific tariff'. For opponents it simply provided a pseudo-scientific gloss for the tariff campaign's proposals. A more reasoned appraisal is that the Tariff Commission was essential because an economic argument, to be politically credible, must possess at least some degree of internal consistency and hold a plausible claim to scientific validity.[22] However, neither of these explanations fully grasps the political importance of the Tariff Commission, which was that a 'scientific tariff' was a political necessity if a realistic attempt was to be made to satisfy the conflicting demands which threatened to open up divisions not only between rural and urban interests but also within those highly-stratified sectors of the economy. British industrialists and agriculturalists, in spite of what has been written about 'entrepreneurial failure' in the late nineteenth century, were not unimaginative, and they held clear and strong views as to whether a particular tariff regime would help or hinder them. The primary task of the Tariff Commission was to construct a tariff regime which would attract as many and offend as few of these diverse interests as possible.

CONCLUDING REMARKS

This brief examination of the main elements of the tariff argument serves to illustrate that there was a clear rationale underpinning tariff reform. It is difficult to understand the evolving structure of the tariff campaign unless one regards it as a British blend of the strategies of *Sammlungspolitik* and 'social imperialism' that were so characteristic of the contemporary Continental Right. First, the tariff campaign attempted to demonstrate the social welfare benefits of Empire and the maintenance of Britain's productive economic base to the working classes. In the initial phase of the tariff campaign, this argument stood as an autonomous Conservative effort to enrol mass support, but its appeal within Conservative circles deepened after 1906, when it was presented as an explicit alternative to Socialist methods of providing social welfare improvements. Second, the tariff campaign attempted to unite propertied interests, not just through a coherent stance against the internal threat posed by Socialism, but through a programme to defend British capital against the external threat of foreign competition. The essence of tariff reform was an attempt to demonstrate the basic harmony and indeed interdependence of classes, sectors and interests within a neo-mercantilist economic framework. In short, the tariff campaign, as the following detailed examination of the tariff programme will demonstrate, represented a political economy of integration, offering the consolidation of the Empire against rival powers, support for British agriculture, British industry and British jobs against foreign competition, and the defence of the existing social fabric against the threat of Socialism.

7

IMPERIAL ORGANIZATION

The era of expansion is over ... the era of organization is just
beginning.

(Lord Milner at Liverpool, 7 June 1910)

my policy, whether it be protectionist or not, in some of its incidents,
is entirely based on my firm belief of its necessity if we are to keep
the Empire together. Rhodes was absolutely right: if we cannot find
a practical tie we shall insensibly drift apart.

(J. Chamberlain to E.B. Iwan-Muller, 11 December 1903)[1]

The tariff campaign began with Joseph Chamberlain's hymn to the Empire
at Bingley Hall, Birmingham on 15 May 1903. For eight years imperial
unity had been a constant theme of Chamberlain's career. In June 1895 he
had refused the positions of Home Secretary and Chancellor of the
Exchequer in Lord Salisbury's third administration in order to take
the post of Colonial Secretary, telling Salisbury, 'I should prefer the
Colonies – in the hope of furthering closer union between them and
the United Kingdom'.[2] That autumn Chamberlain made a number of
speeches calling for closer economic and political unity within the Empire.
In 1897 he floated the idea of an imperial 'Zollverein' at the Imperial
Conference, and when the Colonies proved unreceptive he looked instead
to colonial offers of preferential trade to establish closer imperial relations.
In the light of the colonial contributions to the Boer War and the 'Canadian
offer' at the 1902 Imperial Conference, Chamberlain sought Cabinet
approval for imperial preference, and when his hopes were dashed he
launched the tariff campaign. He was not alone in regarding imperial unity
as central to the tariff campaign. In 1903 the industrial magnate Sir Vincent
Caillard, who was to be closely involved with the tariff campaign, spoke
of his 'intimate conviction that the welfare and prosperity of the United
Kingdom, and of almost all, if not of all, the British colonies, must depend
to an immense extent upon the maintenance of the Empire',[3] whilst the
Rules of the Compatriots' Club stated that '[t]he object of the Club is to
advance the ideal of a United British Empire, and to advocate consistently

those principles of constructive policy on all constitutional, economic, defensive and educational questions which will help towards the fulfilment of that ideal'.[4] The tariff campaign contended that imperial unity was essential to the maintenance of Britain's imperial role and, by implication, crucial to the fortunes of 'the imperial Party'.

SIZE MATTERS

In 1909 Lord Milner noted that 'the time is coming . . . when the United Kingdom *alone* will be hard put to retain its place amongst the foremost nations of the world'.[5] Underpinning this was an argument about the kind of competition Britain faced. In May 1902 Joseph Chamberlain argued that 'The days are for great empires and not for little states',[6] a remark in step with contemporary geopolitical analysis.[7] Developments in world politics over the last quarter of the nineteenth century had, according to the Tariff Commission, been characterized by 'the creation of large states – the United States, Germany etc. – each pursuing its own national policy, conceived in its own individual interest',[8] and demonstrating that 'the tendency everywhere in the world is towards organization'.[9] It seemed clear that 'Providence is on the side of the bigger social batallions'.[10] For Britain, the question was 'how can these little islands hold their own in the long run against such great and rich empires as the United States and Germany are rapidly becoming, or even such as Russia will be when it recovers from its present [1905] disasters',[11] and the answer, according to the tariff argument, was for British statesmen to 'learn to think imperially'.[12]

What 'thinking imperially' meant was explained by Lord Selborne, who told Ernest Pretyman in September 1903 that 'if this country is to maintain herself in the years to come in the same rank with the US, Russia and Germany, the unit must be enlarged from the UK to the Empire'.[13] According to J.L. Garvin protection and imperial preference constituted a single policy, for if 'the maintenance of the Empire must depend to an overwhelming degree upon the power and the wealth of the island' it was also the case that 'the power and wealth of the island must depend . . . upon the maintenance of the Empire'.[14] The key was that 'the physiological system of the Empire . . . must be considered as a whole'.[15] National economic thinking had to be informed by the fact that 'the nation cannot limit its view of economic policy by an insular horizon'.[16] This point was summed up by Arthur Steel-Maitland, who argued that economic thought ought to be 'Nationalistic', but added 'Nation here = British Empire'.[17]

A QUESTION OF URGENCY

'Learning to think imperially' was deemed urgent. Since Britain was confronted not only by large-scale competitors but also 'the adoption by these larger states of scientific tariffs' it was, in the Tariff Commission's view, essential for economic survival that Britain 'find within the Empire new markets for British manufactures'.[18] The economic benefits of imperial preference were reckoned to be self-evident. In 1908 the Commission pointed out that exports to New Zealand, Australia and Canada had a value of £23.75 million per annum in the period 1892–6, but that the preferences granted by Canada in 1897, New Zealand in 1903 and Australia in 1907 had seen this trade's value more than double to £50 million per annum by 1908.[19] Critics pointed out that Britain's imperial trade was still not as great as trade with other nations, but the tariff campaign had three other arguments for imperial preference. The first was that the aggregate totals of foreign and imperial trade did not do justice to the dynamics of British trade: although the volume of Britain's non-colonial trade was higher, colonial trade was growing faster. Colonial markets were presented as markets with a future, as opposed to older markets where tariffs and import substitution precluded any growth of British trade.[20] The second feature of Britain's imperial trade singled out by the tariff campaign was that the Colonies imported 'almost exclusively our fully manufactured goods',[21] which underpinned a contention that 'we must rely upon Imperial markets for the progress of our trade both in *character* and value'.[22] The third advantage of the colonial markets was that they were deemed 'beyond the reach of our rivals' control':[23] close ties with Britain meant imperial markets were more secure. Imperial preference was thus deemed to offer a clear and positive remedy for Britain's economic ills, but the tariff campaign stressed that this remedy had to be taken quickly.

In his Bingley Hall speech Joseph Chamberlain sounded a warning, telling the British people 'Make a mistake in your Imperial policy – it is irretrievable. You have an opportunity, you will never have it again'.[24] The urgent tone of much of the argument for imperial preference was prompted by fear that the internal structure of the Empire was too weak and that it would drift apart unless conscious efforts were made to arrest 'centrifugal' tendencies. In particular the tariff campaign doubted whether the Colonies' enthusiasm for closer ties with the motherland, seemingly so pronounced in the immediate aftermath of the Boer War, could be sustained if their overtures were continually rebuffed. In July 1904 Chamberlain pointedly stated that 'the Colonies will never want for suitors, and if you do not pay your court to them, whilst they are still willing to receive your addresses, you will find that in time to come they will have made some [other] arrangements'.[25]

Concern that the Colonies were becoming more independent arose in the 1890s, when the Colonies began to develop tariff systems of their own and to engage in trade negotiations with a number of countries.[26] Preferences extended to Britain had seemed to indicate that the Colonies had a genuine desire for closer links with Britain, but Canada had, by 1907, signed trade treaties (at that point unratified) with Austria-Hungary, Switzerland and Japan and opened negotiations with France for reciprocal tariff arrangements.[27] The Franco-Canadian negotiations clearly worried Conservative imperialists. Arthur Steel-Maitland described the proposed agreement as 'a nasty treaty', and suggested that the editor of the *Morning Post* write an article praising the Canadians for obtaining a good bargain on the grounds that this might prompt the French to ask for more and wreck the negotiations.[28] Even more disturbing, in 1910 the Liberal government in Canada began discussions with the United States which culminated with a proposal for a trade agreement which would have relegated Britain to a poor second place in terms of entry to the Canadian market.

The Colonies' growing self-assertiveness reinforced a view that, despite abundant pro-Empire sentiment in both in the Motherland and Colonies, 'the sentiments ... which unite us ... are not enough'.[29] Chamberlain's views were echoed by Lord Dunraven, who argued that

sentiment is ... a powerful force of gravitation towards the centre, but conflicting interests are a centrifugal force, and, as the tendency of the former must be weaker with time, and the latter stronger, eventual disruption ... [is] inevitable failing the adoption of means for reconciling the two conflicting forces.[30]

To exploit the Empire's full potential, it was necesary to 'use sentiment ... to remove the difficulties in the way of practical organization' and then 'secure it by bonds of steel, by bonds that are of sentiment *and of interest*'.[31] Economic ties were seen as the best 'practical' complement to ties of sentiment. However, the question remained as to how best to shape these ties.

THE CASE FOR PREFERENCE

The core of the tariff policy for imperial unity was the negotiation of preferential tariff agreements with the Colonies. The tariff controversy began with the 1/- registration duty on imported corn imposed to pay for the Boer War. In Chamberlain's initial schema colonial corn was to be exempted from this duty, but in the autumn of 1903 he argued for a 2/- per quarter duty on imported corn with a 1/- preference for colonial produce. The latter proposal was tariff reform policy until 1910, when it was decided that colonial corn should enter Britain duty-free. In return for preferential treatment of their corn the Colonies were to continue their policy of preferential tariff rates for British manufactured imports.

That *preference*, in the form outlined above, dominated the tariff argument was largely due to two factors. The first was that the only colonial goods which Britain imported were foodstuffs and raw materials. The introduction of a tariff on raw materials was unacceptable to British manufacturers. In the realm of imported foods British farmers were no more thrilled by the prospect of cheap colonial competition than foreign. This provoked a long-running debate as to whether colonial corn in particular would enjoy preferential or free entry to the British market.[32] But, whether or not colonial imports entered free, imperial preference still required some kind of 'food tax'. That the tariff campaign and the Conservative party stuck with the food tax in spite of its well-known electoral drawbacks is in part testimony to the importance of imperial unity to tariff and Conservative politics.[33] The second factor militating in favour of preference was that it was the only policy acceptable to the Colonies. In the 1890s the Colonies had rejected Empire free trade in order to protect their 'infant' domestic industries from British as well as foreign imports, a position well known to those engaged in the tariff programme. In his key Glasgow speech of October 1903 Joseph Chamberlain told his audience that the Colonies were 'all protective countries' because they were not content 'to be what the Americans call a 'one horse country', with a single industry and no diversity of employment'.[34] It was a constant refrain of the tariff campaign that 'Tariff reformers have never urged that it is either possible or even desirable to aim at the present time at Free Trade within the Empire'.[35] Preference was the only viable policy, in that, as the Tariff Commission recognized,

> [t]he development of the autonomous powers of the self-governing Colonies has made it necessary that any commercial arrangement with them should be the result of negotiations between the Imperial and the several Colonial Governments as representatives of co-ordinate British States each having special regard to its own national interests as well as the interests of the Empire as a whole.[36]

The tariff campaign's focus on preference indicated how far colonial national aspirations constrained moves towards imperial economic unity.

A NEW CONCEPTION OF EMPIRE?

The broader significance of the argument for preference was that the imperial aspect of tariff reform marked an important break from previous conceptions of Empire and the role of the Colonies. Writing to Balfour in February 1907, W.A.S. Hewins attacked free trade and old Mercantilist views of the Colonies. 'The Colonies', Hewins wrote,

> had a definite place in this [Mercantilist] system. But it was a subordinate place, both economically and politically . . . they were to supply . . . raw materials . . . which we could not produce and take in our manufactures . . . It is noteworthy that the role played by

198

the Colonies under the Mercantile system was precisely that which Cobden and his followers expected both Colonies and foreign countries to play when the United Kingdom adopted free importation.[37]

Thus the tariff critique of free trade led also to a repudiation of the classical Mercantilist view of Colonies as an appendage of the parent country, on the grounds that to treat Colonies in this manner would be to commit free trade errors through an excess of imperialist zeal. It was essential, Hewins argued, to design a 'new conception' of imperial economic relations which would be 'different from the Mercantilist view of earlier days on the one hand, and from Cobdenism on the other'.[38] The proposal for imperial preference, with its emphasis on the necessity of genuine reciprocity and its concern for colonial development, is thus to be understood as part of an effort to redefine the relationship between Britain and its Colonies in the light of 'recent developments both within and without the Empire'.[39]

The most important aspect of the 'new conception' of Empire was the notion that

> the British Empire is not an Empire in the sense in which that term has been applied before. The British Colonies are no longer Colonies in the sense in which that term was originally applied to them ... We are sister States in which the mother country by virtue of her age, by virtue of all that has been done in the past, may claim to be first, but only first among equals.[40]

This was a vision based on the creation of a system in which member States were regarded as equals. No State within the Empire was to be subordinate to any other individual State; ultimately loyalty lay with the Empire conceived as an organic unity. When Leo Amery asked in 1910 'What do we mean when we speak of Imperial unity?', he answered himself by saying

> we mean that all its [the Empire's] members should remain citizens of a single world State with a duty and a loyalty towards that State, none the less real and intense because of the co-existence with it of a duty and a loyalty towards the particular nation or community within the Empire to which they belong.[41]

This imperial relationship aimed to balance the integrative and disintegrative potential of the Colonies' national aspirations.

Exactly how the national/imperial balance was conceived was outlined in George Wyndham's Rectorial Address to the University of Glasgow in 1904.[42] In the pattern of world events Wyndham discerned 'a continuous trend towards complex political aggregation, so constant as almost to argue a force of human nature which might be called Political

Gravitation'.[43] To Wyndham this 'force' was at work in the British Empire, but 'the birth of an Organic Empire State'[44] required careful midwifery. As an example of what *not* to do Wyndham cited Rome.[45] A fatal flaw in the Roman Imperium, according to Wyndham, had been that 'local colour and feature throughout the vast extension of the Empire' had been 'destroyed', producing a 'baneful tendency towards cosmopolitanism'.[46] The net result had been disintegration, because 'a cosmopolitan world is not a polity and cannot inspire the love or exact the allegiance of men who, by nature, must be members of an organic State'.[47] Wyndham argued that if the British Empire was to avoid Rome's fate it had to allow 'adequate local attachment'[48] and respect the legitimate aspiration to nationhood on the part of the Colonies.[49]

The need to 'revere nationality', George Wyndham argued, should not be allowed to 'harden into Nationalism and oppose obstacles to the further development of the State'.[50] 'The remedy against exaggeration of National sentiment', Wyndham declared, lay in 'preferring ... the two ideas of Empire and of Race'.[51] The imperial idea was necessary because 'the State must be large enough in contour to fire the imagination of all its citizens with faith in the future';[52] only membership of an 'Empire State' could instil such faith. Encouragement of racial pride was healthier than the encouragement of national pride, which could easily lapse into a narrow chauvinism.[53] Because nationality was not 'co-extensive with Race',[54] racial pride did not prevent loyalty on the part of members of a particular race towards the nation in which they happened to dwell. Hence, when Wyndham stated 'let pride be in Race, patriotism for the Empire'[55] he harmonized 'universal allegiance' to the Empire and Race with the 'particular sentiment' of individual nations.[56]

George Wyndham had a reputation for eccentricity and for constructing over-florid and sometimes obscure arguments. But his views on the primacy of 'Race loyalty' were a vital part of the tariff reform conception of imperial relations. In his Bingley Hall speech of May 1903 Joseph Chamberlain made it clear that when he discussed the Empire he wished to consider 'only our relations ... to that white British population that constitutes the majority in the great self-governing Colonies of the Empire',[57] and at Glasgow in October of the same year he stated that the aim of the tariff campaign was 'to consolidate the British race'.[58] J.L. Garvin spoke of the British Empire as 'a dominion that should be secured by the preponderance in numbers of the race that holds it',[59] whilst Lord Milner spoke of the Empire as 'these new lands of immense promise inhabited by men of our race'.[60] Leo Amery took the argument a stage further, telling Alfred Lyttelton[61] that Britain 'shall have to do what the Romans did and divide British subjects into at least two classes, (a) the full British citizen, and (b) the British subject'. The basic distinction, Amery argued, was between 'Communities of full citizens [which] are self-governing and have every right to legislate as regards the admission and exclusion of British subjects' and

> British subjects [who] live in communities not self-governing and though they have every equality of treatment before the law ... yet they have no right to insist on being admitted to any other part of the British Empire or to share its franchise.[62]

Amery's notion of a two-tier imperial citizenship, based on an explicitly racial division, was one of the fullest statements of its kind, but wherever the notion of imperial preference appeared the theme of racial unity was never far behind.

By equating imperial unity with racial unity – and only white settler, self-governing Colonies featured prominently in tariff propaganda – it was possible to avoid an overstress on separate national, and particularly British, interests. The notion of the Empire as a racially unified polity complemented the tariff campaign's description of the Empire's unity of economic interest. Just as imperial preference was to blend national and imperial economics so the idea of 'the Race' was to allow for separate national identities within the broader framework of a supra-national, racial identity. In this way the tariff campaign built up, at a number of levels, a series of arguments designed to show that 'the existence of Empire is reconcilable with the self-development of all its parts',[63] and that there was 'no incompatibility between ... national patriotism and the wider patriotism of Empire'.[64]

By constructing a new conception of Empire based, in the words of the Canadian Conservative Robert Borden, on 'co-operation and autonomy'[65] the tariff campaign could claim two things. First, it could claim to have reconciled colonial nationalism with the needs of the mother country, and thereby provided a means of preventing the disintegration of the Empire. As a consequence it could also claim to have produced a way of allowing Britain and British manufacturers to compete on equal terms with larger States. By drawing together 'territories vaster than have ever owned any common interest before' the new imperial policy was to enable the British Empire to 'stand together ... if necessary against the world'.[66] Imperial preference was to create an Empire-State to match other continental powers in scale and scope.

THE POLITICS OF CONSTRUCTIVE IMPERIALISM

In 1904 the Liberal philosopher L.T. Hobhouse noted, with tariff reform in mind, a 'serious attack' on Liberalism from 'the side of imperial politics'.[67] When Joseph Chamberlain spoke of the possible break-up of the Empire, he placed no blame on the Colonies. 'There has never been', Chamberlain declared, 'any question about the loyalty of the Colonies', but he added that there was 'some question . . . about the loyalty of the motherland'.[68] This was attributed to a discouragement of 'imperial patriotism' in Britain 'by our apparent acceptance of the doctrines of the little Englanders'.[69] Little Englandism meant free trade, as Bernard Wise made clear: 'Free Trade is the enemy; because the crude dogma of free imports is the pervading face of little Englandism'.[70] According to the tariff argument, free trade was inimical to imperial organization not simply because tariffs were required for imperial preference, but because free traders 'hated all that we understand by Imperialism'.[71] That 'the entire Manchester school disliked the Empire and disbelieved in it', wrote J.L. Garvin, was a product of the way their politics had developed from their economics:

> If you thought from the economic point of view that foreign nations were going to throw open their markets more and more widely to British trade, that the connection with the Colonies gave you of itself no special commercial advantage, that separation would promote peace and retrenchment by removing causes of quarrel with foreign nations . . . then it necessarily followed that the existence of the British Empire was a political mistake.[72]

Free trade was hostile to Empire because it thought the Empire served no useful purpose.

The major failing of the free trade position was seen to be its cosmopolitan outlook. 'The Cobdenite', Lord Milner argued, 'only looks at the commercial side, he is a cosmopolitan',[73] which meant that 'To the Cobdenite trade is just trade. It doesn't matter with whom you trade as long as you make a profit out of it. It does not matter from whom you get your goods as long as you get them cheap'.[74] This outlook failed to consider the political importance of trade. In 1905 J.L. Garvin noted that 'though trade with Canada . . . and with Argentina might be of nominally equal worth on the cash reckoning of the orthodox economist, there is no comparison in the political value'.[75] Indeed to Garvin 'a transaction in imperial trade, and, above all, with our white Colonies, gives undoubtedly at least twice the political strength derived from a transaction in foreign trade'.[76] Britain's food supply illustrated this. The tariff programme acknowledged that Britain could not feed itself, but argued it was better to draw supplies from the Colonies instead of relying on the resources of a 'potential enemy'.[77] On a broader level, however, 'a wise policy' would 'help divert commerce into channels which would not only assist the British worker, but also assist colonial development and work for more rapid growth of those countries which not only contain our best customers, but our fellow-citizens'.[78] Instead the cosmopolitan assumption of free trade had ensured that 'we have as a nation committed the error of treating political economy as if it were all economy and no politics'.[79]

The 'constructive imperialist' critique of free trade was suited to Conservative politics in and after 1903. After the Boer War Britain's imperial power status had been called into question, and the Conservative party's claim to be *the* imperial party appeared dubious. The tariff campaign offered Conservatives a chance to reestablish their credentials as the party of Empire. But it also provided a means of renewing the Conservative attack on the Liberal party as the anti-imperial party. Between 1902 and 1906 the Conservatives were clearly on the electoral defensive, but imperial issues seemed to offer a chance for a counter attack. The Liberals' imperial flank had been turned in the mid-1880s, again in 1892–5 and again during the Boer War, and imperial issues were regarded as a major weakness in the Liberal defences. In the 1906 election campaign the Conservatives sought to represent the Liberals as utopian internationalists, arguing that the party of Majuba, Khartoum and pro-Boer sentiment could not be trusted with national and imperial security.[80] Likewise, between 1906 and 1910 Conservatives continually sniped at Liberal defence policy, culminating with the 'we want eight and we won't wait' campaign against supposed Liberal reluctance to match German naval expenditure. The 'responsible', Liberal Imperialist members of the Cabinet were portrayed as 'prisoners' of little Englander Radicalism. The implication, as always, was that only Conservatives could be trusted with matters of national and imperial defence.[81]

The argument for imperial preference enhanced the Conservative attack on the Liberals' fitness (or lack of it) to govern the Empire. The tariff campaign's constant carping at free trade 'cosmopolitanism' broadened and deepened Conservative criticism of the 'anti-national' tenor of Liberal foreign, defence and imperial policy. But the case for preference posited further weaknesses: the Liberals were deemed to have failed to foster imperial unity at both the 1907 and 1911 Imperial Conferences. As a consequence the Conservatives claimed that the Liberals were hastening the break-up of the Empire. Soon after the 1911 Imperial Conference Arthur Balfour remarked

> They [the Dominions] gave you . . . preference even in spite of our neglect and the pressure by foreign countries; but if you tell them that they are to look after themselves commercially, that we will have neither part nor let in their arrangement with other countries . . . we shall awake one morning and find that in these communities, loyal as they are to the core, a system of tariffs has been established in which we shall find that the preference of such immense advantage to us and our manufacturers has been swept away . . . [and] I do not believe any Empire can stand long under a strain like that.[82]

From a general critique of liberal political economy the case for preference had become a specific attack on Liberal government policy and in particular a critique of the Liberals' refusal to respond positively to 'the Colonial offer'.[83]

The Liberals' 'neglect' of the Empire was also seen to have undermined the credibility of their domestic reforms. Writing to Lord Milner in April 1908 Benjamin Kidd linked imperial policy and domestic social and economic issues, saying that he looked forward to the introduction of a 'larger policy at home' which would entail '(1) ... A Ministry of Commerce, (2) State control of the sea roads of the Empire and (3) ... State control or nationalization of the railways'.[84] Of these policies, Kidd continued,

> the first is already practically agreed upon; agreement upon the second in principle followed the practical result of the last Colonial Conference; as to the third you will see from Lloyd George's recent Manchester speech how near we are getting to that. And all this from the Liberal Party. But the final matter behind still remains the reconstruction of our fiscal policy and the social policy of which it forms the only possible base.[85]

Kidd's closing remarks referred to the necessity of tariffs as a source of revenue,[86] but this was not the only reason tariffs, and especially preference, were regarded as essential to domestic social reform. Imperial unity and social reform were described as 'inseparable ideals, absolutely interdependent and complementary'[87] because it was taken as axiomatic that 'no policy of social reform which leaves out of view the British Empire can be in the truest sense constructive'.[88] Britain minus the Empire would be a 'fifth-rate nation' without the resources to promote social reform. This emphasis on the necessity of an imperial dimension represented the most practical expression of a train of thought which, as L.T. Hobhouse remarked, linked 'a positive theory of the State in domestic affairs ... [with] a positive theory of Empire'.[89] Liberals could be criticized as 'false collectivists' for their failure to develop an imperial strategy.

Imperial preference also offered helpful criticisms of Socialism, because Socialism was thought to replicate many of the 'errors' of Liberalism. The Labour Party's support for free trade, its membership of the Second International and its pacifist leanings marked it out as 'Cosmopolitan', but, Socialism was seen to possess a powerful appeal, in that its commitment to social reform played on working-class economic and social insecurity.[90] The beauty of imperial preference, according to its advocates, was that it offered a positive Conservative alternative to Socialism – George Wyndham arguing that

> the conflict is between (1) State directed efforts to improve the condition of life for the people here based on tradition and working towards an organic Empire (2) State directed efforts to improve the

204

condition of the people here based on class antagonism and working towards Socialistic Cosmopolitanism.[91]

Imperial preference, in tandem with tariff protection, appealed 'directly to people's self interest and to their pocket'[92] through a promise of higher and more stable levels of employment.[93] Likewise, the organic link posited between imperialism and social policy offered a distinctively Conservative approach to social issues, and social reform was regarded by many Edwardian Conservatives as the best antidote to Socialism.

But it was not just the claim that imperial unity would bring both direct and indirect material benefits to the working class that marked imperial preference as an anti-Socialist policy. Writing to Edward Goulding in December 1909 J.L. Garvin remarked that 'In the last three weeks I have seen the Socialists face to face for the first time for many years. I am amazed. It is not a new party. It is a new religion'.[94] Against this imperial preference could oppose its own creed and 'Kiplingesque' visions of grandeur. An appeal 'to patriotism as well as the pocket' distinguished Conservatives from both Liberals and Socialists. 'The basis of the radical appeal to the electorate', wrote Lord Selborne, 'is materialism, and it is addressed to them in sections . . . no appeal is made to any section on the score of patriotism'.[95] Class antagonism was portrayed as the quintes-sence of Socialism,[96] whereas the quintessence of imperialism was strident patriotism, but it was not a simple appeal. Socialism may have been dismissed as somehow 'un-British',[97] but committed imperialists did not overstress the 'Britishness' of their cause. Preference, as noted above, stressed the organic unity not of the nation but of the Race, and just as all the white, self-governing nations of the Empire were reckoned to be held by a bond of consanguinity so too all classes within each nation were deemed to share the same bond.[98] So Lord Milner declared

> I do not believe that the working classes are the unpatriotic, anti-national, down-with-the-army, up-with-the-foreigner, take-it-lying-down class of Little Englanders, that they are constantly represented to be.

As 'an antidote to the sort of preaching which we get from the present Labour members' Milner advocated that Conservative MPs and candi-dates employ members of the working class on their political staff – the rationale being that 'there is nothing more calculated to remove class prej-udice and antagonism than the co-operation of men of different classes on the same body for the same public end', and that there was no cause so likely to 'bring home to men of all classes their essential interdependence' than 'the common heritage and traditions of the British race'.[99] In short, the imperialism of the tariff campaign posited a racial solidarity in opposition to the cosmopolitan, internationalist class solidarity offered by Socialism.

CONCLUDING REMARKS

In the early twentieth century imperial relations posed a clear but difficult problem, namely how to reconcile colonial nationalism and economic
development with British political and economic interests. The Empire
was changing; the bonds between Britain and the self-governing
Colonies, *de facto* if not *de jure*, were weakening. Imperial preference
attempted to strike a balance between imperialism and nationalism. It
was thus one of the first attempts to design the co-partnership or
Commonwealth structure of imperial relations that emerged at the
Ottawa Conference in 1932.

Imperial preference was designed to solve an imperial problem, but it
also had a wider significance. In a world of great territorial empires the
Colonies' resources and markets were presented as the only means of
securing Britain's power and prosperity, which was in turn seen as vital
to the preservation of Britain's social fabric, in that the social and
economic security of the masses was bound up with their employment
prospects. Britain's economic difficulties had, it was argued, already
caused enough social distress to fuel class antagonisms and bring about
the emergence of a strong Socialist movement. Socialism was, in effect,
seen to be a product of the fact that the British masses felt little or no
attachment to existing social and political structures. Given this analysis
the only answer to the Socialist threat was to find some means of demonstrating that such loyalty would bring genuine benefits. Imperial preference represented a seemingly perfect mechanism to foster socio-political
integration. By demonstrating the centrality of the Empire to Britain's
prosperity and security it was, so the tariff argument implied, possible to
achieve social harmony based on a common, cross-class sense of loyalty
to the institution which provided the key to that prosperity and security.
In this way the Empire was to cut the ground from underneath Socialism
by providing a focus for a positive, alternative conception of class relations. This required an acceptance of the notion that 'the State . . . has a
positive function'.[100] In the context of Edwardian politics, however, the
only alternative seemed to be a far more socially and politically disruptive conception of a positive State.

8

THE DEFENCE OF
BRITISH AGRICULTURE

If we examine Mr Chamberlain's proposals carefully we shall find that in all probability they will do more for agriculture than is very often supposed to be the case.[1]

(H. Chaplin, July 1904)

I do not think there is any more promising branch of the work than that relating to Agriculture . . . I am sure . . . that we shall probably know more about agriculture, and probably do more to stimulate agriculture in England than has been done in the last 50 years.[2]

(W.A.S. Hewins to H. Chaplin, 22 January 1904)

'1846 is not 1903' J.L. Garvin roundly declared in his book *Imperial Reciprocity*,[3] meaning issues raised by the tariff campaign were wholly different to those which had characterized controversy over the Corn Laws sixty years earlier. Garvin's remarks were endorsed by the Tariff Reform League, whose *Speakers' Handbook* noted that 'Tariff Reform is not a revival of the old controversy between Free Trade and Protection. The beginning of wisdom in regard to the Fiscal question lies in a recognition of this fact'.[4] In 1846 debate had been focused on one issue, whether to retain or repeal the Corn Laws. In 1903 the tariff campaign brought a gamut of questions to the fore: the nature of Britain's relations with its Colonies, the needs of British industry in an increasingly competitive world market, and the role of the State in economy and society. However, the position of agriculture within the British economy and agricultural protection itself were also questions integral to the tariff debate and Conservative politics in the early twentieth century.

'THE GREATEST OF ALL OUR INDUSTRIES'

In the second major speech of the tariff campaign proper, Joseph Chamberlain began a tale of economic woe by stating that 'Agriculture, as the greatest of all trades and industries of this country, has been practically destroyed'.[5] For Chamberlain's contemporaries this was probably one of

207

his least contentious remarks. Two Royal Commissions and a catalogue of complaints from landowners and farmers had ensured that depression and decline had been the watchwords of almost every discussion of farming in Britain in the late nineteenth century. The tariff campaign continued this story of British agriculture. In 1904, in his book *Agriculture and Tariff Reform* J.L. Green, the Secretary of the Rural League,[6] presented a number of indicators of rural decay. In particular Green noted that the rural population had fallen by 50 per cent in the period 1851–1901, that between 1885-1902 farming had never been lower than fourth in the Board of Trade list of annual bankruptcies by occupation, and that between 1866 and 1903 over five million acres of farmland had passed out of cultivation.[7] The accuracy of these figures has been broadly confirmed by historical scholarship, but Green's conclusion that they showed an industry 'seriously depressed . . . for many years'[8] has been disputed. The judgement of economic history is that there was no general depression of agriculture, but that there were significant regional variations in the fortunes of British farming.[9] To those who voiced concern about the condition of British farming, what was most alarming was agriculture's *decline* in terms of the size of the farming sector, its contribution to the national income and the numbers employed on the land.[10] Indeed contemporary comment tended to *equate* depression and decline. In this sense Chamberlain, Green and others in the Conservative ranks who raised the 'plight' of agriculture within the framework of the tariff campaign were not concerned simply with current farming income. The issue they raised was in some respects the reverse of the one at stake in the 1840s. The campaign for the repeal of the Corn Laws had in effect asked whether the 'national interest' was to be sacrificed to the interests of agriculture. The tariff campaign asked whether it was in the 'national interest' to allow a wholesale reduction of the British agricultural sector, and concluded that it was not.

A large and prosperous agricultural sector was deemed essential for three reasons. The first was strategic. By 1903, according to J.L. Green, Britain was importing 70 per cent of its wheat supply and a sizeable, if lesser, percentage of other foodstuffs.[11] The Royal Commission on Food Supply which sat in 1903 produced similar figures and confirmed Britain's dependence on imported food. The strategic implications of this were that Britain was vulnerable to blockade and/or a disruption of its shipping.[12] The Royal Commission Report expressed confidence in the Navy's ability to protect Britain's food supplies, but a substantial body of opinion, including a minority of the Royal Commission, was less sanguine.[13] The deputy editor of the *Daily Mail*, the naval 'expert' H.W. Wilson, noted in February 1904 that 'The world has yet to see what will happen when a state which draws its raw materials and its food from across the sea . . . comes into collision with a strong continental state possessing a good navy', but he left his readers in little doubt as to the probable, unpleasant outcome.[14] Part of the case for agricultural regeneration was thus an argument for increased domestic food production on the grounds that 'a nation which depends for its food on the goodwill of another nation ... practically acknowledges that nation as its suzerain'.[15] It was not suggested that Britain should attempt to become self-sufficient in terms of food production, but that in the interests of security Britain could and should produce more than it did.

The second element of the tariff reform case for reversing agricultural decline was economic. According to W.J. Ashley, one of the key indicators of Britain's decline as a manufacturing power was that 'the value of exports of British produce and manufactures was almost stationary between 1872 and 1899'.[16] British manufacturers could not sell their goods because 'our commercial supremacy in all the great civilized markets outside the flag has disappeared'.[17] Concern over the declining overseas market for British manufactures justified reviving British agriculture 'not only ... in its own interest, but also in the manufacturing and commercial interest of the country'.[18] The economic rationale here was that

> the home market is always the best market for a manufacturer, and [as] the export market is shrinking, and is bound to shrink still further as the energy and cheap productive power of foreign rivals becomes felt increasingly in neutral markets, and ... the development of industrialism in foreign countries makes them more independent ... the English manufacturer will be forced more and more upon the home market, and anything ... which will develop that home market is to his advantage.[19]

As a result of the loss of foreign markets, Britain had to rediscover that 'the most important part of a nation's commerce is that which is carried on between the inhabitants of the town and those of the country'.[20]

The final argument for reviving agriculture was that a farming renaissance would help secure social and political stability. Fostering a large and prosperous rural population was to cure two interrelated social problems. The first was the 'rural exodus'. The reduction of acreage under tillage in Britain had, so the Tariff Commission argued, produced a massive drop in the demand for agricultural labour, with the result that 'from the labourer's point of view ... the absence of permanent employment leads him to seek other industries for more regular work for himself, and also to train his children to regard agriculture as an unprofitable task'.[21] If farming was made a more secure occupation, then migration from the countryside would be halted and even reversed. This would help the second problem, urban unemployment.[22] In 1903 the agricultural writer Harold Tremayne argued that 'to the migration of the rural population to the towns is obviously traceable the overcrowding of our cities and the repletion of our labour market'.[23] Given this assumption, common to

209

'authorities' on unemployment across the political spectrum,[24] *The Tariff Dictionary* argued that 'a healthy agriculture . . . relieves congestion of the labour market in the towns'.[25] The decline of agriculture and the problem of unemployment were deemed to be organically related.

Regenerating and repopulating the countryside was also to cut the ground, literally as well as metaphorically, from under Socialism. Conservative spokesmen in Britain in the late nineteenth and early twentieth century, frequently (if inaccurately) citing the example of continental Europe, saw the existence of a large class of peasant proprietors as a bulwark against political radicalism – as Richard Jebb told Lord Milner in 1907, 'They [small proprietors] are always the sanest . . . section of the democracy whenever trouble comes to the State'.[26] The idea shared by many on the Right (and Left) in continental Europe, was that someone who had a 'stake in society', no matter how small, would be unlikely to desire a drastic change in the social order.[27] In 1886 Henry Chaplin had argued, against the backdrop of the Irish disturbances, that 'a large increase in the number of owners of land . . . [is] the surest and perhaps the only safeguard against the predatory instincts of . . . Socialist schemes',[28] and in 1892 Lord Salisbury commenting on his own government's Small Holdings Act, endorsed these sentiments.[29] In an attempt to 'kill Home Rule with kindness' successive Conservative governments sought to transform the Irish tenantry into a class of small owners, culminating in the Wyndham Act of 1903, which effectively bought out the Irish landlords and turned the land over to the tenants. As it happened Irish enthusiasm for Home Rule remained undiminished, but this should not distract attention from the assumptions which informed the strategy. Conservative policy in Ireland was eloquent testimony to the supposed transforming power of property ownership, and many Conservatives argued that the ramparts of property needed strengthening in the rest of the United Kingdom as well.

In spite of some quite active party support, and Salisbury's own agreement as to the rationale of small holdings, little action was taken by the Conservative administrations of the late nineteenth century. However, in the early twentieth century and especially after 1906, Conservative enthusiasm for peasant proprietorship became pronounced. One symptom of this was the revived political career of the veteran land campaigner Jesse Collings, who was dusted down and wheeled on to lead the Conservative Parliamentary attack on the Liberal Government's Small Holdings legislation of 1907. More important, however, Collings' lifelong crusade for small holdings was finally embraced by the Party. The 'Unauthorized Programme' of 1908 was unequivocal in its support for small holdings, and in late 1908 the Conservatives established a Small Ownership Committee, chaired by another small holdings enthusiast Sir Gilbert Parker, which by 1909 had produced a presentable policy. By late

1909 Conservative proposals for land reform through the spread of small ownership were given official backing by Balfour, who provided the Preface to Sir Gilbert Parker's *The Land for the People*[30] and made a special announcement in favour of small ownership during the January 1910 election campaign. The Edwardian Conservative party clearly thought the ramparts of property worth building.

The scale and scope of British agriculture and the future of rural life in general were thus key issues in the Conservatives' intra-party debates of the early twentieth century. The underlying concern was outlined by W.A.S. Hewins, the Secretary of the Tariff Commission, who noted that 'generally speaking all foreign and European countries accept as the basis of their economic policy the necessity of maintaining a flourishing agriculture ... [and] they have endeavoured to maintain a balance between agriculture and industry'.[31] A major aim of the tariff programme was to provide both an argument and a policy for Britain to do likewise.

A POLICY FOR RURAL REGENERATION

i. Tariffs

Christopher Turnor, a Lincolnshire landowner and one of the Conservative party's leading rural policy experts, wrote in 1911 that 'no agricultural programme can really be complete that does not include Tariff Reform, or rather, that is not based on Tariff Reform'.[32] Tariffs were advocated as a means of giving British farmers at least some protection against foreign competition. When Chamberlain launched the tariff campaign in May 1903, the only 'food tax' on the agenda was the 1/- registration duty on imported corn, but by the time of his Glasgow speech in October Chamberlain was arguing for a 2/- duty on corn and also for duties on imported meat, dairy produce and flour. At Welbeck in August 1904 Chamberlain went into further detail about his 'food taxes' – the 2/- duty on corn was to apply to wheat, barley and rye, there was to be a 5 per cent *ad valorem* duty on imported meat and dairy produce and an unspecified duty on flour.[33] Nor was Chamberlain simply firing blind with these proposals. They were welcomed by J.L. Green (and by implication the Rural League), and the Tariff Commission used them as the basis for the policy laid out in its *Agricultural Report* of 1906, although the Tariff Commission also advocated a 1/- duty on colonial grain as well as preferential rates for other colonial foodstuffs.[34] By 1905, therefore, a fairly broad spectrum of agricultural tariffs was integral to the tariff programme, and the possibility of adding other items to the tariff list was never far away.[35] It was always made clear, as the Conservative Party's Chief Agent stressed in his correspondence with one rural Conservative association, that 'the alteration in the fiscal system proposed by Tariff

Reform does not include the restoration of the protective system which existed in this country prior to the repeal of the Corn Laws',[36] but, it was claimed, 'the agricultural interest ... will gain by some of the tariff proposals made'.[37]

How these tariff proposals were to benefit agriculture was a complex issue, made more complex by the way the case was presented. It was always said that moderate duties, such as those outlined above, would not raise the price of food. Chamberlain told his audience at Welbeck that although his proposals would confer great benefits upon the farmer and 'in all cases extend the production of food and increase the employment of labour [on the land] they would 'not increase the price of food'.[38] These statements seem difficult to reconcile, for the only way Chamberlain's proposals could achieve what he claimed was through creating a situation in which British farmers could compete with the low-cost produce of foreign competitors. A rise in prices thus seemed to be the only way in which Chamberlain's tariffs could aid British agriculture. Yet this was precisely the implication Chamberlain and his supporters wished to avoid. The reasoning which allowed these implications to be skirted had been outlined as early as 1899 by E.E. Williams. Commenting on Henry Chaplin's proposal for a 1/- registration duty on imported corn Williams argued that the duty 'would give a small modicum of protection to the British farmer'.[39] However, this 'modicum of protection' was to have no impact on prices, because rather than the consumer paying the duty 'by far the most likely result [was] that the foreigner would pay the duty'. The reason for this, Williams declared, was that

> England is practically the only market for the world's surplus supply of corn, which is sold here for what it will fetch. Now as the home produced, and I trust the Colonial, would be exempt from the shilling duty imposed on foreign corn, the British articles would be able to maintain the same price as before, and the foreigner would have to conform to it; that is to say to sell wheat he would have to take a shilling a quarter less for it, in order that it might enter the market on equal terms with home and colonial produce.[40]

Williams' line of reasoning, implicitly reproduced by Chamberlain at Welbeck, and popularized in Leo Maxse's slogan 'England Expects that Every Foreigner Shall Pay His Duty', was given the stamp of economic authority by W.A.S. Hewins. In 1907, discussing the effects of existing 'food duties' on coffee, tea and cocoa,[41] Hewins stated that 'there is no doubt that all these duties raise prices' and that there was

> something to be said for the view that, apart from the question of Tariff Reform, it might be advantageous to reduce some of our present revenue duties, all of which are paid by the British consumer,

and substitute revenue duties on imported agricultural produce, some part of which would certainly be paid by foreigners.[42]

Thus the 'protective' effect of agricultural tariffs, particularly corn duties, was not a simple return to traditional protection. The emphasis on 'taxing the foreigner' shifted the argument from the issue of *price* towards the issue of *supply*. This introduced an original, subtle and politically very convenient nuance into the economics of agricultural protection. Prices would remain stable but British producers would be able to capture a larger market share; this argument reconciled direct aid to agriculture with cheap or at least un-dear food. If it allowed Conservatives (as Liberals claimed) to appeal to farmers on the grounds that the proposed tariffs were 'protective', and to everyone else on the grounds that they were not, this was all to the good, but the apparent duplicity of the Conservative argument was sustained by the sophistication of tariff economics.

The Tariff Commission surveyed a broad range of farming opinion, providing Conservatives not only with a clear picture of farming attitudes to tariffs but also with the background for a much more ambitious agricultural policy. In 1904 the Agricultural Committee of the Tariff Commission circulated a questionnaire to over 500 agricultural organizations and individual farmers, asking for their views on Chamberlain's proposals and requesting suggestions as to any other steps which could be taken to assist agriculture. With regard to the proposed duties on corn and flour and the question of preference, the Tariff Commission reported that 'No question was more generally answered than this, proving the great interest which the subject has aroused among agriculturalists ... 483 answers were received on this question alone'.[43] Moreover the response was overwhelmingly positive, for the Commission noted that 'on the subject of Mr Chamberlain's wheat and flour proposals ... farmers of every kind, and in every part of the country, approve the principle . . . [and] objections are confined to details'.[44] There was also great enthusiasm for the proposed 5 per cent duty on meat and dairy produce, which produced 453 answers, 209 expressing approval 'almost without qualification' and only sixty-six stating that it would provide no benefit.[45] Interestingly, unanimity was shown about the non-protective (in the traditional sense) nature of the 2/- corn duty. It was accepted that duties on dairy produce, meat and flour would assist British producers and millers, but a low duty on cereals was expected to have minimal benefit.[46] The reason farmers expressed enthusiasm for the corn duty was in part because they saw it as the thin end of the wedge, but also because they assumed the revenue gained from such a duty would be used to reduce rates on agricultural land.[47] This was underlined by a member of the Tariff Commission's Agricultural Committee, a farmer himself, who stated that whilst these [Chamberlain's] proposals are a step in the right direction, and should be welcomed by all farmers, the immediate advantage will be very small, unless in the allocation of the taxes for the purpose of ridding the land of its many burdens.[48]

The idea that tariff revenues could be used to finance 'secondary' benefits for agriculture soon made the transition from backroom discussion to public pronouncement, with Joseph Chamberlain stating in July 1905 that revenues generated by tariffs would indeed be used to reduce rural rates. Demands for reduced rating levels had been a major feature of agricultural politics for fifty years after the repeal of the Corn Laws, but in the 1890s growing budgetary problems had seemed to rule out any further remission of 'the burdens on agriculture'.[49] However, as an untapped source of revenue, tariffs could fund rating reform.

Between 1906 and 1910 the indirect benefits of tariffs became increasingly important to the Conservative effort to attract agricultural support. The Conservatives wished to maximize their appeal in rural districts whilst minimizing their vulnerability to a 'dear food' cry. This was a difficult circle to square. In 1904 the Tariff Commission demonstrated there was a 'considerable section' of farmers who objected to colonial corn and meat products entering Britain duty free.[50] The Tariff Commission advocated a 1/- per quarter duty on colonial corn, but many Conservatives, even some of the most committed tariff reformers, were unhappy with this proposal. The result was confusion and often contradictory statements.[51] No 'official' pronouncement was made on this question until April 1910, when Balfour, in an open letter to George Courthope, declared that colonial corn would enter duty free. This was welcomed by the Party,[52] as helpful in limiting the scope of 'dear food' accusations. But even a minimal concession to these prejudices could but disappointment agriculturalists. The proposed duty on colonial corn was largely of symbolic value, but symbols, especially for the hard-pressed arable districts, were important. In these circumstances proposals such as tariff-funded rate reductions sugared the pill, convincing farmers that the Conservative party was still serious about giving assistance to its oldest allies.[53]

The Conservatives' desire to avoid 'food tax' opprobrium did not, however, lead them to abandon an ambitious agricultural policy or even protective tariffs. The proposals for a 2/- per quarter duty on foreign corn, the duties on meat, dairy produce and flour remained, in 1906 the Tariff Commission added fruit and vegetables to the tariff 'list', and between 1906 and 1910 there was no sign that these tariffs would would be relinquished. However, after 1906 it was generally acknowledged that in rural areas the Conservatives could not live on tariffs alone. Writing to Balfour in February 1907, W.A.S. Hewins pointed out that 'the

Agricultural Report of the Tariff Commission shows the great need of a non-fiscal agricultural policy ... and the genuine and widespread demand for such a policy throughout the rural districts'. He added 'no Party which has not such a policy, to which practical effect can be given, can hope to win or retain the county seats'.[54] It is difficult to ascertain if Balfour was persuaded, but Conservative proposals after 1906 indicated a more wide-ranging 'rural initiative'.

ii. 'Back to the land'

Conservative development of the broader aspects of agricultural policy only came to fruition after 1910, in the form of a comprehensive discussion document drawn up by Lord Milner, the formation and discussions of the Conservative agricultural policy committee, and the publication in 1913 of *A Unionist Agricultural Policy*.[55] This chapter will occasionally draw upon these, since many of the proposals presented in 1912–13 were refined versions of policies brought forward before 1910.[56] This was particularly true of the policy that was to be the linchpin of the party's alternative to the Liberal Land Campaign in 1913 – namely an argument for 'the building up of a substantial class of small freeholders'.[57] The Land Campaign undoubtedly raised the tempo of Conservative discussion on small holdings,[58] but the principles of Conservative policy were established and endorsed by the party before the January election of 1910.

In the period immediately after the opening of the tariff campaign, Conservative discussion of agricultural policy was concerned almost exclusively with the reaction of Britain's farmers. But another major Conservative worry in rural districts was the labouring vote. From 1900 to 1906 the only positive appeal to the labourers, made by Joseph Chamberlain, was indirect. In Chamberlain's Welbeck scheme agricultural labourers were to gain from tariff reform simply on the basis of their 'corporate' interest. However, the Conservative defeat in 1906 seemed to expose an important weakness in this strategy. The problem was summarized by Ailwyn Fellowes,[59] who told Balfour that the difficulty with tariff reform in the counties was that the farmers were 'out and out protectionists' whilst the labourers would 'not have their bread taxed'.[60] If this was the case, and St John Brodrick had told Austen Chamberlain soon after the election that 'the rural voters were quite shaken about food',[61] then any appeal to the labourers' corporate interests was bound to fail because the labourers appeared to be voting as consumers, not producers.

Small holdings reconciled the full tariff programme with an appeal to the agricultural labourer. 'Food taxes' and small holdings were linked in a kind of political-economic symbiosis. According to Alfred Milner small holdings needed 'a certain measure of protection ... not ... protection of the old type of high duties upon wheat, but rather of moderate duties on those other agricultural products in which small owners are likely in this country to find most profitable scope'.[62] The duties Milner evidently had in mind were those favoured by the Tariff Commission, on dairy produce, fruit and vegetables. Here Milner received support from two Conservative agricultural experts. For George Courthope the beauty of tariffs on a wide range of agricultural imports was that they would enable British agriculture to diversify into new types of crop production particularly suited to small producers.[63] Bevil Tollemache agreed. Noting 'a large and increasing demand for such commodities as fruit, vegetables, flowers, pig-meat, eggs, poultry and dairy produce',[64] Tollemache argued that this demand was being met by foreign imports, but that if enough small holders were created and given a modicum of protection 'there should be no difficulty in adequately supplying this demand at home'.[65]

'Food taxes' were crucial to the economic feasibility of small holdings, and small holdings were essential to the political feasibility of 'food taxes'. In early 1907 Jesse Collings informed the Westminster Branch of the Tariff Reform League that

> the agricultural labourer would never be persuaded to support Tariff Reform unless it was allied to a question which was its complement – a question in which the villagers had a close interest – that of some prospect of a fair number of them being restored to the land.[66]

That small holdings and tariffs were, in tandem, capable of attracting the labourers' vote was not based on the idea of small holdings as a simple *quid pro quo* for tariffs; rather it stemmed from the supposed transformation of the labourers' economic outlook which small ownership would bring about. 'If a constituency boasts small holdings', wrote the Conservative MP Oliver Locker-Lampson, 'the Tariff Reform case is naturally stronger. Because, in a sentence, a small holding converts a labourer from a consumer into a producer'.[67] Through small holdings the agricultural labourers were to be transformed into supporters of 'dear food', simply by reversing their position in relation to the means of production.

Small holdings were also important in their own right. Proposals to make them feasible and attractive included the creation of agricultural co-operatives on the Danish model. In 1904 the Tariff Commission's Agricultural Committee noted that co-operatives were of most interest to small farmers[68] – the growing interest in co-operatives was thus indicative of the increasing importance of small holdings to Conservative thinking. Although it was agreed that 'co-operation is no panacea for agriculture'[69] it was also accepted that even the relatively few co-operatives functioning in Britain had achieved signal benefits. Henry

Chaplin pointed out that their collective bargaining power had, for example, helped in 'compelling railway companies to come to proper arrangements'.[70] Collective buying and selling of plant, fertilizer and produce was to bring small farmers economies of scale in purchasing and distribution which they could not realize as individual economic units. In an age when large-scale enterprise was regarded as the dominant mode of organization, co-operatives were described as a means of enabling small farmers 'to fight scientific competition with its own implements'.[71]

That few co-operatives had emerged in Britain and that they had been relatively unsuccessful, in contrast to the experience of Germany, Denmark and other nations, was attributed in part to divisions within British agriculture, but it was also blamed on a lack of support from the State and British financial institutions. According to many Conservative agricultural spokesmen, the most pressing need of an agricultural co-operative was *credit* 'to enable them to develop the land and tide over bad times'.[72] Sir Gilbert Parker argued that the concentration of Britain's banking system had robbed the localities of sympathetic, local institutions which could provide the relatively small, but critical amounts of capital necessary to stabilize co-operatives. Local credit banks, State sponsored and funded if need be, were to provide capital for agricultural co-operation.[73] Besides financial assistance, the 'Unauthorized Programme' of 1908 argued for demonstration farms to allow 'the dissemination of technical information' on the most up-to-date farming methods.[74] In addition it was suggested that rural schools should have agricultural economics and rural life added to their curricula, so that 'children in rural elementary schools should have their minds directed to rural subjects',[75] and that specially-trained staff provided by a new range of training colleges should offer instruction in these subjects at elementary, secondary and adult level. In short, the State was to provide a range of supporting services to buttress co-operative agricultural production and generally raise the morale and profile of British agriculture.

Lastly, small holdings were to be made attractive by the provision of land and mortgages 'for the creation of occupying ownerships ... at a low rate of interest'.[76] The 'Unauthorized Programme' noted that 'the large number of applications which have been made under the [Liberal] Small Holdings Act of 1907 affords welcome evidence that the deplorable decrease of the rural population is not due to a lack of men willing, if able, to make a home on the land'.[77] The question was how to satisfy this demand and turn it to Conservative purposes. Here the Conservatives drew on the Irish example and looked to the Wyndham Act as a model. Under the Wyndham Act the State had effectively made Irish landlords and tenants an offer that neither could refuse: the State purchased holdings from the landlords and converted this outlay into long-term, low-interest mortgages for the tenantry.[78] By applying the same principles in the rest of Britain, the demand for small holdings could, so it was argued, be rendered fully effective.[79]

There were, however, problems in translating the Irish experience to the rest of Britain. As George Wyndham himself pointed out, there had been 'no market – as a whole – for Irish land except to the tenants'; in England there was 'a general market – sometimes a 'fancy' market'.[80] The stable land market in Ireland had made it relatively easy to establish purchase prices agreeable to vendors and purchasers. In the rest of Britain the land market fluctuated from region to region, making 'fair' purchase prices a complex problem. The solution which Milner and the Conservative Agricultural Policy Committee produced was for the Board of Agriculture to establish local evaluation committees to act in co-operation with Parish and County Councils.[81] Using local knowledge, but under central super-vision, these committees could establish binding 'fair' prices, thus preventing either buyers and sellers from being deterred from entering the market.

Conversion of tenant farmers into owners was one thing, but the argument for small holdings was also based on the premise that it was necessary to encourage people to settle on or return to the land. This entailed, as Sir Gilbert Parker, Jesse Collings and Lord Milner all recognized, 'the purchase of properties by the State with a view to their sub-division and re-sale to a number of small owners'.[82] The State would be taking a far more active role in the land market than in Ireland, although the Irish example still held in terms of the provision of generous mortgages. In effect the State was to act as a central land agent with the express purpose of making small holdings available not only for farmers and labourers already working the land but also for the re-migration of urban dwellers.

The effort, and the estimated cost of such a scheme,[83] indicated the Conservatives' growing desire to identify themselves as a party of land reform. This broadening of agricultural policy was driven by a more general effort to broaden the electoral appeal of Conservatism after 1906. A rural policy was an essential complement to the tariff and social reforming programme adopted by the party between 1906 and 1910. Developments on the other side of British politics also help to account for the Conservatives' commitment to bringing people back to the land. After 1906 the Liberals, as anxious to retain as the Conservatives were to capture the county constituencies, focused a great deal of attention on the 'land question'. In 1907 the Liberal government introduced its own small holdings and allotments legislation, thereby threatening to entrench their hold on the agricultural labourers' vote. Even more important, the long-standing Radical/Socialist critique of the 'land monopoly' began to acquire a legislative cutting edge as the People's Budget singled out landed wealth for special attention. In these circumstances the attraction

THE DEFENCE OF BRITISH AGRICULTURE

of a counter-initiative was very great, with *The Outlook* summing up the feelings of many Conservatives when it noted that

> it is a political necessity to increase the numbers of men having property in land, or at any rate some interest in land other than that of mere wage earners . . . [because] When the land is in the hands of but few it is powerless to defend itself against the attacks of fantastic and predatory doctrines.[84]

In fact by the autumn of 1910 even Walter Long, who was always wary of positive initiatives, was telling Balfour that 'Even with all its risks I personally am a convert to the system of small ownership, for one reason above all others. I believe it is the only way in which we can resist the march of Socialism'.[85] As property came under threat, the notion of heading off the Radical/Socialist challenge through wider dissemination of property was increasingly accepted in the Conservative ranks.

CONCLUDING REMARKS

The prominence accorded to agriculture and rural life in the debates of the tariff campaign and the discussions of the Edwardian Conservative party more generally can be viewed in a number of ways. On the one hand it could be regarded as one last kick by a party in the throes of casting off its old identity as the party of the land. Equally, the Conservative (and Liberal) emphasis on land could be seen as a 'romantic residue',[86] part of a 'rural myth' which regarded country life and values as an antidote to the social and moral problems associated with an increasingly urban society. There is evidence for both views. Both in and outside the Conservative party there were individuals and groups associated with agriculture who saw the debate begun by the tariff campaign as the last chance to turn the clock back to 1846. The fact that Henry Chaplin, whose manner and politics were sometimes reminiscent of the 'booby squires' of old, helped to shape Conservative rural policy appears to confirm atavism at work. Likewise the 'rural myth' was active. Social phenomena and cultural icons as diverse as the Garden City movement, naturism, the cults of Arthurian chivalry and 'Constable country', and George Bernard Shaw (amongst others) tramping through the countryside in Jaeger clothes were all manifestations of a heterogeneous but pervasive belief in the superiority of rural life. But these interpretations only partially explain Conservative interest in rural policy.

The problem with seeing Conservative rural policy as some kind of throwback is that it misconstrues the Edwardian political agenda and ignores some important implications of the evolution of Conservative ideas about British agriculture. It is essential to banish the notion that for Edwardian politicians to think about agriculture and the land was somehow 'backward looking'. It is true that many of the great issues raised in Edwardian political debate, such as social reform and welfare, the rise of Labour, progressive taxation and Britain's industrial performance and competitiveness, are issues which have come to be regarded as the stuff of modern politics, whilst the land and agriculture have been relegated to a separate and largely peripheral sphere.[87] But for Edwardian politicians the land was neither separate nor peripheral – it was regarded as intrinsic to all the great issues of the day. For Progressives the attack on the 'land monopoly', through the People's Budget, the taxation of land values and site-value rating, was one of the most important areas of common ground between Radicalism and Socialism, and provided a significant policy bond between the Liberal and Labour parties. In essence, the land question was central to both the theory and practice of the New Liberalism, providing political, electoral and, it was argued, fiscal support for the Liberal government's Collectivist initiatives. Likewise, the Conservatives' land policy was not simply a counter to Progressive arguments for land reform, but an integral part of a structure designed to allow Conservatives to meet the broad political-economic issues of the day with a positive programme. For both Progessives and Conservatives, therefore, the land question and the role of the agricultural sector were not tangential, but seen to intersect 'modern' issues at every point.

On the structure of British agriculture itself Conservative thinking was definitely shaped by contemporary developments and not by the remembrance of things past. In addition to the basic argument for revitalizing British agriculture, Conservative policy demonstrated a further consistent pattern, an increasing emphasis on expanding the number of small farmers. This carried important implications. In 1904 J.L. Green, commenting on Chamberlain's proposals for a 2/- duty on corn and 5 per cent *ad valorem* on meat and dairy produce, observed that

> [These] proposals are intended, so far as corn-growing is concerned, to give a preference to the Colonies over the foreigner in our markets. It is clearly not intended, or likely, that corn-growing . . . in Great Britain, will receive any particular impetus by their adoption. We agree with the best formed agricultural opinion that the future of British farming will be mainly in a stock-raising and dairying direction, accompanied by a large increase in small holdings for the[ir] production.[88]

The Conservatives' increasing emphasis on small holdings and their desire to play down the domestic impact of the corn duties and play up the importance of other agricultural tariffs/policies were closely related. The Conservative party, through the framework of the tariff campaign, was, in effect, attempting to adjust to changes in the structure of the

British agricultural market. Responding to pressure from foreign competition, this had shifted away from arable farming to mixed and dairy production. But although the process of change was under way and understood, it was neither complete nor accepted. The debate over free colonial corn, and the importance attached to the 2/- corn duty, indicated how arable farmers – traditionally the most loyal sector of Conservative support – still influenced Conservative thinking.[89] The Conservative debate over agricultural policy was, therefore, not only the product of an attempt to address the question of a rural–urban balance, but also an attempt to weigh and reconcile different interests within the agricultural sector. By the early twentieth century it had become clear as never before that British agriculture was not simply a tripartite structure consisting of landlords, farmers and labourers, but that there were regional and product differences to be taken into account as well. The political market had altered too. The enfranchisement of agricultural labourers, and their mobilization in and after 1906, coupled with the emergence of farming organizations less willing to accept the Conservative party as 'the farmers' friend', redrew the map of rural politics. The changing and complex political economy of the Edwardian Conservative party's debate on agricultural policy thus reflected the changing and increasingly complex structure it was supposed to address. The Conservative party's interest in agricultural policy, far from being an attempt to turn the clock back, was an effort to confront immediate problems.

The structure of British agriculture envisaged in the Conservative debate on rural policy was as far removed from political-economic atavism as one could imagine. Equally the method of creating that structure was wholly in keeping with the innovative flavour of Edwardian political controversy. Of particular importance here was the role assigned to the State. In 1906 the Tariff Commission remarked that 'many witnesses ... have drawn attention to the great advantages which have followed [for] agriculture in foreign countries through the organization on a great scale of State departments with extensive powers'.[90] By 1910 the Conservative party had adopted a policy which implied bringing Britain into line with other nations in this area. Agricultural tariffs, and the range of supporting services necessary to support the Conservatives' small holdings schemes, would have entailed extensive research, a large administrative machine, and a central authority endowed with quite wide-ranging powers and a large budget. Small wonder that by 1913 Lord Milner was telling Bonar Law 'I like the idea of a big Land Department ... [with] all the powers of interference, or imprint of Govt., which it is thought desirable to create';[91] the Conservatives' plans would not have been feasible without such a Department. This emphasis on the role of the State was in keeping with both the Conservative analysis of what was wrong with British agriculture and the underlying philosophy of the tariff campaign. According to Christopher Turnor the decline of British agriculture was testimony to the fact that 'generation after generation of politicians ... in their belief in the soundness of Manchester doctrines were led to neglect agriculture'.[92] As a result of this 'lack of interest by the State'[93] a situation was seen to have arisen in which a whole section of British economic and social life had been placed under conditions of great hardship, causing dislocation and discontent in every echelon of rural society. Beginning with Chamberlain's Glasgow proposals, and continuing through the work of the Tariff Commission and the evolution of the Conservatives' small holdings policy, the tariff campaign and the broader policy debates which it prompted, held out the promise of reversing agricultural decline and defusing rural discontent across the board. This was to be achieved by the State abandoning its non-interventionist position and acting for 'the improvement of agriculture as an industry ... [and] giving assistance and encouragement to all those engaged in it'.[94]

9

THE DEFENCE OF BRITISH INDUSTRY

once we were in isolated supremacy over the manufacturing interests of the world. Who will be bold enough to say now that we are first among equals in manufacturing power? In many of the greatest industries ... we are not even second among equals. In some respects we have to rejoice that we are still third among these industrial competitors.

(A.J. Balfour at Birmingham, September 1910)

tariff rates are frequently fixed less out of regard for the technical conditions of production which prevail in particular branches of production, than as the outcome of a political struggle for power among various industrial groups.

(Rudolf Hilferding, *Finance Capital*)

Speaking at Greenock in October 1903 Joseph Chamberlain presented his audience with a depressing list of ailing British industries – 'sugar has gone' , he declared, 'silk has gone; iron is threatened; wool is threatened; cotton will go'.[1] Chamberlain was not the first person to play Cassandra over British industry – nor was he to be the last. Throughout the twentieth century, concern over Britain's apparent economic decline, and the problems of the manufacturing sector in particular, has been arguably *the* central theme of British political debate. But although it drew upon arguments from the economic debates of the 1880s and 1890s it was the tariff campaign which first brought the question of industrial decline to the heart of British politics.

A PORTRAIT OF DECLINE

That the British manufacturing sector was suffering serious difficulties was intrinsic to the rationale of tariffs, and Chamberlain's catalogue of decaying or dying industries was reproduced by many tariff reform spokesmen and publications. However, the task of providing the Conservative party, and through them the public, with the fullest picture of Britain's industrial problems lay with the Tariff Commission.[2] Its evidence and reports presented a gloomy picture of a number of Britain's key industries. Its 1904 *Report on the Iron and Steel Trades* noted that

> At the end of the [eighteen] seventies the total amount of pig iron produced in the United Kingdom was . . . as much as the total of the five iron-producing countries next in importance, and no less than 45 per cent of the total production of the world.

However, the Commission provided figures to show that

> Early in the nineties, the United Kingdom lost the pre-eminence it had enjoyed for more than 100 years, and the United States took the first place. Since then the United Kingdom has been overtaken by Germany.[3]

The same problem had overtaken the steel sector,[4] which was also seen to be suffering from increased import penetration.

With regard to Britain's textile industries the Tariff Commission found cause for concern. It distinguished between the woollen trade, which was suffering, and the cotton trade, which was relatively prosperous. However, optimism was qualified, in that Britain's consumption of raw cotton, a key indicator of output growth, had fallen below that of rival nations, and that British exports of cotton goods had become over-dependent on the Indian market.[5] Overall the Commission concluded that the level of output and world market share enjoyed by Britain's textile industries had, as with iron and steel, fallen from first to third place in an international league table. Thus even the flagship sector of Britain's industrial revolution was experiencing major problems. Further reports by the Commission, on engineering, pottery, glass and confectionery, produced similar gloomy conclusions.

The Tariff Commission sought to establish that the 'decline' of British industry was largely a *relative* slippage in relation to the achievements of rival nations in terms of output and world market share. The Commission and other tariff experts attributed this relative decline to a fall in the level of British manufactured exports. Writing in 1904 the economist R.H.I. Palgrave noted that 'In England it will be observed that within twenty years, from 1880–1899, the exports of manufactured goods dropped three per cent.'[6] A year later Palgrave claimed that between 1890 and 1902 the value of 'exports of "articles wholly or mainly manufactured" . . . diminished from about 226 millions to 222 millions'.[7] A relative fall off in manufactured exports was largely inevitable 'due to the industrialization of other countries . . . in regard to those branches of production in which we once stood almost alone'.[8] But an absolute decline implied a greater problem, raising concern that Britain was losing its 'historic predominance as a country manufacturing for export'.[9]

The root of British industry's export problem was discerned through a close examination of Britain's trade figures. 'In the case of France', wrote R.H.I. Palgrave, 'the value of our exports has ... diminished almost four per cent [in the period 1890–1902]. In the case of Germany, there was likewise a diminution of eleven per cent'.[10] Palgrave's figures were supported by the Tariff Commission, and by other tariff analysts, with the common conclusion being that the fall in the value of manufactured exports was because Britain's traditional markets in Europe and the USA had greatly reduced the volume of their imports from Britain.[11] In part this was explained by import substitution, but it was also seen as 'the result of the excessively high import duties ... on our goods'.[12] The Tariff Commission concluded that British manufactured exports were suffering because the revival of protectionism had 'deprived us of markets we have formerly enjoyed, first by shutting out our goods from the countries which have imposed [tariffs], and, secondly, by stimulating the development of home manufactures in the countries concerned'.[13]

What made the loss of Continental and US markets through tariffs especially damaging was that it was not seen to be a temporary problem brought about by the desire of these countries to protect 'infant industries'. The behaviour of Britain's rivals in continually adding to their tariff barriers indicated to tariff experts that those nations were pursuing a long-term policy to purge all competing manufactures from their domestic markets. In a lecture to the Compatriots' Club in March 1905 the Secretary of the Tariff Commission, W.A.S. Hewins, outlined the ongoing nature of the protectionist revival when he described the new German duties on worsted and woollen goods: 'I do not think the increase in the duties in the class I am considering is excessive, but when you have a duty which already is nearly prohibitive, a very slight increase kept on for a series of years will turn the scale and make it prohibitive'.[14] Hewins argued that British engineering would suffer as well, because 'some of the duties to be levied upon machinery imported into Germany are now so drastic that I do not at present see how the trade in these branches can be continued at all'.[15]

Besides the closing of overseas markets by tariffs, British industry was reckoned to be facing severe import penetration. The Tariff Commission confirmed the 'Made in Germany' scares of the late nineteenth century with regard to the increasing volume of manufactured imports. It noted that 'home consumption [of pig iron] has risen between 1890 and 1902 by no less than two million tons, an increase of 70 per cent ... Our imports during the same time increased by 200 per cent', the conclusion being that 'foreign manufactures have gained far more than British manufacturers from the increase of the British home market'.[16] The engineering sector was also thought to be suffering, with the Commission reporting that 'speaking generally it may be said that foreign competition in engineering products in the United Kingdom is increasing both in area and severity',[17] and the same comment was passed on the woollen trade.[18] In effect the Tariff Commission's prognosis was that British manufacturers faced an assault which was hitting them at home and abroad.

The success enjoyed by foreign producers in penetrating the British market was attributed in part to 'the British policy of free imports', but great emphasis was also placed on 'the [industrial] organization of foreign countries'.[19] Britain's unilateral free trade policy, so it was argued, presented competitors with an open door to the British market. However, it was also contended that Britain's rivals were able to exploit this to an unusual degree, because their forms of industrial organization made it impossible for British manufacturers to compete on equal terms.

The first advantage of foreign industrialists was that their tariff systems had ensured that trusts and cartels had emerged as the dominant industrial structure in their countries – like the German economist Joseph Havermeyer the Tariff Commission believed that 'The Tariff is the mother of trusts'. The advantages of industrial combination were that

> syndicates . . . have diminished the risk to capital, diminished the expenses on management and cost of production, given stability to prices, and increased the profits. Higher organization of industry gives economy and efficiency. A nation whose principal branch of industry is brought to a state of high efficiency by such combination, can compete much better in the markets of the world than the other nations who have not made such progress.[20]

This emphasis on the superior efficiency of 'trusts' was a constant theme in Tariff Commission discussions: referred to most frequently in relation to coal mining and the iron and steel industries,[21] the benefits of industrial combination were regarded as generally applicable.[22]

Tariffs were thought to provide foreign industrialists with a second competitive advantage – the tactic of 'dumping'. Dumping was defined by *The Tariff Dictionary* as 'the sale by foreigners in this country of surplus goods at prices which do not afford a reasonable profit'.[23] The Tariff Commission's *Report on the Iron and Steel Trades* stated that foreign competitors had been dumping cheap iron and steel on the British market as early as the 1890s and that the process was still going on: 'A firm employing 1500 hands, writing in February [1904]', the Commission noted, 'states that the current price of basic pig iron in Germany was 58 Marks per ton. The lowest cost at which this could be converted into steel joists could not be less than 31 M per ton. Yet those German joists, costing no less than 89 M, were being offered . . . at 82.5 M'.[24] Similarly, the Commission reported with regard to the woollen trade that 'importations take place from time to time below British cost, and in a certain proportion of cases it is said that these goods are sold below their cost of production in the country of origin'.[25] It was conceded that dumping was not that widespread in the wool trade,[26] but the Commission was unequivocal that in the engineering sector there were 'many instances of dumping'.[27]

By using 'every means in their power to exclude foreign competition'[28] the protectionist nations, it was felt, were able to secure two requirements for a successful dumping campaign. First of all, by preventing import penetration, Britain's competitors gave their industrialists a guaranteed home market and a guaranteed price level within that market. This, it was contended, gave foreign manufacturers a stable profit margin even before they entered the international markets. The large and secure home market produced by protection allowed foreign manufacturers to lower their costs. 'All manufacturers', the Tariff Commission noted, 'lay the greatest stress upon the importance of the continuous running of the works and a large output as a means of securing the most economical cost';[29] protectionism secured this for Britain's competitors. 'With this system, for securing maximum output and continuous running', the Tariff Commission pointed out, 'foreign countries can produce at lowest cost, keep up their prices at home, and, after supplying the home market, dump their surplus on the British home market at any price irrespective of cost'.[30]

To the Tariff Commission, dumping dealt two blows to British manufacturers. The price of dumped goods was too low for British industry to compete, and this threatened British trade both in the domestic market and in neutral markets not yet closed by tariffs. The Tariff Commission further argued that 'Increasing foreign importations have made it impossible . . . to secure large and continuous orders and have thus increased the cost of production and lessened profits'.[31] In other words, it was reckoned that rival nations 'by . . . attacking our home market . . . have diminished the competitive power of British manufacturers to push their goods in neutral markets'.[32] Dumping damaged British industry by subjecting it to 'unfair' competition, but the insecurity of trade which dumping created prevented British industrialists from developing the same economies of scale available in the protectionist, dumping nations. The result, so it was argued, was that British industry, through no fault of its own, was trapped in a vicious cycle of ever-decreasing competitiveness.

The deleterious effects of dumping were held to have other less obvious but equally harmful long-term consequences for British industry. In 1903 J.L. Garvin argued that 'the key of competitive power in the modern age is the encouragement of capital',[33] a view which was supported by William Cunningham who remarked that the late nineteenth and early twentieth century was 'an age when capital has become the dominating influence in production'.[34] Britain, according to Garvin, should have enjoyed an immense advantage as a result of the reserves of capital it had accumulated in the period of its unchallenged industrial supremacy. However, the insecurity of British industry in the face of closing markets and dumped goods had prevented Britain from taking full advantage of its financial resources, because uncompetitive industries were not attractive to investors. In Garvin's words 'A dumping ground for goods' was 'a slumping ground for capital', because

> making one country the dumping ground for the surplus of all the rest and exposing the home manufacturer to the attack of foreign rivals, who are all protected by their tariffs from . . . counter operations . . . must necessarily mean the minimum of security for capital and the minimum of inducement [to invest].[35]

The Tariff Commission's investigations confirmed this: the *Report on the Textile Trades* noted that in the woollen industry 'the home trade . . . has tended to become more and more insecure during recent years. [And] That state of insecurity makes it more and more difficult to get new capital into the trade, to build new mills, or to maintain in the proper stage of efficiency those that already exist'.[36]

That British industry 'exposed to competition with subsidized rivals'[37] could not attract vital capital investment was considered a serious enough problem, but another aspect was regarded as equally disturbing. Writing to W.J. Ashley in 1904 Joseph Chamberlain stated that, through the tariff campaign, he wished to make clear 'the evil results of the transfer of capital in the shape of investments in foreign countries'.[38] British investors not only ignored British industry, but also invested in the industries of rival nations. The 'evil results' of this were outlined by George Wyndham, who told his father in November 1908 that

> I have studied 'Invisible' Exports and capital investment abroad for some time . . . To account for [the] excess of Imports over Exports they [the Board of Trade] said in the Blue Book for 1903 (a) some pay the freights of our ships, (b) others to the tune of £90,000,000 are interest on capital invested abroad. Schooling in the British trade year book has proved [the] original emphasis that our shipping does not earn the amount credited to it. I think it far more likely that more – much more – than £90,000,000 is interest on capital invested abroad coming back in the shape of articles.[39]

With this statement Wyndham articulated the tariff argument which linked foreign protectionism, dumping, British overseas investment and the poor shape of British industry. That capital was 'pouring out of this country',[40] even before the People's Budget, was because it went to 'take refuge behind tariff walls'.[41] Foreign manufacturers, secure behind their protective tariffs, could offer the assured returns which British industry, in its state of 'chronic insecurity',[42] was unable to guarantee. Thus the tariff argument established yet another vicious cycle destructive of British industry.

Tariff reform analysis of British industrial 'decline' indicated a complex political economy. The importance it attached to trusts and cartels places the tariff argument firmly in the context of contemporary debate about the evolution of modern capitalism. Trusts and cartels were admired, but also feared, across the political spectrum in Britain and many other nations. In the United States the 'trust question' dominated the political scene in the early twentieth century, with some, like Herbert Croly and Theodore Roosevelt, viewing trusts as progressive and potentially bene- ficial forces, and others, such as Louis Brandeis, regarding them as destructive of the virtuous, competitive individualism which supposedly lay at the heart of American values.[43] In Europe Socialist thinkers, most notably Rudolf Hilferding, Rosa Luxemburg and Lenin, took this devel- opment as a sign that capitalism was moving into its terminal 'monopoly' phase. In Germany Liberals, like Max Weber, and Conservatives, like Gustav Schmoller, were equally impressed by the process of cartelization, but regarded it as a sign of capitalism having assumed a more rational and efficient form. In Britain the Fabians were keenly interested in trusts,[44] and viewed the emergence of large-scale capitalism as a welcome abolition of anarchic, individualist enterprise and a prelude to State management of the economy. By way of contrast some free traders, both Liberal and Conservative, argued that one good reason for opposing tariffs was to prevent the emergence of these structures in Britain, with Margaret Hirst noting that 'a Trust has never been formed in an industry exposed to the competition of foreign goods of similar quality'.[45] Whether these varied groups and individuals approved of or were horrified by trusts, they were all agreed that they represented a new, increasingly dominant and highly effective form of economic organization.

The tariff campaign thus found itself in broad agreement with a wide range of contemporary opinion as to the importance of trusts, and tariff reformers could also find support, sometimes from the most unikely sources, for their view as to the significance of dumping. In his book *Finance Capital* the Austrian Marxist Rudolf Hilferding argued that late nineteenth-century protectionism had seen 'a change in the function of the tariff from an "educational" tariff to a protective tariff for cartels'.[46] According to Hilferding, tariff policies in the early part of the century had been designed 'to guard ... developing domestic industry against the danger of being stifled or destroyed by overwhelming competition from a well-developed foreign industry'.[47] However, 'in the age of capitalist monopolies' things were different, and it was 'the most powerful indus- tries, with a high export potential, whose competitiveness on the world market is beyond doubt' which enjoyed tariff protection.[48] The reason for this, Hilferding argued, was that tariff protection allowed a cartel 'to sell

229

below its production price, because it has obtained an extra profit, determined by the level of the protective tariff, from its sales on the domestic market . . . [and] is . . . able to use a part of this extra profit to expand its sales abroad by underselling its competitors'.[49] In Hilferding's view tariffs 'from being a means of defence against the conquest of the domestic market by foreign industries' had become 'a means for the conquest of foreign markets by domestic industry' and thus 'what was once a defensive weapon of the weak [had] become an offensive weapon in the hands of the powerful'.[50] Hilferding's analysis could have been penned by a member of the Tariff Commission. Likewise, evidence emerged from the United States which indicated that below-cost selling was a common practice amongst highly capitalized firms, not always because they wished to undersell competitors but because they were desperate to ensure continuous running to amortize their capital and secure enough current revenue to cover their fixed costs.[51] In short, the link which the tariff campaign discerned between dumping, trusts and tariffs was widely acknowledged as intrinsic to the new world of corporate enterprise.

When tariff reform is viewed in the light of this larger debate, it cannot be seen simply as a platform for moaning industrialists. Rather it must be seen as an attempt to grapple with the trust question, to clarify its significance for British industry and, ultimately, to persuade British industrial interests to support a policy which, by implication at least, would enable them to counter the challenge of corporate competition through imitation. Recent economic history has concluded that one of the major problems facing British industry in the late nineteenth and early twentieth century was that its individualistic structure rendered it highly vulnerable to competition from the corporate giants of the United States and Germany.[52] On these grounds alone there is a plausible case for taking tariff reform economics more seriously than is the wont of most economists,[53] and in this sense the industrial aspect of the tariff campaign could be seen as yet another 'idea ahead of its time', a category of thinking suspiciously well-known to historians of the debate on British decline. However, a more prosaic, but more realistic appraisal of the industrial side of the tariff argument is that it was shaped by the very particular historical problem of constructing a tariff-based Conservative appeal to Britain's industrial constituency.

THE SPLINTERED AUDIENCE

In terms of Conservative politics the industrial aspect of the tariff campaign posed a straightforward question. Was it possible to harness late nineteenth and early twentieth-century rumblings against liberal political economy and secure Conservative appeal in Britain's industrial heartlands? To do so was one of Chamberlain's main aims. In the first major speech of the tariff campaign proper[54] Chamberlain broadened the tariff debate to include a proposal for a 10 per cent *ad valorem* duty on imported manufactured goods, and then delivered this protectionist message to some of Britain's major industrial centres. However, it was also clear from the beginning that uniting British business behind a protectionist crusade was going to be difficult. Divisions of opinion between different sectors of the economy and indeed between and *within* different branches of British manufacturing industry had hamstrung earlier efforts to break with free trade or any other aspect of Britain's liberal economic stance. Similar problems explain the advent of the Tariff Commission.

The personnel assembled in the autumn of 1903 to act as members of the Tariff Commission gave the project a promising start. A wide range of industries was represented on the Commission and, as the most authoritative history of the Commission's work has pointed out, this immediately gave and gives the lie to any suggestion that the Commission and the wider tariff debate were simply reflecting the interests of a narrow group of trades unique in experiencing the blast of foreign competition.[55] But hopes of finding a consensus on tariff reform amongst industrialists were dashed during the Commission's investigations. From December 1903 until the outbreak of the Great War it gathered information both from questionnaires circulated to an impressive range of industrial concerns, and from witnesses questioned by specialist committees.[56] But there were huge problems in formulating a tariff policy with *general* appeal. The cotton industry, for example, refused almost en bloc to co-operate with the Commission's enquiries. In January 1904 Charles Eckersley, a yarn spinner and a member of the Commission, bemoaned the fact that 'When I agreed to become a member, I had no idea that I should be the only representative of the cotton spinning interest',[57] although some company was found for him. Even the Commission's written enquiries were ignored – out of 942 cotton firms which received questionnaires on imperial preference only forty-four replied.[58] In 1905 the Commission's Textile Committee noted, and this was a central conclusion of their *Report*, that the closure of foreign markets by tariffs had affected several branches of the industry, and hence retaliatory tariffs could have some appeal in cotton districts.[59] In early March 1909 W.A.S. Hewins received a plea from E.A. Bagley, the Secretary of the Manchester Tariff Reform league, asking for help to put the tariff reform case to the cotton industry.[60] Later that month Hewins himself lectured 300 Manchester businessmen on the subject of 'Fiscal Reform in Relation to Cotton', and emphasized the damage inflicted by German and US tariff policy and the probable benefits of retaliation.[61] Hewins need not have bothered, for the appeal of retaliation in Lancashire seems to have been limited to a few manufacturers (such as Eckersley), whilst the bulk of

231

producers and more especially the traders and merchants remained loyal to free trade.[62] Furthermore, the cotton districts were openly hostile to protection and imperial preference. The former offered them nothing as there was little or no import penetration by foreign cotton producers; the latter raised 'the greatest fear . . . the cotton industry faced in tariff reform . . . a modification of the Indian tariff'.[63] For the tariff campaign the hostility of the cotton industry seemed insurmountable.

The tariff campaign did not enjoy plain sailing with Britain's other major industries. For example, a leading figure from the woollen industry, W.H. Mitchell, was a founder member of the Tariff Commission. Mitchell was a Bradford mill owner, a senior vice-president of the Bradford Chamber of Commerce and a member of the Executive Council of the UK Chambers of Commerce. In his evidence to the Tariff Commission he argued that 'the history of the trade of Bradford is a record of a long fight against hostile tariffs for the last 25 years', and he called for protective and retaliatory tariffs in order to check imports and re-open overseas markets.[64] However, as Mitchell told Hewins, his position was not representative. In fact, curiously enough, Mitchell pointed out that his firm, chiefly concerned with spinning yarns, had suffered less from tariffs and foreign competition than those producing finished cloths. This could have implied that finished cloth manufacturers were even more likely to support tariffs than Mitchell, and some did, but it also indicated that experiences within the wool industry were diverse enough to encourage differing viewpoints on the tariff question. This last point was confirmed by A.F. Firth, a Bradford carpet manufacturer, who, in returning a Tariff Commission questionnaire to Mitchell, asked that his views on tariffs be kept confidential because 'my father and brother [partners in the family business] take a different view of the fiscal question from what I do'.[65]

The same problem of divided opinion was evident in a sector generally reckoned to be closely associated with the tariff campaign, the iron and steel industry. Again prominent members of the industry, such as Colonel Allen of Bessemers and the Ebbw Vale Steel Company, and Sir Alfred Hickman, president of the British Iron Trade Association, were active members of the Tariff Commission, whilst Sheffield had been one of the most important centres of tariff agitation since the late 1880s. Yet, in spite of the significant degree of support by prominent individuals and firms, the industry was by no means unanimous in its support for tariffs. In 1911, with the Tariff Commission short of funds, an appeal was made to those iron and steel firms employing over 1,000 hands who had provided information for the Commission's enquiries. However, of the six firms approached, three, the North-Eastern Steel Company, Sheepridge, and Dorman Long, did not send contributions on the grounds that 'the Board is divided in opinion'.[66]

The lukewarm response of the iron and steel industry may have been due to disillusion at the apparent failure of tariff reform at the 1910 elections, but this seems unlikely. Divisions of opinion on tariffs not only within sectors of industry but also within individual firms were common before 1910, and were still in evidence in the inter-war years.[67] The divergent and often conflicting views which the Tariff Commission gleaned from British industry made the formulation of a 'scientific tariff' a nightmare: there were enough problems in accurately classifying firms, let alone the class of goods to be subjected to tariffs – one industrialist's 'unfair competition' could be another's cheap input.[68] The Tariff Commission's major discovery was that there was no industrial consensus, and certainly no agreement on a specific tariff policy.

The absence of a tariff consensus in British industry helps to explain some crucial aspects of the tariff campaign. In the first place the campaign, in spite of the Tariff Commission's efforts, did not appeal to industry on the basis of a detailed, 'scientific tariff'. In the end, the proposed industrial tariff was the 10 per cent all round *ad valorem* tariff on manufactured goods first advocated by Chamberlain in October 1903. There were some embellishments, for example a 15 per cent tariff was suggested for certain iron and steel imports,[69] but the basic 10 per cent was presented as adequate for the purposes of both protection and retaliation. By sticking to this broad proposal the tariff campaign effectively conceded that the complexities of a scientific tariff were too difficult to unravel.

More important, however, the lack of agreement within industry over tariffs ensured that the industrial aspect of the tariff campaign progressed not as the product of 'interest group' politics, that is as a passive receiver and transmitter of the views of pressure groups. Diversity of opinion amongst British industrialists meant that it was impossible for the tariff campaign simply to broadcast *the* industrial interest, for there was no coherent view to broadcast. The tariff campaign represented an attempt to *construct* rather than reflect a concept and language of the industrial interest.

CONSTRUCTING AN INDUSTRIAL IDENTITY

There were two central features in the tariff campaign's construction of a general industrial interest. The first was economic nationalism, the second was an ideology of 'producerism'. Economic nationalism was central to the tariff campaign's description of British industrial decline. Damage inflicted by the State-aided foreign industry was seen as evidence that the world had entered 'a period in which the nations of the world have begun to set themselves to maintain their places in the world by the national organization of industry'.[70] The essential argument was that British industrialists were faced by unified, national industrial blocs and were defenceless in 'a commercial war being hotly waged against us'.[71] The implication, and this was reinforced by the use of military metaphors,[72] was that British industry also needed to develop national policies, such as tariff protection and retaliation, in order to defend *itself* rather than remaining defenceless as a multiplicity of individual selves. Joseph Chamberlain's warning at Greenock that 'cotton *will go*' was of course partly apologetic, in that the relative prosperity of the cotton industry was an embarrassment for a campaign predicated on assumptions of industrial decline. But, following as it did a lament for industries already 'going', it was also a statement that no industry could or should regard itself as an island. The decline of one industry, the lost market of another, or the damage inflicted by dumping to another, all the result of nationally-organized foreign competition, were, according to the tariff campaign, an indication that all British industries were threatened by a common foe. The tariff campaign was thus a plea as much as a policy, a plea that the differing opinions and interests of individual industries be subsumed by a common struggle against the threat of an external 'other' in the shape of foreign industry.

The link between economic and industrial nationalism and tariffs was further emphasized by the tariff reform critique of free trade 'cosmopolitanism'. Writing in 1904 Leo Maxse stated that a fatal flaw of free trade thinking was that Cobden 'in his cosmopolitan enthusiasm thought that the principle of the division of labour had international as well as national application'.[73] In Cobden's time an international division of labour had meant Britain supplying the bulk of the world's manufactured goods whilst the world supplied Britain with food and raw materials. However, this state of affairs had proved unacceptable to nations seeking economic self determination, and, according to J.L. Garvin,

> the whole basis of Cobdenism was in reality destroyed by the Treaty of Frankfurt ... [which] opened a new economic epoch; the industrial awakening of the Continent and America was at hand, and with it the end of the manufacturing monopoly we had held for a century.[74]

Garvin concluded that 'the whole theory upon which it [free trade] rested had been destroyed by ... competitive reality'.[75] In short, the internationalist assumptions of free trade were thought to have underestimated the power of nationalist sentiment in general and economic nationalism in particular. 'When we adopted Mr Cobden's policy', wrote Garvin, 'we thought, as he thought, that the world was tending towards an age of cosmopolitan liberalism and free exchange ... when what was really approaching was the age of Bismarck, militarism, universal tariffs and destructive competition'.[76]

234

The critique of economic cosmopolitanism was linked to the second arm of the tariff campaign's attempt to construct an image of an industrial community of interest, its ideology of 'producerism'. According to the tariff argument one major reason why the free trade system had contributed to a deterioration of Britain's economic fortunes was that the assumptions of free trade economics prevented free traders from seeing anything wrong. Here criticism focused on the supposed tendency of free traders to define the condition of the economy by reference to 'a special test based only upon a fraction of our national economic interests – the total of our foreign trade returns'.[77] Even the most committed tariff reformer agreed that if one made an analysis of the aggregate volume of British trade, and indeed British exports, and took the results as an indication of Britain's economic position, it was possible to argue that 'Old England is not going back', that 'every year sees a great increase in our acquired wealth' and that 'exports . . . [are] larger than ever'.[78] But this was seen as irrelevant, because the aggregate value and volume of British trade and exports, and the overall increase in national wealth, were 'no measure of our prosperity'.[79] The great fault of the free trade analysis was seen to be that its fixation with international trade flows allowed no qualitative distinctions to be made. This, in the tariff reform book, was a glaring oversight, in that how much Britain exported was regarded as less important than what Britain exported. J.L. Garvin argued that an examination of Britain's export trade in the late nineteenth century revealed that 'the composition of those exports has undergone a portentous change. We sold to Germany, Holland, Belgium, France and the United States £12,000,000 more raw material . . . [and] £14,000,000 less manufactures'.[80] Furthermore, the Tariff Commission produced evidence that not all manufactured exports told a happy story, in that, for example, woollen exports were tending to consist more of semi-finished goods, that is goods which were low value-added and which employed less labour.[81] This increased dependence on raw material exports, especially coal, and on semi-finished goods was presented as evidence of Britain's decline as a *producing* nation, and stood as an argument for making domestic manufacturing industry the litmus of national economic well-being.

This identification of production as the essence of a national economy, and of manufacturing industry as the essence of production, was underlined by the tariff campaign's contrast between the fortunes of industry and the fortunes of the service sector under free trade. Britain's position as an international finance and banking centre had, according to the tariff argument, waxed as Britain's industrial prowess had waned, with both developments the result of free trade. The reasoning here was straightforward. The interests of the financial sector were cosmopolitan: capital flowed to where it would gain returns, insurance flourished no matter whose trade was insured, and bills of exchange could be profitably discounted no matter who presented them. The City's interests were seen to lie in a net expansion of world trade – anyone's trade – and in a continuation of Britain's role as the world's mart. Hence the tariff campaign was infused with a rhetoric openly contemptuous of Britain's financial sector. In September 1903 Ernest Pretyman told Joseph Chamberlain that 'under the present system [free trade] the proportion of placemen, rentiers, agents and distributors is daily increasing and that of producers daily diminishing'.[82] Chamberlain himself stated at Birmingham in May 1904 that 'Invisible exports are invisible so far as the working man is concerned. What does he see of them?',[83] whilst a few months earlier Sir Gilbert Parker had argued that 'For invisible exports there were only invisible commercial travellers'.[84] Nor did the rhetoric cool, for in 1908 George Wyndham was telling his father that if Britain continued its drift towards dependence on 'invisibles' it would become 'a nation of bankers and commission agents supporting armies of unemployed loafers'.[85]

The tariff campaign argued that 'non-producers' were at best dependent and at worst parasitic upon 'producers'. J.L. Garvin remarked, 'Mr Chamberlain brings the nation back to the main point of national economy when he tells it that successful production and competitive progress are the vital conditions of popular welfare'.[86] This was regarded as essential because the free trade conception of good national house-keeping, namely to 'buy cheap and sell dear', was thought to have encouraged a short-term, 'consumerist' approach to economics which led to a tendency 'to consider too much the advantage of buying cheaply and not to pay sufficient attention to the methods by which we may have the means that will enable us to pay at all'.[87] In this particular context the great failure of free trade was that Britain was no longer paying for goods with goods, but covering its foreign trade imbalance with the income from capital assets accumulated in the past, or in other words that Britain was 'living off its capital'.[88] The question posed by the tariff campaign was 'How did we obtain the immense sums of capital . . . the earnings of which yield this vast income?', and the answer was that 'this . . . capital was the expression and the result of our ascendancy in manufactures in the past . . . [and that] Manufactures have been the principal base from which the supremacy of Great Britain as the chief reservoir of capital in the world has been built up'.[89] Given these assumptions, the decline in Britain's industrial base, as signposted by the increased importance of invisible earnings, could only lead to an erosion of Britain's financial position, in that 'just as our agrarian position has gone and our manu-facturing predominance has been lessened, so also with the gradual diminution of the industrial power of the United Kingdom England will cease to be the great financial and commercial centre of the world'.[90]

Productive, industrial enterprise was deemed essential to the national economy, including its cosmopolitan sector.

The tariff message was clear. The British economy consisted of a productive sector, industry,[91] which would be best served by the national economics of tariff reform, and a non-productive sector, financial services, served by the cosmopolitan economics of free trade. This message reflected the tariff campaign's experiences in dealing with the service sector. Throughout the campaign, relations between the tariff camp and 'the City', in particular the banking sector, were always strained and often hostile. Only eight bankers were listed as co-operating with Commission enquiries.[92] Three of them, Sir Vincent Caillard, Vicary Gibbs and A.L. Jones, were members of the Commission, and Caillard, with his extensive industrial interests, was hardly a typical banker, whilst Jones was a local banker, which left Gibbs as the only real 'City man' on the Commission.[93] This made life very difficult, with W.A.S. Hewins noting that it was almost impossible to obtain data or detailed opinions about Britain's role as a financial centre.[94] This lack of co-operation was put down to outright hostility. At a meeting of the Commission in May 1906 W.A.S. Hewins noted that 'The position of the bankers, I gather, is that any change in our fiscal system would be disastrous to London as a banking centre'.[95] This was certainly a view which had been expressed by Sir Felix Schuster in his address to the Institute of Bankers in December 1903,[96] and that other well-known bastion of free trade, the Treasury, expressed similar concerns that same year.[97] Later assertions at Tariff Commission meetings that 'almost every banker is opposed to tariff reform'[98] were challenged on the basis that 'bankers whose business is largely on the Exchange are against it ... [whilst] those who are doing general business and who would benefit by the increased prosperity to the country more or less favour it',[99] but this turned out to be more an expression of wishful thinking than a statement of fact. Not even the domestic clearing banks provided support for tariff reform.

The experience of the tariff campaign bore out the findings of a survey of 'City' opinion on the tariff question carried out by H.A. Gwynne in late 1903. Gwynne, acting on Chamberlain's behalf, discovered a range of opinion in the City, pointing out that on the Stock Exchange and in the insurance world there was support for tariff reform, but also noting that 'in banking circles ... opposition shows itself very strongly'.[100] One of the most interesting features of the tariff campaign, however, was that the position of 'the City' was conflated with that of the banks. In effect the banking sector's hostility to tariff reform provided a peg on which the tariff campaign sought to hang a more general critique of the service sector's dependence on free trade and, as a consequence, Britain's growing dependence under free trade on a cosmopolitan service sector. By concentrating attention on the banks the tariff campaign directed criticism at the City elite, a sector which was socially, structurally and geographically separated from industry, committed to and known for its cosmopolitan market interests, and which had been the object of much resentment as its corporate and individual wealth had grown during the 'hard times' of the 1880s and 1890s. Just as foreign trusts, tariffs and dumping were the external 'other' confronting British industry so 'the City' became the 'enemy within', an internal 'other' whose non-productive interests marked it out as different from and opposed to the interests of the national productive industrial base. And just as the tariff campaign was a call for British industry to recognize its commonality in the face of the external threat, so too it was a plea for industry to recognize its common cause against internal agents of cosmopolitanism who sought to relegate industry to a subordinate role.

A POLICY FOR NATIONAL PRODUCTION

The tariff campaign's proposals for the defence of British industry were wholly in keeping with its analysis of industrial 'decline' and its emphasis on economic nationalism and production. Tariff reform was to restore two things lost to British industry as a result of free trade, namely 'stable conditions of production and prosperous and expanding markets'.[101] The former was to be furnished by tariff protection which would, it was argued, rectify 'the defenceless position that our present system leaves us in'[102] which 'allowed the foreigner to compete with us at an advantage to himself'.[103] The 10 per cent tariff proposed would defend British manufacturers from foreign competition and dumping – 'Only protection', wrote J.L. Garvin, 'can compete with protection'.[104] Protection was to secure the British home market, and help British industries to compete not just in the domestic market but abroad as well. Quoting Andrew Carnegie, Sir Vincent Caillard noted that 'the most powerful weapon for conquering foreign markets is a profitable home market'.[105]

Protective tariffs were also to make British industry attractive to investors. 'The introduction of . . . a [protective] tariff', so W.A.S. Hewins told Arthur Balfour,

> would give that sense of security which is lacking at the present time, and without which we cannot get that free flow of capital into great industries which is the real basis of their development . . . the existence of even small duties . . . would regulate competition, so that home manufacturers could see more clearly the conditions upon which their business is conducted.[106]

Tariffs would shelter British capital, allowing British industrialists rather than foreign rivals to benefit from Britain's accumulation of capital reserves.

Imperial preference was to provide the second prerequisite for industrial success, viz. prosperous and expanding markets. Retaliation, initially presented as a means of prising open some of Britain's older markets, was downgraded to a secondary role as the tariff campaign progressed.[107] For the most part the old European and US markets were seen as lost to economic nationalism. Imperial preference with the Colonies was, in every respect, the great white hope. At Glasgow in October 1903 Joseph Chamberlain argued that in the last quarter of the nineteenth century 'export of manufactures ... [to] British possessions has increased £40,000,000 ... and it remains at the present day the most rapidly increasing, the most important, the most valuable of the whole of our trade'.[108] Chamberlain exaggerated, but the real essence of the tariff campaign's argument was that the Colonies represented the only fast-growing and, equally important, the most secure markets for British goods. In 1907 the Tariff Commission, more careful with its statistics than Chamberlain, pointed out that in the ten years 1897 to 1907 British trade with Canada, New Zealand and Australia had increased by over 100 per cent to £50,000,000 per annum,[109] whilst the Tariff Reform League *Speaker's Handbook* remarked of the Colonies that 'already these markets buy from us, per head of the population, in pounds whereas foreign and neutral markets buy in shillings'.[110] Imperial preference was to provide British manufacturers with privileged access to a large and ever-increasing market.

Protection and preference, acting in tandem, were the means presented by the tariff campaign for securing the twin goals of stable conditions of production and an expanding market for British goods. Moreover, the logic of the tariff argument was that these two objectives were inseparable. Imperial preference was to secure market opportunities, but at the same time British manufacturing capacity had to be stable and secure enough to take advantage of those opportunities. Thus J.L. Garvin expressed a central tenet of tariff thinking when he wrote in 1905 that 'from our point of view, we can regard a National Tariff on the one hand, and Federal Trade upon the other, as the inseparable factors of a dual apparatus, or rather as the reciprocating parts of a single mechanism'.[111]

The insistence on the need for protection and preference makes it possible to place the industrial aspect of the tariff debate in a much broader context. In his book *Tariff Reform* the Conservative MP G.C. Tryon stated that to escape its economic difficulties Britain had to

adopt a national constructive policy under which the State uses its infuence to develop and strengthen the trade of its citizens, by such measures as the fostering of young industries, by discrimination in its import duties ... by the granting of special privileges to help trade ... and by similar State action for the conscious, deliberate development of trade.[112]

In advocating such an active role for the State in the development of trade and industry Tryon, and all the other Conservatives who took up the tariff argument on this point, fully appreciated that they were preaching economic heresies. The tariff campaign questioned the whole basis of liberal economics by criticizing the overall structure of the British economy as it appeared to have developed under free trade.

One of the most important criticisms that free traders levelled at the tariff campaign was that the imposition of tariiffs would lead to a 'dislocation of trade', in that tariffs would interrupt the natural flow of goods and effectively act as a subsidy to inefficient industries. Against this criticism tariff reformers argued that to speak of a dislocation of trade by tariffs was nonsense, given that 'our trade is not flowing now in those "natural channels" that Free Traders desire; it is checked, controlled or changed in character by the tariffs of our neighbours'.[113] Apart from the fact that Britain's economic destiny under free trade was no longer in its own hands the tariff campaign, as was noted above, also stressed that the diversion of Britain's trade into areas like raw materials and services meant becoming a second-rate industrial power. Implicitly the tariff reform versus free trade debate represented a conflict between those who accepted the structural changes taking place in the British economy and those who did not. Hence Winston Churchill argued against tariffs on the grounds that the abandonment of free trade would mean: 'exit for ever the banking, broking, warehousing predominance of Great Britain',[114] whilst Percy Ashley[115] told Arthur Balfour that if Britain did not impose tariffs 'we may become more and more a creditor country – a banking country rather than an industrial country'.[116]

The issues raised by the call for industrial protection and preference were thus much deeper than is perhaps generally acknowledged. The tariff argument for greater regulation of trade and support for manufacturing industry really revolved around the view that Britain should sever its links with the international economy and reorientate itself towards a more autarkic economic position, and thereby prevent the erosion of its manufacturing base by foreign rivals who had already adopted this stance. Free trade, arguably the most important link in the chain binding Britain to the international economy, was a key target for those favouring a more autarkic approach, and the fact that Britain's 'cosmopolitan' elite, the City bankers, opposed tariffs served simply to reinforce the tariff argument. As a consequence the tariff debate can be seen as another important skirmish in the long-running battle over whether the interests of industry have been sacrificed to the interests of finance.

The national versus cosmopolitan, producer versus non-producer divide posited by the tariff campaign undoubtedly has a longer-term significance, but it also has great importance in the more immediate context of the politics of tariff reform. To understand the purchase of this rhetorical dichotomy for Edwardian Conservatives it is essential to realize that once they had grasped the tariff reform nettle the party was straight-away confronted by the labyrinthine complexities of British industrial politics. If an appeal was to be made to British industrialists, many of whom, as the Tariff Commission confirmed, were indeed complaining of foreign competition and lost markets, then some definition of the industrial interest had to be found and a policy shaped accordingly. But defining the industrial interest, again as the Tariff Commission discovered, was near to impossible. In these circumstances it is unsurprising that the industrial policy of the tariff programme remained somewhat general – an all-round tariff and the promise of imperial markets. Ironically, given the energy devoted to finding a 'scientific tariff', the policy proposals were secondary to the larger promise that the tariff campaign held out to the industrial sector. The identification of production and the health of industry as the test of the national economy's well-being, and the promise of government prioritizing the needs of provincial industry over the demands of London's cosmopolitan financial elite, offered status and recognition as well as material assistance. Tariff reform told British industry that it was important, that it was the nation's key economic resource, and that the Conservative party understood that industry faced difficulties and desired to address them.

10

SOCIAL REFORM

> without a great social programme the Conservative and Unionist
> Parties have never prospered long.
>
> (J.L. Garvin to Lord Northcliffe, 4 August 1909)[1]

To contemporaries the potential appeal of policies designed to defend
British agriculture and industry was fairly obvious. A commitment to
restructuring Britain's trade position and bolstering the domestic market
for Britain's industrial and rural producers made sense: it framed an appeal
both to the Conservative party's traditional rural constituency and to a core
element of its more recently acquired urban support. However, the question remained as to how the Conservative party could attract the key
working-class vote. Imperial unity was thought to offer popular appeal,
but even the most enthusiastic imperialist accepted that 'the Unionist Party
cannot live upon an exclusive diet of imperialism'.[2] Across the spectrum
of Conservative opinion it was admitted, albeit reluctantly by some, that
the main interest of the working class was material improvement in general
and social reform in particular, but could this be provided in a *Conservative*
fashion? Here, once again, tariff reform came into its own. One of the most
important aspects of the political economy of the tariff campaign, and one
of the reasons why it appealed to Conservatives, was that tariffs were the
cornerstone of a distinctive social policy. The link between tariff reform and
social reform was complex, and as the tariff debate evolved there were
shifts in emphasis concerning their exact relationship. But, in the period
1903 to 1910, the argument that 'Fiscal reform . . . is the indispensable
condition of all other reforms'[3] was constantly repeated as the
Conservative party sought to construct a positive social reform policy.

EMPLOYMENT: THE ECONOMIC TAP-ROOT OF SOCIAL REFORM

'Tariff Reform means work for all' was one of the most widely-used
Conservative slogans of the Edwardian period, expressing the party's

claim to a positive outlook on 'the social question'. In the early years of the tariff campaign Joseph Chamberlain repeatedly stressed the employment advantages of tariffs, arguing that

> the question of employment is at the root of all the social reforms of our time ... There is no dole from the State. There is no relief of taxation. There is no legislation which the wit of man can devise, no artificial combination to raise the rate of wages, which will weigh for one moment in the balance against a policy which would give to our people some substantial increase in the demand for their labour.[4]

Nor did such claims diminish. In the run up to the first general election of 1910, Arthur Balfour told the electors of Stockport that 'Tariff Reform will undoubtedly do great things for the unemployed'. Characteristically Balfour qualified his position by adding 'I do not say that Tariff Reform will entirely remove unemployment', but his conclusion that tariffs would 'beyond all question stimulate industry and greatly help the workers' was as close to an unequivocal statement on the subject the ever-cautious Balfour was likely to make.[5] There were 'various means', Alfred Milner argued, of dealing with Britain's social difficulties: 'You can do so by labour registries, you can do so by legislation against sweating. But all such measures, though they minimize the evils, do not go to the heart of them. At the root of them all lies the problem of unemployment'.[6]

The definition of the problem defined the nature of the solution. In 1909 W.J. Ashley argued, in a pamphlet entitled *Social Legislation*, that

> the chief industrial cause [of unemployment], is the fluctuation, both seasonal and cyclical, in the amount of employment. This itself is the outcome of our competitive system; and, of course, the more a country is exposed to the full tide of competition – the freer its trade – the greater this fluctuation must be.[7]

Ashley concluded that it was 'necessary, in the interest of social reform, to exercise control over external commerce as well as over internal industry'. Though 'trusts [were] doing the work of social reformers' in that 'capitalistic combinations' placed helpful limitations on internal competition, he argued that this was inadequate. Tariffs were essential to the creation of efficient trusts,[8] and because import penetration caused more damage than internal competition.[9] With the cause of unemployment described thus the remedy was 'a policy directed to the development of national production, [and] to the maintenance of national trade'.[10] The tariff argument linked Britain's decline as a producing and trading nation to the growth of social distress, with unemployment acting as a barometer of the former and the cause of the latter.

In terms of the burgeoning debate on social reform in the early years of the twentieth century, the Conservative party's emphasis on the employment effects of tariff reform can be interpreted variously. The simplest reading is that it represented an argument for avoiding more State intervention in the workings of the economy.[11] To see this as 'limiting' the social aspect of tariff reform is to misread the way in which contemporaries constructed 'the social question' and defined social policy.[12] In offering tariffs as a cure for unemployment, Conservative advocates of tariff reform could point to foreign examples – in the United States, France and Germany tariffs were often presented as employment policies. In addition there was the supporting testimony of Charles Booth. Writing in the *National Review* in January 1904 Booth argued that free trade, based as it was on cosmopolitan, laissez faire, individualist principles, was 'out of time', and he advocated the introduction of a 5 per cent *ad valorem* tariff on all inter-colonial trade (with reciprocal preferences) and a 5 per cent *ad valorem* duty on foreign manufactured imports. Booth presented these measures in terms of their social effects. He dismissed the 'food tax' scare, arguing that 'neither the proposals I have sketched, nor the more elaborate . . . and in some ways more moderate scheme laid before the country by Mr Chamberlain, would be likely to affect appreciably the cost of life in England'. In any case, 'The interests of the mass of the people, and of the poorest not the least, are found in the regularity of employment more than the cheapness of food'. The aim of tariffs was, he declared, 'to secure a continuance of progressive prosperity, and to lay deeper the foundations and strengthen the structure of national life', with the result that there would be 'more employment from the first, and the employment would be more regular'.[13]

That the tariff campaign secured Booth's support was a major political coup, but it also indicated that the employment aspect of the tariff argument was central to the debate over Britain's social problems. This was confirmed in 1906–07, when Booth's findings were supported by the investigations of Arthur Steel-Maitland[14] and Rose Squire. Acting for the Royal Commission on the Poor Laws, Steel-Maitland and Squire conducted a nationwide survey into 'The Relation of Industrial and Sanitary Conditions to Pauperism'. Drawing on evidence they gathered from Trade Unions and local Poor Law Boards of Guardians, they concluded that casual and irregular employment were indeed the main cause of pauperism.[15] Unemployment was in this sense one of the great 'discoveries' of the late nineteenth and early twentieth century, and was recognized by all social investigators, regardless of political allegiance, as both a major issue in its own right and as a key to other social problems.[16] Tariff reform thus addressed directly a central social concern with one of the few tools of economic intervention known and, in international terms at least, widely practised at the time.

In fact Conservatives acknowledged unemployment as important even before they adopted tariff reform as their 'first constructive plank'. In 1905 the Balfour administration's Unemployed Workmen's Act created a framework under which central government could subsidize counter-cyclical public works directed by local authorities. The scheme was hedged around with administrative and financial constraints, but clearly indicated the growing significance of the issue and the Conservative party's recognition of its political resonance. In this respect the Unemployed Workmen's Act represented the 'official' Conservative effort to gain a political advantage by presenting Conservatism as responsive to social issues. The tariff campaign can be regarded as an 'unofficial' effort to achieve the same end.

In the autumn of 1903 Joseph Chamberlain had attacked the early-Victorian free trade campaign as 'a manufacturers' and middle-class movement'.[17] This remark may seem strange, given Chamberlain's background, but his meaning became clear as the campaign developed:

> the doctrine of Mr Cobden was a consistent doctrine. His view was that there should be no interference by the State in our domestic concerns. He believed that individuals should be left to themselves ... To him protection of labour was quite as bad as protection of trade. To him a trade union was worse than a landord. To him all factory legislation was as bad as the institution of tariffs.[18]

The tariff argument linked the rejection of free trade with a willingness to foster social legislation, whilst at the same time implying that a continued adherence to free trade meant inactivity on social policy.[19] The stress on protecting employment by tariffs offered the Conservatives a powerful negative to place against Liberalism's heritage and the policy tradition of the Liberal party.[20]

After 1906 it was difficult for the Conservative party to argue that the defenders of free trade were opposed to social reform – the Liberal government's legislation rendered the argument untenable. However, this did not rule out the idea that free trade and social reform were irreconcilable. To begin with, the Conservatives contended that the Liberal government's mixing of free trade and social reform was illogical. Liberal welfare reforms such as old age pensions and the 'Children's Charter' indicated that 'This Party in the sphere of social legislation fully admits the right of the government to "interfere" with the play of "natural" forces', whilst in the realm of trade relations it regarded 'the same principle ... as a dangerous heresy'.[21] On this point even the Conservative free traders were in agreement with the rest of their party.[22] The same reasoning led both Conservative free traders and tariff reformers to argue that the Liberals had opened the door to tariffs by conceding the principle of State intervention.

For the Conservative Free Traders *all* measures of State intervention were impractical, not to say immoral and dangerous, because they were Socialist. However, the 'official' Conservative stance after 1906 was that State intervention and social legislation were not Socialist per se: how reforms were financed determined whether they were Socialist. Arthur Balfour never tired of reiterating the statement he had first made in the 1890s that there was all the difference between Socialism and *'practical social reform'*. The Liberals' social reforms were deemed impractical on the basis that 'any scheme . . . which has for its sole object the alleviating of results, without touching the causes' could only be 'a quack remedy . . . an anodyne which will speedily paralyse the patient'.[23] The most important of the 'causes' the Liberals were accused of ignoring was pressure on the labour market caused by foreign competition. A paradigm case of the Conservative stance was one of the most persistent social concerns of the period, the issue of sweated labour. The Conservatives' attitude to anti-sweating legislation in itself will be discussed in more detail below; here it is simply worth noting that when Joseph Chamberlain addressed the question in 1903 he argued

> What is the good . . . in the name of common sense, of prohibiting sweated labour in this country, if you allow sweated goods to come in from foreign countries? If protected labour is good . . . then it is good to protect the results of labour.[24]

The message was clear. Any legislation to protect British workers from having to compete with the low-cost products of sweated labour had, to be effective, to be accompanied by tariffs to keep out imports of such products, otherwise the threat to wages and employment would not be removed, and the Conservatives argued thus when the Liberals introduced their Sweated Industries Bill in 1908, the forerunner to the 1909 Trade Boards Act.[25]

In the period between 1906 and 1910 the contention that Liberal social reforms addressed only symptoms and not the underlying cause of social distress seemed both sensible and effective. It seemed sensible because in the period between late 1907 and mid-1909 there was a severe down-turn in the trade cycle which resulted in 'the most acute commercial depression since 1879'.[26] During this recession some Trade Unions reported unemployment amongst their membership as high as 15 per cent, and although full statistics are not available unemployment was clearly severe and widespread. The claim that 'tariff reform means work for all' could thus be pressed, and by-election results in 1908 appeared to confirm that in these circumstances tariff reform, presented as an employment policy, was an effective electoral weapon. In January 1908 the Conservatives overturned a substantial Liberal majority in Mid-Devon in spite of some factors which normally told against the Conservatives, namely a very high poll and an efficient Liberal organization. Contemporary reports attributed this result to the Conservative candidate's appeal. During the campaign *The Times* remarked that 'the dominating note of all Captain Morrison-Bell's [the Conservative candidate] utterance is that the serious problem of unemployment . . . can to a large extent be solved by . . . safeguarding our great productive industries from unfair competition',[27] and on the eve of polling it added that

> Captain Morrison-Bell's contention that a rearrangement of our fiscal system would ensure more work for the British workman and would also enable money to be found for the inception of social schemes such as housing reform and old age pensions is treated with respect in quarters hitherto impervious to all but free trade propaganda.[28]

It is not certain whether Morrison-Bell's 'pressing tariff reform on the electors almost to the exclusion of everything else'[29] or some other factor[30] secured his victory. What is certain is that Morrison-Bell's insistence that tariff reform would mean work was thought to have been decisive. At the NUCA Conference in November 1908 the National Union Council reported that

> The Nation is now beginning to realise that the Radical policy of Socialism and attacks on capital, together with the continued free importation of foreign manufactured goods, is decreasing the area of employment . . . [and] all classes are beginning to turn their eyes towards the banner of fiscal reform . . . The proof of this is to be found in the year's remarkable by-elections.[31]

Thus in December 1909 Austen Chamberlain, advising a Conservative candidate as to Liberal weaknesses, stressed that Asquith 'had nothing to say on the greatest of the national problems of today – the question of unemployment', and that therefore the candidate should concentrate on the unemployment issue and the remedy the Conservatives had in 'the constructive policy of tariff reform'.[32] The employment aspect of the tariff campaign allowed the Conservative party to present themselves as the 'real' social reformers, prepared to deal with the causes as well as the symptoms of social distress.

There was one more link between tariff reform and social reform in terms of the issue of employment. This was the contention that tariffs were necessary to off-set increases in production costs caused by social and factory reforms.[33] In 1904 W.J. Ashley stated that in Germany the introduction of social legislation had been facilitated because 'Bismarck was enabled to weaken the opposition of the industrialists to what was hardly less than a social revolution . . . by the more or less concurrent gift of a protective tariff'.[34] This may not have been an historically accurate assessment of the German situation, but it drew attention to a potentially fruitful approach to social reform. In the 1890s a major obstacle to social and factory legislation had been employer complaints about the costs of measures like factory, health and unemployment insurance and shorter working hours.[35] In the Edwardian period many employers came to accept the need for such reforms, either as a result of agreeing that a healthy workforce was more likely to be an efficient workforce, or as a result of realizing that these reforms might be the price of social and industrial peace. However, the issue of cost was still an important employer concern, and a number of employers' organizations asked whether they could achieve 'compensation' for raised costs through lower wages or higher prices.[36] Given that a general attempt to cut wages would almost certainly have provoked widespread industrial unrest the only way to mollify employer opinion appeared to be higher prices, and tariffs offered an obvious solution.[37] Whether the promise of tariffs was designed to sell social reform to employers or the promise of social reform was a means of selling tariffs to the working class is a moot but largely irrelevant point. Tariff Reform could satisfy both objects by presenting tariffs and social reform as interlocking aspects of what was known in France, Germany and the United States as 'the protection of national labour'.[38] In short the employment effects of tariff reform provided the Conservatives with an example of the mutual welfare interest of employers and employees as 'producing classes' in the defence of Britain's national productive base.

REVENUE

Tariffs were also crucial to the development of specific Conservative legislative proposals. Speaking in Parliament on 28 May, only two weeks after his Bingley Hall declaration, Chamberlain stated that revenue generated by tariff reform would be used to assist the British working class. He promised to use tariff revenues to reduce or abolish other indirect taxes pressing on working-class incomes, but he also indicated that they could be used to pay for social reform. In early June Chamberlain confirmed this in an open letter to a working man, stating that

> as regards old age pensions I would not myself look at the matter unless I felt able to promise that a large scheme for the provision of such pensions to all who had been thrifty and well-conducted would be assured by a revision of our system of import duties.[39]

In 1903 it seemed quite clear that Chamberlain wished to use the revenue aspect of tariff reform to meld imperialism with social reform and thereby produce a policy with genuine mass appeal. Certainly this was the view of his contemporaries. Ten days after the Bingley Hall speech, and *before*

Chamberlain made his comments in Parliament and to his working-class correspondent, Lord Selborne told Alfred Milner

> You will see what is running in Chamberlain's mind as in Balfour's, a preferential tariff coupled with old age pensions – you will see at once that the connexion is very real. The voters will never agree to a tax on their food unless they are going to benefit by it personally.[40]

But having raised these expectations and fears Chamberlain retreated from this bold and apparently promising attempt to set a new agenda on social policy. After 1903 Chamberlain mentioned few if any legislative proposals for social reform, and no link between such legislation and the revenue potential of tariffs. In fact in May 1906 Chamberlain went so far as to state that he had 'never . . . in the whole course of my life, made any promises of old age pensions'.[41]

Joseph Chamberlain's inconsistency over this matter should not be allowed to obscure the significance of the revenue argument to the social reforming side of the tariff campaign. The notion of using tariff revenues to finance social reform was in circulation both before and after Chamberlain raised and discarded the idea. As early as 1900 Henry Chaplin, acting as Chairman of a Parliamentary Committee on old age pensions, suggested that a pensions system could be financed by a registration duty on imported corn. Commenting on what he called 'Mr Chaplin's Kite' E.E. Williams[42] argued that the imposition of such a duty would be an important step, not only because it could be used to establish imperial preference, but also because

> the political atmosphere is charged with what is known as social reform . . . It is emphatically the note of the age . . . we have to look forward to the establishment of old age pensions and probably a good deal else . . . How are we going to find the money? . . . The Income Tax is at a burdensome rate . . . it could not be increased . . . Our excise is already excessively high . . . Death Duties . . . can not be increased . . . [so] is it possible to devise any better means of getting money than by the taxation of the Customs' House?[43]

These tentative suggestions took on an increased importance after the Boer War. To a number of senior Conservatives, most notably the Chancellor Hicks-Beach, the cost of 'Joe's War' had effectively put an end to any discussion of social reform, but there were others in the Conservative ranks who felt that the war had cleared away obstacles. In particular the way the war was financed seemed to offer a model for social reform. In March 1902 Edward Goulding, introducing a Private Member's Bill for Old Age Pensions, pointed out that 'The only complaint against the scheme is that the cost would be too great'. He countered this by arguing that 'We are now paying extra taxation for the

War without any inconvenience', and that 'One thing ... this war has shown ... is that the nation can bear the necessary taxation required for this purpose'. The taxation to which he referred was the shilling registration duty on corn which had been introduced in 1901 to help pay for the war, for he stated 'If the Chancellor of the Exchequer will follow the policy he inaugurated last year, and boldly broaden the basis of taxation ... then the amount needed [for old age pensions] will be quickly raised'. Goulding concluded that he did not believe 'that even the old theories of free trade would stand in the way' of his scheme as one had only to 'Earmark the taxation for Old Age Pensions' and it would be 'cheerfully paid'.[44]

The concept of 'broadening the basis of taxation' through tariffs was thus quite well developed before Chamberlain deployed it in his initial campaign, and although Chamberlain himself retreated from the idea of using this 'broader' tax base to fund social reforms his 'followers' did not. In fact between 1904 and 1906 some of Chamberlain's associates grew somewhat restive over his neglect of social reform, and in 1904 Edward Goulding and J.F. Remnant brought forward another Old Age Pensions Bill, arguing that revenue tariffs were the only sensible means of financing the measure.[45] As with the employment argument there was 'expert' testimony to support the case for revenue tariffs. In this case Charles Follett, a one-time Permanent Secretary at the Inland Revenue, argued that, with government expenditure set to rise and with existing taxes at the limit of their justice and efficiency, the only way ahead was to find new sources of revenue. Follett concluded that the most efficient and equitable new taxes would be an all-round tariff on manufactured goods and low tariffs on imported foodstuffs.[46] That Follett should have lent his support to the idea of 'broadening the basis of taxation' can in part be attributed to the fact that he had an axe to grind – Follett was an early convert to tariff reform and a founder member of the Compatriots' Club. At the same time it would be a mistake to assess his argument simply in these terms. Follett's conclusions were controversial, but since the late nineteenth century the basic contention that new sources of revenue would have to be found had become increasingly commonplace.

Although one cannot understand the revenue aspect of the tariff campaign without placing it in its proper, long-term perspective it is also the case that short-term considerations, and in particular the dynamics of British political argument between 1906 and 1910, brought revenue tariffs to the centre of Conservative politics. The 1906 general election result convinced the bulk of the Conservative party that appealing to the working class was essential for electoral success, and the Labour by-election victories in 1907 served only to confirm the popular appeal of Collectivist ideas. But the question still remained as to how Collectivist social legislation was to be funded. Tariff reform appeared to give the

Conservatives a chance both to steal a march on the Liberal government and produce a positive counter to Labour's appeal. Writing to Arthur Balfour in May 1907 W.A.S. Hewins argued that Asquith's March budget 'does not provide on sound financial lines for the normal expenditure of the country ... [and] fails to indicate from what new sources of revenue the promises of the government for undertaking certain social reforms can be fulfilled'.[47] Expanding on his ideas in a paper entitled 'The Inelasticity of the Present Revenue' Hewins, adopting a position very similar to that taken by Charles Follett, stated that existing direct and indirect taxes were almost beyond their optimimum level. Since old age pensions, free school meals,[48] and small holdings legislation were certain to be enacted and certain to prove expensive, new demands on the Exchequer could only be met by the adoption of revenue tariffs.[49] Whether or not Hewins' argument persuaded Balfour to commit himself to tariff reform[50] it is certainly the case that Balfour's key-note speech to the NUCA Conference at Birmingham in 1907, which finally placed tariff reform at the heart of official Conservative policy, gave pride of place to the revenue potential of tariffs.[51] The 1907 Conference, in contrast to previous years, saw the main speakers from the floor give equal weight to revenue tariffs as 'the *only* means of providing the necessary funds for old age pensions and other reforms which they desire to effect for the benefit of the working class'.[52]

Various estimates of the revenue to be gleaned from tariffs were put forward, ranging from the £20,000,000 suggested by George Courthope and the *Morning Post* to the £24–30,000,000 estimated by W.A.S. Hewins.[53] However, the quantity was less important than how they would raise it. That tariffs were indirect taxes was important. When the Conservatives faced their high noon at the general election of January 1910, revenue tariffs offered them 'an alternative method of taxation', a way of financing social reforms without recourse to the 'punitive', 'class-jealous' taxes of the 1909 Budget.

That tariffs could offer succour to upper- and middle-class taxpayers threatened by the Liberals' fiscal radicalism was not the main point, for it was assumed that these people were likely to vote Conservative anyway. The importance of the revenue aspect of tariffs was that it seemed to provide a promising mode of appeal to the working class and a means of persuading them that Socialist policies were not in their interest. The tariff argument claimed that Socialist social reforms not only failed to address the issue of unemployment but compounded it through taxation. Writing in 1908 G.E. Raine[54] argued that

> every time that money which would otherwise be employed in production is withdrawn from production, and is treated as income [for tax purposes], so much the worse does our industrial position

251

become. If, instead of allowing capital to be invested in undertakings which give work and wages, we divert it for the endowment of temporary and frequently foolish palliatives, we merely increase the number of the unemployed and swell the army of the discontented.[55]

Socialism mistakenly treated all capital as income, and thus 'confiscated' much-needed investment capital for social reforms. A further charge laid against Socialist taxation was that 'if ... tax ... approaches the figure approved by the Socialists ... businesses will be closed, shareholders will get as much out ... as they can and will hasten to invest ... in some country where the blessings of Socialism are unknown'.[56] By 1908, that is even before the People's Budget, some Conservatives felt that the level of direct taxation in Britain was already producing this effect.[57] Socialism, or so it was argued, not only threatened the confiscation and misuse of capital resources but also caused investors to export their capital to places where it was unavailable to British producers and indeed actively deployed against them as investment capital for competitors. According to the Conservatives a Socialist tax regime could only 'scare capital out of the country and leave labour in the lurch'.[58] In 1909 this argument was central to the Conservative assault on the People's Budget, with F.E. Smith telling the electors of Huddersfield that 'More capital ha[s] gone abroad during one year of the present Government's time in office than in any other single year ... [and] If Capital were driven abroad there was lost the one and only chance of employing labour'.[59] The tariff critique of the Liberals' fiscal strategy thus reinforced the attack on Liberal social reform – whilst the government's social reforms 'ignored' unemployment their tax policies were depicted as exacerbating the problem.

The tariff campaign's critique of Socialism may have imbued it with some appeal for Conservatives, but the Conservative free traders' critique of Socialist taxation was almost identical and yet their arguments were marginalized in the period after 1906. The attraction of the tariff argument was as a positive alternative to the Liberal–Socialist agenda. Just as a dele-terious employment effect was deemed intrinsic to Socialist taxation so a positive employment effect was intrinsic to tariffs. At this point there appeared to be a contradiction in the tariff case. On the one hand it was argued that tariffs on manufactures and foodstuffs would protect domestic producers by shutting out imports, but on the other hand, statements about the revenue potential of tariffs seemed to assume that foreign goods would still enter the British market. This apparent inconsistency was used by, amongst others, the Conservative free trader Lord Cromer in an attempt to discredit tariff reform, but his attack was parried and returned with interest. Replying to Cromer's criticism Leo Amery stated that

> if we tariff reformers proposed that ... the whole of our national revenue should be raised from protective duties only, then Lord

Cromer might have some justification for his challenge. Unfortunately we have never proposed any such thing . . . The real gist of the matter is that the taxable capacity of a nation depends upon its productive power. An increase of production is an increase of taxable capacity, and . . . is felt at once in an increase of our national production . . . To a large extent this increase [in revenue] will come, not through the new tariff directly, but through the greater productivity of the existing sources of revenue.[60]

Nor was Amery isolated in arguing along these lines. In 1910 Arthur Steel-Maitland restated the basic reasoning and went so far as to put some figures forward, stating that

The national revenue (and indeed local rates) is really contributed by men who earn their livelihood and their means to pay taxes by industry, either themselves producing articles, or helping in their distribution. Roughly speaking . . . for every shilling's worth of production in England, rather more than 2d is contributed in rates and taxes.[61]

This allowed Conservatives not only to deny the contradiction between the protective and revenue aspects of tariff reform, but to claim that the two functions were mutually supportive. Tariffs, by securing a 'sound' productive base, were to make social reform feasible in both fiscal and 'real' terms. It was contended that 'Tariff Reform will keep capital in the country and reduce the amount of unemployment',[62] and that increased employment would increase the nation's taxable capacity.

LEGISLATIVE PROPOSALS

i. Old age pensions

For what reforms were tariffs to provide revenue? Old age pensions were perhaps the most discussed reform in the late nineteenth and early twentieth century, and they were the issue first mentioned in connection with the tariff campaign. Pensions had a long-established pedigree in Conservative circles, with, as was noted above, proposals emerging from the Conservative ranks in the period between 1900 and 1903. In May 1904 another scheme was presented by Edward Goulding and J.F. Remnant, which suggested that 'A person who had maintained himself as a good citizen during what might be called the working years of his life would be entitled to a pension . . . of not less than 5/- and not more than 7/- per week'.[63] A comparison with the old age pensions legislation enacted by the Liberal government in 1908 – a 5/- per week pension at the age of 70 – shows that this early 'unofficial' Conservative proposal was relatively generous. It should be noted that this bill allowed for 'certain disqualifications', namely for those who had been in prison or in receipt of Poor Law Relief, and maintained a strict distinction between the 'deserving' and 'undeserving' poor,[64] but these disqualifications featured in other pensions proposals of the time and the Liberal legislation of 1908. Of equal importance in terms of the bill's philosophy was Goulding's insistence that, unlike Poor Law Relief, 'the receipt of this pension' was not to be 'treated as a badge of failure and inferiority' and that it was not to 'disqualify the recipient from exercising the franchise and participating in the privileges of a free citizen'.[65] Since it was the case that 'a large proportion of the wage-earning community were totally unable to provide by financial contribution for old age', the award of a pension had to be treated 'not merely as a charity, but as a right'.[66]

Before 1906 few Conservatives, apart from the free traders, opposed pensions in principle, but few were prepared to commit themselves to legislative action. However, in the wake of the 1906 election defeat pensions became an important part of the Conservative effort to develop a constructive social policy. In January 1907 Austen Chamberlain stated that 'the greatest and most urgent of all social reforms is that of old age pensions',[67] and later in the same year he implored Arthur Balfour to make a clear commitment to pensions legislation.[68] Early in 1908 Chamberlain made further declarations in favour of pensions,[69] and in four by-election campaigns in the early months of the year the victorious Conservative candidates all stressed their commitment to pensions.[70] That Conservative discussion of the pensions question should have been marked by a new urgency was understandable. Apart from the broad assumption that pensions would be a vote winner the Conservatives, courtesy of a 'leak' from Asquith's secretary at the Exchequer, had been informed in April 1907 that the Liberal government was preparing to introduce old age pensions but had 'no idea of the sort of scheme they mean to start'.[71] In these circumstances loud and positive declarations by the Conservatives could at least prevent the party from appearing wholly negative.

In May 1908 the Liberals introduced their old age pensions legislation, but the Conservatives fought hard to avoid being thrown onto the defensive. In Parliament the Conservatives gave pensions a warm welcome. The main Conservative speakers in the Commons debate were Austen Chamberlain, Edward Goulding, Percy Clive and J.W. Hills, men who had established reputations as strong advocates of pensions, and Goulding congratulated the government on their 'courage, foresight and effort to grapple with this problem which had too long been shirked and shelved on account of its great difficulties'.[72] In the general election campaigns of 1910 the Liberal party was to claim that the Conservatives voted against old age pensions, but this was not the case. It was true that a small band of Conservatives, led by the free trade contingent, opposed pensions, but they were a tiny minority. The great majority of Conservative MPs voted in favour of pensions or were 'paired'. Conservatives only expressed concern over *how* pensions were enacted, not whether they should be enacted in the first place. Conservative action, or rather inaction, in the Lords confirmed these sentiments, in that the old age pensions legislation was one of the few Liberal measures not savaged by Mr Balfour's poodle. It was thus typical of the Conservative response to the pensions legislation that the 'Unauthorized Programme' of September 1908 stressed that 'In the field of social reform the most important question now before the country is the *future development* of the system of old age pensions', it being understood that 'we have no desire to reverse what has been done, for we look to the future rather than to the past'.[73]

Exactly how pensions were to be developed was discussed in some detail at the 1909 NUCA Conference. H.K. Newton, a member of the National Union Council, argued that old age pensions could be made more generous by removing the disqualifications which applied to paupers and 'enlarging and extending the size of the benefits'.[74] These improvements were to be made practicable by switching to a contributory structure, to be implemented after consultation with the Friendly Societies who, along with the Trade Unions, were seen as 'a nucleus of a scheme for old age pensions by means of insurance'.[75] This proposal, which received the unanimous backing of the NUCA, expressed the consistent Conservative opinion that a contributory scheme was the most equitable and efficient way of funding a comprehensive pensions system.[76] One attraction of contributory pensions, as a Lancastrian Conservative stated in a letter to Lord Derby in November 1910, was that such a scheme would facilitate

> the offer of a larger old age pension ... say 7/6 or 10/- per week at 60, with the argument that 5/- per week at 70 [the 1908 level] is a charity dole insufficient for proper support, pauperising in its influence and not capable of comparison with a system of contributory pension at 60 of say 7/6 per week.[77]

This would enable the Conservatives to 'outbid' the Liberals. The cost of a contributory system, as Derby's correspondent went on to point out, would be minimal; contributions could be collected through the Post Office by means of special stamps thereby reducing administrative overheads, but, additionally, 'as we know the average life of the working class to be 53 years or less the scheme is almost at once self-supporting'.[78] It is impossible to establish whether it was the cost advantages, or the possible electoral advantage which led Conservatives to advocate contributory pensions. What is certain is that the Conservative discussion of old age

255

pensions indicated a desire to deny the Liberal and Labour parties a clear run on this most publicized of social reforms and to develop a distinctive but positive approach to the pensions issue.

ii. The regulation of labour

Old age pensions were a focus of much Conservative discussion of social reform, but an important aspect of Conservative thinking on social legislation was that pensions 'should be considered and dealt with in relation to other questions of national organization'.[79] In this context a great deal of Conservative attention was devoted to issues of labour regulation. In presenting the case for contributory pensions the 'Unauthorized Programme' noted that 'such a system would carry with it the incidental advantage of effecting the registration of our industrial population . . . a condition essential to the solution of unemployment and other pressing social problems'.[80] The importance of labour registries, according to Arthur Steel-Maitland, was that they would reduce the problems associated with casual labour and help 'regularize employment'. More regular employment was seen as a good thing in itself, but Steel-Maitland contended that a more regularly employed workforce would mean a higher demand for goods and thus a greater demand for labour.[81] The idea of using labour registries to improve the flow of information in the labour market was also part of Fabian thinking, was prominent in the work of the young William Beveridge and had percolated into the 'official mind' of the labour department at the Board of Trade.[82] Conservative thinking was thus in keeping with a broad sweep of contemporary opinion on the 'labour problem', and when the Liberal government introduced legislation to establish Labour Exchanges in 1909 the Conservatives treated the measure as non-controversial, with Bonar Law stating in the Commons that 'The principle of the [Labour Exchanges] Bill . . . [is] one on which certainly everybody is pretty well agreed'.[83] The only issues raised by Conservatives were how the cost of Labour Exchanges was to be met, and, pointing to the German example, argued that the more general security of employment guaranteed by tariffs would allow Labour Exchanges to deal with a smaller problem more effectively.[84]

The Conservative party's positive approach to labour registries was matched by their interest in sweated labour. Sweating had first emerged as a question of major concern in the mid-1880s, and a Parliamentary Select Committee had investigated the problem during Salisbury's second administration. In spite of continued revelations in the 1890s, particularly about working conditions in the clothing trades,[85] sweating remained in the pending file of British political debate until after 1906, when a number of legislative proposals were brought forward, culminating with the 1909 Trade Boards Act. This Act appears to conform to a traditional, 'triumphalist' model of welfare legislation – 'discovery' of a problem, followed by 'scientific investigation', followed by pressure from 'progressive' groups and individuals, followed by action when a progressively-minded government was elected. Revelations about sweating in the 1880s appear as part of the more general 'discovery' of systemic causes of poverty in the late nineteenth century, which in turn led to a disenchantment with laissez faire and a call for government regulation by groups like the National Anti-Sweating League (NASL). The election of a social-reforming Liberal government in 1906, which included some prominent members of the NASL, can thus be seen as the penultimate phase of a process which culminated with the 1909 Act. This description of the emergence of the Trade Boards Act undoubtedly tells part of the story, but only a part. The impetus for anti-sweating legislation came not simply from the development of new knowledge and new theories which provided Progressives with a justification for government intervention. Of equal significance was the party-political struggle after 1906, and the Conservatives' attempt to present themselves as champions of the crusade against sweating.

The part played by the NASL, and in particular the Liberal members of that body, in helping to shape the Trade Boards Act has been acknowledged by historical scholarship.[86] Yet although it would be an exaggeration to call the NASL a 'cross-party' organization, there were Conservatives in its upper echelons, with J.W. Hills, Edward Goulding, Arthur Steel-Maitland, Lord Henry Bentinck and Fabian Ware especially prominent. As a consequence, when the Liberal government made their first attempt to grapple with sweated labour in February 1908, in the shape of a Sweated Industries Bill, the Conservatives were in a good position to offer positive criticism. Indeed, J.W. Hills argued in Parliament that the major problem with the Liberal measure was that its regulatory powers were too limited and that

> all the evils of sweating, low wages, long hours, insanitary dwellings, were forms of the great problem of poverty . . . [and] The only way in which this could be altered was by raising wages . . . artificially . . . by State interference.[87]

Such a policy 'would pay the community over and over again, because they had to regard the race, and if this low standard of living deteriorated then it was bad for the community at large'.[88] Hills' argument was endorsed by the 'Unauthorized Programme', which, in line with stated NASL policy, called for 'the establishment of wages boards for specified industries'.[89] These boards were to be 'formed of an equal number of representatives of employers and employees, with an impartial chairman'; their role would consist of 'fixing from time to time, minimum wage rates for their respective areas'.[90] The idea of 'freedom of contract' was thus abrogated on explicitly Collectivist grounds, and in February 1909 a legislative proposal was presented to Parliament on precisely these lines. The new Sweated Industries Bill was presented by J.W. Hills, but two of the Bill's main sponsors were Sir Charles Dilke and Arthur Henderson.[91] This cross-party support showed it was very difficult to differentiate the Conservative position on sweating from that of many Progressives. In the end Hills' proposal was withdrawn, but largely because the government indicated that it was about to bring forward an almost identical measure,[92] the Trade Boards Bill, which would come into force later in 1909. As was the case with the Labour Exchanges legislation, the Trade Boards Bill was treated by the Conservatives as non-controversial.[93] They tried to introduce only one significant amendment, a proposal to make foreign competition an 'objection' which could be raised by employers and/or employees with the Board of Trade when wage rates were being established for a specific industry.[94] In other words the Conservatives' sole criticism of the Trade Boards Act was that it failed to acknowledge a link between wage rates and foreign competition, a point which they foregrounded two years later with their proposal to restrict the import of foreign sweated goods.[95]

iii. Land reform

It would be wrong to conclude this brief analysis of Conservative views on social reform between 1903 and 1910 without some mention of land reform. The details of the Conservative party's proposals for land reform have been discussed before in terms of 'the defence of British agriculture', but the Conservatives argued that the creation of small holdings would have beneficial social effects. Giving 'Hodge' the opportunity to acquire a small holding was described as one way to improve the lot of the agricultural labourer. The 'new peasantry', supported by co-operative marketing, State-funded education in up-to-date farming techniques, and moderate tariffs, was to enjoy self-sufficiency and a standard of living no longer dependent on an uncertain, seasonal wage system. At the same time, however, small holdings were also presented as a means of solving urban social problems. As Sir Gilbert Parker stated in his 1909 pamphlet *The Land for the People*,

> [L]abour is leaving the fields. The best of it emigrates to develop foreign countries, the worst remains to overcrowd and pauperise our towns. The countryside is lonely, the cities are thronged with the miserable ... we are declining, losing in wealth, in men ... in personal physique ... By losing the proportions between the field and the factory the national equilibrium is violently disturbed, and grave social and economic problems are being created.[96]

In short, unemployment, over-crowding and unsanitary conditions in Britain's towns and cities were products of rural depopulation. The solution, therefore, was to encourage some of those who had abandoned the countryside to return to rural life. To achieve this it was necessary to offer the inducement of a stable rural economy with a higher standard of living than that available in the towns. Small holdings, underpinned by a network of State-encouraged or State-subsidized supporting services, were presented as the inducement which could fulfil these requirements.

As early as 1873 the eugenicist Francis Galton had argued that rural depopulation and the consequent imbalance between rural and urban dwellers in Britain were causing a 'deterioration of the race', and thereafter most discussions of 'the condition of the people' stressed the importance of redressing this imbalance.[97] By the Edwardian period the cry of 'Back to the Land' was voiced in one form or another by an astonishing variety of political and quasi-political organizations. Arguably the most lasting Edwardian tribute to the superiority of the countryside was Ebenezer Howard's garden city movement, which, in the shape of Letchworth, created a *rus in urbe* tabernacle to the joys of rural life. The social benefits of country living were also stressed by the National Service League. In the wake of revelations about the (un)fitness of Boer War recruits drawn from the cities, the NSL argued that a healthy army depended upon recruits who had enjoyed a healthy rural life.[98] Further 'scientific' support came from the Eugenics Society and the findings of the 1904 Parliamentary Committee on Physical Deterioration, both of which agreed that rural dwellers were physically and indeed morally superior to their urban counterparts.[99] Ideas about the social benefits of returning people to the land were politically widespread. In 1904 land reform and repeopling the countryside played a central part in James Keir Hardie's schemes for dealing with unemployment and attendant social problems,[100] and other Labour politicians – George Lansbury, Ben Tillett and Ramsay MacDonald – saw land reform as intrinsic to social reform. Likewise the Land Campaign of 1912 represented the culmination of a long tradition of Liberal thought which linked land reform to social progress and the relief of social ills, a tradition which had found expression not only in Gladstone's Irish land reforms, but in the allotments and small holdings schemes promulgated by Sir William Harcourt in the 1890s and by his son Ludovic in 1908.

In presenting land reform as a key element of their social programme the Conservatives were not promulgating an eccentric view of welfare policy. The only 'peculiarities' of the Conservative case for land reform were the emphasis placed on small *ownership*, which was contrasted with the Liberal–Socialist emphasis on tenancy, and the argument for supporting newly-established small holders with tariffs. A broad range of contemporary opinion tended to see *urbanization* rather than industrialization *per se* as a major cause of Britain's social ills. When seen in this context, Conservative pronouncements and promises on small holdings, from Jesse Collings' perennial proposals, through the statements of the 'Unauthorized Programme', to the commitment made by Arthur Balfour in January 1910, were simply one more part of the Conservatives' effort to establish their credentials as a social-reforming party.

CONCLUDING REMARKS

Between 1903 and 1910 the Conservative party became increasingly receptive to the idea of developing a distinctive policy on social reform. At the outset most of the running was made by a number of committed individuals, but after 1906 the Conservative party as a whole sought to avoid a negative image on issues of social policy. Electoral considerations provided the main impetus for this development. The Conservatives' electoral slump after 1900 and their mini-revival in 1908, when coupled with developments on the Left, resulted in an increased acceptance amongst Conservatives that it was time to act upon the long-established assumption that the way to the mass electorate's heart was through social reform. But although electoral factors can explain the *timing* of the Conservative party's move towards a positive stance on social reform, they do not explain the *nature* of the Conservatives' social policy proposals.

In confronting their electoral problems the Conservatives had to face a number of other difficult questions. In January 1909 the Conservative weekly *The Outlook* noted that

> The new political divisions are growths whose branches touch the firmament, and whose roots strike down to the bedrock of society. The greatest of such divisions is concerned with the relations of the State and the Individual. Does the State exist by and for the citizen, or does the Citizen exist by and for the State? ... In fine, is the State or the Individual to be the unit of our social and economic policy.[101]

This was certainly a fair picture of the 'new political divisions' within the Conservative party. In October 1907 St Loe Strachey, the leading Conservative free trade publicist, denounced Conservative supporters of old age pensions on the grounds that 'a bad proposal like old age pensions is not improved by calling it social reform instead of Socialism'.[102] Strachey's views were contradicted by J.L. Garvin, who declared that 'the *Spectator* ... is wrong in thinking that social reform, even when involving sweeping measures of State intervention is the same thing as Socialism ... they may be as opposite as bane and antidote'.[103] Clearly there was an argument raging within the Conservative party over the proper realm of State activity, but by 1908 one of the more obscure members of the Chamberlain clan felt confident enough to declare gone is the pure Individualism of Lord Morley and Lord Hugh Cecil, with its profound distrust of all State action, and its indifference to the use or waste of national manpower ... [although] a devoted few under the aegis of Lord Hugh and Mr Strachey have raised its last sanctuary in the British Constitutional Association.[104]

Norman Chamberlain's description of the situation was quite accurate. By 1908 the Conservative party's increasingly positive stance on social reform had left the Conservative free traders out in the cold, and the British Constitutional Association had indeed emerged as a last refuge for disgruntled Individualists from both major parties.[105] In effect the swing towards social reform can be seen in terms of the Conservative party's participation in the more general 'Individualist versus Collectivist' debate which was such a characteristic feature of political argument in late Victorian and Edwardian Britain. As the Conservative party struggled to construct a viable electoral strategy so too they were forced to redefine their position on the role of the State in economy and society.

The Edwardian Conservative party gradually accepted an extended, positive role for the State, but how could they justify this as *Conservative*? State intervention was designed to benefit directly one section of society, the working class. Such benefits could be deemed a social good on the grounds that society, considered organically, would be improved by raising the standard of living, quality of life and health of the lower strata. But the fact remained that to speak of class benefits, as Lord Salisbury had recognized, was to risk awakening class antagonisms. Hence, in addressing the question of social reform, and in attempting to use social reform to gain mass support, the Conservative party had to shape a class appeal that eschewed antagonistic class politics. That class was central to Conservative thinking in this context is amply demonstrated by the actions (and inactions) of the House of Lords between 1906 and 1910. The Liberal government's social reform and trade union measures, that is to say legislation designed specifically for the working class as a class, were left untouched. However, measures that could be deemed 'sectional', such as education reform and Irish legislation, were systematically mutilated in the Upper House. The only exception to this rule was the People's Budget, which was deemed unacceptable not because it was designed to benefit the working class, but because it did so at the expense of the upper classes. The key, then, to *Conservative* social reform was to benefit the working class as a class but without 'robbing henroosts', and it was in this context that tariffs became so crucial to the Conservative strategy.

That tariffs could provide a non-punitive means of funding social reform was one way of overcoming its intrinsic class bias, but this was by no means their most significant aspect. In October 1903 Joseph Chamberlain stated 'it is absolutely impossible to reconcile Free Trade

with trade unionism'.[106] Only a month later one of Chamberlain's lieu-
tenants, Leo Amery, asked Benjamin Kidd to produce

> a leaflet or short pamphlet setting forth as succinctly as possible that
> trade unionism and our movement are really one and the same
> thing: that unionism defeats its own ends if it only keeps out the
> home 'blackleg' but pays no heed to the foreign blackleg.[107]

Amery himself was instrumental in establishing one of the most
interesting, if one of the most unsuccessful, Conservative attempts to
appeal to organized labour on the very grounds he had outlined to Kidd
– the Trade Union Tariff Reform Association (TUTRA).[108] The failure of
the TUTRA did not, however, dent Conservative hopes that organized
labour would flock to the banner of tariff reform. These hopes grew: in
January 1906 Bernard Holland, a staunch tariff reformer, stated that he
had 'little doubt that five years hence the Labour party will be in favour
of a general tariff on manufactured goods', whilst the self-professed tariff
'agnostic' E.B. Iwan-Muller argued that 'organised labour is . . . as likely
as not in the future . . . to prove severely protectionist. If it is sincere in its
programme it *must* be protectionist'.[109] Since the aim of trade unions was
to protect the interests of their members, then protectionism, which
would defend jobs, was in harmony with the trade union *raison d'être*. It
was assumed that trade unionists could be persuaded that their interests
as workers and producers stood above all their other interests. In other
words the Conservatives hoped, to use a Marxian distinction, that a tariff
appeal to the interests of the working class as a class *in itself* could be used
to override attempts to mobilize them as a class *for itself*. The argument
that the protection of national production and national labour would
create the revenue to pay for social reform likewise confirms the
Conservative party's determination to present itself as the producers'
party. In this way they sought to speak the language of class with a
Conservative accent. Well-worn Victorian assertions about the unity of
capital and labour and the priority of production over distribution had
been changed. The Victorians had seen the unity of capital and labour in
terms of keeping the State out of social and economic life, but the
Edwardian Conservative party looked to State intervention to demonstrate and promote the harmony of class interests.

The Conservative party's evolving position on the question of social
reform indicates that the tariff campaign was 'instrumental in drawing
the Tory party towards the twentieth-century notion of the State with its
responsibility for managing the economy and maintaining the rising standards of the people'.[110] The political and electoral climate of Edwardian
Britain convinced the Conservatives that it was essential 'to see their way
towards a labour policy which will satisfy some of the demands of the
labour people',[111] and tariff reform was the basis for just such a policy.

The employment and revenue aspects of tariffs provided the Conservatives with a clear critique of Liberal and Labour policies, but more importantly they underpinned the Conservative party's own social reform programme – 'a policy equally removed from individualism and ... demagogic socialism'.[112] In late 1909 the Conservatives' social policies were still evolving, and there was to be renewed intra-party debate on social issues in the wake of the party's two election defeats in 1910. However, as the Conservatives prepared for the January 1910 election they could lay claim to a distinctive, Collectivist approach to 'the social question' based on a positive conception of a producers' State.

Part IV

DISINTEGRATION

11

DISINTEGRATION

Things fall apart; the centre cannot hold.

(W.B. Yeats, *The Second Coming*)

The Conservative party entered the general election campaign of January 1910 with tariff reform the coping stone of an ambitious and radical policy structure. This structure – 'the full tariff programme' – was a product of an attempt to construct a coalition of social forces that could defend the interests and institutions identified with Conservatism against both external threat and internal disruption. Conservatives, grudgingly in some cases, had come to accept this programme as the best hope for Conservatism in the early twentieth century. But between January 1910 and the outbreak of the Great War the unity constructed on the basis of the 'economics of political integration' was destroyed.

The apparent failure of the full programme to deliver electoral success in 1910, and in particular the party's inability to make a breakthrough in the electoral cockpit of England, Lancashire, was a root cause of the party's retreat from the full programme. Even the confidence of some of the most committed Radical Conservatives was dented, with Benjamin Kidd telling Alfred Lyttelton that

> the fighting centre of the opposition to Tariff Reform is the Lancashire cotton trade. It cannot be otherwise for Lancashire must selfishly fight to the death against protection for native manufacturers in India ... Lancashire will fight the case to the bitter end ... [and] all this talk of converting Lancashire is therefore nonsense.[1]

Kidd did not advocate abandonment of the full programme, but the very fact that a 'true believer' could express such doubts is an indication of how far confidence in the Radical Conservative strategy had been shaken. In short, just as the situation between 1903 and 1910 had been increasingly conducive to the purchase of Radical Conservative arguments, so the period after 1910 weakened their purchase. This is not to say that the Conservative party retreated either fully or in a straight line from one position to another between 1910 and 1914. Rather the party became embroiled in a prolonged and inconclusive internal debate. Having entered the January 1910 general election campaign with high hopes and a clear sense of direction, the Conservative party descended into confusion; on the eve of the Great War it was unsure of its future strategy or even its future.

DEFINING THE PROBLEM 1910–14: CONSERVATISM ON THE ELECTORAL AND POLITICAL DEFENSIVE

In the two general elections of 1910 the Conservative party recovered much of the ground lost in 1906. In both elections the Conservatives received the largest share of the popular vote, and in December 1910 they won the same number of seats as the Liberals. However, these results, as many at the time realized, were no cause for Conservative optimism. Electoral history after 1885 showed that the Conservatives were essentially an English party. Scotland and Wales (apart from the narrow Conservative majorities in Scotland in 1895 and 1900) were strongly Liberal, and Ireland was dominated by Irish Nationalists. To win an election, the Conservatives had to obtain a big majority of the 428 English county and borough seats. In particular they had to do well in the 154 seats in the North and the 59 seats in London. But in England, and in the North and London especially, the Labour party, in tandem with the Liberals, had weakened the Conservative position. Conservatives after 1910 frequently referred to the government as 'the Coalition' in recognition that they were faced by an unprecedentedly solid anti-Conservative bloc.

Superficially Conservatives did well at by-elections in the period 1910 to 1914,[2] but their electoral position remained fragile. Between December 1910 and August 1914 they gained 16 seats. Of these, nine were made in three-cornered contests, and in seven the division of the Liberal-Labour vote let them in. The other seven gains were achieved in straight fights with Liberal, and in one case Labour, opponents. In two cases the seats remained highly marginal, with Cheltenham returning a Conservative by four votes in a poll of over 8,000. Nor were the remaining five 'good' Conservative gains unequivocal successes: the North-West Manchester victory of August 1912 was achieved on a poll reduced by 1,000 from that recorded in January 1910; East Cambridgeshire in May 1913 saw the Conservatives recapture a seat they had won in January 1910 and lost in December, whilst in November 1912 the Conservatives won Bow and Bromley in most peculiar circumstances.[3] Thus only two by-election gains, South Manchester and South Somerset, could offer comfort. Ultimately, these results showed that the electoral fate of the Conservative party hung on the state of relations between the Liberal and Labour parties, and reports of the Progressive Alliance's death before

1914 have been greatly exaggerated.[4] Neither Steel-Maitland, the Conservative party chairman after 1911, nor the Conservative Whips, had any deep confidence in a Conservative electoral victory.[5] A CCO memorandum prepared as late as 1916 produced, albeit in retrospect, a gloomy analysis of pre-war electoral prospects. According to this, the best that could have been hoped for was a swing of 5 per cent against the Liberals and a Conservative majority of twelve in a winter 1914 election. But CCO acknowledged that this was an unlikely scenario, as the Liberals would not have held an election before they had abolished plural voting (as they had intended) and on that basis CCO estimated that the Liberals would have achieved a majority over the Conservatives of 38 to 40 seats in a May 1915 election.[6]

In the period 1910 to 1914 the situation was made worse, in that the Conservatives faced continued onslaughts on their cherished institutions. To begin with, there was the House of Lords. The election of January 1910 had been called after the Lords rejected the 1909 Budget. The Liberals fought on a 'Peers versus People' cry, and it was clear that the outcome of the election would determine the future of the Upper Chamber's legislative function. The Liberals' return to office in both January and December 1910, and the failure of the 'Truce of God' occasioned by Edward VII's death to produce a compromise between the major parties, resulted in the Liberals moving to abolish the Lords' legislative veto. By means of the Parliament Bill, introduced in February 1911, 'Mr Balfour's poodle' was to be neutered.

The abolition of the Lords' veto powers was a serious blow to the Conservatives. For decades, and in particular since the mid-1880s, the House of Lords had provided the Conservative party with a last line of defence against unsavoury legislation.[7] Lord Selborne argued that 'the principal function of a second chamber is to protect the essential interests and institutions of the country against hasty and ill-considered legislation',[8] and the in-built Conservative majority in the Lords was able to define which legislation was 'hasty and ill-considered'. Selborne stressed financial legislation: 'To deprive the second chamber of all financial powers would leave private property at the mercy of any chance majority elected to the House of Commons.'[9] For the party of property 'single chamber government' based on the principles of the People's Budget was a threatening prospect.

Nor was private property the only institution close to Conservative hearts threatened by the abolition of the Lords' veto. The elections of 1910 had left the Liberals dependent not only upon the 'Socialist' contingent, but also upon the Irish Nationalists, and the obvious price for that support was Home Rule. With the Labour party also supporting the Irish cause there was, after 1910, an overwhelming Commons majority in favour of Home Rule. The abolition of the Lords' veto thus implied an end to the Union with Ireland. Sure enough, in April 1912, less than a year after the Parliament Act was passed, Asquith's government introduced a new Home Rule Bill, and the Conservatives' worst fears were realized.

In terms of the more general political context the Conservatives also continued to find themselves on the defensive. Between 1906 and 1910 the Liberals' social-reforming initiatives had, so Conservatives thought, underpinned the government's popular appeal and helped prevent a Conservative electoral breakthrough. In the period 1910 to 1914 such Liberal initiatives were more limited, but the National Insurance legislation of 1911 threw Conservatives into confusion, and Lloyd George's Land Campaign, launched in 1913, induced panic in the Conservative ranks. Some historians have argued that the Liberal party's reforming impetus was lost after 1910, but to the Conservative party at the time, Asquith's government seemed innovative and dangerous. Indeed Liberal reliance on Labour and Irish support after 1910 made the government appear even more radical. Besides Irish Home Rule there were the demands of Socialists and militant trade unions, made all the more alarming by widespread labour unrest in the period. Wherever the Conservatives looked the political situation seemed potentially disastrous.

SHAPING THE CONSERVATIVE RESPONSE, 1910–14: THE POLITICS OF CONFUSION

Conflict between advocates of different responses to the party's problems meant that from the first months of 1910 to the outbreak of the Great War the Conservative party found it difficult to establish a consensus on any major issue; the party's disagreements led to the resignation of one leader and the threatened resignation of his successor. Between 1906 and 1910 there had been general agreement that the full tariff programme was a plausible solution to the party's various problems, but between 1910 and 1914 the Conservatives found problems and no solutions. The years immediately before the Great War saw a continuance and in some ways a deepening of the crisis of Conservatism.

Internecine strife was renewed in earnest in 1910, when the party failed to win either of the general elections of that year. In the immediate aftermath of the election defeats there was one point agreed, namely the need to overhaul party organization. But this was the limit of consensus as only a minority of Conservatives blamed their electoral difficulties solely on inefficient organization. In February 1911 Arthur Steel-Maitland indicated where deeper disgreements in the party lay when he declared 'the Archangel Gabriel would be a failure as Chief Agent unless he had a policy for which to organize', and he underlined this point in July the same year, stating that 'organization, by itself, is not enough' and arguing that the party needed 'a coherent and democractic policy for which to organize'.[10] The question Conservatives faced was what represented a 'coherent and democratic policy', and between January 1910 and the outbreak of the Great War they could not produce a clear or united answer.

THE HOUSE OF LORDS

After the 1910 elections, the Liberal government's determination to reduce the powers of the House of Lords produced deep fissures in the Conservative ranks.[11] The party split into three camps: the 'Diehards' or 'Ditchers' wanted to reject the Parliament Bill, the 'Hedgers' favoured abstention, and the 'Rats' were for acquiescence. Disagreement thus appeared straightforward, but more than the Lords' veto was at stake.

The 'Hedgers', with whom Arthur Balfour had most sympathy, took the view that the Parliament Bill was a *fait accompli*, but that the delaying powers left to the Lords would, in the hands of a Conservative majority in the Upper House, represent a still useful weapon.[12] The Diehards felt that a Second Chamber without veto powers was worthless. Their strategy was to counter-attack by offering an alternative reform of the Upper House. In February 1911 a meeting of 180 Conservatives proposed the reconstruction of the Lords as a 300-member chamber, consisting of 100 members elected from and by the peerage, 100 nominated by the Prime Minister of the day, and 100 directly elected by popular vote.[13] The hereditary element was thus to be preserved, but the directly elected members were to bring a 'democractic' element to the Upper Chamber and thereby justify its retention of a veto. This counter-offensive to the Radical attack was designed to forestall more damaging changes.

After the passage of the Parliament Bill, the Diehards created an organization – the Halsbury Club – to 'keep our force intact ... [and] put forward a true Tory policy'.[14] The kind of policy they sought was outlined by Neville Chamberlain, who told his half-brother soon after the inaugural meeting of the Halsbury Club that 'Milner, Carson, Selborne, Willoughby de Broke and other Diehards [have] met and decided to act together and *go for a forward policy*'.[15] The Diehard movement represented one more effort in the long-running attempt to equip the Conservatives with a positive stance.

Conservative convulsions over the Parliament Bill showed the party was deeply troubled. The Liberals had always had the upper hand: they possessed a Commons majority in favour of abolishing the Lords' veto, and had George V's promise to create enough Liberal peers to pass the Parliament Bill if it were defeated in the Lords. Perhaps the Conservatives' hopeless position was responsible for their shambolic response to the Parliament Bill, but it is also the case that divisions on this issue reflected deeper divisions of opinion within both the party and the peerage.

The 'constitutional crisis' had arisen because the Lords rejected the People's Budget. At the time, this had seemed a reckless act, running counter to Salisbury's maxim that the Lords avoid appearing as a class-biased institution. Such intemperate behaviour could be attributed to poor leadership. But Balfour's problems were more the product of the situation he faced. Salisbury had dealt with a divided and irresolute Liberal party neither able nor willing to confront the Lords. Moreover, Conservative electoral success in the 1880s and 1890s meant that the Lords had not faced an extended period of Radical legislation. After 1906 the situation changed. The Liberals were possessed of a large Commons majority and united behind a Radical, even Socialistic programme. In short, what had been only a Salisburyian nightmare became a reality for Balfour's party. Many peers, especially the 'backwoodsmen' who emerged from rural exile in 1909 to fight Lloyd George, saw the People's Budget as a spiteful assault on an already 'beleaguered' class. Their veto was a product of fear and frustration brewing over twenty or so years.[16] In these circumstances it would have been difficult to control the Lords' reaction. Salisbury had had to work hard, even when things were quiet, to get 'their Lordships' to adhere to the rules of his 'long game', but the People's Budget represented the apogee of anti-landlord political economy – for the peerage there was no 'long game' left to play. Furthermore, the People's Budget and the land taxes were seen by all Conservatives, not just the peers, as a dangerous threat to property. The party as a whole, especially the rank and file, approved of the Lords' 'intemperate' action.[17]

Had the Conservatives won in 1910 all would have been well. However, having lost a 'Peers versus People' contest their problems multiplied. The peers had been almost unanimous in rejecting the Budget, seeking to provoke an election in the hope of a Conservative victory. When this gamble failed, the peers had to find some way of accommodating themselves to a new tax regime. In the 1880s, as noted earlier,[18] the political as well as the economic situation had helped to determine the financial dispositions of some aristocrats.[19] As early as the 1890s Oscar Wilde's Lady Bracknell had preferred 'the funds' to land, and many non-fictional members of her class, especially after the 1909 Budget, felt the same. In January 1912 the Duke of Portsmouth told Law that the Budget had been

> the adoption of a system through which the State . . . could from
> time to time turn the thumb screw on the capital and savings of the
> individual . . . Ever since that Budget, I have, as indeed have many
> others, guiltily been transferring our old and making our new

investments in securities outside this country, and where the Dividends need not be collected here.[20]

For many aristocratic families, especially those of middling and lower rank, a combination of economic hardship and political insecurity prompted them to downgrade their interests in the land or even leave the country.[21] Many large estates continued to flourish, but enough 'broad acres' were traded for securities,[22] and sufficient country homes exchanged for places like Kenya's 'Happy Valley', to register a class no longer confident of its place in society.

The Parliament Bill threatened a further double blow to the aristocracy's status. In itself the abolition of the Lords' veto threatened to end the aristocracy's privileged role in the constitution. In addition, the Liberals' statement that they would create 500 new peers if the Bill were rejected threatened the social homogeneity of the British peerage. Thus the peers confronted a painful dilemma in 1910–11. If they accepted the Bill their special constitutional status was gone, but if they defied the government they would lose their constitutional authority *and* their social exclusivity. That the Lords passed the Parliament Bill seems to indicate that they preferred the latter to the former. This was the Diehards' interpretation of events. They felt that the Hedgers and Rats simply wished to prevent 'the wrong sort' from being ennobled.[23] There was certainly much talk in aristocratic circles of the Liberals trying to 'vulgarize our order', and Balfour noted that Diehard action would mean that if 'you object to your tailor being made a peer, you mean to vote in such a way that your hatter and barber shall be ennobled also'.[24] Hedger and Rat behaviour cannot be attributed solely to politically supine snobbery, but in a broader sense there is something in the notion that the peerage – some reluctantly, others more willingly – *chose* to abandon their political role in 1911. By 1917 the Duke of Northumberland told his Diehard leader Lord Halsbury that 'I have almost abandoned politics as hopeless – at any rate for a peer'.[25] For Northumberland, whose family had exercised political authority for centuries, the notion that a peer's involvement in politics was no longer automatic had obviously been difficult to accept. Others, notably Hedgers and Rats accepted it more easily. Ultimately, the division of opinion amongst the peers over the Parliament Bill was an argument between those who felt they could do nothing but retreat from the centre of politics with the dignity of their titles intact, and those who raged against the dying of the light.

For the Conservative party the Parliament Bill, and the divisions it opened up within the peerage, had important consequences. The Upper Chamber had been the means of making good Balfour's boast of 1906 that whoever had a majority in the Commons the Conservatives governed the Empire, but after 1911 that was no longer the case. However, the

Conservatives were not only defeated in 1911, they were divided. The majority of the party supported the Diehard attempt to preserve Britain's *ancien régime*, but not a large enough majority to force a final showdown over the creation of Liberal peers. This created great bitterness. Just before the Lords voted on the Parliament Bill, Lord Selborne told his wife 'If they [the Rats] beat us . . . there will be a very serious position in the party',[26] and his views were confirmed by the party's Chief Whip.[27] Most of the 'deep-rooted animus'[28] was directed at the Rats, but the Hedgers did not escape Diehard wrath. Balfour also became a target for criticism, in part because of his enigmatic stance on the Parliament Bill, but also because his absence from the country on the day of the vote was interpreted as at best negligent and at worst cowardly.[29] Becoming the first Conservative leader since Peel to be, in effect, driven from his post, Balfour resigned because neither his party nor his class could be united against the challenge of democracy represented by the Parliament Bill.

THE 'FOOD TAX' CONTROVERSY

Two months before the January 1910 election J.P. Hughes, the Conservative chief agent, predicted the party would make gains in London, the Home Counties, East Anglia and the West Country, but that the North, Yorkshire and Lancashire would produce disappointing results. Hughes also reported that the electorate's response to the House of Lords, abuse of the People's Budget, and opposition to Home Rule was luke-warm or hostile, but that 'the proposal to take full toll of the foreigner and to produce . . . a rapid expansion of trade within the Empire commands an instant and genuine audience'.[30] However, Hughes also indicated that the popularity of tariffs was confined largely to areas where he predicted Conservative gains.[31] The conflicting signals Hughes received during the election, and the regional disparities in the results that he accurately predicted, were to shape one of the most important debates in the Conservative party over the next four years – whether to press on with the 'food tax' element of the tariff programme.

The 'food tax' debate has been studied extensively,[32] and there is little to be gained from a further detailed account here. Briefly, the critics of food taxes went on the offensive after the January 1910 election, and secured in the first instance a pledge that a Conservative government would admit colonial corn duty free. During the December 1910 election, Balfour, under pressure from Conservatives in Lancashire in particular, declared that food taxes would be submitted to referendum, and, as a consequence, alienated supporters of the full programme. Balfour's resignation in October 1911, and his replacement by Law, seemed to indicate a renewed commitment to the full programme, but over the next year Law came under pressure, much of it emanating from Lancashire, to drop the food taxes. The crisis point was reached in the winter of 1912–13. In early December Lord Lansdowne publicly repudiated a food tax referendum, provoking outcry in Lancashire. Law attempted to calm the situation in a speech at Ashton-Under-Lyne, where he stated that any initiative for food taxes would have to come from the Colonies. Following furious debate, which saw tempers at boiling point and Law threatening to resign, the leadership found party opinion moving against food taxes, and in January 1913 Law announced that a future Conservative government would not impose food taxes without holding a general election – the so-called 'Edinburgh compromise'.

So much for the basic story. But what was all the arguing and intrigue about? One answer is the Empire. The food tax debate had begun with Joseph Chamberlain's call for imperial preference, and this was still central to the full programme after 1910. Indeed, for committed supporters imperial preference was regarded as more important than ever. Reciprocal trade negotiations between Canada and the USA had raised the spectre of Britain's most prosperous and valued dominion moving out of the imperial trade orbit. That Canada was even contemplating a treaty with the USA was seen as a result of negligence on the part not only of the British government but also the Conservative party. The Liberals' failure to respond to the 'Colonial Offer' at the Imperial Conferences of 1907 and 1911 was roundly condemned.[33] However, Conservative indecision was also deprecated, with Arthur Steel-Maitland arguing that 'the present Canadian Reciprocity agreement is just the result of the previous unbusinesslike behaviour of our party'.[34] The electoral victory of the Anglophile Canadian Conservatives in September 1911 was thought to have saved the day, with Sir Vincent Caillard summing up the euphoric response of British imperialists when he declared 'What a "Glory Be" victory Canada has won for our cause'.[35] Yet little over a year later the British Conservatives were turning their backs on preference in a manner which could but 'offend the Colonies'.[36] For imperial enthusiasts in the Conservative camp the 'postponement' of the food taxes sent the Colonies the wrong signals at the wrong time.

Domestic considerations also shaped the food tax debate. The core issue was made clear during the 1910 election campaigns. In January 1910 advocates of the full programme complained that mere opposition to the People's Budget had been too prominent a feature of the Conservative campaign, with the result that 'nine out of ten working men' saw the election as about 'coronets and landowners against the people's budget'[37] rather than the merits of the tariff programme. In contrast, their opponents argued that the party had failed simply because of the food taxes.

That critics of food taxes were able to attack after January 1910 was due to Conservatives agreeing on one reason for their party's failure, namely the lack of a breakthrough in Lancashire. In April 1910 *The Outlook*, always sympathetic to the full programme, conceded that 'the Cotton districts . . . remain the great electoral problem of the Unionist Party', and in October Balfour told Lord Derby 'I regard Lancashire as the very key and centre of the next electoral battle-field'.[38] But the question remained as to how this breakthrough was to be secured. For Lord Derby, the 'King of Lancashire', the party's failings in the Duchy were the result of the food taxes, and immediately after the January 1910 election he and other Lancashire party bosses pressed for them to be 'postponed' or abandoned.[39]

The decision to send Law to fight North-West Manchester in December 1910 confirmed Lancashire's importance to the Conservative cause, and his contest became a litmus test of the full tariff programme's viability in this crucial region. From the time he arrived in Manchester Law came under pressure from local grandees to soft-pedal the food taxes.[40] In particular, local opinion argued that 'Lancashire can be won only if Balfour announces that Tariff on passing would be submitted to a referendum'.[41] Law appears to have been persuaded to accept this argument, and in turn his views influenced Balfour, for in December 1910 Balfour announced that a Conservative administration would submit a tariff budget to a referendum if Asquith pledged to do the same with Home Rule.

This 'referendum pledge' appears to have had little electoral impact – it certainly did not prevent Law from losing in North-West Manchester – but it provoked a storm in the party. 'Our mutual friend', Leo Maxse told Edward Goulding, 'has done more harm to tariff reform during the past two months than he did good in the past five years . . . I calculate that Balfour's . . . speech cost us 40–50 seats'.[42] Maxse's distrust of Balfour was well known, but his views were supported by Radical Conservatives who had been close to the party leader. For example Hewins referred to 'the disastrous Albert Hall speech',[43] and told Balfour that 'the false impression as to the meaning of your speech lost me hundreds of votes among the working men'.[44] In Austen Chamberlain's view the only people who welcomed the 'referendum pledge' were 'the little band of free fooders who have done nothing to help and much to hinder us since 1903';[45] as Joseph Lawrence told Balfour, 'some people interpret your latest declaration as an indefinite "shelving" of the issue at the bidding of Free Trade Unionists and Ex-Liberals'.[46]

The reaction of most Radical Conservatives was that Balfour had chosen, through the 'referendum pledge', to address the wrong audience.[47] Law had sent a telegram to Balfour indicating that the popularity of the 'pledge' was seen to lie with wealthy Conservatives, whereas 'all working class audiences [are] only interested in tariff reform'.[48] Subsequent criticisms confirmed that Balfour was felt to have accorded priority to a predominantly middle-class, free trade vote. Radical Conservatives like Viscount

Wolmer agreed that the party's electoral problems in Lancashire were 'very serious', but he also argued that 'without Tariff Reform we should not have stood a chance'. Instead Wolmer blamed the defeat on 'class feeling' and the fact that 'the working men do not trust us'.[49] Wolmer remained confident, however, that 'If Trade Unionists are ever going to desert their Socialist leaders they will do so on the Tariff Question'.[50]

The Conservative leadership in Lancashire took a different view. In the Duchy, and especially in Manchester, most Conservatives had always been luke-warm about the full programme, even between 1906 and 1910. In 1908, when the Conservatives won a famous by-election victory in Manchester North-West, the Conservative candidate had fought almost exclusively on an 'anti-Socialist' message.[51] The apparent success of this defensive approach had reinforced opinion against the full programme amongst leading Lancashire Conservatives, and explains their support for the 'referendum pledge'. In December 1910 Derby reacted violently – 'damn these Chamberlains' – to Austen Chamberlain's statement that the referendum applied to the one election only,[52] and the following October he threatened to withdraw from party activity and 'begin a crusade of my own against the imposition of these [food] taxes'.[53] Finally, in December 1912, after both Lansdowne and Law had repudiated the 'referendum pledge', Derby argued that 'the result of abandoning it is that all those free traders who were joining us owing to their detestation of the present Government and owing to a feeling of security by reason of the Referendum, are dropping out not in ones and twos but literally I should say in hundreds'.[54]

At one level the conflict over the food taxes was straightforward – could the Conservative party win an election whilst advocating duties on foodstuffs? But advocates of the full programme held that electoral progress was dependent upon a pro-active course of action, and that the Conservatives required a constructive policy to mobilize working-class votes, whereas critics of the food taxes looked to a more defensive strategy: the 4th Marquis of Salisbury told Austen Chamberlain in February 1910 that the difference between them was that 'To you it must always be something positive upon which you seek to attract support; to me it is the rallying of cautious men who will join with me to resist restless change'.[55] The food tax dispute was thus a clash of ideas over what Conservatism stood for and to whom it should appeal. But this problem was further complicated by regional differences within the party. When Lansdowne made his declaration in favour of abandoning the referendum in early December 1912 Robert Sanders remarked that 'In the South and West and Home Counties I don't think any harm will be done by it; but it is generally agreed that the effect will be very bad in the North ... [where] the agents are a good deal troubled by it'.[56] A survey of party opinion in Bradford, Liverpool, Bristol, Newcastle and Manchester confirmed this, although in Bradford there was the further complication of local party leaders opposing food taxes whilst the rank and file supported them.[57] Ideological conflicts were thus informed and complicated by disagreements between different levels and regions of party activity. The food tax debate revealed a remarkably complex spectrum of Conservative thought.

Although the food tax controversy seemed to be settled in January 1913 it would be a mistake to underestimate the depth of the divisions it caused, or to assume that the debate had concluded. After Law's speech at Ashton, Sir Almeric Fitzroy noted that 'No opposition leader now makes a speech without giving the lie to one of his colleagues, not infrequently to himself, and their followers are at sixes and sevens'.[58] Likewise, Lord Derby confessed 'I am miserable at the outlook and do not see a single bright spot relieving the darkness'.[59] Even allowing for hyperbole one can understand why a sense of *Götterdämmerung* gripped the Conservative party around Christmas 1912. Supporters of the full programme, like Austen Chamberlain, seemed prepared to defend food taxes at all costs, whilst their opponents seemed equally unwilling to give ground. Moreover, there was evidence, especially in the case of Lord Derby and the anti-food tax lobby in Lancashire, that the leaders of the conflicting factions could not fully control their rank and file supporters.[60] By early January 1913 the party's situation was grave. On 3 January 1913 Lord Balcarres, the Conservative Chief Whip, remarked that Law's resignation was a real possibility, and three days later he noted that Lansdowne was speaking of Law and himself resigning together.[61] On 7 January Balcarres felt that the situation had become 'A real crisis – for we are not only in danger of losing our leaders, but equally of losing the Union, the Welsh Church, and Tariff Reform into the bargain'.[62] H.A. Gwynne's view was, if anything, even more gloomy – 'the party', Gwynne argued, 'is heading straight not merely for disaster, but for splitting up into little bits which will take at least a couple of generations to piece together again'.[63]

In the end the Conservatives drew back from the brink. The party Memorial presented to Law on 10 January expressed confidence in his (and Lansdowne's) leadership. The signatories – 231 of 280 Conservative MPs[64] – accepted Law's 'Ashton formula': the Colonies would have to take the initiative on Imperial Preference and the party would make no unilateral commitment to impose duties on the 'basic foodstuffs' of the working class.[65] Thus Law was able to make his 'double-election' pledge at Edinburgh in the knowledge that there would be no major revolt in his parliamentary party. But the Conservatives had courted disaster – as J.S. Sandars put it,

> Lansdowne and B.L. have had a very severe trial. I cannot remember
> any political leaders being called upon to take back a policy which

has been so recently announced under circumstances of imposing seriousness. [The] inclination to resign must have been – as indeed we know – very difficult to resist. And yet what a situation would have arisen had they yielded to it![66]

That the Conservatives avoided a major split in the winter of 1912–13 was in large part due to concessions by Radical Conservatives. This is important, for the fact that they, and not the anti-food tax lobby, were forced to give ground for the 'greater good' of party unity indicated how far the position had changed since 1910. However, although the 'Christmas crisis' resulted in a retreat from the full programme, the Conservatives had not constructed a new basis for unity in January 1913. It is true that only eight MPs refused to sign the party Memorial to Law, but this was hardly surprising given that MPs were effectively told to sign or risk the destruction of their party. Faced with such pressure most politicians would compromise, but it is important to realize that a *compromise* was precisely what had been produced. Lord Balcarres noted that the Memorial was 'adjusted to meet every gradation of opinion' and represented 'a real potpourri of compromises'.[67] The question after January 1913 was whether this potpourri could continue to satisfy every taste, and in April 1913 H.A. Gwynne indicated that the Memorial did not represent a definitive settlement, for he told Robert Cecil that

The Memorial I disliked and still dislike . . . I accepted it loyally . . . [but] it is only in respect of its securing or helping to secure unity that the thing has any value whatever [and] I take it that you and your section of the Party liked it as little as I did. In fact it was a compromise . . . [and] I am quite convinced that unless both sides keep to the contract the Unionist Party will be split from top to bottom.[68]

It seems that an armed truce rather than a full peace treaty had been implemented in early 1913.

The threat of Home Rule and the gathering European crisis undoubtedly put the food tax question in the shade in 1913–14, but it would be wrong to assume that the debate was over. From 1910 on, the hallmarks of the Conservative party's position on this issue had been volatility and ambiguity. By 1912 it was clear there was strong opposition to food taxes, but many Conservatives were determined to resist any dilution of the full programme. Lord Stamfordham recorded that he had been told in July 1912 that 'the anti-food taxers were in the minority and that they would have either to follow the majority or GO!',[69] and if this information was accurate it indicated that there was a rapid and marked shift in party opinion in the last half of 1912. W.C. Bridgeman noted that in October the Parliamentary party had been six to four against the food taxes, but that by December this had turned into a four to one majority.[70] However, this meant that one-fifth of the Parliamentary party (about sixty MPs) were still committed to the full programme, and they possessed powerful organizational resources, in the shape of the TRL, the Imperial Mission, the Compatriots Club and the bulk of the NUCA, to support any renewal of their campaign.

That supporters of the full programme were still willing to fight their corner was demonstrated by an eruption of Conservative in-fighting over the Kendal by-election of March 1913. The candidate nominated by the retiring Conservative MP was rejected by the local Conservative association, who wished to run a local businessman, one Colonel Weston. The problem was that the initial candidate, a Mr Aigle, supported the full programme, whilst Colonel Weston, although 'right on Home Rule and the Welsh Church',[71] was a free trader. Fearful that supporters of the full programme would look upon a free trade candidacy as a breach of the 'Edinburgh compromise', CCO, in the shape of the party chairman himself, tried to persuade the Kendal Conservative association to revert to Mr Aigle, but to no avail. Tariff reform opinion was outraged: 'Law was told he must either withdraw the Central Office support and recognition of Col. Weston or . . . the worst [i.e. an independent tariff reform candidate] would happen'.[72] Colonel Weston fought and won the seat, but without CCO endorsement. The annual meeting of the TRL saw the Kendal situation discussed at length, with George Wyndham reportedly stating that he would 'prefer Tariff Reform' to plain Unionism, and Austen Chamberlain insisting that there be no more 'concessions' to free trade opinion.[73] The Kendal episode was followed by further outbursts of strong tariff sentiment later in the year.[74]

Supporters of the full programme were put on the defensive in the winter of 1912–13, but it seems to have rendered them even more determined to defend the elements of the tariff programme that remained after the 'Edinburgh compromise'. It is difficult to see how the Conservatives could have avoided renewed controversy had it not been for the war – after all the party continued to debate the merits of tariffs and imperial preference after 1918, when their political and electoral position had become much stronger. If, as seemed likely, the Conservatives had been defeated in 1915, the volatile state of party opinion would probably have seen arguments over the food taxes erupt once again.

THE POSITION OF AGRICULTURE

The decision to 'postpone' the food taxes made the Conservatives party's relationship with Britain's farming interests difficult. Shelving food taxes did not mean abandoning tariff reform. Duties on imported manufactured goods remained central to Conservative policy, and the party had to face the issue of whether farmers would accept a tariff regime which offered them no direct benefits and possibly some harm.

The Conservatives had ample warning of the farming community's sensitivity over food taxes. Farming clubs and associations around the country had made it clear that agriculture had to share equally in any benefits that tariffs might bring.[75] In 1910 this had caused the Conservative leadership some difficulty when they debated whether to continue advocating an import duty on colonial corn. Dropping this duty diluted the 'dear bread' problem, but caused consternation in agricultural circles. Austen Chamberlain outlined a solution to the problem: he told Balfour

> There may be a few parts of the country where the agriculturalists would like Colonial corn taxed, but the representatives which have come to see me on the subject come largely from county members who find the proposed tax on Colonial wheat unpopular with labourers and farmers. We grow so little wheat in these days that even the farmer in most parts of the country is to be reckoned a consumer rather than a producer of wheat.[76]

Food taxes in their broader aspect were to be retained, whilst the 'dear loaf' tax, insofar as it related to colonial wheat, was to be jettisoned, thereby accommodating agricultural interests and electoral expediency in a subtle compromise.

The proposed duty on colonial wheat was discarded without major upset, but the compromise represented a significant retreat from the full programme. In particular the justification Austen Chamberlain produced for dropping the duty was that Britain no longer had a large wheat-producing sector, or, as *The Outlook* argued, that it was 'no use complaining of the lopsidical development of this country during the era of free imports ... [or complaining that] Throughout the whole or greater part of that period the village has been ruthlessly sacrificed to the town'.[77] Yet a central argument of the full tariff programme had been that there was every need to complain about the rural–urban imbalance, and that the fall-off in British wheat production was bad not only for Britain's farmers but for the country as whole. To accept the market's decision, as Chamberlain suggested, went against the national economic logic of the full programme. That there was no major party upset was almost certainly due to the fact that the proposed two-shilling duty on foreign corn and the broader range of food taxes on both foreign and colonial meat, dairy produce, fruit and vegetables were retained. Nevertheless in October 1910 the burgeoning National Farmers' Union (NFU) underlined its commitment to obtaining a fair share of any tariff benefits,[78] and Acland-Hood warned that 'If we drop these [food] taxes we lose the counties'.[79]

The concerns prompted by the decision to go for 'free Colonial corn' were small beer compared to the alarums that greeted Law's full-scale 'postponement' of the food taxes three years later. Following Law's speech at Ashton, Leo Amery warned Austen Chamberlain that

> the speech unless re-explained ... would seem to preclude all protection of any sort to British Agriculture. It ... is essential to make clear that 'food' in the Ashton speech only referred to bread and meat in the ordinary sense of the food of the masses, and that we are not precluded from protective as well as preferential duties on barley and oats, fruit, hops, poultry and, I should like to add, dairy products.

Without such a 're-explanation', Amery argued, the party would have no positive appeal to British, Irish and Dominion farmers.[80] The question Radical Conservatives asked was whether it was politically feasible to 'offer a policy which claims to be beneficial to national industries, and leave out of your policy the most ancient, the most extensive, the most important socially, and the least prosperous'.[81]

Summing up the developments that led to the 'Edinburgh compromise', Earl Crawford (formerly Balcarres) noted that although the immediate crisis had passed, 'the agricultural difficulty will remain'.[82] He was quite right. As soon as it became clear that the food taxes were to be shelved Law received messages from a number of Conservative party agricultural spokesmen indicating displeasure at the decision and warning that it would cause trouble with the farmers.[83] The next few months saw evidence of significant farming discontent over the 'Edinburgh compromise'. In mid-January the Lincolnshire Farmers' Union provided Law with a copy of their resolution that they would 'be no party to any changes in ... fiscal policy that excludes Agriculture from its benefits',[84] and in the same month the NFU passed a similarly strong-worded resolution. In the autumn Christopher Turnor told Law's Parliamentary secretary that

> the farmers are beginning to feel generally ... that though they have suffered under free trade they have at all events been upon the same footing as all other industries: but that now their position will only be made worse by any measure of protection being granted to any of the other industries

and he warned that 'an important group of men, who really are Unionists, are about to start an organization for the purpose of inclining farmers throughout the country to vote against the Unionists'.[85] This was the Farmers' Tariff Union (FTU), which warned that it would

> advise every farmer to abstain from taking part in the next Election unless the Conservative candidate has pledged himself to vote against any scheme of Tariff Reform that does not carry out the full policy of Mr Joseph Chamberlain.[86]

Law received reassurance that the FTU was not representative of farming opinion, and that the NFU had distanced itself from FTU activities.[87] The FTU seemed largely a Lincolnshire phenomenon, but it would be a mistake to see farming disgruntlement with the Conservatives as either confined to a specific area or short-lived.[88] In January 1910 Law was warned by the chairman of the Hop Growers' Defence League, whose membership was drawn mainly from Kent, Sussex and Herefordshire, that

> a storm is brewing, which may increase to a whirlwind, unless the position of the Unionist Party towards agriculture is shown to be quite satisfactory ... To put the matter plainly, it will be necessary to give agriculture the benefit of some large scheme of betterment at *one and the same time* that manufacturers are given the benefit of a scheme of tariffs.[89]

Law heard similar complaints from North Devon, and Austen Chamberlain was lobbied by the Essex Farmers' Association, whose leading spokesman also demanded that 'agriculture should have ... the [same] advantages as others'.[90]

What made the situation worse in 1913–14 were the Liberals' 'skilful attempts ... to turn the farmers'[91] through ground level activism in the counties. In late October 1913 Steel-Maitland drew Law's attention to developments in Northamptonshire, where 'a Radical farmer' had 'captured' the Chamber of Agriculture and was bringing motions to the CCA on matters of tenant compensation for disturbance and related questions. Steel-Maitland felt that on these issues, which the Land Campaign was also promoting, the CCA might fall into Radical hands. Though he was 'not by nature panicky' he was 'frightened at the prospects of the farmers being turned against us *on yet another account*'.[92]

The Conservatives' desire to limit the damage caused by the 'Edinburgh compromise' and thwart Liberal attempts to sway the farming vote led to a frenetic policy debate. The most straightforward suggestion, to return to the direct tariff appeal of the full programme, was advanced in the *Second Agricultural Report* of the Tariff Commission, published in June 1914. According to the Tariff Commission agricultural imports, especially of dairy produce, had risen markedly since the publication of their first report, and hence they contended that there was an even stronger case for a comprehensive agricultural tariff schedule of the kind they had laid out in 1906.[93] A more subtle argument for a tariff appeal was that the 'Edinburgh compromise' formula – no tariffs on the 'basic foodstuffs of the people' – should be interpreted literally, in that cereals like barley and oats, and other items like hops, were not foodstuffs and it was thus possible to advocate tariffs on such goods without breaching the compromise.[94] These arguments received strong support from Radical Conservatives, but the party hierarchy refused to consider them.[95] Instead the Conservatives fell back on rate relief. Immediately Law's decision to drop the food taxes became known, Conservative agricultural spokesmen began to press for a commitment on rates.[96] Its necessity was urged by the agricultural committee of the Tariff Commission and the party's Land Policy Comittee,[97] and in November 1913, Law stated that revenues raised by industrial tariffs would indeed be used to fund rate relief on agricultural land.[98]

That the Conservatives were so concerned to appease farming opinion was understandable. In March 1913 one NFU representative pointed out to Austen Chamberlain that there were

> 170 constituencies with under 500 majorities, which on a mean average of 250 votes, an average of only 125 ... transferred is required to change these seats over to the other side, [and] slightly over half of these are Unionist and about 80 Government members.

Chamberlain's correspondent concluded, 'the agricultural vote is at present the main stay of Conservatism, [and] failure to retain ... [it] must mean disaster'.[99] Farmers turning Liberal seemed unlikely, but this was not the Conservatives' main fear. In January 1913 one leading tariff campaigner told Austen Chamberlain that dropping the food taxes would be safe, because farmers would be 'dead against' the Land Campaign and would continue supporting Conservatives.[100] In an apparently similar vein another of Chamberlain's correspondents stated that 'I don't think the farmers will readily turn against us', but this individual also stressed that '*in order to keep [the farmers] ... as really helpful supporters* we must have something to offer them, for there can be no doubt that they will strongly resent agriculture being sacrificed a second time in the interests of the manufacturing community'.[101] The Conservatives' concern was that disillusioned farmers would either abstain or not render the party full assistance.

The 'Edinburgh compromise' seemed to many to signal that the Conservatives had opted for an 'urban' strategy, but the Conservatives worked hard to reassure farming opinion. Law's speech to the NUCA in November 1913, promising rate relief to agriculture, went some way towards pacifying farmers,[102] but they were not wholly satisfied. In January 1914 the General Secretary of the NFU was pressing Law for further concessions on local taxation, railway rates, issues relating to the break-up of estates, and on agricultural wages,[103] and the Liberal Agricultural Holdings Bill in 1914 saw the Conservatives still desperate to demonstrate their sympathy with tenant farmers.[104] As late as May 1914 Walter Long, who in 1912 had been sanguine about farming support, was still bemoaning the fact that the 'Edinburgh compromise has alarmed and distressed many ... farmers'.[105] Neither the farmers' confidence in the Conservative party nor the Conservatives' confidence in the farmers had been fully restored.

SOCIAL REFORM

Writing to J.S. Sandars to express disappointment at the January 1910 election result, J.L. Garvin stated that 'a strong and definite policy of social reform ... would have made a Great Difference in Lancashire'.[106] Arthur Steel-Maitland also pressed constantly for a more ambitious approach to social questions. For example, in February 1911 Steel-Maitland asked Lord Northcliffe to 'help us by giving general instructions [to your newspapers] to emphasize the need that the Unionist Party should take up certain social reforms with a real wish to get them carried', and in April he criticized the party's official journal *The Conservative and Unionist* for its negative outlook, and drew a reassurance that the editor would 'make the paper a better instrument of *construction*'.[107] His most significant initiative, however, was the establishment of the USRC. In October 1910 Steel-Maitland asked Sidney Rosenbaum, the assistant secretary of the Tariff Commission, to chair a proposed committee of Conservative social reformers. Rosenbaum refused, but agreed that 'certain lines' of social policy had to be placed on the Conservative agenda and that 'our ... side should be permeated with the knowledge and the desire of carrying them out'.[108] There was no time for Steel-Maitland to find an alternative chairman or to get this committee working before the December 1910 election, but in early 1911 he reactivated the idea, and on 28 February 1911 the USRC held its first meeting.[109] The key address was presented by the historical economist and secretary of the Tariff Commission, W.A.S. Hewins. Hewins outlined a dual role for the USRC. First, it was to provide 'a definite Conservative theory of the State' and, second, it was to draw up specific proposals for social and economic reforms based upon that theory.[110] Over the next three years the USRC more than adequately fulfilled both functions.

The USRC's 1914 pamphlet *Industrial Unrest* provided the clearest exposition of its conception of 'a definite Conservative theory of the State'. It declared that

> We have in this country now outlived that curious philosophic conception of the relation between the State and the individual which finds its origins in Rousseau and its most powerful exponents on this side of the channel in Bentham, the two Mills, Herbert Spencer and Cobden ... [and] the view of modern as of ancient Toryism is that the interests of the State and the community must at all costs be safeguarded, but that the interests of the [individual] worker must not be sacrificed in the process, for the worker is an integral portion of the State.[111]

285

This organic conception of the relationship between the State and the Individual, based on ideas of reciprocal obligation and duty, was contrasted both with the outlook of mid-Victorian Liberalism and Socialist conceptions of the State. According to the USRC, Socialists saw the State as an instrument of class rather than of national progress and were hostile to 'any measure of social reform which is not recommended by the spirit of class hatred'.[112] The USRC conception occupied a clear, and convenient, middle-ground between the Old Liberals' Individualism and the 'Socialism' of the New Liberals and their Labour allies.

The USRC's conceptual framework was supported by detailed policy proposals. There were six areas of social policy where the USRC was active: the Poor Law, agriculture, education, housing, industrial unrest and health.[113] As well as producing reports and policy documents, it introduced a number of private member's Bills of its own and supported other proposals, including some individual Liberal and Labour measures. One USRC proposal, twice brought before Parliament, was Arthur Griffiths-Boscawen's housing Bill, which sought to provide Exchequer grants to enable, and even compel, local councils to clear slums and construct working-class housing, especially in rural areas.[114] Working conditions were another area of USRC interest. In 1911 the USRC supported E.A. Goulding's proposal to provide a compulsory rest day for railway clerks,[115] and at the same time backed the Liberal MP Herbert Samuel's Shops Bill.[116] The USRC also supported the Labour MP Will Crooks' Minimum Wage Bill, since 'the regulation of a minimum wage by law was entirely in harmony with the whole of Unionist Socialist policy from the days of Bolingbroke down to Beaconsfield'.[117] After the withdrawal of Crooks' measure the USRC backed Conservative MP Sir Richard Cooper's Minimum Wage Bill[118] and, as will be seen below, some USRC members advocated special minimum wage legislation for agricultural labourers.

The USRC's efforts have been described as 'a synthesis of traditional Toryism, Fabian socialism and contemporary ideas about rural regeneration'.[119] But the USRC located itself within a tradition of Conservative statism – hence Steel-Maitland's remark about Conservative 'Socialism' from Bolingbroke to Beaconsfield, and the frequent USRC references to Shaftesbury, Young England and even Randolph Churchill. But there were important differences between the USRC's statism and that of their Conservative predecessors. The Young England movement, for example, had advocated State intervention to cure the excesses of industrialism, but its viewpoint had been anti-industrial. Like Young England, the USRC criticized the problems caused by industrial society but they aimed to modernize British industrial life in order to equip it for survival in a new era. Like Disraeli and Randolph Churchill the USRC argued for State intervention, but the USRC had a clear theory of the State and produced a coherent programme. In short, the USRC were the first Conservatives to address systematically the role of the State in a mature economy, and their dirigiste ideas, rather than echoing the romanticism and vagueness of Young England, Disraeli and Randolph Churchill, anticipated the Conservative statist thought of the inter-war years and Macmillan era. The USRC defined itself in terms of an old Conservative tradition, but, true to much late-Victorian and Edwardian practice, it helped 'invent' a new tradition.

The USRC drew on advice from various sources, but was a specifically Conservative intellectual project. Though the USRC shared with the Fabians a desire to rationalize the administrative structure of social provision, and leading Fabians commented upon and even helped to compose some USRC policy documents,[120] the Fabian input should not be overestimated. The USRC had a number of external expert advisors, with no one source being more influential than any other.[121] More important, the USRC had its own experts on social policy, and the framework, and some detailed proposals, for a positive Conservative social policy were in place before the USRC was created.[122] The key intellectual input came from the historical economists W.A.S. Hewins and W.J. Ashley, and from Conservative politicians like J.W. Hills, F.E. Smith, Arthur Steel-Maitland and Maurice Woods. These individuals were all committed tariff reformers, and had been prominent in the effort to graft social reform to the tariff campaign before 1910.[123] The USRC was extending Radical Conservative collectivist ideas developed in the period 1903–10.

Before and after 1910 collectivist-minded Conservatives found areas of affinity with the Fabians, but this did not mean they adopted Socialism. Contemporaries distinguished between 'Socialism' as a technical term to describe State intervention and Socialism as a political term to describe class-based and class-biased State intervention. Historians should also register this distinction and avoid the error of equating Socialism with Collectivism. At no point did the USRC adopt the Fabian theory of rent to justify progressive taxation as a fiscal basis for social reform, and USRC members heaped invective on the Liberals' Socialist (i.e. redistributive) fiscal policies. The USRC's idea of 'redistribution' was to pay for social reform through Exchequer grants-in-aid to local government, the idea being to relieve ratepayers by transferring some of their burden to central taxation.[124] Clearly this demanded a boost to Exchequer funds, but the USRC shaped their proposals within the context of a continued adherence to tariff reform, assuming that both indirect tax receipts and the taxable capacity of the nation would increase and thereby obviate any recourse to increased direct taxation.[125]

These links between the USRC and the tariff campaign establish the USRC as part of an ongoing Conservative, anti-Socialist social reform project. They also confirm the continued centrality of tariff reform to

Radical Conservatism. In spite of the fact that some leading USRC figures, notably F.E. Smith, supported Balfour's 'Referendum Pledge', others, like Hewins, Ashley and J.W. Hills, were reluctant to depart from the 'full programme'. Moreover, even if there was some flexibility on the question of food taxes, this left the proposed duty on manufactured goods. Far from suggesting that this should be modified, the party chairman argued that 'The duty on manufactured imports is . . . our sheet anchor and should be pressed more earnestly'.[126] The USRC did not see social policy as a substitite for tariff reform, but saw tariffs as necessary to a viable social programme, with Philip Lloyd-Greame stating that 'Unemployment insurance under free imports . . . [is] like drawing water in a sieve' and that Conservatives had to 'resist Socialism . . . by a strong and balanced process of social reform joined to a vigorous Imperialism'.[127] Even as opinion in the Conservative party began to shift towards a 'postponement' of the food taxes, the USRC, for the most part, continued to support the full programme.

The USRC ensured there was a comprehensive social reform package available to the Conservative party between 1911 and 1914. But in fact the Conservative party as a whole was divided over questions of social reform. The Liberal government's National Insurance (NI) legislation of 1911 typified their difficulties. When the Liberals introduced their insurance scheme it received, as W.C. Bridgeman noted, 'the most fulsome and effusive adulation from our front bench',[128] with Austen Chamberlain greeting it as 'the foundation stone of a work which every Party desired to see carried to a successful conclusion'.[129] However, by the time of the Bill's third reading in December 1911 the Conservative stance was less straightforward, with Robert Sanders noting that 'we have had a good deal of trouble in the party on the subject. Some of our people said they must vote against it. Others equally determined to vote for it'.[130] As the debate on NI developed, the Conservative position became more complicated.

Only a week before the NI Bill was introduced Arthur Steel-Maitland sought advice from a number of leading Conservative businessman as to the probable effects of such legislation on British business.[131] Over the next few months significant business opposition surfaced. In June the South Staffordshire Ironmasters' Association told Steel-Maitland that NI contributions would increase costs at a time when they were already struggling to compete in the world's markets, and, in August, the Birmingham Chamber of Commerce demanded that unemployment insurance be dropped from the Bill and referred to a Royal Commission.[132] Nor was it only large, organized business lobbies that expressed concern. In late May and early June 1911 Steel-Maitland received a large number of letters from representatives of various industrial insurance and general assurance companies, all expressing concern at the threat posed by NI to their livelihoods and urging either that the Bill be resisted or that their companies be made 'Approved Societies' under the NI system.[133] W.C. Bridgeman's prediction that the friendly societies 'and other thrift organizations' would not take kindly to NI thus proved to be well-founded.[134] There was also opposition from the working-class clientele of the friendly societies and industrial insurance companies, who looked upon employee contributions to the NI fund as akin to a new form of taxation.[135]

The opposition to NI led the Conservatives to adopt an increasingly critical stance. The Conservative response to the business community's objections was that 'if we were going to have insurance and other great schemes we were bound to help industry by protecting it against unfair competition from outside';[136] the 'burdens laid upon industry' were to be compensated 'by imposing some moderate duties ... equivalent to the increased charges'.[137] The Conservatives also embraced some working-class objections to NI, and opposed the financial structure of the Liberal legislation on the grounds that it exacted 'a poll tax from the whole of the wage-earning class'.[138] Such criticisms allowed the Conservative party to adopt the lofty stance of 'upholding the principle' of State insurance[139] whilst mobilizing hostility towards the government's legislation.

To anyone with a brief acquaintance of the rough and tumble of politics, the Conservatives' blatant desire to have their NI cake and eat it will come as no surprise. However, cynicism should not be allowed to conceal the very real confusions in the Conservative position. When NI was introduced, the Conservatives were anxious to avoid suggestions that they were opposed to a new measure of social reform, and they gained the confidence to criticize the government scheme only when it became evident that there was significant opposition. But their own warm welcome prevented them from root and branch criticism and forced them to seek a positive alternative. This in turn led Conservatives to confront questions which had bedevilled Lloyd George when he constructed the government's scheme, namely how to balance the often conflicting interests which were touched by NI. By 1914 *some* Conservatives had made *some* advances in dealing with these questions, but the party's immediate reaction to the NI issue revealed indecision in the Conservative ranks.

It may be that the Conservative party's failure to produce a definite position on NI was no bad thing, for NI posed problems for the government as well as Conservatives. However, this cannot be said about the Liberals' other main social policy initiative between 1910 and 1914 – the Liberal Land Campaign, officially launched in October 1913. The Land Campaign caused concern in Conservative circles because its proposals incorporated most of the goals for which Radical land reformers had been campaigning since the 1840s.[140] It called for a Ministry of Land to supervise land usage in the United Kingdom. The new Ministry's powers were to be exercised by a body of Land Commissioners with authority to intervene in all aspects of rural, and many aspects of urban, life. With regard to landlord–tenant relations, the Land Commissioners were to be empowered to fix rents, set rates of compensation for tenant improvements and disturbance of leases, and to nullify evictions. With regard to the position of agricultural labour, they were to have powers to fix wage rates (for which farmers would be able to claim rent abatement), reduce working hours, and acquire land, if necessary by compulsory purchase, for allotments and small holdings. These proposals were ambitious and politically astute, targeting that *bête noire* of Radical politics, the landlord, but offering benefits to both farmers and labourers. The Land Campaign thus saw the Liberals attempting to mobilize the labouring vote and drive a wedge between farmers and landlords.

The Conservative party viewed the Land Campaign as a major threat, and small wonder given that, as the former Conservative chief whip remarked in August 1912, 'The present strength of [the] party in the House of Commons comes largely from the agricultural districts'.[141] In May 1912 a Liberal land reformer won a by-election in North-West Norfolk, and almost simultaneously came the Liberal announcement that they would hold a 'Land Enquiry'. After the launch of the Land Campaign proper, Conservative concern increased. In December 1913 Charles Bathurst, a leading spokesman of rural Conservatism, told Law that Lloyd George's programme was making rapid strides in the Southern counties, and anxious messages to CCO from local party activists in the South confirmed this.[142] In January 1914 a worried Arthur Steel-Maitland ordered an investigation into 'the effect of Lloyd George's propaganda',[143] and by April he noted that, although he had no conclusive evidence, 'scattered reports . . . support the view that Lloyd George's proposals propagated by local lectures etc. are having an effect'.[144]

For Radical Conservatives the answer to this threat was to present an alternative programme of land reform. According to men like J.L. Green and Sir Gilbert Parker, Conservative success in the counties in 1910 had been due to the agricultural side of the 'full programme', particularly 'the policy of land reform set forth by Mr Balfour, and explained in detail by the Small Ownership Committee'.[145] To consolidate the Conservative position in the counties it was essential, Radical Conservatives argued, to confirm the party's commitment to land reform, but by mid-1912 there was concern that the party had failed to take the necessary steps. Writing to Law in May 1912 Jesse Collings noted, on the evidence of the North-West Norfolk by-election campaign, that

> the chief difficulty . . . [our agents] find is that the voters of the division – labourers – cannot be got to believe that the Unionists intend to carry out the land purchase scheme which is so attractive to them.[146]

Likewise Lord Malmesbury warned Law 'the working classes are growing more and more concerned that the Unionist party is not sincere in its attempt to deal with the Land Question',[147] and J.L. Green concluded that 'unless our party leaders come out with some bold policy of land reform, as well as Housing Reform, in the country districts, we shall lose very heavily indeed at the next election'.[148]

People like Collings, Green and Parker had devoted most of their political lives to the land question, and their demands could be seen as simply a continuance of their careers as 'land cranks'. However, from mid-1912 through to the outbreak of the Great War there was constant discussion of land reform in the Conservative ranks, and many prominent land 'cranks' were co-opted onto the burgeoning Conservative land committees. The Lincolnshire land 'expert' Christopher Turnor was a key member of the USRC Agriculture Committee, which began work on land policy in the summer of 1912 and published *A Unionist Agricultural Policy* in September 1913. Turnor's advice was also sought by Lord Milner when, in the late summer of 1912, he was commissioned by the Conservative party chairman to produce a land reform package. Collings and Parker too were in close contact with Milner throughout the preparation of his 'Agricultural Memorandum', produced in the Spring of 1913, and another land 'expert', H. Trustram Eve, was in effect the joint author of Milner's proposals. Furthermore, Milner, Turnor, and another land reform specialist, Beville Stanier, were all members of a larger 'official' Conservative Land Policy Committee which produced a major report for the party leader in August 1913.[149]

The Conservatives' activity on the land question produced one area of consensus as the party committed itself to a small holdings policy. The rationale of small holdings, as described by Milner, was that

If the present Social Order is to endure, it is simply necessary, at whatever the cost, to effect a great increase in the number of people who have a direct interest in the maintenance of private property ... One man may own 5,000 acres, another only five, but as long as he owns anything, he will, in 99 cases out of 100, be on the side of private property against nationalisation.[150]

There was some dispute in the party as to whether the creation of these 'ramparts of property' meant simply giving existing tenants the right to buy or whether it meant purchasing land for sale to new occupants – Walter Long, for example, supported the former but was sceptical about the latter.[151] Part of the problem was the issue of whether local authorities would be granted powers of compulsory purchase, for such a proposal would have offended the sensibilities of some Conservative grandees.[152] The issue of compulsory purchase was never fully resolved, but, in spite of this, the broad definition of land purchase was accepted. Furthermore, in both 1912 and 1913 the NUCA unanimously supported proposals for a Conservative initiative on small holdings, and Law endorsed the policy in his speech to the NUCA at Norwich in November 1913.

The Conservatives' consensus on small holdings was difficult to carry over into other areas of rural policy, a problem made particularly clear by the issue of agricultural wages. In August 1912 Law was informed that 'the Chancellor of the Exchequer has his attention directed to the question of Agricultural Wages, and contemplates steps to raise them by Act of Parliament'.[153] For some Radical Conservatives the best way to tackle the wages question was to pre-empt Lloyd George. By the summer of 1913 the USRC had approved in principle the idea of a minimum wage, and in Septmber 1913 it published proposals calling for the establishment of rural wages boards – to be appointed by County Councils – to indicate and if neccessary enforce a minimum wage for agricultural labourers. Under the USRC scheme farmers were to be compensated for any increased costs by a reduction of local taxation financed by grants-in-aid from central Exchequer funds.[154] But in spite of this attempt to balance farmers' and labourers' interests, quietists in the party voiced strong opposition, and Walter Long warned Law of 'the danger of estranging or even alarming the Land owner & Farmer who are the backbone of our Party'.[155] A compromise proposal was brought forward by Lord Alexander Thynne,[156] who suggested a voluntary minimum wage,[157] but even this mild proposal faced objections.[158] The difficulty was succinctly outlined by the party's Land Policy Committee. In a memorandum designed as a guide for Law as he prepared to meet the 1913 NUCA Conference, the Committee noted that there were regions where agricultural wages were 'too low for a proper standard of decent and healthy living' and was 'unanimously of [the] opinion that the present agreed policy of the Party does not take into sufficient consideration the gravity of the problem of agricultural wages'; but there was 'considerable divergence of opinion in the Party' over whether wages boards or any other form of intervention was desirable.[159] The issue could not be ignored because '[t]he number of people deeply interested' was 'so large', but any attempt to grapple with it meant incurring the risk of serious intra-party disputes. In November 1913 Law understandably postponed the issue by telling the NUCA that the subject of agricultural wages demanded a full enquiry.[160]

Law's attempt to prevent an internal party feud failed almost immediately. Less than two weeks after Law's speech to the NUCA Walter Long referred to the idea of a minimum wage as 'a disaster',[161] and Law was immediately informed by a leading USRC advocate of minimum wages that

> The suggestion for an enquiry afforded a reasonable compromise ... certainly [it] satisfied supporters of Wages Boards; but if

opponents of them do not accept such a compromise, and feel at liberty to attack them, their supporters will inevitably claim an equal freedom in their defence.[162]

Liberal action intensified the pressure. In October the Land campaign included explicit proposals for an agricultural minimum wage, an initiative widely regarded as a major vote-winner.[163] By January 1914 even some high-ranking Conservative quietists were alarmed. The party whip R.A. Sanders was

> of the opinion that in some constituencies where wages are low and majorities are small, we ought even now to say something which will prevent those labourers who have been on our side from thinking that we are not prepared to do anything about wages. Otherwise . . . we shall lose these seats.[164]

Likewise Lord Salisbury admitted 'profound discontent amongst agricultural labourers' made it 'very difficult to resist the demand for some sort of State interference with the rate of agricultural wages'.[165] But there were still major points of dispute. For example Steel-Maitland, assessing Salisbury's views on wages, was highly critical; he dismissed Salisbury's assertion that a minimum wage would cause unemployment and expressed scepticism about the effectiveness of the voluntary scheme that Salisbury offered as an alternative.[166] However, when a USRC-sponsored book advocating Wages Boards appeared in February 1914,[167] it was subjected to equally pungent criticism by Salisbury and other quietists.[168] This conflict at the centre mirrored contradictory signals from the grass roots. On the one hand the Central Office Agent for several Southern counties asked 'Why cannot our people tack a Minimum Wage clause on to our land scheme?', but on the other hand Law was faced, one month later, with a deputation from the Cornwall Farmers' Union expressing opposition to a minimum wage.[169] Almost every Conservative recognized the threat posed by the Land Campaign, but the party continued to speak with a babel of voices on 'the wages question' through the Spring and Summer of 1914, and was still unable to reconcile conflicting approaches when the European crisis curtailed the argument.[170]

In the 1890s Lord Salisbury had predicted that 'social questions' would 'break up' the Conservative party, and between 1910 and 1914 he was close to being proved right. In the 1890s Salisbury had opposed social programmes because they would alienate old friends without winning new ones: the constructive Conservatives' 'full programme' had been designed to square this particular circle. After 1910 there were doubts about the effectiveness of either strategy. The agricultural wages issue was a paradigm case of the problems facing the Conservatives. In response to constructive Conservative proposals on wages, quietists like

St Audries argued the party should 'stick to the farmer who is on our side and never mind the labourer whose vote you won't get anyhow'.[171] This was quintessential Salisburyian advice, but whether it was as useful in 1913 as it had been in 1892 was in doubt. In the 1890s Salisbury had faced a demoralized Liberal party which seemed incapable of mobilizing the mass rural vote. Moreover, Salisburyian Conservatives had been for the most part confident, although by no means cocksure, about the farming vote. In 1913, however, the Liberal party had an apparently successful strategy for winning the mass vote in the counties. In addition, there was some question as to whether the Conservatives could rely on an increasingly independent-minded farming lobby. In these circumstances the USRC and its supporters felt the Conservative party should design a policy that could broaden the party's support. To do anything else was, in their view, to leave the field clear for Lloyd George to roll up the counties. But although many Conservatives shared their fears they could not agree on a response.

The Conservatives' debate on social reform and State intervention was bound in with a continuing internal controversy over the kind of audience the party needed to attract. This debate had moved through various stages since the advent of the mass electorate, but the Conservative party was not much closer to resolving the issues in 1914 than it had been in 1884. In the late nineteenth century the Conservatives had been fortunate insofar as their opponents had found these questions even more problematic, but between 1906 and 1914 it was the Liberals who were most at ease with problems of State and society and the mass electorate. For a while the 'full tariff programme', with its structure designed to harmonize social classes and economic interests through State action, appeared to fulfil the dream of a Conservative social policy that was both 'popular and safe'. But after 1910 the Conservatives showed themselves to be unsure of how to address 'the social question' and produced no clear response to Liberal initiatives. Conservatives were confused as to their position on the role of the State in society and the economy, and divided over the kind of audience they needed to attract. This confusion helps to explain the contradictory position adopted by Law, who allowed and even encouraged groups like the USRC to think out loud, and yet sought wherever possible to postpone decisions on social policy. By allowing Radical Conservatives to develop their ideas Law left open the possibility of a more positive approach to the mass electorate, but by refusing to endorse their programme he reassured quietists that he would not embark on any 'adventures' that would offend the party's core support. In this respect Law's 'paralysis' on social policy cannot be attributed simply to quietist leanings of his own. Rather it reflected a broader 'indecision' affecting the Conservative party.

TAMING THE MASSES

The Conservatives' internal debate on the social question was clearly driven by the issue of whether a commitment to social reform would overcome the apparent alienation of the British working class from the Conservative party. But social reform was also discussed within the context of how to reconcile the masses more generally to British social and political institutions.

The party was agreed that if the masses were to accept the political structure, and in particular the Parliamentary system, as legitimate then the working class had to have direct representation – writing to Austen Chamberlain in October 1910 Law argued that 'the country has become accustomed to direct representation of working men in the House of Commons, and there is not . . . any doubt that the working class approve of it'.[172] As Law pointed out, however, the Osborne Judgement of 1909, which had rendered the Trade Union political levy illegal, had 'destroy[ed] the means by which this representation in the past has been secured'.[173] After some debate the Conservatives' official stance was that, to allow adequate working-class political representation, the Osborne Judgement should be upheld and MPs should be paid, and the reasoning behind this offers intriguing insights into the way the Edwardian party perceived labour politics.

In September 1910 both Lord Selborne and H.A. Gwynne told Austen Chamberlain that, as trade unionists did not wish to see their funds wasted on futile political activities, 'reversal of the Osborne Judgement is undoubtedly very unpopular with the majority of Trade Unionists'.[174] However, Selborne and Gwynne also argued, and here they were supported by Law, F.E. Smith, and Joseph Chamberlain, that 'If we fight payment of Members and oppose the reversal of the judgement, we lay ourselves open to the taunt that we do not desire labour representation'.[175] Although payment of MPs was undesirable in principle it was deemed preferable to reversal of the Osborne Judgement.[176] The implicit strategy here was to *depoliticize* trade unions by severing their financial links with the Labour party. The assumptions underlying this strategy were almost Leninist, for it was assumed that one had only to remove the institutional link with the Socialist Labour party and trade unions would revert to a narrow, 'economist', 'trade union consciousness' interested only in 'safe' bread and butter issues of pay and conditions. The logic of supporting both payment of members and the Osborne Judgement was that such a strategy would ensure the election of genuinely independent working-class MPs – representative, as it were, of their class in itself rather than for itself.

With a few notable exceptions[177] the Conservative party was united on the question of labour representation, but there was less unity on display during the labour unrest between 1911 and 1914. In these four years an average of ten million working days per year were lost, and in some disputes, notably the dock strike at Hull, Manchester transport strike and Liverpool rail strike in the summer of 1911, and the widespread miners' strike of 1912, the level of violence was disturbingly high. In addition, there was concern that these disputes were not 'normal' worker unrest. The fact that British Socialism had established a significant presence, and that a less prominent but more incendiary Syndicalist ideology had permeated sections of the trade union movement, meant that the labour unrest of 1911–14 had threatening political implications. Obviously the Liberal government faced the immediate problem of dealing with the unrest, but the Conservative party also had to construct a response, for it was their propertied supporters who were worst affected and most frightened by industrial strife and public disorder.

The party was broadly agreed on one point concerning labour unrest. During the miners' strike of 1912 Law was told 'It is a leader's strike. The men have little or no interest in it, & they only remain "out" from loyalty to their union . . . the leaders are Socialists &. . . have for some time been anxious for a general strike'.[178] The notion that trade unions were characterized by a divorce between a highly-politicized Socialist leadership and an apolitical and therefore moderate rank and file was largely an extension of themes that had emerged from Conservative discussion of labour representation. Hence Conservatives developed what was to be a leitmotif of Conservative politics for the next seventy years, namely a call for unions to hold secret ballots on strike action in order to empower the supposedly silent, moderate majority.[179] Agreed on a mechanism to prevent unions from calling strikes so easily in the future, the party was divided on how to resolve existing disputes.

For Individualist Conservatives like Lords Hugh and Robert Cecil and Frederick Banbury trade union militancy was a question of discipline. For them the solution to labour unrest lay in firm resistance to strike action, secret ballots to reduce the power of the Socialist trade union leadership, and voluntaryist measures at the factory level, such as profit-sharing and perhaps industrial co-partnership, to weaken the idea of class tension in the productive process.[180] At the other end of the scale Radical Conservatives, such as the USRC, looked to a more dirigiste approach. The USRC publication *Industrial Unrest* conceded the principle of the minimum wage and called for the State to establish compulsory arbitration and an independent industrial court as a mechanism for settling disputes. Here the USRC cited the New Zealand and Australian models as exemplars of enlightened labour law, and argued that only through State-fostered conciliation could national interests, as opposed to the particular interests involved in any dispute, be considered properly.[181] Neither of these strategies commanded majority support within the party.

On the one hand there was antagonism to anything that looked like a concession to strike demands.[182] On the other hand there were Conservatives who accepted that industrial peace was unlikely unless some trade union demands were met.[183] This conflict was overlaid by confusion within the two bands of opinion. For example Charles Bathurst told Law that he was opposed to minimum wage legislation, and yet he was a member of the USRC sub-committee on industrial unrest which produced the 1914 publication in favour of minimum wages.

With confusion prevailing in the party ranks, Law and the party hierarchy opted for a 'wait and see' approach. Law's 'in-tray' during the unrest, especially during the miners' strike of 1912, indicated that Conservatives, and Conservative businessmen in particular, had an almost 'grand peur' conception of this bout of industrial strife. But Conservatives could not unite either in criticism of the government's approach or in favour of an alternative. Conservative industrialists railed against the fact that the Trades Disputes Bill had conferred 'enormous power for mischief ... upon organized labour', and that trade unions were 'allowed to preach violence and intimidation and to keep up a constant state of unrest',[184] but neither they nor their party could agree on a strategy for the management of industrial unrest. By 1914 the Liberal government had introduced payment of members and reversed the Osborne judgement, presenting the Conservatives with the worst of both worlds in terms of labour representation. At the same time the labour unrest had exposed, or so it seemed, Conservative impotence in the face of Lloyd George and G.A. Askwith's settlement of the conflicts. The USRC's pamphlet on *Industrial Unrest* was published only a few months before the outbreak of the Great War, but although some of its key proposals had been endorsed by the party chairman it was still a discussion document rather than a definitive statement of party policy. When the European crisis broke, the Conservative party was still locked in debate over how to control the excesses of industrial conflict and how best to integrate organized labour into the modern State.

IRELAND

After 1910, and especially after 1912, Ireland became once more a focal point of political controversy. To some Conservatives at the time, and to some historians since,[185] this appeared to benefit the Conservative party. Conservatives may have been at sixes and sevens over the House of Lords, social policy, food taxes and the land campaign, but surely they could rally to the cause of the Union: after all, Home Rule was the issue which had brought the early twentieth-century configuration of Conservative forces into existence. Furthermore, Ireland was seen as the Liberals' great weakness – here it seemed was a chance for the

Conservatives to counter the Liberal court cards of social reform and the land campaign with the low trumps of popular Protestantism and 'the Union in danger'. But although Ireland presented the Liberal government with serious difficulties, it proved equally problematic for the Conservatives.

The notion that the Irish question offered Conservatives a means of escape from their ten-year debate over tariff reform, on the grounds that defence of the Union was the Conservative party's *raison d'être* and tariff reform its hobby, is problematic. According to many Radical Conservatives, Home Rule could only be defeated if Ireland was offered the benefits of the full tariff programme. In January 1910 Garvin told Balfour's Parliamentary secretary that 'Our agricultural policy is more essential to Irish interests than ... anything else' and he described the Irish peasantry as 'food taxers to a man'.[186] That Irish farmers were protectionist was no secret, and some Conservatives felt that an offer of tariff benefits was perhaps the one positive means of countering the appeal of Home Rule.[187] In February 1910 Robert Sanders met with the moderate Irish Nationalist William O'Brien, and reported that the O'Brienite faction might accept the maintenance of the Union if 'the Tariff Reform party ... establish[ed] a friendly attitude towards Ireland by admitting that Ireland has a grievance under the present Fiscal System and that she would be considered under Fiscal Reform'.[188] There was no problem with conceding Irish grievances under free trade, for the leading architect of the 1903 Land Purchase Act, George Wyndham, told one Irish audience that for Ireland 'the curse of Cobden' was greater than 'the curse of Cromwell'.[189] What Ireland could gain by tariff reform was outlined by Leo Amery. Writing to Law after a two-week tour of Ireland in early 1912, Amery told his new party leader that

> If you could [make] some definite declaration that the tariff policy of the Unionist Party will be framed with a special regard to the needs of Ireland, not only in the matter of store cattle, but as regards poultry and eggs and dairy products, possibly also barley and oats, sugar beet and tobacco . . . it would have a very great effect and help most materially in killing the Home Rule Bill in Ireland . . . [We] should make everybody in Ireland realise that the Union means inclusion in the future British tariff and inclusion with specially favourable consideration not only for Irish agriculture but also for such Irish industries as it may be possible to foster.[190]

For people like Amery, Austen Chamberlain, W.A.S. Hewins and Lord Milner[191] the full tariff programme could demonstrate a Conservative commitment to 'a really rapid economic development in Ireland following our return to power'.[192] Their contention was that the economic interests of Irish producers, especially farmers, would override their sentimental support for Irish Nationalism, and that tariff reform would enable Home Rule to be 'killed for good'.[193] Austen Chamberlain summed up the view of many Radical Conservatives when he told St Loe Strachey in December 1913 that 'If I had to choose between Home Rule and Tariff Reform I presume that I should try to defeat Home Rule first and turn to TR afterwards; but to understand my position . . . you must understand that in my opinion there is no such choice'.[194]

By itself the Radical Conservatives' criticism of Law's stance on Ireland was irksome to the party leader, but it was only one of a variety of criticisms of Law's Irish policy. Perhaps the most ambitious Conservative scheme for defending the Union was the idea of so-called 'Home Rule All Round'. The idea was to construct a federal constitution for the United Kingdom, with regional assemblies in England, Wales and Scotland, as well as Ireland. These assemblies were to have control over local taxation, education, the poor law, local agricultural development and other matters of 'local concern'. Westminster, however, was to retain control over foreign and imperial policy, military and naval planning, central taxation, and trade policy.[195] This 'Home Rule All Round' would preserve the Union because the Irish question would lose its 'special case' status if it was placed in a broader framework of constitutional reform, and because if Ireland was granted sufficient autonomy to decide matters important to local Irish interests, then the Irish would not wish to leave the Union. According to Lord Milner, one of the leading advocates of 'Home Rule All Round', this devolution of power would 'carry out the Union effectively' by abolishing Dublin Castle, the Vice-Royalty, the Irish Secretaryship and 'all the apparatus of official and executive separatism which is the real root of the demand for legislative separatism'.[196] For the first time Ireland, it was argued, would be 'a free country under the Union',[197] governed and treated no differently from any other part of the United Kingdom.

The 'federalists', in spite of the cross-party appeal of their ideas,[198] did not cause immediate problems for the Conservative leader. Far more serious was the attack launched on Law's 'Ulsterization' of the Irish question. The existence of Protestant Ulster had long been a vital part of the case against the Gladstonian model of Home Rule, but prior to the Edwardian period Ulster had been just that, a part, but not the whole, of the Unionist argument. However, Law's response to the Home Rule crisis of 1912–14 saw a crucial and controversial shift of emphasis, with Ulster emerging as the focus of attention. As a result some elements of the Conservative party sought to mobilize party opinion against their leader's policy.

The issue that symbolized Law's 'narrow' view of the Irish problem was the proposal to exclude Ulster from Home Rule. Law himself appears to have been in favour of exclusion almost from the beginning, but it was from the autumn of 1913 onwards that Law and Lansdowne grew increasingly committed to the idea. A number of factors propelled the Conservative leaders towards exclusion. In Law's case his own background in the Ulster-orientated politics of Glasgow Protestantism may well have been an influence, but this would not account either for Lansdowne's stance, or for that of Sir Edward Carson[199] – one must look to more than biographical influences to understand the 'Ulsterization' of the Conservative leadership's position. To some extent it seems to have been the case that Law, Lansdowne, and those Conservatives that followed their lead, accepted Carson's argument that exclusion was 'the best settlement if Home Rule is inevitable'.[200] With the Lords' veto gone there was little the Conservatives could do to prevent Home Rule in some form, and Ulster was acknowledged as the weakest link in the Home Rule case. For the Liberals, exclusion offered an increasingly attractive means of avoiding the moral and practical problems of coercing Ulster.[201] Redmond's Irish Nationalists were naturally reluctant to accept exclusion, but if Liberal and Conservative leaders moved towards agreement, Redmond's political leverage on this point was reduced.[202] From a 'high political' point of view, Ulster's exclusion seemed a plausible solution to the 'Damnable Question'.

Developments 'on the ground' in Ireland were of equal importance. In September 1913 Lansdowne told Law '[W]e have to be extremely careful in our relations with Carson and his friends. They are "running their own show"'.[203] Lansdowne pointed out that there was 'some advantage' in being able to deny responsibility for Ulster's actions, but this was to admit that the situation was not under central control. That the Conservative leadership could not exercise full authority in Ulster was a product of changes in Ulster politics in the late nineteenth and early twentieth century.[204] At the time of the first Home Rule Bill Ulster Conservatives had been a landlord-dominated grouping with close social, economic and kinship ties with mainland Conservatism. From the 1890s onwards, however, the social and political influence of landlords in Ulster, and indeed Ireland generally, had been eroded, in part as a result of successive Conservative land purchase schemes which saw many landlords leave. As a result Ulster Conservatism became dominated by farmers, industrialists and professionals, who had fewer associational links with the mainland and whose political and electoral strategy was based on local economic and sectarian issues. The increasingly parochial nature of Conservatism in Ulster was thus part of a process which saw Unionism in Northern Ireland draw away from mainland Conservative Unionism. The Conservative leadership had to cope with the fact that Unionism in Ireland tended to speak with an Ulster accent, and that Ulster would offer violent resistance to Home Rule come what may. In such circumstances exclusion was the line of least resistance, for the ability of Ulster Unionists to act as an autononous group left Law and Lansdowne little room for manoeuvre.

The still sizeable rump of Southern Irish Unionists provided vocal opposition to exclusion, with Lord Midleton, the former Conservative War Minister, their main spokesman. In October 1913 Midleton told Law there was unease amongst Unionists in the South and West of Ireland over the implications of the 'Covenanter' movement in mainland Britain. According to Midleton 'The Solemn League and Covenant' – in effect a mass petition against the government's Irish policy – was worded in such a way as to imply it was a pro-Ulster campaign, whereas Southern Unionists wished to see the Covenant as an anti-Home Rule movement *tout court*.[205] Over the next six months Southern Unionist concern escalated. In January 1914 Sir Edward Carson stated that Southern Unionists would be able to get better terms for themselves if they separated their interests from those of Ulster, and by the Spring rumours of a cross-party compromise based on Ulster's exclusion were commonplace. Southern Unionists felt increasingly unable to trust the Conservative leadership, and in April Midleton informed Law that a Southern Unionist committee had been formed to safeguard their interests.[206] By May Midleton was issuing warnings to the party leadership, arguing that if the government and opposition reached a compromise on the basis of Ulster's exclusion there would be the danger of 'a serious split in the Party'.[207]

Of course Midleton had good reason to 'talk up' the level of opposition to exclusion, but his warnings were not unjustified. In October 1913 Lansdowne told Law that although the Southern Unionists were themselves 'feeble folk' they would 'find their voices if they were to discover that they had been left in the lurch, and their cry would find a vociferous response amongst our own "Diehards"'.[208] There was indeed strong Conservative support for the Southern Unionists. As early as September 1912 Thomas Comyn-Platt[209] complained

> The question of Home Rule is regarded almost entirely as one that concerns Ulster alone. That to my mind is absolutely wrong. It is a question of the Union ... my contention is that this Party, and also the electors ... have lost sight of this. Either we are a Party that stands for the Union, the whole Union and nothing else but the Union, or else we are for disintegration, there is no half-way house.[210]

This stance was institutionalized in the Union Defence League (UDL). Led by Walter Long,[211] the UDL was from an early stage opposed to compromise on Home Rule[212] and, in spite of its strong Conservative Parliamentary cohort, distanced itself from the party leadership in the period 1911–14.[213] The League for the Support of Ulster and the Union, led by the colourful Diehard peer Lord Willoughby de Broke, took a similar stance against compromise, and was supported at one stage by 100 Conservative peers and 120 Conservative MPs.[214] In November 1913 Walter Long told his leader that a compromise would be 'followed by a schism, even greater and more deep-seated than that which occurred at the time of the passage of the Parliament Act',[215] and as late as June 1914 Balfour noted that 'As regards Unionist opinion, the chief peril to be feared is the notion that the leaders of the party have compromised their Unionist principles for the sake of Ulster'.[216]

The opposition of Southern Unionists and their supporters to Home Rule of any kind was not the only problem Law had to deal with on his own side. By the summer of 1914 there were some indications that Law had 'educated' perhaps even a majority of his party to accept exclusion as the 'best possible settlement' or at any rate as the best possible *tactic*.[217] The Home Rule Bill had its third reading in the House of Commons on 26 May; thereafter, Conservative attention focused on attempts to amend the measure in the Lords. In particular, in early July, the Lords proposed to exclude nine Northern Irish counties from Home Rule on a permanent basis, whereas the Bill as it stood was to exclude four counties for a period of six years. Conservatives seemed to be united behind Law's approach, but there were still differences of opinion over the meaning and interpretation of the Lords' amendment. Two weeks before the Home Rule Bill passed the Commons, Law was visited by back-benchers seeking to clarify the party's position on exclusion. Leo Amery informed Law that if he wished to satisfy this deputation he had to point out that exclusion was not a final settlement. Amery argued that exclusion was acceptable as a temporary expedient, but that if Law wanted to 'allay the anxiety in the rank and file in the House and rally the party throughout the country', he had to make it clear that the Conservatives remained opposed to Home Rule and would repeal it if returned to office.[218] However, the Lords' amendment, sanctioned by Law and Lansdowne, seemed to advocate permanent partition of Ireland, and for those Conservatives who had seen exclusion as an expedient, but not a principle, this was unacceptable, with Lord Selborne baldly stating that he could 'never follow Law . . . in accepting the complete exclusion of the six counties *as a final settlement* of the Irish constitutional question'.[219] A section of Conservative opinion clearly did not wish to see exclusion become partition.

Law even had problems with those in his party who were willing to accept the permanent exclusion of Ulster. Here there were two main difficulties. The first was that there was some confusion as to what constituted 'Ulster'. Shortly before the Buckingham Palace conference of 21–24 July 1914 Earl Crawford (formerly Lord Balcarres) expressed concern that Law misunderstood and, as a consequence, over-simplified the Ulster issue – Crawford noted that

Law seems to assume that the position of Tyrone is the only outstanding problem. And moreover it would appear that Carson takes the same view. Is this conceivable? What about our Unionists in Fermanagh, and the Covenanters in Donegal and Cavan? What becomes of Carson's bellicose speeches a week old, and of the strong attitude taken up by the whole party and the press in support of the Lords' decision to exclude the whole of Ulster? I can already hear the cry of those who say they are betrayed.[220]

Likewise H.A. Gwynne told Law that much of the party was committed to the demand for a 'clean cut' for Ulster, but went on to point out that by this some party members meant a partition based on the exclusion of six counties and others up to nine.[221] The Conservatives were confused, in more ways than one, about where to draw the line in Ireland.

Far from unifying the Conservatives, the Home Rule crisis of 1912–14 demonstrated that on Ireland, as on most of the great early twentieth-century issues, the Conservative party was home to divergent and often conflicting views. In Ireland there was rivalry between Southern and Ulster Unionists, and neither group trusted, nor did they always obey, the Conservative leadership at Westminster. Amongst the Conservative elite, opinion on Ireland ranged from Law and Carson's single-minded support for Ulster to Milner and Austen Chamberlain's constructive federalism, whilst the party rank and file pursued options that encompassed gun-running to the Ulster Volunteer Force and support for a negotiated settlement. Law may well have possessed a clear personal vision as to the best way forward on Ireland, but opinion in his party was so fragmented that it was not possible for him either to shape or impose a unity based on that vision. Leo Amery perhaps exaggerated when he stated that the Buckingham Palace conference had almost led to 'an open explosion' in the party, but it is difficult to contest his view that in July 1914 the Conservative party was in 'a state of suspense and uncertainty' over Ireland.[222]

Between 1910 and 1914 the Conservative party expended much energy on the Irish question, but not all well spent. Effort went not into attacks on the Liberal government but into attempts to reconcile conflicting interests within the Conservative party. In this respect its fixation on the Irish question was a continuation of its search for an issue or programme that would bind the forces of Conservatism together, and by the outbreak of the Great War it had proved as ineffective as all their other efforts in this direction. Moreover, the Irish question also failed to restore the Conservative party's electoral fortunes. In the summer of 1912 Arthur Steel-Maitland, reviewing the party's options, noted that Home Rule seemed to excite very little popular interest, and that Ireland, unless Ulster actually decided to fight, was an unpromising issue upon which to concentrate an autumn campaign.[223] Later that same year Walter Long surveyed opinion in five major towns, Bradford, Bristol, Newcastle, Liverpool and Manchester, and reported to Law that in the first three Home Rule was greeted with apathy, and that only in Liverpool, already a Conservative stronghold, and Manchester was opposition to Home Rule a popular stance.[224] Of course this was at the beginning of the Home Rule controversy, but in late 1913, after the debate had been running for a year, Neville Chamberlain, writing on behalf of Conservatives in Birmingham, stated that attacks on Home Rule were not enough for working-class voters in the Midlands who were 'accustomed to a positive and definite policy' and wished to hear about social reform.[225] Likewise William Hayes Fisher[226] argued that in London 'however much we may endeavour to force the electors to vote on the Home Rule issue only they will not be deterred from supporting a candidate who promises them speedy relief from a position of financial injustice'.[227] Not for the first time the ideological map of early twentieth-century Conservatism was made more complex by different regional experiences. As the Home Rule crisis moved towards a climax it became evident that the Conservative party had walked or at least been drawn into a political minefield. In these circumstances many Conservatives greeted the European crisis and outbreak of the Great War with an almost audible sigh of relief.

CONCLUDING REMARKS

Between 1910 and the outbreak of the Great War the Conservative party was in a mess. In 1909–10 its main aims had been to win an electoral victory, defeat the People's Budget and secure the position of the House of Lords. By the summer of 1911 it had failed on all three counts. The subsequent resignation of the party leader led in turn to what was, in effect, the first contest for the Conservative leadership. What has often been emphasized about the 1911 'contest' is that the vulgarity of a vote was avoided, and that the leadership question was settled with as much goodwill as could be mustered – the implication being that 1911 saw Conservatives display their 'natural' tendency to 'pull together' in a crisis. This 'optimistic' interpretation is largely the result of 1911 being viewed in the light of later developments. In and immediately after 1911, feelings were running high in the party, and relations between the main rivals for the leadership were marked by obvious bitterness.[228] Furthermore, in his first three years in the post, Law, like his predecessor, found the leadership of the Conservative party to be something of a poisoned chalice. Apart from snide whispers about the unsuitability of his house on the 'wrong side of the park' and the inadequacy of his catering,[229] Law faced constant criticism from a variety of quarters on almost every major issue. Of course party leaders invariably complain that their followers' indiscipline renders the 'burden of leadership' almost too great to bear – such complaints are stock-in-trade for encouraging party discipline – but in Law's case the complaints were more than justified. Between 1911 and 1914 hardly six months went by without Law threatening to resign. In March 1913, for example, Law was reported to be 'hankering after his bridge and golf' and complaining to the party's chief whip that 'the glory of his position is much diminished ... by reason of the discordant cries of his followers and the difficulty of satisfying his adherents',[230] and this only two months after Law's authority had supposedly been renewed by the party 'Memorial' and the 'Edinburgh compromise'. Far from looking like a leader incrementally asserting his authority, Law looked like what he was: a second-choice incumbent, inexperienced at the highest levels of politics, beleaguered by the strain of managing a divided party, and living from crisis to crisis.

For the most part Law was not to blame either for his own troubles or the party's. The problems the Conservative party faced were deep-seated and made decisions difficult. The food tax question is a prime example. Law may have been right to abandon this aspect of the tariff programme, but this was not clear at the time. The balance of Conservative opinion had swayed away from food taxes, but there were still many Conservatives who adhered to the full programme, and they made life difficult for Law at both the centre and periphery of Conservative politics. The decision offended the most committed constructive imperialists, and further implied that the Conservative party had decided to prioritize urban interests. Perhaps this was sensible, given that the farming interest and rural vote was shrinking. However, in pre-1914 electoral terms the over-represented English counties were still crucial for the Conservative party, and it remained to be seen whether the risk of alienating even a portion of the farming interest would be compensated by significant returns in the towns. Moreover, it was not clear that all urban centres felt the same about the food tax question.

Social reform, like the food tax issue, showed the Conservative party to be racked by divisions. Indeed, the internal party tensions on this ensured the Conservative party's position remained ill-defined. On certain issues, such as National Insurance, indecision may well have been a blessing in disguise, but it left the Conservative party in a difficult situation. Arthur Steel-Maitland summed up despairingly

> We cannot outbid the Liberals or Socialists, but we ought to realise that the bulk of the population are alive to their own interests, and have an exaggerated belief that these can be bettered by legislation to an extent that no one could have dreamed of fifteen years ago. Even if we cannot outbid, we ought to show them that we sympathise, and are sincere in a desire to act along sound lines; and yet this is just what we do not do.[231]

There is some evidence that State intervention was not always received warmly by the mass electorate, but if Steel-Maitland did err on this point he erred in good company. The general assumption of Edwardian politicians was that the masses had an interest in social reform: whether this interest was 'real' or not, the Conservative party felt obliged to address social legislation, and the controversies this provoked were real enough. The supposed electoral purchase of social reform lent weight to the arguments and activities of groups like the USRC, but at the same time there were those in the party who 'pointed to the growing expenditure of the country and the extravagance of the Government' and argued that a future Conservative administration should 'avoid any fresh taxation and ... not propose schemes of so called Social Reform which would throw fresh burdens upon the rich'.[232] In both town and country the Conservatives faced the question of how to reconcile their propertied supporters to any positive appeal to the propertyless mass electorate. The issue Joseph Chamberlain had raised in the 1890s of how to be both 'popular and safe' was still unresolved.

'The duty of an Opposition is to oppose.' This was an oft-repeated maxim of Edwardian Conservatives who sought to escape the toils of internal strife, and a maxim Andrew Bonar Law sought to act upon. In particular the Irish question seemed to offer Law a chance to rally his forces in a simple rearguard action against Home Rule. But even on this question Conservative opinion was divided. In the end the Conservatives disagreed over what they should defend, was it to be the Union or Ulster, and over the best kind of defence, was it to be a positive or negative, peaceful or violent campaign. Equally important, however, they disagreed over whether their emphasis on defeating Home Rule was effective politically and electorally. A common message in 1913–14 was that the Conservatives were backing the wrong horse, for the simple reason that the campaign against Home Rule was not drawing widespread popular support. At the same time both the party chairman and the chief whip indicated that there could be a popular backlash against the party if it seemed to support extremist opposition to Home Rule, with Steel-Maitland warning that if civil war broke out then the party held responsible would be 'slaughtered' by public opinion.[233] Far from leading the party out of its travails, Law's high-risk strategy of focusing attention on Ireland served to exacerbate them. By 1914 it seems that the Conservatives were engaged in placing all their eggs in a very precariously balanced basket.

CONCLUSION

The peculiarities of Edwardian Conservatism and problems of Conservative historiography

A QUESTION OF LEADERSHIP, OR MEASURES NOT MEN

The historiography of the Conservative party has seen great emphasis placed on the role of individual politicians. Most Conservative leaders have been the subject of several biographies, and many other major party figures have enjoyed similar close attention. In part this reflects the fact that biography, especially political biography, is the most popular form of historical literature in Britain. Many leading figures of the Liberal and Labour parties have also been placed under the biographical spotlight, but what makes the historiography of the Conservative party stand out is that biographies and autobiographies far outweigh monographs and general studies of the party. By way of contrast, histories of the Left have attached primary importance to an analysis of the structures, constituencies and ideas of the Liberal and Labour parties and even fringe groups. Thus the emphasis on biography in Conservative history is due not simply to the popularity of the genre, but is indicative of a tendency to study the Conservative party through the lives and works of its 'great men' or women. Histories of the Conservative party, like the party itself, have tended to establish a close link between its fortunes and the successes or failures of its leaders.

The problems of the Edwardian Conservative party have tarnished the reputation of Arthur Balfour, who suffers from unfavourable comparisons with both his predecessor and successor. The party flourished under Salisbury, languished under Balfour and enjoyed a resurgence under Law, but was the Edwardian party's poor performance largely a result of Balfour's ineptitude? Balfour certainly had his critics at the time. He was seen as indecisive by all sides in the tariff controversy, and regarded as too remote to combat effectively the popular 'demagoguery' of Lloyd George, Churchill and their Labour allies. By 1911 there were few in the Conservative party, outside his personal friends and family, who mourned his resignation.[1] Historical scholarship has, at least for the period between 1903 and 1906, confirmed Balfour's indecision over tariff reform, although it has been 'excused' as the product of a desire to avert an irreparable split in the party.[2] Likewise his apparent inability to assert himself either over his party or opponents has in part been attributed to his intellectual style of politics, which rendered his views too complex and his personality too cool for both the party and the public. The general impression of Balfour presented by his biographers and students of the Edwardian period is that of a clever and able politician who was unsuited to the task of guiding the Conservative party through the political storms of the early twentieth century.

Yet it is not at all clear that Balfour's problems were the product of personal failings. His successful career as Salisbury's Leader of the House of Commons in the 1890s, and his achievements as a Cabinet Minister both before and after his period as party leader, indicate that he was by no means intrinsically incompetent or indecisive either as a party manager or as a policy-maker. There may be something in the idea that Balfour was more comfortable lower down in the chain of responsibility, but it seems equally if not more plausible to argue that Balfour's problems as Conservative leader were the product of circumstances largely beyond his control, and that unfavourable comparisons with Salisbury and Law are misplaced.

Balfour inherited from Salisbury a range of assumptions and practices as well as the party leadership, and many of his actions can be read as an attempt to pursue the same forms of political strategy that had worked for his predecessor. In the autumn of 1903, Balfour's manoeuvres with regard to the various Cabinet resignations over the tariff issue were as Machiavellian as Salisbury's at the time of Randolph Churchill's resignation in 1887. In November 1905, Balfour's decision to resign rather than call a general election was based on the hope that Liberal party divisions would be exposed when they attempted to form a government. Between 1906 and 1910 Balfour deployed the House of Lords against 'sectional' Liberal legislation, seeking to undermine the Liberals' legislative programme and provoke a general election. The problem for Balfour, however, was that these quintessentially Salisburyian strategies failed, not because he implemented them poorly but because the circumstances were utterly different from those of the late nineteenth century. In 1887 Salisbury had outmanoeuvred a reckless opponent on an issue which had very little resonance in the Conservative ranks. In 1903 Balfour was faced with a dispute over an issue which had been bubbling beneath the surface of Conservative politics for almost twenty years and which touched upon core party concerns. In the late nineteenth century Salisbury had benefited from facing a divided Liberal party which had indeed fallen apart when called to office. In 1905–6 the Liberal party was no longer the fissiparous grouping it had been before the turn of the century. This in turn dealt a blow to the strategy of using the Lords to harry the Liberal party. In the late nineteenth century the Liberal party had been neither able nor willing to force a 'peers versus the people' election. But in 1909–10 a cohesive, radical and angry Liberal party was prepared to confront the Second Chamber. Equally important in this context, the weakness of the Liberals in the 1880s and 1890s had allowed Salisbury, not without difficulty, to keep the more intemperate members of his own class and party on a tight rein and thus use the Lords' powers sparingly. But in 1909–10 the Liberals' budgetary raid on wealth and the land inflamed aristocratic opinion in particular and Conservative opinion more generally. It is doubtful whether Balfour, or anyone else, could have prevented the Lords from the 'tactical error' of vetoing the People's Budget – the issues at stake were regarded as too great for compromise and the feelings they aroused were too strong to be controlled. Salisbury's success had been in part based upon his skills as a political operator and party manager. However, his aim had been to avoid difficult questions rather than to confront them, and here he had been assisted by Liberal weakness. As a consequence Balfour inherited a some-what mixed legacy of postponed problems and a political and electoral strategy designed to contain a divided and inert opposition. He could have been forgiven for feeling that Salisbury had retired at the right time, before, in the words of Lord Callaghan, the skies were darkened with chickens coming home to roost.

That neither Balfour's nor his party's problems were the result of poor leadership is to some extent confirmed by the fact that his successor fared little better. Every student of Edwardian politics is familiar with Lloyd George's comment that in electing Andrew Bonar Law leader in 1911 the Conservative party had 'stumbled on the right man by accident'.[3] However, the 'prophetic wisdom' of this statement is clear only with hindsight, and in particular as a result of developments *after* 1914 when Law, as a result of war-time political upheavals, brought the Conservative party back into power. Before the war intervened, however, Law was making no better fist of solving the Conservative party's difficulties than Balfour. The party was still electorally weak and likely to grow weaker with the abolition of plural voting. It was running scared in the face of the Land Campaign, divided over social reform, tariffs and even Ireland. Law's leadership was subjected to constant criticism from a variety of directions, and Law himself frequently mentioned resignation. There was no clear indication that either Law or the Conservative party were secure before the outbreak of the Great War.

If Balfour's failings seem less apparent when placed in context the same thing can be said of the Conservative party as a whole. The Conservatives' success over the last century has led to an assumption that if they are not doing well then it must be because they have done some-thing wrong. But it could be that the Conservatives' opponents have, for once, got something right, and this was the case in the early twentieth century. The Edwardian period is one of the few periods in the last century when the Conservative party faced dynamic, well-led, well-organized and cohesive opponents. Ideologically and electorally the Liberal party, Labour and the Irish Nationalists produced an effective anti-Conservative bloc. Moreover, the Liberal governments' conduct of policy gave the Conservatives relatively little lee-way for driving wedges into this bloc. In particular, the Liberals' most radical innovation, the use of the Budget explicitly to engineer social change through redistributive progressive taxation, was carefully targeted at the upper echelons of a narrow band of direct taxpayers. These people were more than likely to be Conservative supporters already, and thus the Liberals, having lost the bulk of their grandee and *grand bourgeois* support in the 1880s, were not in danger of alienating large numbers of Liberal voters through the impact of their new tax regime. The Conservatives played this issue to the utmost in the 1910 elections, but although it seems to have helped them gain some seats in the South and South-East it did not give them victory. Indeed, even the Liberal seat they had won on an 'anti-Socialist' appeal in 1908 – the celebrated by-election victory over Winston Churchill at Manchester North-West – returned to the Liberal fold in 1910. The Conservatives also found it difficult to turn the Liberals' imperial flank. They raised the naval question in no uncertain terms in 1909 – 'we want eight and we won't wait' – but the government built twelve dreadnoughts, and demonstrated that it was possible for Liberals, contra Conservative claims, to be radical, produce social reforms *and* defend the Empire. The Salisburyian strategy of portraying the Conservatives' opponents as a radical and irresponsible threat to economic, social and imperial security, and organizing a defensive coalition against a fragmenting Left, simply did not work in the early twentieth century. As a consequence Balfour and his colleagues were forced to confront the difficult task of restructuring their party's strategy.

Rather than speaking of the failures of Conservatism in the Edwardian period it is perhaps more accurate to speak of the success of Liberalism, the Progressive Alliance and Irish Nationalism. Electorally the Progressive Alliance undermined the Conservatives' position in England whilst the Celtic fringe remained committedly anti-Conservative, thereby forcing the Conservatives to rely largely upon what was at that point a minority enclave in the South and South-East of England. At the same time the Liberal governments' innovatory but careful and wide-ranging policy priorities satisfied the bulk of their own and their allies' supporters. That between 1911 and 1914 the Conservatives and their new leader were drawn towards extremes of speech and action was an eloquent expression of the frustration which the party's impotence had induced, and in turn spoke volumes for the way in which their opponents had thwarted them at every turn. It was not until after the Great War, when the Liberal party and the Progressive Alliance had been shattered, the Irish Nationalists had been removed from the scene, and the whole shape of British politics changed by electoral reform and the social, economic and fiscal impact of war, that the Conservative party escaped from its thralldom.

THE PROBLEM OF CONSERVATIVE IDEOLOGY

In January 1906, Leo Maxse, the tariff reforming editor of the *National Review* told his counterpart at the *Daily Telegraph* that 'it is on great public issues that we differ and not on any personal questions at all'.[4] This feeling of fundamental difference was reciprocated by Conservative free traders, with Lord Hugh Cecil telling his brother Robert in January 1915 that

> there is a section [of the party] ... with whom I do not think it would be ever possible for me to work ... This is the section represented by the *Morning Post* and Leo [Maxse] at the *National Review* ... it is not a single issue but the whole attitude they adopt towards problems which is intolerable. I cannot read either the *National Review* or the *Morning Post* without being driven into violent antagonism. Even when I agree with the conclusion, the reasons and method of argument are such as to make me hate my own opinions.[5]

On this evidence F.E. Smith was correct when he wrote in 1913 that 'It is abundantly clear that there exist in the Conservative party quite distinct schools of political thought',[6] for the tariff debate was clearly not just an argument over trade policy but part of a broader controversy over what the Conservative party stood for, to whom it should appeal and on what grounds. In short, the tariff debate and the Edwardian Conservative party's more general convulsions were the product of an argument over the nature of Conservatism itself.

One conclusion of this study is, therefore, that the history of the Edwardian Conservative party should help dispose of one of the most curious, but most persistent, themes in Conservative historiography, namely that the Conservative party is not an ideological party and that 'Conservatism is not a political system, and certainly not an ideology'.[7] This is a position which many Conservatives have held over the years. For example in the 1920s John Buchan and Walter Elliot were agreed that Conservatism was 'above all things a spirit ... and not an abstract doctrine', and that it was based on 'an observation of life and not a priori reasoning',[8] and in the 1970s Ian Gilmour declared that whatever else it was Conservatism was 'not an ideology or a doctrine'.[9] It is also a view

311

which informs the semi-official *History of the Conservative Party*, especially the volume dealing with the Edwardian period, which explicitly rejects any discussion of the party's internal debates in terms of ideas or ideology on the grounds that 'a *History of the Conservative Party* . . . does not owe much to the work of philosophers'.[10]

This view of Conservatism and the Conservative party as somehow 'non-ideological', and that Conservatives are in some fundamental sense untheoretical, is radically fallacious. In the first instance it is based on a pejorative use of the concept of ideology which equates ideological thought with 'dogma' and contrasts it with 'common sense' or 'empirical wisdom'. However, this overlooks the fact that one can be dogmatically anti-dogma, that 'common sense' is, to say the least, a contestable notion and that empiricism is in itself a theory. Even if it is the case that Conservatism is based on 'a distrust of the purely intellectual approach to politics',[11] this represents an important ideological statement with immense implications for the nature of Conservative political ideas. The notion of Conservatism as a 'non-ideology' should be taken seriously only insofar as it is in itself an aspect of Conservative ideology. Likewise any rejection of 'abstract debate' as a factor of any import in Conservative politics is based on an over-formalistic notion of what constitutes 'political ideas'. It may be the case that the Conservatives have not produced a plethora of 'great thinkers' and do not habitually refer to a canon of 'great works', but beyond such formal contributions to political thought lies the realm of rhetoric, received ideas and common values. Conservatives always possess a clearly definable frame of reference which informs their vision of and response to issues and events. Without such a frame of reference there would be nothing to indicate what made their views, arguments and activities *Conservative*.

The view of Conservatism as a non-ideology has not gone unchallenged, and several scholars of political philosophy have between them produced an impressive corpus of work which has traced continuities of Conservative thought and argument through the modern era, and identi- fied some of the central tenets of Conservative philosophy.[12] Likewise a number of historians, and in particular historians of the Edwardian period, have begun to 'take Conservatism seriously' in terms of the complexities not only of its institutional but also ideological development.[13] And rightly so, for the history of the Edwardian Conservative party indicates that the idea of Conservatism and the Conservative party as 'non-ideological' should, as one commentator has recently put it, 'be delivered, if necessary by private contractors, to the rubbish heap of history'.[14]

Some might be tempted to argue that the behaviour of the Edwardian party was simply exceptional, and that whilst Edwardian Conservatives were ideologically animated, neither their predecessors nor successors engaged in ideological disputes. However, such an argument would misunderstand the nature of political parties and political ideologies and distort the history of the Conservative party. There has never been a period in any party's history when its identity and outlook have been undisputed by its membership and supporters. Political parties are not monolithic institutions expressing uniform views, no matter how frequently party leaders might wish that they were. Parties are always to a greater or lesser extent coalitions of groups, interests and ideas, and a party's identity is constantly being debated and negotiated between and within its representatives and its core and potential constituency. One conception of a party's identity will normally be ascendant at any given point, having secured majority support and the authority to act as the basis for the party's view of and response to issues and events, but although internal debates may be constrained they are never absent. Thus, for example, in the late nineteenth century there were those who argued against the prevailing Salisburyian quietism for a Radical Conservative strategy to attract mass support. In the inter-war years, dirigiste-minded Conservatives such as the YMCA and those Conservative supporters of the 'Next Five Years' group were critical of their party's adherence to liberal economic orthodoxies and called for a more positive response to Britain's economic and social problems. Conversely, in the 1950s and 1960s, the Conservatives' apparent acceptance of the mixed economy and the welfare state was challenged by numerous Conservative critics of the post-war settlement. These debates cannot be dismissed as disagreements over individual aspects of policy – they were disputes about the direction of Conservative politics and about the nature and condition of the interests, institutions and values that Conservatism was supposed to uphold. What made the Edwardian period distinctive, therefore, was not that the Conservative party engaged in a debate over the nature of Conservatism, but that the debate was so intense that it prevented the emergence of anything but a fragile working consensus between 1906 and 1910 when the party temporarily adopted the Radical Conservative strategy.

If the Edwardian Conservative party's engagement in ideological debate cannot in itself be seen as in some fundamental sense 'un-Conservative', neither can the Radical Conservative strategy be seen as beyond the pale of the basic tenets of Conservatism. Drawing on the work of Anthony Quinton[15] it is possible to see Conservatism as based on four closely related principles. At the core of Conservatism is the notion of *intellectual imperfection*. Related to but distinct from the idea of 'original sin', the concept of intellectual imperfection rests on the premise that human rational faculties are inadequate to the task of comprehending the complexities of social development, and that abstract reasoning cannot be trusted as a guide for social and political organization. Three other tenets follow on from this. First, *traditionalism*, by which is meant that Conservatives have a reverence for established customs and institutions, and, as a corollary, a hostility to 'sudden, precipitate and revolutionary change'.[16] Second, *organicism*, that is to say that Conservatives regard society as a 'unitary, natural growth, an organized living whole not a mechanical aggregate' composed of 'social beings, related to one another within a texture of inherited customs and institutions which endow them with their specific social nature'.[17] Third, *political scepticism*, or the belief 'that political wisdom, the kind of knowledge that is needed for the successful management of human affairs, is not to be found in the theoretical speculations of isolated thinkers, but in the historically accumulated social experience of the community as a whole'.[18]

On the basis of these principles, Conservatives set limits to the kind of knowledge available to politicians. In particular Conservatism holds that political knowledge can be established only on an empirical basis, through an examination of the experiences of a given society. This position is reinforced by the Conservative stress on the complex nature of any given society, which implies that only gradual, evolutionary forms of social change are acceptable, because society's complexities are too great for any short-lived social 'plan' to produce practicable, comprehensive schemes of change. Finally, any change carried out must, in Conservative eyes, be implemented through existing customs and institutions, which in themselves represent the organic structure and development of society. What this means is that for Conservatives 'the real', broadly speaking, is 'the ideal', in that social and political relationships *as they exist* are regarded as essentially 'natural' inasmuch as they are seen as a product of society's evolution as a living organism. Conservatives are not opposed to social and political change *per se*, but they would contend that such change must be evolutionary and organic. For Conservatives there are necessary limits to what political action can achieve.

The Radical Conservative strategy developed in the Edwardian period conforms to the principles of Conservatism and their implications, and in terms of both ends and means it was genuinely Conservative. With regard to ends, the Radical Conservative strategy was designed to preserve existing institutions and patterns of social and political authority. The Empire was to be saved from disintegration and Britain's global status preserved, and private property was to be protected more effectively against predatory Socialism and disruptive social conflict averted. The means whereby these goals were to be achieved, the tariff programme, was based on an historical, relativist outlook, which argued that economic and social policy had to be tailored to the immediate needs of a given polity considered as an organic unit. Here the Neo-Mercantilist rationale of the tariff programme was deliberately contrasted with the abstract prescriptions and Individualist, cosmopolitan assumptions of liberal economics and the equally abstract and cosmopolitan class-based approach of Socialism. The Radical Conservative strategy thus stressed the organic structure of society, sought to prevent social conflict and to safeguard existing social relations, refused to countenance abstract social and economic reasoning, and was committed to the preservation of property and Empire, the twin pillars of late-Victorian Conservatism. On this basis there are no grounds for seeing the Radical Conservative strategy as 'un-Conservative' in either its theory or practice.

The only way in which the Radical Conservative strategy can be depicted as 'un-Conservative' is if one accepts the position adopted by some Conservative free traders, and groups such as the LPDL and the BCA, who argued that the Statism of the Radical Conservative strategy was counter to 'genuine Conservatism'.[19] These critics contended that the Radical Conservative strategy was closer to Socialism than Conservatism, on the grounds that by accepting the need for State intervention the Radical Conservative strategy conceded the basis of the Socialist case. This position is similar to the one adopted by free-market Conservative critics of the mixed economy and the welfare state in the 1950s and 1960s and by Thatcherite critics of the so-called 'ratchet' effect of twentieth-century legislation. According to these schools of thought the Conservatives, by accommodating themselves to State intervention, abandoned their principles to a creeping Socialism. This viewpoint equates Socialism with Collectivism, and, as a necessary corollary, equates Conservatism with anti-Collectivist or even Individualist politics, and on this basis the Edwardian Radical Conservative strategy can be expelled from the Conservative pantheon for having embraced rather than opposed State intervention.

It seems somewhat difficult to reconcile the Collectivist and anti-Collectivist conceptions of Conservatism. However, this circle can be squared if one accepts that Conservatism, like Faust, has two souls dwelling within its breast, with a philosophy of a paternalist, statist authority competing with a libertarian, non-interventionist stance.[20] Such a frame of reference allows space both for the Radical Conservative strategy, as a manifestation of the paternalist approach, and for its Conservative free trade critics and their supporters, as a manifestation of the libertarian stance. When viewed in this light the two schools' denunciations of one another as 'un-Conservative' can be regarded simply as part of the rhetorical rough and tumble of political debate, and the conflicts and controversies within the Edwardian Conservative party, especially the tariff issue, can be understood as part of an ongoing Conservative debate over the role of the State, or perhaps more accurately over the relationship and proper balance between State and civil society.

The notion of a long-standing dichotomy in Conservative conceptions of State–civil society relations appears to have a great deal of explanatory power, but there are problems with it. The basic difficulty is one of chronology. The libertarian trend of Conservatism has been traced to

Adam Smith, Edmund Burke and to the Liberal Toryism of the early nineteenth century which reached its apogee with the premiership of Sir Robert Peel.[21] Yet it is difficult to establish Smith, let alone Burke, as clear libertarians. The conception of State–civil society relations that underpinned Burke's and also Smith's thought was very complex, and certainly Burke was too much of an organicist to be cast as even an unconscious prophet of Individualist thinking.[22] It is equally difficult to see Lord Liverpool, Peel or Liberal Toryism as indicative of a libertarian Conservative tradition. Lord Liverpool was many things, but he was no Individualist, and his concept of limited politics was not based on a hostilty to State intervention in principle. Peel's interest in economic liberalism, and in particular free trade, seems at first glance more promising, but in terms of his relationship to Conservatism two things are worth noting: first, Peel's espousal of free trade led to the bulk of the Conservative party deserting and denouncing him; second, the Peelites as a group were absorbed into the Liberal party, and the most recent appraisal of Peel's career has concluded that 'Peel was not the founder of the Conservative party but was the progenitor of Gladstonian Liberalism'.[23] Attempts to locate libertarian Conservatism in the late eighteenth and early to mid-nineteenth century founder on the rocks of an a-historical or reductionist teleology.

The first time that clear anti-Collectivist, libertarian arguments were deployed on the Right was in the late nineteenth and early twentieth century, in the writings and activities of groups and individuals like the LPDL, the BCA, Lord Wemyss, Herbert Spencer, A.V. Dicey, Ernest Benn, and St Loe Strachey. However, a pertinent fact to remember about these people and their ideas is that they were drawn largely from mid-Victorian Liberalism. It is true that the LPDL, Wemyss, Dicey *et al.* allied with the Conservative party, but this was not because they considered themselves Conservatives. This alliance was a product of their disgust with the Liberal party, which they felt had abandoned Liberalism. They had no great love for Conservatism,[24] but, given the tenor of Liberal politics, saw the Conservative party as a last hope in their struggle to preserve their brand of old Liberalism.[25] It was a hope that was, in the first instance, disappointed. Even Lord Salisbury's quietism made too many concessions to 'Socialism' for the liking of the LPDL and Dicey,[26] but the Edwardian Conservatives made Salisbury appear a paragon of libertarian virtue. It was this sense of 'betrayal' by a Conservative party that had seemingly embraced Collectivism which imbued someone like Dicey's writings with such bitterness. Having deserted the Liberal cause because of the Liberal party's growing Collectivist tendencies, Dicey *et al.* found themselves allied with what seemed to them to be a party of Collectivist Quislings. This is not to argue that there were no Conservative libertarians, for the LPDL and the BCA found support, especially from

316

some notable individuals in the party hierarchy, within the Conservative fold. However, the fact remains that libertarians were marginalized in Conservative politics in the late nineteenth and early twentieth century, and the core of their intellectual position was founded on conceptions of State–civil society relations that had underpinned mid-Victorian Liberalism.

The Edwardian Conservative party's internal debates also point to more specific developments within Conservatism. If it is the case that *in the twentieth century* a key issue for Conservatives has been the role of the State in economy and society, and that the party has broadly speaking been split into paternalist and libertarian camps – and this model does work well for the century as a whole – then the starting point for that dichotomy appears to have been the 1880s. This has important implications. It seems that the emergence of libertarian Conservatism was associated with the Conservative party's absorption of a significant portion of the mid-Victorian Liberal constituency. Here it must be stressed that this study does not seek to argue that the libertarian argument was promulgated solely by ex-Liberals. Rather this study would contend that the developments which led many Liberals to defect to the Conservatives created a context in which a libertarian strategy and vocabulary, once associated with Liberalism, was made available to and appropriated by the Right. However, it is worth noting that if one seeks a correlation between the defection of Liberal support to the Conservative party and an ideological transformation of Conservatism then, in the long run, the development of libertarian Conservatism is a better candidate than the tariff campaign's dirigisme.

TARIFF REFORM, THE BRITISH ECONOMY AND THE TRANSFORMATION OF CONSERVATISM

The tariff debate has great significance in terms of the social history of Conservative politics, and in particular sheds a great deal of light on the so-called 'transformation of Conservatism'. In the end this study would argue that those historians who have discerned a link between the tariff campaign and the *embourgeoisement* of the Conservative party are correct, but for wholly the wrong reasons. The structure and content of the tariff debate show that tariff reform cannot be seen in a straightforwardly instrumentalist or determinist light. Tariff reform was not an industrial, urban policy; imperial preference and industrial tariffs were only two aspects of a much broader policy structure. It is true that when the Conservative party 'postponed' the food taxes in 1913 the tariff policy began to look more like an industrial policy, but the fact that it ended up as an industrially-oriented policy is not the same thing as it having started out that way. To see the tariff debate simply in terms

317

of its end result is to confuse an historical moment with an historical process.

To make proper sense of the tariff campaign it must be viewed as part of a fractured Conservative contribution to a much broader debate about patterns of British economic and social development. This debate encompassed a range of issues, the most important of which concerned the short and long-term development of the British economy, the effect of any changes in its structure on various economic and social classes, interests and groups, and the ramifications of all this for the shape of British politics. The tariff campaign and the Radical Conservative strategy were part of the Conservative party's attempt to get to grips with these issues and to define the party's task in relation to them. In this sense the tariff controversy was symptomatic of the Conservative party's difficulty in constructing a stable coalition of forces in the changing economic environment of the late nineteenth and early twentieth century. The Radical Conservative 'full tariff programme' represented one Conservative perception of the optimum path for British economic development, of how this would affect various interests, and of the political alignments which would be produced by following this path. Implicit in this was a definition of the audience(s) which the Conservative party should address – the priorities of policy reflecting perceived priorities of appeal. That the Conservative party turned away from the 'full tariff programme' after 1910, and especially after 1913, implied that it had rejected the Radical Conservative definition of the party's audience(s). The 'postponement' of the food taxes in particular seemed to indicate a willingness to concentrate on urban interests and accept the market verdict on the future of Britain's agricultural sector.

However, if the tariff debate witnessed a symbolic break in the Conservative party's special relationship with British agriculture, it is difficult to argue convincingly that it saw a political triumph on the part of Britain's provincial industrial elites. Indeed, viewed in terms of the future development of both the British economy and Conservative politics, the tariff campaign looks less like a reflection of the assertiveness of Britain's industrial provinces and more like a desperate and ultimately unsuccessful effort to construct a unified and effective industrial lobby. Between 1880 and 1914 the British economy developed into what one economic historian has called 'an import economy'.[27] In part this was a product of the comparative advantage enjoyed by foreign agricultural producers, which led Britain to become dependent on imported foodstuffs. However, it was also a product of Britain's vast overseas investment portfolio and income from services, which led Britain to import visible goods, industrial as well as agricultural, in payment for its invisible earnings.[28] This trend pointed not only to a shrinkage of Britain's agricultural sector, but also to a relative decline in Britain's industrial position as Britain grew increasingly reliant upon service sector income. The tariff campaign, as Elie Halevy pointed out many years ago, saw an attempt by 'national' producers to rebel against Britain's links to the international economy,[29] and the underlying rationale of the 'full tariff programme' was to construct a national producers' alliance against the cosmopolitan, 'gentlemanly capitalism' of the service sector. A weakness in the Radical Conservative strategy, however, was that the service sector was not the only cosmopolitan economic interest in Britain. Important parts of the export sector and Britain's working classes, the latter benefiting from cheap imported food, also linked their interests to Britain's cosmopolitical economy. Thus although the tariff debate may have seen the Conservative party reorientate itself towards towns, it still had to discover which urban interests it could attract and how. In the short term the tariff debate may have shown that the shrunken agricultural sector no longer carried enough political clout to enjoy special status with the Conservative party. Arguably, however, the stratification of Britain's urban elites and interests revealed by the tariff debate were to have a longer term significance for the development of both the British economy and Conservative politics.

BRITISH CONSERVATISM IN A EUROPEAN CONTEXT

Comparative history is always a risky business, especially in Britain where the 'Fog in Channel – Continent Cut Off' tradition of political history is still strong. The danger of comparative history is that it frequently takes the similar for the same, and reduces complex phenomena into simple, formulaic patterns. One important thing to remember, therefore, is that comparative history is as helpful in illustrating the differences as well as the similarities between various national experiences. Bearing this in mind, this study would conclude that to understand fully British Conservative politics in the late nineteenth and early twentieth century, and the genesis and development of the tariff debate in particular, it is helpful, even essential, to place developments on the British Right in a European perspective.

Between 1880 and 1914 the forces of Conservatism (loosely defined) in Europe faced a clutch of interrelated problems as they sought to adjust to a volatile climate. In the sphere of international relations the last quarter of the nineteenth century saw a major shift in world affairs, in that the unification of Germany, Italy and, in effect, the United States led to their emerging, along with Russia and France, as challengers to Britain's imperial and economic hegemony. Leaving aside the more complex and tense international relations problems that it created, this global shift posed a number of domestic problems for politicians in all major states. The development of great power rivalry was itself largely the result of the spread of industrialization, which provided the economic base upon which armies, navies and great power status were built. But industrialization, as well as helping to create new (and reinvigorate old) powers, created new forces and problems that had to be addressed and solved, namely the interests, needs and governance of large and growing urban populations. These questions confronted all politicians, but they posed particular problems for European Conservatives, who for the most part represented landed elites and were associated with forms of political authority based on rural societies. This last problem was compounded by the fact that most major European nations had moved, by the 1880s, to a system of mass participatory politics that was far removed from the world of court factions and elite manoeuvre. Although they could not absolve themselves from some of the responsibility for creating it, the world that Europe's Conservatives faced in the last quarter of the nineteenth century seemed increasingly alien to them.

With European societies becoming more urban, and with mass politics becoming the norm, European Conservatives confronted two major questions. To begin with the advent of the 'age of the masses' raised the issue of whether political organizations and structures associated with elite politics could survive the growth and spread of 'democracy'.[30] A seemingly related issue here was whether elite institutions, representing existing power and property relations, could withstand the challenge of the Socialist and organized labour movements which burgeoned as an apparent corollary to mass politics. These two problems together constituted what is perhaps best termed the question of *vertical integration*, that is whether the forces of Conservatism could shape an effective top-down appeal and secure popular acquiescence in the existing distribution of power and resources. There was, however, another vital aspect of the general 'Conservative dilemma'. As Europe's elites sought to construct alliances against the challenge of the 'great unwashed', the question arose as to whether all forms of property and social authority, old and new, urban and rural, industrial and professional, aristocratic and bourgeois, could act in harmony. This problem was made especially difficult by the cyclical downturn of the late nineteenth century – once known as the 'Great Depression' – which saw many of these disparate interests competing to gain privileged access to State support. This constituted what may be termed the question of *horizontal integration*, that is whether it was possible to structure an appeal that could traverse and pull together the middling and upper echelons of society. These problems were extant in most European countries, and lay at the heart of a general 'crisis of Conservatism' in late nineteenth- and early twentieth-century Europe.

The response that the 'crisis of Conservatism' elicited varied across the continent, but a number of common themes can be discerned. In the first place there was imperialism. The complex phenomenon known as the 'new imperialism', which saw all the major (and some of the minor) industrialized nations engage in imperial expansion in the late nineteenth century, has attracted much scholarly attention. For this study the significance of the new imperialism lies in its importance to the European Right. With regard to vertical integration, imperialism offered the Right two kinds of appeal to the masses. First, there were promises of material benefits, in the form either of emigration to new lands, or secure employment attendant on the prosperity that new markets would bring. Thus, for example, in Germany in the late 1870s and 1880s the idea of using colonial migration to defuse social tension permeated business circles and the National Liberal and Free Conservative parties, and provided a rationale for Bismarck's colonial ventures.[31] In France in the 1890s the Parti Colonial and leading figures on the Right like Jules Ferry and Méline stressed the employment benefits of Colonial expansion.[32] Second, there was a general populist appeal, with 'popular imperialism' acting as an extended nationalism. Here imperialism was designed to foster a sense of national or racial solidarity in opposition to an Other. The Other could be a rival nation or a 'subject' people, but it was often linked with an 'enemy within', generally citizens of a different ethnic origin/religion or of an 'anti-nationalist' political persuasion.[33] In France the Boulangists linked demands for imperial expansion and anti-German sentiment,[34] whilst in the 1890s and 1900s Royalists, the Ligue des Patriots and the Action Français all sought to secure popular support for the Right through a mixture of imperialism, 'revanchism' and anti-semitism.[35] In Germany the most obvious, of many, attempts to mobilize mass support from the Right through this form of appeal were the nationalist *Verbanden* that emerged in the early twentieth century, the Navy League, Army League, Pan-German League and Society for the Eastern Marches, all of which campaigned on the basis of German expansion abroad and antagonism to 'un-German' influences – Jews, Socialists, Poles – at home.[36] Together or separately the imperialist approaches described here represent what has been termed 'social imperialism', that is a strategy for defusing a society's internal tensions by diverting them towards external conflicts and questions.[37] This strategy had a particular resonance in terms of concern over the growth of Socialism, in that the emphasis on nationality and imperial rivalry was deliberately opposed to the class politics and internationalism associated with Socialist movements. It should be noted that in Germany and Italy in particular, but also in France and the USA, the idea of constructing a national identity that would override regional loyalties also informed imperialist ideologies, but the fundamental assertion remained the same, namely that imperialism could attract broad, popular support and would produce a socially and politically integrative effect.

The assertion that imperialism would have mass appeal was, however, not necessarily designed for the consumption of the masses alone, but also for those frightened by the masses. Social imperialism could appeal to middling and upper-class groups on the grounds that it seemed to offer a means of heading-off Socialism with a 'safe' counter-mobilization.[38] Certainly the bulk of activists in the German nationalist leagues and colonial societies, and in the French Parti Colonial and other such groups tended to be middle and lower middle class.[39] Thus the proliferation of imperialist arguments, groups and agitations associated with the Right can be seen as part of the problem of horizontal integration facing European Conservatives – an attempt to reassure propertied groups that there was a plausible strategy for defending their interests. At the same time imperialism offered a means of satisfying the demands of particular interests. From the mid-1870s on, when the 'Great Depression' hit the European economies, business lobbies across the continent could be found demanding various forms of State assistance. One persistent demand was for new markets in hitherto unexploited parts of the globe. This may not have been wholly 'rational', but most governments faced strong pressures from influential business interests, and with protectionism rife it seemed that not to act might result in potentially valuable territories becoming the preserve of rival powers. 'Fear of the closing door', and, equally important, fear of the political consequences of not responding to it, are important factors in explaining the 'new imperialism'.[40] Nor should it be overlooked that certain interests did benefit significantly from expansionary policies, either from trade or from providing the military hardware to maintain an imperial presence: in France for example the cotton industry found valuable markets in Indo-China,[41] and in Germany the steel and shipbuilding industries profited from the construction of the German fleet after 1898.[42] The idea that business interests might benefit from and therefore support imperialism, and the notion that the masses could be 'bought off' by the profits of Empire, were not invented by Marxist thinkers and historians, but were rooted in the reaction of European chambers of commerce, trade associations and political groups on the Right to the cyclical downturns and increasingly competitive world markets of the late nineteenth century.

In March 1892 Jules Ferry wrote that 'an active Colonial policy' was essential to the interests of French workers, but he also described it as a 'counterpart of the policy of protection for national labour'.[43] Ferry was referring to the protective tariffs for which the French Right campaigned in the 1880s and 1890s. With industrial unrest rife through this period, and with Socialist groups gathering strength, tariffs, it was argued, would preserve social peace and forestall the rise of Socialism. *Travail National* argued in 1884 that 'our guiding principle is the solidarity of *patron* and worker ... we propose solidarity of all French workers in the face of foreign competition', whilst Jules Méline declared in 1891 that 'the best form of socialism ... would be that of producing work for our workers, of improving their conditions and . . . of raising their wages and improving their welfare'.[44] Tariffs were the instrument designed to achieve these goals, in that they were to foster a 'producers' alliance' of workers and employers by emphasizing their joint interest in securing French industry against import penetration. Tariffs were to guarantee profits for employers and allow them to pay higher wages and improve working conditions, thereby removing the grievances which sparked industrial unrest and fuelled the growth of Socialism. At the same time class antagonisms were to be submerged as French producers concentrated on the 'real' enemy, the foreign competitor.[45] Similar arguments were deployed in Germany in the 1870s, and also in the United States throughout the late nineteenth century,[46] the underlying message being that the priority of the working class was secure employment and that they should and would support measures to defend their trade and hence their jobs against imports.

In terms of appealing to the industrial working class, protective tariffs made sense as a complement to imperial expansion. The latter could only appeal to workers in export industries whereas the former promised benefits to the home market sector as well. But the political economy of tariffs was also linked to the problem of horizontal integration. The most persistent demands for protective tariffs in the late nineteenth century came from European agriculturalists, particularly arable farmers, who faced severe competition from North American foodstuffs. In most continental countries, notably France, Germany and Italy, rural inhabitants made up almost half of the population, and landed notables were the most powerful force in the governing elites and representative institutions. The European agricultural sector thus had a great deal of political leverage, which was reflected in the widespread introduction of agricultural protection in the last quarter of the century. It is significant, however, that governments, even those dominated by landed notables, rarely granted protection to agriculture without offering similar benefits to industry: in Germany in 1879 and again in 1902, in France in 1896 and in Italy in 1878 and 1887 the national tariff structure was designed to balance the benefits for both rural and urban producers.

Agricultural protection was for the most part designed to raise food prices, but this raised concern that urban workers would demand higher wages to compensate for the rise in the cost of living, which in turn would antagonize employers. In short, agricultural protection by itself would, it was thought, alienate urban communities en bloc, and similarly, industrial protection alone threatened to antagonize the farm sector. One seemingly plausible way of overcoming this problem was for agricultural tariffs to be matched by industrial protection – thereby matching higher prices for the farm sector with higher profits and more secure employment for the industrial sector. A balanced tariff equation held out the possibility of reconciling rural and urban interests. Indeed the argument was taken a stage further, with advocates of both agricultural and industrial protection stating that the policies and interests were mutually sustaining, in that a prosperous rural sector would provide a buoyant market for protected manufacturers and vice versa. The most cogent formulation of this argument came from German Neo-Mercantilist economists like Adolph Wagner and Gustav Schmoller, but it was also stated clearly by French protectionist politicians like Ferry and Méline and by Crispi in Italy. Likewise this notion of rural–urban balance informed the attempts by Bismarck and his successors to construct an 'iron and rye' alliance or *Sammlungspolitik* in Germany, the Méline government's essay at forging an 'iron and wheat' alliance in France in the 1890s, and Crispi's 'trasformismo' in Italy. The creation of a general producers' alliance, incorporating and integrating rural and urban interests, within the framework of a protected national economy was at the heart of tariff debates across Europe between 1870 and the outbreak of the Great War.

Tariffs also offered one further boon in terms of both vertical and horizontal integration. Almost without exception Europe's major States in the late nineteenth and early twentieth century were faced with fiscal crises. There were a number of reasons for this. Government bureaucracies at both central and local levels were expanding to keep pace with the administrative responsibilities and burdens of governing increasingly complex, more densely-populated societies. In addition the 'search for social peace' led to demands for State-funded measures to ameliorate the conditions of the lower orders – Germany for example introduced old age pensions and industrial insurance in 1888, and France saw numerous pensions proposals in the 1890s and 1900s which finally produced legislation in 1910.[47] Imperial expansion and great power rivalry fuelled the growth of Europe's military establishments, with the 'Navy Race' and conscript armies demanding large-scale expenditure. The question of how to cope with these seemingly ever-escalating costs caused concern not only in Europe's finance ministries but amongst Europe's propertied elites, who worried that they would become the source of revenue to close the fiscal gap. In particular the growth of Radical and Socialist movements threatened the emergence of 'confiscatory' tax regimes based on progressive direct taxes. In these circumstances tariffs had the attraction of being a non-Socialist source of public revenue – a means of spreading an increased tax burden across the whole of a society through indirect taxes. In German revenue tariffs were always important, for the Imperial Government was constitutionally forbidden to impose direct taxes, but the growth of the SPD made revenue tariffs even more attractive. Likewise in France, where budgetary problems were escalating for a decade before the Great War, the customs house offered a way of avoiding an income tax. In the late nineteenth and early twentieth century tariffs offered a fiscal underpinning for a Conservative vision of 'social solidarity' – benefits for everyone but paid for by everyone.

On the face of it the European Right responded resourcefully to its problems, producing a plethora of new ideas, policies and institutions designed to harness both popular and propertied support. However, the variety of responses produced by the Right, in spite of shared themes of imperialism, nationalism and anti-Socialism, reflected discord rather than harmony. A good example of the problem is the role of populist movements on the Right. In Germany the nationalist leagues, such as the Navy League and Pan-German League seemed to offer Germany's traditional ruling elites a means of broadening and deepening support for the social and political status quo. Viewed in this light the nationalist leagues appear as part of a new 'technique of rule' whereby Germany's patrician governing class attempted to mobilize middle-, lower middle-class and even mass support. However, the nationalist leagues were by no means pliant tools of the German governing elite. They were often critical of the ability of these old notables to confront the external and internal challenges to Germany and German propertied interests, and considered themselves better judges of Germany's military needs and better anti-Socialists than the Kaiser's Junker ministers.[48] Likewise the Agrarian League, which emerged in the 1890s to press the demands of Germany's peasant farmers, was not a product of traditional elites constructing an organizational complement to the 'politics of notables' in rural areas, but an indication of the frustration and anger of many German farmers and a desire on their part to organize independent political action.[49] Similar problems emerged in France during the Boulanger affair.[50] Following their rout in the 1886 elections, French Royalist groups were in desperate need of a strategy that would broaden their appeal and legitimize the institutions they sought to restore and/or defend. In these circumstances Boulangism, with its populist nationalism, and its organizational strength in towns and cities, especially Paris, seemed capable of providing indians for the Royalist chiefs. However, many Royalists disapproved of links with Boulanger and his followers on both social and political grounds. Boulangism may have brought new social groups, especially urban *petit bourgeois* and working-class elements, into an alliance with Royalism, but this prompted concern that Royalist elites might be usurped by political and social arrivistes. There was also concern that the mobilization of mass support was inherently dangerous, in that once roused the masses might prove difficult to control. For many Royalists an alliance with Boulanger was too much like taking a tiger by the tail. Likewise there were many Boulangists who were uneasy about allying with Royalism, which they saw as an ineffective political force with an effete leadership neither willing nor able to cope with the demands of mass politics. Alliances between traditional, predominantly landed elites and populist movements seemed to offer European Conservatives a means of harnessing new sources of support, but such alliances, even if they could be realized, were fraught with tension.

Tariffs too were often a source of conflict. In France, after more than a decade of debate, industrial and agricultural interests agreed on the tariff schedules introduced by the Méline administration in 1896, which seems to have been a successful horizontal integration strategy.[51] However, in Germany it was a different story. The much vaunted alliance of 'iron and rye' arguably held for the latter part of Bismarck's Chancellorship, but thereafter serious disputes arose. During Caprivi's period in office, reductions in agricultural tariffs and moves towards bilateral trade negotiations to open markets for German export industries led to divisions between rural and urban interests.[52] Miquel and Bulow attempted to bring these interests together again after the turn of the century, but not always successfully.[53] The complexity of interests that had to be satisfied by tariff policies, both within as well as between the industrial and agricultural sectors, ensured that tariff policies would never be anything but controversial. As a consequence tariffs could and often did provoke rather than harmonize conflicts of interest between various propertied groups. Nor did they seem to attract mass support or forestall the popularity of Socialism. In Germany the SPD was initially divided over the issue of protecting national labour, but when it became clear that a tariff schedule would include agrarian protection they expressed opposition, and this did not prevent their growth as a significant force. Similarly in France the Méline tariffs did not halt the march of the French Socialist groups, and trade unions in France were also tariff sceptics.

Even imperialism could be a source of tension. There may have been widespread support for the general idea of imperial expansion, but when it came to details there was often disagreement. In Germany there were two contrasting conceptions of expansion. On the one hand there was a call for Germany to expand and establish settlers in Eastern Europe, the aim being to export German farm communities. The underlying themes of this colonial ideology were anti-modern and anti-industrial, in that they eulogized the cultural and social value of a German peasant life seemingly threatened by external competition and by internal industrialization and rural depopulation. On the other hand there were demands for German annexation of new territories in Africa, Asia and the Pacific, explicitly depicted as an engine for trade and industrial growth, that is a means of accelerating the trends which 'settler' colonialism so disliked. It was not impossible to reconcile these viewpoints, but the fact remains that 'imperialism' in Germany was a contested concept.[54] French imperialism was similarly stratified, with, in particular, clear differences between domestic interests seeking to exploit the trade potential of Colonies in mercantilist fashion and French colonists who in some cases sought to develop their own productive capabilities.[55]

The story of European Conservatism in the period between 1870 and 1914 is an increasingly unhappy one. In France neither the Royalist nor Republican Right established itself as an effective electoral force over the long term. Between 1877 and 1900 the Royalists, largely as a result of their own internal divisions, declined from being a majority in the Chambre des Députés to the position of a fringe group. The Republican Right, briefly ascendant in the 1890s, was damaged by the Dreyfus Affair and excluded from government thereafter. This left the Church to be defeated by Radical anti-clericalism in 1906, and in 1914 the likely introduction of an income tax threatened French propertied elites with a 'confiscatory' fiscal regime. In the decade before the Great War the French Right was losing on all fronts. The failure to establish a mainstream Conservative force that could challenge the ascendancy of the Left led to the growth of extremist groups. The activities of the Ligue des Patriots, the abortive Déroulède coup of 1899, Royalist and Church involvement with anti-semitic politics, and the emergence of the Action Français were all symptomatic of frustration, confusion and conflict on the French Right. Likewise in Germany the forces of Conservatism were increasingly divided. The German Conservative party was after the 1880s split over whether to turn itself into a popular, national party or remain an essentially East Elbian, elite organization,[56] but this in itself reflected divisions within the German and especially Prussian nobility.[57] The National Liberal party, whose gravitation to the Right in the late 1870s had provided part of the basis for Bismarck's 'iron and rye' alliance, was in decline electorally from the 1880s,[58] and showed no signs of adapting to the exigencies of mass politics. Then there were the nationalist leagues, whose disruptive potential has already been noted. The social constituency and political structures of the German Right showed serious fractures by the turn of the century, and in the decade before the outbreak of the Great War there was no lasting agreement on a process of reintegration. Between 1910 and 1914 the SPD became the largest single party in the Reichstag, and posed a seemingly powerful threat to values, institutions and interests associated with the Right. However, rather than closing ranks in the face of the challenge from the Left the German Right lapsed into further internecine strife and confusion, with the result that there was a serious danger of a general fragmentation of the forces of Conservatism.[59]

Until the 1870s the identity of European Conservatives had been clear. For the most part they were associated with the defence of monarchy, aristocracy, armed forces, church and the land, and the often interlocking cultural, economic and social authority wielded by these institutions had been the basis of Conservative political authority and organization. However, from the 1870s to the outbreak of the Great War the identity of European Conservatives became confused as they were confronted with a changing political and public sphere which necessitated a search for

327

new allies, new methods of political organization, and new sources of authority and legitimation. Confusion arose because old elite groups often disagreed on either the desirability or the best method of incorporating new audiences and institutions within the Conservative fold, and, likewise, not all of the new potential Conservative forces and interests were agreed either on the efficacy of allying with old elites or on how best to realize such an alliance. Imperialism, tariffs and anti-Socialism were common parameters as Europe's Conservatives sought to construct a calculus of social and political integration, but the often conflicting definitions of these variables were just as likely to produce differentiation. The outcome of Conservative integration strategies thus rarely matched their intentions, with the result that doubts emerged over the general effectiveness of Conservative politics. This in turn raised concern about whether Conservatism could adequately respond to the needs and aspirations of either its old constituents or potential new adherents, which led many to look to alternative forms of Right politics. One historian of the French Right has noted that 'the Radical Right will multiply to critical strength only when the health of moderate Conservatism begins to fail and a Left can present itself as a serious alternative',[60] and this was increasingly the situation in many European countries between 1880 and 1914. The apparent creeping failure of established elites, parties and institutions to fulfil such tasks as thwarting the rise of Socialism and defending and furthering the interests of propertied and professional groups led to the emergence of philosophies and organizations which explicitly rejected established structures and values. This 'Revolt from the Right' has been described as the last kick of Europe's *ancien régime* – produced and led by aristocrats raging against the passing of their social and political authority and indeed of their world in general.[61] But the appearance of Radical Right, proto-Fascist groups in Europe before 1914 was the product of problems that affected Conservatism generally and not just its oldest leaders and representatives. Both the Radical Right and aristocratic anger were symptoms of a crisis of support, cohesion, legitimacy and identity that faced European Conservatism in the late nineteenth and early twentieth century.

In Britain, as in all countries, the 'crisis of Conservatism' was refracted through a prism of particular national institutions and political traditions, but there are some striking similarities with the European experience. In Britain, as on the Continent, Victorian Conservatism was associated with elites and institutions that appeared to be residues of the *ancien régime*. In the late nineteenth and early twentieth century, however, British Conservatism had to adapt to a new social and political world. In particular the Conservative party had to assimilate new, urban elites as part of its core constituency, and find a way of securing mass support. Thus British Conservatives, like their continental counterparts, were faced with the problems of constructing horizontal and vertical integration strate-gies. This was never an easy task, and the notion that the Conservative party seamlessly absorbed and attracted new forms of political organiza-tion and new sources of support is palpably false. The 'transformation of Victorian Conservatism' was a process fraught with tension. Likewise the Conservatives' adjustment to mass politics produced an ongoing debate over the party's strategy and structure. That the internal tensions gener-ated by these problems did not sunder the Conservative party in the Salisburyian era does not indicate that they had been resolved. Alternative conceptions of the Conservative identity and constituency bubbled beneath the surface of Salisburyian Conservatism, and burst into the open when the party's fortunes dipped and its very *raison d'être* was threatened in the early twentieth century. The tariff debate and the other controversies which disrupted Edwardian Conservatism were a product of the break-down, for a variety of reasons, of the Salisburyian integra-tion strategy and the (ultimately unsuccessful) search for a workable alternative approach. The appeal of tariffs for British Conservatives, as for their continental counterparts, was that they seemed in various ways to offer a means of constructing a coalition of forces broad enough to legitimize and defend existing patterns of social, economic and political authority. The tariff programme was the social imperialism and *Sammlungspolitik* of the British Right.

The British variant of the tariff-based integration strategy was no more successful than the continental versions. As a result British Conservatism in the early twentieth century, like its continental counterparts, was also in danger of fragmenting, with the problem growing particularly acute in the period 1910–14. As the party of Empire the Conservatives were unable to agree on a conception of imperial relations and development that either met the internal and external challenges to Empire or satisfied the different sections of imperialist opinion. As the party of property the Conservatives were confused by the conflicting claims of Britain's highly-stratified propertied interests, and although there seemed to be the potential to construct a defensive coalition of propertied interests on the basis of 'anti-Socialism', the fact was that Conservative opinion was divided both as to what Socialism was and how best to combat it. To cap it all even Unionism proved to be a divisive issue, with Conservatives unsure over whether to defend the Union, Ulster, nine counties, six counties or pursue some other strategy be it violent or non-violent.

At first glance what seems to separate the pre-1914 British 'crisis of Conservatism' from the continental experience is the relative weakness of extreme, Radical Right, proto-Fascist movements. There is much to be said for playing down the impact of the Radical Right in Britain before 1914, and indeed for exercising great care in using the term Radical Right in the British context. Here the role played by someone like Leo Maxse in

329

Conservative politics before 1914 illustrates the pit-falls of clumsy analysis. Maxse has been described by some historians as the epitome of the Radical Right in pre-1914 Britain.[62] He was often contemptuous of Britain's governmental structures, expressed often violently nationalist emotions, flirted with anti-semitism and was deeply critical of the Conservative hierarchy. At the same time Maxse also tended to lapse into what Richard Hofstadter described as the chief characteristic of Radical Right politics, namely a 'paranoid style'.[63] The most obvious expression of this was Maxse's 'radical plutocracy' enquiry, launched in the wake of the Marconi scandal,[64] when he came close to depicting the Liberal government as tools of a shadowy 'cosmopolitan finance'. Maxse's obsession with corruption in high places was, however, part of his more general suspicion of the closed world of Westminster politics. Maxse believed that politicians, once inside Westminster, tended to 'go native' and become interested solely in their own advancement inside this exclusive club. His attacks on 'Mugwumps', 'Tadpoles' and 'Tapers' were a regular feature of his editorials in the *National Review*, and he blamed many of the ills of the Conservative party on the 'self-serving' apparatchiks of CCO, and many of the ills of the country on the 'petty-fogging' of parliamentary life. These jibes at the 'old gang', a phrase Maxse used frequently, are reminiscent of Oswald Mosley, and on occasion Maxse did veer towards a rather Fascistic Caesarism, calling for 'a Leader' to save the nation.

Maxse's views could easily be dismissed as the rantings of a political eccentric who enjoyed, through his ownership of a major periodical, the benefit of a national medium to express his peculiar views. The product of an eccentric family, Maxse had started his political life as a Liberal Unionist and developed a reputation as a maverick. In short, his profile was of a kind not normally associated with mainstream Conservatism, and both his background and 'quirky' views seem to fit with the idea of his being on the political fringe. However, it is instructive to compare Maxse's views with those of the rising young Conservative MP W.C. Bridgeman, who was to be described in his obituary as 'an admirable type of the English country gentleman . . . [who] did much . . . for the Church, for education, especially in rural districts, for the Navy . . . for agriculture . . . and for sport'.[65] In other words Bridgeman was a man of impeccable Conservative credentials, and yet, at the special NUCA Conference in July 1906, he seconded Maxse's motion calling for the reform of CCO, a motion which stemmed from Maxse's 'paranoid', 'outsider's' view of the obstructiveness of the party mandarins towards tariff reform. Moreover, Bridgeman justified his actions to Balfour in terms which Maxse would have approved, arguing that Balfour seemed to be 'surrounded by men who are not in touch with the mass of the party', complaining of the 'extraordinary difference in perspective which party questions assume inside the House from that presented by them to the man in the street' and voicing suspicions about the 'pourparlers of the whips of both sides'.[66]

The similarity of outlook which marked the views of Maxse, who was temperamentally if not socially an outsider, and Bridgeman, the quintessential insider, is significant. Clearly something strange was happening to the Edwardian Conservative party, but is it helpful to see it in terms of the emergence of Radical Right, proto-Fascist ideas? The frustrations which people like Maxse and Bridgeman expressed towards the party hierarchy were the product of their belief that the leadership was not responding adequately to the problems facing the party, and on this point Maxse was expressing a position held by a majority of the Conservative party. Where Maxse did find himself more or less isolated was in allowing his frustrations to lead him, along with Lord Willoughby de Broke and a handful of other Diehards, to consider the formation of an alternative party of the Right in 1911–12. Here otherwise close associates like Bridgeman, F.E. Smith, and Selborne distanced themselves from Maxse, and his fellow editor and friend H.A. Gwynne pointedly told him that the Conservative party was

> the only weapon we have with which to achieve our purpose and help on the causes which both you and I have strongly at heart ... and anything that tends to disorganize it or to destroy the efficacy of that weapon seems to me to postpone the fulfillment of our desires.[67]

In other words when Maxse was at his most extreme he was at his most isolated, and in this sense it was Maxse's Radical *Conservatism* not his more dangerous views that brought him so close to people like Bridgeman and to the hub of Edwardian Conservative politics. That the views of mainstream Conservatives elided so easily with those expressed by a maverick like Maxse is evidence of how threatened the Conservative party felt and of how far they were preprared to use a radical voice to pursue Conservative ends. That they were not prepared to countenance Maxse at his most radical confirms that those ends were indeed Conservative.

If the constraints on Leo Maxse's extremism lead one to downplay the significance of Radical Right ideas in Britain the same thing is true of Radical Right institutions. Unlike their continental counterparts, Britain's populist, radical nationalist, anti-Socialist leagues did not attract mass support and seem to have been confined to the political margins.[68] This in itself is important, in that it may help to explain one of the key features of inter-war British politics – the failure of Fascism. The development of extreme Right politics on the continent after 1918 was in many cases a continuation of trends that had existed before the Great War. Germany is a good example, for it has been convincingly argued that the emergence of proto-Fascist traditions and organizations before 1914 was symptomatic of a failure of mainstream Conservatism to cope with the general social and political splintering of the German Right.[69] With this splintering even more pronounced in the Weimar period, the failure of a moderate Conservatism to act as an effective ideological and institutional rallying point for the Right created the political space for the rise of the Nazis. Thus the fact that the British 'legion of leagues' failed to present a similar disruptive threat in Britain before 1914 seems to indicate that the Right was not as socially or politically fissiparous as on the continent, and that the political space for extremism was limited.

This argument is strengthened if one sees the British 'legion of leagues' not as a threat but as a complement to Conservatism, pointing to 'new sources of support whose eventual accommodation, and to new issues whose eventual resolution, would ultimately modify the [Conservative] party and help equip it for the challenges of post-war politics'.[70] Research into the social constituency of the 'legion of leagues' has indicated an overwhelmingly middle and lower middle-class base for these organizations. This, along with the fact that some Conservative MPs and activists took part in the leagues' activities and that the party was on occasion able to work with these organizations, seems to indicate that groups like the ASU, NL, NSL etc. were one of the means whereby the Conservative party broadened its support amongst middle- and lower middle-class voters. On this basis the leagues may well have been part of the process which assisted in the party's transformation from 'a loose conglomeration of agrarian interests to the predominant Party of government in urban, industrial Britain'.[71] Such an analysis indicates that in Britain the legion of leagues were not in the long run an alternative to moderate Conservatism but part of that mainstream, loyal to and even dependent upon the Conservative party.

The implication of all of this is that the Radical Right in Britain before 1914 was not a powerful force ideologically or institutionally, and that there was limited potential for a radical disruption of British politics in general and Conservative politics in particular from the Right. The Conservative party it seems was able to constrain and contain the kind of political fragmentation of the Right that led to the growth of extremism on the continent. At this point, however, a codicil must be inserted. The idea that the Radical Right had been successfully contained is based on the assumption that the disruptive potential of Radical Right ideas and organizations had been exhausted by 1914, which in turn assumes that the 'crisis of Conservatism' was over by that date. Yet it is not at all obvious that this was the case. Between 1910 and 1914 the Conservative party was very unsettled. Disgruntled agriculturalists and imperialists resented the party's back-pedalling on the food taxes, whilst the Land

Campaign threw the party into fresh panics and disagreements. The party's tendency to endorse violent resistance in Ulster, and Law's much-vaunted 'new style', which seemed to consist largely of abusing Asquith, were symptomatic of the Conservatives' inability to discover a real sense of direction. Had the Conservatives lost another general election in 1915 they might well have lost credibility as a potential party of government, and this would have damaged their position as the integrating force of the political Right. As it happened the Great War intervened and provided the Conservatives with an opportunity to confirm what had been an *uncertain* trend towards a reshaping and consolidation of the Right. Just as many historians have stressed the importance of the Great War in the decline of the Liberal party, one should be aware that it may well have played an equally significant role in saving the Conservative party from disintegration.

APPENDIX 1

CONSERVATIVE MP SUPPORTING FAIR TRADE IN THE 1880s

H.J. Atkinson (Boston)
Sir E. Bates (Plymouth)
A.A. Baumann (Peckham)
W.J. Beadel (Essex)
G. Bentinck (Whitehaven)
Lord Henry Bentinck (Norfolk N.W.)
Sir A. Borthwick (Kensington South)
Col. Bridgeman (Bolton)
Col. A. Brookfield (Rye)
Sir W.C. Brooks (Altrincham)
Sir A. Campbell (Renfrewshire West)
H. Chaplin (Sleaford)
E. Clarke (Plymouth)
J. Colomb (Bow)
Adm. Sir J. Commerell (Southampton)
Baron de Worms (Liverpool Toxteth)
Baron Dimsdale (Hitchin)
F. Dixon-Hartland (Uxbridge)
Sir W.H. Dyke (Dartford)
H.W. Eaton (Coventry)
W.J. Evelyn (Deptford)
G.H. Finch (Rutland)

Lord Folkestone (Enfield)
Gen. Fraser (Lambeth North)
L.H. Isaacs (Newington)
F.W. Isaacson (Stepney)
L. Jennings (Stockport)
W. Kenyon-Slaney (N. Shrops.)
H. Kimber (Wandsworth)
Col. King-Harman (Thanet)
W. Knatchbull-Hugesson (N.-E. Kent)
G. Kynoch (Aston)
A. Lafone (Bermondsey)
Sir R. Lethbridge (N. Kensington)
Vct. Lewisham (Lewisham)
W. Long (East Wilts.)
Sir H. Maxwell (Wigtown)
T. Milvain (Durham)
Lord Newark (Newark)
W.P. Pomfret (Ashford)
A.K. Rollitt (S. Islington)
J.M. Sandys (Bootle)
J. Spencer (West Bromwich)
W. Tomlinson (Preston)
C.E.H. Vincent (C. Sheffield)
R. Webster (St Pancras East)
R. Winn (Pontefract)

APPENDIX 2

Conservative representatives of middle- and mixed-class London and South-East Suburban seats, 1885–1910 (as defined in H. Pelling, *Social Geography of British Elections 1885–1910*)

MIDDLE-CLASS SEATS

Battersea (Clapham)
J.S. Gilliat: banker/merchant, Bank of England director
P.M. Thornton: writer
G.D. Faber: barrister, Privy Council Registrar, related by marriage to gentry

Camberwell (Dulwich)
J.M. Howard, QC.: barrister, manufacturer
J.B. Maple (Bart. 1895): furniture business
Dr F.R. Harris: legal family, doctor, secretary to Cecil Rhodes and Chartered Company
A. Bonar Law: ironmaster

Chelsea
C.A. Whitmore: barrister, civil service
S. Hoare: banker, married into aristocracy

Finsbury (Holborn)
Col. F. Duncan: military/gentry
B. Gainsford,QC. (Kt 1892): barrister

Sir Chas. Hall, QC: barrister, Attorney Gen. to Prince of Wales, Recorder of London
J.F. Remnant: barrister, military, LCC whip for party

Hackney (North)
Sir L. Pelly: military
W.R. Bousfield, QC: engineer cum barrister specializing in engineering patents
W.R. Greene: scion of the E. Anglian brewing family

Hampstead
Sir H.T. Holland (peer 1888): aristocracy/military
C.E.B. Hoare (CH 1902): banker
T. Milvain, KC: barrister, Judge Advocate 1905
J.S. Fletcher: barrister (non-practising)

Kensington (South)
Sir A. Borthwick (peer 1895): gentry/merchant
Lord Warkworth (Earl Percy): aristocracy/military

335

Lambeth (Brixton)
E. Baggalley: barrister
Marquis of Carmarthen:
    aristocracy/military
Hon. E. Hubbard: City merchant,
    Bank of England director,
    aristocracy (brother of
    Carmarthen)
Sir R.G.C. Mowbray: barrister,
    judge, gentry
D. Dalziel: Chairman Motor Cab
    Co., director Pullman Co.

Lambeth (Norwood)
T.E. Bristowe: stockbroker
C.E. Tritton (Kt 1900): Bill broker,
    London Chamber
G.F.S. Bowles: barrister
Sir H.S. Samuel: law/finance

Lewisham
Viscount Lewisham:
    aristocracy/military
J. Penn: Chairman marine
    engineering co. in Greenwich
Maj. E.F. Coates: stockbroker,
    military

Marylebone East
Lord Charles Beresford:
    aristocracy, navy
E. Boulnois: Vice Pres. London
    Life Assoc., director
    Westminster electric co.,
    merchant
Lord Robert Cecil: aristocracy
J. Boyton: auctioneer and
    surveyor (senior partner), one-
    time Pres. of Institute of Estate
    Agents

Marylebone West
Sir F.S. Hunt: railway contractor
    and shipbuilder
Sir H. Farquar: aristocracy/
    gentry/military
Sir S.E. Scott: aristocracy/
    military

Paddington North
L.L. Cohen: stockbroker
J. Aird (Bart. 1901): building
    contractor
A. Strauss: metal merchant and
    mine-owner (tin)

Paddington South
Lord Randolph Churchill:
    aristocracy
T.G. Fardell (Kt. 1895): barrister
H.P. Harris: barrister

St George's Hanover Square
Lord A. Percy: aristocracy/
    military
G.J. Goschen: banker
Col. H. Legge: aristocracy/
    military
A. Lyttelton: aristocracy

Strand
W.H. Smith: retailer
W.F.D. Smith: retailer
W. Long: gentry

Wandsworth
H. Kimber (Kt 1900): solicitor,
    colonial railway and banking
    interests

Westminster
W.A. Burdett-Coutts:
    aristocracy/finance

MIXED-CLASS SEATS

Deptford
W.J. Evelyn: gentry
C.T. Darling, QC (Kt 1895):
  barrister
A.H.A. Morton: academic

Fulham
W.H. Fisher: barrister/gentry

Greenwich
T.W. Boord (Kt 1892): local
  distiller
Lord Hugh Cecil: aristocracy
I.H. Benn: ironmaster, one-time
  Mayor of Greenwich, Board
  member of the Port of London
  Authority

Hackney Central
Sir W.G. Hunter: army surgeon
Sir A.R. Scobie: barrister
A.H.A. Allhusen: chemical
  manufacturer, married to
  gentry

Hackney South
T.H. Robertson: barrister, Irish
  gentry

Hammersmith
Maj.-Gen.W. Goldsworthy:
  military
W.J. Bull: solicitor

Islington East
C. Lambert: barrister
B.L. Cohen: stockbroker

Islington North
G.C.T. Bartley: civil service,
  founder of a savings bank

Islington South
Sir A.K. Rollitt: merchant,
  manufacturer

Kensington North
Sir R. Lethbridge: gentry/
  military
W.E.T. Sharpe: barrister, Ceylon
  civil service
A. Burgoyne: colonial merchant

Lambeth (Kennington)
R. Gent-Davis: barrister
F.L. Cook: warehouseman

St Pancras North
Hon. W. Baillie-Cochrane:
  aristocracy/military
E.R.P. Moon: barrister

St Pancras South
J. Goldsmid: solicitor/finance
H. Jessel: barrister, military
  (married Goldsmid's
  daughter)

St Pancras West
H.R. Graham: barrister

Woolwich
E. Hughes (Kt 1900): solicitor,
  party agent for region
Lord Charles Beresford:
  aristocracy, navy
Maj. W.A. Adams: military

SOUTH-EAST SUBURBAN SEATS

Croydon

W. Grantham, QC: barrister, judge

S. Herbert: aristocracy, barrister

C.T. Ritchie: merchant

H.O. Arnold-Forster: barrister, gentry

Hornsey

Sir J. Hogg: aristocracy, one-time Chairman Metropolitan Board of Works, military

H.C. Stephens: ink maker and supplier

C.B. Balfour: aristocracy/military

Earl Ronaldshay: aristocracy/ military

Harrow

W. Ambrose, QC: barrister

I.E.B. Cox: barrister and legal publications

H.C. Mallaby-Deeley: barrister, board of Norwich Union Life Assurance

Ealing

Lord G. Hamilton: aristocracy/military

H. Nield: barrister

Brentford

O.E. Coope: brewer

J. Bigwood: solicitor

Lord A.F. Compton: aristocracy/military

Surrey North-East (Kingston)

Sir J.W. Ellis: barrister/gentry/military

Sir R. Temple: barrister, finance

T. Skewes-Cox: solicitor

G. Cave: barrister

Wimbledon

H.C.O. Bonsor: brewer, Bank of England Director

C.E. Hambro: banker

H. Chaplin: gentry

Kent West (Sevenoaks)

C.W. Mills: banker

H.W. Forster: barrister

APPENDIX 3

MEMBERS OF THE COMPATRIOTS' CLUB

L.S. Amery*
J.S. Arkwright*
P. Arnold
W.J. Ashley
Sir A. Baines
C.A.M. Barlow
Duke of Bedford
C.F. Moberly Bell
J.H. Birchenough
H. Blakiston
A.G. Boscawen*
C.W. Boyd
F.E. Bray
W.C. Bridgeman*
J. Buchan
Sir Vincent Caillard*
J. Cator*
Evelyn Cecil*
A. Chamberlain*
J. Chamberlain*
N. Chamberlain*
H. Chisholm
Sir John Cockburn*
A. Colefax
J.G. Colmer
Sir T. Cuninghame
W. Cunningham
L.R. Davies*
H.N. Dickenson
Sir Arthur Conan Doyle*

H.E. Duke*
C.R. Dunlop
J.L. Garvin
C.S. Goldmann*
E.A. Goulding*
Earl Grey
H.A. Gwynne
Sir Alfred Harmsworth
F. Leverton Harris*
W.A.S. Hewins*
E.H. Hills*
J.W. Hills*
C.H. Hoare*
H. Hodge
B. Holland
R.H. Holland
G.T. Hutchison
R. Jebb*
J.H. Keeling
B. Kidd
A.W. Kirkaldy
C.C. Lance
A.B. Law*
Sir Walter Lawrence*
T.V. Lees
P.H. Lockhart
H. Lygon*
A.S. MacDowall
H.J. Mackinder*
M. Macmillan

L.J. Maxse
F.H. Medhurst*
J. Menzies
J. Saxon Mills
Viscount Milner
W.F. Moneypenny
T. Morrison
Viscount Morpeth*
F.S. Oliver
E.B. Osborn
C.S. Parker
Sir Gilbert Parker*
C. Arthur Pearson
H. Pike Pease*
Sir Westby Perceval
R.B. Philpotts
J.R.L. Rankin*
W.L. Richards
Viscount Ridley*
S. Roberts*
C. Ross
G.G. Russell
V. Russell

J. Holt Schooling
G. Craig Sellar
A.J.H. Smith
F.E. Smith*
J. Parker Smith*
E.J. Solano
G. Speir
A. Steel-Maitland*
W. Burton Stewart*
W.R. Sullivan
R.H. Tatham
J.W. Taverner
G.C. Tryon
Viscount Turnor*
J.D. Walker*
J. Walter
A. Ward
J.H. Welsford*
C.A. Whitmore*
H.W. Wilson
B.R. Wise*
W.H. Wood

* = Conservative MP/candidate

APPENDIX 4

MEMBERS OF THE UNIONIST SOCIAL REFORM COMMITTEE

Executive Committee

F.E. Smith †
C.S. Goldman †
Viscount Wolmer
Maurice Woods
E.A. Goulding †

A. Griffiths-Boscawen †
J.W. Hills †
A. Steel-Maitland † *
L. Worthington-Evans

General Committee

W.W. Astor
Almeric Paget
L.S. Amery †
C. Montagu Barlow †
H.W. Forster
W.A.S. Hewins †
H. Hodge †
Earl of Malmesbury *
Duke of Marlborough

W. Ormsby-Gore
Sir Gilbert Parker † *
H. Page-Croft *
S. Rosenbaum
W. Watson Rutherford
H. Smith
Earl Winterton † *
Lord Willoughby de Broke
Walter Guinness

Associate Members

I.H. Benn
A.S. Benn
Sir William Bull
N. Craig
J.F. Hope
F. Cassell
B.E. Peto
B. Archer-Shee
R. Hunt

C. Bathurst
W.C. Bridgeman †
R.A. Cooper
J. Craig
B. Eyres-Monsell
W. Faber
V. Fleming
A. St G. Hamersley

Associate members cont.

R. Hunt
H.A. Jessell
W. Joynson Hicks
H.W. Lawson
G. Locker-Lampson
O. Locker-Lampson
C. Lowther
H.C. Mallaby-Deeley
E.C. Meysey-Thompson
W. Mitchell-Thompson
J. Norton-Griffiths
W.R.W. Peel

E.M. Pollock
R.H. Rawson
J. Remnant
L.N. de Rothschild
L. Scott
B. Stanier
A. Strauss
Lord A. Thynne
G.C. Tryon †
S.A. Ward
Fabian Ware

* = member of Confederacy
† = member of Compatriots

NOTES

INTRODUCTION

1 In five of their twelve defeats – 1923, 1929, 1950, 1964, and February 1974 – the Conservatives either remained the largest party, or confined their opponents to reliance upon third-party support or single-figure Parliamentary majorities. In simple numerical terms this was also the case in the January and December 1910 elections, but the situation in 1910 was less helpful to the Conservatives than would at first seem to be the case. See pp. 136–42, 267–70.

2 Only two Conservative victories, 1885 and 1951, left the party with a difficult Parliamentary situation.

3 For the Conservatives' pessimistic view of their pre-1914 electoral position see pp. 269–70.

4 For an eloquent statement of puzzlement at the Edwardian party's behaviour see R. Blake, *The Conservative Party From Peel to Thatcher* (London 1985), pp. 167–95.

5 The period after 1979 may seem at first glance to be an exception to this rule, but two points are worth noting: first, the 'Thatcherite' Conservative party, as a number of commentators have pointed out, moved more cautiously than was sometimes supposed; second, and this is a subject which I will deal with at greater length elsewhere, the pre-1970s Conservative party, especially in the middle and lower ranks, was already sympathetic to much of the 'Thatcherite' project.

6 Unsigned Memorandum (probably from the Chief Whip, Acland-Hood) to Balfour, n.d. May (?) 1905, BP, 47980, fos 231–5. This Memo. also concluded that 'The Unionist rank and file . . . have shown themselves overwhelmingly in favour of the views taken by Tariff Reformers'.

7 Acland-Hood to Sandars, 16 Dec. 1905, JSSP, MS Eng. Hist. c. 750, fos 245–6.

8 Lord Robert Cecil told H.A. Gwynne in 1909 that although he remained opposed to preference and protection he felt that there was a good case for the revenue, retaliation and anti-dumping aspects of tariff reform, see R. Cecil to Gwynne, 14 Nov. 1911, HAGP, MS Gwynne, Box 27. See also pp. 152–4.

9 See N. Blewett, *The Peers, The Parties and the People* (London 1971), p. 317.

10 With regard to old age pensions, Acland-Hood told Balfour that any objections had to be carefully handled on the grounds that 'our men will be very shy of voting on any amendment on the Second Reading – for fear of being accused of voting against', Acland-Hood to Balfour, 7 June 1908, BP, 49771, fos 175–8.

11 See pp. 242–63.

12 For attempts by some of Chamberlain's supporters to keep this aspect of tariff reform active before 1906 see pp. 248–50.

13 For the NFTL's activities see B.H. Brown, *The Tariff Reform Movement in Great Britain*, 1881–95 (New York 1943), and S.H. Zebel, 'Fair Trade', *JMH*, xii, 1940. See also pp. 186, 248–9.

14 Zebel, 'Fair Trade', p. 174.

15 Chamberlain to Balfour, 19 July 1892, BP, 49773, fos 53–4.

16 See S.H. Zebel, 'Joseph Chamberlain and the Genesis of Tariff Reform', *JBS*, vii, 1967, and R.V. Kubicek, *The Administration of Imperialism: Joseph Chamberlain at the Colonial Office* (Durham NC 1969).

17 Blake, *Conservative Party*, p. 182.

18 For this interpretation see A. Sykes, *Tariff Reform in British Politics* (Oxford 1979).

19 R. Jebb to F. Ware, 30 July 1912, JP. Ware had been removed from the editorship of the *Morning Post* the previous Spring. The historian who has attached most significance to this quotation is Alan Sykes, see his *Tariff Reform*, p. 294.

20 Asquith to Lyttelton, 16 Dec. 1894, ALP, CHAN 2/1, fos 9–10.

21 'A Conservative MP', 'Reasons for a Coalition', *NR*, cxxxiii, Mar. 1895, pp. 16–30.

22 Balfour to G.C. Bartley, 28 Aug. 1895, BP, 49850, fos 253–4.

23 ibid.

24 See J. Chamberlain to Salisbury, 16 Nov. 1891, SP, outlining problems in Liberal Unionist–Conservative relations in Birmingham, and A.J. Balfour to Lord James of Hereford, 14 Apr. 1895, BP, 49850, fos 200–3, discussing a dispute in Leamington Spa. Chamberlain added that in Birmingham the local leaders got on well and that the problems were with the local rank and file.

25 Balfour to Colonel Milward, n.d. (Feb./Mar.?) 1892, BP, 49850, fos 44–51.

26 See pp. 145–6.

27 See Chamberlain to *The Times*, 24 Apr. 1902, and Chamberlain to J.S. Sandars, 9 Oct. 1902, both letters are cited in J.E.B. Munson, 'The Unionist Coalition and Education, 1895–1902', *HJ*, xv, 1977.

28 For an examination of this cordiality at the 'high political' level see J. France, 'Personalities and Politics in the Formation of the Unionist Alliance, 1885–95' unpublished Cambridge University PhD thesis, 1987.

29 It should be pointed out that tariff reform was one such issue, in that, for example, Liberal Unionists like the Duke of Devonshire and Lord James of Hereford opposed tariff reform and sided with the Conservative free traders, but Lord Selborne, another Whig scion, was an ardent tariff reformer. Likewise, although Lords Hugh and Robert Cecil were free traders, their brothers, the 4th Lord Salisbury and Lord Evelyn Cecil, were, respectively, sympathetic and ardently committed to the tariff cause.

30 See pp. 129–31.

31 By 1906 there was already a strong body of Conservative opinion that wished to see an amalgamation of the parties, see W.C. Bridgeman, Diary, 10 Feb. 1906, in P. Williamson (ed.), *The Modernization of Conservative Politics: The Diaries and Letters of William Bridgeman, 1904–35* (London 1988).

32 See A. Adonis, *Making Aristocracy Work*, (Oxford 1993), pp. 25–6.

33 For the prominence of tariff reform in aristocratic politics in the Edwardian period see ibid., pp. 27, 144–57 and also G. Phillips, *The Diehards* (Cambridge, Mass. 1979).

34 See pp. 187–90, 211–15.

35 `Jebb to R.(?) Pringle, 25 Jan. 1912, JP.

36 Indeed the Chairman of the Tariff Reform League wrote to congratulate Gwynne on his appointment, describing it as 'a very good thing for tariff reform', Lord Ridley to Gwynne, 12 July 1911, HAGP, MS Gwynne, Box 27.

37 For an introduction to this episode see D. Dutton, 'Unionist Politics and the Aftermath of the General Election of 1906: a Reassessment', *HJ*, xxii, 1979.

38 Balcarres, Diary, 5 Feb. 1906, CP, p. 90.

39 ibid.

40 For this interpretation see D. Porter, 'The Unionist Tariff Reformers, 1903–14', unpublished Manchester University PhD thesis, 1976, and also, D. Porter and S. Newton, *Modernization Frustrated* (London 1984), G. Ingham, *Capitalism Divided* (London 1984), pp. 152–9.

41 For an introduction to the issue of the tariff campaign's finances see F. Coetzee, 'Pressure Groups, Tory Businessmen and the Age of Corruption Before the First World War', *HJ*, xxix, 1986.

42 Lord Cecil of Chelwood, *All The Way* (London 1949), p. 88.

43 For an introduction to the Confederacy and its activities see A. Sykes, 'The Confederacy and the Purge of the Unionist Free Traders', *HJ*, xvii, 1975.

44 B. Wise to Milner, 30 Dec. 1906, MP, MS Milner Dep. 218, fos 241–2. See also H. Page-Croft, *My Life of Strife* (London 1948), p. 43 for a description of the 'country' origins of the Confederacy.

45 For a full discussion of the agricultural aspect of the tariff campaign see pp. 187–90, 207–22.

46 J.R. Seeley, *The Expansion of England* (London 1883), p. 317.

47 See W.C.B. Tunstall, 'Imperial Defence, 1870–97', in *The Cambridge History of the British Empire*, iii, ch. 7.

48 See R.H. Williams, *Defending the Empire* (New Haven 1991).

49 On naval problems in general see A. Marder, *From Dreadnought to Scapa Flow* (2 vols, Oxford 1961–9), i, *The Path to War 1900–14*. In 1893 two of the navy's capital ships, *Victoria* and *Camperdown*, had collided during an exercise, and one had sunk.

50 The Navy Estimates were a constant source of controversy in the late nineteenth and early twentieth century. See for example B. Semmel, *Liberalism and Naval Strategy* (London 1986), pp. 124–9.

51 See I.F. Clarke, *Voices Prophesying War* (London 1966) and also A.J.A. Morris, *The Scaremongers* (London 1983).

52 It is interesting, however, that H.O. Arnold-Forster, the Conservative War Minister and military reformer between 1902 and 1905 was himself an author of an 'invasion' novel, *In A Conning Tower*.

53 See ch. 1.

54 RCDTI, *Final Report*, 1886, p. 519.

55 See J. Harris, 'The Transition to High Politics in British Social Policy, 1880–1914' in M. Bentley and J. Stevenson, *High and Low Politics in Modern British History* (Oxford 1984).

56 See B. Hilton, *The Age of Atonement* (Oxford 1989). In this context it is noteworthy that even an Anglican divine like William Cunningham (Vicar of Great St Mary's, Cambridge and Dean of Ely), who made a major formal contribution to the tariff debate, discussed tariff issues in largely secular terms. For Cunningham's ideas see ch. 5.

57 For an introduction to this development see J. Cornford, 'The Transformation of Victorian Conservatism', *VS*, vii, 1963–4.

58 See pp. 125–7.

59 R. Kipling, 'The Islanders', 1902, in T.S. Eliot (ed.) *A Choice of Kipling's Verse* (London 1979 edition).

60 H.G. Wells, *The Wife of Sir Isaac Harmon* (London 1914).

61 Milner to C. Dawkins, 4 Jan. 1902, MP, MS Eng. Hist. c. 68 fos 4–6.

62 See G. Searle, *The Quest for National Efficiency* (Oxford 1971), pp. 34–53.

63 See A.L. Friedberg, *The Weary Titan* (Princeton 1989), pp. 174–81, 187–8, 292–303.

64. See Williams, *Empire*, Morris, *Scaremongers*.

65. See A. Summers, 'Militarism in Britain Before the Great War', *HWJ*, ii, 1976, idem, 'The Character of Edwardian Nationalism', in P. Kennedy and A. Nicholls (eds), *Nationalist and Racialist Movements in Britain and Germany Before 1914* (London 1981), F. Coetzee, *For Party or Country* (Oxford 1989).

66 Balfour to Lady Salisbury 17 Jan. 1906, in B. Dugdale, *Arthur James Balfour*, (2 vols, London 1939) i, p. 329.

67 See pp. 142–4.

68 For a comprehensive and stimulating analysis of the milieu of these organizations see Coetzee, *Party or Country*.

69 ibid., p.3.

70 For example in 1911 the Chairman of the IML, Rowland Hunt, a Conservative MP, denounced the Conservative party and called for 'the formation of a new Patriotic Party', Hunt to Willoughby de Broke, 14 Aug. 1911, WDBP, WB/3/34.

71 See pp. 184–93.

72. See pp. 207–22.

73 See pp. 215–19.

74 For further comparative analysis see pp. 326–31.

75 See P. Kennedy and A. Nicholls (eds), *Nationalist and Racialist Movements in Britain and Germany Before 1914* (London 1980), G. Eley, *Reshaping the German Right in Wilhelmine Germany* (New Haven 1981), H. Rogger and E. Weber (eds), *The European Right* (London 1966), F.L. Carsten, *The Rise of Fascism* (London 1965).

76 See for example F. Stern, *The Politics of Cultural Despair* (Berkeley 1961), E. Nolte, *Three Faces of Fascism* (London 1963).

77 See pp. 329–32.

1 THE POLITICAL ECONOMY OF DECLINE

1 JCP, JC 18/18/22.

2 JCP, JC 9/7/16.

3 See ch. 5.

4 See R. Betts, 'The Allusion to Rome in British Imperialist Thought in the Late Nineteenth Century', *VS*, 1971.

5 Some of the domestic political ramifications of Britain's military concerns are dealt with in Morris, *The Scaremongers*, Semmel, *Naval Strategy* and P.M. Kennedy, *The Realities Behind Diplomacy* (London 1981). For a stimulating treatment of the Conservative viewpoint see Williams, *Defending the Empire*.

6 The most concise treatment of the changes in the agricultural sector is C. O'Grada, 'Agricultural Decline 1860–1914', in R. Floud and D.N. McCloskey (eds), *The Economic History of Britain Since 1700*, (2 vols, Cambridge 1980) ii, pp. 175–97.

7 RCDTI. *Final Report* (London 1886), p. 519.

8 O'Grada, 'Agricultural Decline', p. 189.

9 ibid., *passim* and also F.M.L. Thompson, 'An Anatomy of English Agriculture, 1870–1914' in B. Holderness and M. Turner (eds), *Land, Labour and Agriculture, 1700–1920* (London 1991).

10 These figures are taken from P.J. Cain, 'Political Economy and the Tariff Reform Controversy', in A. O'Day (ed.), *The Edwardian Age: Conflict and Stability* (London 1979), p. 36.

11 For a summary of this viewpoint see R. Floud, 'Britain 1860–1914: A Survey'

in Floud and McCloskey, *Economic History*, ii, pp. 1–26, V. Creuzot, *The Victorian Economy* (London 1982), pp. 185–277, S. Pollard, *Britain's Prime and Britain's Decline* (London 1988), pp. 18–54, 260–71.

12 D. McCloskey and C.K. Harley, 'Foreign Trade, Competition and the Expanding International Economy' in Floud and McCloskey, *Economic History*, ii, pp. 50–69 and D. Aldcroft (ed.), *British Industry and the Growth of Foreign Competition* (London 1968).

13 McCloskey and Harley, 'Foreign Trade'.

14 Pollard, *Prime and Decline*, pp. 19–45.

15 See Floud, 'Britain 1860–1914', and Harley and McCloskey 'Foreign Trade', ibid.

16 It has, however, been convincingly argued that the late Victorian economy was showing signs of an 'institutional rigidity' which hampered technological and structural change within industries – see in particular B. Elbaum and W. Lazonick (eds), *The Decline of the British Economy* (Oxford 1986), A. Chandler, *Scale and Scope* (Cambridge, Mass. 1989).

17 Cain, 'Political Economy', p. 36.

18 RCDTI *First Report*, 1886, Appendix A, p. 89.

19 For an account of the founding of the NFTL see S.H. Zebel, 'Fair Trade: An English Reaction to the Breakdown of the Cobden Treaty System', *JMH*, xii, 1940, pp. 161–85.

20 Lord Dunraven, 6 Nov. 1884, *PD*, Third Series, ccxliii, cc. 1044–5.

21 A list of the Chambers consulted can be found in RCDTI, *First Report*, Appendix A, p. 73. For some typical answers see Aberdeen Chamber of Commerce to RCDTI, 21 Oct. 1885, Birmingham Chamber of Commerce to RCDTI, 30 Sept. 1885, Manchester Chamber of Commerce to RCDTI, n.d. Oct. 1885, ibid., pp. 74, 77, 97–104.

22 For a concise summary of the fair traders' diagnosis of Britain's economic ills see 'To the Electors of the United Kingdom', *FT* , 16 Oct. 1885.

23 See ibid., and also W.F. Ecroyd, *Self Help* (London 1881), *passim*.

24 See F. Brittain, *Sham Free Trade: What It Has Done For England* (Sheffield 1885), a pamphlet in SCCP, LD/107/14. At the Annual General Meeting of the Sheffield Chamber in 1876 it was argued that because of US tariffs 'it was not at all likely that Sheffield would ever again have anything like the trade with the United States that it had had in the past', ibid., LD/1986/1. The SCCP also reveal great concern over the breakdown of the Cobden Treaty and the new French tariffs of 1881, cf ibid., LD/1989/4/192, 212, 213.

25 *The Times*, 3 Aug. 1881.

26 The RCDTI concluded that 'the extreme lowering of prices brought about by the extension of American farming appears to be the main factor of the present agricultural position', *Final Report*, p. 515.

27 See O'Grada, 'Agricultural Decline', pp. 179–82.

28 See *FT*, 12 Mar. 1886.

29 See the comments by W.J. Beadel, MP and F.S. Brereton, farming spokesman from, respectively, Essex and Kent, at the Quarterly Meeting of the NFTL in July 1886. Both men were opposed to 'free imports' of colonial as well as foreign grain. *FT* 6 Aug. 1886.

30 Nottingham Chamber of Commerce to RCDTI, 23 Sept. 1885, RCDTI *First Report*, Appendix A, p. 108.

31 Halifax Chamber of Commerce to RCDTI, n.d. Oct. 1885, RCDTI *First Report*, Appendix A, p. 86.

32 For example, the reply of the Birmingham Chamber was very hostile to free trade, but a full meeting of the Chamber, in early October 1885, rejected a fair trade motion by 62 votes to 49. *FT*, 30 Oct. 1885.

NOTES

33 Both S.H. Zebel, 'Fair Trade', and B.H. Brown, *The Tariff Reform Movement in Britain 1880–95* (Columbia 1945) suggest that retaliation was really just a sop to free trade opinion.

34 E.W. Hamilton, Diary 7 Oct. 1881, 7 Oct. 1882 in D.W.R. Bahlmann (ed.), *The Diary of Sir Edward Hamilton*, 2 vols (Oxford 1972), i, pp. 173, 346.

35 Hamilton, Diary 27 Oct. 1884, ibid p. 718.

36 W.F. Ecroyd, 31 Oct. 1884, *PD*, Third Series, ccxliii, c. 681.

37 C.T. Ritchie, 24 Mar. 1882, *PD*, Third Series, cclxviii, c. 1827.

38 Sir J. Clapham, *An Economic History of Modern Britain* (3 vols, Cambridge, 19863), ii, p. 251.

39 'The Past and the Future', *FT*, 16 Oct. 1885.

40 Dunraven, 6 Nov. 1884, *PD*, Third Series, ccxliii, cc. 1047–8.

41 J.M. Keynes, Private Evidence to the Macmillan Committee, 28 Feb. 1930, in *The Collected Writings of John Maynard Keynes*, 30 vols (London 1973–82), xx, p. 117. See also the striking comment in *FT*, 21 May 1886 which states that 'By displacing the home product, "something else" not being substituted in its place, not only is the first home production lost, but a valuable customer at home has been lost also'.

42 Dunraven, 6 Nov. 1884. *PD*, Third Series, ccxliii, c. 1045.

43 RCDTI, *First Report*, Appendix A, p. 79.

44 Chamberlain at Birmingham, 25 Jan. 1889, in *IF*, iv, no. 2, Feb. 1889, pp. 35–6.

45 This point is made by B. Porter, *The Lion's Share* (London 1975), pp. 75–151.

46 J. Gallagher and R. Robinson, 'The Imperialism of Free Trade', *EcHR*, vi, 1953.

47 See W.G. Hynes, *The Economics of Empire* (London 1979), *passim*.

48 The correspondence between the Liverpool Chamber and the Foreign Office is recorded in the Minutes of the Liverpool Chamber for 8 Oct. and 29 Oct. 1884, LCCP, 380 COM 1/2, fos 53, 56. For the general lobbying that took place see Hynes, *Economics*, pp. 40–54.

49 RCDTI, *Final Report*, p. 530.

50 Special General Meeting of the Liverpool Chamber, 19 Feb. 1890, LCCP, 380 COM 1/3 fos 3–4.

51 Special General Meeting of the Liverpool Chamber, 18 Nov. 1891, ibid., fo. 54.

52 See Hynes, *Economics*, pp. 109–29.

53 A concise statement of the IFL argument on this point can be found in S. Bourne, 'Imperial Federation in Its Commercial Aspect', *IF*, i. no. 1 Jan. 1886, pp. 8–10.

54 For a contemporary statistical analysis see S. Bourne, 'The Relative Importance to the Mother Country of Her Colonial Trade', ibid., i, no. 3, pp. 70–2.

55 In 1892 the Méline tariff signalled the victory of the protectionists in France. In the USA the McKinley tariffs of 1890 struck 'a heavy blow at British industry', *The Times*, 9 Oct. 1890.

56 'Imperial Federation and the Trade of Wakefield', *IF*, ii, no. 1 Jan. 1887, p. 14.

57 'The Lords of Trade and Imperial federation', *IF*, ii, no. 3, Mar. 1887, p. 51. See also further references to support for imperial federation from the Associated Chambers in the IFL *Annual Report*, 19 May 1890, IFLP, 62779.

58 'The Cutlers' Feast At Sheffield', *IF*, iii, no. 10, Oct. 1888, p. 204.

59 On 16 Dec. 1889 The Liverpool Chamber held a special meeting which was addressed by the IFL's 'star' speaker G.R. Parkin. Other special meetings were held on, for example, 19 Feb. 1890, 18 Nov. 1891, 30 Nov. 1892, and the question of imperial federation was also discussed at normal meetings. For the special meetings discussed here see LCCP, 380 COM 1/2, fos 61–2, and 380 COM 1/3, fos 3–4, 54, 82.

348

60 Birmingham Chamber of Commerce, *Annual Report*, (Birmingham 1893), p. 3.
61 See the report on a special meeting of the Blackburn Chamber of 6 Mar. 1893 which adopted the identical motion, word for word, as that passed by the Birmingham Chamber, Blackburn Chamber of Commerce, *Annual Report*, (Blackburn 1893), p. 17. For the similar action of the Bradford and London, and indeed other Chambers, see Hynes, *Economics*, pp. 109–29.
62 IFL General Committee, Minutes 24 Feb. 1885, IFLP, 62778.
63 IFL Special Executive Committee, Minutes 17 July 1886, ibid.
64 IFL Executive Committee, Minutes 20 Dec. 1886, ibid.
65 Rosebery at Leeds, 11 Oct. 1888, *IF*, iii, no. 11, pp. 213–15.
66 'Imperial Federation', *FT*, 9 July 1886.
67 For discussion of this episode and the general problem of imperial preference see R.V. Kubicek, *The Administration of Imperialism*, (Durham, NC 1975), ch. viii.
68 See ibid., p. 155.
69 Minute by Selborne, 29 July 1895, PRO, CO 323/403/13432, in ibid.
70 Hamilton, Diary, 9 June 1896, EHP, 47669.
71 H.O. Arnold-Forster at Manchester, 30 Jan. 1887 *IF*, ii, no. 3, Mar. 1887.
72 Sir L. Playfair at Leeds, n.d. Dec. 1891, *IF*, vii, no. 1, Jan. 1892.
73 In the late 1880s the fair traders shifted the emphasis of their arguments away from retaliation and began to concentrate much more on imperial preference, see *FT* 1887, 1888 *passim*. Similarly, when Samuel Cunliffe-Lister, a leading fair trader, was challenged by Randolph Churchill in December 1887 to state exactly what fair trade was, he replied that it was 'tariff federation of the Empire'. See the report of this exchange in 'The Fair Trade Scheme of Commercial Federation', *IF*, ii, no. 12, Dec. 1887.
74 Secretary of IFL to Council of IFL, 24 Apr. 1893, IFLP, 62780.
75 ibid.
76 The free trade concerns of the BEL are revealed in the correspondence at the time of the formal founding of the League between R. Herbert and Sir John Lubbock, on 16 Apr. 1895 and 15 June 1895, AP, 49661, fos 26–7, 53–4. The preferentialist leanings of the UETL were made very clear by the leadership of the well-known fair trader Sir C.E.H. Vincent.
77 For the City's commitment to free trade and the BEL see S.R.B. Smith, 'British Nationalism, Imperialism and the City of London, 1880–1900', unpublished London University PhD thesis, 1985, pp. 207–17. For Birmingham and Sheffield's support for preference and the UETL see respectively Hynes, *Economics*, pp. 113–14 and Sheffield Chamber of Commerce, Annual Report of the Council to the Chamber (Sheffield 1899), pp. 8–9. Sir John Lubbock, a member of a prominent City family, was president of the BEL, and Sir Howard Vincent, the MP for Sheffield Central, led the UETL.
78 J.E. Cairnes, *Essays in Political Economy* (London 1873), pp. 311–12.
79 For a discussion of this tradition see J.C. Wood, *British Economists and The Empire* (London 1983), pp. 1–180.
80 W.J. Courthope to Carnarvon, 17 Apr. 1887, CP, 60775, fos 190–3.
81 For a more detailed discussion of the bimetallic debate see E.H.H. Green, 'Rentiers v Producers: The Political Economy of the Bimetallic Controversy 1880–98', *EHR*, cii, 1988.
82 See RCC, *Final Report*, (London 1888), pp. 11–12 for a rehearsal of the bimetallists' arguments on these points. For a further exposition see also H.S. Foxwell, *A Criticism of Lord Farrer on the Monetary Standard* (London 1896).
83 See RCC, *First Report* (London 1887): evidence of A.D. Provand, examined 28 Feb. 1887, Q. 3320 for a description of this problem.

84 Bimetallists believed that an international agreement was necessary: they did 'not think any legislative action . . . we could take . . . would have much effect on the value of silver except in conjunction with other Goverments', RCC *First Report*, evidence of A.D. Provand, Q. 3384. With regard to the 'legal ratio', the first such ratio preferred was 15.5:1, but later 17:1 was posited, and by the mid-1890s 22:1.

85 See RCAD, *First Report*, p. 33.

86 S. Williamson in *Proceedings of the Bimetallic League* (1888), p. 13.

87 ibid., *passim*.

88 See RCC, *Final Report*. The evidence of A.D. Provand and J.C. Fielden is representative of the general view expressed by the cotton interest.

89 See the reference to this development by H. Macniel in *Proceedings of the Bimetallic League* (1893), p. 13.

90 For the importance of the bimetallic issue at the 1895 election in Lancashire see Green, 'Rentiers', pp. 596–7.

91 H.H. Gibbs, *Address on Bimetallism* (London 1885), p. 5.

92 J.C. Fielden in *Proceedings* (1888), p. 82.

93 H.R. Beeton, 'The Currency Question for Laymen', *NR*, cliii, Nov. 1885, pp. 385–401, 389.

94 Sir G.L. Molesworth in *Proceedings* (1893), p. 29.

95 In fact there were a number of City banking firms, including of course H.H. Gibbs' own concern, who supported bimetallism, but it was always a minority taste in the City.

96 L.J. Maxse, 'Episodes of the Month – The Money Power', *NR*, no. clxxviii, Dec. 1897, pp. 509–12.

97 F.A. Walker, *International Bimetallism* (London 1896), p. 50.

98 H.H. Gibbs to T.H. Farrer, 5 Oct. 1892, HHGP, MS 11,021, fos 561–3.

99 A Senior Optime, *Monometallism Unmasked* (London 1895), p. 27.

100 H.S. Foxwell, *Irregularity of Employment and Fluctuations in Prices* (Edinburgh 1886), pp. 43–4.

101 Sir J. Rolleston in *Proceedings* (1893), p. 101.

102 H.S. Foxwell in *Proceedings* (1888), p. 76.

103 R. Chalmers to T.H. Farrer, 19 Nov. 1898, FP, i. fo. 28.

104 For these debates and their relationship see B. Hilton, *Corn, Cash, Commerce* (Oxford 1979).

105 This point is established somewhat opaquely by K. Williams, *From Pauperism to Poverty* (London 1981).

106 For Foxwell and Dunraven's views see pp. 34–5, 44–5. For Hobson's analysis of unemployment see J. Allett, *New Liberalism: The Political Economy of J.A. Hobson* (Toronto 1981), pp. 99–118.

107 For a summary of this development see J. Harris, *Private Lives, Public Spirit* (Oxford 1993), pp. 237–41.

108 Harris, *Unemployment*, pp. 75–9.

109 G. Stedman Jones, *Outcast London* (Oxford 1974).

110 Harris, 'Transition', *passim*.

111 ibid.

112 F.W. Hirst, *Gladstone as Financier and Economist* (Oxford 1929).

113 This description was Lord Salisbury's, see Salisbury to Chamberlain, 13 Dec. 1896, JCP, JC 5/7.

114 See J. Cronin, *The Politics of State Expansion* (London 1991), pp. 52–4.

115 Hamilton, Diary, 2 Apr. 1889, EHP, 48650.

116 Hicks-Beach, 18 Apr. 1901, *PD*, 4th series, xcii, cc. 616–52.

117 Hamilton, Diary, 3 Apr. 1894, EHP, 48663.

118 Hamilton, Diary, 5 Apr. 1894, ibid.
119 Hamilton, Diary, 6 Dec. 1894, ibid., 48665.
120 Hamilton, Diary, 18 June 1895, ibid., 48667.
121 Hamilton, Some remarks on Public Finance, Cabinet Memorandum, July 1895, in H. Roseveare, *The Treasury* (London 1969), pp. 220–1. Hamilton's comment on the incoming Conservative Government are in Hamilton, Diary, 23 July 1895, EHP, 48667.
112 ibid.
123 Hamilton, Diary, 9 Jan. 1896, EHP, 48668.
124 Salisbury in Parliament, 30 Jan. 1900, in Roseveare, *Treasury*, p. 183.
125 Military expenditure was the area of the largest growth in government expenditure, see J. Cronin, *The Politics of State Expansion* (London 1991), pp. 51–2.
126 For the local government fiscal crisis see ibid., pp. 52–4 and A. Offer, *Property and Politics*, pp. 201–20.
127 See Cronin, *State Expansion*, pp. 51–4, Offer, *Property and Politics*, pp. 201–41.
128 See ibid., and also pp. 113–14.
129 For Chamberlain's problems with the Treasury see Kubicek, *Administration*, pp. 70–90.
130 Hamilton, Diary, 2 Apr. 1899, EHP, 48650.
131 For the controversy over the 1894 Budget see D.A. Hamer, *Liberal Politics in the Age of Gladstone and Rosebery* (Oxford 1972), pp. 223–5.
132 Hamilton, 'Some Remarks'.
133 Sir W. Harcourt in Parliament, 1895, in B.K. Murray, *The People's Budget* (Oxford 1980), p. 21.
134 Hicks-Beach to Salisbury, 27 Jan. 1899, SP.
135 Hicks-Beach to Salisbury, 13 Sept. 1901, ibid.
136 ibid.
137 For the effective mid-Victorian budgetary consensus see H.C.G. Matthew, 'Disraeli, Gladstone and the Politics of the Mid-Victorian Budget', *HJ*, xxii, 1979, pp. 417–42.
138 For this point see Roseveare, *Treasury*, pp. 186–8.
139 ibid., p. 223.
140 For the significance of this aspect of Treasury thinking see R. Middleton, *Towards the Managed Economy* (London 1984), pp. 144–72.
141 H.H. Gibbs to W.H. Smith, 1 June 1889, HHGP, MS 11,021, fos 671–83.
142 Edgeworth to Foxwell, 26 Jan. 1888, HSFP.
143 The best description of the divisions within the agricultural community can be found in J.R. Fisher, 'Agriculture and British Public Opinion', unpublished Hull University PhD thesis, 1973, esp. pp. 18, 177–231. See also below pp. 89–101.
144 For an interesting description of the lack of any institutional framework for the expression of united industrial interests see R.W.D. Boyce, *British Capitalism at the Crossroads*, (Cambridge 1986), pp. 8–12.
145 See Fisher, 'Agriculture', pp. 223–6.

2 CONSERVATISM AND THE EMPIRE

1 Quoted in W.F. Moneypenny and G.E. Buckle, *The Life of Benjamin Disraeli* (London 1929 edn, 2 vols), ii, p. 534.
2 For example P. Smith in his *Disraelian Conservatism*, R. Blake in *Disraeli* and more recently H. Cunningham in 'Jingoism in 1877–78', *VS*, xiv, 1971, pp. 429–54, and 'The Conservative Party and Patriotism' in R. Colls and

P. Dodd (eds), *Englishness: Politics and Culture 1880–1920* (London 1986).

3 For the significance of the 1870s to this development see in particular H. Cunningham, 'The Language of Patriotism 1750–1914', *HWJ*, xii, 1981.

4 For the important link between Palmerston's approach to foreign policy and the broader context of Liberal and Radical politics see M. Taylor, 'Patriotism and Radicalism in Mid-Victorian Britain', unpublished Cambridge University PhD thesis, 1989.

5 Dilke remained in the Liberal fold throughout his career, but Seeley, like many Liberal imperialists, abandoned the Liberal party over Home Rule.

6 Chamberlain to Stead, 10 Aug. 1878, in A. Porter, *The Origins of the South African War* (Manchester 1980), p. 35.

7 See T. Lloyd, *The General Election of 1880* (London 1968).

8 See especially Cunningham, 'Jingoism', *passim*.

9 See R.T. Shannon, *Gladstone and the Bulgarian Agitation, 1876* (London 1963).

10 The most comprehensive treatment of the subject is D.M. Schreuder, *Gladstone and Kruger* (London 1969).

11 See ibid., pp. 169–224 for a description of the genesis and ambiguous nature of the Pretoria Convention.

12 Salisbury, 31 Mar. 1881, in ibid., pp. 221–2.

13 ibid., pp. 134–46.

14 H.C.G. Matthew, 'Introduction' to idem (ed.), *The Gladstone Diaries*, vols x and xi (Oxford 1990), lxxviii.

15 Gladstone to Wolverton, 22 Mar. 1884, in ibid., xi, p. 128. As Matthew points out the Sudan was often referred to as 'Egypt', an indication not of ignorance but of the fact that the situation there was seen to be a sub-set of the involvement in Egypt.

16 Gladstone to Northbrook, 6 Jan. 1885, in ibid., p. 272.

17 Salisbury, 26 Feb. 1885, *PD*, 3rd series, ccxciv, c. 1311.

18 ibid., c. 1312.

19 ibid., c. 1317.

20 Richmond, 26 Feb. 1885, ibid., c. 1346.

21 H. Chaplin, 26 Feb. 1885, ibid., c. 1437.

22 See the analysis in R.A. Huttenback and L.E. Davis, *Mammon and the Pursuit of Empire* (Cambridge 1986), pp. 235–61.

23 A. Milner to H.S. Foxwell, 15 July 1884, HSFP. In 1884 Oxford Liberal Association refused to adopt Milner as a candidate because of his criticisms of the government's Egyptian policy. See Oxford Liberal Association to Milner, 10 July 1884, MP, MS Milner Dep. 25.

24 For this episode see P. Marshall, 'The Imperial Factor in the Liberal Decline, 1880–85', in J.E. Flint and G. Williams (eds), *Perspectives on Empire* (London 1973), p. 138.

25 In December 1885 Chamberlain warned Gladstone that the Conservatives were going to use the Irish Question to raise a cry of 'Empire in Danger', and he noted that 'it will not be possible to satisfy the Irish party with any proposals that are likely to secure the general support of English Liberals', Chamberlain to Gladstone, 19 Dec. 1885, Gladstone papers, BL, Add. MSS 49, 126, fos 127–9.

26 D.G. Hoskin, 'The Genesis and Significance of the 1886 "Home Rule" Split in the Liberal Party', unpublished Cambridge University PhD thesis, 1964, p. 16.

27 For a full discussion of the Irish–South Africa link established by contemporaries see Schreuder, *Gladstone and Kruger*, pp. 180–1, 229–36.

28 For the role of the Irish Nationalists in these episodes see R. Robinson, 'Imperial Problems in British Politics 1880–95', in E.A. Benians, Sir J. Butler and C.E. Carrington (eds), *The Cambridge History of the British Empire*, (4 vols.

Cambridge 1959), III, pp. 134–57.

29 See Robinson, 'Imperial Problems', pp. 131–58, Marshall, 'Imperial Factor', pp. 139–40.

30 Lyall to Morley, n.d. 1882, in M. Durand, *The Life of Sir A.C. Lyall* (Edinburgh 1913), in Marshall, 'Imperial Factor', p. 136.

31 For Gladstone's acknowledgement of the strength of feeling against the Ilbert Bill see Gladstone to Sir H. Ponsonby, 22 Oct. 1883, in Matthew (ed.), *Gladstone Diaries*, xi, pp. 45–6.

32 J.F. Stephen to *The Times*, n.d. 1883, in Marshall, 'Imperial Factor', p. 138.

33 Gladstone to Spencer, 3 Dec. 1883, in Matthew (ed.), *Gladstone Diaries*, xi, pp. 71–2.

34 Gladstone, 10 May 1886, *PD*, 3rd Series, cccv, c. 576.

35 W.S. Shirley, 8 Apr. 1886, *PD*, 3rd Series, ccciv, cc. 1100–1.

36 Spencer to Ponsonby, 9 May 1886, in P. Gordon (ed.), *The Red Earl: The Papers of the 5th Earl Spencer, 1835–1910*, 2 vols (Northampton 1981), ii, p. 118.

37 Spencer to Monck, 28 Apr. 1886, ibid., pp. 116–17.

38 See, for example, the speech of W.S. Shirley, 8 Apr. 1886, *PD*, 3rd Series, vol. ccciv, cc. 1100–1

39 W. Long, 8 Apr. 1886, ibid., cc. 1101–4.

40 Hartington, 9 Apr. 1886, ibid., c. 1263, G.J. Goschen, 13 Apr. 1886, ibid., c. 1477.

41 See pp. 85–7.

42 See H.C.G. Matthew, *The Liberal Imperialists* (Oxford 1973).

43 As Miles Taylor has demonstrated even the supposed patron saints of Little Englandism, Cobden and Bright, were not hostile to the Empire as such, they simply wished to see the Empire open to democratic control and managed more effectively for the general good of Britain and the Colonies alike. See M. Taylor 'Patriotism and Radicalism', and also E.H.H. Green and M. Taylor, 'Further Thoughts on Little Englandism' in R. Samuel (ed.), *Patriotism* (3 vols. London 1989), i, pp. 103–9.

44 For example, the IFL's first President was the Liberal statesman and author of the famous 1870 Education Act W.E. Forster.

45 An examination of the IFL Executive Committee Minutes for the period 1886–92 reveals 52 MPs strongly involved with League business (Peers were not included in this survey). Of these 33 were Conservatives, 12 were Liberal Unionists and 9 Liberals.

46 Rosebery to A. Loring, 30 Apr. 1890, IFLP, 62779.

47 It should be noted, however, that in 1894 Austen Chamberlain expressed concern that Rosebery's succession to the Liberal leadership would make it difficult 'to make . . . party capital out of Uganda, South Africa etc.' and that 'We shall . . . not get some votes that Mr G's weakness on these points would have driven over to us'. Chamberlain to Maxse, 9 Mar. 1894, LJMP 443 W 664.

48 See Cannadine, *The Decline and Fall of the British Aristocracy* (New Haven 1990), pp. 133–4, 444–5, 588–605, Huttenback and Davis, *Mammon*, pp. 210–12.

49 See Cannadine, *British Aristocracy*, p. 588.

50 See below pp. 35–7 and for a more detailed survey see Hynes, *Economics of Empire, passim*.

51 See de Cecco, *Money and Empire*, and also Huttenback and Davis, *Mammon*.

52 See R. Price, 'Society, Status and Jingoism: the Social Roots of Lower Middle Class Patriotism, 1870–1900' in G. Crossick (ed.), *The Lower Middle Class in Britain* (London 1977), pp. 89–112 and idem, *An Imperial War and the British Working Class* (London 1972).

53 As the replies of the various Chambers of Commerce and Trade Associations to the RCDTI made very clear, there was a basic agreement over the economic

utility of Colonies but there were also very important differences over the optimum imperial economic relationship. See pp. 32–3, 37.

54 See A.L. Friedberg, *The Weary Titan* (Princeton 1988) for a stimulating analysis of the debate over Britain's military–imperial resources.

55 Seeley, *Expansion of England*, p. 88.

56 See for example the remark in the Imperial Federation League Annual Report that 'The action of the *laws of polotical development* as exemplified in such orderly, though almost unconscious growth, emphasises the need for the deliberate adoption of [the] federal principle', (my emphasis) IFL Annual Report, 24 Mar. 1887, IFLP, 62779.

57 See pp. 32–3, 40–1.

58 See pp. 133–4.

59 See in particular K. Williams, 'The British State, Social Imperialism and Emigration from Britain, 1900–22', unpublished London University PhD thesis (1985), and idem, 'A Way Out of Our Troubles: The Politics of Empire Settlement, 1900–22' in S. Constantine (ed.), *Emigrants and Empire: British Settlement in the Dominions Between the Wars* (Manchester 1990), pp. 22–44.

60 For the concept of imperial overstretch see Kennedy, *Great Powers*. For plans to raise funds for imperial defence from the Colonies, and especially the proposal by the Cape Premier Jan Hofmeyr to use an imperial tariff for this purpose, see Kubicek, *Administration of Imperialism*.

61 See in particular Cunningham, 'Conservative Party and Patriotism', *passim*.

62 See pp. 133–4.

63 Salisbury at Carnarvon, 10 Apr. 1888, cited in A. Porter, 'Lord Salisbury, Foreign Policy and Domestic Finance, 1860–1900', in R. Blake and H. Cecil (eds), *Salisbury: The Man and His Policies* (Basingstoke 1987), p. 170.

64 For a summary of these challenges see Porter, *Lion's Share*, pp. 119–51.

65 Salisbury to Baring, 11 Feb. 1887, quoted in Porter, 'Lord Salisbury', p. 172.

66 For the constraints on Chamberlain's schemes see p. 51. For the Treasury's concern over Kitchener's campaigns see M. Hicks-Beach to Salisbury, 1 Nov. 1897, SP. For the financial constraints placed on foreign and imperial policy in general see Porter, 'Lord Salisbury', *passim*.

67 See Porter, 'Lord Salisbury', pp. 165–6.

68 See Huttenback and Davis, *Mammon*, pp. 183–214, and also P.K. O'Brien, 'The Costs and Benefits of British Imperialism, 1846–1914', *P and P*, cxx, 1988.

69 'Commercial Union Between the United Kingdom and the Colonies', Memo by 'R.G.' to the Cabinet, 9 Feb. 1891, PRO CAB 37/29 (7).

70 Memorandum for 1905 NUCA meeting, n.d. Sept. (?) 1905, JCP, JC 5/13/14.

71 For this interpretation see in particular P. Fraser, *Joseph Chamberlain: Radicalism and Empire*, (London 1966).

72 Chamberlain at Walsall, 15 July 1895, *The Times*, 16 July 1895.

73 Selborne to Chamberlain, 3 July 1899, JCP, JC 10/4/2/47.

74 In his study of the popular reaction to the war, *An Imperial War and the British Working Class* (London 1973), Richard Price concluded that the masses were not swept off their feet by jingoistic fervour, but more recently his conclusions have been challenged by, amongst others, M. Blanch, in his essay 'British Society and the War' in P. Warwick (ed.) *The South African War* (London 1980).

75 J. Bryce to Goldwin Smith, 23 Jan. 1900, cited in Kennedy, *Anglo-German Antagonism*, p. 362.

76 See J.A. Hobson, *The Psychology of Jingoism* (London 1901).

77 Salisbury to Hicks-Beach, 14 Sept. 1901, in Marsh, *The Discipline*, p. 309.

78 Chamberlain at Stourbridge, 9 Oct. 1900, in J.L. Garvin, *Joseph Chamberlain*, iii, p. 598.

79 Chamberlain to Beauchamp, 5 Mar. 1900, in ibid., p. 629.
80 Chamberlain at Birmingham, 15 May 1903, in Boyd (ed.), *Speeches*, ii, p. 127.
81 Maxse, 'Episodes of the Month', *NR*, cclxxvii, Mar. 1906, p. 8.
82 Chamberlain to Beauchamp, 5 Mar. 1900, in Garvin, *Joseph Chamberlain*, iii, p. 629.
83 Proceedings of the Imperial Conference, 1902, Cmnd. 1299, ix–x.
84 Dudley to Churchill, 9 Nov. 1902, in R.S. Churchill, *Winston S. Churchill*, companion volume ii, part i, pp. 171–2.
85 See E.H.H. Green, 'Arthur Balfour and the Genesis of the Tariff Reform Campaign – a Reappraisal', (forthcoming).
86 See pp. 49, 51–2.
87 Sir William Harcourt, 23 Apr. 1903, *PD*, 4th Series, cxxi, c. 266.

3 CONSERVATISM AND THE PROPERTIED

1 RCP 1/14/91.
2 See Cornford, 'Transformation', *passim*.
3 Northcote, Diary 28 Apr. 1880, IP, 50063A, fos 324–8. Salisbury also felt that this was 'not an unlikely occurrence', Salisbury to Balfour, 5 Oct. 1880, 49688, fos 33–6.
4 This legislation gave tenants the right to hunt and kill ground game on their farms; previously these rights had been vested solely in the landlord.
5 Northcote, Diary, 20 June 1880, IP, 50063A, fos 347–57.
6 W.E. Gladstone, Memorandum 9 Dec. 1880, circulated to Cabinet 11 Dec. 1880, cited in Hoskin, 'Home Rule Split', p. 82.
7 See in particular W.H. Smith, 2 May 1881, *PD*, 3rd Series, cclx, cc. 1571–81, and Balfour's denunciation of the Bill's 'Socialist principles', ibid., c. 1611.
8 Salisbury, 1 Aug. 1881, *PD*, 3rd Series, cclxiv, c. 259.
9 Salisbury, 'Disintegration', p. 344. A leading farming journal, *The Mark Lane Express* had noted (17 Jan. 1881) that the idea of 'dual ownership' intrinsic to the '3 Fs' could be transferred to the United Kingdom as a whole. See J.R. Fisher, 'The Farmers' Alliance: An Agricultural Protest Movement of the 1880s', *AgHR*, xxvi, 1978, p. 19.
10 Although *The Radical Programme* was not published until 1885 the first instalment had appeared in the *Fortnightly Review* in the summer of 1883.
11 The Agricultural Holdings Act of 1883, which made it obligatory for landlords to provide compensation for improvements carried out by their tenants, and which represented an intervention in landlord–tenant relations, was regarded as one result of Farmers' Alliance agitation. For the Agricultural Holdings Act and the activities of the Farmers' Alliance see Fisher, 'Farmers' Alliance', *passim*, and also idem, 'Public Opinion and Agriculture', unpublished University of Hull PhD thesis, 1972, pp. 176–230.
12 Salisbury, 'Disintegration', pp. 345, 354.
13 See T. Knowles, 3 June 1880, *PD*, 3rd Series, cclii, cc. 1100–1. Knowles represented the mining seat of Wigan, and was acknowledged by Joseph Chamberlain, the Minister (President of the Board of Trade) responsible for the Bill, to be genuinely representative of the coal-mining interest, see J. Chamberlain, 6 July 1880, *PD*, 3rd Series, ccliii, c. 1764.
14 W.Y. Craig, 3 June 1880, ibid., c. 1105, see also Balfour, 2 July 1880, *PD*, 3rd Series, ccliii, c. 1407.
15 Salisbury, 'Disintegration', p. 343.
16 ibid., p. 356.
17 *The Radical Programme* (London 1885), p. 13. H.M. Hyndman, the leader of the Social Democratic Federation, also assisted the Conservatives in this context

when he argued that Radicals were doing the Socialists' work for them, and that Chamberlain's arguments 'which he uses against the landowners will be turned against himself as a capitalist and the class to which he belongs'. H.M. Hyndman, 'The Radicals and Socialism', *Nineteenth Century*, Nov. 1885, quoted in H. Perkin, 'Land Reform and Class Conflict in Victorian Britain' in idem, *The Structured Crowd* (Brighton 1981), p. 125.

18 Salisbury, 'Disintegration', p. 356.

19 ibid., p. 349.

20 Halsbury, 31 March 1887, *PD*, 3rd Series, ccxiii, c. 31.

21 For a suggestive treatment of the overlap between threats to landed and other forms of property see Perkin, 'Land Reform', *passim*.

22 Lansdowne, 1 Aug. 1881, *PD*, 3rd Series, cclxiv, cc. 280, 301. Argyll told Earl Spencer that 'The universal, indiscriminate right of sale to *all* tenants is quite monstrous ... How would you like it at your gate at Althorp?', Argyll to Spencer, 18 Apr. 1881, in P. Gordon (ed.), *The Red Earl: The Papers of the 5th Earl Spencer, 1835–1910* (2 vols, Northampton 1981), i, p. 191. Even Spencer, who supported the Irish land legislation confessed that the measure was 'an ugly thing for English landlords to swallow', that he was not wholly smitten with such legislation and agreed that 'the Bill approaches ... those principles [the '3 Fs']', Spencer to Earl Cowper, 3 Apr. 1881, ibid., p. 170.

23 Craig was President of the North Staffordshire Institute of Mining and Engineering.

24 Apart from Craig, the Liberals who voted against the Bill were A. Barnes, an 'extensive coal owner' (according to *Dod's Parliamentary Companion*) and MP for the mining constituency of Chesterfield, J.C. Bolton, an East India merchant and vice-chairman of the Glasgow Chamber of Commerce, A. Brogden, an ironmaster, S.C. Glyn, a son of the banker and Liberal Whip Lord Wolverton, H.M. Jackson, a prominent lawyer, J. Pender, chairman of the Eastern Telegraph Company, H. Robertson, a civil engineer, ironmaster, locomotive engine maker and builder of three railway lines, C. Russell, a lawyer, Sir John St Aubyn, a Deputy Warden of the Cornish Stannaries, C.R.M. Talbot, MP for the coal-mining county of Glamorganshire, A.P. Vivian, another Deputy Warden of the Cornish Stannaries and MP for the tin-mining West Cornwall constituency, and E. Watkin, the chairman of the South Eastern Railway Co.

25 For example, H.H. Vivian, another Liberal coal owner and MP for Glamorganshire spoke against the measure in the Commons but did not vote in the crucial division. It is possible that other Liberal MPs expressed their disquiet through abstention rather than direct opposition.

26 The Marquis of Zetland left the Liberal party as a result of this dispute, whilst two other Whig landowners in the North Riding, Earl Grey and the Duke of Cleveland, both publicly supported the Conservative candidate. For this episode see T.A. Jenkins, *Gladstone, the Whigs and the Liberal Party, 1874–86* (Oxford 1989), pp. 163–4.

27 It is worth noting that the Liberal motion concerned the failure of the Queen's Speech to deal with the questions of allotments and small holdings and the 'fairness' of rents and security of tenure of English tenants.

28 For a discussion of this phenomenon and an analysis of the contemporary viewpoint see Shannon, *Age of Disraeli*, pp. 66–9, 162–3, 180–1.

29 For a contemporary report of concern amongst employers about growing trade union power see the Earl of Derby's Diary, 23 Sept. 1873, cited in ibid., pp. 162–3.

30 See J.P. Parry, 'Religion and the Collapse of Gladstone's First Government, 1870–74', *HJ*, xxv, 1982.

31 The 1871 Trade Union legislation had given trade unions legal recognition as corporate bodies, but made picketing illegal – seemingly giving with one hand and taking with another. Likewise the 1870 Education Act had failed to establish a compulsory, secular national education system as desired by militant Noncomformity. For these tensions in the Liberal ranks see Parry, *Democracy and Religion*.

32 Goschen's remarks are reported in W.C. Cartwright's Diary, 31 Oct. 1882, in Jenkins, *Liberal Party*, p. 174.

33 G.J. Goschen, 'Since 1880', *Nineteenth Century*, xvii, 1885. The title of the essay is significant in terms of establishing a contemporary view of the 'turning point' in Liberal politics.

34 Goschen, ibid., p. 728, cited in Taylor, *Men Versus the State*, p. 10.

35 ibid. To some degree Gladstone shared Goschen's view of the 'New Radicalism', insofar as he saw 'the pet idea' of 'the Liberalism of today' as 'taking into the hands of the State the business of the individual man', see Gladstone to H. Acton, 11 Feb. 1885, in Matthew (ed.), *Gladstone Diaries*, xi, pp. 294–5.

36 [H. Maine], 'Hares and Rabbits', *St James's Gazette*, i, 1880, p. 76, in Taylor, *Men Versus the State*, p. 9.

37 G.J. Goschen, 'Since 1880', Nineteenth Century, xvii, 1885, p. 727, in ibid., pp. 9–10.

38 The concerns of some prominent Liberal intellectuals on these questions are dealt with in ibid., pp. 1–35. Lord Southesk left the Liberal party in 1885. He complained that Liberal legislation was 'driving into the Rights of property' and expressed fear at the probable 'socialistic government of the future', Southesk to Gladstone, 27 Oct. 1885, in Matthew (ed.), *Gladstone Diaries*, xi, p. 417, n. 6.

39 See D. Southgate, *The Passing of the Whigs* (London 1962), Hamer, *Liberal Politics*, M. Barker, *Gladstone and Radicalism* (Brighton 1975), Jenkins, *Liberal Party*, and H.C.G. Matthew, 'Introduction' to idem (ed.), *The Gladstone Diaries*, vols x, xi, (Oxford 1990).

40 Spencer to Lansdowne, 16 Aug. 1885, in Gordon (ed.), *Red Earl*, ii, p. 72.

41 See, for example, E. Hardcastle to Salisbury, 27 July 1885, SP – calling for 'a straightforward, national policy which will draw to us all moderate men disgusted and alarmed as they are at Gladstone – Chamberlainism', quoted in Lubenow, *Home Rule Crisis*, p. 85.

42 Salisbury, 'Disintegration', p. 358.

43 See W.C. Lubenow, 'Irish Home Rule and The Social Basis of the Great Separation of the Liberal Party in 1886', *HJ*, xxviii, 1985.

44 See, for example, Spencer to Lansdowne, 16 Aug. 1885, and Spencer to Lansdowne, 2 Feb. 1886, which reveal a clear understanding of Lansdown's concerns: these letters are in Gordon (ed.), *Red Earl*, i, pp. 70–4, 107–9.

45 Argyll to Spencer, 18 Apr. 1881, in Gordon (ed.), *Red Earl*, i. p. 171, Lansdowne, 1 Aug. 1881, *PD*, Third Series, cclxiv, c. 300.

46 Salisbury to Carnarvon, 29 July 1882, CARP, 60759, fos 85–6.

47 Sir Michael Hicks-Beach argued that 'power in Ireland will be handed over by this Bill ... [to those] in apostolic succession to the Land League ... [whose] doctrines ... were doctrines of assassination and treason'. Sir Michael Hicks-Beach, 13 Apr. 1886, *PD*, ccciv, c. 1521. A meeting of senior Liberal Home Rulers – Gladstone, Grenville, Spencer, Harcourt and Morley

– also concluded that 'It is doubtful whether an Irish chamber could be trusted to treat him [the Irish landlord] fairly', and they also noted 'It is hardly doubtful that he would persuade powerful parties and interests in this country that it would not treat him fairly', Memorandum of a Conclave at the House of Commons, 23 Mar. 1886, in Matthew (ed.), *Gladstone Diaries*, xi, p. 516.

48 Gladstone to R.H. Hutton, 24 May 1886, in Matthew (ed.), *Gladstone Diaries*, xi, p. 560.

49 NLF, *Report*, 1889, quoted in Hamer, *Liberal Politics*, p. 147.

50 For a breakdown of the social make up of the Liberal and Conservative/Liberal Unionist Parties in the House of Commons see Perkin, 'Land Reform', pp. 124–5, 130–1.

51 See below.

52 For further discussion of the importance of MPs representing local interests see below.

53 See J. Cornford, 'The Parliamentary Foundations of the Hotel Cecil', in R. Robson (ed.), *Ideas and Institutions of Victorian Britain*.

54 Arthur Steel-Maitland, the first party Chairman, appointed W. Jenkins, a Birmingham businessman who had previously been secretary of Joseph Chamberlain's Imperial Tariff Committee, to the post of Chief Organization Secretary at CCO with authority for 'the immediate management ... of the Conservative associations in the constituencies ... [and] control of the District Agents of the Central Office', Steel-Maitland to Jenkins, 10 Aug. 1911, SMP, GD 193/151/1/86.

55 Balcarres to E. Talbot, n.d. Feb. 1913, JSSP, MS Eng. Hist. c. 765, fo. 87.

56 See, for example, the complaint in *The Farmer*, 7 Dec. 1876, about the appearance 'in certain agricultural districts, [of] men from the Stock Exchange, capitalists and other clearly non-agricultural gentry', cited in Fisher, 'Public Opinion and Agriculture', p. 316. A quarter of a century later Lord Balcarres noted that 'Acland-Hood is furious at the desire of county constituencies to have semitic candidates – Van Raalte, Marks, Ashley, Van Laun, and so forth, in preference to good old-fashioned Tory country gentlemen ... Our Party will suffer severely through this type of cosmopolitan candidate ... The number of Jews is considerable, but as a rule they represent towns *which does not signify so much'*, Balcarres, Diary, 3 Mar. 1904, in Vincent (ed.), *CP*, p. 72 (my emphasis).

57 See W.D. Rubinstein, *Men of Property, passim*.

58 See F.M.L. Thompson, 'Britain' in D. Spring (ed.), *European Landed Elites in the 19th Century*, Cannadine, *Aristocracy*, pp. 9, 55–6.

59 See Adonis, *Making Aristocracy Work*, pp. 54–5.

60 Thompson, *Landed Society*, pp. 292–326, Cannadine, *Aristocracy*, p. 92.

61 See Williams, *Defending the Empire*, pp. 138–40.

62 For details see below, pp. 98–9, 113–15.

63 See Adonis, *Making Aristocracy Work*, pp. 117–124.

64 Montagu to Salisbury, 22 Feb. 1894, in ibid., p. 122.

65 ibid., pp. 117–154.

66 A. Adonis, 'The survival of the Great Estates: Henry, 4th Earl of Carnarvon and his dispositions in the 1880s', *HR*, lxiv, 1991.

67 Hamilton, Diary, n.d. 1896, in Adonis, *Making Aristocracy Work*, p. 132. Aristocratic opposition, mobilized in the Lords and in the country, was also a major feature of the campaign against, and ultimate destruction of, Arnold-Forster's proposed army reforms in the period 1902–4. See Williams, *Defending the Empire*, pp. 41–58.

68 Salisbury (4th Marquis) to Law, 1 Aug. 1912, BLP, 27/1/2/. Salisbury was referring here to his non-objection to the 1903 Irish Land Purchase Act.
69 Adonis, *Making Aristocracy Work*, p. 26.
70 See ibid., pp. 189–92.
71 Lansdowne to Selborne, 4 July 1907, SELP, MS Selborne 79, fos 20–1.
72 Salisbury to Carnarvon, 8 Oct. 1881, CARP, 60759, fos 64–5.
73 See J.P.D. Dunbabin, *Rural Discontent in Nineteenth Century Britain* (London 1974).
74 See A. Howkins, *Poor Labouring Men* (London 1986).
75 See Thompson, *Landed Society*, pp. 232–7.
76 For a contemporary statement of the problem from the point of view of a 'straitened landlord' see 'Letters from Ruricola' [Earl Carnarvon], *National Review*, xiv, Apr. 1884, xxiii, Jan. 1885, xxvi, Apr. 1886. For Carnarvon's own problems see Adonis, 'Great Estates'.
77 Northcote, Diary, 20 June 1880, IP, 50063A, fos 347–57.
78 ibid.
79 ibid.
80 For a discussion of Conservative problems with this legislation see March, *The Discipline*, pp. 29–30.
81 H. Chaplin to Salisbury, 7 July 1887, SP. This Committee had probably existed for some time, but I have not found any earlier references to its activities.
82 In spite of intense lobbying the committee was unable to force amendment to the Agricultural Holdings Act in 1890 and, in the same year, was further disappointed in its efforts to obtain regulation of cattle-ship loading.
83 Chaplin to Salisbury, 7 July 1887, SP.
84 *The Agricultural Gazette*, 30 Nov. 1891, quoted in fisher, 'Public Opinion', p. 125.
85 Chaplin to Salisbury, 9 Dec. 1892, SP.
86 Chaplin to Akers-Douglas, 26 Dec. 1892, ADP, U564 c. 122/10.
87 See A. Howkins, *Reshaping Rural England: A Social History, 1850–1925* (London 1991), pp. 157–61.
88 ibid., p. 161.
89 Balfour, Memorandum to Salisbury, n.d. June 1895, SP.
90 Chaplin to Salisbury, 1 June 1895, SP.
91 That this occurred as a result of the pressures described here is confirmed by Almeric Fitzroy's memoirs. In February 1905, remarking on the question as to who was to succeed Walter Long at the Board of Agriculture, Fitzroy noted that 'it was practically laid down *in 1895* that the President of the Board of Agriculture should necessarily be in the Cabinet', Sir Almeric Fitzroy, *Memoirs of Sir Almeric Fitzroy* (2 vols, London 1923), i, p. 236 (my emphasis).
92 For a contemporary account of these episodes see C. Turnor, *Land Problems and the National Welfare* (London 1911), pp. 297–326.
93 G.L. Courthope was MP for East Sussex, Chairman of the Central Chamber of Agriculture, and Chairman of various Conservative back-bench committees dealing with agricultural questions.
94 Courthope to A. Chamberlain, 6 Feb. 1910, ACP, AC 8/5/9.
95 Howkins, *Rural England*, p. 138.
96 ibid., esp. pp. 138–65.
97 Quoted in Lubenow, *Home Rule Crisis*, p. 185.
98 See M. Kinnear, *The British Voter* (Ithaca 1968), p. 13.
99 See below pp. 120–2.
100 E.J. Feuchtwanger, *Disraeli, Democracy and the Tory Party* (Oxford 1968), pp. 80–3, Shannon, *Age of Disraeli*, pp. 180–1.

101 This will be remedied by Franz Coetzee's forthcoming study of Villa Toryism.

102 See for example P. Joyce, 'Popular Toryism in Lancashire, 1860–90', unpublished Oxford University D.Phil thesis, 1975 for Conservatism in Lancashire cotton towns, P. Waller, *Democracy and Sectarianism*, (Liverpool 1981) for Conservatism in Liverpool, and J. Lawrence, 'Party Politics and the People: Continuity and Change in the Political History of Wolverhampton, 1815–1914', unpublished Cambridge University PhD thesis, 1989.

103 Of course there were some exceptions to this rule. Occasionally 'outsiders' were chosen to fight supposedly near to hopeless causes. An interesting example of the latter is Sir Howard Vincent's candidacy for Sheffield Central in 1885. Vincent was chosen to stand against the supposedly 'unbeatable' Samuel Plimsoll, but having achieved a most unexpected victory Vincent went on to forge very close links with his constituency. Alternatively, some constituencies would occasionally adopt figures of genuinely national standing. One example of this is Arthur Balfour's adoption by East Manchester in 1885, although, as will be seen below, this may not have been the only reason Balfour stood in that constituency.

104 It is worth noting that many of these individuals, or their family predecessors, had in fact been Liberals.

105 For example Paddington South (Lord Randolph Churchill 1885–94), Marylebone East (Lord Charles Beresford, 1885–9, Lord Robert Cecil, 1906–10), South Kensington (Earl Percy, 1895–1910), St George's, Hanover Square (Lord Algernon Percy, 1885–7, The Hon. H. Legge, 1900–06, Alfred Lyttelton 1906–14), Lembeth, Brixton (Marquis of Carmarthen, 1887–96) Lewisham (Viscount Lewisham 1885–6). All of the seats are classified as 'predominantly middle class' in Pelling, *Social Geography*, p. 30. Lewisham was perhaps a special case in that the constituency bordered on the Kent estates of the Earls of Dartmouth, to which Viscount Lewisham was the heir.

106 R. Bell (Vice-President Southampton Conservative Association) to Salisbury, 17 May 1892, SP. The irate burgesses evidently had their way, for in 1895 the Conservative candidate for Southampton was a local barrister.

107 R.H.Trainor, 'Peers on an Industrial Frontier: the Earls of Dartmouth and Dudley in the Black Country, c. 1810–1914', in D. Cannadine (ed.), *Patricians, Power and Politics in Nineteenth Century Towns* (Leicester 1982), pp. 69–122. It is noticeable, however, that Dudley and Dartmouth's presence in the politics of Wolverhampton, the largest conurbation, was kept to a minimum by local Conservatives in the last quarter of the century: for this information I am grateful to Dr John Lawrence.

108 See Shannon, *Age of Disraeli*, pp. 193–5, 223–59.

109 T. Freston to Balfour, 3 Jan. 1883, quoted in R.F. Foster, 'Tory Democracy and Political Elitism: Provincial Conservatism and Parliamentary Tories in the Early 1880s', in A. Cosgrove and J. McGuire (eds), *Parliament and Community* (Belfast 1983), pp. 147–75, 154.

110 ibid., esp. pp. 161–4, and also idem, *Lord Randolph Churchill*, (Oxford 1985) esp. pp. 98–127.

111 For Disraeli's extreme reluctance to visit the provinces see Shannon, *Age of Disraeli*, p. 325.

112 W.L. Jackson to Salisbury 29 July 1884, SP.

113 Conservative MP for Islington South, Rollit was a solicitor and shipowner with extensive interests in London, Newcastle and Hull. Rollit was Sheriff of Hull, his birthplace, in 1875–6 and Mayor from 1883–5. At the peak of his career in the 1890s Rollit was a vice-president of the Law Society, president of the Associated Chambers of Commerce of the UK, and of London and Hull

Chambers of Commerce, and president of the Municipal Corporations Association.

114 A.K. Rollit to Salisbury, 27 Feb. 1893, 13 May 1895, 21 Jan. 1896, SP.

115 Jackson was a leather merchant and tanner in Leeds, and became Chairman of the Great Northern Railway. He was President of Leeds Chamber of Commerce in the 1880s and Mayor of Leeds in 1895–6.

116 W.L. Jackson to Salisbury, 14 Dec. 1888, SP.

117 W.L. Jackson to Salisbury, 31 May 1897, SP.

118 See Cannadine, *British Aristocracy*, pp. 300–15 for details of the expanding number of honours made available for disbursement in the late nineteenth and early twentieth century and their accelerated use.

119 Schomberg McDonnell to A. Akers-Douglas, ADP, U564 c. 24/23.

120 It is interesting to note that the candidate for a knighthood if Goldsworthy turned down the honour was Joseph Addison, the Conservative MP for the cotton town of Ashton-Under-Lyne, ibid. A similar argument for offering a general acknowledgement through an individual honour was made by H. Seton-Karr when he suggested in 1889 and 1892 that Roby Pilkington be considered for a baronetcy. He stated that in addition to his services to the Conservative cause in St Helens 'no glass maker had yet been honoured'. Seton-Karr to Salisbury, 21 July 1889, 29 July 1892, quoted in T.C. Barker, *The Glassmakers* (London 1977), p. 234.

121 Balfour to Schomberg McDonnell, 11 Apr. 1892, SP.

122 Balfour to Schomberg McDonnell, 12 Apr. 1892, SP.

123 It seems likely that the proliferation of awards and initials that began in the 1880s was in part a product of a need to find more things to give away whilst maintaining a clear award hierarchy.

124 McDonnell to Akers-Douglas, 27 Dec. 1898, ADP, U564 c. 24/34.

125 This delayed W.L. Jackson's elevation in 1895. See Salisbury to Akers-Douglas, 7 Dec. 1898, ADP, U564 c. 18/50.

126 For example in December 1890 Schomberg McDonnell, discussing the forth-coming New Year's Honours, stated that there was no justification for 'promoting' Henry Howorth, the Salford MP, and that if he was promoted 'Maclean [MP for Oldham], King [MP for Hull Central] and Howard Vincent would be frantic', McDonnell to Akers-Douglas, 27 Dec. 1890, ADP, U564 c. 24/13. In the end Howorth and Vincent were both knighted, but Maclean missed out.

127 See M. Pugh, *The Tories and the People* (Oxford 1985).

128 For a discussion of the Primrose League's role in terms of 'popular Toryism' see chapter 4.

129 The fact that they were given the titles of 'Knights and Dames' seems in this context less of an attempt to conjure up a chivalric past and more a means of providing proxy titles for Conservative social climbers.

130 The 'Society' aspect of Conservative politics was also important at the highest level of politics. Lady Salisbury, for example, sought the advice of the Chief Whip when she held parties, for she was 'anxious to ask any one who would be of use to the Party' and particularly wanted to know if they had wives and daughters to impress and entertain. Lady Salisbury to Akers-Douglas, 24 Apr. n.d. ante-1900, ADP, U564 c. 19/5.

131 Cranborne to Akers-Douglas, 26 July 1886, ADP, U564 c. 20/1.

132 J.E. Gorst (?), *Vanity Fair*, May, Oct. 1880, quoted in Shannon, *Age of Disraeli*, p. 398.

133 Balfour to Salisbury, 27 Aug. 1891, SP.

134 Balfour to Akers-Douglas, 2 Jan. 1888, ADP, U564 c. 22/3.

135 Balfour to Schomberg McDonnell, 12 Apr. 1892, SP.
136 Chaplin to Salisbury, 9 Dec. 1892, SP.
137 ibid.
138 See J.H. Round, 'The Protectionist Revival', *NR*, cxlviii, June 1895, pp. 497–511.
139 Quoted in Fisher, 'Public Opinion', p. 249.
140 See Brown, *Tariff Reform Movement*, and for fair trade activity in Manchester see *Fair Trade*, li, 1 Oct. 1886. In 1885 both Altrincham and Bolton elected fair trade Conservative MPs.
141 See esp. W.E. Gladstone to R. Grosvenor, 21 Nov. 1885, and to G.J. Goschen, 26 Nov. 1885, in Matthew (ed.), *Gladstone diaries*, xi, pp. 435–6.
142 See pp. 30–5.
143 Hamilton, Diary, 19 Sept. 1881, Bahlmann (ed.), *Hamilton Diary*, i, p. 169.
144 C.T. Ritchie, 24 Mar. 1882, *PD*, 3rd Series, cclxvii, cc. 1823–4. Edward Hamilton remarked with disgust that 'Northcote and his supporters all supported Ritchie', Diary, 26 Mar. 1882, Bahlmann (ed.), *Hamilton Diary*, i, p. 242.
145 See for example Lord Dunraven's motion in the House of Lords, 6 Nov. 1884, and the proposed Commons' amendments to the Queen's Speech by David McIver, 31 Oct. 1884, James Lowther, 9 Feb. 1892, and Howard Vincent, 12 Mar. 1894. Edward Hamilton noted in the case of McIver's motion that it was 'supported by the Front Opposition Bench', Diary, 1 Nov. 1884, Bahlmann (ed.), *Hamilton Diary*, ii, p. 723.
146 Edward Hamilton saw Salisbury's sympathy for a Royal Commission as a product of his 'coquetting' with fair trade, Diary, 24 Dec. 1885, ibid., ii, p. 718.
147 See Foster, *Randolph Churchill*, pp. 91–2, 134–40.
148 For Salisbury's Hastings speech see Marsh, *Discipline*, p. 129.
149 *The Times*, 30 Dec. 1887, quoted in Fisher, 'Public Opinion', p. 765.
150 Chaplin to Salisbury, 9 Dec. 1892, SP. Middleton was the Conservative party's Chief Agent and played a decisive role in determining the electoral acceptability of statements by the Conservative leadership.
151 Hamilton, Diary, 24 Dec. 1884, Bahlmann (ed.), *Hamilton Diary*, ii, pp. 755–6.
152 *The Times*, 7 Nov. 1887.
153 See pp. 30–5.
154 The proposal was made by Joseph Chamberlain, who argued that bounties were encouraging British sugar importers to buy from France and Germany rather than the British West Indies.
155 Hicks-Beach to Salisbury, 24 Nov. 1897, SP.
156 Salisbury to McDonnell, 20 Dec. 1892, McDonnell papers, quoted in Marsh, *Discipline*, p. 129, (my emphasis).
157 See Offer, *Property and Politics*, esp. pp. 162–200.
158 ibid., pp. 200–13.
159 Salisbury at Trowbridge, 27 June 1894, *The Times*, 30 June 1894.
160 For a Liberal critique of the Act on these grounds see for example D.F. Goddard, 20 Apr. 1896, *PD*, 4th series, xxxix, cc. 1300–2. For a general discussion of this problem see Offer, *Property*, chapter xiv.
161 This was the main Liberal amendment as proposed by Sir Henry Fowler, 30 Apr. 1896, *PD*, 4th series, xl, c. 240.
162 ibid., cc. 241–2.
163 G. Whiteley, 20 Apr. 1896, *PD*, 4th series, xxxix, cc. 1327–8.
164 For more details see Offer, *Property*, esp. pp. 221–40.
165 See pp. 41–6 and also Green, 'Rentiers', *passim*.
166 Evidence of Churchill's intentions at this point can be found in L. Courtney to Churchill, 17 Dec. 1886, RCP, RCHL 1/17.

167 See in particular the NUCA Conference Minutes for the 1892 meeting in Sheffield and the 1894 meeting at Newcastle, CPP, NUA 2/1/12, fos 102–5, 151–2, NUA 2/2/2, fos 24–5.

168 J. Chamberlain to G.J. Goschen, 17 Jan. 1895, BP, 49706, fo. 160.

169 L.J. Maxse, 'Episodes of the Month', *NR*, cl, Aug. 1895.

170 Chaplin to Salisbury, 27 Dec. 1887, SP.

171 The phrase is Henry Chaplin's.

172 See Green, 'Rentiers', pp. 605–7.

173 See Green, 'Rentiers', pp. 609–11 and idem, 'Empiricism Belimed', pp. 680–3.

174 See Howe, 'Bimetallic Controversy'.

175 For City lobbying with the Treasury and the outlook of the Bank see Green, 'Rentiers', pp. 605–6, 611–12. For Salisbury's general reliance on City figures for economic advice see Marsh, *The Discipline*, p. 41 and for their advice to the government on this particular issue see for example N.M. Rothschild to Hicks-Beach, 27 July 1897, SP.

176 J. Chamberlain to Gladstone, 3 June 1881, GP, 44125, fos 69–70.

4 CONSERVATISM AND THE PROPERTYLESS

1 Quoted in A.B. Cooke and J.R. Vincent, *The Governing Passion* (Brighton 1974), p. 3.

2 For the effects of the 1884 Act see C. Seymour, *Electoral Reform in England and Wales*, (London 1929), p. 482n, and N. Blewett, 'The Franchise in the United Kingdom', 1885–1918, *P and P*, xxxii, 1965.

3 On the basic stability of county elections see in particular D.C. Moore, *The Politics of Deference* (London 1976), and for the crucial role of local 'notables' in this context see H.J. Hanham, *Elections and Party Management* (Brighton 1959).

4 See P. Smith, *Disraelian Conservatism and social Reform*, (London 1967), Feuchtwanger, *Tory Party*, and Shannon, *Age of Disraeli*.

5 Lord Salisbury (then Lord Cranborne) had resigned his Cabinet post in 1867 in protest at the proposed extension of the franchise.

6 G. Smith to M. Gibson, 31 July 1883, in A.P.W. Malcomson (ed.), *The Ashbourne Papers* (London 1974), p. 174. Hicks-Beach to Salisbury, 22 Dec. 1886, SP.

7 Under the 1867 electoral system there had been 172 English county seats, of which the Conservatives won 127 in 1868, 145 in 1874 and 118 in 1880. The Redistribution Act of 1885 had boosted county representation to 234 seats, of which the Conservatives only won 101 in 1885. For further details of the Conservatives' county position in 1885 see P. Clarke with K. Langford, 'Hodge's Politics: The Agricultural Labourers and the Third Reform Act in Suffolk', in R. Quinault and N. Harte (eds), *Land and Society* (Manchester 1995 forthcoming).

8 H. Howorth to A.J. Balfour, 16 June 1885, Balfour papers (Whittinghame collection), National Library of Scotland. (I am grateful to Dr John France for providing me with a transcript of this quotation.)

9 Lady Wolmer to Lord Wolmer, 25 Sept. 1885, SELP, MS Selborne, adds. 1, fo. 76.

10 Lady Salisbury to E. Cecil, n.d. Apr. 1885, Cecil-Maxse papers, West Kent Record Office, U1599/c/709/2.

11 Chamberlain to Sir William Harcourt, 6 Dec. 1885, JCP, JC5/38/152, R. Brett to Chamberlain, 9 Dec. 1885, ibid., JC5/2/3.

12 E. Hamilton, Diary, 4 Dec. 1885, EHP, 48650.

13 Chaplin to Salisbury, 7 July 1887, ibid.

14 H.R. Farquarson, 'More Tillage: A Plea for the Farm Labourer', *NR*, xlvi, Aug. 1888, pp. 762–3.
15 Curzon, in Lord Ronaldshay, *The Life of Lord Curzon*, p. 100.
16 A. Milner, 'A View of Socialism', lectures at Toynbee Hall, May 1882, reprinted in *NR*, dlxxxvi, Jan. 1931, p. 240.
17 J. Kirkup, *A History of Socialism*, (London 1892), in Wolfe, *Radicalism*, p. 16.
18 Thus Socialism in Britain was described by the visiting French scholar André Métin in 1897 as 'any doctrine opposed to laissez faire'. A. Metin, *Le Socialisme en Angleterre* (Paris 1897), in E.J. Hobsbawm, *Labouring Men* (London 1964), p. 261.
19 Collini, *Liberalism and Sociology*, pp. 13–50.
20 Taylor, *Men Versus the State*, *passim*.
21 L.J. Maxse, 'Episodes of the Month', *NR*, ci, July 1891, p. 589 (my emphasis).
22 A. Oldham, 'The History of Socialism', ibid., xciii, Nov. 1890, p. 311.
23 See Salisbury, 'Disintegration', pp. 355–6.
24 ibid., p. 347.
25 See pp. 46–8.
26 For example the Royal Commission on the Aged Poor and the well-publicized researches of Charles Booth and Seebohm Rowntree.
27 J. Chamberlain to E. Russell, 22 Jan. 1882, in Jay, *Chamberlain*, p. 73.
28 For the so-called 'doctrine of ransom' see J. Chamberlain at Birmingham, 5 Jan. 1885, in C. Boyd (ed.), *Speeches of the Right Honourable Joseph Chamberlain*, 2 vols (London 1913), i, pp. 131–40.
29 Salisbury, 'Disintegration', p. 343.
30 For the most comprehensive analysis of Salisbury's political outlook see Marsh, *Discipline*, *passim*.
31 For an analysis of the Salisburyian outlook on this point see J. France, 'Salisbury and the Unionist Alliance', in Blake and Cecil (eds), *Salisbury*.
32 For a discussion of some important aspects of the Middleton machine see Marsh, *Discipline*, ch. 6.
33 Some short cuts were available, with the secretary of one local association pointing out that the knowledge of local political opinion possessed by postmen and schoolmasters was well worth exploiting. Minutes of the General Committee Meeting, NHCA, 15 Apr. 1889, Secretary's Report, CPA, NHCA 1/1.
34 Lady Knightley, Diary, 12 May 1885, in Pugh, *Tories*, p. 48.
35 For an acknowledgement of the Primrose League's contribution at elections see R.W. Middleton to Lord Harris, 17 Apr. 1888, ADP, U564 CLp1, fo. 393.
36 See Blewett, 'The Franchise' and also D.M. Tanner, 'The Parliamentary Electoral System, the "Fourth" Reform Act and the Rise of Labour in England and Wales', *BIHR*, lvi, 1983.
37 For example the NHCA decided, in 1887, to employ a paid secretary at a salary of £175 per annum, plus £50 expenses, see Minutes of a Special Committee Meeting, NHCA, 2 Dec. 1887, CPA, NHCA 1/1. In 1904 the Secretary noted that CCO guidelines for payment were £200–300 per annum, plus expenses, 'for a gentleman', and that a number of local associations paid at the top end of the scale – Minutes of the General Committee Meeting, NHCA, 1 Feb. 1904, Secretary's Report, ibid., NHCA 1/3.
38 For a particularly good example of the Primrose League being deployed in this way see Secretary's Report, Minutes of the General Committee, NHCA, 25 Jan. 1889.
39 Minutes of the General Committee, NHCA, 15 Apr. 1889, Secretary's Report, ibid.

40 Marsh, *Discipline*, pp. 195–6.
41 Their views were shared by the Liberal Unionist Whips, see J. Powell-Williams to Chamberlain, 15 May 1892, BP, 49773, fo. 41.
42 Wolmer to Salisbury, 9 Jan. 1891, SP.
43 Rowe, Note on the Rossendale by-election, 22 Jan. 1891, SP.
44 Rossendale was not, technically, a borough seat, but its electorate was largely made up of urban, working-class voters from the industrial towns it contained. In fact the constituency was lost on a 92 per cent poll.
45 E. Hamilton, Diary, 24 July 1892, EHP, Add. MSS 48657.
46 Hamilton wrote that 'the general impression, if not conviction, in Tory circles seems to be that the General Election will take place in July next'. He gave four reasons, the third of which was that 'the agricultural labourers will be too busy occupied in harvesting to care about the poll', Diary, 15 Jan. 1892, EHP, 48657. See also F.J. Woods (Balfour's private secretary) to Schomberg McDonnell, 15 Mar. 1892, with notes by Salisbury on a letter from J.K. Wingfield-Digby to E. Cecil, n.d. Mar. 1892, SP. Wingfield-Digby, a county MP (Dorsetshire), and President of his local Chamber of Agriculture, had asked that Parliament be dissolved in mid-July in order that polling run through late July and early August, i.e. harvest time.
47 See P. Joyce, 'Popular Toryism in Lancashire, 1860–90', unpublished Oxford University D.Phil thesis, 1975, Clarke, *Lancashire*, R.L. Greenall, 'Popular Conservatism in Salford, 1868–1886', *Northern History*, ix, 1974.
48 See J. Lawrence, 'Class and Gender in the Making of Urban Toryism: 1880–1914', *EHR*, cviii, 1993, and idem, 'Party, Politics and the People: Continuity and Change in the Political History of Wolverhampton, 1815–1914', unpublished Cambridge University PhD thesis, 1989.
49 See P. Waller, *Democracy and Sectarianism: A Political and Social History of Liverpool, 1868–1939* (Liverpool 1981).
50 See Joyce, 'Popular Toryism' and idem, *Work, society and Politics*, and Lawrence, 'Urban Toryism'.
51 See Pugh, *Tories*, and also Lawrence, 'Urban Toryism'.
52 See Waller, *Liverpool*.
53 Lawrence, 'Urban Toryism'.
54 There were also some manifestations of this phenomenon in rural districts – see Clarke, 'Hodge's Politics'. It is, however, difficult to assess how widespread rural working-class Conservatism was, for Alun Howkins' work on rural politics has indicated that agricultural labourers showed a very marked tendency to Liberal and often Radical politics – Howkins, *Poor Labouring Men*, and idem, *Rural Society*.
55 See Clarke, *Lancashire*, pp. 53–80.
56 Disraeli referred to social reform on a number of occasions and certainly shared the assumption that such reforms would be popular, but, as Paul Smith had demonstrated, he was never interested in any attempt to make a systematic appeal on this basis, see Smith, *Disraelian Conservatism, passim*.
57 See Foster, *Churchill*, pp. 105–19.
58 See also Lord Dunraven, 'The Real Truth About Tory Democracy', *NR*, li, May 1887, p. 311, for a similar argument before the Spalding by-election.
59 Chaplin to Balfour, 25 Dec. 1891, BP, 49772, fos 70–4; Chaplin told Salisbury that the Conservatives would 'lose four seats in Lincolnshire alone . . . unless we can manage to arrest the present drift of rural feeling', Chaplin to Salisbury, 25 Dec. 1891, SP.
60 See, for example, Northbrook to Salisbury, 8 Jan. 1890, SP.
61 See Marsh, *Discipline*, pp. 51–2.

62 Edward Goulding, later Lord Wargrave. At this point Goulding was Conservative MP for Devizes, and like many who took a positive stance on social reform in the late nineteenth century, he was to become, as will be seen below, one of the most forceful advocates of a wide-ranging Conservative social and economic reform programme in the Edwardian period.

63 E.A. Goulding, 18 May 1897, *PD*, 4th series, xlix, c. 766.

64 J. Chamberlain in Parliament, 18 May 1897, ibid., c. 810.

65 For this interpretation see P. Davis, 'The Liberal Unionist Party in British Politics, 1886–1895', unpublished London University PhD thesis, 1976, I. Gilmour, *Inside Right*, p. 31, and Blake, *Conservative Party*, pp. 159–61.

66 See below, pp. 129–32.

67 In this context the Liberal Unionists' chief contribution was, arguably, organizational, in that it was Joseph Chamberlain and Jesse Collings who brought about the creation of the Rural Labourers' League (later the Rural League) in 1888. The purpose of this organization being to counter the 'action of the Gladstonians on the Allotments Association' and to match Radical propaganda and agitation in the counties with 'equal activity on the Unionist side'. J. Chamberlain to Lord Wolmer, 13 Mar. 1888, SELP, MS Selborne 8, fo. 1, Rural Labourers' League to Lord Carnarvon, 20 May 1890, CARP, 60852.

68 J. Chisholm to R. Churchill, 5 Feb. 1892, in A. Hutchison, *A Political History of Scotland, 1832–1924* (Edinburgh 1986), p. 201.

69 Chamberlain told Balfour that to wring concessions from the Duke of Devonshire he had to threaten 'to commit suicide in his presence' whilst the Conservatives had passed legislation on Small Holdings and Free Education, see Balfour's Memo. on a discussion with Chamberlain, Balfour to Salisbury, 26 July 1892, BP, 49690, fos 55–64. Beatrice Webb also noted that 'the majority of the Liberal Unionists in the H of C have been anti-Chamberlainite, more hostile in their hearts to Joe than the bigoted Tories', B. Webb, Diary, 8 July 1895, N. and J. Mackenzie (eds), *The Diary of Beatrice Webb*, (4 vols, London 1988), ii, pp. 76–7.

70 For example, Sir Howard Vincent, Edward Goulding, Sir Benjamin Stone and Henry Chaplin.

71 For an outline of the Scottish NUCA programme see *The Times*, 31 Oct. 1894. The programme is below.

72 For example, Workmen's Dwelling Bill (sponsored by Hickman and Vincent) 1897, Extension of the Factory Acts to Fishing Trades (sponsored by A.K. Rollitt and G. Doughty) 1897, Workmen's Dwelling Bill (sponsored by T. Wrightson) 1894.

73 See Taylor, *Men Versus the State*. See also N. Soldon, 'Laissez-Faire as Dogma: The case of the Liberty and Property Defence League' in K.D. Brown (ed.), *Essays in Anti-Labour History* (London 1974), and E. Bristow, 'The Liberty and Property Defence League and Individualism', *HJ*, xviii, 1975.

74 See *The Times*, 31 Oct. 1894.

75 See speeches of Sir T. Wrightson and Sir A.K. Rollit, NUCA Conference, Sheffield 13–14 Dec. 1892, NUCA Conference Minutes, CPA, NUA 2/1/2, fos 45–62.

76 ibid., fos 120–30.

77 For the details of Chamberlain's programme see his speech at Brighton, in *The Times* 12 Oct. 1894.

78 Chamberlain to Chaplin, 19 Apr. 1895, JCP, JC 5/13/13.

79 ibid.

80 Significantly, Chamberlain chose the *National Review*, a journal which had

been founded as a 'Disraelian' Conservative organ in 1883. See his article 'Old Age Pensions', *NR*, cviii, Feb. 1892, pp. 720–36.

81 Chamberlain to Strachey, 18 Dec. 1894, STRP, S/4/6/5.

82 Salisbury to B. Maple, 14 Mar. 1892, BP, 49690, fos 6–8.

83 Salisbury to Balfour, 26 July 1892, BP, 49690, fos 65–6.

84 For the importance of the Friendly Societies in the debates on social policy see E.P. Hennock, *British Social Reform and German Precedents* (Oxford 1987), pp. 140–1, 174–5, 188–95. For Chamberlain's circumspection see his 'Old Age Pensions', p. 734.

85 J.S. Sandars, Memorandum on 'The Eight Hours Question', Mar. 1891, JSSP, MS Eng. Hist. c. 724, fos 152–88.

86 G. Wyndham to C. Wyndham, 22 May 1892, in J.W. Mackail and G. Wyndham, *Life and Letters of George Wyndham*, 2 vols (London 1925), i, pp. 260–1.

87 See, for example, the comments of the ironmaster Alfred Hickman, 5 May 1897, *PD*, 4th Series, xlviii, cc. 1562–3. See also Hennock, *British Social Reform*, pp. 59–61.

88 The Workmen's Compensation Act of 1897 was also supported by many employers because they saw it as preferable to the litigation that Employers' Liability could produce.

89 Balfour at Manchester, 22 Mar. 1894, *The Times*, 23 Mar. 1894.

90 Ritchie to Salisbury, 7 Mar. 1888, SP.

91 ibid.

92 Sir J.F.S. Rolleston, *Proceedings of the Bimetallic League* (Manchester 1888), p. 101.

93 See pp. 147–8.

94 For example, Sir Howard Vincent, a leading advocate of fair trade and imperial preference, was closely associated, both personally and through his constituency, with the steel industry.

95 'The Value of the Colonies', *Imperial Federation*, i, March 1886, p. 78.

96 See Sir H. Vincent at Sheffield, NUCA Conference, 13–14 Dec. 1892, NUCA Conference Minutes, CPA, NUA 2/1/2.

97 J. Chamberlain at Birmingham, 9 May 1895, in P. Fraser, *Joseph Chamberlain: Radicalism and Empire* (London 1966), p. 166 (my emphasis).

98 Chamberlain in London, 16 July 1895, in S. Zebel, 'Joseph Chamberlain and the Genesis of Tariff Reform', *JBS*, vii, 1967–8, p. 138.

99 'Should We Re-impose the Corn Duties?', *Fair Trade*, 6 Nov. 1885.

100 For a cogent expression of this argument see Sir Howard Vincent at the NUCA Conference, Sheffield, 13 Dec. 1892, NUCA Conference Minutes, 1892, CPA, NUA 2/1/12 fos 80–94.

101 'A.G.' to the Editor of *Fair Trade*, 4 Dec. 1885.

102 M. Anderson to Salisbury, 6 Feb. 1886, in Harris, *Unemployment*, p. 51.

103 For example Chamberlain, Reginald Brett and Gladstone himself felt Fair Trade had been crucial.

104 See Ashmead-Bartlett to Salisbury, 7 Nov. 1885, and Herbert to Salisbury, 2 Dec. 1885, SP.

105 For the role of leading Socialists in the strikes of 1888–9 see H. Pelling, *The Origins of the Labour Party* (London, 2nd edition 1965). For the success of the employer offensive see R. Price, *Labour in British Society* (London 1983), pp. 112–36.

106 W.E.H. Lecky, *Democracy and Liberty*, 2 vols, (London 1895, 1989 edition), i, p. 437. Lecky, one of a number of Liberal intellectuals who abandoned the Liberal party as a result of its 'Leftward' drift, was also an Irish landlord and became the Liberal Unionist MP for Dublin University in 1895. Lecky

evidently felt he had got carried away in his 1895 'optimism', for he was careful to state in the Introduction to the 1898 edition of *Democracy and Liberty* that the 1895 result did not necessarily represent a conclusive rejection of Socialism.

107 BLP, 18/2/12.

108 In Dugdale, *Balfour*, i, p. 381.

109 Maxse, 'Episodes of the Month', *NR*, cclxxvi, Feb. 1906, p. 949.

110 See Ramsden, *Balfour and Baldwin*, esp. ch. iii.

111 See E.H.H. Green, 'Radical Conservatism: The Electoral Genesis of Tariff Reform', *HJ*, xxviii, 1985, pp. 671–3.

112 F.W.S. Craig, *British Parliamentary Election Results 1885–1918* (Brighton 1974).

113 The problems this was causing the Liberals were already evident in North Hampshire in 1893. The secretary of NHCA reported that 'the registration courts are over and I think that we have done very well. The opposition did not even put in an appearance and our friend Mr Munn [the Liberal agent] I have not seen or heard of for ages', Minutes of the General Committee Meeting, NHCA, 27 Oct. 1893, Secretary's Report, CPA, NHCA 1/2.

114 In the end the total of unopposed Conservative returns in 1900 was a remarkable 163, and the percentage of the electorate represented by unopposed returns was 35.1 per cent.

115 ibid. – all of these figures are taken from Craig's work.

116 For the most interesting discussion of the overall electoral situation in the late nineteenth and early twentieth century see N. Blewett, *The Peers, The People and the Parties* (London 1971), pp. 3–24.

117 For the fullest discussion of the Liberal revival see Clarke, *Lancashire, passim*.

118 See Blewett, *Peers*, pp. 16–35.

119 The following discussion is based on P.F. Clarke, 'British Politics and Blackburn Politics, 1900–1910', *HJ*, xii, 1969, pp. 302–27.

120 Blackburn Conservatism has also been strong in the 1860s and 1870s, with always one of the borough's seats, and often both, being held by the Conservatives.

121 See Clarke, *Lancashire*, pp. 45–50, 244–8, and Lawrence, 'Urban Toryism'. An important exception to this rule was Liverpool.

122 Balcarres, Diary, 15 Mar. 1912, in Vincent (ed.), *Crawford Papers*, pp. 267–8.

123 ibid.

124 See A. Fox, *History and Heritage* (London 1986 edition), K. Burgess, *The Challenge of Labour* (London 1980), H.F. Gospel and C.R. Littler (eds), *Managerial Strategies and Industrial Relations* (London 1983).

125 A well-documented example is the cotton industry, and in particular the spinning sector, see W. Lazonick, *Competitive Advantage on the Shop Floor* (Cambridge, Mass. 1990), esp. pp. 154–72.

126 For one example of the problems see the situation in St Helens described in T.C. Barker, *The Glassmakers: Pilkington: The Rise of an International Company* (London 1977), pp. 230–1.

127 For these decisions see Fox, *History and Heritage*, pp. 179–87.

128 See Tanner, *Political Change*, pp. 165–96.

129 ibid., and also Clarke, *Lancashire*, ch. 12.

130 Chamberlain to Law, BLP, 21/1.

131 Salisbury to Selborne, 19 Jan. 1906, SELP, MS Selborne 5, fos 110–17.

132 E.B. Iwan-Muller, 'Some Thoughts on the Present Discontents', 13 Feb. 1906, BP, 49796, fos 117–59.

133 ibid.

134 ibid.
135 ibid.
136 Balfour to Chamberlain, 15 Jan. 1906, JCP, JC 21/11.
137 Chamberlain to Balfour, 24 Oct. 1907, BP, 49736, fos 21–32.
138 See below for a more detailed discussion of this development.
139 Amery to Northcliffe, 26 Nov. 1910, NP, 62157, fo. 159.
140 Amery to Northcliffe, 12 Dec. 1910, ibid., fo. 161.
141 Chamberlain to Balfour, 24 Jan. 1910, BP, 49736, fos 21–32.
142 Stanley to A. Chamberlain, 15 Jan. 1906, ACP, AC 7/2/2.
143 Garvin to Maxse, 4 Apr. 1906, LJMP, 455 S 295.
144 Holland to Lyttelton, 17 Jan. 1906, ALP, CHAN 5/13.
145 Salisbury to Selborne, 19 Jan. 1906, SELP, MS Selborne 5 fos 110–17.
146 ibid.
147 Balfour to Northcliffe, 17 Jan. 1906, BP, 49858, fo. 47.
148 W. Lawler-Wilson, *The Menace of Socialism* (London 1909), p. 17. Lawler Wilson was one of the founder members of the Anti-Socialist Union.
149 Balfour to Chamberlain, 17 Jan. 1906, ACP, AC 7/2/1.
150 Maxse, 'Episodes of the Month', *NR*, cclxxviii, Apr. 1906.
151 See W. Barry, 'Liberals or Jacobins', *NR*, cclxxxi, July 1906, *passim*.
152 A. Chamberlain to M.E. Chamberlain, 25 May, 1907, in A. Chamberlain, *Politics From Inside* (London 1936), p. 89.
153 Maxse, 'Episodes of the Month', *NR*, cccxx, Oct. 1909, p. 196.
154 J.L. Garvin, 'Free Trade as a Socialist Policy', *NR*, cclxxxxv, Sept. 1907, p. 53.
155 Murray, *People's Budget*, pp. 82–5.
156 For the significance and details of Asquith's budget see ibid., pp. 45–7.
157 'The Coming Fiscal Reform', *The Outlook*, 6 June 1908, p. 782.
158 For one of the most interesting interpretations of this development see Wolfe, *Radicalism to Socialism, passim*.
159 For discussion of this concept in differing radical contents see Allett, *New Liberalism*, and D.M. Ricci, 'Fabian Socialism, A Theory of Rent as Exploitation', *JBS*, ix, 1969.
160 See Blewett, *Peers*, p. 323.
161 P. Lloyd-Greame, 'Memorandum on Social Policy', n.d. 1912, SMP, GD 193/80/5/50. In 1912 a Conservative Committee investigating questions of local and imperial taxation noted that 48 members of the English League for the Taxation of Land Values had stood for election in January 1910 and that 38 had been elected, Memorandum, n.d. 1911 (?), ibid., GD 193/80/3/1–6.
162 It only served to reinforce the Conservatives' view of the Budget and to confirm all their fears that the Labour leadership welcomed it as Socialist.
163 H. Dendy, 'The Socialist Propaganda', *NR*, cli, Sept. 1895, p. 747.
164 Lawler-Wilson, *The Menace*, p. 180.
165 C.A. Gregg to Steel-Maitland, n.d. Jan. 1910, SMP, GD 193/147/7/1.
166 N. and J. Mackenzie (eds), *Webb Diary*, ii, p. 120.
167 For Chamberlain's concerns see Chamberlain to Balfour, 4 Aug. 1902, BP, 49774, fos 7–12, and Chamberlain to Balfour, 9 Sept. 1902, JCP, JC 11/5/10.
168 Chamberlain to J.S. Wood, 27 Nov. 1903, JCP, JC 18/18/125.
169 Chamberlain to Maxse, 13 Mar. 1905, LJMP, 453 S 25.
170 Chamberlain to Selborne, 3 Sept. 1904, SELP, MS Selborne 73, fos 29–30.
171 Chamberlain to Maxse, 13 Mar. 1905, LJMP, 453 S 25.
172 Morpeth to Maxse, 25 Jan. 1906, LJMP, 455 S 295.
173 Chamberlain to Deakin, 26 Apr. 1906, in Jay, *Joseph Chamberlain*, p. 305.
174 Law to Maxse, 30 Jan. 1906, LJMP, 454 S 334.
175 R. Hunt in Parliament 18 Feb. 1907, *The Times*, 19 Feb. 1907.

176 Maxse, 'Episodes of the Month', *NR*, ccclxxxii, Oct. 1910, p. 213.
177 For a discussion of these changes see Ramsden, *Balfour and Baldwin*, pp. 26–7.
178 The NUCA Conferences had seen heavy support for Chamberlain's programme from 1903 on.
179 Chamberlain to Chaplin, 9 Jan. 1906, JCP, JC 21/2/22.
180 J. Chamberlain to A. Chamberlain, 4 May 1906, ACP, AC/8/2/18.
181 Wise to Milner, 30 Dec. 1906, MP, MS Milner Dep. 18, fos 241–2.
182 On the Confederacy's activities see A. Sykes, 'The Confederacy and the Purge of the Unionist Free Traders', *HJ* xviii, 1975.
183 Law to Maxse, 5 Jan. 1907, LJMP, 457 S 463.
184 Ware to Chamberlain, 12 Dec. 1910, ACP, AC 8/7/27.
185 For a full discussion of the Conservative debate on social reform and their development of a comprehensive programme after 1906 see ch. 10.
186 Chamberlain to Balfour, 24 Oct. 1907, BP, 49736, fos 21–32.
187 ibid.
188 Drawn up by a number of Conservative 'experts' in the field of social policy – in particular Milner, Leo Amery, Fabian Ware, W.J. Ashley and J.W. Hills – the programme was published in the *Morning Post* a few weeks before the NUCA conference of 1908. Two drafts of the programme are to be found in the BLP, 18/4/75.
189 Milner *et al.*, 'Unionism' (the working title of the programme), ibid.
190 Garvin to Maxse, 4 Apr. 1906, LJMP, 455 S 295.
191 Chamberlain to Balfour, 24 Oct. 1907, BP, 49736, fos 21–32.
192 Arnold-Forster, *English Socialism*, p. 11.
193 N. Chamberlain, 'The New Imperialism and the Old Parties', *NR*, ccciv, June 1908, p. 644.
194 Sanderson to Chamberlain, 8 Feb. 1906, ACP, AC 7/2/8. For a general endorsement of this view see the special discussion of Socialism at the NUCA Conference of 1907.
195 The Conservatives had lost Woolwich to the Labour candidate Will Crooks in March 1903 and Rye to the Liberals in the same month.
196 B. Webb, Diary, 27 Mar. 1903, N. and J. Mackenzie (eds), *Webb Diary*, ii, pp. 275–6.
197 Sandars to Balfour, 4 Sept. 1902, BP, 49631, fos 26–9.
198 That the tariff campaign, in its early stages, appeared to produce an electoral respite increased its credibility as a potential vote-winner. Even some Liberals, notably Asquith, felt, in late 1903, that Chamberlain's bandwagon might prove difficult to stop.
199 Balfour's key statement in this context was his speech at Sheffield in September 1903, the arguments of which he later expanded and published as *Economic Notes on Insular Free Trade* (London 1903).
200 Lord Cecil of Chelwood, *All The Way* (London 1949), p. 109.
201 ibid.
202 Currie to Lonsdale, 7 Jan. 1904, JCP, JC 19/7/15.
203 See for example Stanley to Chamberlain, 27 Jan. 1906, ACP, AC 7/2/8.
204 In September 1903 Wyndham had in fact sent a lengthy Memorandum to Chamberlain, and concluded that 'I find myself very far from desiring to see any fundamental or even substantial change in our fiscal policy.' G. Wyndham to Chamberlain, 9 Sept. 1903, JCP, JC 18/18/129.
205 For example see Wyndham's speeches at Dover, on 6 Jan. 1906, and at Crewe on 10 Jan. 1906, *The Times*, 7 Jan. 1906, 11 Jan. 1906. For Wyndham's admission that he had departed from the 'official' line see G. Wyndham to M. Wyndham, 24 Jan. 1906, in Mackail and Wyndham, *Life and Letters*, ii, p. 539.

206 G. Wyndham to M. Wyndham, 27 Jan. 1906, in Mackail and Wyndham, ibid., p. 542.

207 G. Wyndham to C. Wyndham, 24 Jan. 1906, in ibid., p. 540.

208 For the most rigorous Conservative analysis of free trade as a complete system see the views of the historical economists outlined in ch. 5 of this study.

209 J.H. Balfour Browne, 'The Coming Social Revolution', *NR*, cclxxv, Nov. 1906, p. 247.

210 The fact that the organization the Conservative free traders set up to fight the tariff campaign was called the Free Food League was indicative of the emphasis they placed on this point.

211 For an analysis of the Conservative free traders' ideas on this point see Morris, 'Strachey', pp. 58–86.

212 At most the free traders numbered about 40 MPs, many of whom were either to retire or be defeated in 1906. For an estimation of the Conservative free trade numbers see N. Blewett, 'Free Fooders, Balfourites and Whole-Hoggers', *HJ*, xxi, 1968.

213 See Arthur Elliott's remark that 'The Confederates count for little. It is the countenance they get from the Leaders and officials of the Conservative Party that is important'. Elliott to Cromer 17 July 1909, CROP, FO 633/18.

214 Long to Cecil, 2 Feb. 1908, COCP, Add. MSS 51072, fos 62–4.

215 It should be noted that Long himself had no great sympathy for the tariff cause, and thus had no axe to grind in defending the tariff reformers from charges of conspiracy.

216 James to Elliott, 20 Feb. 1908, CROP, FO 633 18.

217 Strachey to Welby, 29 June 1908, STRP, S/16/2/31.

218 Strachey to Elliott, 20 Jan. 1908, ibid., S/16/2/4.

219 Cromer, Memorandum, Dec. 1908, CROP, FO 633/18.

220 The two MPs in question were Sir Robert Perks, a leading Liberal Imperialist, and Harold Cox, the one-time President of the Cobden Club.

221 Cromer to R. Cecil, 28 May 1909, COCP, 51072, fos 40–1.

222 The 'near miss' was Wolverhampton East, where the Conservative candidate was Leo Amery. For Amery's discussion of the campaign, see L.S. Amery, *My Political Life*, 3 vols (London 1953), i, *England Before the Storm*, pp. 285–9.

223 Lord Milner *et al.*, 'Unionism', BLP, 18/4/75.

224 'At present, Tariff Reformers, by means of general promises and assertions attract many classes', Lord James of Hereford to A. Elliott, 20 Feb. 1908, CROP, FO 633/18. This letter was written only one month after Radical Conservative candidates had made impressive gains at Mid-Devon and South Hereford.

225 W.J. Courthope, 'Party Government and the Empire', *NR*, cccxxxi, Sept. 1910, p. 65 (my emphasis).

226 Chamberlain to Goulding, 23 Jan. 1906, WARP, WAR 2.

5 INTELLECTUAL PRELUDE

1 The work which has appeared has tended to fall into one of two categories: biographical essays, such as those by D.P. Crook on *Benjamin Kidd* (Cambridge 1981), L. Parker on *Halford Mackinder* (Oxford 1982), or thematic studies, such as G. Jones, *Social Darwinism and English Thought* (Brighton 1980), G.R. Searle, *The Quest for National Efficiency*, (Oxford 1971) and idem *Eugenics and Politics* (London 1976). But neither the biographical nor the thematic studies relate their subject matter to the specific context of Conservative politics.

2 The notable exceptions are A. Quinton, *The Politics of Imperfection* (London 1978), N. O'Sullivan, *Conservatism* (London 1976) and the sections devoted to Conservatism in W.H. Greenleaf, *The British Political Tradition* (4 vols, London 1983–7), ii, *The Ideological Heritage*.

3 The amount of work on these questions is too vast to be listed in full here, but see especially P.F. Clarke, *Liberals and Social Democrats* (Cambridge 1979), S. Collini, *Liberalism and Sociology* (Cambridge 1980), M. Freeden, *The New Liberalism* (Oxford 1977), W. Wolfe, *From Radicalism to Socialism* (Brighton 1977), A. MacBriar, *Fabian Socialism and British Politics* (London 1965).

4 See especially Clarke, *Lancashire*, idem, *Liberals*, Freeden, *New Liberalism*, Collini, *Liberalism*.

5 For example, the standard work on the Conservative party in this period, Ramsden, *Balfour and Baldwin*, deliberately avoids discussion of Conservative intellectual developments. B. Semmel, *Imperialism and Social Reform* (London 1962), and R.J. Scally, *The Origins of the Lloyd George Coalition* (Princeton 1975), engage with 'social imperialist' thought, but not within the context of Conservatism.

6 For a survey of Dicey's ideas see R. Cosgrove, *A.V. Dicey: Victorian Jurist* (London 1979). Dicey's ideas are treated in a most stimulating manner by Greenleaf, *British Political Tradition*, i, *The Rise of Collectivism*. Undoubtedly Dicey's ideas had a great deal of purchase amongst certain Conservatives, most notably with the Conservative free traders, but his ideas were essentially those of a disillusioned Mid-Victorian Liberal. For the fullest treatment of Individualist Liberal thinkers who ended up in the Conservative camp see Taylor, *Men Versus the State*.

7 B. Kidd, *Social Evolution* (London 1894), p. 18.

8 ibid., p. 23.

9 ibid.

10 J.R. MacDonald to B. Kidd, 9 Aug. 1894, KP, 8069.

11 The Rainbow Circle had been established as a seminary for the modification of Liberal ideas which allowed the New Liberalism to meet the challenges of the early twentieth century with a Collectivist face. See in particular, Clarke, *Liberals*, pp. 56–61 and M. Freeden (ed.), *Minutes of the Rainbow Circle, 1894–1924* (London 1989), pp. 1–16.

12 B. Kidd, *Individualism and After* (London 1908), p. 13.

13 L.C.M.S. Amery to Kidd, 4 March 1904, KP, 8069.

14 Apart from Amery and Kidd other notable Compatriots were Alfred Milner, Leo Maxse, W.A.S. Hewins, H.W. Wilson, J.L. Garvin, A. Steel-Maitland, J.W. Hills, H.A. Gwynne, W.J. Ashley and others.

15 L.L.Price, review of *Compatriots' Club Lectures*, EcR, xv, 1905, pp. 362–7.

16 See G.R. Searle, *National Efficiency* for the best discussion of this development, although an illuminating fictional account of the Coefficients can be found in H.G. Wells, *The New Machiavelli* (London 1911) where the club appears as the 'Pentagram Circle'.

17 See pp. 71–2, 108–13.

18 For background to the historical economists' views outside their political context see in particular J. Burrow, S. Collini, and D. Winch, *That Noble Science of Politics* (Cambridge 1985), ch. 7, and G.M. Koot, *The English Historical Economists* (Cambridge 1988).

19 H.S. Foxwell, 'The Economic Movement in England', *Quarterly Journal of Economics*, ii, Oct. 1887, pp. 84–103, 89.

20 W. Cunningham, 'A Plea for Pure Theory', EcR, ii, Jan. 1892, pp. 25–41, 34.

21 W. Cunningham, *Politics and Economics* (London 1885), p. 3.

22 W.J. Ashley, *An Introduction to English Economic History and Theory* (2 vols London 1893), i, x.
23 W. Cunningham, 'The Progress of Economic Doctrine in England in the Eighteenth Century', *EcJ*, i, March 1891, pp. 73–94.
24 ibid. and also idem, 'The Relativity of Economic Doctrine', *EcJ*, ii, pp. 1–16.
25 Ashley, *Introduction*, x.
26 Cunningham, 'The Progress', p. 88.
27 Cunningham, *Politics*, vii.
28 Foxwell to Seligman, 23 Feb. 1888, Misc. Economists' papers, Marshall Library, Cambridge, Misc 2, fo. 8.
29 H.S. Foxwell, 'The Growth of Monopoly, and its Bearing on the Functions of the State', 1888, reprinted in his *Papers on Current Finance* (London 1919), pp. 262–80, 264.
30 Ashley to M. Ashley, n.d. June (?) 1886, in A. Ashley, *W.J. Ashley: A Life* (London 1925), p. 34.
31 Ashley to M. Ashley, n.d. July (?) 1886, in ibid., p. 36.
32 Foxwell, 'Growth of Monopoly', p. 266. See also Ashley's remark that 'society is feeling its way ... towards a corporate organization of industry', Ashley, *The Economic Organization of England* (London 1914), p. 190.
33 W. Cunningham, *The Wisdom of the Wise* (London 1904), p. 19.
34 ibid.
35 L.L. Price, 'Economic Theory and Fiscal Policy', *EcJ*, xiv, Sept. 1904, pp. 372–87, 383.
36 Cunningham, *Politics*, p. 14.
37 W. Cunningham, *Christianity and Socialism* (London 1909), p. 9.
38 Cunningham, *Wisdom*, p. 18.
39 Cunningham, *Politics*, p. 135.
40 W. Cunningham, *Political Economy and Practical Life* (London 1893), p. 28.
41 ibid., p. 24.
42 Cunningham, *Wisdom*, p. 61.
43 W. Cunningham, *The Rise and Decline of the Free Trade Movement* (London 1904), p. 11.
44 W.J. Ashley, *The Tariff Problem* (1903 edition), p. 1.
45 L.L. Price, 'Economic Theory', p. 379.
46 Cunningham, *Christianity*, p. 9.
47 Cunningham, *Politics*, p. 108.
48 Cunningham, *Free Trade Movement*, p. 90.
49 This had, of course, been the complaint of a number of commentators in countries deluged with British manufactured goods. In particular Friedrich List, in Germany, and Henry Carey, in the United States, depicted Britain's commitment to free trade as simply naked national interest masquerading as 'God's diplomacy'.
50 Cunningham, *Politics*, p. 16.
51 ibid., p. 87.
52 L.L. Price, 'The Fiscal Question – Retrospect and Prospect', *EcR*, xvi, pp. 129–55, 154. See also Cunningham's hostile review of Norman Angell's *The Great Illusion*, *EcR*, xxiii, pp. 7–13, in which Cunningham recanted his own statement, made to the British Association in 1891, that economic Cosmopolitanism was a growing force and nationalism in retreat. Why Cunningham had made this earlier statement, which conflicted with his other writings at the time, is somewhat of a mystery.
53 W. Cunningham, *The Alternative to Socialism in England* (Cambridge 1885), pp. 1–2.

54 See ch. 1.

55 Ashley, *The Tariff Problem*, (1903 edition), p. 51.

56 ibid., pp. 60–5.

57 See Cunningham, *Free Trade Movement*, pp. 138–40. Hewins felt that Britain's manufacturing sector had been in decline since 1888, see W.A.S. Hewins, 'Notes' for 26 May 1888, Hewins papers, Sheffield University Library, Box MSS 141.

58 Ashley, *The Tariff Problem* (1903 edition), p. 68.

59 L.L. Price, 'Free Trade and Protection', *EcJ*, xii, 1902, pp. 305–19, 310.

60 L.L. Price, 'Economic Theory', p. 384. See also Ashley, *Tariff Problem* (1903 edition), p. 131.

61 Ashley, *Economic Organization*, p. 90.

62 Cunningham, *Free Trade Movement*, p. 136.

63 Ashley, *The Tariff Problem* (1905 edition), pp. 212–15.

64 E.W. Hamilton, notes on 'Excess of Imports over Exports', 28 Nov. 1898, E.W. Hamilton, Private Office papers, PRO, T 168/39.

65 Cunningham, *The Case Against Free Trade* (London 1911), p. 37.

66 Sir R. Giffen to J. Chamberlain, 26 Oct. 1903, JCP, JC 18/18/64.

67 Foxwell, *Irregularity of Employment*, p. 7.

68 Cunningham, *Wisdom*, p. 66.

69 ibid.

70 ibid.

71 Cunningham, *Politics*, pp. 144–5.

72 ibid., pp. 98–9.

73 ibid., pp. 170–4.

74 ibid., p. 117.

75 For Cunningham's support for pensions and his comments on trade unions see, respectively, his *Political Economy and Practical Life* (London 1893), p. 17 and *Politics*, pp. 98–9. For Price on industrial arbitration and wages boards see in particular his 'Methods of Industrial Reform' in idem, *Economic Science* (London 1896). For the activities of Hewins and Ashley in the USRC and their broad commitment to social reform see below pp. 242–3, 247–8, 285–9.

76 Foxwell, 'Growth of Monopoly', p. 277.

77 Cunningham, *Socialism in England*, p. 5.

78 ibid., p. 11.

79 H.S. Foxwell, 'Introduction' to A. Menger, *The Right to the Whole Produce of Labour* (London 1899), lxxxiii.

80 ibid., xl–xli.

81 ibid.

82 W.J. Ashley, 'The Rehabilitation of Ricardo', *EcJ*, i, 1891, pp. 474–89.

83 L.L. Price, 'Some Aspects of the Theory of Rent', in idem, *Economic Science*, p. 213.

84 For more detailed comment on the 1909 Budget as a Socialist measure see pp. 143–4.

85 Foxwell to Seligman, 23 June 1909, Miscellaneous Economists' papers, Misc. 2, i, fo. 13.

86 L.L. Price, 'The Relation of Economic Science to Practical Affairs', in idem, *Economic Science*, p. 371.

87 L.L. Price, 'Methods of Industrial Reform', ibid., p. 125.

88 Cunningham, *Christianity*, p. 9.

89 Cunningham, *The Causes of Labour Unrest* (London 1912), p. 16.

90 This was, of course, the same distinction which the historical economists had been keen to make when they drew the line between national (domestic

industry and agriculture) and cosmopolitan (international commerce and banking) economic interests.

91 Ashley to M. Ashley, n.d. June (?) 1886, in A. Ashley, *W.J. Ashley*, p. 35.
92 Cunningham, *Christianity*, p. 9.
93 W. Cunningham, *Why Had Roscher So Little Influence in England?* (London 1894), p. 2.
94 ibid.
95 ibid., p. 3.
96 ibid.
97 W.J. Ashley, 'Political Economy and the Tariff Problem', *EcR*, xiv, 1904, pp. 257–78, 263.
98 W.A.S. Hewins described how, in the late nineteenth century, he 'took up ... the working of the old national system of economics' in *The Apologia of an Imperialist* (2 vols, London 1929), ii, p. 35.
99 W.J. Ashley, 'Commercial Education' in *National Education: A Symposium* (London 1901), pp. 182–94.
100 Cunningham, *Free Trade Movement*, p. 150.
101 Cunningham, *Wisdom*, p. 53.
102 Hewins, *Apologia*, i, p. 31.
103 Ashley, 'Political Economy', p. 263.
104 See in particular A.W. Coats, 'Political Economy and the Tariff Reform Campaign of 1903', *JLE*, ii, 1968, pp. 181–229.
105 On the work of the Tariff Commission see below pp. 190–2, 221–41 and also A.J. Marrison, 'British Businessmen and the Scientific Tariff: A Study of Joseph Chamberlain's Tariff Commission 1903–21', unpublished Hull University PhD thesis, 1976.
106 For Hewins' influence on Balfour see Sykes, *Tariff Reform*, pp. 129–31.
107 Chamberlain to Ashley, 26 Apr. 1904, JCP, JC 19/7/2.
108 One of Cunningham's contemporaries noted that 'he was ... above all things a "good Party man" ', F.R. Salter, 'Preface' to A. Cunningham, *William Cunningham: Teacher and Priest* (London 1953).
109 Foxwell's espousal of bimetallism marked him as dangerously unorthodox in the eyes of Alfred Marshall, who recommended Pigou over Foxwell for the Chair of Economics in Cambridge in 1908.
110 Law to Ashley, n.d. Dec. 1904, in Ashley, *W.J. Ashley*, p. 135.
111 J. Chamberlain, oral communication to W.A.S. Hewins, 12 June 1903, in Hewins, *Apologia*, i, p. 60.
112 See Cunningham, *William Cunningham*, pp. 12–16 and Ashley *W.J. Ashley*, pp. 25–40.
113 J.C. Wood, *British Economists and the Empire* (London 1983), p. 218.
114 Ashley, *Introduction*, ix.
115 Lujo Brentano, for example, was never used as a government 'propagandist', nor any of the other Liberal economists who were also State employees.
116 See Collini, *Liberalism*, pp. 51–78, Richter, *Politics of Conscience*, *passim*, Clarke, *Liberals*, pp. 9–27, Freeden, *New Liberalism*, pp. 1–24, 52–60.
117 Undated remark by Cunningham, cited in Cunningham, *William Cunningham*, p. 50.
118 See, for example, Foxwell's remark to J.N. Keynes that 'there seems to be no real interest taken in Cambridge in any practical Economic question ... the contrast between Cambridge and Oxford is very striking', Foxwell to J.N. Keynes, 14 Dec. 1894, J.N. Keynes papers, Marshall Library, Cambridge, JNK Box 1, fo. 35.
119 The fact that Ashley and Hewins' views were from the start almost

impossible to differentiate from those of the staunch Conservative Cunningham is significant in this context.

120 For the most cogent statement of the historical economists' position on the importance of the Empire see W.A.S. Hewins, 'Imperialism and its Probable Effects on the Commercial Policy of the United Kingdom'. This article was published in Schmoller's *Jahrbuch* in 1899. MS copies of it can be found in the Hewins papers, Box MSS 19.

121 L.T. Hobhouse, *Democracy and Reaction*, p. 12.

122 Clarke, *Liberals*, pp. 66–74.

123 W. Clarke to Kidd, 15 Feb. 1898, KP, 8069.

124 ibid.

125 See Clarke, *Liberals*, pp. 84–8.

126 S. Webb to E.R. Pease, 30 May 1903, in N. Mackenzie (ed.), *Letters of Sidney and Beatrice Webb*, (3 vols, Cambridge 1976), ii, p. 184.

127 Hobhouse, *Democracy and Reaction*, p. 5.

128 B. Webb to Russell, n.d. May (?) 1903, in Mackenzie (ed.) *Letters*, ii, p. 185.

129 Russell left the Co-Efficients Club because of what he saw as its increasingly anti-free trade direction.

130 B. Webb to Russell, n.d. May (?) 1903, in Mackenzie (ed.) *Letters*, ii, p. 185.

131 S. Webb to Hewins, 30 May 1903, in ibid.

132 Another point of departure was the Fabian theory of rent and the taxation policies which it implied. This difference appears, however, not to have surfaced in the period 1900–4, which indicates the importance of the imperial issue at this time.

133 A. Milner, *The Nation and the Empire*, (London 1913), xxxii.

134 ibid.

135 Milner at Liverpool, 7 June 1910, in ibid., p. 466.

136 'The Principles of Constructive Economics as Applied to the Maintenance of Empire', *Compatriots' Club Lectures* (London 1905), p. 55.

137 G. Myrdal, *The Political Element in the Development of Economic Thought* (London 1953), p. 192.

6 THE ECONOMICS OF POLITICAL INTEGRATION

1 Chamberlain to Devonshire, 21 Sept. 1903, JCP, JC 18/18/47. for an analysis of Chamberlain's career that emphasizes his imperial interests see R. Quinault, 'Joseph Chamberlain: A reassessment' in A. O'Day and T. Gourvish (eds), *Later Victorian Britain* (London 1990).

2 J. Chamberlain in Parliament, 28 May 1903, *PD*, 4th series, cxxiii, c. 185.

3 C.T. Ritchie noted that 'Originally old age pensions were to form an important part of the proposal. I understand that has now been abandoned', Ritchie, Memorandum, 9 Sept. 1903, JCP, JC 18/16/2.

4 Ashley to Bonar Law, 21 Dec. 1904, BLP, 18/1/5.

5 W.J. Ashley, 'Unionist Principles and Social Reform', *The Outlook*, 20 Oct. 1906.

6 Chamberlain to the 1900 Club, 25 June 1906, in Murray *People's Budget*, p. 25.

7 See pp. 211–12.

8 Between May and September 1903 Chamberlain had abandoned the reimposition of the 1/- registration duty in favour of a 2/- per quarter duty on foreign corn with a 1/- preference for colonial corn.

9 Chamberlain to Devonshire, 21 Sept. 1903, JCP, JC 18/18/47.

10 Chamberlain at Welbeck, 4 Aug. 1904, *The Standard*, 5 Aug. 1904.

11 For Hewins' particular interest in agriculture see his *Apologia*, i, pp. 102–7.

12 ibid., p. 102.

13 Garvin to Maxse, 8 Dec. 1906, LJMP, 456 S 432 (my emphasis).

14 Robert and Hugh Cecil described tariff reform in these terms.

15 Wyndham to Balfour, 8 Nov. 1905, in Mackail and Wyndham, *Life*, ii, p. 517 (my emphasis).

16 Pretyman to Selborne, 18 Sept. 1903, SP, MS Selborne 73, fos 3–4 (my emphasis).

17 Chaplin to Chamberlain, 20 Sept. 1903, in Garvin and Amery, *Chamberlain*, iv, p. 4.

18 A.H.H. Matthews to TC, 28 Mar. 1906, TCP, TC6 1/23, citing E. Suffolk Chamber of Agriculture resolution, n.d. Oct. 1903 (?), Milborne Farmers' Club resolution, 5 Oct. 1903, Lincs. Chamber of Agriculture resolution, 9 Dec. 1903.

19 TC, Minutes of a meeting to discuss the Preliminary Report on the Iron and Steel Trades, comments of H. Chaplin, 28 June 1904, TCP, TC2 1/8.

20 TC Agricultural Committee, Notes on its 1st Meeting, 8 Mar. 1904, TCP, TC2 2/1; see also TC Memorandum MM14, 'On the Work of the Agricultural Committee', 24 Apr. 1904, TCP, TC1 8/1.

21 W.A.S. Hewins at a meeting of the Tariff Commission, TC, Minutes of Proceedings, 23 May 1907, TCP, TC2 1/4.

22 A.J. Marrison, 'British Businessmen and the Scientific Tariff: a Study of Joseph Chamberlain's Tariff Commission, 1903–21' (With Special Reference to the Period 1903–13), unpublished Hull University PhD thesis, 1976, p. 1.

7 IMPERIAL ORGANIZATION

1 Iwan-Muller papers, BL, Add MSS, 51,316.

2 J. Chamberlain, Memorandum of a Meeting between himself, Lord Salisbury, Arthur Balfour and the Duke of Devonshire, 24 June 1895, in Garvin, *Chamberlain*, iii, p. 5.

3 Sir Vincent Caillard, *Imperial Fiscal Reform* (London 1903), p. 31.

4 'Rules of the Compatriots' Club', copy in SMP, GD193/129/133x.

5 Milner at Bath, 30 Apr. 1909, *Nation and the Empire*, p. 376 (my emphasis).

6 Chamberlain at Birmingham, 16 May 1902, in Garvin, *Chamberlain*, iv, p. 177.

7 See pp. 164–5.

8 TC Memorandum MM35, 'Colonial Preference and Imperial Reciprocity', 22 July 1908, LSE pamphlet collection fHJ/51–70.

9 B. Kidd, 'Colonial Preference and Free Trade', (2nd article, section i), KP, 8069.

10 C.S. Goldman, 'Introduction', in idem (ed.), *The Empire and the Century*, xix.

11 L.C.M.S. Amery, 'The Case for Tariff Reform', quoted in Kennedy, *Anglo-German Antagonism*, p. 308.

12 Selborne at Handsworth, 4 Jan. 1905, *The Times*, 5 Jan. 1905.

13 Selborne to Pretyman, 19 Sept. 1903, SELP, MS Selborne 73, fos 5–9.

14 J.L. Garvin, 'The Principles of Constructive Economics as Applied to the Maintenance of the Empire' in *Compatriots' Club Lectures*, p. 44.

15 Garvin, 'Constructive Economics', p. 45.

16 ibid.

17 A. Steel-Maitland, 'The Economics of Modern Industry and Imperialism', MP, MS Milner Dep. 34, fos 179–97.

18 'Colonial Preference and Imperial Reciprocity', TC Memorandum, MM35, 22 July 1908, p. 2.

19 ibid. Likewise, the Bradford woollen manufacturer W.H. Mitchell told W.A.S. Hewins that there had been a 'steady and profitable' increase in trade with Canada following the Canadian preference, see Mitchell to Hewins, 9 Jan. 1907, TCP, TC6 1/24.

20 For this argument see for example Caillard, *Imperial Fiscal Reform*, pp. 31–2.

21 TRL, *Speakers' Handbook* (1908 edition), xvi.
22 Garvin, 'Economics of Empire', i, pp. 88–9 (my emphasis).
23 Tryon, *Tariff Reform*, p. 53.
24 Chamberlain at Birmingham, 15 May 1903, in Boyd (ed.), *Speeches*, ii, p. 128.
25 Chamberlain at the Hotel Cecil, 8 July 1904, in Dowding, *Tariff Reform Mirage*, p. 136.
26 See pp. 71–2.
27 TC Memorandum MM 35, 'Colonial Preference and Imperial Reciprocity'.
28 Steel-Maitland to F. Ware, 4 Jan. 1909, SMP, GD193/141/298.
29 Chamberlain at the Hotel Cecil, 8 July 1904, in Dowding, *Tariff Reform Mirage*, p. 135.
30 Dunraven to Chamberlain, 23 Sept. 1910, JCP, JC 18/17/8.
31 Chamberlain at Preston, 11 Jan. 1905, in Boyd (ed.), *Speeches*, ii, p. 294 (my emphasis).
32 See pp. 214–15.
33 As ch. 8 makes clear the food taxes were also important as a tariff appeal to British agriculture.
34 Chamberlain at Glasgow, 6 Oct. 1903, in Boyd (ed.), *Speeches*, ii, p. 159.
35 TC Memo., 'The New Australian Tariff', n.d. 1907 (?), TCP, TC8 2/3. Sir Vincent Caillard advocated Imperial Free Trade in *Imperial Fiscal Reform*, he was out of step with other leading tariff campaigners. If Imperial Free Trade was mentioned in connection with tariff reform disclaimers soon appeared. For example, in October 1908 the *Morning Post* carried a statement by one writer that 'the ultimate ideal is Inter-Imperial Free Trade', but the next day the notion was repudiated, and it was made clear that 'It is not . . . part of the policy of Preferential Trade to suggest to any overseas Dominion a limitation of its industries present or future', the *Morning Post*, 6, 7 Oct. 1908.
36 TC Memo., MM 35, 'Colonial Preference and Imperial Reciprocity'.
37 Hewins to Balfour, 18 Feb. 1907, BP, 49779, fos 61–70.
38 ibid.
39 ibid.
40 Chamberlain at Birmingham, 27 July 1905, in Boyd (ed.), *Speeches*, ii, p. 329.
41 L.C.M.S. Amery, 'Imperial Unity', a speech to the Chatham Club, 15 July 1910, in idem, *Union and strength* (London 1912), p. 2.
42 Wyndham, as Irish secretary, was well attuned to conceptualizing and wrestling with the problem of containing national aspirations within an imperial framework.
43 G. Wyndham, *The Development of the State* (London 1904), p. 32.
44 ibid., p. 49.
45 Again Wyndham was not alone in citing this example – the fate of Rome was a fixation of many Edwardian imperialists. For an outline of this phenomenon see S. Hynes, *The Edwardian Turn of Mind* (New Haven 1968), pp. 15–26.
46 Wyndham, *Development of the State*, p. 36.
47 ibid., p. 7.
48 ibid., p. 36.
49 One cannot help wondering whether Wyndham's argument for conceding 'adequate local attachment' may have helped lead him into the 'Irish devolution' crisis of 1905 which brought about his resignation. For the best discussion of Wyndham's period as Chief Secretary and the devolution imbroglio see A. Gailey, 'Unionist Policy in Ireland 1895–1906', unpublished Cambridge University PhD thesis, 1985.
50 Wyndham, *Development*, p. 45.
51 ibid., p. 56.

52 ibid., p. 11.
53 ibid., p. 48.
54 ibid., p. 47.
55 ibid., p. 49.
56 ibid., p. 58.
57 Chamberlain at Birmingham, 15 May 1903, in Boyd (ed.), *Speeches*, ii, p. 2.
58 Chamberlain at Glasgow, 6 Oct. 1903, ibid., p. 142.
59 Garvin, 'Economics of Empire', p. 57.
60 Milner at the Authors' Club, 2 Dec. 1912, *The Nation and the Empire*, p. 490.
61 Chamberlain's successor as Colonial Secretary.
62 Amery to Lyttelton, 20 Aug. 1904, ALP, CHAN 2/1, fos 2–7. The particular context within which Amery raised this idea was that of ensuring a white predominance in South Africa: 'If you want to grow a special kind of flower in a garden you keep out the weeds. If you want a white population in South Africa you must keep out Asiatics.'
63 B. Wise, 'The Problem of Empire', in Malmesbury (ed.), *The New Order*, p. 101.
64 Milner at Vancouver, 9 Oct. 1908, *Nation and Empire*, p. 310.
65 R. Borden, quoted in B. Holland, *The Fall of Protection* (London 1904), p. 392.
66 Chamberlain at Gainsborough, 1 Feb. 1905, and at Birmingham, 15 May 1903, in Boyd (ed.), *Speeches*, ii, pp. 295, 127.
67 Hobhouse, *Democracy and Reaction*, p. 12.
68 Chamberlain at the Hotel Cecil, 8 July 1904, in Dowding, *Tariff Reform Mirage*, p. 136.
69 Chamberlain at Birmingham, 15 May 1903, in Boyd (ed.), *Speeches*, ii, p. 128.
70 Wise, 'Problem of Empire', p. 103.
71 Garvin, *Imperial Reciprocity*, p. 63.
72 Garvin, 'Constructive Economics', pp. 56–7.
73 Milner at Edinburgh, 15 Nov. 1907, *Nation and Empire*, p. 241.
74 Milner at Nottingham, 19 Apr. 1909, ibid., p. 372.
75 Garvin, 'Constructive Economics', p. 110.
76 ibid.
77 Caillard, *Imperial Fiscal Reform*, pp. 121–5.
78 Milner at Edinburgh, 15 Nov. 1907, *Nation and Empire*, p. 241.
79 Sir Vincent Caillard, 'Imperial Preference and the Cost of Food', in *Compatriots' Club Lectures*, p. 145.
80 See Election Materials, Jan. 1906, JSSP, MS Eng. Hist. c. 751, fos 1–8, and also see Williams, *Defending the Empire*, pp. 77–83.
81 The 'high politics' of the Conservative attack on Liberal policies for imperial defence is dealt with at length by Williams, *Defending the Empire*, pp. 84–199; the 'low politics' is dealt with in Coetzee, *Party or Country*, and Summers, 'Edwardian Nationalism'.
82 Balfour at the Albert Hall, 7 Oct. 1911, in TC Memo. MM 50, 'The Abandonment of Cobdenism', LSE pamphlet collection fHJ/51–70.
83 See the amendment to the King's Speech by J.W. Hills, 19 Feb. 1907, expressing 'regret that no reference is made ... to the approaching Colonial Conference and to the opportunity thereby offered for promoting freer trade within the Empire and closer commercial relations with the Colonies on a preferential basis', *PD*, 4th series, clxix, c. 732.
84 Kidd to Milner, 25 Apr. 1908, MP, MS Milner Dep. 35, fo. 86.
85 ibid.
86 For the importance of tariffs as a revenue source for social reform see pp. 248–53.
87 Milner at Manchester, 14 Dec. 1906, *Nation and Empire*, p. 139.

88 *The Outlook*, 9 Nov. 1907.

89 Hobhouse, *Democracy and Reaction*, p. 12.

90 See pp. 148–50.

91 Wyndham to Balfour, 28 Jan. 1906, Balfour papers, Whittinghame (I am grateful to Dr Andrew Gailey for providing me with a transcript of this letter).

92 G.F. Shee to L.J. Maxse, 19 May 1910, LJMP, 461 R 642–5.

93 See pp. 242–8 for discussion of the supposedly beneficial employment effects of tariffs.

94 Garvin to Goulding, 5 Dec. 1909, WP, WAR 2.

95 Selborne, typescript of two articles written for the *Morning Post*, July 1912, SP, MS Selborne 79, fos 80–94.

96 See p. 144.

97 For a discussion of this kind of Conservative attack on Socialism see Coetzee, *Party or Country*, pp. 98–103.

98 For a stimulating treatment of this question, albeit with a different emphasis, see W. Mock, 'The Function of "Race" in Imperial Ideologies: the Example of Joseph Chamberlain', in Kennedy and Nicholls (eds), *Nationalist and Racialist Movements*, pp. 190–203.

99 Milner at Rugby, 19 Nov. 1907, *Nation and Empire*, pp. 252–3.

100 Garvin, 'Constructive Economics', p. 9.

8 THE DEFENCE OF BRITISH AGRICULTURE

1 H. Chaplin, opening address to the Agricultural Committee of the Tariff Commission, n.d. July 1904, TCP, TC6 1/2.

2 ibid., TC6 1/2.

3 J.L. Garvin, *Imperial Reciprocity* (London 1903), p. 84.

4 TRL, *Speakers' Handbook* (5th edition, London 1908), v.

5 J. Chamberlain at Greenock, 7 Oct. 1903, in Boyd (ed.), *Speeches*, ii, p. 177.

6 Previously the Rural Labourers' League.

7 J.L. Green, *Agriculture and Tariff Reform* (London 1904), pp. 23–9. Green's figures were supported by *The Tariff Commission Report on Agriculture* (London 1906).

8 Green, ibid., p. 9.

9 The most comprehensive survey to date is Thompson, 'Anatomy of English Farming'.

10 On this point contemporary opinion and recent scholarship are in complete agreement, for no economic historian would dispute the fact that the agricultural sector was shrinking – for the most recent discussion see ibid., pp. 218–19.

11 Green, *Agriculture and Tariff Reform*, p. 18 – these figures were quite accurate.

12 For the Royal Commission on Food Supply and the long-running debate/concern over the vulnerability of Britain's food supplies see A. Offer, *The First World War: An Agrarian Interpretation* (Oxford 1989), pp. 81–92, 217–32.

13 One Conservative front-bench member of the Royal Commission, the one-time Secretary for War George Wyndham, concluded that Britain was 'a raft moored in the Atlantic with a fortnight's food on board'. See C. Gatty, *George Wyndham: Recognita* (London 1914), p. 143.

14 H.W. Wilson, 'A National Tariff for National Defence', *NR*, ccvii, Feb. 1904, p. 887. See also the Assistant Editor [J.L. Garvin], 'The Economics of Empire', *NR*, Special Supplement for the year 1903–4, 2 vols, ii, p. 2.

15 E.E. Williams, *The Case for Protection* (London 1899), p. 6.

16 W.J. Ashley, *The Tariff Problem* (1st edition, London 1903), p. 53.
17 Garvin, 'Economics of Empire', i, p. 44.
18 Williams, *Case for Protection*, p. 77.
19 E.E. Williams, 'A Countryside Reborn', *NR*, ccxxxviii, Dec. 1902, p. 562.
20 C. Turnor, 'A Constructive Agricultural Policy', *NR*, cccxxii, Dec. 1909, p. 543. 'Unionists and Land Policy', *The Outlook*, 7 May 1910.
21 *Tariff Commission Report on Agriculture*, para. 342.
22 For a more detailed discussion of this point see pp. 258–60.
23 H. Tremayne, *Protection and the Farmer*, p. 3.
24 See pp. 258–60.
25 'Agriculture', *The Tariff Dictionary*, p. 3.
26 Jebb to Milner, 12 Oct. 1907, JP.
27 Perhaps the best known comment about the 'innate' Conservatism of peasants was Marx's likening the French peasantry to a sack of potatoes in *The Eighteenth Brumaire of Louis Bonaparte*, a comment which fitted well with his general contempt for 'the idiocy of rural life'. Marx's views on this point at least were, however, shared by, in France, Jules Méline and Jules Ferry, in Germany by Bismarck, Hohenlohe and Bulow, and in Russia by Count Stolypin, whose land reforms were based squarely on this assumption.
28 H. Chaplin, 26 Jan. 1886, *Times*, 27 Jan. 1886.
29 Salisbury at Exeter, 2 Feb. 1892, *Times*, 3 Feb. 1892.
30 Parker, the Conservative MP for Gravesend, was Chairman of the Small Ownership Committee.
31 W.A.S. Hewins, Memorandum on Agriculture, n.d. 1905 (?), TCP, TC8 2/7.
32 Turnor, *Land Problems*, p. 299.
33 Chamberlain at Welbeck, 4 Aug. 1904, *The Standard*, 5 Aug. 1904.
34 Green, *Agriculture and Tariff Reform*, p. 76, The Tariff Commission, *Report on Agriculture*.
35 In particular there was a great deal of pressure for the Party to propose duties on imported hops – for example see F. Neame (Hop Farmer of E. Kent), evidence to the Agricultural Committee of the Tariff Commission, 10 Jan. 1905, TCP, TC3 1/181.
36 J.P. Hughes to T. Davies (Secretary, Cirencester Conservative Association), 21 Dec. 1909, TCP, TC8 2/18.
37 W.A.S. Hewins, Memorandum of conversations with A.J. Balfour of 1, 3, 4, Nov. 1907, BP, 49779, fos 117–28.
38 Chamberlain at Welbeck, 4 Aug. 1904, *The Standard*, 5 Aug. 1904.
39 Williams, 'Mr Chaplin's Kite', p. 223.
40 ibid., p. 224.
41 These duties did not contravene free trade precepts because they were non-protective.
42 Hewins to Balfour, 11 Feb. 1907, BP, 49779, fos 37–40.
43 Tariff Commission, Memorandum on the Report on Answers to the Inquiry Form Issued by the Agricultural Committee, n.d. Oct. (?) 1904, TCP, TC 1/81.
44 ibid.
45 The only criticism made by those who responded positively was that the duty should be higher, perhaps 10–15 per cent *ad valorem*. ibid.
46 ibid.
47 Sixty-six of the respondents to the Tariff Commission Questionnaire rested approval of Chamberlain's proposals on this assumption.
48 J.W. Dennis, evidence to the Agricultural Committee of the Tariff Commission, 14 Nov. 1904, TCP, TC6 1/3. Dennis was a farmer, a fruit and potato broker and a merchant, chiefly in agricultural products.

49 See pp. 113–14.

50 Tariff Commission, Inquiry, para. 88.

51 At the City Carlton Club in March 1910 the Conservative MP Major E.F. Coates noted that, during the January election campaign, 'in one place he was told to say nothing about such taxes; in another, to declare that no duty would be put on colonial corn; and in a third, that a 1/- duty would be placed on that corn', quoted in Dowding, *Tariff Reform Mirage*, p. 108.

52 The fact that Austen Chamberlain accepted this pronouncement without demur is an indication of its largely non-controversial status, for Chamberlain was perhaps the leading senior advocate of a positive agricultural policy. For his views see his correspondence with Balfour on the subject cited below p. 281.

53 This was the approach adopted by W.A.S. Hewins when in 1908 he addressed the Lincolnshire Farmers' Union, one of the most militant arable farming organizations in the country. Hewins told his audience that there was no prospect of a return to high corn duties, and the focus of his speech was the revenue potential of tariffs. Hewins' arguments are outlined in Dowding, *Tariff Reform Mirage*, p. 107.

54 Hewins to Balfour, 11 Feb. 1907, BP, 49779, fos 37–40.

55 Copies of 'Lord Milner's Agricultural Memorandum' can be found in the private papers of a number of leading Conservatives, but the best record of the Memorandum's genesis and the intra-party discussion of its proposals is in the MP, see MS Milner Dep. 159 for the Memorandum itself, and MS Milner Dep. 38 and 40 for party discussions. Documents relating to the discussions of the Conservative Agricultural Policy Committee can also be found in MS Milner Dep. 38.

56 There were a few innovations between 1910 and 1913, and they will be discussed in the following chapter.

57 'Agrarian Juggling', *The Outlook*, 6 Nov. 1909.

58 For the impact of the Land Campaign see pp. 289–93.

59 Fellowes was a Conservative Whip and MP, until his defeat in 1906, for the mainly agricultural constituency of North Huntingdonshire.

60 Fellowes to Balfour, 24 Oct. 1907, BP, 49858, fos 183–5.

61 St John Brodrick to A. Chamberlain, 28 Jan. 1906, ACP, AC 7/2/2.

62 Milner at the Constitutional Club, 26 June 1908, in *The Nation and the Empire*, p. 301.

63 G. Courthope, 'Land' in Malmesbury (ed.), *The New Order*, p. 301.

64 Tollemache, *Ownership of Land*, p. 38.

65 ibid.

66 J. Collings at Westminster, 7 Feb. 1907, *The Times*, 8 Feb. 1907.

67 O. Locker-Lampson, 'Food Duties and the County Elections', *NR*, cccxxvii, May 1910, p. 478.

68 Minutes of the 3rd Meeting of the Tariff Commission Agricultural Committee, 1 Nov. 1904, TCP, TC2 2/5.

69 Minutes of the 3rd Meeting of the Tariff Commission Agricultural Committee, remarks of J.W. Dennis, TCP, TC2 2/5.

70 ibid.

71 Sir Gilbert Parker, *The Land for the People* (London 1909), p. 11.

72 ibid., p. 11. See also Lord Milner *et al.*, 'Unionism', BLP, 18/4/75, C. Turnor, 'A Constructive Agricultural Policy', *NR*, cccxxii, Dec. 1909, p. 599, idem, *Land Problems and the National Welfare* (London 1911), B. Tollemache, *The Occupying Ownership of Land* (London 1913), pp. 56–9, 'Lord Milner's Agricultural

Memorandum', A Group of Unionists, *A Unionist Agricultural Policy*, pp. 25–6.

73 Parker, *Land for the People*, p. 11. The models here were undoubtedly the Danish and German local *Sparkassen* and the French *Crédit Agricole*.

74 Lord Milner *et al.*, 'Unionism', BLP, 18/4/74.

75 Lord Onslow, 'Suggestions for an Agricultural Policy' a memorandum sent to A. Chamberlain, 24 Mar. 1909, ACP, AC 8/1/1–3. For similar ideas about rural education see Turnor, 'Constructive Agricultural Policy', pp. 598–9, and idem, *Land, Labour and the Unionist Party* (London 1912), p. 9.

76 Onslow, 'Suggestions for an Agricultural Policy'. Onslow hoped that mortgages could be advanced at 3 per cent.

77 Milner *et al.*, 'Unionism'.

78 The fullest treatment of the Wyndham Act can be found in A. Gailey, 'Unionist Policy in Ireland, 1886–1905', unpublished Cambridge University PhD thesis, 1985.

79 For references to the Wyndham Act in this context see Lord Onslow, 'Suggestions for an Agricultural Policy'. Likewise Jesse Collings argued that 'tenant farmers should be enabled to purchase their holdings by the aid of the State on the Irish lines', J. Collings to R.D. Blumenfeld, 4 Apr. 1910, RDBP, Coll 2, whilst Lord Milner argued in 1912 that 'there is nothing to prevent an immediate declaration, to the effect that the Unionist party desires to see a great increase in the number of owners of land, brought about by State aid *on the Irish principle*', Milner to J. Collings, 12 July 1912, MP, MS Milner Dep. 38, fos 170–2 (my emphasis). Milner's 'Agricultural Memorandum' also continually referred to the Irish model, and it is worth noting that this memorandum was submitted to George Wyndham, the author of the eponymous act, for close scrutiny and amendment, see G. Wyndham, 'Notes on Lord Milner's Agricultural Memorandum', n.d. Mar. (?) 1913, MP, MS Milner Dep. 38 fos 144–54.

80 G. Wyndham 'Notes on Lord Milner's Agricultural Memorandum', n.d. Mar. (?) 1913, MP, MS Milner Dep. 38, fo. 153.

81 Milner, 'Agricultural Memorandum', A Group of Unionists, *A Unionist Agricultural Policy*.

82 The quotation is taken from Milner, 'Agricultural Memorandum', but see also J. Collings, *Land Reform* (London 1906) and Parker, *Land for the People*, p. 22.

83 In July 1912 Jesse Collings estimated that the Conservative scheme would cost £12,000,000, J. Collings to Milner, 10 July 1912, MP, MS Milner Dep. 38, fos 162–7.

84 'The People on the Land', *The Outlook*, 6 Nov. 1909.

85 W. Long to A.J. Balfour, n.d. 1909 (?) in Offer, *Property*, p. 362.

86 For a discussion of Edwardian debates on the land in these terms see Offer, *Property and Politics*, pp. 329–47.

87 At this point it is worth remembering that in the early twentieth century agriculture, in spite of its decline, was still one of the largest single employers in the country.

88 Green, *Agriculture and Tariff Reform*, p. 76.

89 As will be seen in Part IV of this book the arable sector was still capable of presenting a powerful and disruptive case for itself as late as 1913. See pp. 280–5.

90 *Tariff Commission Report on Agriculture*, para. 359.

91 Milner to Bonar Law, 24 Oct. 1913, BLP, 30/3/50.

92 Turnor, *Land Problems*, p. 285.

93 Tremayne, *Protection and the Farmer*, p. 60.

94 Milner to Bonar Law, 24 Oct. 1913, BLP, 30/3/50.

9 THE DEFENCE OF BRITISH INDUSTRY

1 Chamberlain at Greenock, 7 Oct. 1903, in Boyd (ed.), *Speeches*, ii, p. 177.
2 This was not a self-appointed task, the Commission received requests, sometimes passed on by CCO, for assistance from local Conservative groups and
individual MPs. See for example the request from the Lancashire NUCA
Committee for 'educative' material about tariff reform and the cotton
industry, forwarded by the Conservative Chief Whip to the Commission –
J. Eastham to A. Acland-Hood, 3 Mar. 1909, TCP, TC8 2/5.
3 TC, *Report on the Iron and Steel Trades* (London 1904), para. 33.
4 ibid., para. 40.
5 TC, *Report on the Textile Trades*, (7 vols, London 1904–5), ii, para. 13, para. 45.
6 R.H.I. Palgrave, 'Colonial Friends and Foreign Rivals', *NR*, cclii, Feb. 1904,
p. 983.
7 R.H.I. Palgrave, 'The Industrial Condition of the Country', *NR*, cclxv, Mar.
1905, p. 161.
8 P. Ashley to Balfour, 4 July 1903, BP, 49870, fos 38–45.
9 Garvin, *Imperial Reciprocity*, p. 40.
10 Palgrave, 'Colonial Friends', pp. 985–6.
11 See for example TC, *Textile Trades*, para. 68.
12 Palgrave, 'Colonial Friends, p. 986.
13 TC, *Textile Trades*, para. 101.
14 W.A.S. Hewins, 'The Influence of the New German Commercial Treaties on
British Industries', *NR*, cclxviii, p. 698.
15 ibid., p. 700.
16 TC, *Iron and Steel Trades*, para. 42.
17 TC, *Report on the Engineering Trades* (London 1904), para 25.
18 TC, *Textile Trades*, ii, para. 1456.
19 TC, *Iron and Steel Trades*, para. 54.
20 TC Memorandum MM1, Memorandum on German Kartells in the Iron and
Steel Industries, 10 Mar. 1904, TCP, TC1 8/1.
21 See for example TC, *Iron and Steel Trades*, paras 60–1, TC Memorandum
MM9.
22 Here it is important to note that the Tariff Commission's discussion of cartels
and combinations was part of a much wider national and international
debate on 'the trust question'. See below for a discussion of the broader
context of this debate.
23 'Dumping', *The Tariff Dictionary*, p. 69.
24 TC, *Iron and Steel Trades*, para. 63.
25 TC, *Textile Trades*, ii, para. 1451.
26 However, the Commission felt that it was a growing problem and that
the future would see more evidence of dumping in this sector, ibid., paras
73–4.
27 TC, *Engineering Trades*, para. 7.
28 TC, *Iron and Steel Trades*, para. 46.
29 TC, *Iron and Steel Trades*, para. 55.
30 ibid., para 62.
31 TC, *Textile Trades*, ii, para. 1456.
32 TC, *Iron and Steel Trades*, para. 46.
33 Garvin, *Imperial Reciprocity*, p. 37.
34 Cunningham, *Free Trade Movement*, p. 33.
35 Garvin, *Imperial Reciprocity*, p. 37.
36 TC, *Textile Trades*, ii, para. 1449.

37 Cunningham, *Free Trade Movement*, p. 33.

38 Chamberlain to Ashley, 26 Apr. 1904, JCP, JC 18/18/7.

39 G. Wyndham to C. Wyndham, 4 Nov. 1908, in Mackail and Wyndham, *Life and Letters*, ii, pp. 620–1.

40 ibid.

41 ibid. The Tariff Commission provided some evidence to support Wyndham's assertion, noting that, for example, several sewing cotton firms had 'migrated' to tariff protected nations and were enjoying a virtual monopoly of their newly-adopted home market, TC, *Textile Trades*, ii, para. 65.

42 Cunningham, *Free Trade Movement*, p. 33.

43 The literature on the trust issue in the USA is vast, but some helpful contributions are G. Kolko, *The Triumph of Conservatism* (New York 1963), N.R. Lamoreaux, *The Great Merger Movement in American Business* (Cambridge 1985), M. Sklar, *The Corporate Reconstruction of American Capitalism* (Cambridge 1987), M. Keller, *Regulating a New Economy* (Harvard 1989).

44 In fact the Fabians commissioned a special study of trusts, see H.W. Macrosty, *The Trust Movement in Britain* (London 1907).

45 M. Hirst, *The Story of Trusts* (London 1913), p. 189.

46 R. Hilferding, *Finance Capital*, (Vienna 1905, London 1981 edition), p. 305.

47 ibid., p. 307.

48 ibid.

49 ibid., pp. 308–9.

50 ibid., p. 310.

51 See the evidence presented to the Federal Trade Commission in 1902, cited in Lamoreaux, *Great Merger Movement*, pp. 34–5.

52 See B. Elbaum and W. Lazonick (eds), *The Decline of the British Economy* (Oxford 1986), A. Chandler, *Scale and Scope* (Cambridge, Mass. 1990).

53 In fact there are wider grounds for taking tariff reform economics seriously. For a full and sympathetic treatment of the economics of tariff reform see A.J. Marrison, *British Businessmen and Protection, 1903–32* (forthcoming).

54 Chamberlain at Glasgow, 6 Oct. 1903, in Boyd (ed.), *Speeches*, ii, pp. 140–64.

55 See Marrison, 'Tariff Commission', *passim*.

56 The period of the Commission's greatest activity was January 1904 to December 1905, the period which saw the preparation of the main Commission *Reports*, but the Commission continued to gather evidence and provide advice to the Conservative leadership. In 1907 the Commission stated that it had gathered information from 15,000 firms, see 'A Brief Account of the Work of the Tariff Commission', 4 Nov. 1907, TC Memorandum MM 32, LSE pamphlet collection fHJ/f51.

57 C. Eckersley to W. Harrison, 1 Jan. 1904, TCP, TC6 1/5.

58 See Marrison, 'Tariff Commission', p. 333.

59 Minutes of the Textile Committee of the Tariff Commission, 18 May 1905, TCP, in ibid., p. 331.

60 Bagley to Hewins, 1 Mar. 1909, TCP, TC8 2/5.

61 W.A.S. Hewins, 'Fiscal Reform in Relation to Cotton', n.d. Mar. 1909, TCP, TC8 2/5.

62 Hewins had been advised of the 'cosmopolitan' leanings of cotton merchants and traders five years earlier: see S. Levinstein to Hewins, 8 Feb. 1904, TCP, in Marrison, 'Tariff Commission', p. 302.

63 ibid., p. 340.

64 T.H. Mitchell, evidence to the Tariff Commission, 8 June 1904, TCP, TC6 1/24.

65 A.F. Firth to W.H. Mitchell, 11 Feb. 1904, TCP, TC6 1/24.
66 P.A. Hurd to Sir Vincent Caillard, 19 July 1911, TCP, TC6 1/1.
67 See A.J. Marrison, 'Businessmen, Industries and Tariff Reform in Great Britain, 1903–30', *Business History*, xxv, 1983.
68 A good example was the ship-building industry, which benefited from the import of German steel plate at 'dumped' prices.
69 TC, *Iron and Steel Trades*, para. 77.
70 B. Kidd, 'Colonial Preference and Free Trade', (2nd Article, Section ii), from the proof copy of a series of articles on this subject, later published in the *Daily Mail*, KP, 8069.
71 Lord Dudley to W.S. Churchill, 9 Nov. 1902, in R. Churchill, *Winston Churchill*, companion volume II, part 1, pp. 171–2.
72 Joseph Camberlain, according to Henry Page-Croft, once remarked 'why do people not realize that Germany is making war on us, that here economic attack is just as surely an overt act of aggression as if she had declared hostilities?', in Page-Croft, *Life*, p. 47.
73 L.J. Maxse, 'Cobdenism and its Fallacies', *NR*, ccliii, Mar. 1904, p. 54.
74 J.L. Garvin, 'The Economics of Empire', I, p. 24.
75 ibid., p. 28.
76 ibid., p. 4.
77 G.C. Tryon, *Tariff Reform* (London 1909), p. 62.
78 Chamberlain to Lord Forrest, 1 Apr. 1903, in Garvin and Amery, *Chamberlain*, iv, p. 169.
79 ibid.
80 Garvin, *Imperial Reciprocity*, p. 57.
81 S. Rosenberg (Tariff Commission Statistician) to H. Chaplin, 29 Apr. 1904, TCP, TC6 1/2.
82 E.G. Pretyman to Chamberlain, 22 Sept. 1903, JCP, JC 18/17/23.
83 Chamberlain at Birmingham, 12 May 1904, in Dowding, *Tariff Reform Mirage*, p. 236.
84 Parker at Bristol, 20 Feb. 1904, in ibid.
85 G. Wyndham to C. Wyndham, 4 Nov. 1908, in Mackail and Wyndham, *Life and Letters*, ii, pp. 620–1.
86 Garvin, 'Economics of Empire', i, p. 23.
87 J. Chamberlain to W.E. Lovsey, 19 May 1903, JCP, JC 18/18/92.
88 For a succinct summary of this criticism see the book by the Conservative MP Arthur Fell, *The Failure of Free Trade* (London 1904), pp. 48–50.
89 B. Kidd, 'Colonial Preference' (5th Article, Section i), KP, 8069.
90 W.A.S. Hewins, Memorandum of Conversations with A.J. Balfour on 1, 3, and 4 Nov. 1907, BP, 49779, fos 117–28.
91 Agriculture also qualified as a 'productive' sector, but interestingly enough the divide between its interests and those of finance was not so sharply drawn or so frequently stated by the tariff campaign.
92 Miscellaneous Lists, n.d. TCP, TC8 2/17.
93 Vicary Gibbs was a merchant banker, a partner in Antony Gibbs and Son. It is perhaps also worth noting that his father, Lord Aldenham (H.H. Gibbs) had been President of the Bimetallic League, and whose views on the issue of 'national/productive versus cosmopolitan/financial' economics are discussed in ch. 1 of this study. Of the other five who co-operated none was a City figure of the front rank.
94 See Tariff Commission, Minutes of Proceedings, 17 May 1906, 31 May 1906, and 23 May 1907, for Hewins' statement of the problem, TCP, TC2 1/12, 13, 14.
95 Tariff Commission, Minutes of Proceedings, 17 May 1906, TCP, TC2 1/12.

96 Schuster was later to become Chairman of the Committee of London Clearing Banks.
97 'The Fiscal Problem', Unsigned Treasury memorandum (sent to E.W. Hamilton), 8 Aug. 1903, copy in SMP, GD 193/88/1/147.
98 Tariff Commission, Minutes of Proceedings, 31 May 1906, Statement by C.J. Phillips, TCP, TC2 1/13.
99 ibid., Statement by A. Mosely.
100 H.A. Gwynne, Memorandum on 'Arguments Against Mr Chamberlain's Policy', n.d. Dec (?) 1903, MAGP, MS Gwynne, Box 27.
101 V. Caillard, *Imperial Fiscal Reform* (London 1903), p. 227.
102 Lord Dudley to W.S. Churchill, 9 Nov. 1902, in R.S. Churchill, *Winston S. Churchill*, companion volume ii, part i, pp. 171–2.
103 Chamberlain to E.A. Goulding, 3 Feb. 1908, WARP, WAR 2.
104 Garvin, 'Economics of Empire', i, p. 44.
105 Caillard, *Imperial Fiscal Reform*, p. 229.
106 Hewins to Balfour, 26 July 1909, BP, 49779, fos 214–16.
107 As noted above, retaliation was looked upon as a possible means of 'selling' tariff reform to the cotton industry, which did not suffer from import penetration, but it was one of the few occasions after 1906 that retaliation played an important role in tariff discussions.
108 Chamberlain at Glasgow, 6 Oct. 1903, in Boyd (ed.), *Speeches*, ii, p. 158.
109 'Colonial Preference and Imperial Reciprocity', Tariff Commission memorandum MM 33, 22 July 1907, LSE pamphlet collection fHJ/51–70.
110 Tariff Reform League, *Speaker's Handbook* (5th edition, London 1908), xvi.
111 J.L. Garvin, 'The Principles of Constructive Economics as Applied to the Maintenance of the Empire', in *Compatriot's Club Lectures* (London 1905), p. 10.
112 Tryon, *Tariff Reform*, pp. 12–13.
113 ibid., p. 7, see also Caillard, *Imperial Fiscal Reform*, p. 226.
114 Churchill to J. Moore Bayley, 20 May 1903, in R.S. Churchill, *Winston Churchill*, companion volume ii, part i, pp. 182–3.
115 Percy Ashley was a Board of Trade official and brother of the tariff reforming historical economist W.J. Ashley.
116 P. Ashley to Balfour, 4 July 1904, BP, 49870, fos 38–45.

10 SOCIAL REFORM

1 JSSP, MS Eng. Hist. c. 759, fos 64–70.
2 W.J. Ashley, 'Unionist Principles and Social Reform', *The Outlook*, 20 Oct. 1906.
3 'The Conflict of Policies', *The Outlook*, 23 Oct. 1909.
4 J. Chamberlain at the Albert Hall, 7 July 1905, in W.E. Dowding, *The Tariff Reform Mirage* (London 1913), p. 255.
5 Balfour at Stockport, 8 Nov. 1909, *The Times*, 9 Nov. 1909. This was not simply Balfourian evasion. Bonar Law had been similarly cautious, telling the NUCA Conference in 1908 that 'None of the leaders had ever said that a change of fiscal policy would do away with all fluctuations of employment ... but they did believe that Tariff Reform would tend ... to minimize the effect of bad trade [and] ... steady the employment of the working classes'. Bonar Law at the NUCA Conference, Cardiff, 19 Nov. 1908, NUCA Conference Minutes, CPA, (Microfilm Card no. 59).
6 Milner at Cardiff, 23 Dec. 1909, *The Nation and the Empire*, p. 451.

7 W.J. Ashley, *Social Legislation* (Oxford 1909), p. 7.

8 ibid.

9 ibid.

10 Milner at Cardiff, 23 Dec. 1910, *The Nation and the Empire*, p. 451.

11 P.A. Gourevitch, *Politics in Hard Times* (Ithaca 1986), pp. 46–8.

12 In the 1920s and 1930s tariffs, the empire, emigration, hours of work and the school-leaving age were as important to contemporary conceptions of (un)employment policy as 'Keynesian' demand management and other recognizably 'modern' elements of economic policy. See W.R. Garside, *British Unemployment 1919–69*, (Cambridge 1990).

13 C. Booth, 'Fiscal Reform', *NR*, ccli, Jan. 1904, pp. 686–700.

14 That Steel-Maitland, the future Conservative party Chairman and leading light of the Unionist Social Reform Committee, was so actively engaged in these investigations is important.

15 A full record of Steel-Maitland's part in the investigation survives in the SMP, GD 193/131. For the significance of this investigation as part of an evolving debate on unemployment see Harris, *Unemployment and Politics*, pp. 36–41.

16 Seebohm Rowntree and William Beveridge, two of the most prominent Liberal experts on social issues, placed great emphasis on unemployment and irregular employment as central to any discussion of poverty, whilst at the 1905 meeting of the Labour Representation Committee, James Keir Hardie stated that unemployment was 'the root cause from which most of the troubles in the labour world sprang'. Labour Representation Committee, Report of the 5th Annual Conference, Appendix 1, p. 63, cited in Harris, *Unemployment*, p. 236.

17 J. Chamberlain at Liverpool, 27 Oct. 1903, in Boyd (ed.), *Speeches*, ii, p. 202.

18 J. Chamberlain at Limehouse, 15 Dec. 1904, in ibid., p. 259.

19 An interesting formal statement of this contention was made by W.J. Ashley, who argued that 'in a very real sense Germany can be said to owe its insurance system to its protective system. For ... it was in large measure the outcome of that revolt against the doctrine of laissez faire among economists and administrators which also led them to favour or acquiesce in a return to protection. As an example, per contra, it was the eloquent Professor Brentano, now the leading advocate of free trade, who, when compulsory insurance was first mooted, offered the most brilliant opposition to it in the name of liberty'. W.J. Ashley, *The Progress of the German Working Class in the Last Quarter of a Century* (London 1904), p. 19.

20 It is interesting to note that some leading Liberals feared that Chamberlain had found an effective criticism. In late 1903 Lord Ripon informed Campbell-Bannerman that the working class were being seduced by the tariff campaign, and in the same vein Herbert Gladstone stressed the importance of the Liberal party developing a positive alternative to tariff reform. See Ripon to Campbell-Bannerman, 18 Oct. 1903, and H. Gladstone to Campbell-Bannerman, 5 Dec. 1903, cited in Harris, *Unemployment*, pp. 215–16.

21 *The Outlook*, 25 Jan. 1908.

22 See above pp. 247–8.

23 'The Out-of-Work Problem', *The Outlook*, 31 Oct. 1908.

24 J. Chamberlain at Liverpool, 27 Oct. 1903, in Boyd (ed.), *Speeches*, ii, p. 206.

25 E.A. Goulding in Parliament, 21 Feb. 1908, *Morning Post*, 22 Feb. 1908.

26 Harris, *Unemployment and Politics*, p. 273.

27 *The Times*, 16 Jan. 1908.

28 ibid., 17 Jan. 1908.

29 *Daily Chronicle*, 31 Dec. 1907. A comprehensive record of press coverage of this by-election can be found in the Morrison-Bell papers, Devon County Record Office.

30 For example the local branch of the ILP advised working men in the district to abstain, whilst the Suffragettes, and Mrs Pankhurst in person, campaigned for Morrison-Bell.

31 National Union Council, Report to the NUCA Conference, Cardiff, 19 Nov. 1908, NUCA Conference Minutes, CPA, (Microfilm Card no. 58).

32 Chamberlain to M. Woods, 15 Dec. 1909, ACP, AC 8/3/2.

33 For this argument in the specific context of anti-sweating see J.F. Remnant in Parliament, 12 May 1911, *The Times*, 13 May 1911.

34 Ashley, *German Working Class*, p. 19.

35 See pp. 130–2.

36 See R. Hay, 'Employers and Social Policy in Britain', in P. Thane (ed.), *Essays in Social History*, (2 vols, Oxford 1986), ii.

37 The Conservatives continued to press this argument in relation to all the Liberals' most ambitious industrial social reforms, with the NUCA Central Committee reporting to the NUCA Conference of 1912 that 'The new burdens placed upon industry – the Insurance Act, the Minimum Wages [Trade Boards] Act, the Eight Hour Day for Coal Miners Act ... have impressed upon people ... the necessity of putting British industries on a par with their foreign competitors by imposing some moderate duties, which should be equivalent to the increased charges'. National Union Council, Report to NUCA Conference, London, 14 Nov. 1912, NUCA Conference Minutes, CPA, (Microfilm Card no. 64).

38 For comparative examples see, for France, H. Lebovics, 'Protection Against Labour Troubles' IRSH, 1986, for the USA T.E. Terrill, *The Tariff, Politics and US Foreign Policy* (Westport, Conn. 1973), pp. 170–90.

39 J. Chamberlain to an unnamed working man, 3 June 1903, cited in Dowding, *Tariff Reform Mirage*, p. 282.

40 Selborne to Milner, 25 May 1903, MP MS Milner Dep. 216, fos 168–9.

41 J. Chamberlain, 1 May 1906, PD, 4th Series, clvi, c. 456.

42 Williams, of course, had already established his reputation as a tariff sympathizer through his books *Made in Germany* (London 1896) and *The Foreigner in the Farmyard* (London 1897). It is also worth noting that in 1903 he became Secretary of the Imperial Tariff Committee, a body set up by Chamberlain in Birmingham to co-ordinate tariff reform activities in the Midlands in particular and to assist more generally with tariff propaganda.

43 E.E. Williams, 'Mr Chaplin's Kite', NR, cc, Oct. 1900, pp. 227–8.

44 Goulding, 19 Mar. 1902, PD, 4th Series, cv, cc. 495–8.

45 See Goulding, 6 May 1904, PD, 4th series, cxxxiv, cc. 669–70.

46 C.J. Follett, 'The Revenue Aspects of Fiscal Reform', NR, cclxxi, Sept. 1905, pp. 145–57.

47 Hewins to Balfour, 13 May 1907, BP, 49779, fos 85–6.

48 The Liberal government had in fact already enacted free school meals legislation in 1906.

49 W.A.S. Hewins, 'The Inelasticity of the Present Revenue', sent to Balfour 13 May 1907, BP, 49779, fos 90–9.

50 For an interpretation of Balfour's position which places emphasis on Hewins' influence see Sykes, *Tariff Reforms*, pp. 129–31.

51 For Balfour's speech see the NUCA Conference Minutes for 1907, CPA, NUA 2/2/3.

52 W. Palmer (London University Conservative Assoc.) to NUCA Conference

1907, ibid. (my emphasis). For similar statements see the speeches by Henry Chaplin, F.E. Smith and Edward Goulding.

53 G. Courthorpe at Little Common, 20 Sept. 1908, *Morning Post*, 22 Sept. 1908, *Morning Post*, 5 July 1909, W.A.S. Hewins at Lincoln, 16 Oct. 1909, cited in Dowding, *Tariff Reform Mirage*, p. 282.

54 Raine was the Secretary of the London Municipal Society, the organization which represented the Conservative cause at local government level in London.

55 G.E. Raine, *Present Day Socialism and the Problem of the Unemployed* (London 1908), p. 2.

56 H.O. Arnold-Forster, English Socialism, p. 113. See also W.A.S. Hewins' paper 'Possibilities of Increasing the Yield of the Income Tax', sent to Balfour, n.d. July (?) 1907, BP, 49779, fos 104–7, in which Hewins noted that if there was an increase in the income tax 'Investments would be diverted from home to foreign. Investments in foreign bearer bonds would be distinctly encouraged'.

57 See for example G. Wyndham to C. Wyndham, 4 Nov. 1911, Mackail and Wyndham, *Life and Letters*, ii, p. 318.

58 G. Wyndham at Cardiff, 18 Nov. 1908, *The Times*, 19 Nov. 1908. See also NUCA Central Committee, Report to NUCA Conference, Cardiff, 19 Nov. 1909, NUCA Conference Minutes, CPA, (Microfilm Card no. 80).

59 F.E. Smith at Huddersfield, 21 Sept. 1909, *The Times*, 22 Sept. 1909.

60 'Tariff Reformer' [L. Amery], *The Times*, 28 Mar. 1908.

61 A. Steel-Maitland to C. (?) Booth, 27 July 1910, SMP, GD 193/148/2/27.

62 NUCA Central Committee, Report to NUCA Conference, Cardiff, 19 Nov. 1909, CPA, NUCA Conference Minutes (Microfilm Card no. 61).

63 Goulding, 6 May 1904, PD, 4th Series, cxxxiv, cc. 669–70.

64 ibid.

65 ibid.

66 ibid.

67 A. Chamberlain at Walsall, 31 Jan. 1907, *The Times*, 1 Feb. 1907.

68 Chamberlain to Balfour, 24 Oct. 1907, BP, 49736, fos 21–32.

69 See for example his speeches at Birmingham, 19 Jan. 1908 and at Hay Mills, 20 Jan. 1908, *The Times*, 20, 21 Jan. 1908.

70 The candidates in question were Clive Morrison-Bell (Mid-Devon), Edward Goulding (Worcester), Percy Clive (South Hereford) and Leo Amery (Wolverhampton). Goulding's commitment to pensions was already well-established; Morrison-Bell's election address declared strong support for pensions and other social reforms, *Western Morning News*, 5 Jan. 1908; For Clive and Amery's position see, respectively, *The Times*, 10 Jan. 1908, and *The Times*, 27, 28, 29 Apr. 1908.

71 R. Meiklejohn to A. Steel-Maitland, 26 Apr. 1907, SMP, GD 193/135/171.

72 Goulding, 16 June 1908, PD, 4th Series, cxc, cc. 744–88.

73 Milner *et al.*, 'Unionism' (my emphasis).

74 H.K. Newton at the NUCA Conference, Manchester, 16 Nov. 1909, NUCA Conference Minutes, CPA, (Microfilm Card no. 62).

75 L. Worthington-Evans at the NUCA Conference, Manchester, 16 Nov. 1909, ibid.

76 In 1908 Conservative spokesmen on pensions, from the Front Bench to the 'Unauthorized Programme', had, with the exception of Edward Goulding, argued in favour of contributory pensions.

77 Unnamed Lancashire Conservative to Lord Derby, 12 Nov. 1910, enclosed with Derby to J.S. Sandars, 13 Nov. 1910, JSSP, MS Eng. Hist. c. 762, fos 34–9.

78 ibid.

79 Milner *et al.*, 'Unionism'.
80 ibid.
81 A. Steel-Maitland, 'Labour' in Malmesbury (ed.), *The New Order*, pp. 358–9.
82 See R. Davidson, *Whitehall and the Labour Problem* (London 1985).
83 Bonar Law, 16 June 1909, PD, 5th Series, vi, c. 1045.
84 ibid.
85 See J. Schmiechen, *Sweated Industries and Sweated Labour: the London Clothing Trades, 1860–1914* (London 1984).
86 See S. Blackburn, 'Ideology and Social Policy: The Origins of the Trade Boards Act', HJ, xxxiv, 1991, pp. 43–64, 53–64. The most prominent Liberal figures in the NASL were Percy Alden, Leo Chiozza Money, Charles Masterman and the NASL Secretary J.J. Mallon.
87 Hills, 21 Feb. 1908, PD, 4th Series, clxxxiv, cc. 1219–20.
88 ibid.
89 Milner *et al.*, 'Unionism'.
90 ibid.
91 A copy of the Bill can be found in the SMP, GD 193/352/7.
92 The Trade Boards Bill was in fact introduced in March.
93 The only Conservative voice raised in opposition was that of the extreme Individualist Sir Frederick Banbury, whose speeches were interrupted by general laughter.
94 See PD, 5th Series, vii, cc. 2443–50.
95 See pp. 246, 286.
96 Parker, *Land for the People*, p. 32.
97 See pp. 219–20.
98 For the views of the National Service League see Summers, 'Militarism'. On this point British militarists were in set with much continental thought. For a similar stress on the military need for a rural population in the German context see the influential text by General F. Von Bernhardi, *Germany and the Next War* (London 1912), which was translated into English and widely circulated amongst British advocates of increased military 'preparedness'.
99 See G.R. Searle, *Eugenics and Politics* (London 1976), pp. 20–5.
100 J. Keir Hardie, *The Unemployed Problem* (London 1904), pp. 4–5, 10.
101 'The New Leaf', *The Outlook*, 2 Jan. 1909.
102 J. St Loe Strachey to Lady Londonderry, 8 Oct. 1907, STRP, S 9/15/3.
103 Garvin, 'Free Trade as a Socialist Policy', p. 51.
104 N[orman] Chamberlain, 'The New Imperialism and the Old Parties', NR, ccciv, June 1908, p. 646.
105 Apart from Lords Hugh and Robert Cecil, St Loe Strachey and A.V. Dicey, the other prominent members of the BCA were the old-style Liberals Arthur Elliot, Harold Cox and sir Robert Perks.
106 Chamberlain at Liverpool, 17 Oct. 1908, in Boyd (ed.), *speeches*, ii, p. 204.
107 L. Amery to B. Kidd, n.d. Nov. (?) 1903, KP, 8069.
108 For the TUTRA see K.D. Brown, 'The Trade Union Tariff Reform Association', *JBS*, ix, 1970, pp. 141–73.
109 B. Holland to A. Lyttelton, 17 Jan. 1906, ALP, CHAN 2/13, E.B. Iwan-Muller, 'Some Thoughts on the Present discontents', n.d. Jan. 1906, BP, 49706, fos 117–59.
110 M. Pugh, 'Popular Conservatism in Britain: Continuity and Change, 1880–1987', *JBS*, xxvii, 1988.
111 W.J. Ashley to Bonar Law, 19 Jan. 1906, BLP, 21/1.
112 Steel-Maitland to Milner, n.d. Oct 1907, SMP, GD 193/135/187.

11 DISINTEGRATION

1 Kidd to Lyttelton, 4 Oct. 1911, ALP, CHAN 2/15, fos 28–9.
2 For an optimistic view of the Conservatives' electoral 'improvement' see Ramsden, *Balfour and Baldwin*, pp. 85–6. Conservative gains at municipal elections could also be seen as a sign of revival, but for the caution necessary when using municipal results see D. Tanner, 'Electoral Statistics and the Rise of the Labour Party, 1906–31', *HJ*, xxxiv, 1991.
3 The sitting Labour MP, George Lansbury, resigned his seat to fight as a 'Women's Suffrage' candidate, behaviour which did not endear him to many of his supporters or local organizers.
4 See Tanner, *Political Change*, pp. 317–50.
5 Steel-Maitland stated in December 1913 that 'there is absolutely no enthusiasm for us', Steel-Maitland to A.C. Glazebrook, 24 Dec. 1913, SMP, GD 193/159/6/9. Robert Sanders noted in February 1914 that 'On the whole the [by-] elections show a turn in our favour, but it cannot be called a great wave', Diary, 24 Feb. 1914, *RSD*, p. 73.
6 Memorandum to the NUCA Executive Committee on the Report of the Speaker's Conference [on electoral reform], n.d. 1916, SMP, GD 193/202/11x.
7 For an overview of the House of Lords' importance see Adonis, *Making Aristocracy Work, passim*.
8 'House of Lords Reform and the Constitution', unsigned memorandum, almost certainly written by Selborne, n.d. May (?) 1910, SELP, MS Selborne 74, fos 34–5.
9 ibid.
10 Steel-Maitland to Northcliffe, 18 Feb. 1911, SMP, GD 193/151/4/88x, Steel-Maitland to J.W. Martin, 12 July 1911, ibid., GD 193/154/4/67. See also the views of Lord Balcarres that 'It is Radical policy, not Conservative organisation which produced the debacle. An inferior organisation will secure victory for a popular policy – but no organisation, however excellent, can combat a popular policy', Balcarres, Diary, 11 May 1911, CP, p. 183.
11 See in particular G.D. Phillips, *The Diehards* (Cambridge, Mass. 1979).
12 See Balcarres, Diary, 21 July 1911, CP, p. 196.
13 For the full details of the discussions and draft proposals see SELP, MS Selborne 75.
14 G. Wyndham to Lord Willoughby de Broke, 15 Aug. 1911, WDBP, WB 3/40.
15 N. Chamberlain to A. Chamberlain, 7 Oct. 1911, ACP, AC 9/3/4 (my emphasis). The only Diehards who were out of step on the need for a positive policy were Lords Hugh and Robert Cecil.
16 See Thompson, *Landed Society*, pp. 314–25, D. Spring, 'Land and Politics', Adonis, *Making Aristocracy Work*, pp. 240–73, Cannadine, *British Aristocracy*, pp. 35–70.
17 See Balcarres, Diary, 9, 20 Sept. 1909, CP, pp. 132, 134, and also Adonis, *Making Aristocracy Work*, pp. 144–57.
18 See pp. 88–94.
19 See Cannadine, *British Aristocracy*, pp. 88–138.
20 Portsmouth to Law, 29 Jan. 1912, BLP, 26/1/68.
21 Cannadine, *British Aristocracy*, pp. 429–43.
22 ibid., Thompson, *Landed Society*, pp. 321–4.
23 For a good example of Diehard opinion on this subject see Amery, *My Political Life*, i, p. 381.
24 Balcarres, Notes, 1 Aug. 1911, CP, pp. 208–9.
25 Northumberland to Halsbury, 30 Mar. 1917, HP, 56375.

26 Selborne to Lady Selborne, 9 Aug. 1911, SELP, MS Selborne 102, fos 23–4.
27 Balcarres to Lady Wantage, 13 Aug. 1911, CP, p. 217.
28 ibid.
29 Balcarres, Diary, 16 Aug. 1911, ibid., p. 219.
30 J.P. Hughes, 'A Note on the General Election', n.d. Nov. 1909, marked 'STRICTLY CONFIDENTIAL', issued by J.S. Sandars, GP, MS Gwynne, Box 27.
31 ibid.
32 See in particular Sykes, *Tariff Reform*, pp. 258–84, Dutton, *Loyal Opposition*, pp. 181–202.
33 See pp. 203–4, and also R. Jebb, *The Imperial Conference* (London 1911).
34 Steel–Maitland to Northcliffe, 7 Feb. 1911, SMP, GD193/151/4/1–2x.
35 Caillard to Hewins, 24 Sept. 1911, TCP, TC6/1/1. See also H. Page-Croft, *The Path of Empire* (London 1912), pp. 1–2 for further celebration of this event.
36 F.S. Oliver to Milner, 17 Dec. 1912, MP, MS Milner Dep. 13, fo. 15.
37 Winterton to Maxse, 18 Aug. 1910, LJMP, 460 R 353.
38 'The New Campaign', *The Outlook*, 9 Apr. 1910, Balfour to Derby, 6 Oct. 1910, BP, 49743, fos 17–18.
39 See Sykes, *Tariff Reform*, pp. 267–71.
40 See ibid., and Dutton, *Loyal Opposition*,pp. 182–92.
41 E.E. Marsden (editor of *The Textile Mercury*) to Sandars, n.d. Nov. 1910, in A.M. Gollin, *The Observer and J.L. Garvin*, (London 1960), p. 260.
42 Maxse to Goulding, 10 Dec. 1910, WARP, WAR 2.
43 Hewins to Chamberlain, 14 Dec. 1910, ACP, AC 8/7/23.
44 Hewins to Balfour, 11 Dec. 1910, BP, 49779, fos 253–5.
45 Chamberlain to Lansdowne, 18 Dec. 1910, ACP, AC 8/7/6.
46 Lawrence to Balfour, 5 Dec. 1910, BP, 49791, fos 271–2.
47 Some prominent Radical Conservatives – Selborne, J.L. Garvin and F.E. Smith – supported the referendum, which muddied the waters on this issue. However, they saw the referendum not as a means of postponing the food taxes but as a means of confirming popular support for the full programme, see Selborne to Lady Selborne, 16 Dec. 1910, SELP, MS Selborne 101, fos 235–6.
48 Law to Sandars, 29 Nov. 1910, BP, 49693, fos 6–8.
49 Wolmer to Chamberlain, 1 Nov. 1910, ACP, AC 9/3/64.
50 Wolmer to Steel–Maitland, 30 July 1910, SMP, GD193/149/8/64.
51 See P.F. Clarke, 'The End of Laissez Faire and the Politics of Cotton', *HJ*, xv, 1972.
52 Derby to Sandars, 15 Dec. 1910, BP, 49743, fo. 19.
53 Derby to Long, WLP, 62405.
54 Derby to Gwynne, 19 Dec. 1912, HAGP, MS Gwynne, Box 22.
55 Salisbury to Chamberlain, 12 Feb. 1910, ACP, AC 8/5/10.
56 Sanders, Diary, 8 Dec. 1912, RSD, p. 53.
57 Long to Law, n.d. Sept. (?) 1912, BLP, 26/1/76.
58 Fitzroy, *Memoirs*, ii, p. 501.
59 Derby to Balfour, 22 Dec. 1912, BP, 49473, fo. 36.
60 See Balcarres, Diary 7 Jan. 1913, CP, p. 298, and see also Derby to Gwynne, 31 Dec. 1912, HAGP, MS Gwynne Box 22.
61 Balcarres, Diary, 3 Jan. 1913, 6 Jan. 1913, CP, pp. 296–7.
62 ibid., p. 298.
63 Gwynne to Amery, 7 Jan. 1913, in Dutton, *Loyal Opposition*, p. 191.
64 The front bench (27 MPs) were not asked to sign. For these figures see Balcarres, Diary, 10 Jan. 1913, CP, p. 302.

65 ibid.
66 Sandars to Gwynne, 15 Jan. 1913, HAGP, MS Gwynne, Box 15.
67 Balcarres, Diary, 8 Jan. 1913, CP, pp. 300–1.
68 Gwynne to Cecil, 21 Apr. 1913, HAGP, MS Gwynne, Box 17. See also T.G. Bowles to Law, 2 Aug. 1913 – Bowles, a free trader, referred specifically to the 'Edinburgh compromise' and compained that tariff reformers were not sticking to it, BLP 30/1/4.
69 Stamfordham to Sandars, 27 Jan. 1913, JSSP, MS Eng. Hist. c. 765, fos 84–5. In May 1912 Law had told Salisbury that the food taxes were essential to the maintenance of party unity, Law to Salisbury 3 May 1912, BLP 33/4/34.
70 Bridgeman, Diary, 30 Dec. 1912, in Williamson (ed.), *Modernization*, pp. 65–6.
71 J.S. Sandars to Balfour, 23 Mar. 1913, BP, 49768, fos 42–5. This letter, marked 'Private, Destroy' contains a detailed account of the row provoked by events in Kendal.
72 ibid.
73 ibid. Robert Sanders noted 'our tariff reformers are furious', Sanders, Diary, 16 Mar. 1913, RSD, p. 62.
74 The TRL called upon Law to confirm tariff reform as the 'first constructive policy of the party', see Lord Duncannon to Law, 11 Nov. 1913, BLP, 30/4/25. Nine Conservative MPs, all signatories of the January Memorial, were listed as supporting this call. The NUCA conference, somewhat ambiguously, passed motions in support of Law's position, but at the same time confirmed its commitment to imperial preference.
75 See pp. 187–92.
76 Chamberlain to Balfour, 9 Mar. 1910, BP, 49736, fos 69–82.
77 ibid.
78 See *The Times*, 6 Oct. 1910.
79 Acland-Hood to Sandars, 6 Nov. 1910, JSSP, MS Eng. Hist. c. 762, fos 6–11.
80 Amery to Chamberlain, 27 Dec. 1912, 5 Jan. 1913, ACP, AC10/3/1, 9/5/9.
81 C.A. Vince to Amery, 4 Jan. 1913, BLP, 28/2/32.
82 Crawford, Diary, 19 Jan. 1913, CP, pp. 304–6.
83 Bathurst to Law, 12 Jan. 1913, and C.S. Parker to Law, 16 Jan. 1913, BLP, 28/2/55, 28/2/65.
84 H.W. Palmer to Law, 16 Jan. 1913, BLP, 28/2/66.
85 C. Turnor to J. Baird, 28 Sept. 1913, BLP, 30/2/32.
86 B. Gilbert to G. Lloyd, 2 Dec. 1913, GLP, GLLD 16/15.
87 A. Weigall to Law, 17 Jan. 1914, BLP, 31/2/47.
88 For this interpretation see Fforde, *Conservatism and Collectivism*, pp. 144–5.
89 A. Bannister to Law, 10 Jan. 1913, BLP, 28/2/45.
90 C. Wing-Gray at a meeting of Essex Farmers and Employers, 14 Apr. 1913, *East Anglian Daily Times*, 15 Apr. 1913, enclosed with Chamberlain to J. Farrow and the Essex Farmers Association, n.d. Apr. 1913, ACP, AC9/5/20.
91 Steel-Maitland, Memorandum on the Land Question, n.d. Nov. (?) 1913, SMP, GD193/119/5/139–43.
92 Steel-Maitland to Law, 28 Oct. 1913, BLP, 30/3/62 (my emphasis).
93 TC Memorandum MM53, Second Report of the Agricultural Committee, 22 June 1914, TCP, TC1/8/3.
94 For this suggestion see, for example, H. Page-Croft to Law, 8 Nov. 1913, R. Hunt to Law, 26 Mar. 1914, BLP, 30/4/17, 32/1/68.
95 See Page-Croft to Law, 11 Nov. 1913, BLP, 30/4/26.
96 Bathurst to Law, 12 Jan. 1913, A. Colefax to Law, 15 Jan. 1913, BLP, 28/2/55, 28/2/62.
97 See TC Agricultural Committee, Minutes, 22 Apr. 1913, Draft Memorandum

on Agricultural Rates, TCP2/2/2. The Tariff Commission called for agricultural land to be taxed on only one quarter of its rateable value, with an estimated cost to the Exchequer of £1.9 million, see 'The Budget and Agriculture', TC Memorandum, MM52, 15 May 1914. For the Land Policy Committee's position see 'Report of the Committee Appointed to Consider the Land Policy of the Unionist Party', n.d. Aug. 1913, MP, MS Milner Dep. 40, fos 91–183.

98 Law at NUCA Conference, 13 Nov. 1913, NUCA Conference Minutes, CPA, NUA 2/2/4.

99 S. Hole to Chamberlain, 24 Mar. 1913, ACP, AC9/5/37.

100 F. Leverton Harris to Chamberlain, 4 Jan. 1913, ACP, AC9/5/33.

101 A. Colefax to Chamberlain, 14 Jan. 1913, ACP, AC9/5/14 (my emphasis).

102 For this view see Fforde, *Conservatism and Collectivism*, p. 144.

103 H.W. Palmer to Law, 12 Jan. 1914, BLP, 31/2/32.

104 See Fforde, *Conservatism and Collectivism*, p. 144. Fforde's reference to this episode in 1914 partially contradicts his view that the Conservative leadership was not concerned about hostile farming opinion after October 1913.

105 Long to Law, 6 May 1914, BLP, 32/3/13–16.

106 Garvin to J.S. Sandars, 29 Jan. 1910, JSSP, MS Eng. Hist. c. 760, fos 29–30.

107 Steel-Maitland to Northcliffe, 7 Feb. 1911, H. Richardson to Steel-Maitland, 26 Apr. 1911, SMP, GD193/151/4/1–2x, GD193/151/6/21 (original emphasis).

108 S. Rosenbaum to Steel-Maitland, 23 Oct. 1910, SMP, GD193/149/4/28.

109 For the Minutes of this meeting see SMP, GD193/108/1/159.

110 ibid.

111 These quotations are taken from the published report of the USRC's industrial unrest sub-committee, J.W. Hills, W.J. Ashley and M. Woods, *Industrial Unrest* (London 1914), vi.

112 F.E. Smith, *Unionist Policy*, p. 310.

113 For the details of the USRC's work see J. Ridley, 'The Unionist Social Reform Committee, 1911–14: Wets Before the Deluge', *HJ*, xxx, 1987.

114 For the full details of this proposal see Ridley, 'Social Reform', pp. 402–3.

115 For this proposal see E.A. Goulding in Parliament, 4 Apr. 1911, *The Times*, 5 Apr. 1911.

116 This Bill proposed compulsory Sunday closing and one half-day closing per week for all shops. The USRC was aware of its popularity with shopworkers – see, for example, Birmingham and District Boot Trades Association to Steel-Maitland, 30 Oct. 1911, and L. Blakemore (Secretary of the National Amalgamated Union of Shop Assistants, Watchmen and Clerks) to Steel-Maitland, 12 Nov. 1911, SMP, GD193/153/2/208, GD193/154/5/25.

117 Steel-Maitland in Parliament, 26 Apr. 1911, *The Times*, 27 Apr. 1911.

118 For this proposal see R. Cooper, 13 May 1914, *PD*, 4th Series, ccxlii, cc. 1134–7.

119 Ridley, 'Social Reform', p. 391.

120 ibid., pp. 400–1.

121 For example Sir Robert Morant, the Civil Servant who had played such an important part in shaping the 1902 Education Act, offered advice on health and education policy, whilst members of the Royal College of Surgeons and the British Medical Association were also used as advisors.

122 See pp. 242–66.

123 See pp. 242–3, 247–8.

124 See Ridley, 'Social Reform', pp. 405–6.

125 See pp. 248–53.

126 Steel-Maitland, Memorandum on 'Suggested Policy', n.d. June (?) 1912, SMP,

GD193/80/5/43–9. In the same document Steel-Maitland argued that 'it is imperative that candidates be made to toe the line on the food taxes, while they are part of the Party programme', and stated that the party should develop a land policy and then 'tack it on to our Tariff policy'.

127 P. Lloyd-Greame, Memorandum 'Upon the Necessity, the Method and the Limits of Social Reform Considered as a Part of Unionist Policy', n.d. Aug (?) 1912, SMP, GD193/80/5/50.

128 Williamson (ed.), *Bridgeman Diary*, p. 40.

129 Chamberlain in Parliament, 4 May 1911, *The Times*, 5 May 1911.

130 Sanders, Diary, 6 Dec. 1911, RSD, p. 37.

131 See J.M. Mckillop to Steel-Maitland, 26 Apr. 1911, SMP, GD193/152/3/28. The men contacted included Sir Thomas Wrightson, a coalowner, chairman of an engineering company and previously Conservative MP for Stockton (1892–5) and St Pancras (1899–1906), and Dudley Docker, chairman of the Metropolitan Carriage company (Britain's largest single employer in 1911), and a leading figure in Midlands Conservatism.

132 South Staffs. Ironmasters Assoc. to Steel-Maitland, 19 June 1911, Birmingham Chamber of Commerce to Steel-Maitland, 26 Aug. 1911, SMP, GD193/152/1/36, GD193/155/5/67. For further indications of business concern over NI see Hay, 'Employers and Social Policy'.

133 See, for example, J.E. Durant *et al.* to Steel-Maitland, 19–25 May, 1911, SMP, GD193/151/1/99–111. There was also a petition against the NI Bill by pharmacists in East Birmingham, concerned that they would lose their income from providing medicines to the Poor Law authorities, J. Laing to Steel-Maitland, 14 June 1911, SMP, GD193/151/1/119–20.

134 See Williamson (ed.), *Bridgeman Diary*, p. 40.

135 See B.J. Williams (Railway Clerks Assoc.) to Steel-Maitland, n.d. May 1911, SMP GD193/151/1/115.

136 Hewins to NUCA Conference, Leeds, 16 Nov. 1911, NUCA Conference Minutes, CPA.

137 NUCA Council, 'Report' to NUCA Conference, 14 Nov. 1912, NUCA Conference Minutes, ibid.

138 ibid. The Conservatives gave no details of their 'alternative' proposals for financing NI.

139 See NUCA Council, 'Report' to the NUCA Conference, 16 Nov. 1911, NUCA Conference Minutes, 1911, CPA.

140 The fullest examination of the Land Campaign is to be found in I. Packer, 'Liberalism and the Land Campaign', unpublished Oxford University D.Phil thesis (forthcoming).

141 St Audries to Law, 21 Aug. 1912 (?), BLP, 27/1/48.

142 C.H. Simpson (Sec. E. Dorset Conservative and Unionist Assoc.) to J. Boraston, 21 Jan. 1914, E. Hely (Central Office Agent for Gloucs., Wilts., Mons., Hants., Isle of Wight and Dorset) to J. Boraston, 12 Jan. 1914, SMP, GD193/119/5/59–60.

143 Bathurst to Law, 4 Dec. 1913, BLP, 31/1/6, Steel-Maitland to Salisbury, 20 Jan. 1914, SMP, GD193/119/5/61–2.

144 Steel-Maitland, Memorandum, 6 Apr. 1914, SMP, GD193/119/5/1.

145 Here Green emphasized the work of his own organization, the Rural League, in the campaigns, Green to Milner, 1 July 1910, MP, MS Milner Dep. 36, fo. 213. Sir Gilbert Parker, *The Times*, 24 Jan. 1910.

146 Collings to Law, 17 May 1912, BLP, 26/3/28.

147 Malmesbury to Law, 1 July 1912, BLP, 26/5/1.

148 Green to Malmesbury, 29 June 1912, BLP, 26/5/1.

149 A summary of the origins and activities of these initiatives can be found in Fforde, *Conservatism and Collectivism*, pp. 126–59. The Land Policy Committee was chaired by Lord Salisbury, with the other members being Milner, Stanier, Turnor, and the MPs Lord Alexander Thynne, Sir Mark Sykes, Sir John Spear, E.A. Fitzroy, G.L. Courthope, J.F. Hope, E.G. Pretyman, F.B. Mildmay, C. Bathurst, A. Weigall and J.W. Hills. See Salisbury *et al.*, 'Report of the Committee Appointed to Consider the Land Policy of the Unionist Party', n.d. Aug. 1913, MP, MS Milner Dep. 40, fos 91–183.

150 Milner, 'Agricultural Memorandum'.

151 Long to Law, 1 Aug. 1912, BLP, 27/1/17.

152 See for example St Audries (Acland-Hood) to Law, 21 Aug. 1912, BLP, 27/1/48, Lansdowne to A. Chamberlain, 18 Apr. 1913, ACP, AC9/5/45.

153 B. Peto *et al.*, 'Memorandum on Land Policy', n.d. July (?) 1912, enclosed with W. Long to Law, 1 Aug. 1912, BLP, 27/1/17.

154 *Unionist Agricultural Policy*, pp. 11–13.

155 Long to Law, 31 Oct. 1913, BLP, 30/3/77.

156 Thynne, the heir to the Marquis of Bath, was a member of the USRC Land Committee, but had distanced himself from the proposal for wages boards.

157 Thynne, 'Memorandum [on agricultural wages]', n.d. Aug. 1913, enclosed with E. Talbot to Law, 29 Aug. 1913, BLP, 30/1/31.

158 See Lansdowne to Law, 4 Sept. 1913, BLP, 30/2/7.

159 Salisbury *et al.* to Law, n.d.

160 This was the strategy advocated by E.G. Pretyman, the President of the Land Union, who told Law that as opinion in the party was divided between constructive and quietist groups, and as neither side would hold back, an enquiry was the only way of keeping the lid on the argument, Pretyman to Law, 29 Oct. 1913, BLP, 30/3/66.

161 Long at Bristol, 25 Nov. 1913, *The Times*, 26 Nov. 1913.

162 J.W. Hills to Law, 29 Nov. 1913, BLP, 30/4/60.

163 See for example H. Trustram Eve to Steel-Maitland, 2 Nov. 1913, SMP, GD193/119/5/83–8, C. Bathurst to Law, 4 Dec. 1913, BLP, 31/1/16, anon. to Steel-Maitland, 6 Dec. 1913, and C.H. Simpson (Sec. E. Dorset Conservative and Unionist Assoc.) to J. Boraston, 21 Jan. 1914, SMP, GD193/119/5/77, GD193/119/5/59.

164 Sandars' views are reported in Steel-Maitland to Lansdowne, 22 Jan. 1914, SMP, GD193/119/5/54–6.

165 Salisbury, 'Memorandum on the Agricultural Labourers' Wages Question' to Steel-Maitland, 20 Jan. 1914, SMP, GD193/119/5/34–46.

166 Steel-Maitland, 'Notes on Lord Salisbury's Memorandum', 17 Feb. 1914, SMP, GD/193/119/5/15.

167 The book in question was G.E. Raine, *Lloyd George and the Land* (London 1914).

168 See for example Salisbury to Steel-Maitland, 10 Feb. 1914, and J.M. Fraser to Steel-Maitland, 6 Feb. 1910, SMP, GD193/119/5/47, 49.

169 E. Hely to Steel-Maitland, 12 Jan. 1914, SMP, GD193/119/5/60, *Morning Post*, 24 Feb. 1914.

170 For an example of the continuing debate see Long 'Memorandum on the Wages Question' to Law, 6 May 1914, BLP, 32/3/13–16.

171 This comment is noted in Sanders, Diary, 13 Nov. 1913, RSD, pp. 66–7.

172 Law to Chamberlain, 1 Oct. 1910, BLP, 18/8/12.

173 ibid.

174 Selborne to Chamberlain, 15 Sept. 1910, ACP, AC8/6/8, Gwynne to Chamberlain, 30 Sept. 1910, HAGP, MS Gwynne Box 17.

175 Gwynne to Chamberlain, 30 Sept. 1910, ibid.

176 See A. Chamberlain to Law, 29 Sept. 1910, BLP, 18/6/125.

177 Leo Maxse, for example, denounced payment of members, see Maxse to Law, 29 Sept. 1910, BLP, 18/6/124.

178 R.T. Moore to Law, 9 Mar. 1912, BLP, 25/3/20. Law's correspondence files on the labour unrest are filled with similar assertions.

179 See for example Selborne to Law, 14 Mar. 1914, Tullibardine to Law, 19 Mar. 1912, BLP, 25/3/31, 25/3/47.

180 See E. Bristow, 'Profit Sharing and Labour Unrest' in Brown (ed.), *Anti-Labour History*.

181 USRC, *Industrial Unrest*, pp. 7–20.

182 See for example A. Lupton (Engineer and Surveyor) to Law, 19 Mar. 1912, BLP, 25/3/48.

183 See F.W. Wybrew (Secretary of the National Conservative Labour Party) to Law, 9 Mar. 1912, BLP, 25/3/17.

184 J. Gardiner (Chairman and owner of a Glasgow shipping and iron company) to Law, 7 Mar. 1912, W.H. Raeburn (shipowner) to Law, 25 Mar. 1912, BLP, 25/3/13, 26/1/58.

185 See Blake, *Conservative Party*, pp. 194–5 and idem, *Unknown Prime Minister*, pp. 149–201, Ramsden, *Balfour and Baldwin*, pp. 77–86, Sykes, *Tariff Reform*, pp. 258–72.

186 Garvin to Sandars, 27 Jan. 1910, BP, 49795, fos 44–57.

187 Even Conservative politicians who were pessimistic about Ireland conceded that in principle 'the Irish would probably vote for Tariff Reform', Steel-Maitland to C.A. Gregg, 9 Mar. 1910, SMP, GD 193/147/7/14.

188 Sandars to Chamberlain, 18 Feb. 1910, ACP, AC 9/3/53.

189 Wyndham at Limerick, 10 Oct. 1912, *The Times*, 11 Oct. 1912.

190 Amery to Law, 17 Jan. 1912, BLP, 25/1/33. For further details of Amery's position see his *The Case Against Home Rule* (London 1912), esp. pp. 1–45.

191 For Hewins' views see his *Tariff Reform and Home Rule* (London 1912). For Milner's position see below.

192 Amery to Chamberlain, 27 Dec. 1912, ACP, AC 10/3/1.

193 ibid.

194 Chamberlain to Strachey, 26 Dec. 1913, STRP, S 4/5/3.

195 See in particular J. Kendle, *The Round Table Movement* (Toronto 1968) and idem, 'The Round Table Movement and "Home Rule All Round" ', *HJ*, xi, 1968.

196 Milner, 'Notes'.

197 ibid.

198 For example Winston Churchill flirted with the 'federalist solution'. See P. Addison, *Churchill and the Home Front*, (London 1992), pp. 171–2.

199 Although he championed Ulster's cause Carson was a Southern Unionist and not an Ulsterman.

200 Lansdowne to Law, quoting a letter from Carson, 26 Sept. 1913, BLP, 30/2/27.

201 See P. Jalland, *The Liberals and Ireland* (Brighton 1980), pp. 158–75, 194–210.

202 In fact recent research suggests that Redmond had, *sotto voce*, acknowledged that exclusion was almost inevitable.

203 Lansdowne to Law, 26 Sept. 1913, BLP, 30/2/27.

204 The most thorough examination of these developments is A. Jackson, *The Ulster Party* (Oxford 1989): this interpretation of Ulster politics is based on his analysis.

205 Midleton to Law, 11 Oct. 1913, BLP, 30/3/20. See also Lord Ashtoun to Law, 1 Dec. 1913, complaining that Law's speech in Dublin in late November had given no comfort to Unionists in the South and West of Ireland, BLP, 31/1/1.

206 Midleton to Law, 13 Apr. 1914, BLP, 32/2/31.
207 Midleton to Law, 14 May 1914, ibid., 32/3/28.
208 Lansdowne to Law, 10 Oct. 1913, ibid., 30/3/16.
209 Comyn-Platt had been Conservative candidate for Louth in 1906, but, more significantly, he was also the secretary of the Confederacy and a Diehard.
210 Comyn-Platt to Selborne, n.d. Sept. 1912, SELP, MS Selborne 77, fos 14–17.
211 Long, a candidate for the Conservative leadership in 1911, had been Balfour's Irish Secretary in 1905–6, was MP for Dublin in 1906–10, and had family connections with the Southern Irish gentry.
212 See Long to Law, 4 June 1912, BLP, 26/4/7.
213 See R. Murphy, 'Faction in the Conservative Party and the Home Rule Crisis, 1912–14', History, lxxi, 1986.
214 ibid., pp. 226–8.
215 Long to Law, 20 Nov. 1913, WLP, BL, Add. MSS, 62416.
216 Balfour, Memorandum on Ireland, sent to Lansdowne 12 June 1914, BLP, 32/4/17.
217 For the importance of this distinction see below.
218 Amery to Law, 13 May 1914, BLP, 32/3/25.
219 Selborne to A. Chamberlain, 12 Aug. 1914, SELP, MS Selborne 77, fo. 184 (my emphasis).
220 Crawford, Diary, 17 July 1914, CP, p. 339.
221 Gwynne to Law, 20 July 1914, BLP, 33/1/39.
222 ibid.
223 Steel-Maitland, notes on 'Suggested Policy', n.d. May (?) 1912, SMP, GD193/80/5/43–9.
224 Long to Law, n.d. Sept. (?) 1912, BLP, 26/1/76.
225 N. Chamberlain to Law, 6 Sept. 1913, and 14 Nov. 1913, ibid., 30/2/9, 30/4/34.
226 Conservative MP for Fulham, one-time Parliamentary Whip and a London County Council Alderman.
227 Hayes Fisher to Lansdowne, 16 Dec. 1913, WLP, 947/441.
228 For the bad relations between Austen Chamberlain and Walter Long see A. Chamberlain, Politics From Inside (London 1936), pp. 345, 383–5.
229 Balcarres, Diary, 12 Nov. 1911, 8 July 1912 CP, pp. 249, 277.
230 The report of this conversation between Law and Edmund Talbot is in J.S. Sandars to Balfour, 23 Mar. 1913, BP, 49768, fos 42–5.
231 Steel-Maitland to A.C. Glazebrook, 24 Dec. 1913, SMP, GD193/159/6/9.
232 H.C. Gibbs (City Conservative Assoc.) to Law, 28 Mar. 1912, BLP, 26/1/70.
233 Steel-Maitland to A.C. Glazebrook, 24 Dec. 1913, SMP, GD193/159/6/9, the views of Edmund Talbot, the new chief whip, are recorded in Crawford, Diary, 13 Oct. 1913, CP, p. 318.

CONCLUSION

1 Even Lord Selborne, who was married to Balfour's cousin, was one of his strongest critics.
2 See Ramsden, Balfour and Baldwin, pp. 10–15, 29–30 and A.M. Gollin, Balfour's Burden (London 1965), pp. 256–85, R. Rempel, Unionists Divided (Newton Abbot 1972), pp. 115–33.
3 Quoted in Ramsden, Balfour and Baldwin, p. 91.
4 Maxse to E.B. Iwan-Muller, 13 Jan. 1906, Iwan-Muller papers, BL, Add MSS, 52914.
5 Lord Hugh Cecil to Lord Robert Cecil, 10 Jan. 1915, COCP, 51157.

6 F.E. Smith, *Unionist Policy and Other Essays* (London 1913), p. 5.

7 R. Kirk, 'Preface' to idem (ed.), *A Conservative Reader* (Harmondsworth 1982), xiv.

8 J. Buchan, 'Preface' to A. Bryant, *The Spirit of Conservatism* (London 1929), vii.

9 I. Gilmour, *Inside Right* (London 1980 edition), p. 121.

10 Ramsden, *Balfour and Baldwin*, ix.

11 'Conservatism' in *The Fontana Dictionary of Modern Thought* (London 1980 edition).

12 See in particular W.H. Greenleaf, *The British Political Tradition* (3 vols London 1984–8), ii, *The Ideological Heritage*, N. O'Sullivan, *Conservatism* (London 1976), A. Quinton, *The Politics of Imperfection* (London 1978), P. Norton and A. Aughey, *Conservatives and Conservatism* (London 1981), R. Eccleshall, *English Conservatism Since the Restoration* (London 1990). Other earlier studies include the fascinating work of Karl Mannheim, *Conservatism* (London 1983 edition) and S.P. Huntington, 'Conservatism as an Ideology', *American Political Science Review*, li, 1957.

13 See in particular Coetzee, *Party or Country*, Fforde, *Conservatism and Collectivism*.

14 T. Honderich, *Conservatism* (London 1990), p. 38.

15 See Quinton, *Imperfection*. The detailed reasons for preferring Quinton's definitional framework are explained in E.H.H. Green, 'The Strange Death of Tory England', *TCBH*, 2, 1991.

16 Quinton, *Imperfection*, p. 16.

17 ibid.

18 ibid., p. 17.

19 For a study of Edwardian Conservatism which effectively takes this position see Fforde, *Conservatism and Collectivism*.

20 See in particular Greenleaf, *Ideological Heritage*, pp. 189–308 and R. Eccleshall, *English Conservatism Since the Restoration* (London 1990).

21 Eccleshall, *English Conservatism*, pp. 39–44, 79–86, and D. Willetts, *Modern Conservatism* (Harmondsworth 1992), pp. 7–10.

22 On Smith see, for example, M. Ignatieff and I. Hont (eds), *Wealth and Virtue* (Cambridge 1982), and on Burke see J.G.A. Pocock, 'The Political Economy of Burke's *Reflections on the Revolution in France*', *HJ*, xxv, 1982.

23 B. Hilton, 'Peel: a Reappraisal', *HJ*, xxii, 1979.

24 In this classic defence of Individualism, *The Man Versus the State*, the guru of the LPDL, and of many other libertarians then and since, Herbert Spencer, referred to Socialism as 'the New Toryism' on the grounds that Conservatism had always been sympathetic to State intervention.

25 See Taylor, *Men Versus the State*.

26 In his famous 'Introduction' to the 1914 edition of his *Law and Public Opinion*, Dicey placed the onset of the 'age of Collectivism' in the late nineteenth century, that is in a period when Salisbury was Prime Minister for the greater part of the time.

27 Offer, *First World War*, pp. 81–92.

28 Pollard, *Prime and Decline*, pp. 107–10, and also P. Cain and A.G. Hopkins, *British Imperialism, 1688–1970* (2 vols London 1993), i, pp. 161–98.

29 E. Halevy, *Imperialism and the Rise of Labour* (London 1961 edition), pp. 335–44.

30 I use this term in its contemporary (i.e. very loose) sense as a short-hand for large-scale enfranchisement. As far as I am aware there were no countries which before 1914 conformed to the modern model of 'one person, one vote'.

31 See Smith, *Nazi Imperialism*, pp. 32–6, H.U. Wehler, 'Bismarck's Imperialism', *P and P*, 1969.

32 See H. Lebovics, *The Alliance of Iron and Wheat in the Third French Republic* (Baton Rouge 1988), pp. 143–57.
33 For the importance of 'the Other' to the language of imperialism see for example B. Anderson, *Imagined Communities* (London 1987), *passim*.
34 For the most comprehensive analysis of Boulangism see W. Irvine, *The Boulanger Affair Reconsidered* (Oxford 1989).
35 See S. Wilson, 'The Anti-Semitic Riots of 1898 in France', *HJ*, xvi, 1973, idem, 'Catholic Populism in France at the Time of the Dreyfus Affair', *JCH*, x, 1975, M. Larkin, 'La République en Danger? The Pretenders, the Army and Déroulède, 1898–99', *EHR*, c, 1985.
36 See G. Eley, *Reshaping the German Right* (New Haven 1980).
37 See G. Eley, 'Defending Social Imperialism: Use and Abuse of an Idea', *SH*, 1976.
38 See Smith, *Nazi Imperialism*, esp. pp. 21–50.
39 See for example Eley, *Reshaping, passim*, and L. Abrams and D.J. Miller, 'Who Were the French Colonialists? A Reassessment of the Parti Colonial, 1890–1914', *HJ*, xix, 1976.
40 D.K. Fieldhouse, *Economics and Empire* (London 1984 edition), pp. 19–34, G.N. Sanderson, 'The European Partition of Africa', *JICH*, 1975, H.A. Turner, 'Bismarck's Imperial Venture: Anti-British in Origin?' in P. Gifford and W.R. Louis (eds), *Britain and Germany in Africa* (London 1967).
41 Lebovics, *Alliance*, pp. 152–3.
42 The classic study is E. Kehr, *Battleship Building and Party Politics in Germany 1894–1901* (Chicago 1975 edition).
43 *Travail National*, 27 Mar. 1892, in Lebovics, *Alliance*, p. 149.
44 *Travail National*, 6 July 1884, J. Méline, *Journal Officiel*, Chambre des Députés, 12 May 1891, in H. Lebovics, 'Protection Against Labour Troubles', *IRSH*, xxxi, 1986.
45 ibid.
46 In Germany the 'protection of national labour' argument was less in evidence, in part because unemployment and labour unrest, save for the Ruhr coal strike of 1905, were not a significant problem. for the US position see Terrill, *The Tariff*, esp. pp. 160–200, E.P. Crapol, *America for Americans* (Westport, Conn. 1973), pp. 170–90.
47 For an overview of welfare developments see P. Baldwin, *The Politics of Social Solidarity* (Cambridge 1990). For Germany see G.A. Ritter, *Social Welfare in Germany and Britain* (Leamington Spa 1986) and for France see J.F. Stone, *The Search for Social Peace* (Albany, NY 1983).
48 See Eley, *German Right, passim*.
49 See J. Retallack, *Notables of the Right* (London 1988), esp. pp. 100–15, D. Blackbourn, 'Peasants and Politics in Germany, 1871–1914', in idem, *Populists and Patricians* (London 1987).
50 My analysis of the Boulanger affair is based largely on Irvine, *Boulanger* and M. Burns, *Rural Society and French Politics* (Princeton, NJ 1984).
51 Lebovics, *Alliance*, pp. 186–9.
52 K. Barkin, *The Conflict Over German Industrialization, 1890–1902* (Chicago 1970), pp. 41–93.
53 ibid., pp. 211–73.
54 Smith, *Nazi Imperialism*, pp. 20–41.
55 C. Andrew and A. Kanya-Forstner, 'French Business and the French Colonists', *HJ*, xix, 1976.
56 Retallack, *Notables, passim*.
57 R.M. Berdahl, 'Conservative Politics and Aristocratic Landowners in Bismarckian Germany', *JMH*, xliv, 1972.

58 J.J. Sheehan, *German Liberalism in the Nineteenth Century* (London 1982 edition), pp. 184–270, D.S. White, *The Splintered Party* (Cambridge, Mass. 1976).
59 Eley, *German Right*, pp. 293–334.
60 Lebovics, *Alliance*, p. 9.
61 A. Mayer, *The Persistence of the Old Regime* (London 1981).
62 J.A. Hutcheson, *Leopold Maxse and the National Review* (New York, 1989), G.R. Searle, 'Critics of Edwardian Society: The Case of the Radical Right' in O'Day (ed.), *Edwardian Age* and idem, 'The Revolt from the Right in Edwardian Britain', in Kennedy and Nicholls (eds), *Nationalist Movements*.
63 R. Hofstadter, *The Paranoid Style in American Politics* (Columbia 1965).
64 See G.R. Searle, *Corruption in British Politics, 1890–1935* (Oxford 1989).
65 Obituary of W.C. Bridgeman, *The Times*, quoted in Williamson (ed.), *Bridgeman Diary*, p. 1.
66 Bridgeman to Balfour, 2 Aug. 1906, quoted in ibid., pp. 30–1.
67 Gwynne to Maxse, 19 July 1911, LJMP, 463 T 99–101a. See also Selborne to Willoughby de Broke, 18 Nov. 1911, WDBP, WB 3/46 for a similar scouting of the idea of a new party.
68 A. Sykes, 'The Radical Right and the Crisis of Conservatism in the Early Twentieth Century', *HJ*, xxvi, 1983.
69 See for example Eley, *German Right*.
70 Coetzee, *Party or Country*, p. 6.
71 ibid., p. 5.

BIBLIOGRAPHY

(For reasons of cost this bibliography omits published contemporary sources and secondary literature. Much of this detail is, however, contained in the notes to the text.)

MANUSCRIPT SOURCES

Akers-Douglas papers, West Kent Record Office
Arnold-Forster papers, British Library
Astor papers, Reading University Library
Asquith papers, Bodleian Libray, Oxford
Avebury papers, British Library
Balfour papers, British Library
Blumenfeld papers, House of Lords Record Office
Cabinet Minutes and Memoranda (CAB 37), Public Record Office
Cannan papers, London School of Economics
Carnarvon papers, British Library
Cecil of Chelwood (Robert Cecil) papers, British Library
Cecil-Maxse papers, West Kent Record Office
A. Chamberlain papers, Birmingham University Library
J. Chamberlain papers, Birmingham University Library
N. Chamberlain papers, Birmingham University Library
Randolph Churchill papers, Churchill College, Cambridge
Conservative party archive, Bodleian Library, Oxford
Cromer papers, Public Record Office
Farrer papers, London School of Economics
Gibbs papers, Guildhall Library, London
Giffen papers, London School of Economics
W.E. Gladstone papers, British Library
Gwynne papers, Bodleian Library, Oxford
Halsbury papers, British Library
E.W. Hamilton papers (Private), British Library
E.W. Hamilton papers (Office), Public Record Office
Harcourt papers, Bodleian Library, Oxford
Hewins papers, Sheffield University Library
Iddesleigh (Stafford Northcote) papers, British Library
Imperial Federation League papers, British Library
Iwan-Muller papers, British Library
Jebb papers, Institute of Commonwealth Studies Library
J.N. Keynes papers, Marshall Library, Cambridge

Kidd papers, Cambridge University Library
Law papers, House of Lords Record Office
Liverpool Chamber of Commerce papers, Liverpool Central Library
Lloyd papers, Churchill College, Cambridge
Long papers, British Library
Lyttelton (Chandos) papers, Churchill College, Cambridge
Maxse papers, West Sussex Record Office
Milner papers, Bodleian Library, Oxford
Miscellaneous Economists' papers, Marshall Library, Cambridge
C. Morrison-Bell papers, Devon County Record Office
Northcliffe papers, British Library
Onslow papers, Guildford Record Office
Page-Croft papers, Churchill College, Cambridge
Ritchie papers, British Library
St Aldwyn (Hicks-Beach) papers, Gloucester Record Office
Salisbury papers, Hatfield House, Hertfordshire
Sandars papers, Bodleian Library, Oxford
Selborne papers, Bodleian Library, Oxford
Sheffield Chamber of Commerce papers, Sheffield Central Library
Steel-Maitland papers, Scottish Record Office
Strachey papers, House of Lords Record Office
Tariff Commission papers, London School of Economics
Wargrave (E.A. Goulding) papers, House of Lords Record Office
Willoughby de Broke papers, House of Lords Record Office

PARLIAMENTARY PAPERS

Royal Commission on the Depression of Trade and Industry
(First Report, 1886, Cmnd. 4621)
(Final Report, 1886, Cmnd. 4893)

Royal Commission on Currency
(First Report, 1887, Cmnd. 5099)
(Second Report, 1888, Cmnd. 5248)
(Final Report, 1888, Cmnd. 5512)

Royal Commission on Agricultural Depression
(First Report, 1894, Cmnd. 7400)
(Second Report, 1896, Cmnd. 7981)
(Final Report, 1897, Cmnd. 8540)

NEWSPAPERS AND PERIODICALS

(Dates indicate where systematic study has been undertaken)
The Bimetallist (1895–1901)
The Contemporary Review (1880–1914)
The Economic Journal (1891–1914)
The Economic Review (1891–1914)
Fair Trade (1885–6)
The Fortnightly Review (1880–1914)
Imperial Federation (1886–93)
The Morning Post (1900–14)
The National Review (1882–1914)
The Outlook (1904–14)
The Times

INDEX